Fodor's 2013

HAWAII

Fodor's Travel Publications · New York, Toronto, London, Sydney, Auckland

www.fodors.com

FODOR'S HAWAII 2013

Editors: Jess Moss, Linda Cabasin, Mark Sullivan
Writers: Karen Anderson, Kristina Anderson, Melissa Chang, Lois Ann Ell, Eliza Escaño-Vasquez, Bonnie Friedman, Michael Levine, Heidi Pool, Joana Varawa, Charles E. Roessler, David Simon, Cynthia Sweeney, Catherine E. Toth

Production Editor: Evangelos Vasilakis
Maps & Illustrations: David Lindroth and Mark Stroud, *cartographers;* Rebecca Baer, *map editor;* William Wu, *information graphics*
Design: Fabrizio La Rocca, *creative director;* Tina Malaney, Chie Ushio, Jessica Walsh, *designers;* Melanie Marin, *associate director of photography;* Jennifer Romains, *photo research*
Cover Photo: (Bird of Paradise, Big Island) Wasmac/eStock Photo
Production Manager: Angela L. McLean

ISBN 978-0-307-92927-3

ISSN 0071-6421

SPECIAL SALES
This book is available at special discounts for bulk purchases for sales promotions or premiums. Special editions, including personalized covers, excerpts of existing books, and corporate imprints, can be created in large quantities for special needs. For more information, write to Special Markets/Premium Sales, 1745 Broadway, MD 3-1, New York, NY 10019, or e-mail specialmarkets@randomhouse.com.

AN IMPORTANT TIP & AN INVITATION
Although all prices, opening times, and other details in this book are based on information supplied to us at press time, changes occur all the time in the travel world, and Fodor's cannot accept responsibility for facts that become outdated or for inadvertent errors or omissions. So **always confirm information when it matters,** especially if you're making a detour to visit a specific place. Your experiences—positive and negative—matter to us. If we have missed or misstated something, **please write to us.** Share your opinion instantly through our online feedback center at fodors.com/contact-us.

PRINTED IN CHINA

10 9 8 7 6 5 4 3 2 1

CONTENTS

ABOUT
THIS GUIDE

Fodor's Ratings

Everything in this guide is worth doing—
we don't cover what isn't—but exceptional sights, hotels, and restaurants are
recognized with additional accolades.
Fodor's Choice★ indicates our top recommendations; **★** highlights places we
deem **Highly Recommended**; and **Best Bets**
call attention to notable hotels and restaurants in various categories. Care to
nominate a new place? Visit Fodors.com/
contact-us.

Trip Costs

We list prices wherever possible to help
you budget well. Hotel and restaurant
price categories from **$** to **$$$$** are noted
alongside each recommendation. For
hotels, we include the lowest cost of a
standard double room in high season.
For restaurants, we cite the average price
of a main course at dinner or, if dinner
isn't served, at lunch. For attractions,
we always list adult admission fees; dis-
counts are usually available for children,
students, and senior citizens.

Hotels

Our local writers vet every hotel to recom-
mend the best overnights in each price cat-
egory, from budget to expensive. Unless
otherwise specified, you can expect pri-
vate bath, phone, and TV in your room.
For expanded hotel reviews, facilities, and
deals visit Fodors.com.

TripAdvisor ⊙⊙

Our expert hotel picks are reinforced by
high ratings on TripAdvisor. Look for rep-
resentative quotes in this guide, and the
latest TripAdvisor ratings and feedback
at Fodors.com.

Restaurants

Unless we state otherwise, restaurants are
open for lunch and dinner daily. We men-
tion dress code only when there's a specific

Ratings		Hotels &
★	Fodor's Choice	**Restaurants**
★	Highly recommended	🏨 Hotel
☾	Family-friendly	⇗ Number of rooms
		⎰⎱ Meal plans
Listings		✕ Restaurant
⊠	Address	⌂ Reservations
⊠	Branch address	🏛 Dress code
⌨	Mailing address	⊟ No credit cards
☎	Telephone	$ Price
🖷	Fax	
⊕	Website	**Other**
✎	E-mail	⇨ See also
✑	Admission fee	☞ Take note
☉	Open/closed times	🏌 Golf facilities
Ⓜ	Subway	
✛	Directions or Map coordinates	

requirement and reservations only when
they're essential or not accepted. To make
restaurant reservations, visit Fodors.com.

Credit Cards

The hotels and restaurants in this guide
typically accept credit cards. If not, we'll
say so.

Experience
Hawaii

WHAT'S WHERE

Hanalei

Mt. Waialeale
5,148 ft. ▲   Kapaa

Kaulakahi Channel

Waimea   Lihue

NIIHAU   Poipu   KAUAI   5

Kauai Channel

Kauai Channel

Kahuku Pt.

OAHU

Haleiwa   Laie

Kaena Pt.

Kaneohe

Pearl Harbor   2

HONOLULU   Waikiki

PACIFIC

Kaiwi Channel

OCEAN

*Numbers correspond to
chapters in this book.*

2 Oahu. Honolulu and
Waikiki are here—and it's a
great big luau. It's got hot
restaurants and lively nightlife
as well as gorgeous white-
sand beaches, knife-edged
mountain ranges, and cultural
sites including Pearl Harbor.

3 Maui. The phrase *Maui no
ka oi* means Maui is the best,
the most, the tops. There's
good reason for the superlatives. It's got a little of everything, perfect for families with
divergent interests.

4 Big Island of Hawaii. It
has two faces, watched over
by snowcapped Mauna Kea
and steaming Mauna Loa. The
Kona side has parched, lava-
strewn lowlands, and eastern
Hilo is characterized by lush
flower farms and waterfalls.

5 Kauai. This is the "Garden Isle," and it's where
you'll find the lush, green
folding sea cliffs of Napali
Coast, the colorful and
awesome Waimea Canyon,
and more beaches per mile
of coastline than any other
Hawaiian island.

6 Molokai. It's the least
changed, most laid-back
of the Islands. Come here
to ride a mule down a cliff
to Kalaupapa Peninsula;
experience the Kamakou
Preserve, a 2,774-acre wildlife refuge; and for plenty of
peace and quiet.

7 Lanai. For years there
was nothing here except
for pineapples and red-dirt
roads. Today it attracts the
well-heeled in search of
privacy, with a few upscale
resorts, archery and shooting, four-wheel-drive excursions, and superb scuba
diving.

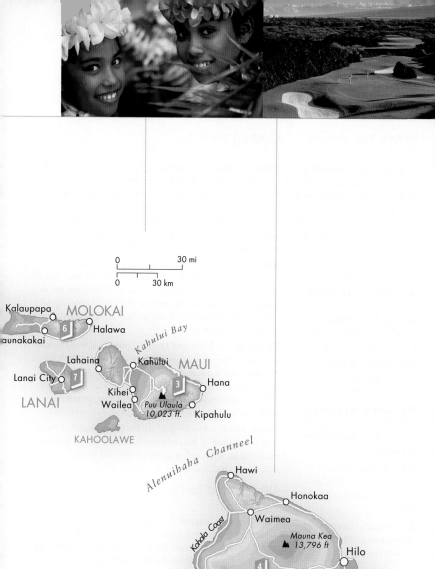

0   30 mi
0   30 km

Kalaupapa   MOLOKAI
aunakakai   6   Halawa

Lanai City   7
LANAI   Lahaina   Kahului   MAUI
                                              Hana
             Kihei   3
             Wailea   Puu Ulaula   Kipahulu
                       10,023 ft.

KAHOOLAWE

Kahului Bay

Alenuihaha Channeel

Hawi

                    Honokaa

            Waimea
                    Mauna Kea
                    13,796 ft.
                              Hilo

Kailua-Kona   Kona Coast
               Captain Cook   Pahoa
HAWAII   Mauna Loa
(The Big Island)   13,677 ft.   Volcano

               Pahala
Hoopuloa

               Naalehu

Kohala Coast

HAWAII PLANNER

When You Arrive

Honolulu's International Airport is the main stopover for most domestic and international flights, but all of Hawaii's major Islands have their own airports. Flights to the Neighbor Islands leave from Honolulu almost every half hour daily.

Visitor Information

Oahu Visitors Bureau
☏ 808/524-0722, 877/525-6248 ⊕ www.visit-oahu.com.

Maui Visitors Bureau
☏ 808/244-3530, 800/525-6284 ⊕ www.visitmaui.com.

Big Island Visitors Bureau
☏ 808/961-5797, 800/648-2441 ⊕ www.gohawaii.com/big-island.

Kauai Visitors Bureau
☏ 808/245-3971, 800/262-1400 ⊕ www.kauaidiscovery.com.

Hawaii Island Chamber of Commerce ☏ 808/935-7178 ⊕ www.hicc.biz.

Hawaii Beach Safety
⊕ www.hawaiibeachsafety.org.

Hawaii Department of Land and Natural Resources
☏ 808/587-0400
⊕ www.hawaii.gov/dlnr.

Hawaii Visitors and Convention Bureau ☏ 808/923-1811, 800/464-2924
⊕ www.gohawaii.com.

Getting Here

Oahu: Honolulu International Airport is 20 minutes (40 during rush hour) from Waikiki. Car rental is across the street from baggage claim. An inefficient airport taxi system requires you to line up to a taxi wrangler who radios for cars (about $30 to Waikiki). Other options: TheBus ($2.50, one lap-size bag allowed), SpeediShuttle ($14.55), and the Roberts Hawaii Express Shuttle ($12).

Maui: Most visitors arrive at Kahului Airport in Central Maui. For trips to Molokai or Lanai, ferries are available to both islands and have room for your golf clubs and mountain bike. If you prefer to travel to Molokai or Lanai by air, and you're not averse to flying on four- to 12-seaters, your best bet is a small air taxi.

Big Island: The Big Island's two airports are directly across the island from each other. Kona International Airport on the west side is about a 10-minute drive from Kailua-Kona and 30 to 45 minutes from the Kohala Coast. On the east side, Hilo International Airport, 2 miles from downtown Hilo, is about 40 minutes from Volcanoes National Park.

Kauai: All commercial flights use the Lihue Airport, 2 miles east of the town of the same name. It has just two baggage-claim areas, each with a visitor information center.

Dining and Lodging

Hawaii is a melting pot of cultures, and nowhere is this more apparent than in its cuisine. From luau and "plate lunch" to sushi and steak, there's no shortage of interesting flavors and presentations. As for lodging, there are many top-notch resorts in Hawaii, as well as a wide variety of condos and vacation rentals to choose from.

Getting Around

Oahu: If you want to travel around the island on your own schedule, renting a car is a must. Heavy traffic toward downtown Honolulu begins as early as 6:30 am and lasts until 9 am. In the afternoon, expect traffic departing downtown to back up beginning around 3 pm until approximately 7 pm.

Maui: Driving from one point on Maui to another can take longer than the mileage indicates. It's 52 miles from Kahului Airport to Hana, but the drive can take three hours. As for driving to Haleakala, the 38-mile drive from sea level to the summit will take you about two hours. Traffic on Maui's roads can be heavy, especially during the rush hours of 6 am to 8:30 am and 3:30 pm to 6:30 pm.

Big Island: It's a good idea to rent a car with four-wheel drive, such as a Jeep, on the Big Island. Some of the island's best sights (and most beautiful beaches) are at the end of rough or unpaved roads. Most agencies make you sign an agreement that you won't drive on the path to Mauna Kea and its observatories. Keep in mind that, while a good portion of the Saddle Road is smoothly paved, it is also remote, winding, and bumpy in certain areas, unlighted, and bereft of gas stations.

Kauai: A rental car is the best way to get to your hotel, though taxis and some hotel shuttles are available. From the airport it will take you about 15 to 25 minutes to drive to Wailua or Kapaa, 30 to 40 minutes to reach Poipu, and 45 minutes to an hour to get to Princeville or Hanalei. Kauai roads are subject to some pretty heavy traffic, especially going through Kapaa and Lihue.

Island Driving Times

Oahu: Waikiki to Downtown Honolulu	4 miles/10 min
Oahu: Waikiki to Hololulu Int'l Airport	12 miles/25 min
Oahu: Waikiki to Haleiwa	34 miles /45 min
Maui: Kahului to Wailea	17 miles /30 min
Maui: Kahului to Kaanapali	25 miles /45 min
Maui: Kahului to Kapalua	36 miles /1 hr 15 min
Big Island: Kailua-Kona to Kohala Coast	32 miles /50 min
Big Island: Kailua-Kona to Hilo	86 miles /2.5 hr
Kauai: Hanalei to Lihue	32 miles /1 hr 5 min
Kauai: Lihue to Poipu	13 miles /25 min

Hawaii's Best Festivals and Events

February: Chinese New Year: Lahaina, Maui, and in Chinatown on Oahu. Waimea Town Celebration: Waimea, Kauai.

March: Prince Kuhio Day Celebration: Lihue, Kauai.

April: Merrie Monarch Hula Festival: Hilo, Big Island. East Maui Taro Festival: Hana, Maui. Kona Chocolate Festival: Big Island.

May: World Fire-Knife Dance Championships & Samoa Festival: Polynesian Cultural Center, Laie, Oahu. Maui Onion Festival: Kaanapali, Maui.

June: Hawaiian Slack-Key Guitar Festival: Kahului, Maui. King Kamehameha Hula Competition: Honolulu, Oahu. Flavors of Honolulu: Honolulu, Oahu. Maui Film Festival: Wailea and other locations, Maui.

July: Fourth of July celebrations: Magic Island, Kailua Beach, and at Pearl Harbor's Schofield Barracks, Oahu. In Honolulu, displays light up the skies.

October: Ironman Triathalon World Championship: Kailua-Kona, Big Island. Halloween festivities: Lahaina, Maui, and Chinatown and Waikiki on Oahu. Plantation Days: Lahaina, Maui.

November: Kona Coffee Cultural Festival: Kona, Big Island. Triple Crown of Surfing: North Shore, Oahu.

HAWAII TODAY

Hawaiian culture and tradition here have experienced a renaissance over the last few decades. There's a real effort to revive traditions and to respect history as the Islands go through major changes. New developments often have a Hawaiian cultural expert on staff to ensure cultural sensitivity and to educate newcomers.

Nonetheless, development remains a huge issue for all Islanders—land prices are skyrocketing, putting many areas out of reach for the native population. Traffic is becoming a problem on roads that were not designed to accommodate all the new drivers, and the Islands' limited natural resources are being seriously tapped. The government, though sluggish to respond at first, is trying to make development in Hawaii as sustainable as possible.

Sustainability

Although sustainability is an effective buzzword and authentic direction for the Islands' dining establishments, 90% of Hawaii's food and energy is imported.

Most of the land was used for mono-cropping of pineapple or sugarcane, both of which have all but vanished. Sugarcane is now produced in only two plants on Kauai and Maui, while pineapple production has dropped precipitously. Dole, once the largest pineapple company in Hawaii, closed its plants in 1991, and after 90 years, Del Monte stopped pineapple production in 2008. The next year, Maui Land and Pineapple Company also ceased its Maui Gold pineapple operation, although in early 2010 a group of executives took over one third of the land and created a new company. Low cost of labor and transportation from Latin American and Southeast Asian pineapple producers are factors contributing to the industry's

demise in Hawaii. Although this proves daunting, it also sets the stage for great agricultural change to be explored.

Back-to-Basics Agriculture

Emulating how the Hawaiian ancestors lived and returning to their simple ways of growing and sharing a variety of foods has become a statewide initiative. Hawaii has the natural conditions and talent to produce far more diversity in agriculture than it currently does.

The seed of this movement thrives through various farmers' markets and partnerships between restaurants and local farmers. Localized efforts such as the Hawaii Farm Bureau Federation are collectively leading the organic and sustainable agricultural renaissance. From home-cooked meals to casual plate lunches to fine-dining cuisine, these sustainable trailblazers enrich the culinary tapestry of Hawaii and uplift the Islands' overall quality of life.

Tourism and the Economy

The over-$10 billion tourism industry represents a third of Hawaii's state income. Naturally, this dependency causes economic hardship as the financial meltdown of recent years affects tourists' ability to visit and spend.

One way the industry has changed has been to adopt more eco-conscious practices, as many Hawaiians feel that development shouldn't happen without regard for impact to local communities and their natural environment.

Belief that an industry based on the Hawaiians' *aloha* should protect, promote, and empower local culture and provide more entrepreneurial opportunities for local people has become more important to tourism businesses. More companies are incorporating authentic

Hawaiiana in their programs and aim not only to provide a commercially viable tour but also to ensure that the visitor leaves feeling connected to his or her host.

The concept of *kuleana*, a word for both privilege and responsibility, is upheld. Having the privilege to live in such a sublime place comes with the responsibility to protect it.

Sovereignty

Political issues of sovereignty continue to divide Native Hawaiians, who have formed myriad organizations, each operating with a separate agenda and lacking one collectively defined goal. Ranging from achieving complete independence to solidifying a nation within a nation, existing sovereignty models remain fractured and their future unresolved.

The introduction of the Native Hawaiian Government Reorganization Act of 2009 attempts to set up a legal framework in which Native Hawaiians can attain federal recognition and coexist as a self-governed entity. Also known as the Akaka Bill after Senator Daniel Akaka of Hawaii, this pending bill has been presented before Congress and is still awaiting a vote at the time of this writing.

Rise of Hawaiian Pride

After Hawaii became a state in 1959, a process of Americanization began. Traditions were duly silenced in the name of citizenship. Teaching Hawaiian language was banned from schools and children were distanced from their local customs.

But Hawaiians are resilient people, and with the rise of the civil rights movement they began to reflect on their own national identity, bringing an astonishing renaissance of the Hawaiian culture to fruition.

The people rediscovered language, hula, chanting, and even the traditional Polynesian arts of canoe building and wayfinding (navigation by the stars without use of instruments). This cultural resurrection is now firmly established in today's Hawaiian culture, with a palpable pride that exudes from Hawaiians young and old.

The election of President Barack Obama definitely increased Hawaiian pride and inspired a ubiquitous hope for a better future. The president's strong connection and commitment to Hawaiian values of diversity, spirituality, family, and conservation have restored confidence that Hawaii can inspire a more peaceful, tolerant, and environmentally conscious world.

HAWAII TOP EXPERIENCES

Hit the Road to Hana on Maui

(A) Spectacular views of waterfalls, lush forests, and the sparkling ocean are part of the pleasure of the twisting drive along the North Shore to tiny, timeless Hana in East Maui. The journey is the destination, but once you arrive, kick back and relax.

Visit Oahu's Pearl Harbor

(B) This top Honolulu site is not to be missed—spend the better part of a day touring the *Missouri,* the *Arizona* Memorial, and, if you have time, the *Bowfin.*

See a Lava Show on the Big Island

(C) At Hawaii Volcanoes National Park, watch as fiery red lava pours, steaming, into the ocean; stare in awe at nighttime lava fireworks; and hike across the floor of a crater.

Explore Kauai's Napali Coast

(D) Experiencing Kauai's emerald green Napali Coast is a must-do. You can see these awesome cliffs on the northwest side of the island by boat, helicopter, or by hiking the Kalalau Trail. Whichever you pick, you won't be disappointed.

Hike Maui's Haleakala

(E) Trek down into Maui's Haleakala National Park's massive bowl and see proof, at this dormant volcano, of how very powerful the earth's exhalations can be. You won't see landscape like this anywhere, outside of visiting the moon. The barren terrain is deceptive, however—many of the world's rarest plants, birds, and insects live here.

Surf at Waikiki Beach on Oahu

(F) Waikiki, with its well-shaped but diminutive waves, remains the perfect spot for grommets (surfing newbies), though surf schools operate at beaches (and many hotels) around the island. Most companies guarantee at least one standing ride in the course of a lesson. And catching your first wave? We guarantee you'll never forget it.

Catch the Views at Kauai's Waimea Canyon

(G) From its start in the west Kauai town of Waimea to the road's end some 20 uphill miles later at Puu O Kila Look-out, you'll pass through several microclimates—from hot, desertlike conditions at sea level to the cool, deciduous forest of Kokee—and navigate through the traditional Hawaiian system of land division called *ahupuaa*.

Drive Big Island's Hamakua Coast

The views of the Pacific are absolutely breathtaking along this stretch of road between Kohala and Hilo. Make sure to take the Old Mamalahoa Highway's scenic four-mile detour off Hawaii Belt Road.

Enjoy Oahu After Hours

(H) Yes, you can have an umbrella drink at sunset. But in the multicultural metropolis of Honolulu, there's so much more to it than that. Sip a glass of wine and listen to jazz at The Dragon Upstairs in Chinatown, join the beach-and-beer gang at Duke's Canoe Club, or head to Zanzabar, where DJs spin hip-hop and techno.

Whale Watch on Maui

(I) Maui is the cradle for hundreds of humpback whales that return every year to frolic in the warm waters and give birth. Watch a mama whale teach her one-ton calf how to tail wave. You can eavesdrop on them, too: book a tour boat with a hydrophone or just plunk your head underwater to hear the strange squeaks, groans, and chortles of the cetaceans.

Watch a Luau

(J) There are luau that are spectacles and those that lean toward the more authentic. Both have their merits, depending on the experience you're after. Two that are worthy of mention are the Old Lahaina Luau on Maui and the thrilling performances at the Polynesian Cultural Center on Oahu.

THE HAWAIIAN ISLANDS

Oahu. The state's capital, Honolulu, is on Oahu; this is the center of Hawaii's economy and by far the most populated island in the chain—953,000 residents add up to 71% of the state's population. At 597 square miles Oahu is the third largest island in the chain; the majority of residents live in or around Honolulu, so the rest of the island still fits neatly into the tropical, untouched vision of Hawaii. Situated southeast of Kauai and northwest of Maui, Oahu is a central location for island hopping. Pearl Harbor, iconic Waikiki Beach, and surfing contests on the legendary North Shore are all here.

Maui. The second largest island in the chain, Maui is northwest of the Big Island and close enough to be visible from its beaches on a clear day. The island's 729 square miles are home to only 155,000 people but host more than 2 million tourists every year. With its restaurants and lively nightlife, Maui is the only island that competes with Oahu in terms of entertainment; its charm lies in the fact that although entertainment is available, Maui's towns still feel like island villages compared to the heaving modern city of Honolulu.

Hawaii (The Big Island). The Big Island has the second largest population of the Islands (almost 190,000) but feels sparsely settled due to its size. It's 4,038 square miles and growing—all the other Islands could fit onto the Big Island and there would still be room left over. The southernmost island in the chain (slightly southeast of Maui), the Big Island is home to Kilauea, the most active volcano on the planet. It percolates within Volcanoes National Park, which draws nearly 3 million visitors every year.

Kauai. The northernmost island in the chain (northwest of Oahu), Kauai is, at approximately 622 square miles, the fourth largest of all the Islands and the least populated of the larger Islands, with 64,000 residents. Known as the Garden Isle, this island is home to lush botanical gardens as well as the stunning Napali Coast and Waimea Canyon. The island is a favorite with honeymooners and others wanting to get away from it all—lush and peaceful, it's the perfect escape from the modern world.

Molokai. North of Lanai and Maui, and east of Oahu, Molokai is Hawaii's fifth-largest island, encompassing 260 square miles. On a clear night, the lights of Honolulu are visible from Molokai's western shore. Molokai is sparsely populated, with about 7,300 residents, the majority of whom are Native Hawaiians. Most of the island's 79,000 annual visitors travel from Maui or Oahu to spend the day exploring its beaches, cliffs, and former leper colony on Kalaupapa Peninsula.

Lanai. Lying just off Maui's western coast, Lanai looks nothing like its sister Islands, with pine trees and deserts in place of palm trees and beaches. Still, the tiny 140-square-mile island is home to about 3,200 residents and draws an average of 75,000 visitors each year to two resorts (one in the mountains and one at the shore), both operated by Four Seasons.

Hawaii's Geology

The Hawaiian Islands comprise more than just the islands inhabited and visited by humans. A total of 19 islands and atolls constitute the State of Hawaii, with a total landmass of 6,423.4 square miles.

The Islands are actually exposed peaks of a submersed mountain range called the Hawaiian Ridge-Emperor Seamounts

chain. The range was formed as the Pacific plate moves very slowly (around 32 miles every million years—or about as much as your fingernails grow in one year) over a hot spot in the Earth's mantle. Because the plate moves northwestwardly, the Islands in the northwest portion of the archipelago (chain) are older, which is also why they're smaller—they have been eroding longer and have actually sunk back into the sea floor.

The Big Island is the youngest, and thus the largest, island in the chain. It is built from five different volcanoes, including Mauna Loa, which is the largest mountain on the planet (when measured from the bottom of the sea floor). Mauna Loa and Kilauea are the only Hawaiian volcanoes still erupting with any sort of frequency. Mauna Loa last erupted in 1984. Kilauea has been continuously erupting since 1983.

Mauna Kea (Big Island), Hualalai (Big Island), and Haleakala (Maui) are all in what's called the post-shield-building stage of volcanic development—eruptions decrease steadily for up to a million years before ceasing entirely. Kohala (Big Island), Lanai (Lanai), and Waianae (Oahu) are considered extinct volcanoes, in the erosional stage of development; Koolau (Oahu) and West Maui (Maui) volcanoes are extinct volcanoes in the rejuvenation stage—after lying dormant for hundreds of thousands of years, they began erupting again, but only once every several thousand years.

There is currently an active undersea volcano to the south and east of the Big Island called Kamaehu that has been erupting regularly. If it continues its current pattern, it should breach the ocean's surface in tens of thousands of years.

Hawaii's Flora and Fauna

More than 90% of native Hawaiian flora and fauna are endemic (they evolved into unique species here), like the koa tree and the yellow hibiscus. Long-dormant volcanic craters are perfect hiding places for rare native plants. The silversword, a rare cousin of the sunflower, grows on Hawaii's three tallest peaks: Haleakala, Mauna Kea, and Mauna Loa, and nowhere else on Earth. Ohia trees— thought to be the favorite of Pele, the volcano goddess—bury their roots in fields of once-molten lava, and one variety sprouts ruby pom-pom–like lehua blossoms. The deep yellow petals of ilima (once reserved for royalty) are tiny discs, which make the most elegant lei.

But most of the plants you see while walking around, however, aren't Hawaiian at all and came from Tahitian, Samoan, or European visitors. Plumeria is ubiquitous; alien orchids run rampant on the Big Island; bright orange relatives of the ilima light up the mountains of Oahu. Though these flowers are not native, they give the Hawaiian lei their color and fragrance.

Hawaii's state bird, the nene goose, is making a comeback from its former endangered status. It roams freely in parts of Maui, Kauai, and the Big Island. Rare Hawaiian monk seals breed in the northwestern Islands. With only 1,500 left in the wild, you probably won't catch many lounging on the beaches, though they have been spotted on the shores of Kauai in recent years. Spinner dolphins and sea turtles can be found off the coast of all the Islands; and every year from November to April, the humpback whales migrate past Hawaii in droves.

CHOOSING YOUR ISLANDS

You've decided to go to Hawaii, but should you stay put and relax on one island or try sampling more than one? If all you have is a week, it is probably best to stick to just one island. You traveled all this way, why spend your precious vacation time at car rental counters, hotel check-in desks, and airports? But, with seven or more nights, a little island hopping is a great way to experience the diversity of sights and experiences that are packed into this small state. Here are some of our favorite island-pairing itineraries for every type of trip.

Family Travel: Oahu and Maui

If you're traveling with children, Oahu and Maui have the most options.

Why Oahu: Oahu is by far the most kid-friendly island. For sea life, visit the Wakiki Aquarium and Sea Life Park or let the little ones get up close and personal with fish at Hanauma Bay. At Pearl Harbor you can visit an aircraft carrier or, if the kids are at least four, a World War II submarine. Then there's the Honolulu Zoo and a slippery slide–filled water park, not to mention some very family-friendly and safe beaches. *Plan to spend 4 nights.*

Why Maui: Whales! Though you can see whales from any island between November and April, there's no better place than Maui. If your visit doesn't fall during peak whale-watching season, visit the Whalers Village Museum, the Hawaiian Islands Humpback Whale National Marine Sanctuary or the Maui Ocean Center (to get an up close look at some of Hawaii's smaller sea creatures). Away from the water, there's the Sugar Cane Train. *Plan to spend at least 3 nights.*

Romance: Maui and Kauai

If you're getting away for seclusion, romantic walks along the beach, and the pampering at world-class spas, consider Maui and Kauai.

Why Maui: You'll find waterfalls, salt-and-pepper sand beaches, and incredible views as you follow the twisting turning Road to Hana. The luxury resorts in Wailea or Kaanapali provide lots of fine dining and spa treatment options. And for those who want to start their day early, there's the drive up to Haleakala to see the sun rise— or for couples who prefer to sleep in, there's the arguably even more spectacular sunset from the summit. *Plan to spend 4 nights.*

Why Kauai: The North Shore communities of Hanalei and Princeville provide the opportunity to get away from crowds and indulge in some spectacular beaches, hiking, and helicopter rides. At Princeville you can experience views straight out of *South Pacific* as well as excellent dining and spas at the St. Regis Hotel, while a drive to Kee Beach at the end of the road provides innumerable options for pulling over and grabbing a beach, all for just the two of you. *Plan to spend at least 3 nights.*

Golf, Shopping, and Luxury: Maui and the Big Island

For luxurious travel, great shopping, restaurants, and accommodations you can't beat Maui and the Big Island.

Why Maui: The resorts at Wailea and Kaanapali have endless options for dining, shopping, and spa treatments. And, the golf on Maui can't be beat with Kapalua, the Dunes at Maui Lani, and Makena Resort topping the list of spectacular courses. *Plan to spend 4 nights.*

Why the Big Island: In addition to having incredible natural scenery, the Big Island offers world-class resorts and golfing

along the Kohala Coast. The Mauna Kea and Hapuna golf courses rank among the top in state while the courses at Mauna Lani Resort and Waikoloa Village allow the unusual experience of playing in and around lava flows. Gourmet dining and spa treatments are readily available at the top resorts and you'll find shopping opportunities at King's Shops at Waikoloa Village as well as within many of the resorts themselves. Or, travel to Hawi or Waimea (Kamuela) for original island boutiques. *Plan to spend at least 3 nights.*

Natural Beauty and Pristine Beaches: The Big Island and Kauai

Really want to get away and experience nature at its most primal? The Big Island is the place to start, followed by a trip to Kauai.

Why the Big Island: Home to 11 different climate zones, the Big Island is large enough to contain all the other Hawaiian Islands inside it. There are countless options for those who want to get off the beaten track and get their hands (and feet) dirty—or sandy as the case may be. See lava flowing or steam rising from Kilauea. Visit beaches in your choice of gold, white, green, or black sand. Snorkel or dive just offshore from an ancient Hawaiian settlement. Or, hike through rain forests to hidden waterfalls. The choices are endless on this island. *Plan to spend at least 4 nights.*

Why Kauai: The Napali Coast is the main draw for those seeking secluded beaches and incredible scenery. If you're interested in hiking to otherwise inaccessible beaches along sheer sea cliffs, this is as good as it gets. Or, head up to Waimea Canyon to see the "Grand Canyon of the Pacific." Want waterfalls? Opaekaa Falls

outside Lihue is one of the state's most breathtaking. And there's no better place for bird-watching than Kilauea Point National Wildlife Refuge. *Plan to spend at least 3 nights.*

Volcanic Views: The Big Island and Maui

For those coming to Hawaii for the volcanoes, there are really only two options: The Big Island and Maui.

Why the Big Island: Start by flying into Hilo and head straight to Hawaii Volcanoes National Park and Kilauea Volcano. Plan to spend at least two days at Kilauea—you'll need time to really explore the caldera, drive to the end of Chain of Craters Road, and have some time for hiking in and around this active volcano. While eruptions are unpredictable, helicopter companies can get you views of otherwise inaccessible lava flows. You can also make a visit up to the summit of Mauna Kea with a tour company. From here you'll see views not only of the observatories (Mauna Kea is one of the best places in the world for astronomy), but also Kilauea and Haleakala volcanoes, which loom in the distance. *Plan to spend at least 4 nights.*

Why Maui: Though all the islands in Hawaii were built from the same hot spot in Earth's crust, the only other island to have had volcanic activity in recorded history was Maui, at Haleakala. The House of the Sun (as Haleakala is known) has great hiking and camping opportunities. *Plan to spend 3 nights.*

ISLAND-FINDER CHART

Not sure which Hawaiian island is your kind of paradise? Any island would make a memorable vacation, but not every one has that particular mix of attributes that makes it perfect for you. Use this chart to compare how each island measures up to your vacation dreams. Looking for great nightlife and world-class surfing? Oahu would fit the bill. Hate crowds but love scuba? Lanai is your place. You can also consult What's Where to learn more about the specific attractions of each island.

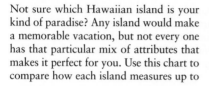

	OAHU	MAUI	BIG ISLAND	KAUAI	MOLOKAI	LANAI
Beaches						
Activities & Sports	●	●	●	◐	◐	◐
Deserted	◐	◐	◐	●	●	◐
Party Scene	●	◐	◐	○	○	○
City Life						
Crowds	●	◐	◐	◐	○	○
Urban Development	●	◐	◐	◐	○	○
Entertainment						
Hawaiian Cultural Events	●	●	●	◐	◐	○
Museums	●	◐	◐	◐	○	○
Nightlife	●	◐	○	○	○	○
Performing Arts	●	◐	○	○	○	○
Shopping	●	●	◐	◐	○	○
Lodging						
B&Bs	◐	◐	●	●	○	○
Condos	●	●	●	●	◐	○
Hotels & Resorts	●	●	●	●	○	●
Vacation Rentals	◐	●	◐	●	◐	○
Nature						
Rainforest Sights	◐	◐	◐	●	◐	○
Volcanic Sights	○	◐	●	○	○	○
Wildlife	○	◐	●	●	◐	◐
Sports						
Golf	●	●	●	◐	○	●
Hiking	◐	●	●	●	◐	◐
Scuba	◐	●	●	◐	○	◐
Snorkeling	◐	●	●	◐	◐	◐
Surfing	●	●	◐	◐	◐	○
Windsurfing	◐	●	◐	◐	◐	○

KEY: ● Noteworthy ◐ Some ○ Little or None

WHEN TO GO

Long days of sunshine and fairly mild year-round temperatures make Hawaii an all-season destination. Most resort areas are at sea level, with average afternoon temperatures of 75°F to 80°F during the coldest months of December and January; during the hottest months of August and September the temperature often reaches 90°F. Only at high elevations does the temperature drop into the colder realms, and only at mountain summits does it reach freezing.

Most travelers head to the Islands in winter. From mid-December through mid-April, visitors find Hawaii's sun-splashed beaches and balmy trade winds appealing. This high season means that fewer travel bargains are available; room rates average 10% to 15% higher during this season than the rest of the year. The highest rates you're likely to pay are between Christmas and New Year. Spring break (the month of March) and even summer can be pricey. A general rule of thumb: When kids are on recess from school, it's high season in Hawaii.

Rainfall can be high in winter, particularly on the north and east shores of each island. Generally speaking, you're guaranteed sun and warm temperatures on the west and south shores no matter what time of year.

Only-in-Hawaii Holidays

If you happen to be in the Islands on March 26 or June 11, you'll notice light traffic and busy beaches—these are state holidays not celebrated anywhere else. March 26 recognizes the birthday of Prince Jonah Kuhio Kalanianaole, a member of the royal line who served as a delegate to Congress and spearheaded the effort to set aside homelands for Hawaiian people. June 11 honors the first island-wide monarch, Kamehameha the Great;

locals drape his statues with lei and stage elaborate parades.

May 1 isn't an official holiday, but it's the day when schools and civic groups celebrate the quintessential Islands gift, the flower lei, with lei-making contests and pageants.

Statehood Day is celebrated on the third Friday in August (Admission Day was August 21, 1959).

Another holiday much celebrated is Chinese New Year, in part because many Hawaiians married Chinese immigrants. Homes and businesses sprout bright red good-luck mottoes, lions dance in the streets, and everybody eats *gau* (steamed pudding) and *jai* (vegetarian stew).

The state also celebrates Good Friday as a spring holiday.

Climate

Moist trade winds drop their precipitation on the north and east sides of the Islands, creating tropical climates, while the south and west sides remain hot and dry with desertlike conditions. Higher "Upcountry" elevations typically have cooler, and often misty conditions.

Average maximum and minimum temperatures for Honolulu are listed here; temperatures throughout the Hawaiian Islands are similar.

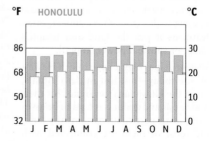

HAWAIIAN PEOPLE AND THEIR CULTURE

By October 2010, Hawaii's population was more than 1.3 million with the majority of residents living on Oahu. Nine percent are Hawaiian or other Pacific Islander, almost 40% are Asian American, 9% are Latino, and about 25% Caucasian. Nearly a fifth of the population list two or more races, making Hawaii the most diverse state in the United States.

Among individuals 18 and older, about 84% finished high school, half attained some college, and 26% completed a bachelor's degree or higher.

The Role of Tradition

The kingdom of Hawaii was ruled by a spiritual class system. Although the *alii*, or chief, was believed to be the direct descendent of a deity or god, high priests, known as *kahuna*, presided over every imaginable aspect of life and *kapu* (taboos) that strictly governed the commoners.

Each part of nature and ritual was connected to a deity—Kane was the highest of all deities, symbolizing sunlight and creation; Ku was the god of war; Lono represented fertility, rainfall, music, and peace; Kanaloa was the god of the underworld or darker spirits. Probably the most well known by outsiders is Pele, the goddess of fire.

The kapu not only provided social order, they also swayed the people to act with reverence for the environment. Any abuse was met with extreme punishment, often death, as it put the land and people's *mana*, or spiritual power, in peril.

Ancient deities play a huge role in Hawaiian life today—not just in daily rituals, but in the Hawaiians' reverence for their land. Gods and goddesses tend to be associated with particular parts of the land, and most of them are connected with many places, thanks to the body of stories built up around each.

One of the most important ways the ancient Hawaiians showed respect for their gods and goddesses was through the hula. Various forms of the hula were performed as prayers to the gods and as praise to the chiefs. Performances were taken very seriously, as a mistake was thought to invalidate the prayer, or even to offend the god or chief in question. Hula is still performed both as entertainment and as prayer; it is not uncommon for a hula performance to be included in an official government ceremony.

Who Are the Hawaiians Today?

To define the Hawaiians in a page, let alone a paragraph, is nearly impossible. Those considered to be indigenous Hawaiians are descendants of the ancient Polynesians who crossed the vast ocean and settled Hawaii. According to the government, there are Native Hawaiians or native Hawaiians (note the change in capitalization), depending on a person's background.

Federal and state agencies apply different methods to determine Hawaiian lineage, from measuring blood percentage to mapping genealogy. This has caused turmoil within the community because it excludes many who claim Hawaiian heritage. It almost guarantees that, as races intermingle, even those considered Native Hawaiian now will eventually disappear on paper, displacing generations to come.

Modern Hawaiian Culture

Perfect weather aside, Hawaii might be the warmest place anyone can visit. The Hawaii experience begins and ends with *aloha*, a word that envelops love, affection, and mercy, and has become a

salutation for hello and good-bye. Broken down, *alo* means "presence" and *ha* means "breath"—the presence of breath. It's to live with love and respect for self and others with every breath. Past the manicured resorts and tour buses, aloha is a moral compass that binds all of Hawaii's people.

Hawaii is blessed with some of the most unspoiled natural wonders, and aloha extends to the land, or *aina*. Hawaiians are raised outdoors and have strong ties to nature. They realize as children that the ocean and land are the delicate source of all life. Even ancient gods were embodied by nature, and this reverence has been passed down to present generations who believe in *kuleana*, their privilege and responsibility.

Hawaii's diverse cultures unfold in a beautiful montage of customs and arts—from music, to dance, to food. Musical genres range from slack key to *Jawaiian* (Hawaiian reggae) to *hapa-haole* (Hawaiian music with English words). From George Kahumoku's Grammy-worthy laid-back strumming to the late Iz Kamakawiwoole's "Somewhere over the Rainbow" to Jack Johnson's more mainstream tunes, contemporary Hawaiian music has definitely carved its ever-evolving niche.

The Merrie Monarch Festival is celebrating almost 50 years of worldwide hula competition and education. The fine-dining culinary scene, especially in Honolulu, has a rich tapestry of ethnic influences and talent. But the real gems are the humble hole-in-the-wall eateries that serve authentic cuisines of many ethnic origins in one plate, a deliciously mixed plate indeed.

And perhaps, the most striking quality in today's Hawaiian culture is the sense of family, or *ohana*. Sooner or later, almost everyone you meet becomes an uncle or auntie, and it is not uncommon for near strangers to be welcomed into a home as a member of the family.

Until the last century, the practice of *hanai*, in which a family essentially adopts a child, usually a grandchild, without formalities, was still prevalent. While still practiced to a somewhat lesser degree, the *hanai*, which means to feed or nourish, still resonates within most families and communities.

How to Act Like a Local

Adopting local customs is a firsthand introduction to the Islands' unique culture. So live in T-shirts and shorts. Wear cheap rubber flip-flops, but call them slippers. Wave people into your lane on the highway, and, when someone lets you in, give them a wave of thanks in return. Never, ever blow your horn, even when the pickup truck in front of you is stopped for a long session of "talk story" right in the middle of the road.

Holoholo means to go out for the fun of it—an aimless stroll, ride, or drive. "Wheah you goin', braddah?" "Oh, holoholo." It's local speak for Sunday drive, no plan, it's not the destination but the journey. Try setting out without an itinerary. Learn to *shaka*: pinky and thumb extended, middle fingers curled in, waggle sideways. Eat white rice with everything. When someone says, "Aloha!" answer, "Aloha no!" ("And a real big aloha back to you"). And, as the locals say, "No make big body" ("Try not to act like you own the place").

THE HISTORY OF HAWAII

Hawaiian history is long and complex; a brief survey can put into context the ongoing renaissance of native arts and culture.

The Polynesians

Long before both Christopher Columbus and the Vikings, Polynesian seafarers set out to explore the vast stretches of the open ocean in double-hulled canoes. From western Polynesia, they traveled back and forth between Samoa, Fiji, Tahiti, the Marquesas, and the Society Isles, settling on the outer reaches of the Pacific, Hawaii, and Easter Island, as early as AD 300. The golden era of Polynesian voyaging peaked around AD 1200, after which the distant Hawaiian Islands were left to develop their own unique cultural practices and subsistence in relative isolation.

The Islands' symbiotic society was deeply intertwined with religion, mythology, science, and artistry. Ruled by an *alii,* or chief, each settlement was nestled in an *ahupuaa,* a pie-shaped land division from the uplands where the alii lived, through the valleys and down to the shores where the commoners resided. Everyone contributed, whether it was by building canoes, catching fish, making tools, or farming land.

A United Kingdom

When the British explorer Captain James Cook arrived in 1778, he was revered as a god upon his arrival and later killed over a stolen boat. With guns and ammunition purchased from Cook, the Big Island chief, Kamehameha the Great, gained a significant advantage over the other alii. He united Hawaii into one kingdom in 1810, bringing an end to the frequent interisland battles that dominated Hawaiian life.

Tragically, the new kingdom was beset with troubles. Native religion was abandoned, and *kapu* (laws and regulations) were eventually abolished. The European explorers brought foreign diseases with them, and within a few short decades the Native Hawaiian population was decimated.

New laws regarding land ownership and religious practices eroded the underpinnings of pre-contact Hawaii. Each successor to the Hawaiian throne sacrificed more control over the Island kingdom. As Westerners permeated Hawaiian culture, Hawaii became more riddled with layers of racial issues, injustice, and social unrest.

Modern Hawaii

Finally in 1893, the last Hawaiian monarch, Queen Liliuokalani, was overthrown by a group of Americans and European businessmen and government officials, aided by an armed militia. This led to the creation of the Republic of Hawaii, and it became a U.S. territory for the next 60 years. The loss of Hawaiian sovereignty and the conditions of annexation have haunted the Hawaiian people since the monarchy was deposed.

Pearl Harbor was attacked in 1941, which engaged the United States immediately into World War II. Tourism, from its beginnings in the early 1900s, flourished after the war and naturally inspired rapid real estate development in Waikiki. In 1959, Hawaii officially became the 50th state. Statehood paved the way for Hawaiians to participate in the American democratic process, which was not universally embraced by all Hawaiians. With the rise of the civil rights movement in the 1960s, Hawaiians began to reclaim their own identity, from language to hula.

HAWAII AND THE ENVIRONMENT

Sustainability—it's a word rolling off everyone's tongues these days. In a place known as the most remote island chain in the world (check your globe), Hawaii relies heavily on the outside world for food and material goods—estimates put the percentage of food arriving on container ships as high as 90. Like many places, though, efforts are afoot to change that. And you can help.

Shop Local Farms and Markets

From Kauai to the Big Island, farmers' markets are cropping up, providing a place for growers to sell fresh fruits and vegetables. There is no reason to buy imported mangoes, papayas, avocadoes, and bananas at grocery stores, when the ones you'll find at farmers' markets are not only fresher and bigger but tastier, too. Some markets allow the sale of fresh-packaged foods—salsa, say, or smoothies—and the on-site preparation of food—like pork *laulau* (pork, beef and fish or chicken with taro, or luau, leaves wrapped and steamed in *ti* leaves) or roasted corn on the cob—so you can make your run to the market a dining experience.

Not only is the locavore movement vibrantly alive at farmers' markets, but Hawaii's top chefs are sourcing more of their produce—and fish, beef, chicken, and cheese—from local providers as well. You'll notice this movement on restaurant menus, featuring Kilauea greens or Hamakua tomatoes or locally caught mahimahi.

And while most people are familiar with Kona coffee farm tours on Big Island, if you're interested in the growing slow-food movement in Hawaii, you'll be heartened to know many farmers are opening up their operations for tours—as well as sumptuous meals.

Support Hawaii's Merchants

Food isn't the only sustainable effort in Hawaii. Buying local goods like art and jewelry, Hawaiian heritage products, crafts, music, and apparel is another way to "green up" the local economy. The County of Kauai helps make it easy with a program called **Kauai Made** (⊕ *www.kauaimade.net*), which showcases products made on Kauai, by Kauai people, using Kauai materials. The Maui Chamber of Commerce does something similar with **Made in Maui** (⊕ *www.madeinmaui.com*). Think of both as the Good Housekeeping Seal of Approval for locally made goods.

Then there are the crafty entrepreneurs who are diverting items from the trash heap by repurposing garbage. Take Oahu's **Muumuu Heaven** (⊕ *www.muumuuheaven.com*). They got their start by reincarnating vintage aloha apparel into hip new fashions. **Kini Beach** (⊕ *www.kinibeach.com*) collects discarded grass mats and plastic inflatables from Waikiki hotels and uses them to make pricey bags and totes.

Choose Green Tour Operators

Conscious decisions when it comes to Island activities go a long way to protecting Hawaii's natural world. The **Hawaii Ecotourism Association** (⊕ *www.hawaiiecotourism.org*) recognizes tour operators for, among other things, their environmental stewardship. The **Hawaii Tourism Authority** (⊕ *www.hawaiitourismauthority.org*) recognizes outfitters for their cultural sensitivity. Winners of these awards are good choices when it comes to guided tours and activities.

TOP 10 HAWAIIAN FOODS TO TRY

Food in Hawaii is a reflection of the state's diverse cultural makeup and tropical location. Fresh seafood, organic fruits and vegetables, free-range beef, and locally grown products are the hallmarks of Hawaii regional cuisine. Its preparations are drawn from across the Pacific Rim, including Japan, the Philippines, Korea, and Thailand—and "local food" is a cuisine in its own right. Don't miss Hawaiian-grown coffee, either, whether it's smooth Kona from the Big Island or coffee grown on other islands.

Saimin

The ultimate hangover cure and the perfect comfort food during Hawaii's mild winters, *saimin* ranks at the top of the list of local favorites. In fact, it's one of the few dishes deemed truly local, having been highlighted in cookbooks since the 1930s. Saimin is an Asian-style noodle soup so ubiquitous, it's even on McDonald's menus statewide. In mom-and-pop shops, a large melamine bowl is filled with homemade *dashi*, or chicken broth, and wheat-flour noodles and then topped off with strips of omelet, green onions, bright pink fish cake and *char siu* (Chinese roast pork) or canned luncheon meat, such as SPAM. Add shoyu and chili pepper water, lift your chopsticks and slurp away.

SPAM

Speaking of SPAM, Hawaii's most prevalent grab-and-go snack is SPAM *musubi*. Often displayed next to cash registers at groceries and convenience stores, the glorified rice ball is rectangular, topped with a slice of fried SPAM and wrapped in *nori* (seaweed). Musubi is a bite-sized meal in itself. But just like sushi, the rice part hardens when refrigerated. So it's best to gobble it up, right after purchase.

Hormel Company's SPAM actually deserves its own recognition—way beyond as a mere musubi topping. About 5 million cans are sold per year in Hawaii and the Aloha State even hosts a festival in its honor. It's inexpensive protein and goes a long way when mixed with rice, scrambled eggs, noodles or, well, anything. The spiced luncheon meat gained popularity in World War II days, when fish was rationed. Gourmets and those with aversions to salt, high cholesterol, or high blood pressure may cringe at the thought of eating it, but SPAM in Hawaii is here to stay.

Manapua

Another savory snack is *manapua*, fist-sized dough balls fashioned after Chinese *bao* (a traditional Chinese bun) and stuffed with fillings such as *char siu* (Chinese barbeque) pork and then steamed. Many mom-and-pop stores sell them in commercial steamer display cases along with pork hash and other dim sum. Modern-day fillings include curry chicken.

Fresh Ahi or Tako Poke

There's nothing like fresh ahi or *tako* (octopus) *poke* to break the ice at a backyard party, except, of course, the cold beer handed to you from the cooler. The perfect pupu, poke (pronounced poh-kay) is basically raw seafood cut into bite-sized chunks and mixed with everything from green onions to roasted and ground kukui nuts. Other variations include mixing the fish with chopped round onion, sesame oil, seaweed, and chili pepper water. Shoyu is the constant. These days, grocery stores sell a rainbow of varieties such as kimchi crab and anything goes, from adding mayonnaise to tobiko caviar. Fish lovers who want to take it to the next level order sashimi, the best cuts of ahi sliced and dipped in a mixture of shoyu and wasabi.

Tropical Fruits

Tropical fruits such as apple banana and strawberry papaya are plucked from trees in Island neighborhoods and eaten for breakfast—plain or with a squeeze of fresh lime. Give them a try; the banana tastes like an apple and the papaya's rosy flesh explains its name. Locals also love to add their own creative touches to exotic fruits. Green mangoes are pickled with Chinese five spice, and Maui Gold pineapples are topped with li hing mui powder (heck, even margarita glasses are rimmed with it). Green papaya is tossed in a Vietnamese salad with fish paste and fresh prawns.

Plate Lunch

It would be remiss not to mention the plate lunch as one of the most beloved dishes in Hawaii. It generally includes two scoops of sticky white rice, a scoop of macaroni or macaroni-potato salad, heavy on the mayo, and perhaps kimchi or *koko* (salted cabbage). There are countless choices of main protein such as chicken *katsu* (fried cutlet), fried mahimahi and beef tomato. The king of all plate lunches is the Hawaiian plate. The main item is laulau or kalua pig and cabbage along with poi, *lomilomi* salmon, chicken long rice, and sticky white rice.

Bento Box

The bento box gained popularity back in the plantation days, when workers toiled in the sugarcane fields. No one brought sandwiches to work then. Instead it was a lunch box with the ever-present steamed white rice, pickled *ume* (plum) to preserve the rice, and main meats such as fried chicken or fish. Today, many stores sell prepackaged bentos or you may go to an *okazuya* (Japanese deli) with a hot buffet counter and create your own.

Malasadas

The Portuguese have contributed much to Hawaii cuisine in the form of sausage, soup, and sweetbread. But their most revered food is *malasadas*, hot, deep-fried doughnuts rolled in sugar. Malasadas are crowd-pleasers. Buy them by the dozen, hot from the fryer, placed in brown paper bags to absorb the grease. Or bite into gourmet malasadas at restaurants, filled with vanilla or chocolate cream.

Shave Ice

Much more than just a snow cone, shave ice is what locals crave after a blazing day at the beach or a hot-as-Hades game of soccer. If you're lucky, you'll find a neighborhood store that hand-shaves the ice, but it's rare. Either way, the counter person will ask you first if you'd like ice cream and/or adzuki beans scooped into the bottom of the cone or cup. Then they shape the ice to a giant mound and add colorful fruit syrups. First-timers should order the Rainbow, of course.

Crack Seed

There are dozens of varieties of crack seed in dwindling specialty shops and at the drug stores. Chinese call the preserved fruits and nuts *see mui* but somehow the Pidgin English version is what Hawaiians prefer. Those who like hard candy and salty foods will love li hing mangoes and rock salt plums, and those with an itchy throat will feel relief from the lemon strips. Peruse large glass jars of crack seed sold in bulk or smaller hanging bags—the latter make good gifts to give to friends back home.

BEST FARMERS' MARKETS IN HAWAII

Oahu

Although there are exceptions, the **People's Open Market** dominates farmers' markets on Oahu. Others include the **Saturday Farmers' Market** at Kapiolani Community College on Diamond Head Road in Honolulu, **Thursday Kailua Farmers' Market** at Kailua Square Shopping Center, **Restaurant Row Farmers' Market** right on Ala Moana Boulevard in Honolulu (buy produce after you eat a restaurant meal!), **Waikiki Farmers' Market** at the Waikiki Community Center, and the **North Shore Country Market at Sunset** in Haleiwa. The Hawaii Farm Bureau (⊕ *whfbf.org/markets*) has information and weekly tip sheets about farmers' markets on O'ahu.

Maui

Exotic oddities and fresh organic produce are wowing attendees of the **Ono Organic Farms** farmers' market near Hasegawa General store in Hana, where you can taste from durian to star apple to egg fruit. **Maui Swap Meet** on Kahului Beach Road at Maui Community College is a great way to spend your Saturday. Peruse coconuts sliced open for you by a machete-wielding Tongan, banana bread just out of the oven, and much more. There are plenty of crafts as well. **The Upcountry Farmers' Market**, near the Longs Drug Center in Pukalani, sells wonderful local produce every Saturday morning.

Those just heading back to the condo from the beach on Saturday morning will want to make leisurely pit stops at Maui farmers' markets in **Kihei** (on Lipoa Street) and **Honokowai** (at Hawaiian Motors parking lot).

Big Island

Each Hawaiian Island has its own flavor when it comes to farmers' markets. Because of its vast size, the Big Island even boasts specialties from its various regions. For instance, those who shop at **Naalehu Farmers' Market,** in front of Ace Hardware at South Point, will find the best local Kau oranges.

Head to **Hilo Farmers' Market** on the corner of Kamehemeha Avenue and Mamo Street along with Keaau Village Farmers' Market on Old Volcano Road and you'll get the ripest and most colorful papaya displayed at the state's lowest prices, along with jams, salsas, and an incredible variety of Asian street-food treats and gorgeous local flowers.

Kailua Village Farmers' Market, at the corner of Alii Drive and Hualalai Road, has produce, macadamia nuts and, of course, Kona coffee. For a taste of things "hippie" and "New Age," **Pahoa Village Farmers' Market** in eccentric Pahoa can't be beat. On Saturday morning **The Hawaiian Homesteaders Association Farmers' Market** is a lively stop if you're in Waimea.

Kauai

Sunshine Markets almost has a monopoly on Kauai with weekly displays all over the island. Luckily, the selection is good and the produce is quality. **Kekaha Neighborhood Center** on Elepaio Road in Kekaha is just one of six produced by Sunshine Markets. Others include **Kalaheo Neighborhood Center** on Papalina Road in Kalaheo, **Kapaa New Town Park** on Kahau Road in Kapaa, **Kilauea Neighborhood Center** off Lighthouse Road in Kilauea, **Koloa Ball Park** on Maluhia Road in Koloa, and **Vidinha Stadium** in Lihue.

The independent **Kauai Community Market** thrives on the campus of the local community college across from Grove Farm.

KIDS AND FAMILIES

With dozens of adventures, discoveries, and fun-filled beach days, Hawaii is a blast with kids. Even better, the things to do here do not appeal only to small fry. The entire family, parents included, will enjoy surfing, discovering a waterfall in the rain forest, and snorkeling with sea turtles. And there are plenty of organized activities for kids that will free parents' time for a few romantic beach strolls.

Choosing a Place to Stay

Resorts: All the big resorts make kids' programs a priority, and it shows. When you are booking your room, ask about "kids eat free" deals and the number of kids' pools at the resort. Also check out the size of the groups in the children's programs, and find out whether the cost of the programs includes lunch, equipment, and activities.

Condos: Condo and vacation rentals are a fantastic value for families vacationing in Hawaii. You can cook your own food, which is cheaper than eating out and sometimes easier (especially if you have a finicky eater in your group), and you'll get twice the space of a hotel room for about a quarter of the price. If you decide to go the condo route, be sure to ask about the size of the complex's pool (some try to pawn a tiny soaking tub off as a pool) and whether barbecues are available.

Ocean Activities

Hawaii is all about getting your kids outside—away from TV and video games. And who could resist the turquoise water, the promise of spotting dolphins or whales, and the fun of boogie boarding or surfing?

On the Beach: Most people like being in the water, but toddlers and school-age kids are often completely captivated by Hawaii's beaches. The swimming pool at your condo or hotel is always an option, but don't be afraid to hit the beach with a little one in tow. There are several in Hawaii that are nearly as safe as a pool—completely protected bays with pleasant white-sand beaches. As always, use your judgment, and heed all posted signs and lifeguard warnings.

On the Waves: Surf lessons are a great idea for older kids, especially if Mom and Dad want a little quiet time. Beginner lessons are always on safe and easy waves and last anywhere from two to four hours.

The Underwater World: If your kids are ready to try snorkeling, Hawaii is a great place to introduce them to the underwater world. Even without the mask and snorkel, they'll be able to see colorful fish darting this way and that, and they may also spot turtles and dolphins at many of the island beaches.

Land Activities

In addition to beach experiences, Hawaii has rain forests, botanical gardens, aquariums (Oahu and Maui), and even petting zoos and hands-on children's museums that will keep your kids entertained and out of the sun for a day.

After Dark

At night, younger kids get a kick out of luau, and many of the shows incorporate young audience members, adding to the fun. The older kids might find it all a bit lame, but there are a handful of new shows in the Islands that are more modern, incorporating acrobatics, lively music, and fire dancers. If you're planning on hitting a luau with a teen in tow, we highly recommend going the modern route.

ONLY IN HAWAII

Traveling to Hawaii is as close as an American can get to visiting another country while staying within the United States. There's much to learn and understand about the state's indigenous culture, the hundred years of immigration that resulted in today's blended society, and the tradition of aloha that has welcomed millions of visitors over the years.

Aloha Shirt

To go to Hawaii without taking an aloha shirt home is almost sacrilege. The first aloha shirts from the 1920s and 1930s—called "silkies"—were classic canvases of art and tailored for the tourists. Popular culture caught on in the 1950s, and they became a fashion craze. With the 1960s' more subdued designs, Aloha Friday was born, and the shirt became appropriate clothing for work, play, and formal occasions. Because of its soaring popularity, cheaper and mass-produced versions became available.

Hawaiian Quilt

Although ancient Hawaiians were already known to produce fine *kapa* (bark) cloth, the actual art of quilting originated from the missionaries. Hawaiians have created designs to reflect their own aesthetic, and bold patterns evolved over time. They can be pricey because the quilts are intricately made by hand and can take years to finish. These masterpieces are considered precious heirlooms that reflect the history and beauty of Hawaii.

Popular Souvenirs

Souvenir shopping can be intimidating. There's a sea of Islands-inspired and often kitschy merchandise, so we'd like to give you a breakdown of popular and fun gifts that you might encounter and consider bringing home. If authenticity is important to you, be sure to check labels and ask shopkeepers. Museum shops are good places for authentic, Hawaiian-made souvenirs.

Fabrics. Purchased by the yard or already made into everything from napkins to bedspreads, modern Hawaiian fabrics make wonderful keepsakes.

Home accessories. Deck out your kitchen or dining room in festive luau style with bottle openers, pineapple mugs, tiki glasses, shot glasses, slipper and surfboard magnets, and salt-and-pepper shakers.

Lei and shell necklaces. From silk or polyester flower lei to kukui or puka shell necklaces, lei have been traditionally used as a welcome offering to guests (although the artificial ones are more for fun, as real flowers are always preferable).

Lauhala products. *Lauhala* weaving is a traditional Hawaiian art. The leaves come from the hala, or pandanus, tree and are hand-woven to create lovely gift boxes, baskets, bags, and picture frames.

Spa products. Relive your spa treatment at home with Hawaiian bath and body products, many of them manufactured with ingredients found only on the Islands.

Vintage Hawaii. You can find vintage photos, reproductions of vintage postcards or paintings, heirloom jewelry, and vintage aloha wear in many specialty stores.

Luau

The luau's origin, which was a celebratory feast, can be traced back to the earliest Hawaiian civilizations. In the traditional luau, the taboo or *kapu* laws were very strict, requiring men and women to eat separately. However, in 1819 King Kamehameha II broke the great taboo and shared a feast with women and commoners ushering in the modern-era luau. Today, traditional luau usually commemorate a

child's first birthday, graduation, wedding, or other family occasion. They also are a Hawaiian experience that most visitors enjoy, and resorts and other companies have incorporated the fire-knife dance and other Polynesian dances into their elaborate presentations.

Nose flutes

The nose flute is an instrument used in ancient times to serenade a lover. For the Hawaiians, the nose is romantic, sacred, and pure. The Hawaiian word for kiss is *honi*. Similar to an Eskimo's kiss, the noses touch on each side sharing one's spiritual energy or breath. The Hawaiian term, *ohe hano ihu*, simply translated to "bamboo," with which the instrument is made; "breathe," because one has to gently breathe through it to make soothing music; and "nose," as it is made for the nose and not the mouth.

Slack-Key Guitar and the Paniolo

Kihoalu, or slack-key music, evolved in the early 1800s when King Kamehameha III brought in Mexican and Spanish vaqueros to manage the overpopulated cattle that had run wild on the Islands. The vaqueros brought their guitars and would play music around the campfire after work. When they left, supposedly leaving their guitars to their new friends, the Hawaiian *paniolo,* or cowboys, began to infuse what they learned from the vaqueros with their native music and chants, and so the art of slack-key music was born.

Today, the paniolo culture thrives where ranchers have settled.

Ukulele

The word *ukulele* literally translates to the "the jumping flea" and came to Hawaii in the 1880s by way of the Portuguese and Spanish. Once a fading art form, today it brings international kudos as a solo instrument, thanks to tireless musicians and teachers who have worked hard to keep it by our fingertips.

One such teacher is Roy Sakuma. Founder of four ukulele schools and a legend in his own right, Sakuma and his wife Kathy produced Oahu's first Ukulele Festival in 1971. Since then, they've brought the tradition to the Big Island, Kauai, and Maui. The free event annually draws thousands of artists and fans from all over the globe.

Hula

"Hula is the language of the heart, therefore the heartbeat of the Hawaiian people." —Kalakaua, the Merrie Monarch. Thousands—from tots to seniors—devote hours each week to hula classes. All these dancers need some place to show off their stuff. The result is a network of hula competitions (generally free or very inexpensive) and free performances in malls and other public spaces. Many resorts offer hula instruction.

BEST BEACHES

No one ever gets as much beach time in Hawaii as they planned to, it seems, but it's a problem of time, not beaches. Beaches of every size, color (even green), and description line the state's many shorelines.

They have different strengths: some are great for sitting, but not so great for swimming. Some offer beach-park amenities like lifeguards and showers, whereas others are more private and isolated. Read up before you head out.

Oahu

Makapuu Beach. Quite possibly Oahu's most breathtaking scenic view—with a hiking trail to a historic lighthouse, offshore views of two rocky islets, home to thousands of nesting seabirds, and hang gliders launching off nearby cliffs.

While the white-sand beach and surroundings adorn many postcards, the treacherous ocean's currents invite experienced body boarders only.

Kailua Beach Park. This is a true family beach, offering something for everyone: A long stretch of sand for walking, turquoise seas set against cobalt skies for impressive photographs, a sandy-bottom shoreline for ocean swimming, and grassy expanses underneath shade trees for picnics.

You can even rent a kayak and make the short paddle to Popia (Flat) Island. This is Windward Oahu, so expect wind—all the better if you're an avid windsurfer or kiteboarder.

Waimea Bay. This is the beach that makes Hawaii famous every winter when monster waves and the world's best surfers roll in.

Show up to watch, not partake. If the rest of us want to get in the water here, we have to wait until summer when the safe, onshore break is great for novice bodysurfers.

White Plains. This beach is equal parts Kailua Beach Park with its facilities and tree-covered barbecue areas and Waikiki with its numerous surf breaks—minus the crowds and high-rises.

Pack for the day—cooler with food and drink, snorkel gear, inflatables, and body board—as this destination is 35 minutes from downtown Honolulu.

Maui

Napili Beach. There is much to love about this intimate, crescent-shaped beach. Sunbathing, snorkeling, swimming, bodysurfing, and—after a full day of beach fun—startling sunsets. Bring the kids; they'll love the turtles that nosh on the *limu* (seaweed) growing on the lava rocks.

Makena (Big Beach). Don't forget the camera for this one. A bit remote and tricky to find, the effort is worth it—a long, wide stretch of golden sand and translucent offshore water. It's beautiful, yes, but the icing on the cake is this beach is never crowded. Use caution for swimming because the steep, onshore break can get big.

Waianapanapa State Park. The rustic beauty will capture your heart here—a black-sand beach framed by lava cliffs and backed by bright green *naupaka* bushes. Ocean currents can be strong, so cool off in one of two freshwater pools.

Get an early start, because your day's destination is just shy of Hana and requires a short, quarter-mile walk.

Big Island

Hapuna Beach State Recreation Area. It's hard to know where to start with this beach—the long, perfect crescent of sand, the calm, turquoise waters, rocky points for snorkeling, even surf in winter. Just about everyone can find something to love

here. With its west-facing views, this is a good spot for sunsets.

Kaunaoa Beach (Mauna Kea Beach). This is like the big brother, more advanced version of Hapuna Beach with snorkeling, bodysurfing, and board surfing but trickier currents, so be careful. Still, it's worth it. Try them both and let us know which you prefer. For most, it's a toss-up.

Papakolea Beach (Green Sand Beach). Papakolea makes our list, because, really, how often do you run across a green-sand beach? That's right, green. The greenish tint here is caused by an accumulation of olivine crystals that formed in volcanic eruptions.

This isn't the most swimmable of beaches, but the sand, sculpted cliffs and dry, barren landscape make it quite memorable. A steep, 2-mile hike is required to access the beach.

Punaluu Beach Park (Black Sand Beach). This might as well be called Turtle Beach. Both the endangered Hawaiian green sea turtle and hawksbill turtle bask on the rocky, black-sand beach here.

We prefer to stay dry at this beach—due to strong rip currents—and snap pictures of the turtles and picnic under one of the many pavilions.

Kauai

Haena Beach Park (Tunnels Beach). Even if all you do is sit on the beach, you'll leave here happy. The scenic beauty is unsurpassed, with verdant mountains serving as a backdrop to the turquoise ocean.

Snorkeling is the best on the island during the calm, summer months. When the winter's waves arrive, surfers line up on the outside break.

Hanalei Bay Beach Park. When you dream of Hawaii, this is what comes to mind: a vast bay rimmed by a wide beach and waterfalls draping distant mountains. Everyone finds something to do here—surf, kayak, swim, sail, sunbathe, walk and celebrity-watch.

Like most north shore beaches in Hawaii, Hanalei switches from calm in summer to big waves in winter.

Poipu Beach Park. The *keiki* (child's) swimming hole makes Poipu a great family beach, but it's also popular with snorkelers and moderate-to-experienced surfers. And while Poipu is considered a tourist destination, the Kauai residents come out on the weekends, adding a local flavor.

Be mindful of the endangered Hawaiian monk seals; they like it here, too.

Polihale State Park. If you're looking for remote, if you're looking for guaranteed sun, or if you're thinking of camping on the beach, drive the 5-mile-long cane-haul road to the westernmost point of Kauai. Be sure to stay for the sunset.

Unless you're an experienced water person, we advise staying out of the water due to a steep, onshore break. You can walk for miles along this beach, the longest in Hawaii.

BEST OUTDOOR ADVENTURES

In a place surrounded by the ocean, water sports like surfing, snorkeling, and scuba diving abound. Hawaii has it all—and more. But that's just the sea. Interior mountains and valleys offer a never-ending stream of other outdoor adventures. Here are our picks for the best water and land adventures around the state.

Oahu

Dive and snorkel at Shark's Cove. Some of the best things in life require a wait. That's the case with Shark's Cove—you have to wait for summer until it's safe to enter the water and swim with an amazing array of marine life thanks to the large boulders and coral heads dotting the sea floor and forming small caves and ledges. This is both a spectacular shore dive and snorkeling destination in one—perfect for the diver-snorkeler couple.

Bike the Aiea Loop Trail. This 4.5-mile, single-track, loop trail offers some of the most fun mountain biking in central Oahu. Although it's listed as an intermediate trail, some sections are a bit more difficult, with steep drop-offs. We recommend it for the weekend warrior who has a bit more experience. Caution: Do not attempt in wet weather.

Golf at the Royal Hawaiian Golf Club. Carved out of the middle of a tropical rain forest, this peaceful setting offers an antidote to the hustle and bustle of Waikiki. Bring your "A" game and a full bag, because club selection is key here. You'll want to hit each and every fairway.

Learn to surf at Waikiki Beach. You've heard the age-old saying that goes, "When in Rome, do as the Romans do." Well, when in Hawaii, surf. The sport that was once reserved for *alii*, or royalty, knows no class barrier these days. And there is no better place to learn than Waikiki, with its long and gentle rolling swells.

Hike to Kaena Point. For a raw and rugged look at Oahu's coastline, head to hot, dry Kaena Point. Head out early in the morning as Kaena Point is situated at the northwestern tip of the island (about 45 minutes from Waikiki). The 5-mile round-trip hike—rather, walk—ends at the westernmost tip of the island.

Maui

Explore Molokini Crater. Snorkeling here is like swimming in a tropical-fish aquarium. Molokini is a crescent-shaped crater that barely peeks its ridged spine above the ocean's surface, and the reef fish love it. If you're not comfortable leaping off the side of a boat into the open ocean, you may not go for this. Go early before the winds pick up.

Golf at Kapalua Resort. Geoff Ogilvy and Rory Sabbatini know a thing or two about the Plantation Course at Kapalua, the site of the PGA Tour's first event each January. You can take them on—sort of—by playing in their footsteps. Sabbatini owned the course on his fourth round in 2010, shooting a 63. Slope and wind will challenge the best of golfers here.

Hike in Haleakala Crater. How about hiking on black sand on the top of a mountain? There aren't many places you can do that. Thirty miles of trails await here—everything from day hikes to multiday pack trips. At 10,000 feet and summit temperatures ranging from 40 to 60 degrees, you'll forget you're in Hawaii.

Snorkel at Kekaa. We like Kekaa Point for its big marine life: a turtle the size of a small car, eagle rays with three-foot wingspans, and all kinds of Hawaii's colorful endemic fish. But keep an eye

out above, too, because this is a popular cliff-diving spot.

Big Island

Bike Kulani Trails. Stands of 80-foot eucalyptus. Giant tree ferns. The sweet song of honeycreepers overhead. Add single-track of rock and root—no dirt here—and we're talking a technically difficult ride. Did we mention this is a rain forest? That explains the perennial slick coat of slime on every possible surface. Advanced cyclists only.

Snorkel at Kealakekua Bay. Yes, the snorkeling here is tops for Big Island but, to be real, the draw here are the Hawaiian spinner dolphins that rest in the bay during the daytime. While it's enticing to swim with wild dolphins, doing so can disrupt their sleep patterns and make them susceptible to predators—aka sharks—so stick to an early morning or late afternoon schedule and give the dolphins their space between 9 and 3.

Search for lava at Volcanoes National Park. It isn't too often that you can witness the creation of rock in action. That's just what happens at Volcanoes National Park. The most dramatic example occurs where lava enters the sea. While Mother Nature rarely gives her itinerary in advance, if you're lucky, a hike or boat ride may pay off with spectacular views of nature's wonder. Sunrise and sunset makes for the best viewing opportunities.

Go horseback riding in Waipio Valley. The Valley of the Kings owes its relative isolation and off-the-grid status to the two-thousand-foot cliffs book-ending the valley. Really, the only way to explore this sacred place is on two legs—or four. We're partial to the horseback rides that wend deep into the rain forest to a series of waterfalls and pools—the setting for a perfect romantic getaway.

Kauai

Tour Napali Coast by boat. Every one of the Hawaiian Islands possesses something spectacularly unique to it, and this stretch of folding cliffs is it for Kauai. To see it, though, you'll want to hop aboard a boat. You may opt for the leisurely ride aboard a catamaran or the more adventurous inflatable raft. You can even stop for snorkeling or a walk through an ancient fishing village. Whatever you do, don't forget your camera.

Kayak the Wailua River. The largest river in all Hawaii, the Wailua River's source is the center of the island—a place known as Mt. Waiaheale—the wettest spot on Earth. And yet it's no Mighty Mississippi. There are no rapids to run. And that makes it a great waterway for learning to kayak. Guided tours will take you to a remote waterfall. Bring the whole family on this one.

Hike the Kalalau Trail. The Sierra Club allegedly rates this famous, cliff-side trail a difficulty level of 9 out of 10. But don't let that stop you. You don't have to hike the entire 11 miles. A mile hike will reward you with scenic ocean views—where in winter you might see breaching whales—sights of soaring seabirds and tropical plant life dotting the trail sides. Wear sturdy shoes, pack your camera, and be prepared to "ooh" and "aah."

Enjoy a Helicopter Ride. If you drive from Kee Beach to Polihale, you may think you've seen all of Kauai, but we're here to tell you there's more scenic beauty awaiting you. Lots more. Save up for this one. It's not cheap, but a helicopter ride over the Garden Island will make you think you're watching a movie with 3-D glasses.

TOP SCENIC SPOTS

Oahu

Nuuanu Pali Lookout. With sweeping views of the verdant Koolau Mountains and Kaneohe Bay, the point where Kamehameha I forced enemy warriors over the cliff is a must-stop on any tour around the island.

Waikiki Beach at sunset. This is quintessential Oahu: sailboats and catamarans cruise offshore, Diamond Head glows magenta in the last rays of sunlight while the turquoise Pacific washes gently up to pristine beaches.

Bellows Beach Park. With sugary coral sand and jade green waters this giant arc of a beach is why people come to Hawaii. While the colors of the sea and sand and few crowds are its best features, the jagged Koolau Mountains provide a backdrop for this idyllic tropical spot.

Maui

The Road to Hana. Calling the Road to Hana a "scenic spot" may be playing it down. With innumerable waterfalls, black-sand beaches, views over taro patches, and the sheer engineering involved in the narrow bridges and switchback curves, this stretch of highway in a tropical paradise provides scenic views around every corner.

Haleakala. Most known for its views at sunrise, the summit of Haleakala volcano is equally spectacular at sunset. On clear days the Big Island, Molokai, Lanai, Kahoolawe, and Molokini Crater are visible.

Makena Beach. Rolling waves, views of Kahoolawe, and golden sand make this wide beach a weekend favorite for locals.

The Big Island

Top of Mauna Kea at sunset. At almost 14,000 feet, a view from this cinder-covered summit at sunset provides an opportunity not only to see the sun slip into the Pacific through the pristine alpine atmosphere but also fabulous views of Maui's Haleakala.

Waipio Valley Overlook. The road along the Hamakua Coast ends with a view into one of the Big Island's most remote areas. From this point, view sheer black cliffs and the wide green valley that was once home to between 4,000 to 20,000 Hawaiians.

Hawaii Tropical Botanical Garden. Drive past waterfalls, ponds, orchids, and lush green vegetation on one of the Big Island's most scenic roads.

Kauai

Waimea Canyon. The oft-used term *breathtaking* does not do justice to your first view of Waimea Canyon (otherwise known as the Grand Canyon of the Pacific). Narrow waterfalls tumble thousands of feet to streams that cut through the rust-colored volcanic soil. Continue on to the end of the road for a view through the clouds of otherworldly Kalalau Valley.

Hanalei Valley Lookout. On the way to Hanalei (just past the Princeville shops), this pull-out provides views of Hanalei River winding its way through wet *loi* (taro patches) framed by jagged green mountains.

Kee Beach. At the end of the road on the North Shore, Kee Beach is as far as you can drive and as close as you can get to the fabled cliffs of Bali Hai. Surrounded by palm and almond trees, this stretch of white-sand beach is a great spot for viewing sunsets or even the occasional sea lion.

ULTIMATE HAWAIIAN INDULGENCES

Many indulgences in Hawaii don't require reservations, appointments, or making a serious dent in your credit card. They can be as simple as lingering a bit longer in a botanical garden, smelling the plumeria or ginger flowers, or stealing a bit of time away for yourself and a book under an umbrella at one of countless secluded beaches. However, because of Hawaii's world-class spas, chefs, and scenery, extravagant indulgences for the hedonist or gastronome abound.

Oahu

SpaHalekulani at the Halekulani Hotel in Waikiki offers a truly indulgent experience for two. Its Romance Remembered package is a six-hour experience which features massage, steam shower, a champagne lunch in a terrace setting, and concludes with a manicure and pedicure in the salon. For individuals, the four-hour Heavenly Journey offers a scrub and wrap, a soak in a deep Japanese soaking tub, a light lunch on their terrace, and a facial.

Looking for a gastronomic experience? **La Mer** in Waikiki offers a gourmet menu degustation including cherrywood-smoked foie gras and sweet potato gnocchi with duck jus.

Maui

The traditional lomilomi massage at the **Spa at the Four Seasons Resort Wailea** is given in their *hale* (a small replica of an ancient Hawaiian home) overlooking Wailea Bay. The pair of therapists works in unison as they chant and dance while providing a restorative treatment that seeks to unite both mind and body.

Or, have your own personal chef prepare the decadent chocolate and berries dessert to cap off your meal in the private Il Teatro dining room at **Capische at the Hotel Wailea**.

For those with a bit less time and money, the decadent mango margarita at **Polli's Mexican Restaurant** in Makawao is a frozen tropical twist on a traditional favorite. Stop in on your way to or from your trip to Haleakala.

Big Island

Mauna Lani Spa has a unique Lava Watsu treatment that features pressure point techniques and stretching, but the treatment itself is only the beginning. Built inside a natural lava tube, this saltwater Watsu pool is heated to body temperature. Clients float weightlessly throughout a treatment experience that is enhanced by a waterfall and underwater music.

Kauai

Kauai's natural wonders are a perfect opportunity to indulge in a helicopter ride. **Jack Harter Helicopters** offers an aerial tour of dramatic waterfalls and the spectacular Napali coastline—to avoid reflections in your photos, opt for a doors-off trip.

For those who prefer a more soothing experience; relax in your own private cabana in a tropical garden setting of orchids, ti, and other tropical greenery, as you experience the Kauai Clay detoxifying facial treatment at **ANARA Spa**. This treatment features a kava root scrub and mask made from local clays of Kauai.

WEDDINGS AND HONEYMOONS

There's no question that Hawaii is one of the country's foremost honeymoon destinations. Romance is in the air here, and the white, sandy beaches, turquoise water, swaying palm trees, balmy tropical breezes, and perpetual sunshine put people in the mood for love. It's easy to understand why Hawaii is fast becoming a popular wedding destination as well, especially as the cost of airfare is often discounted, new resorts and hotels entice visitors, and as of January 2012 the state now recognizes and grants civil unions. A destination wedding is no longer exclusive to celebrities and the superrich. You can plan a traditional ceremony in a place of worship followed by a reception at an elegant resort, or you can go barefoot on the beach and celebrate at a luau. There are almost as many wedding planners in the Islands as real estate agents, which makes it oh-so-easy to wed in paradise, and then, once the knot is tied, stay and honeymoon as well.

The Big Day

Choosing the Perfect Place. When choosing a location, remember that you really have two choices to make: the ceremony location and where to have the reception, if you're having one. For the former, there are beaches, bluffs overlooking beaches, gardens, private residences, resort lawns, and, of course, places of worship. As for the reception, there are these same choices, as well as restaurants and even luau. If you decide to go outdoors, remember the seasons—yes, Hawaii has seasons. If you're planning a winter wedding outdoors, be sure you have a backup plan (such as a tent), in case it rains. Also, if you're planning an outdoor wedding at sunset—which is very popular—be sure you match the time of your ceremony to the time the sun sets at that time of year. If

you choose an indoor spot, be sure to ask for pictures of the location when you're planning. You don't want to plan a pink wedding, say, and wind up in a room that's predominantly red. Or maybe you do. The point is, it should be your choice.

Finding a Wedding Planner. If you're planning to invite more than a minister and your loved one to your wedding ceremony, seriously consider an on-island wedding planner who can help select a location, help design the floral scheme and recommend a florist as well as a photographer, help plan the menu and choose a restaurant, caterer, or resort, and suggest any Hawaiian traditions to incorporate into your ceremony. And more: Will you need tents, a cake, music? Maybe transportation and lodging? Many planners have relationships with vendors, providing packages—which mean savings.

If you're planning a resort wedding, most have on-site wedding coordinators; however, there are many independents around the Islands and even those who specialize in certain types of ceremonies—by locale, size, religious affiliation, and so on. A simple "Hawaii weddings" Google search will reveal dozens. What's important is that you feel comfortable with your coordinator. Ask for references—and call them. Share your budget. Get a proposal—in writing. Ask how long they've been in business, how much they charge, how often you'll meet with them, and how they select vendors. Request a detailed list of the exact services they'll provide. If your idea of your wedding doesn't match their services, try someone else. If you can afford it, you might want to meet the planner in person.

Getting Your License. The good news about marrying in Hawaii is that no waiting period, no residency or citizenship

requirements, and no blood tests or shots are required. However, both the bride and groom must appear together in person before a marriage-license agent to apply for a marriage license. You'll need proof of age—the legal age to marry is 18. (If you're 19 or older, a valid driver's license will suffice; if you're 18, a certified birth certificate is required.) Upon approval, a marriage license is immediately issued and costs $60, cash only. After the ceremony, your officiant will mail the marriage license to the state. Approximately four months later, you will receive a copy in the mail. (For $10 extra, you can expedite this process. Ask your marriage-license agent when you apply.) For more detailed information, visit ⊕ *www.ehawaii.gov.*

Also—this is important—the person performing your wedding must be licensed by the Hawaii Department of Health, even if he or she is a licensed minister. Be sure to ask.

Wedding Attire. In Hawaii, basically anything goes, from long, formal dresses with trains to white bikinis. Floral sundresses are fine, too. For the men, tuxedos are not the norm; a pair of solid-colored slacks with a nice aloha shirt is. In fact, tradition in Hawaii for the groom is a plain white aloha shirt (they do exist) with slacks or long shorts and a colored sash around the waist. If you're planning a wedding on the beach, barefoot is the way to go.

If you decide to marry in a formal dress and tuxedo, you're better off making your selections on the mainland and hand-carrying them aboard the plane. Yes, it can be a pain, but ask your wedding-gown retailer to provide a special carrying bag. After all, you don't want to chance losing your wedding dress in a wayward piece of luggage. And when it comes to fittings, again, that's something to take care of before you arrive in Hawaii.

Local customs. The most obvious traditional Hawaiian wedding custom is the lei exchange in which the bride and groom take turns placing a lei around the neck of the other—with a kiss. Bridal lei are usually floral, whereas the groom's is typically made of *maile*, a green leafy garland that drapes around the neck and is open at the ends. Brides often also wear a *lei poo*—a circular floral headpiece. Other Hawaiian customs include the blowing of the conch shell, hula, chanting, and Hawaiian music.

The Honeymoon

Do you want champagne and strawberries delivered to your room each morning? A breathtaking swimming pool in which to float? A five-star restaurant in which to dine? Then a resort is the way to go. If, however, you prefer the comforts of a home, try a bed-and-breakfast. A small inn is also good if you're on a tight budget or don't plan to spend much time in your room. On the other hand, maybe you want your own private home in which to romp naked—or just laze around recovering from the wedding planning. Maybe you want your own kitchen so you can whip up a gourmet meal for your loved one. In that case, a private vacation-rental home is the answer. Or maybe a condominium resort. That's another beautiful thing about Hawaii: the lodging accommodations are almost as plentiful as the beaches, and there's one that will perfectly match your tastes and your budget.

CRUISING THE HAWAIIAN ISLANDS

Cruising has become extremely popular in Hawaii. For first-time visitors, it's an excellent way to get a taste of all the Islands; and if you fall in love with one or even two Islands, you know how to plan your next trip.

Cruising to Hawaii

Carnival Cruises. They call them "fun ships" for a reason—Carnival is all about keeping you busy and showing you a good time, both on board and on shore. Great for families, Carnival always plans plenty of kid-friendly activities, and their children's program rates high with the little critics. Carnival offers itineraries starting in Los Angeles, Ensenada, Vancouver, and Honolulu. Their ships stop on Maui (Kahului), the Big Island (Kailua-Kona and Hilo), Oahu, and Kauai. ☎ 888/227–6482 ⊕ www.carnival.com.

Holland America. The grande dame of cruise lines, Holland America has a reputation for service and elegance. Holland America's Hawaii cruises leave from and return to San Diego, California, with a brief stop at Ensenada. In Hawaii, the ship ties up at port in Maui (Lahaina), the Big Island (Hilo), Oahu, and Kauai (Nawiliwili). Holland America also offers longer itineraries (30-plus days) that include Hawaii, Tahiti, and the Marquesas and depart from or return to San Diego, Seattle, or Vancouver. ☎ 877/932–4259 ⊕ www.hollandamerica.com.

Princess Cruises. Princess strives to offer affordable luxury. Their prices start out a little higher, but you get more bells and whistles (affordable balcony rooms, nicer decor, more restaurants to choose from, personalized service). They're not fantastic for kids, but they do a great job of keeping teenagers occupied. *Golden Princess, Sapphire Princess,* and *Star Princess*

sail from Los Angeles on a 14-day round-trip voyage with calls at Hilo on the Big Island, Honolulu, Kauai, and Lahaina on Maui, plus Ensenada, Mexico. There are also 15-day cruises out of San Francisco. In addition, the line offers longer cruises—up to 29 day—that include stops in Hawaii and the South Pacific. ☎ 800/774–6237 ⊕ www.princess.com.

Cruising within Hawaii

American Safari Cruises. Except for the summer months when its yachts cruise Alaska, American Safari Cruises offers round-trip, eight-day, seven-night interisland cruises departing from Lahaina, Maui. The *Safari Explorer* accommodates only 36 passengers; its smaller size allows it to dock at Molokai and Lanai, in addition to a stop on the island of Hawaii. The cruise is all-inclusive, with even shore excursions, water activities, and a massage included as part of the deal. ☎ 888/862–8881 ⊕ www.americansafaricruises.com.

Hawaii Nautical. Offering a completely different sort of experience, Hawaii Nautical provides private multiple-day interisland cruises on their catamarans, yachts, and sailboats. Prices are higher, but service is completely personal, right down to the itinerary. ☎ 808/234–7245 ⊕ www.hawaiinautical.com.

Norwegian Cruise Lines. Norwegian is the only major operator to offer interisland cruises in Hawaii. *Pride of America* sails year-round and offers seven-day itineraries within the Islands stopping on Maui, Oahu, the Big Island (Hilo), and overnighting on Kauai. The ship has a vintage Americana theme and a big family focus with lots of connecting staterooms and suites. ☎ 800/327–7030 ⊕ www.ncl.com.

Oahu

WORD OF MOUTH

"[W]e rented a car for just one day and were able to drive all the way around the island, stopping here and there. [We w]ent to the pineapple plantation, Haleiwa, Waimea, then around the other side and back to Honolulu. [It was w]orth the time to see more than just the million souvenir shops in Waikiki."

—oregonmom

WELCOME TO OAHU

TOP REASONS TO GO

★ **Waves:** Boogie board or surf some of the best breaks on the planet.

★ **Pearl Harbor:** Remember Pearl Harbor with a visit to the *Arizona* Memorial.

★ **Diamond Head:** Scale the crater whose iconic profile looms over Waikiki.

★ **Nightlife:** Raise your glass to the best party scene in Hawaii.

★ **The North Shore:** See Oahu's countryside—check out the famous beaches from Sunset to Waimea Bay and hike to the remote tip of the island.

1 Honolulu. The vibrant capital city holds the nation's only royal palace, free concerts under the tamarind trees in the financial district, and the art galleries, hipster bars, and open markets of Nuuanu and Chinatown.

2 Waikiki. This is the city from postcards, dressed in lights at the base of Diamond Head, famous for its world-class shopping, restaurants, and surf.

3 Pearl Harbor. Hawaii's largest natural harbor is also the resting place of the USS *Arizona*, sunk on December 7, 1941. A memorial pays tribute to the 2,390 dead and hundreds wounded in the attack that led the United States into World War II.

4 Southeast Oahu.
Honolulu's main bedroom communities crawl up the steep-sided valleys that flow into Maunalua Bay. Also here are snorkelers' favorite Hanauma Bay and a string of wild and often hidden beaches.

5 Windward Oahu. The sleepy neighborhoods at the base of the majestic Koolau Mountains offer a respite from the bustling city with long stretches of sandy beaches, charming eateries, ancient Hawaiian fishponds, and offshore islands to explore.

6 The North Shore. Best known for its miles of world-class surf breaks and green-sea-turtle sightings, this plantation town also boasts farms, restaurants, and hiking trails.

7 Central Oahu. Though the interstate cuts through much of this fertile region, it's an integral part of Hawaii's rich cultural history. This valley, between the Waianae and Koolau mountains, is an eclectic mix of farms, planned communities, and strip malls.

8 West (Leeward) Oahu. This rugged part of the island is finding a new identity as a "second city" of suburban homes, golf courses, and tech firms.

GETTING ORIENTED

Oahu, the third largest of the Hawaiian Islands, is not just Honolulu and Waikiki. It's looping mountain trails on the western Waianae and eastern Koolau ranges. It's monster waves breaking on the golden beaches of the North Shore. It's country stores and beaches where turtles are your swimming companions.

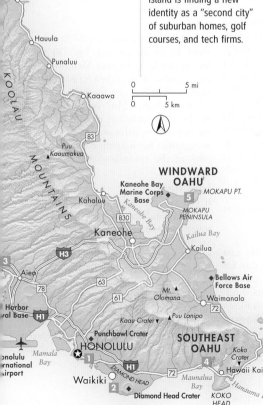

GREAT ITINERARIES

To experience even a fraction of Oahu's charms, you need a minimum of four days and a bus pass. Five days and a car is better: Waikiki is at least a day, Honolulu and Chinatown another, Pearl Harbor the better part of another. Each of the rural sections can swallow a day each, just for driving, sightseeing, and stopping to eat. And that's before you've taken a surf lesson, hung from a parasail, hiked a loop trail, or visited a botanical garden. The following itineraries will take you to our favorite spots on the island.

First Day in Waikiki

You'll be up at dawn due to the time change and dead on your feet by afternoon due to jet lag. Have a dawn swim, change into walking gear, and head east along Kalakaua Avenue to Monsarrat Avenue toward Diamond Head. Either climb to the summit (about 1½ hours round-trip) or enjoy the view from the lookout. After lunch—there are plenty of options along Monsarrat—take a nap in the shade, do some shopping, or visit the nearby East Honolulu neighborhoods of Moiliili and Kaimuki, rife with small shops and quaint restaurants. End the day with an early and inexpensive dinner at one of these neighborhood spots.

Southeast and Windward Exploring

For sand, sun, and surf, follow H1 east to the keyhole-shaped Hanauma Bay for picture-perfect snorkeling, then round the southeast tip of the island with its windswept cliffs and the famous Halona Blowhole. Watch bodysurfers at Sandy Beach or walk up the trail leading to the Makapuu Point Lighthouse. If you like, stop in at Sea Life Park. In Waimanalo, stop for local-style plate lunch or punch on through to Kailua, where there's intriguing shopping and good eating. Lounge at Lanikai Beach until sunset, then grab dinner at one of the area's many restaurants.

The North Shore

Hit H1 westbound and then H2 to get to the North Shore. You'll pass through pineapple fields before dropping down a scenic winding road to Waialua and Haleiwa. Stop in Haleiwa town to shop, enjoy shave ice, and pick up a guided dive or snorkel trip. On winding Kamehameha Highway, stop at famous big-wave beaches, take a dip in a cove with a turtle, and buy fresh island fruit from roadside stands.

Pearl Harbor

Pearl Harbor is almost an all-day investment. Be on the grounds by 7:30 am to line up for USS *Arizona* Memorial tickets. Clamber all over the USS *Bowfin* submarine. Finally, take the free trolley to see the "Mighty Mo" battleship. If it's Wednesday, Saturday, or Sunday, make the five-minute drive *mauka* (toward the mountains) for bargain-basement shopping at the sprawling Aloha Stadium Swap Meet.

Town Time

If you are interested in history, devote a day to Honolulu's historic sites. Downtown, see Iolani Palace, the Kamehameha Statue, and Kawaiahao Church. A few blocks east, explore Chinatown, gilded Kuan Yin Temple, and artsy Nuuanu with its galleries. On the water is the informative Hawaii Maritime Center. Hop west on H1 to the Bishop Museum, the state's anthropological and archaeological center. And 1 mile up Pali Highway is Queen Emma Summer Palace, whose shady grounds were a royal retreat.

2

Oahu is one-stop Hawaii—all the allure of the Islands in a chop-suey mix that has you kayaking around offshore islets by day and sitting in a jazz club 'round midnight, all without ever having to take another flight or repack your suitcase. It offers both the buzz of modern living in jam-packed Honolulu (the state's capital) and the allure of slow-paced island life on its northern and eastern shores. It is, in many ways, the center of the Hawaiian universe.

There are more museums, staffed historic sites, and walking tours here than you'll find on any other island. And only here do a wealth of renovated buildings and well-preserved neighborhoods so clearly spin the story of Hawaii's history. It's the only place to experience island-style urbanity, since there are no other true cities in the state. And yet you can get as lost in the rural landscape and be as laid-back as you wish.

Oahu is home to Waikiki, the most famous Hawaiian beach, as well as some of the world's most famous surf on the North Shore and the Islands' best known historical site—Pearl Harbor. If it's isolation, peace, and quiet you want, Oahu might not be for you, but if you'd like a bit of spice with your piece of paradise, this island provides it.

GEOLOGY

Encompassing 597 square miles, Oahu is the third-largest island in the Hawaiian chain. Scientists believe the island was formed about 4 million years ago by two volcanoes: Waianae and Koolau. Waianae, the older of the two, created the mountain range on the western side of the island, whereas Koolau shapes the eastern side. Central Oahu is an elevated plateau bordered by the two mountain ranges, with Pearl Harbor to the south. Several of Oahu's most famous natural landmarks, including Diamond Head and Hanauma Bay, are tuff rings and cinder cones formed during a renewed volcanic stage (roughly 1 million years ago).

Koko Head in Hawaii Kai is a volcanic cinder cone near Hanauma Bay.

FLORA AND FAUNA

The eastern (Koolau) side of Oahu is much cooler and wetter than the western side of the island, which tends to be dry and arid. The island's official flower, the little orange *ilima*, grows predominantly in the east, but lei throughout the island incorporate *ilima*. Numerous tropical fish call the reef at Hanauma Bay home, migrating humpback whales can be spotted off the coast past Waikiki and Diamond Head from December through April, spinner dolphins pop in and out of the island's bays, and dozens of islets off Oahu's eastern coast provide refuge for endangered seabirds.

HISTORY

Oahu is the most populated island because early tourism to Hawaii started here. Although Kilauea volcano on Hawaii was a tourist attraction in the late 1800s, it was the building of the Moana Hotel on Waikiki Beach in 1901 and subsequent advertising of Hawaii to wealthy San Franciscans that really fueled tourism in the Islands. Oahu was drawing tens of thousands of guests yearly when, on December 7, 1941, Japanese Zeros appeared at dawn to bomb Pearl Harbor. Though tourism understandably dipped during the war (Waikiki Beach was fenced with barbed wire), the subsequent memorial only seemed to attract more visitors, and Oahu remains hugely popular with tourists—especially the Japanese—to this day.

CLOSE UP

Seeing Pearl Harbor

Pearl Harbor is a must-see for many, but there are things to know before you go.

Consider whether you want to see only the USS *Arizona* Memorial, or the USS *Bowfin* and USS *Missouri* as well. Allow approximately an hour and 15 minutes for the USS *Arizona* tour, which includes a 23-minute documentary of the Pearl Harbor attack and a ferry ride to the memorial itself.

Plan to arrive early—tickets for the USS *Arizona* Memorial are free and given out on a first-come, first-served basis. They can disappear within an hour. Take some time to enjoy the newly upgraded visitor center, which houses two exhibits using state-of-the-art technology to tell the story of the attack on December 7, 1941.

Strict security measures prohibit purses, backpacks, diaper bags, and camera cases (although cameras are allowed). Strollers are allowed in the visitor center but not in the theaters or on the shuttle boats. Baggage lockers are available for a small fee. Also, don't forget your ID.

Children under four years of age are not allowed on the USS *Bowfin* for safety reasons, and may not enjoy the crowds or waiting in line at other sights.

Older kids are likely to find the more experiential, hands-on history of the USS *Bowfin* and USS *Missouri* memorable.

For more information, visit ⊕ *www.nps.gov/valr.*

OAHU PLANNER

GETTING HERE AND AROUND

AIR TRAVEL

Honolulu International Airport is 20 minutes (40 during rush hour) from Waikiki. Car-rental companies have booths at baggage claim; shuttle buses then take you to the car pickup areas.

GROUND TRANSPOR-TATION An inefficient airport taxi system requires you to line up to a taxi wrangler who radios for cars (about $25 to Waikiki). Other options include the city's reliable bus system ($2.50) with stops throughout Honolulu and Waikiki, or the Airport Waikiki Express shuttle ($9), which transports you to any hotel in Waikiki. Ask the driver to take Interstate H1, not Nimitz Highway, or your introduction to paradise will be via Honolulu's industrial backside.

CAR TRAVEL

You can get away without renting a car if you plan on staying in Waikiki. But if you want to explore the rest of the island, there's no substitute for having your own wheels. Avoid the obvious tourist cars—candy-colored convertibles, for example—and never leave anything valuable inside, even if you've locked the car. Get a portable GPS navigator, as Oahu's streets can be confusing.

Reserve your vehicle in advance, especially when traveling during the Christmas holidays and summer breaks. This will not only ensure that you get a car but also that you get the best rates. *See Travel Smart Hawaii for more information on renting a car and driving.*

ISLAND DRIVING TIMES Don't let maps fool you. While the distance between Waikiki and, say, the North Shore is roughly 40 miles, it may take more than an hour to get there, thanks to heavy traffic, construction, and other factors. Many of Oahu's main roads are a single lane in each direction, with no alternate routes. So if you're stuck behind a slow-moving vehicle, you may have no other choice than to hope it turns soon. Heavy traffic moving toward downtown can begin as early as 6 am, with after-work traffic starting at 3 pm.

Here are average driving times—without traffic—that will help you plan your excursions accordingly.

DRIVING TIMES	
Waikiki to Ko Olina	1 hour
Waikiki to Haleiwa	45 minutes
Waikiki to Hawaii Kai	25 minutes
Waikiki to Kailua	30 minutes
Waikiki to downtown Honolulu	10 minutes
Waikiki to airport	25 minutes
Kaneohe to Turtle Bay	1 hour
Hawaii Kai to Kailua	25 minutes
Haleiwa to Turtle Bay	20 minutes

RESTAURANTS

Honolulu is home to some of the world's most famous chefs, from Sam Choy and his down-home cooking to the artistic Roy Yamaguchi. While there are plenty of glitzy and recognizable names, some of the best cuisine is off Waikiki's beaten path. Look to Kapahulu and Waialae Avenues for fantastic hole-in-the-wall sushi joints and local favorites. *Prices in the reviews are the average cost of a main course at dinner or, if dinner is not served, at lunch.*

HOTELS

Most of Oahu's lodging options are located in Waikiki. While the Royal Hawaiians and Hilton Hawaiian Villages get most of the airtime when TV shows try to capture this resort area, most of us stay at places that are a bit less flashy but still have their charms. *Prices in the reviews are the lowest cost of a standard double room in high season. Prices for rentals are the lowest per-night cost for a one-bedroom unit in high season.*

GUIDED TOURS

Guided tours are convenient; you don't have to worry about finding a parking spot or getting admission tickets. Most of the tour guides have taken special classes in Hawaiian history and lore, and many are certified by the state of Hawaii. On the other hand, you won't have the freedom to proceed at your own pace, nor will you have the ability to take a detour trip if something else catches your attention.

BUS AND VAN TOURS

Polynesian Adventure. This company leads tours of Pearl Harbor and also offers a circle-island tour by motor coach, van, and minicoach. Best of all, kids are free on many tours. ☎ *808/833–3000* ⊕ *www.polyad.com.*

Roberts Hawaii. Choose from a large selection of tours, including downtown Honolulu ghost tours, underwater submarine tours, and the more traditional Pearl Harbor excursions. Tours are conducted via everything from vans to president-worthy limousines. ☎ *808/539–9400* ⊕ *www. robertshawaii.com.*

THEME TOURS

Discover Hawaii Tours. In addition to circle-island and other Oahu-based itineraries on motor and minicoaches, this company can also get you from Waikiki to the lava flows of the Big Island or to Maui's Hana Highway and back in one day. ☎ *808/690–9050* ⊕ *www. discoverhawaiitours.com.*

E Noa Tours. Certified tour guides conduct circle-island, Pearl Harbor, and shopping tours. ☎ *808/591–2561* ⊕ *www.enoa.com.*

Home of the Brave Hawaii Victory Tour. Perfect for military history buffs, these narrated tours visit Oahu's military bases and the National Memorial Cemetery of the Pacific. Tours also include a visit to the company's private museum, which displays artifacts and memorabilia from World War II. ☎ *808/396–8112* ⊕ *www.pearlharborhq.com.*

VISITOR INFORMATION

Before you go, contact the Oahu Visitors Bureau (OVB). For general information on all the Islands, contact the Hawaii Visitors & Convention Bureau. The HVCB website has a calendar section that shows what local events will be taking place during your stay.

Contacts

Hawaii Visitors & Convention Bureau ✉ *2270 Kalakaua Ave., Suite 801, Honolulu* ☎ *808/923-1811, 800/464-2924 for brochures* ⊕ *www.gohawaii. com.* **Oahu Visitors Bureau** ✉ *733 Bishop St., Suite 1520, Downtown Honolulu, Honolulu* ☎ *877/525-6248* ⊕ *www.gohawaii.com/oahu.*

EXPLORING

HONOLULU

Updated by Michael Levine

Here is Hawaii's only true metropolis, its seat of government, center of commerce and shipping, entertainment and recreation mecca, a historic site and an evolving urban area—conflicting roles that engender endless debate and controversy. For the visitor, Honolulu is an everyman's delight: hipsters and scholars, sightseers and foodies, nature lovers and culture vultures all can find their bliss.

Once there was the broad bay of Mamala and the narrow inlet of Kou, fronting a dusty plain occupied by a few thatched houses and the great Pakaka *heiau* (shrine). Nosing into the narrow passage in the early 1790s, British sea captain William Brown named the port Fair Haven.

Later, Hawaiians would call it Honolulu, or "sheltered bay." As shipping traffic increased, the settlement grew into a Western-style town of streets and buildings, tightly clustered around the single freshwater source, Nuuanu Stream. Not until piped water became available in the early 1900s did Honolulu spread across the greening plain. Long before that, however, Honolulu gained importance when King Kamehameha I reluctantly abandoned his home on the Big Island to build a chiefly compound near the harbor in 1804 to better protect Hawaiian interests from the Western incursion.

Two hundred years later, the entire island is, in a sense, Honolulu—the City and County of Honolulu. The city has no official boundaries, extending across the flatlands from Pearl Harbor to Waikiki and high into the hills behind.

DOWNTOWN HONOLULU

Honolulu's past and present play a delightful counterpoint throughout the downtown sector, which is approximately 6 miles east of Honolulu International Airport. Postmodern glass-and-steel office buildings look down on the Aloha Tower, built in 1926 and, until the early 1960s, the tallest structure in Honolulu. Hawaii's history is told in the architecture of these few blocks: the cut-stone turn-of-the-20th-century storefronts of Merchant Street, the gracious white-columned American-Georgian manor that was the home of the Islands' last queen, the jewel-box palace occupied by the monarchy before it was overthrown, the Spanish-inspired stucco and tile-roofed Territorial Era government buildings, and the 21st-century glass pyramid of the First Hawaiian Bank Building.

GETTING HERE AND AROUND

To reach downtown Honolulu from Waikiki by car, take Ala Moana Boulevard to Alakea Street and turn right; three blocks up on the right, between South King and Hotel, there's a municipal parking lot in Alii Place on the right. There are also public parking lots (75¢ per half hour for the first two hours) in buildings along Alakea, Smith, Beretania, and Bethel streets (Gateway Plaza on Bethel Street is a good choice). The best parking downtown, however, is metered street parking along Punchbowl Street—when you can find it.

Another option is to take Route 19 or 20 of highly popular and convenient TheBus to the Aloha Tower Marketplace, or take a trolley from Waikiki.

WALKING TOURS

American Institute of Architects (AIA) Downtown Walking Tour. See downtown Honolulu from an architectural perspective. Advance reservations are required. Tours are offered only on Saturday. ☎ 808/545–4242 ⊕ www.aiahonolulu.org.

Hawaii Geographic Society. A number of downtown Honolulu historic-temple and archaeology walking tours are available from the society. Email the organization for more information. ☎ 808/538–3952 ✎ hawaiigeographicsociety@gmail.com ⊠ $15.

TIMING

Plan a couple of hours for exploring downtown's historic buildings, more if you're taking a guided tour or walk. The best time to visit is in the cool and relative quiet of morning or on the weekends when downtown is all but deserted except for the historic sites.

TOP ATTRACTIONS

Fodor'sChoice ★ **Iolani Palace.** America's only royal residence was built in 1882 on the site of an earlier palace, and it contains the thrones of King Kalakaua and his successor (and sister) Queen Liliuokalani. Bucking the stereotype of simple island life, the palace had electricity and telephone lines installed even before the White House. Downstairs galleries showcase the royal jewelry and kitchen and offices restored to the glory of the monarchy. The palace is open for guided or self-guided audio tours, and reservations are recommended. ■ TIP→ **If you're set on taking a guided tour, call for reservations a few days in advance.** The gift shop was formerly the Iolani Barracks, built to house the Royal Guard. ✉ *King and Richards Sts., Downtown Honolulu* ☎ *808/522–0832* ⊕ *www.iolanipalace. org* 💰 *$20 guided tour, $12 audio tour, $6 downstairs galleries only* ⊙ *Mon.–Sat. 9–4, guided tours every 15 min 9–11:15, self-guided audio tours 11:45–3:30.*

Kamehameha I Statue. Paying tribute to the Big Island chieftain who united all the warring Hawaiian Islands into one kingdom at the turn of the 18th century, this statue, which stands with one arm outstretched in welcome, is one of three originally cast in Paris, France, by American sculptor T. R. Gould. The original statue, lost at sea and replaced by this one, was eventually salvaged and is now in Kapaau, on the Big Island, near the king's birthplace. Each year on the king's birthday, June 11, the more famous copy is draped in fresh lei that reach lengths of 18 feet and longer. A parade proceeds past the statue, and Hawaiian civic clubs, the women in hats and impressive long *holoku* dresses and the men in sashes and cummerbunds, pay honor to the leader whose name means "The Lonely One." ✉ *417 S. King St., outside Aliiolani Hale, Downtown Honolulu.*

Kawaiahao Church. Fancifully called Hawaii's Westminster Abbey, this 14,000-coral-block house of worship witnessed the coronations, weddings, and funerals of generations of Hawaiian royalty. Each of the building's coral blocks was quarried from reefs offshore at depths of more than 20 feet and transported to this site. Interior woodwork was created from the forests of the Koolau Mountains. The upper gallery has an exhibit of paintings of the royal families. The graves of missionaries and of King Lunalilo are adjacent. Services in English and Hawaiian are held each Sunday, and the church members are exceptionally welcoming, greeting newcomers with lei; their affiliation is United Church of Christ. Although there are no guided tours, you can look around the church at no cost. ✉ *957 Punchbowl St., at King St., Downtown Honolulu* ☎ *808/522–1333* 💰 *Free* ⊙ *Service in English and Hawaiian Sun. at 9 am.*

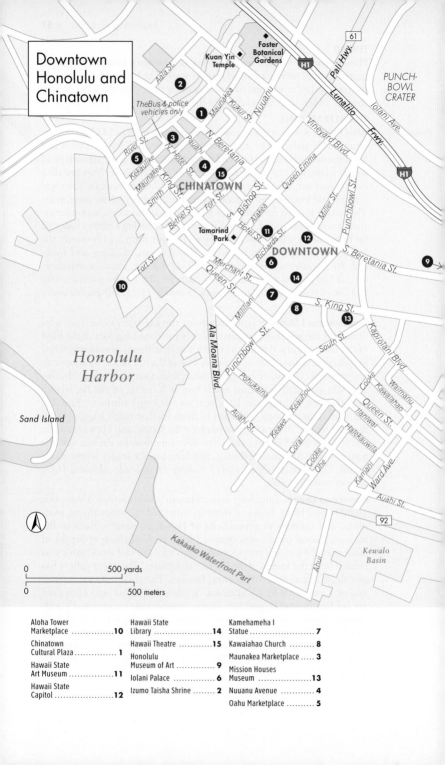

Downtown Honolulu and Chinatown

PUNCH-BOWL CRATER

Foster Botanical Gardens

Kuan Yin Temple

TheBus & police vehicles only

CHINATOWN

Tamarind Park

DOWNTOWN

Honolulu Harbor

Sand Island

Kewalo Basin

Kakaako Waterfront Park

0 _____ 500 yards
0 _____ 500 meters

WORTH NOTING

☪ **Aloha Tower Marketplace.** In two stories of shops and kiosks you can find island-inspired clothing, jewelry, art, and home furnishings. The marketplace also has indoor and outdoor restaurants and live entertainment. For a bird's-eye view of this working harbor, take a free ride up to the observation deck of Aloha Tower. Cruise ships dock at piers 9 and 10 alongside the marketplace and are often greeted and sent out to sea with music and hula dancing at the piers' end. ☒ *1 Aloha Tower Dr., at Piers 10 and 11, Downtown Honolulu* ☎ *808/528–5700 entertainment info* ⊕ *www.alohatower. com* ☙ *Mon.–Sat. 9–9, Sun. 9–6; restaurants open later.*

Hawaii State Art Museum. Hawaii was one of the first states in the nation to legislate that a portion of the taxes paid on commercial building projects be set aside for the purchase of artwork. A few years ago, the state purchased an ornate period-style building (built to house the headquarters of a prominent developer) and dedicated 12,000 feet on the second floor to the art of Hawaii in all its ethnic diversity. The **Diamond Head Gallery** features new acquisitions and thematic shows from the State Art Collection and the State Foundation on Culture and the Arts. The **Ewa Gallery** houses more than 150 works documenting Hawaii's visual-arts history since becoming a state in 1959. Also included are a sculpture gallery as well as a café serving tasty, locally-grown food, a gift shop, and educational meeting rooms. Check for occasional evening events. ☒ *250 S. Hotel St., 2nd fl., Downtown Honolulu* ☎ *808/586–0900 museum, 808/536–5900 restaurant* ⊕ *www.hawaii.gov/sfca* ☒ *Free* ☙ *Tues.–Sat. 10–4.*

Hawaii State Capitol. The capitol's architecture is richly symbolic: the columns resemble palm trees, the legislative chambers are shaped like volcanic cinder cones, and the central court is open to the sky, representing Hawaii's open society. Replicas of the Hawaii state seal, each weighing 7,500 pounds, hang above both its entrances. The building, which in 1969 replaced Iolani Palace as the seat of government, is surrounded by reflecting pools, just as the Islands are embraced by water. A pair of statues, often draped in lei, flank the building: one of the beloved queen Liliuokalani and the other of the sainted Father Damien de Veuster. ☒ *415 S. Beretania St., Downtown Honolulu* ☎ *808/586–0178* ☒ *Free* ☙ *Guided tours Mon., Wed., Fri. 1:30.*

Hawaii State Library. This beautifully renovated main library was built in 1913. Its Samuel M. Kamakau Reading Room, on the first floor in the Mauka (Hawaiian for "mountain") Courtyard, houses an extensive

Hawaii and Pacific book collection and pays tribute to Kamakau, a missionary student whose 19th-century writings in English offer rare and vital insight into traditional Hawaiian culture. ⊠ 478 King St., Downtown Honolulu ☎ 808/586–3500 ⊠ Free ⊙ Mon. and Wed. 10–5, Tues., Fri., and Sat. 9–5, Thurs. 9–8.

Honolulu Museum of Art. Originally built around the collection of a Honolulu matron who donated much of her estate to the museum, the academy is housed in a maze of courtyards, cloistered walkways, and quiet, low-ceilinged spaces. There's an impressive permanent collection that includes Hiroshige's *ukiyo-e* Japanese prints, donated by James Michener; Italian Renaissance paintings; and American and European art. The newer Luce Pavilion complex, nicely incorporated into the more traditional architecture of the place, has a traveling-exhibit gallery, a Hawaiian gallery, an excellent café, and a gift shop. The Academy Theatre screens art films. This is also the jumping-off place for tours of Doris Duke's estate, Shangri-La (these tours are very much in demand and should be reserved far in advance). Call or check the website for special exhibits, concerts, and films. ⊠ 900 S. Beretania St., Downtown Honolulu ☎ 808/532–8700 ⊕ www.honolulumuseum.org ⊠ $10, free 1st Wed. and 3rd Sun. of month; tours of Shangri-La $25 (includes transportation) ⊙ Tues.–Sat. 10–4:30, Sun. 1–5; Shangri-La tours Wed.–Sat. 8:30–1:30 by reservation only.

Mission Houses Museum. The determined Hawaii missionaries arrived in 1820, gaining royal favor and influencing every aspect of island life. Their descendants became leaders in government and business. You can walk through their original dwellings, including Hawaii's oldest wooden structure, a white-frame house that was prefabricated in New England and shipped around the Horn. Certain areas of the museum may be seen only on a one-hour guided tour. Costumed docents give an excellent picture of what mission life was like. Rotating displays showcase such arts as Hawaiian quilting, portraits, even toys. ⊠ 553 S. King St., Downtown Honolulu ☎ 808/531–0481 ⊕ www.missionhouses.org ⊠ $10 ⊙ Tues.–Sat. 10–4; guided tours hourly 11–3.

CHINATOWN

Chinatown's original business district was made up of dry-goods and produce merchants, tailors and dressmakers, barbers, herbalists, and dozens of restaurants. The meat, fish, and produce stalls remain, but the mix is heavier now on gift and curio stores, lei stands, jewelry shops, and bakeries, with a smattering of noodle makers, travel agents, Asian-language video stores, and dozens of restaurants.

The name *Chinatown* here has always been a misnomer. Though three-quarters of Oahu's Chinese lived closely packed in these 25 acres in the late 1800s, even then the neighborhood was half Japanese. Today, you hear Vietnamese and Tagalog as often as Mandarin and Cantonese, and there are voices of Japan, Singapore, Malaysia, Korea, Thailand, Samoa, and the Marshall Islands, as well.

Perhaps a more accurate name is the one used by early Chinese: *Wah Fau* ("Chinese port"), signifying a landing and jumping-off place. Chinese laborers, as soon as they completed their plantation contracts, hurried into the city to start businesses here. It's a launching point for today's immigrants, too: Southeast Asian shops almost outnumber Chinese; stalls carry Filipino specialties like winged beans and goat meat; and in one tiny space, knife-wielding Samoans skin coconuts to order.

In the half century after the first Chinese laborers arrived in Hawaii in 1851, Chinatown was a link to home for the all-male cadre of workers who planned to return to China rich and respected. Merchants not only sold supplies, they held mail, loaned money, wrote letters, translated documents, sent remittances to families, served meals, offered rough bunkhouse accommodations, and were the center for news, gossip, and socializing.

Though much happened to Chinatown in the 20th century—beginning in January 1900, when almost the entire neighborhood was burned to the ground to halt the spread of bubonic plague—it remains a bustling, crowded, noisy, and odiferous place bent primarily on buying and selling, and sublimely oblivious to its status as a National Historic District or the encroaching gentrification on nearby Nuuanu Avenue.

GETTING HERE AND AROUND
Chinatown occupies 15 blocks immediately north of downtown Honolulu—it's flat, compact, and very walkable.

TIMING
This area is easily explored in half a day. The best time to visit is morning, when the *popos* (grandmas) shop—it's cool out, and you can enjoy a cheap dim-sum breakfast. Chinatown is a seven-days-a-week operation. Sundays are especially busy with families sharing dim sum in raucous dining hall–size restaurants.

If you're here between January 20 and February 20, check local newspapers for Chinese New Year activities. Bakeries stock special sweets, stores and homes sprout bright-red scrolls, and lion dancers cavort through the streets feeding on *li-see* (money envelopes). The Narcissus Queen is chosen, and an evening street fair draws crowds.

GUIDED TOURS
Matthew Gray's Hawaii Food Tours. Gray's "Hole in the Wall Tour" culinary tour includes discussion of Hawaiian culinary history and the diversity of the food culture on the island, along with enjoying samples of local favorites from a variety of ethnic restaurants, markets, and bakeries as you walk through Chinatown. It's a great way to get a delicious taste of Hawaii's culture. ☎ 808/926–3663 ⊕ *www.hawaiifoodtours.com*.

TOP ATTRACTIONS
Chinatown Cultural Plaza. This sprawling multistory shopping square surrounds a courtyard with an incense-wreathed shrine and Moongate stage for holiday performances. The Chee Kung Tong Society has a beautifully decorated meeting hall here; a number of such *tongs*

(meeting places) are hidden on upper floors in Chinatown. Outside, near the canal, local members of the community play cards and mah-jongg. ✉ *100 N. Beretania, Chinatown* ⊕ *http://www.chinatownhi.com/.*

Izumo Taisha Shrine. From Chinatown Cultural Plaza, cross a stone bridge to visit Okuninushi No Mikoto, a *kami* (god) who is believed in Shinto tradition to bring good fortune if properly courted (and thanked afterward). ✉ *N. Kukui and Canal, Chinatown* ☎ *No phone.*

Kuan Yin Temple. A couple of blocks *mauka* (toward the mountains) from Chinatown is the oldest Buddhist temple in the Islands. Mistakenly called a goddess by some, Kuan Yin, also known as Kannon, is a *bodhisattva*—one who chose to remain on earth doing good even after achieving enlightenment. Transformed from a male into a female figure centuries ago, she is credited with a particular sympathy for women. You will see representations of her all over the Islands: holding a lotus flower (beauty from the mud of human frailty), as at the temple; pouring out a pitcher of oil (like mercy flowing); or as a sort of Madonna with a child. Visitors are permitted but be aware this is a practicing place of worship. ✉ *170 N. Vineyard, Chinatown* ☎ *No phone.*

Maunakea Marketplace. On the corner of Maunakea and Hotel streets is this plaza surrounded by shops, an indoor market, and a food court. ■ TIP→ If you appreciate fine tea, visit the Tea Hut, an unpretentious counter inside a curio shop.

Hawaiian Chinese Cultural Museum and Archives. Within the Maunakea Marketplace, the Hawaiian Chinese Cultural Museum and Archives displays historic photographs and artifacts. ✉ *Maunakea Marketplace, 1120 Maunakea St., Chinatown* ☎ *808/524-3409* ✑ *$2* ☉ *Mon.–Sat. 10–2* ✉ *1120 Maunakea St., Chinatown* ☎ *808/524-3409.*

★ **Oahu Marketplace.** Here is a taste of old-style Chinatown, where you're likely to be hustled aside as a whole pig (dead, of course) is wrestled through the crowd and where glassy-eyed fish of every size and hue lie stacked forlornly on ice. Try the bubble tea (juices and flavored teas with tapioca bubbles inside) or pick up a bizarre magenta dragonfruit for breakfast. ✉ *N. King St. at Kekaulike, Chinatown.*

WORTH NOTING

Hawaii Theatre. Opened in 1922, this theater earned rave reviews for its neoclassical design, with Corinthian columns, marble statues, and plush carpeting and drapery. Nicknamed the "Pride of the Pacific," the facility was rescued from demolition in the early 1980s and underwent a $30 million renovation. Listed on both the State and National Register of Historic Places, it has become the centerpiece of revitalization efforts of Honolulu's downtown area. The 1,200-seat venue hosts concerts, theatrical productions, dance performances, and film screenings. ✉ *1130 Bethel St., Chinatown* ☎ *808/528-0506* ⊕ *www.hawaiitheatre. com* ✑ *$10* ☉ *1-hr guided tours Tues. at 11 am.*

Nuuanu Avenue. Here on Chinatown's main mauka–makai (mountain-to-ocean) drag and on Bethel Street, which runs parallel, are clustered art galleries, restaurants, a wine shop, an antiques auctioneer, a dress shop or two, one tiny theater space (the Arts at Mark's Garage), and one historic stage (the Hawaii Theatre). **First Friday** art nights, when

SHOPPING IN CHINATOWN

Chinatown is rife with ridiculously inexpensive gifts: folding fans for $1 and coconut purses for $5 at **Maunakea Marketplace,** for example.

Curio shops sell everything from porcelain statues to woks, ginseng to Mao shoes. If you like to sew, or have a yen for a brocade cheongsam, visit the Hong Kong Supermarket in the Wo Fat Chop Sui building (at the corner of N. Hotel and Maunakea) for fresh fruit, crack seed (Chinese dried fruit popular for snacking), and row upon row of boxed, tinned delicacies with indecipherable names.

Chinatown Cultural Plaza offers fine-quality jade. Chinatown is Honolulu's lei center, with shops strung along Beretania and Maunakea; the locals have favorite shops where they're greeted by name. In spring, look for gardenia nosegays wrapped in ti leaves.

galleries stay open until 9 pm, draw crowds. Many stay later and crowd Chinatown's bars. If you like art and people-watching and are fortunate enough to be on Oahu the first Friday of the month, this event shouldn't be missed. ⊠ *Nuuanu Ave., Chinatown.*

GREATER HONOLULU AND DIAMOND HEAD

Downtown Honolulu and Chinatown can easily swallow up a day's walking, sightseeing, and shopping. Another day's worth of attractions surrounds the city's core. To the north, just off H1 in the tightly packed neighborhood of Kalihi, explore a museum given to the Islands in memory of a princess. Immediately *mauka,* off Pali Highway, are a renowned resting place and a carefully preserved home where royal families retreated during the doldrums of summer. To the south, along King Street and Waialae Avenue, are a pair of neighborhoods chockablock with interesting restaurants and shops. Down the shore a bit from Diamond Head, visit Oahu's ritziest address and an equally upscale shopping center.

One reason to venture farther afield is the chance to glimpse Honolulu's residential neighborhoods. Species of classic Hawaii homes include the tiny green-and-white plantation-era house with its corrugated tin roof, two windows flanking a central door and small porch; the breezy bungalow with its swooping Thai-style roofline and two wings flanking screened French doors through which breezes blow into the living room. Note the tangled "Grandma-style" gardens and many *ohana* houses—small homes in the backyard of a larger home or built as apartments perched over the garage, allowing extended families to live together. Carports, which rarely house cars, are the island's version of rec rooms, where parties are held and neighbors sit to "talk story." Sometimes you see gallon jars on the flat roofs of garages or carports: these are pickled lemons fermenting in the sun. Also in the neighborhoods, you find the folksy restaurants and takeout spots favored by the islanders.

GETTING HERE AND AROUND

For those with a Costco card, the cheapest gas on the island is at the Costco station on Arakawa Street between Dillingham Boulevard and Nimitz Highway.

EXPLORING

★ **Bishop Museum.** Founded in 1889 by Charles R. Bishop as a memorial to his wife, Princess Bernice Pauahi Bishop, the museum began as a repository for the royal possessions of this last direct descendant of King Kamehameha the Great. Today it's the Hawaii State Museum of Natural and Cultural History. Its five exhibit halls house almost 25 million items that tell the history of the Hawaiian Islands and their Pacific neighbors. The latest addition to the complex is a 16,500 square-foot natural-science wing with a three-story simulated volcano at its center. The recently renovated Hawaiian Hall, with state-of-the art and often-interactive displays, teaches about the Hawaiian culture. Spectacular Hawaiian artifacts—lustrous feather capes, bone fish hooks, the skeleton of a giant sperm whale, photography and crafts displays, and an authentic, well-preserved grass house—are displayed inside a three-story 19th-century Victorian-style gallery. The building alone, with its huge Victorian turrets and immense stone walls, is worth seeing. Also check out the planetarium, daily tours, hula and science demonstrations, special exhibits, and the Shop Pacifica. ⊠ *1525 Bernice St., Kalihi* ☎ *808/847–3511* ⊕ *www. bishopmuseum.org* ⌨ *$17.95* ⊙ *Wed.–Mon. 9–5.*

Diamond Head State Monument and Park. Panoramas from this 760-foot extinct volcanic peak, once used as a military fortification, extend from Waikiki and Honolulu in one direction and out to Koko Head in the other, with surfers and windsurfers scattered like confetti on the cresting waves below. This 360-degree perspective is a great orientation for first-time visitors. On a clear day, look east past Koko Head to glimpse the outlines of the islands of Maui and Moloka'i. To enter the park from Waikiki, take Kalakaua Avenue east, turn left at Monsarrat Avenue, head a mile up the hill, and look for a sign on the right. Drive through the tunnel to the inside of the crater. The ¾-mile trail to the top begins at the parking lot. New lighting inside the summit tunnel and a spiral staircase eases the way, but be aware that the hike to the crater is an upward climb; if you aren't in the habit of getting occasional exercise, this might not be for you. At the top, you'll find a somewhat awkward climb out into the open air, but the view is worth it. Take bottled water with you to stay hydrated under the tropical sun. ■TIP→ **To beat the heat and the crowds, rise early and make the hike before 8 am.** As you walk, note the color of the vegetation; if the mountain is brown, Honolulu has been without significant rain for a while; but if the trees and undergrowth glow green, you'll know it's the wet season (winter) without looking at a calendar. This is when rare Hawaiian marsh plants revive on the floor of the crater. Keep an eye on your watch if you're here at day's end: the gates close promptly at 6. ⊠ *Diamond Head Rd. at 18th Ave., Waikiki* ☎ *808/587–0300* ⊕ *www.hawaiistateparks.org/ parks/oahu* ⌨ *$1 per person, $5 per vehicle* ⊙ *Daily 6–6.*

National Memorial Cemetery of the Pacific. Nestled in the bowl of Puowaina, or Punchbowl Crater, this 112-acre cemetery is the final resting place

for more than 50,000 U.S. war veterans and family members and is a
solemn reminder of their sacrifice.
Among those buried here is Ernie
Pyle, the famed World War II cor-
respondent who was killed by a
Japanese sniper on Ie Shima, an
island off the northwest coast of
Okinawa. There are intricate stone
maps providing a visual military
history lesson. Puowaina, formed

> **WORD OF MOUTH**
>
> "Since you are visiting the Iolani
> Palace, you might also enjoy a tour
> of Queen Emma Summer Palace.
> If you go to the Pali (it is quite an
> experience), it is near the summer
> palace and could be combined."
> —Giovanna

75,000–100,000 years ago during a period of secondary volcanic activity, translates as "Hill of Sacrifice." Historians believe this site once
served as an altar where ancient Hawaiians offered sacrifices to their
gods. ■ TIP➡ The entrance to the cemetery has unfettered views of Waikiki
and Honolulu—perhaps the finest on Oahu. ⊠ *2177 Puowaina Dr., Nuuanu*
☎ *808/532–3720* ⊕ *www.cem.va.gov/cem/cems/nchp/nmcp.asp* ⊠ *Free*
⊙ *Mar.–Sept., daily 8–6:30; Oct.–Feb., daily 8–5:30.*

★ **Queen Emma Summer Palace.** Queen Emma and her family used this
stately white home, built in 1848, as a retreat from the rigors of court
life in hot and dusty Honolulu during the mid-1800s. It has an eclectic
mix of European, Victorian, and Hawaiian furnishings and has excellent examples of Hawaiian quilts and koa-wood furniture. ⊠ *2913 Pali
Hwy., Nuuanu* ☎ *808/595–3167* ⊕ *www.queenemmasummerpalace.
org* ⊠ *$6* ⊙ *Self-guided or guided tours daily 9–4.*

Spalding House. In the exclusive Makiki Heights neighborhood, just
minutes from downtown Honolulu, the Spalding House houses collections of modern art dating from 1940. Situated in the 3.5-acre Alice
Cooke Spalding home and estate (built in 1925), the museum boasts
ever-changing exhibitions as well as a peaceful sculpture garden with
breathtaking views of Diamond Head and Waikiki. A fun gift shop
features jewelry and other art by local artists. The Contemporary Café
is popular with locals for lunch. It recently merged with the Honolulu
Academy of Arts to become the Honolulu Museum of Art, so a single
admission gets you into both museums. ⊠ *2411 Makiki Heights Dr.,
Makiki Heights* ☎ *808/526–1322* ⊕ *www.honolulumuseum.org* ⊠ *$10*
⊙ *Tues.–Sat. 10–4, Sun. noon–4.*

WAIKIKI

Waikiki is approximately 3 miles east of downtown Honolulu.

A short drive from downtown Honolulu, Waikiki is Oahu's primary
resort area. A mix of historic and modern hotels and condos front the
sunny 2-mile stretch of beach, and many have clear views of Diamond
Head to the west. The area is home to much of the island's dining,
nightlife, and shopping scene—from posh boutiques to hole-in-the-wall
eateries to craft booths at the International Marketplace.

Waikiki was once a favorite retreat for Hawaiian royalty. In 1901
the Moana Hotel debuted, introducing Waikiki as an international
travel destination. The region's fame continued to grow when Duke

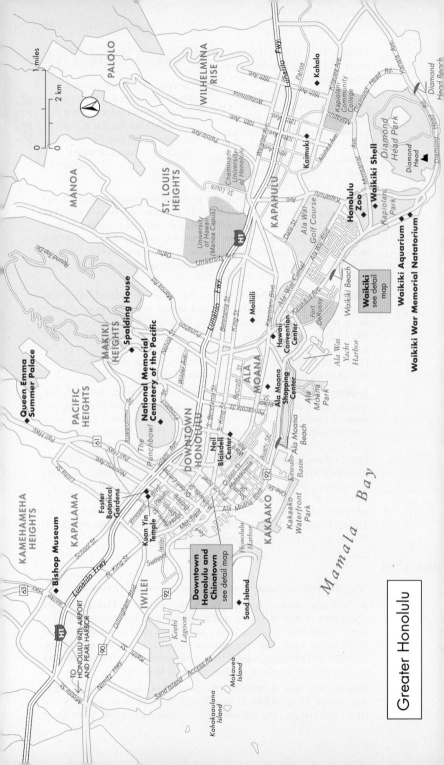

Greater Honolulu

Mamala Bay

PALOLO

WILHELMINA RISE

Kahala

Kapiolani Community College

Diamond Head Rd.

Kaimuki

Diamond Head Park

MANOA

ST. LOUIS HEIGHTS

Chaminade University of Honolulu

Diamond Head

KAPAHULU

Honolulu Zoo

Waikiki Shell

University of Hawaii (Manoa Capus)

Ala Wai Golf Course

Diamond Head Park

University Ave.

Kapiolani Park

Waikiki Aquarium

Waikiki War Memorial Natatorium

MAKIKI HEIGHTS

Spalding House

Moiliili

Hawaii Convention Center

Waikiki
see detail map

Waikiki Beach

Queen Emma Summer Palace

National Memorial Cemetery of the Pacific

Fort DeRussy

Ala Wai Yacht Harbor

PACIFIC HEIGHTS

The Punchbowl

ALA MOANA

Ala Moana Shopping Center

KAMEHAMEHA HEIGHTS

61

DOWNTOWN HONOLULU

Neil Blaisdell Center

Ala Moana Park

Ala Moana Beach

Foster Botanical Gardens

Bishop Museum

KAPALAMA

Kuan Yin Temple

92

KAKAAKO

Kakaako Waterfront Park

Downtown Honolulu and Chinatown
see detail map

Honolulu Harbor

Mamala Bay

IWILEI

63

Lunalilo Frwy.

92

Sand Island

90

TO HONOLULU INTL. AIRPORT AND PEARL HARBOR

Keehi Lagoon

Sand Island Access Rd.

Mokauea Island

Kahakaaulana Island

1 miles

2 km

0

2

Kahanamoku helped popularize the sport of surfing, offering lessons to visitors at Waikiki. You can see Duke immortalized in a bronze statue, with a surfboard, on Kuhio Beach. Today, there is a decidedly "urban resort" vibe here; streets are clean, gardens are manicured, and the sand feels softer than at beaches farther down the coast. There isn't much of a local culture—it's mainly tourist crowds—but you'll still find the relaxed surf-y vibe that has drawn people here for more than a century.

Diamond Head Crater (*see Greater Honolulu and Diamond Head*) is perhaps Hawaii's most recognizable natural landmark. It got its name from sailors who thought they had found precious gems on its slopes; these later proved to be calcite crystals, or fool's gold. Hawaiians saw a resemblance in the sharp angle of the crater's seaward slope to the oddly shaped head of the ahi fish and so called it Leahi, though later they Hawaiianized the English name to Kaimana Hila. It is commemorated in a widely known hula—"*A ike i ka nani o Kaimana Hila, Kaimana Hila, kau mai i luna*" ("We saw the beauty of Diamond Head, Diamond Head set high above").

Kapiolani Park lies in the shadow of the crater. King David Kalakaua established the park in 1887, named it after his queen, and dedicated it "to the use and enjoyment of the people." Kapiolani Park is a 500-acre expanse where you can play all sorts of field sports, enjoy a picnic, see wild animals at the Honolulu Zoo, or hear live music at the Waikiki Shell or the Kapiolani Bandstand.

GETTING HERE AND AROUND

Bounded by the Ala Wai Canal on the north and west, the beach on the south, and the Honolulu Zoo to the east, Waikiki is compact and easy to walk around. TheBus runs multiple routes here from the airport and downtown Honolulu. By car, finding Waikiki from H1 can be tricky; look for the Punahou exit for the west end of Waikiki, and the King Street exit for the eastern end.

EXPLORING

Honolulu Zoo. To get a glimpse of the endangered *nene,* the Hawaii state bird, check out the zoo's Kipuka Nene Sanctuary. Though many animals prefer to remain invisible, particularly the elusive big cats, the monkeys appear to enjoy being seen and are a hoot to watch. It's best to get to the zoo right when it opens, since the animals are livelier in the cool of the morning. There are bigger and better zoos, but this one, though showing signs of neglect due to budget constraints, is a lush garden and has some great programs. There is lots of work going on, including the creation of a new elephant enclosure with more space for the pachyderms to roam. The Wildest Show in Town, a series of concerts ($2 donation), takes place on Wednesday evenings in summer. You can have a family sleepover inside the zoo during Snooze in the Zoo on a Friday or Saturday night every month. Or just head for the petting zoo, where kids can make friends with a llama or stand in the middle of a koi pond. There's an exceptionally good gift shop. On weekends, the Zoo Fence Art Mart, on Monsarrat Avenue on the Diamond Head side outside the zoo, has affordable artwork by contemporary artists. Metered parking is available all along the *makai* (ocean) side of the park and in the lot next to the zoo—but it can fill up early. TheBus, Oahu's only form of public transportation, makes stops here along the way to and from Ala Moana Center and Sea Life Park (routes 22 and 58). ✉ *151 Kapahulu Ave., Waikiki* ☎ *808/971–7171* ⊕ *www.honoluluzoo.org* 🎟 *$14* ⊗ *Daily 9–4:30.*

Kapiolani Bandstand. Victorian-style Kapiolani Bandstand, which was originally built in the late 1890s, is Kapiolani Park's stage for community entertainment and concerts. The nation's only city-sponsored band, the Royal Hawaiian Band, performs free concerts on Sunday afternoon. Local newspapers list event information. ✉ *2805 Monsarrat Ave., Waikiki* ☎ *808/922–5331* ⊕ *www.rhb-music.com.*

© **Waikiki Aquarium.** This amazing little attraction harbors more than 3,000 organisms and 500 species of Hawaiian and South Pacific marine life, endangered Hawaiian monk seals, sharks, and the only chambered nautilus living in captivity. The Edge of the Reef exhibit showcases five different types of reef environments found along Hawaii's shorelines. Check out the small new Northwestern Hawaiian Islands exhibit that explains the formation of the island chain, the Ocean Drifters jellyfish exhibit, outdoor touch pool, and the self-guided audio tour, which is included with admission. The aquarium offers programs of interest to adults and children alike, including the Aquarium After Dark when visitors grab a flashlight and view fish going about their rarely observable nocturnal activities. Plan to spend at least an hour at the aquarium, including 10 minutes for a film in the Sea Visions Theater. ✉ *2777 Kalakaua Ave., Waikiki* ☎ *808/923–9741* ⊕ *www.waquarium. org* 🎟 *$9* ⊗ *Daily 9–4:30.*

Waikiki Shell. Locals bring picnics and grab one of the 6,000 "grass seats" (lawn seating) for music under the stars (there are actual seats, as well). Concerts are held May 1 to Labor Day, with a few winter dates, weather permitting. Check newspaper entertainment sections to see who is performing. ✉ *2805 Monsarrat Ave., Waikiki* ☎ *808/768–5252* ⊕ *www.blaisdellcenter.com.*

Waikiki War Memorial Natatorium. This 1927 World War I monument, dedicated to the 102 Hawaiian servicemen who lost their lives in battle, stands proudly—its 20-foot archway, which was completely restored in 2002, is floodlit at night. Despite a face-lift in 2000, the 100-meter saltwater swimming pool, the training spot for Olympians Johnny Weissmuller and Buster Crabbe and the U.S. Army during World War II, is closed as the pool needs repair. The city has commissioned a study of the natatorium's future while a nonprofit group fights to save the facility. ✉ *2777 Kalakaua Ave., Waikiki.*

Continued on page 69

INS & OUTS OF WAIKIKI

Waikiki is all that is wonderful about a resort area, and all that is regrettable. It's where beach culture meets city life, with water sports, dining, shopping, and hotels—and crowds, too.

On the wonderful side: swimming, surfing, parasailing, and catamaran-riding steps from the street; the best nightlife in Hawaii; shopping from designer to dime stores; and experiences to remember: the heart-lifting rush the first time you stand up on a surfboard, and eating fresh grilled snapper as the sun slips into the sea. As to the regrettable: clogged streets, body-lined beaches, $5 cups of coffee, tacky T-shirts, $20 parking stalls, schlocky artwork, drunks, ceaseless construction—all rather brush the bloom from the plumeria.

Modern Waikiki is nothing like its original self, a network of streams, marshes, and islands that drained the inland valleys. The Ala Wai Canal took care of that in the 1920s. More recently, new landscaping, walkways, and a general attention to infrastructure have brightened a façade that had begun to fade.

But throughout its history, Waikiki has retained its essential character: an enchantment that cannot be fully explained and one that, though diminished by highrises, traffic, and noise, has not yet disappeared. Hawaiian royalty came here, and visitors continue to follow, falling in love with sharp-prowed Diamond Head, the sensuous curve of shoreline with its babysafe waves, and the strong-footed surfers like moving statues in the golden light.

WAIKIKI WEST

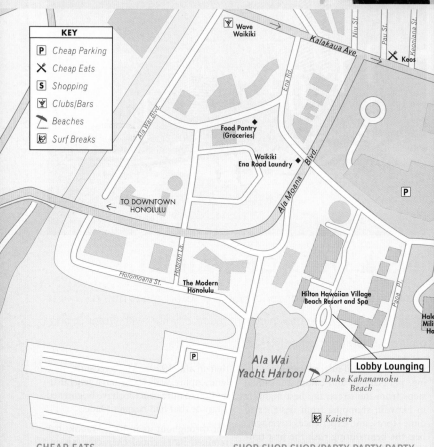

KEY

P	*Cheap Parking*
X	*Cheap Eats*
S	*Shopping*
Y	*Clubs/Bars*
🏄	*Beaches*
🏄	*Surf Breaks*

Wave Waikiki

Kalakaua Ave.

Niu St.

Pau St.

Keoniana St.

Keos

Ena Rd.

Ala Wai Blvd.

Food Pantry (Groceries)

Waikiki Ena Road Laundry

Ala Moana Blvd.

TO DOWNTOWN HONOLULU

P

Holomoana St.

Hobron La.

The Modern Honolulu

Hilton Hawaiian Village Beach Resort and Spa

Paoa Pl.

Hale Mili Ho

Ala Wai Yacht Harbor

P

Lobby Lounging

Duke Kahanamoku Beach

🏄 *Kaisers*

CHEAP EATS

Keo's, 2028 Kuhio: Breakfast.

Pho Old Saigon, 2270 Kuhio: Vietnamese.

Japanese noodle shops: Try Menchanko-Tei, Waikiki Trade Center; Ezogiku, 2164 Kalakaua.

■ TIP→ Thanks to the many Japanese nationals who stay here, Waikiki is blessed with lots of cheap, authentic Japanese food, particularly noodles. Plastic representations of food in the window are an indicator of authenticity and a help in ordering.

SHOP, SHOP, SHOP/PARTY, PARTY, PARTY

2100 Kalakaua: Select high-end European boutiques (Chanel, Gucci, Yves Saint Laurent).

Waikiki Beach Walk: Dine and shop for gifts and apparel from locally-owned stores. 227 Lewers St. 808/931-3591.

Zanzabar: Upscale Zanzabar is a different club every night—Latin, global, over 30. Waikiki Trade Center, 2255 Kuhio Ave. 808/924-3939. Check www.zanzabarhawaii. com for events or call.

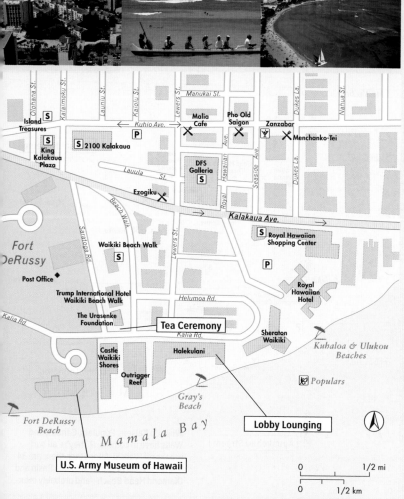

RAINY DAY IDEAS

Bliss Out: Relax at one of Waikiki's luxurious hotel spas. Most treatments feature Hawaiian ingredients.

Lobby Lounging: Among Waikiki's great gathering spots are Halekulani's tranquil courtyards with gorgeous flower arrangements and glimpses of the famous and the Hilton Hawaiian Village's flagged pathways with koi ponds, squawking parrots, and great shops.

Tea Ceremony, Urasenke Foundation: Japan's mysterious tea ceremony is demonstrated. 245 Saratoga Rd. 808/923-3059. $3 donation. Wed., Fri. 10–11 AM.

U.S. Army Museum of Hawaii: Exhibits, including photographs and military equipment, trace the history of Army in the Islands. Battery Randolph, Kalia Rd., Fort DeRussy. 808/955-9552. Free. Tues.–Sat. 9-5.

WAIKIKI EAST

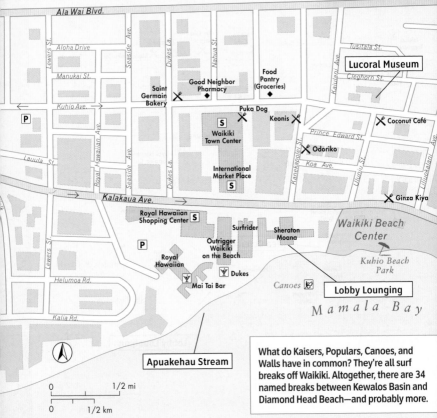

Ala Wai Blvd.

Aloha Drive

Manukai St.

Lewers St.

Seaside Ave.

Dukes La.

Nahua St.

Tusitala St.

Kaiulani Ave.

Cleghorn St.

Lucoral Museum

Saint Germain Bakery

Good Neighbor Pharmacy

Food Pantry (Groceries)

Kuhio Ave.

P

Puka Dog

Keonis

Prince Edward St.

Coconut Café

S

Waikiki Town Center

Odoriko

Kanekapolei St.

Uluniu St.

Lauula St.

Royal Hawaiian Ave.

Seaside Ave.

Dukes La.

International Market Place

S

Koa Ave.

Ginza Kiya

Kalakaua Ave.

 Uluhalani St.

Royal Hawaiian Shopping Center

S

Surfrider

Sheraton Moana

Waikiki Beach Center

Lewers St.

P

Outrigger Waikiki on the Beach

Kuhio Beach Park

Royal Hawaiian

Mai Tai Bar

Dukes

Canoes

Lobby Lounging

Helumoa Rd.

Mamala Bay

Kalia Rd.

0   1/2 mi

0   1/2 km

Apuakehau Stream

What do Kaisers, Populars, Canoes, and Walls have in common? They're all surf breaks off Waikiki. Altogether, there are 34 named breaks between Kewalos Basin and Diamond Head Beach—and probably more.

CHEAP EATS

Coconut Café, 2441 Kuhio: Burgers, sandwiches under $5; fresh fruit smoothies.

Ginza Kiya, 2464 Kalakaua: Japanese noodle shop.

Keoni's, Outrigger East Hotel, 150 Kaiulani Ave.: Breakfasts at rock-bottom prices.

Odoriko, King's Village, 131 Kaiulani Ave.: Japanese noodle shop.

Puka Dog, 2301 Kuhio #334: Delicious hot dogs baked into their buns.

■ TIP→ To save money, go inland. Kuhio, one block toward the mountains from the main drag of Kalakaua, is lined with less expensive restaurants, hotels, and shops.

SHOP, SHOP, SHOP/PARTY, PARTY, PARTY

Sheraton Moana Surfrider: Pick up a present at Nohea Gallery or Sand People. Then relax with a drink at the venerable Banyan Veranda. The radio program *Hawaii Calls* first broadcast to a mainland audience from here in 1935.

Duke's Canoe Club, Outrigger Waikiki: Beach party central.

Mai Tai Bar at the Royal Hawaiian: Birthplace of the Mai Tai.

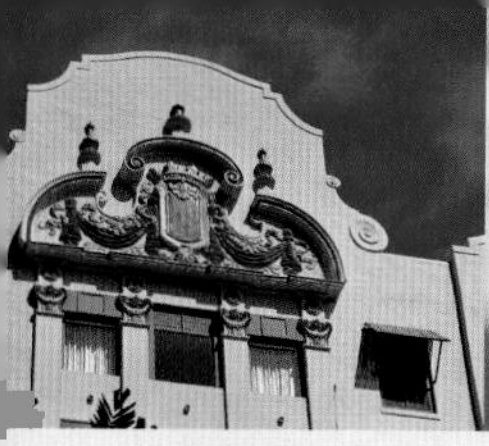

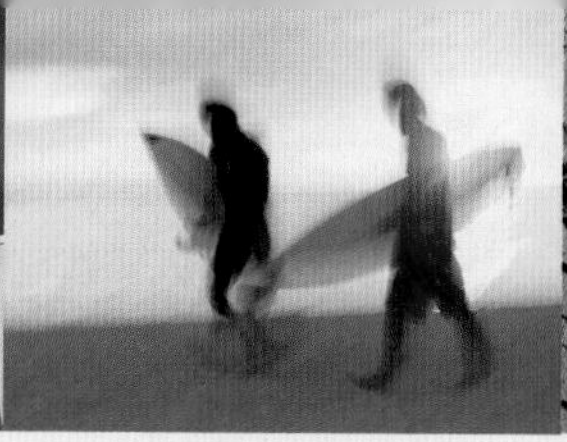

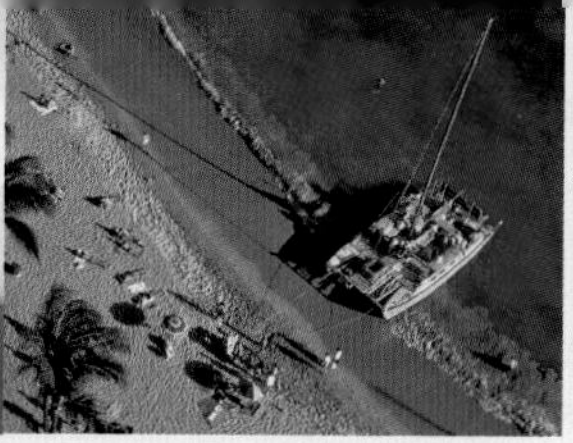

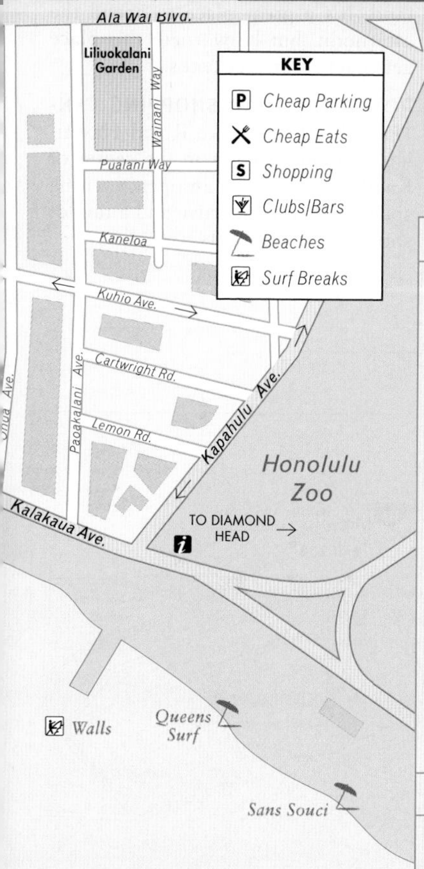
Ala Wai Blvd.
Liliuokalani Garden
Wainani Way
Pualani Way
Kaneloa
Kuhio Ave.
Cartwright Rd.
Paoakalani Ave.
Lemon Rd.
Kapahulu Ave.
Kalakaua Ave.
Honolulu Zoo
TO DIAMOND HEAD
Walls
Queens Surf
Sans Souci
KEY
Cheap Parking
Cheap Eats
Shopping
Clubs/Bars
Beaches
Surf Breaks

WHAT THE LOCALS LOVE

Paid-parking–phobic Islanders usually avoid Waikiki, but these attractions are juicy enough to lure locals:

- **Royal Hawaiian Park Band,** free concerts every Sunday at the Kapiolani Bandstand.
- **Pan-Pacific Festival-Matsuri in Hawaii**, a summer cultural festival that's as good as a trip to Japan.
- **Aloha Festivals in September**, the legendary floral parade and evening show of contemporary Hawaiian music.
- **The Wildest Show in Town**, $1 summer concerts at the Honolulu Zoo.
- **Sunset on the Beach**, free films projected on an outdoor screen at Queen's Beach, with food and entertainment.

APUAKEHAU STREAM

Wade out just in front of the Outrigger Waikiki on the Beach and feel a current of chilly water curling around your ankles. This is the last remnant of three streams that once drained the inland valleys behind you, making of Waikiki a place of swamps, marshes, taro and rice paddies, and giving it the name "spouting water." High-ranking chiefs surfed in a legendary break gouged out by the draining freshwater and rinsed off afterward in the stream whose name means "basket of dew." The Ala Wai Canal, completed in the late 1920s, drained the land, reducing proud Apuakehau Stream to a determined phantom passing beneath Waikiki's streets.

RAINY DAY IDEAS

Lobby lounging: Check out the century-old, period-furnished lobby and veranda of the Sheraton Moana Surfrider Hotel on Kalakaua.

Lucoral Museum: Exhibit and shop explores the world of coral and other semi-precious stones; wander about or take $2 guided tour and participate in jewelry-making activity. 2414 Kuhio.

WHAT'S NEW & CHANGING

Waikiki, which was looking a bit shop-worn, is in the midst of many makeovers. Ask about noise, disruption, and construction when booking.

In addition to fresh landscaping and period light fixtures along Kalakaua and a pathway that encircles Ala Wai Canal, expect:

BEACH WALK: After ten years of planning, the Waikiki Beach Walk—a pedestrian walkway lined with restaurants and shops—opened in 2007 to rave reviews. It was a massive project for the city, costing about $535 million and taking up nearly 8 acres of land. It's a great place to spend the afternoon, but be warned: this place gets packed on weekends.

ROYAL HAWAIIAN SHOPPING CENTER: The fortress-like Royal Hawaiian Shopping Center in the center of Kalakaua Avenue is an open, inviting space with a palm grove and a mix of shops and restaurants.

GETTING THERE

It can seem impossible to figure out how to get to Waikiki from H-1. The exit is far inland, and even when you follow the signs, the route jigs and jogs; it sometimes seems a wonder that more tourists aren't found starving in Kaimuki.

FROM EASTBOUND H-1 (COMING FROM THE AIRPORT):
1. To western Waikiki (Ft. DeRussy and most hotels): Take the Punahou exit from H-1, turn right on Punahou and get in the center lane. Go right on Beretania and almost immediately left onto Kalakaua, which takes you into Waikiki.

2. To eastern Waikiki (Kapiolani Park): Take the King Street exit, and stay on King for two blocks. Go right on Kapahulu, which takes you to Ala Wai Boulevard.

FROM WESTBOUND H-1:
Take the Kapiolani Boulevard exit. Follow Kapiolani to McCully, and go left on McCully. Follow McCully to Kalakaua, and you're in Waikiki.

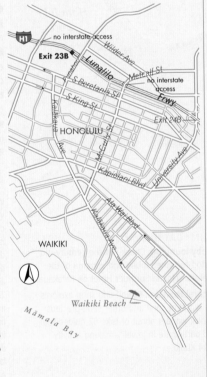

PEARL HARBOR

December 7, 1941. Every American then alive recalls exactly what he or she was doing when the news broke that the Japanese had bombed Pearl Harbor, the catalyst that brought the United States into World War II. More than 2,000 people died that day, and a dozen ships were sunk.

Here, in what is still a key Pacific naval base, the attack is remembered every day by thousands of visitors. In recent years, the memorial has been the site of reconciliation ceremonies involving Pearl Harbor veterans from both sides.

Fodor's Choice ★ **Pearl Harbor National Memorial Museum and Visitor Center.** The Pearl Harbor visitor center, recently reopened after a $58 million renovation and now part of the World War II Valor in the Pacific National Monument, is open from 7 am to 5 pm. For more information, visit ⊕ *www. nps.gov/valr/index.htm.* The site is a must-see for many, but there are things to know before you go. Consider whether you want to see only the *Arizona* Memorial, or the USS *Bowfin* and USS *Missouri* as well (the latter two sights charge admission fees). Allow approximately an hour and 15 minutes for the USS *Arizona* tour. Arrive early—the free, first-come, first-served tickets for the *Arizona* Memorial can disappear within an hour. There are restrictions on what you can bring with you, including purses, backpacks, and camera cases (although cameras are allowed). Baggage lockers are available for a small fee. Also, don't forget ID. *For much more detailed information, see the Pearl Harbor feature.* ⊠ *World War II Valor in the Pacific National Monument, 1 Arizona Memorial Pl., Pearl Harbor* ☎ *808/422–3300* ⊕ *www.nps.gov/ valr/index.htm* ✎ *Free (timed tickets required for Arizona Memorial)* ☉ *Daily 7–5; Arizona Memorial tours daily 8–3.*

SOUTHEAST OAHU

Approximately 10 miles southeast of Waikiki.

Driving southeast from Waikiki on busy four-lane Kalanianaole Highway, you'll pass a dozen bedroom communities tucked into the valleys at the foot of the Koolau Range, with fleeting glimpses of the ocean from a couple of pocket parks. Suddenly, civilization falls away, the road narrows to two lanes, and you enter the rugged coastline of Koko Head and Ka Iwi.

This is a cruel coastline: dry, windswept, and rocky shores, with untamed waves that are notoriously treacherous. While walking its beaches, do not turn your back on the ocean, don't venture close to wet areas where high waves occasionally reach, and be sure to heed warning signs.

At this point, you're passing through Koko Head Regional Park. On your right is the bulging remnant of a pair of volcanic craters that the Hawaiians called Kawaihoa, known today as Koko Head. To the left is Koko Crater and an area of the park that includes a hiking trail, a dryland botanical garden, a firing range, and a riding stable. Ahead is a sinuous shoreline with scenic pullouts and beaches to explore. Named the Ka Iwi Coast (*iwi*, "ee-vee," are bones—sacred to Hawaiians and full of symbolism) for the channel just offshore, this area was once home to a ranch and small fishing enclave that were destroyed by a tidal wave in the 1940s.

GETTING HERE AND AROUND

Driving straight from Waikiki to Makapuu Point takes from a half to a full hour, depending on traffic. There aren't a huge number of sights per se in this corner of Oahu, so a couple of hours should be plenty of exploring time, unless you make a lengthy stop at a particular point.

EXPLORING

Halona Blowhole. Below a scenic turnout along the Koko Head shoreline, this oft-photographed lava tube sucks the ocean in and spits it out. Don't get too close, as conditions can get dangerous. ■TIP→ **Look to your right to see the tiny beach below that was used to film the wave-washed love scene in** *From Here to Eternity.* In winter this is a good spot to watch whales at play. Offshore, the islands of Molokai and Lanai call like distant sirens, and every once in a while Maui is visible in blue silhouette. Take your valuables with you and lock your car, because this scenic location is overrun with tourists and therefore a hot spot for petty thieves. ⊠ *Kalanianaole Hwy., 1 mile east of Hanauma Bay.*

Makapuu Point. This spot has breathtaking views of the ocean, mountains, and the Windward Islands. The point of land jutting out in the distance is **Mokapu Peninsula,** site of a U.S. Marine base. The spired mountain peak is **Mt. Olomana.** In front of you on the long pier is part of the **Makai Undersea Test Range,** a research facility that's closed to the public. Offshore is **Manana Island (Rabbit Island),** a picturesque cay said to resemble a swimming bunny with its ears pulled back. Ironically enough, Manana Island was once overrun with rabbits, thanks to a rancher who let a few hares run wild on the land. They were eradicated in 1994 by biologists who grew concerned that the rabbits were destroying the island's native plants.

Nestled in the cliff face is the **Makapuu Lighthouse,** which became operational in 1909 and has the largest lighthouse lens in America. The lighthouse is closed to the public, but near the Makapuu Point turnout you can find the start of a mile-long paved road (closed to traffic). Hike up to the top of the 647-foot bluff for a closer view of the lighthouse and, in winter, a great whale-watching vantage point. ⊠ *Ka Iwi State Scenic Shoreline, Kalanianaole Hwy., at Makapuu Beach, Kaneohe* ⊕ *www.hawaiistateparks.org.*

WINDWARD OAHU

Approximately 15 miles northeast of downtown Honolulu (20–25 minutes by car), approximately 25 miles southeast of downtown Honolulu via Ka Iwi and Waimanalo (35–45 minutes by car).

Looking at Honolulu's topsy-turvy urban sprawl, you would never suspect the windward side existed. It's a secret Oahuans like to keep, so they can watch the awe on the faces of their guests when the car emerges from the tunnels through the mountains and they gaze for the first time on the panorama of turquoise bays and emerald valleys watched over by the knife-edged Koolau ridges. Jaws literally drop. Every time. And this just a 15-minute drive from downtown.

Continued on page 77

USS *West Virginia* (BB48), 7 December 1941

PEARL HARBOR

December 7, 1941. Every American then alive recalls exactly what he or she was doing when the news broke that the Japanese had bombed Pearl Harbor, the catalyst that brought the United States into World War II.

Although it was clear by late 1941 that war with Japan was inevitable, no one in authority seems to have expected the attack to come in just this way, at just this time. So when the Japanese bombers swept through a gap in Oahu's Koolau Mountains in the hazy light of morning, they found the bulk of America's Pacific fleet right where they hoped it would be: docked like giant stepping stones across the calm waters of the bay named for the pearl oysters that once prospered there. More than 2,000 people died that day, including 49 civilians. A dozen ships were sunk. And on the nearby air bases, virtually every American military aircraft was destroyed or damaged. The attack was a stunning success, but it lit a fire under America, which went to war with "Remember Pearl Harbor" as its battle cry. Here, in what is still a key Pacific naval base, the attack is remembered every day by thousands of visitors, including many curious Japanese, who for years heard little World War II history in their own country. In recent years, the memorial has been the site of reconciliation ceremonies involving Pearl Harbor veterans from both sides.

GETTING AROUND

Pearl Harbor is both a working military base and the most-visited Oahu attraction. Four distinct destinations share a parking lot and are linked by footpath, shuttle, and ferry.

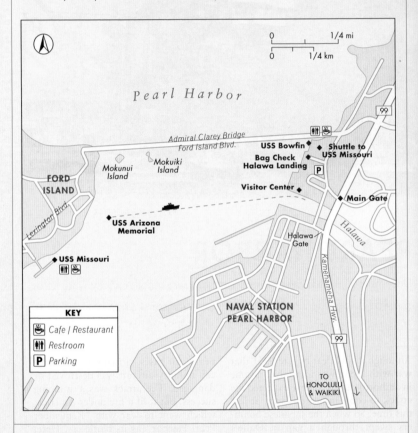

The visitor center is accessible from the parking lot. The USS *Arizona* Memorial itself is in the middle of the harbor; get tickets for the ferry ride at the visitor center. The USS *Bowfin* is also reachable from the parking lot.

The USS *Missouri* is docked at Ford Island, a restricted area of the naval base. Vehicular access is prohibited. To get there, take a shuttle bus from the station near the *Bowfin*.

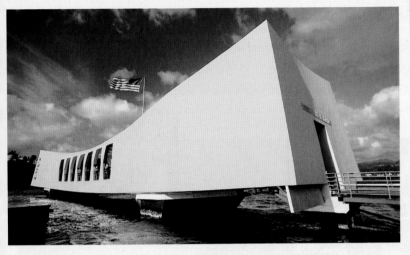

ARIZONA MEMORIAL

Snugged up tight in a row of seven battleships off Ford Island, the USS *Arizona* took a direct hit that December morning, exploded, and rests still on the shallow bottom where she settled.

The swooping, stark-white memorial, which straddles the wreck of the USS *Arizona*, was designed to represent both the depths of the low-spirited, early days of the war, and the uplift of victory.

A visit here begins at the Pearl Harbor Visitor Center, which recently underwent a $58 million renovation. High definition projectors and interactive exhibits were installed, and the building was modernized. From the visitor center, a ferry takes you to the memorial itself, and a new shuttle hub now gives access to sites that were previously inaccessible, like the USS *Utah* and USS *Oklahoma*.

A somber, contemplative mood descends upon visitors during the ferry ride to the *Arizona*; this is a place where 1,177 crewmen lost their lives. Gaze at the names of the dead carved into the wall of white marble. Scatter flowers (but no lei—the string is bad for the fish). Salute the flag. Remember Pearl Harbor.

☎ *808/422–0561*
⊕ *www.nps.gov/valr*

USS *MISSOURI* (BB63)

Together with the *Arizona* Memorial, the *Missouri's* presence in Pearl Harbor perfectly bookends America's WWII experience that began December 7, 1941, and ended on the "Mighty Mo's" starboard deck with the signing of the Terms of Surrender.

Surrender of Japan, USS *Missouri*, 2 September 1945

In the parking area behind the USS *Bowfin* Museum, board a shuttle for a breezy, eight-minute ride to Ford Island and the teak decks and towering superstructure of the *Missouri*, docked for good in the very harbor from which she first went to war on January 2, 1945. The last battleship ever built, the *Missouri* famously hosted the final act of WWII, the signing of the Terms of Surrender. The commission that governs this floating museum has surrounded her with buildings tricked out in WWII style—a canteen that serves as an orientation space for tours, a WACs and WAVEs lounge with a flight simulator the kids will love ($10 per person), Truman's Line restaurant serving Navy-style meals, and a Victory Store housing a souvenir shop and covered with period mottos ("Don't be a blabateur").
■TIP→ Definitely hook up with a tour guide (additional charge) or audio tour —these add a great deal to the experience.

The *Missouri* is all about numbers: 209 feet tall, six 239,000-pound guns, capable of firing up to 23 mi away. Absorb these during the tour, then stop to take advantage of the view from the decks. The Mo is a work in progress, with only a handful of her hundreds of spaces open to view.

☎808/423–2263 or ☎888/877–6477
⊕*www.ussmissouri.com*

USS *BOWFIN* (SS287)

SUBMARINE MUSEUM & PARK

Launched one year to the day after the Pearl Harbor attack, the USS *Bowfin* sank 44 enemy ships during WWII and now serves as the centerpiece of a museum honoring all submariners.

Although the *Bowfin* no less than the *Arizona* Memorial commemorates the lost, the mood here is lighter. Perhaps it's the childlike scale of the boat, a metal tube just 16 feet in diameter, packed with ladders, hatches, and other obstacles, like the naval version of a jungle gym. Perhaps it's the World War II-era music that plays in the covered patio. Or it might be the museum's touching displays—the penciled sailor's journal, the Vargas girlie posters. Aboard the boat nicknamed "Pearl Harbor Avenger," compartments are fitted out as though "Sparky" was away from the radio room just for a moment, and "Cooky" might be right back to his pots and pans. The museum includes many artifacts to spark family conversations, among them a vintage dive suit that looks too big for Shaquille

O'Neal. A caution: The *Bowfin* could be hazardous for very young children; no one under four allowed.

☏ *808/423–1341*
⊕ *www.bowfin.org*

THE PACIFIC AVIATION MUSEUM

This museum opened on December 7, 2006, as phase one of a four-phase tribute to the air wars of the Pacific. Located on Ford Island in Hangar 37, an actual seaplane hangar that survived the Pearl Harbor attack, the museum is made up of a theater where a short film on Pearl Harbor kicks off the tour, an education center, a shop, and a restaurant. Exhibits—many of which are interactive and involve sound effects—include an authentic Japanese Zero in a diorama setting a chance to don a flight suit and play the role of a World War II pilot using one of six flight simulators. Various aircrafts are employed to narrate the great battles: the Doolittle Raid on Japan, the Battle of Midway, Guadalcanal, and so on. The actual Stearman N2S-3 in which President George H. W. Bush soloed is another exhibit. ☏ 808/441–1000 ⊕ www.pacificaviationmuseum.org ▱ $20.

PLAN YOUR PEARL HARBOR DAY
LIKE A MILITARY CAMPAIGN

DIRECTIONS

Take H–1 west from Waikiki to Exit 15A and follow signs. Or take The-Bus route 20 or 47 from Waikiki. Beware high-priced private shuttles. It's a 30-minute drive from Waikiki.

WHAT TO BRING

Picture ID is required during periods of high alert; bring it just in case.

You'll be standing, walking, and climbing all day. Wear something with lots of pockets and a pair of good walking shoes. Carry a light jacket, sunglasses, hat, and sunscreen.

No purses, packs, or bags are allowed. Take only what fits in your pockets. Cameras are okay but without the bags. A private bag storage booth is located in the parking lot near the visitors' center. Leave nothing in your car; theft is a problem despite bicycle security patrols.

HOURS

Hours are 7 AM to 5 PM for the visitor center, though the attractions open at 8 AM. The *Arizona* Memorial starts giving out tickets on a first-come, first-served basis at 7:30 AM; the last tickets are given out at 3 PM. Spring break, summer, and holidays are busiest, and tickets sometimes run out by noon or earlier.

TICKETS

Arizona: Free. Add $7.50 for museum audio tours.

Aviation: $20 adults, $10 children. Add $10 for aviator's guided tour.

Missouri: $20 adults, $10 children. Add $25 for in-depth, behind-the-scenes tours.

Bowfin: $10 adults, $4 children. Add $2 for audio tours. Children under 4 may go into the museum but not aboard the *Bowfin*.

KIDS

This might be the day to enroll younger kids in the hotel children's program. Preschoolers chafe at long waits, and attractions involve some hazards for toddlers. Older kids enjoy the *Bowfin* and *Missouri,* especially.

MAKING THE MOST OF YOUR TIME

Expect to spend at least half a day; a whole day is better if you're a military history buff.

At the *Arizona* Memorial, you'll get a ticket, be given a tour time, and then have to wait anywhere from 15 minutes to 3 hours. You must pick up your own ticket so you can't hold places. If the wait is long, skip over to the *Bowfin* to fill the time.

SUGGESTED READING

Pearl Harbor and the USS Arizona Memorial, by Richard Wisniewski. $5.95. 64-page magazine-size quick history.

Bowfin, by Edwin P. Hoyt. $14.95. Dramatic story of undersea adventure.

The Last Battleship, by Scott C. S. Stone. $11.95. Story of the Mighty Mo.

The Byodo-In Temple on the windward side of Oahu is a replica of an 11th-century temple in Japan.

It's on this side of the island where many native Hawaiians live. Evidence of traditional lifestyles is abundant in crumbling fishponds, rock platforms that once were altars, taro patches still being worked, and thrownet fishermen posed stock-still above the water (though today, they're invariably wearing polarized sunglasses, the better to spot the fish).

Here, the pace is slower, more oriented toward nature. Beach-going, hiking, diving, surfing, and boating are the draws, along with a visit to the Polynesian Cultural Center, and poking through little shops and wayside stores.

GETTING HERE AND AROUND

For a driving experience you won't soon forget, take the H3 freeway over to the windward side. As you pass through the tunnels, be prepared for one of the most breathtaking stretches of road anywhere. Flip a coin before you leave to see who will drive and who will gape.

TIMING

You can easily spend an entire day exploring Windward Oahu, or you can just breeze on through, nodding at the sights on your way to the North Shore. Waikiki to Windward is a drive of less than half an hour; to the North Shore via Kamehameha Highway along the Windward Coast is one hour, minimum.

TOP ATTRACTIONS

Byodo-In Temple. Tucked away in the back of the Valley of the Temples cemetery is a replica of the 11th-century Temple at Uji in Japan. A 2-ton carved wooden statue of the Buddha presides inside the main temple building. Next to the temple building are a meditation pavilion and gardens set dramatically against the sheer, green cliffs of the Koolau

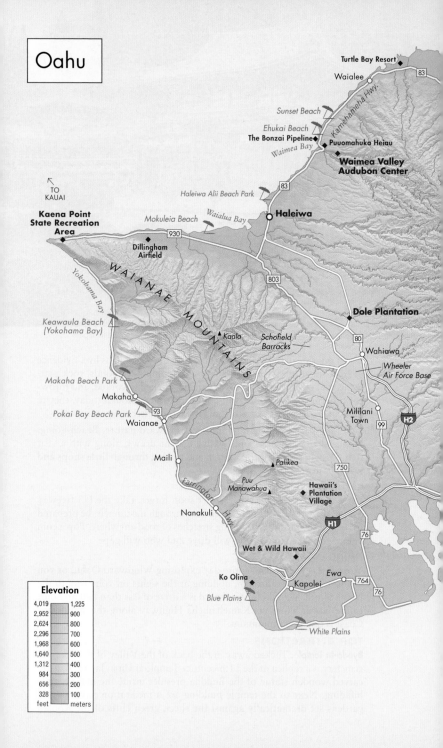

Oahu

Turtle Bay Resort

Waialee

Sunset Beach

Ehukai Beach
The Bonzai Pipeline

Kamehameha Hwy.

Puuomahuka Heiau

Waimea Bay

**Waimea Valley
Audubon Center**

Haleiwa Alii Beach Park

↖
TO
KAUAI

Mokuleia Beach

Waialua Bay

Haleiwa

**Kaena Point
State Recreation
Area**

930

**Dillingham
Airfield**

Yokohama Bay

W A I A N A E

803

Dole Plantation

80

*Keawaula Beach
(Yokohama Bay)*

▲ *Kaala*

*Schofield
Barracks*

M O U N T A I N S

Wahiawa

*Wheeler
Air Force Base*

Makaha Beach Park

Makaha

99

Mililani
Town

H2

93

Pokai Bay Beach Park

Waianae

Maili

▲ *Palikea*

750

*Puu
Manawahua* ▲

**Hawaii's
Plantation
Village** ◆

Farrington Hwy.

Nanakuli

H1

76

Wet & Wild Hawaii ◆

Ewa

764

Ko Olina ◆

Kapolei

76

Blue Plains △

White Plains

Elevation	
4,019	1,225
2,952	900
2,624	800
2,296	700
1,968	600
1,640	500
1,312	400
984	300
656	200
328	100
feet	meters

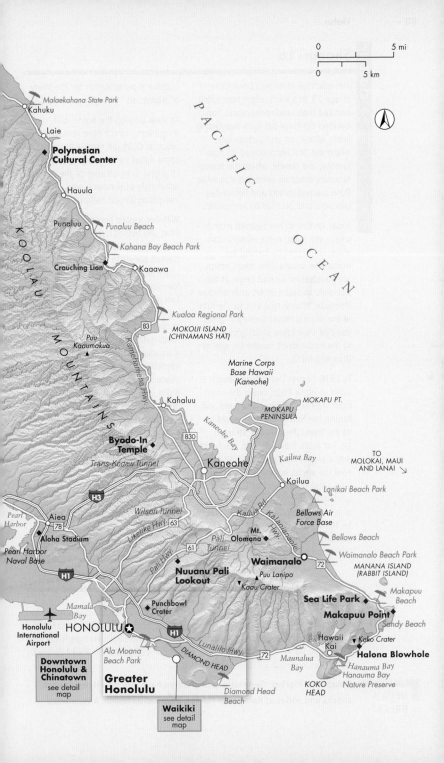

5 mi
5 km

P A C I F I C

O C E A N

Kahuku
Malaekahana State Park
Laie
Polynesian Cultural Center
Hauula
Punaluu
Punaluu Beach
Kahana Bay Beach Park
Crouching Lion
Kaaawa
Kualoa Regional Park
MOKOLII ISLAND (CHINAMANS HAT)

K O O L A U   M O U N T A I N S

Puu Kaaumakua

83
Kamehameha Hwy.

Kahaluu
Marine Corps Base Hawaii (Kaneohe)
MOKAPU PT.
MOKAPU PENINSULA
830
Byodo-In Temple
Trans-Koolau Tunnel
Kaneohe Bay
Kaneohe
Kailua Bay
TO MOLOKAI, MAUI AND LANAI
Kailua
Lanikai Beach Park

Pearl Harbor
Aiea
78
Wilson Tunnel
Likelike Hwy.
63
Kailua Rd.

H3

Kalanianaole Hwy.
Bellows Air Force Base
Bellows Beach

Aloha Stadium
Pearl Harbor Naval Base
H1
61
Mt. Olomana
Pali Tunnel
Pali Hwy.
Waimanalo
Waimanalo Beach Park
MANANA ISLAND (RABBIT ISLAND)

Mamala Bay
Honolulu International Airport
Punchbowl Crater
Nuuanu Pali Lookout
Puu Lanipo
Kaau Crater
Sea Life Park
Makapuu Beach

HONOLULU ★
H1
Lunalilo Hwy.
Makapuu Point
Sandy Beach
Koko Crater

Ala Moana Beach Park
DIAMOND HEAD
72
Hawaii Kai
Halona Blowhole

Downtown Honolulu & Chinatown see detail map

Diamond Head Beach
Maunalua Bay
Hanauma Bay
Hanauma Bay Nature Preserve
KOKO HEAD

Greater Honolulu

Waikiki see detail map

Shangri La

The marriage of heiress Doris Duke, at age 23, to a much older man didn't last. But their around-the-world honeymoon did leave her with two lasting loves: Islamic art and architecture, which she first encountered on that journey; and Hawaii, where the honeymooners made an extended stay while Doris learned to surf and befriended Islanders unimpressed by her wealth.

Today visitors to her beloved Islands—where she spent most winters—can share both loves by touring her home. The sought-after tours, which are coordinated by and begin at the Honolulu Museum of Art in downtown Honolulu, start with a visit to the Arts of the Islamic World Gallery. A short van ride then takes small groups on to the house itself, on the far side of Diamond Head.

In 1936, heiress Doris Duke bought 5 acres at Black Point, down the coast from Waikiki, and began to build and furnish the first home that would be all her own. She called it **Shangri La**. For more than 50 years, the home was a work in progress as Duke traveled the world, buying art and furnishings, picking up ideas for her Mughul garden, for the Playhouse in the style of a 17th-century Irani pavilion, and for the water terraces and tropical gardens. When she died in 1993, Duke left instructions that her home was to

become a public center for the study of Islamic art.

To walk through the house and its gardens—which have remained much as Duke left them with only some minor conservation-oriented changes—is to experience the personal style of someone who saw everything as raw material for her art.

With her trusted houseman, Jin de Silva, she helped build the elaborate Turkish Room, trimming tiles and painted panels to retrofit the existing space (including raising the ceiling and lowering the floor) and building a fountain of her own design. Among many aspects of the home inspired by the Muslim tradition is the entry: an anonymous gate, a blank white wall, and a wooden door that bids you "Enter herein in peace and security" in Arabic characters. Inside, tiles glow, fountains tinkle, and shafts of light illuminate artworks through arches and high windows. This was her private world, entered only by trusted friends.

Guided tours take 2½ hours including transportation from the Honolulu Museum of Art (*see the listing in Exploring Honolulu*). Children under 12 are not admitted. The tours cost $25 and are offered Wednesday–Saturday (first tour 8:30 am, last tour 1:30 pm). They should be reserved far in advance. For more information, see ⊕ *www.shangrilahawaii.org.*

Mountains. You can ring the 5-foot, 3-ton brass bell for good luck and feed some of the hundreds of carp, ducks, and turtles that inhabit the garden's 2-acre pond. Or, you can enjoy the peaceful surroundings and just relax. ⊠ *47-200 Kahekili Hwy., Kaneohe* ☎ *808/239–9844* ⊕ *www. byodo-in.com* ☑ *$3* ⊗ *Daily 9–5.*

NEED A BREAK?

Kalapawai Market. Generations of children have purchased their beach snacks and sodas at Kalapawai Market, near Kailua Beach. A Windward

landmark since 1932, the green-and-white market has distinctive charm. You'll see slipper-clad locals sitting in front sharing a cup of coffee and talking story at picnic tables or in front of the market. It's a good source for your carryout lunch, since there's no concession stand at the beach. With one of the better selections of wine on the island, the market is also a great place to pick up a bottle. ✉ *306 S. Kalaheo Ave., Kailua* ☎ *808/262-4359* ⊕ *www.kalapawaimarket.com* ☉ *Daily 6 am–9 pm; deli closes at 8 pm.*

Nuuanu Pali Lookout. This panoramic perch looks out to Windward Oahu. It was in this region that King Kamehameha I drove defending forces over the edges of the 1,000-foot-high cliffs, thus winning the decisive battle for control of Oahu. ■ TIP➔ From here you can see views that stretch from Kaneohe Bay to Mokolii (little lizard), a small island off the coast, and beyond. Temperatures at the summit are several degrees cooler than in warm Waikiki, so bring a jacket along. And hang on tight to any loose possessions; it gets extremely windy at the lookout. Lock your car; break-ins have occurred here (this lookout is in the most trafficked state park in Hawaii). ✉ *Top of Pali Hwy., Kaneohe* ⊕ *www.hawaiistateparks.org/ parks/oahu/nuuanu.cfm* ☉ *Daily during daylight hours.*

■ EN
ROUTE

Mokolii. As you drive the Windward and North shores along Kamehameha Highway, you'll note a number of interesting geological features. At Kualoa look to the ocean and gaze at the uniquely shaped little island of Mokolii (little lizard), a 206-foot-high sea stack also known as Chinaman's Hat. According to Hawaiian legend, the goddess Hiiaka, sister of Pele, slew the dragon Mokolii and flung its tail into the sea, forming the distinct islet. Other dragon body parts—in the form of rocks, of course—were scattered along the base of nearby Kualoa Ridge. ■ TIP➔ In Laie, if you turn right on Anemoku Street, and right again on Naupaka, you come to a scenic lookout where you can see a group of islets, dramatically washed by the waves. ✉ *49-479 Kamehameha Highway, Kaneohe* ⊕ *www1.honolulu.gov/parks/programs/ beach/kualoa.htm.*

☺ **Polynesian Cultural Center.** Re-created individual villages showcase the lifestyles and traditions of Hawaii, Tahiti, Samoa, Fiji, the Marquesas Islands, New Zealand, and Tonga. Focusing on individual Islands within its 42-acre center, 35 miles from Waikiki, the Polynesian Cultural Center was founded in 1963 by the Church of Jesus Christ of Latter-day Saints. It houses restaurants, hosts luau, and demonstrates cultural traditions such as tribal tattooing, fire dancing, and ancient customs and ceremonies. The expansive open-air shopping village carries Polynesian handicrafts. ■ TIP➔ If you're staying in Honolulu, see the center as part of a van tour so you won't have to drive home late at night after the two-hour evening show. More than 10 different packages are available, from basic admission to an all-inclusive deal. Every May, the PCC hosts the World Fire-Knife Dance Competition, an event that draws the top fire-knife dance performers from around the world. Get tickets for that event in advance. ✉ *55-370 Kamehameha Hwy., Laie* ☎ *808/293-3333, 800/367-7060* ⊕ *www.polynesia.com* 🎫 *$45–$225* ☉ *Mon.–Sat. noon–9:30. Islands close at 6.*

Windward Oahu Villlages

Tiny villages—generally consisting of a sign, store, a beach park, possibly a post office, and not much more—are strung along Kamehameha Highway on the windward side. Each has something to offer. In **Waiahole,** look for fruit stands and an ancient grocery store. In **Kaaawa,** there's a lunch spot and convenience store–gas station. In **Punaluu,** stop at the gallery of fanciful landscape artist Lance Fairly and the woodworking shop, Kahaunani Woods & Crafts, plus venerable Ching General Store or the Shrimp Shack. Kim Taylor Reece's photo studio, featuring haunting portraits of hula dancers, is between Punaluu and Hauula. **Hauula** has Hauula Gift Shop and Art Gallery, formerly yet another Ching Store, now a clothing shop where sarongs wave like banners, and, at Hauula Kai Shopping Center, Tamura Market, with excellent seafood and the last liquor before Mormon-dominated Laie.

WORTH NOTING

Sea Life Park. Dolphins leap and spin and penguins frolic at this marine-life attraction 15 miles from Waikiki at scenic Makapuu Point. The park has a 300,000-gallon Hawaiian reef aquarium, the Hawaiian Monk Seal Care Center, and a breeding sanctuary for Hawaii's endangered *honu* sea turtle. Join the Stingray or Dolphin Encounter and get up close and personal in the water with these sea creatures (don't worry, the rays' stingers have been removed) or go on an underwater photo safari. ⊠ *41-202 Kalanianaole Hwy., Waimanalo* ☎ *808/259–2500, 866/365–7446* ⊕ *www.sealifeparkhawaii.com* ✉ *$30* ☉ *Daily 10:30–5.*

Waimanalo. This modest little seaside town flanked by chiseled cliffs is worth a visit. Home to more local families than Kailua to the north or Hawaii Kai to the south, Waimanalo's biggest draws are its beautiful beaches, offering glorious views to the windward side. **Bellows Beach** is great for swimming and bodysurfing, and **Waimanalo Beach Park** is also safe for swimming. Down the side roads, as you head *mauka* (toward the mountains), are little farms that grow a variety of fruits and flowers. Toward the back of the valley are small ranches with grazing horses. ■TIP→ If you see any trucks selling corn and you're staying at a place where you can cook it, be sure to get some in Waimanalo. It may be the sweetest you'll ever eat, and the price is the lowest on Oahu. ⊠ *Kalanianaole Hwy., Waimanalo.*

THE NORTH SHORE

Approximately 35 miles (one hour) north of downtown Honolulu, approximately 25 miles (one hour by car) from Kualoa Regional Park (Chinaman's Hat) in Windward Oahu.

An hour from town and a world away in atmosphere, Oahu's North Shore, roughly from Kahuku Point to Kaena Point, is about small farms and big waves, tourist traps and otherworldly landscapes. Parks and beaches, roadside fruit stands and shrimp shacks, a bird sanctuary, and a valley preserve offer a dozen reasons to stop between the onetime plantation town of Kahuku and the surf mecca of Haleiwa.

Haleiwa has had many lives, from resort getaway in the 1900s to plantation town through the 20th century to its life today as a surf and tourist magnet. Beyond Haleiwa is the tiny village of Waialua, a string of beach parks, an airfield where gliders, hang gliders, and parachutists play, and, at the end of the road, Kaena Point State Recreation Area, which offers a brisk hike, striking views, and whale-watching in season.

Pack wisely for a day's North Shore excursion: swim and snorkel gear, light jacket and hat (the weather is mercurial, especially in winter), sunscreen and sunglasses, bottled water and snacks, towels and a picnic blanket, and both sandals and close-toed shoes for hiking. A small cooler is nice; you may want to pick up some fruit or fresh corn. As always, leave valuables in the hotel safe and lock the car whenever you park.

GETTING HERE AND AROUND

From Waikiki, the quickest route to the North Shore is H1 east to H2 north, and then the Kamehameha Highway past Wahiawa; you'll hit Haleiwa in less than an hour. The windward route (H1 east, H3, Like Like or Pali Highway, through the mountains, or Kamehameha Highway north) takes at least 90 minutes to Haleiwa, but the drive is far prettier.

TIMING

It's best to dedicate an entire day for an excursion to the North Shore, as it's about an hour from downtown Honolulu, depending on traffic.

TOP ATTRACTIONS

Haleiwa. During the 1920s this seaside hamlet boasted a posh hotel at the end of a railroad line (both long gone). During the 1960s, hippies gathered here, followed by surfers from around the world. Today Haleiwa is a fun mix, with old general stores and contemporary boutiques, galleries, and eateries. Be sure to stop in at **Liliuokalani Protestant Church,** founded by missionaries in the 1830s. It's fronted by a large, stone archway built in 1910 and covered with night-blooming cereus. ⊠ *Haleiwa* ✛ *Follow H1 west from Honolulu to H2 north, exit at Wahiawa, follow Kamehameha Hwy. 6 mi, turn left at signaled intersection, then right into Haleiwa.*

NEED A BREAK?

Matsumoto's. For a real slice of Haleiwa life, stop at Matsumoto's, a family-run business in a building dating from 1910, for shave ice in every flavor imaginable. For something different, order a shave ice with adzuki beans—the red beans are boiled until soft, mixed with sugar, and then placed in the cone with the ice on top. ⊠ *66-087 Kamehameha Hwy., Haleiwa* ☎ *808/637–4827* ⊕ *www.matsumotoshaveice.com* ☉ *Daily, 9–6.*

Kaena Point State Recreation Area. The name means "the heat" and, indeed, this windy barren coast lacks both shade and fresh water (or any man-made amenities). Pack water, wear sturdy closed-toed shoes, don sunscreen and a hat, and lock the car. The hike is along a rutted dirt road, mostly flat and 3 miles long, ending in a rocky, sandy headland. It

See colorful wildlife at the Waimea Valley Audubon Center on Oahu's North Shore.

is here that Hawaiians believed the souls of the dead met with their family gods, and, if judged worthy to enter the afterlife, leaped off into eternal darkness at Leinaakauane, just south of the point. In summer and at low tide, the small coves offer bountiful shelling; in winter, don't venture near the water. Rare native plants dot the landscape. November through March, watch for humpbacks, spouting and breaching. Binoculars and a camera are highly recommended. ⊠ *69-385 Farrington Hwy., Makua* ⊕ *www.hawaiistateparks.org/parks/oahu/index.cfm?park_id=19.*

Puuomahuka Heiau. Worth a stop for its spectacular views from a bluff high above the ocean overlooking Waimea Bay, this sacred spot was once the site of human sacrifices. It's now on the National Register of Historic Places. ⊠ *Pupukea Rd., ½ mile north of Waimea Bay, Haleiwa* ✛ *From Rte. 83, turn right on Pupukea Rd. and drive 1 mile uphill.*

★ **Waimea Valley Park.** Waimea may get lots of press for the giant winter
Ⓒ waves in the bay, but the valley itself is a newsmaker and an ecological treasure in its own right. The Office of Hawaiian Affairs is working to conserve and restore the natural habitat. Follow the Kamananui Stream up the valley through the 1,800 acres of gardens. The botanical collections here include more than 5,000 species of tropical flora, including a superb gathering of Polynesian plants. It's the best place on the island to see native species, such as the endangered Hawaiian moorhen. You can also see the remains of the Hale O Lono *heiau* (temple) along with other ancient archaeological sites; evidence suggests that the area was an important spiritual center. Daily activities between 10 and 2 include hula lessons, native plant walks, lei-making lessons, kapa cloth-making demonstrations, depending on how many

staff members are working on a given day. At the back of the valley, **Waihi Falls** plunges 45 feet into a swimming pond. ■TIP➔ Bring your board shorts—a swim is the perfect way to end your hike. Be sure to bring mosquito repellent, too; it gets buggy. ✉ 59-864 *Kamehameha Hwy., Haleiwa* ☎ 808/638-7766 ⊕ *www.waimeavalley.net* ✉ $15 ◷ *Daily 9–5.*

QUICK BITES

Ted's Bakery. The chocolate *haupia* (coconut pudding) pie at Ted's Bakery is legendary. Stop in for a take-out pie or for a quick plate lunch or sandwich. ✉ *59-024 Kamehameha Hwy., near Sunset Beach, Haleiwa* ☎ *808/638-8207* ⊕ *www.tedsbakery.com* ◷ *Mon.–Tues. 7–6, Wed.–Sun. 7 am–8 pm.*

CENTRAL OAHU

Wahiawa is approximately 20 miles (30–35 minutes by car) north of downtown Honolulu, 15 miles (20–30 minutes by car) south of the North Shore.

Oahu's central plain is a patchwork of old towns and new residential developments, military bases, farms, ranches, and shopping malls, with a few visit-worthy attractions and historic sites scattered about. Central Oahu encompasses the Moanalua Valley, residential Pearl City and Mililani, and the old plantation town of Wahiawa, on the uplands halfway to the North Shore.

GETTING HERE AND AROUND

For central Oahu, all sights are most easily reached by either the H1 or H2 freeway.

TIMING

In Central Oahu, check out the Dole Plantation for all things pineapple. This area is about 35 minutes' drive from downtown Honolulu and might make a good stop on the drive to the North Shore or after a morning at Pearl Harbor, but the area is probably not worth a separate visit, particularly if you're short on time.

EXPLORING

Dole Plantation. Celebrate Hawaii's famous golden fruit at this promotional center with exhibits, a huge gift shop, a snack concession, educational displays, and the world's largest maze. Take the self-guided Garden Tour, plant your own pineapple, or hop aboard the *Pineapple Express* for a 20-minute train tour to learn a bit about life on a pineapple plantation. Kids love the more than 3-acre Pineapple Garden Maze, made up of 14,000 tropical plants and trees. This is about a 40-minute drive from Waikiki, a suitable stop on the way to or from the North Shore. ✉ *64-1550 Kamehameha Hwy., Wahiawa* ☎ *808/621-8408* ⊕ *www.dole-plantation.com* ✉ *Pavilion free, maze $6, train $8, garden tour $5* ◷ *Daily 9:30–5:30; train, maze, and garden 9:30–5.*

WEST (LEEWARD) OAHU

2

Kapolei is approximately 20 miles (30 minutes by car) west of downtown Honolulu, and 12 miles (20 minutes by car) from Mililani; traffic can add significantly to driving time.

West (or Leeward) Oahu has the island's fledgling "second city"—the planned community of Kapolei, where the government hopes to attract enough jobs to lighten inbound traffic to downtown Honolulu—then continues on past a far-flung resort to the Hawaiian communities of Nanakuli and Waianae, to the beach and the end of the road at Keaweula, aka Yokohama Bay.

A couple of cautions as you head to the leeward side: Highway 93 is a narrow, winding, two-lane road notorious for accidents. There's an abrupt transition from freeway to highway at Kapolei, and by the time you reach Nanakuli, it's a country road, so *slow down.* ⚠ Car break-ins and beach thefts are common here.

GETTING HERE AND AROUND

West Oahu begins at folksy Waipahu and continues past Makakilo and Kapolei on H1 and Highway 93, Farrington Highway.

TIMING

If you've got to leave one part of this island for the next trip, this is the part to skip. It's a longish drive to West Oahu by island standards—45 minutes to Kapolei from Waikiki and 90 minutes to Waianae—and Central Oahu has little to offer. The Waianae Coast is naturally beautiful, but the area doesn't have the tourist amenities you'll find elsewhere on the island. The attraction most worth the trek to West Oahu is Hawaii's Plantation Village in Waipahu, about a half hour out of town; it's a living-history museum built from actual homes of turn-of-the-20th-century plantation workers.

Hawaii's Plantation Village. Starting in the 1800s, immigrants seeking work on the sugar plantations came to these Islands like so many waves against the shore. At this living museum 30 minutes from downtown Honolulu, visit authentically furnished buildings, original and replicated, that re-create and pay tribute to the plantation era. See a Chinese social hall; a Japanese shrine, sumo ring, and saimin stand; a dental office; and historic homes. The village is open for guided tours only. ✉ *Waipahu Cultural Gardens Park, 94-695 Waipahu St., Waipahu* ☎ *808/677–0110* ⊕ *www.hawaiiplantationvillage.org* 💰 *$13* 🕓 *Tours on the hr, Mon.–Sat. 10–2.*

BEACHES

Updated by
Michael Levine

Tropical sun mixed with cooling trade winds and pristine waters make Oahu's shores a literal heaven on earth. But contrary to many assumptions, the island is not one big beach. There are miles and miles of coastline without a grain of sand, so you need to know where you're going to fully enjoy the Hawaiian experience.

Much of the island's southern and eastern coast is protected by inner reefs. The reefs provide still coastline water but not much as far as sand is concerned. However, where there are beaches on the south and east shores, they are mind-blowing. In West Oahu and on the North Shore you can find the wide expanses of sand you would expect for enjoying the sunset. Sandy bottoms and protective reefs make the water an adventure in the winter months. Most visitors assume the seasons don't change a bit in the Islands, and they would be mostly right—except for the waves, which are big on the South Shore in summer and placid in winter. It's exactly the opposite on the north side, where winter storms bring in huge waves, but the ocean becomes glasslike come May and June.

HONOLULU

Downtown Honolulu has only one beach, the monstrous Ala Moana. It hosts everything from Dragon Boat competitions to the Aloha State Games.

Ala Moana Beach Park. Ala Moana has a protective reef, which makes it essentially a ½-mile-wide saltwater swimming pool. Very smooth sand and no waves make it a haven for families and stand-up paddle surfers. After Waikiki, this is the most popular beach among visitors, and the free parking area can fill up quickly on sunny weekend days. On the Waikiki side is a peninsula called Magic Island, with shady trees and paved sidewalks ideal for jogging. Ala Moana also has playing fields, tennis courts, and a couple of small ponds for sailing toy boats. This beach is for everyone, but only in the daytime. It's a high-crime area, with lots of homeless people, after dark. **Amenities:** food and drink; lifeguards; parking (no fee); showers; toilets. **Best for:** swimming; walking. ⊠ *1201 Ala Moana Blvd., Downtown Honolulu ✢ From Waikiki take Bus 8 to Ala Moana Shopping Center and cross Ala Moana Blvd.*

WAIKIKI

Duke Kahanamoku Beach. Named for Hawaii's famous Olympic swimming champion, Duke Kahanamoku, this is a hard-packed beach with the only shade trees on the sand in Waikiki. It's great for families with young children because it has both shade and the calmest waters in Waikiki, thanks to a rock wall that creates a semiprotected cove. The ocean clarity here is not as brilliant as most of Waikiki because of the stillness of the surf, but it's a small price to pay for peace of mind about youngsters. The beach fronts the Hilton Hawaiian Village Beach Resort and Spa. **Amenities:** food and drink; showers; toilets. **Best for:** walking; sunset. ⊠ *2005 Kalia Rd.*

Fort DeRussy Beach Park. This is one of the finest beaches on the south side of Oahu. A wide, soft, ultrawhite beachfront with gently lapping waves makes it a family favorite for running-jumping-frolicking fun (this also happens to be where the NFL holds its rookie sand football game every year). The new, heavily shaded grass grilling area, sand volleyball courts, and aquatic rentals make this a must for the active visitor. The beach fronts Hale Koa Hotel as well as Fort DeRussy. **Amenities:** food and drink; lifeguards; showers; toilets; water sports. **Best for:** swimming; walking. ⊠ *2161 Kalia Rd.*

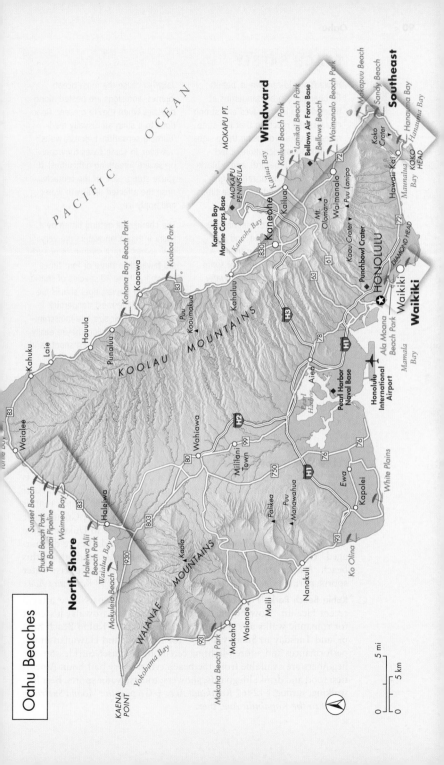

Oahu Beaches

PACIFIC OCEAN

Windward

Southeast

Mokapu Beach
Sandy Beach
Mokapu Point
Makapuu Beach
Lanikai Beach Park
Kailua Beach Park
Bellows Air Force Base
Waimanalo Beach Park
Kailua Bay
Waimanalo Beach
Koko Crater
Kailua
Waimanalo
72
Hanauma Bay
KOKO HEAD
Koko Head
Hawaii Kai
Maunalua Bay
Kaneohe Bay Marine Corps Base
MOKAPU PENINSULA
Mt. Olomana
Puu Lanipo
Kaau Crater
Kaneohe Bay
Kaneohe
830
Puu Kaumakua
Punchbowl Crater
61
63
HONOLULU
Waikiki
DIAMOND HEAD
Waikiki
Ala Moana Beach Park
H3
78
Mamala Bay

Kahana Bay Beach Park
Kaaawa
Kualoa Park
Kahaluu
83

Hauula
Punaluu

Kahuku
Laie

KOOLAU MOUNTAINS

H1
Aiea
Pearl Harbor Naval Base
Honolulu International Airport
H2
Wahiawa
99
Mililani Town
80
750
H1
Puu Manawahua
Ewa
76
White Plains
Kapolei
Waialee
83

North Shore
Sunset Beach
Ehukai Beach Park
The Banzai Pipeline
Waimea Bay
Haleiwa Alii Beach Park
Waialua Beach
Haleiwa
Mokuleia Beach
930
83
803

Waialua Bay
Poliaia
Kaala

WAIANAE MOUNTAINS

Kapolei
Ko Olina
93

Nanakuli
Maili
Waianae
Makaha
Makaha Beach Park
99
Yokohama Bay

KAENA POINT

MOKAPU PT.

5 mi
5 km
0
0

BEACH SAFETY

Hawaii's world-renowned, beautiful beaches can be dangerous at times due to large waves and strong currents—so much so that the state rates wave hazards using three signs: a yellow square (caution), a red stop sign (high hazard), and a black diamond (extreme hazard). Signs are posted and updated three times daily or as conditions change.

Visiting beaches with lifeguards is strongly recommended, and you should swim only when there's a normal caution rating. Never swim alone or dive into unknown water or shallow breaking waves. If you're unable to swim out of a rip current, don't fight the pull but instead tread water and wave your arms in the air to signal for help.

Even in calm conditions, there are other dangerous things in the water to be aware of, including razor-sharp coral, jellyfish, eels, and sharks.

Jellyfish cause the most ocean injuries, and signs are posted along beaches when they're present. Reactions to a sting are usually mild (burning sensation, redness, welts); however, in some cases they can be severe (breathing difficulties). If you're stung, pick off the tentacles, rinse the affected area with water, and apply ice.

The chances of getting bitten by a shark in Hawaiian waters are very low; sharks attack swimmers or surfers fewer than three or four times per year. Of the 40 species of sharks found near Hawaii, tiger sharks are considered the most dangerous because of their size and indiscriminate feeding behavior. They're easily recognized by their blunt snouts and vertical bars on their sides.

The website ⊕ oceansafety.soest. hawaii.edu provides statewide beach-hazard maps as well as weather and surf advisories, listings of closed beaches, and safety tips.

Kahaloa and Ulukou Beaches. The beach widens back out here, creating the "it" spot for the bikini crowd. Beautiful bodies abound. This is where you find most of the sailing catamaran charters for a spectacular sail out to Diamond Head, or surfboard and outrigger canoe rentals for a ride on the rolling waves of the Canoe surf break. Great music and outdoor dancing beckon the sand-bound visitor to Duke's Canoe Club, where shirt and shoes not only aren't required, they're discouraged. The Hawaiian Hotel and the Moana Surfrider are both on this beach. **Amenities:** food and drink; lifeguards; showers; toilets; water sports; parking (fee). **Best for:** partiers; surfing. ⊠ 2259 Kalakaua Ave..

Ⓒ **Kuhio Beach Park.** This beach has experienced a renaissance after a recent face-lift. Now bordered by a landscaped boardwalk, it's great for romantic walks any time of day. Check out the Kuhio Beach hula mound Tuesday to Sunday at 6:30 for free hula and Hawaiian-music performances and a torch-lighting ceremony at sunset. Surf lessons for beginners are available from the beach center every half hour. **Amenities:** food and drink; lifeguards; showers; toilets; water sports. **Best for:** walking, surfing. ⊠ 2461 Kalakaua Ave. ⊹ Go past the Moana Surfrider Hotel to the Kapahulu Ave. pier.

🐚 **Queen's Surf.** So named as it was once the site of Queen Liliuokalani's beach house, this beach draws a mix of families and gay couples—and it seems as if someone is always playing a steel drum. Many weekends, movie screens are set up on the sand, and major motion pictures are shown after the sun sets (⊕ *www.sunsetonthebeach.net*). In the daytime, there are banyan trees for shade and volleyball nets for pros and amateurs alike (this is where Misty May and Kerri Walsh play while in town). The water fronting Queen's Surf is an

BEACHES KEY	
🚻	*Restroom*
🚿	*Showers*
🏄	*Surfing*
🤿	*Snorkel/Scuba*
👫	*Good for kids*
🅿	*Parking*

aquatic preserve, providing the best snorkeling in Waikiki. **Amenities:** lifeguards; showers; toilets. **Best for:** snorkeling, swimming, walking. ✉ *2598 Kalakaua Ave., across from the entrance to Honolulu Zoo.*

🐚 **Sans Souci.** Nicknamed Dig-Me Beach because of its outlandish display of skimpy bathing suits, this small rectangle of sand is nonetheless a good sunning spot for all ages. Children enjoy its shallow, safe waters, which are protected by the walls of the historic natatorium, an Olympic-size saltwater swimming arena that's been closed for decades. Serious swimmers and triathletes also swim in the channel here, beyond the reef. Sans Souci is favored by locals wanting to avoid the crowds while still enjoying the convenience of Waikiki. The New Otani Kaimana Beach Hotel is next door. **Amenities:** lifeguards; showers; toilets; parking (fee and no fee). **Best for:** swimming; walking. ✉ *2776 Kalakaua Ave., across from Kapiolani Park, between the New Otani Kaimana Beach Hotel and the Waikiki War Memorial Natatorium.*

SOUTHEAST OAHU

Much of Southeast Oahu is surrounded by reef, making most of the coast uninviting to swimmers, but the spots where the reef opens up are true gems. The drive along this side of the island is amazing, with its sheer lava-rock walls on one side and deep-blue ocean on the other. There are plenty of restaurants in the suburb of Hawaii Kai, so you can make a day of it, knowing that food isn't far away.

🐚 **Hanauma Bay Nature Preserve.** Picture this as the world's biggest open-air aquarium. You go here to see fish, and fish you'll see. Due to their exposure to thousands of visitors every week, these fish are more like family pets than the skittish marine life you might expect. An old volcanic crater has created a haven from the waves where the coral has thrived. There's an educational center where you must watch a nine-minute

Southeast Oahu

Kaiwi Channel

Hanauma Bay Nature Preserve

Sandy Beach

72

Hawaii Kai

Kahala

72

0   10 miles
0   15 km

video about the nature preserve before being allowed down to the bay. ■TIP→ **The bay is best early in the morning (around 7), before the crowds arrive; it can be difficult to park later in the day.** There's an entry fee for nonresidents. Smoking is not allowed, and the beach is closed on Tuesday. Wednesday to Monday, the beach is open from 6 am to 6 pm. There's a tram from the parking lot to the beach. Need transportation? Hanauma Bay Dive Tours runs snorkeling, snuba, and scuba tours to Hanauma Bay with transportation from Waikiki hotels on Monday, Wednesday, Thursday, and Friday only. *See Scuba Diving in Water Sports and Tours.* **Amenities:** food and drink; lifeguards; parking (fee); showers; toilets. **Best for:** snorkeling; swimming. ⊠ *7455 Kalanianaole Hwy., Hawaii Kai* ☎ *808/396–4229* ⊠ *Nonresident fee $7.50; parking $1; mask, snorkel, and fins rental $12; tram from parking lot to beach $1.75 round-trip* ☉ *Wed.–Mon. 6–6.*

★ **Sandy Beach.** Probably the most popular beach with locals on this side of Oahu, the broad, sloping beach is covered with sunbathers there to watch the "Show" and soak up rays. The Show is a shore break that's like no other in the Islands. Monster ocean swells rolling into the beach combined with the sudden rise in the ocean floor cause waves to jack up and crash magnificently on the shore. Expert surfers and body boarders young and old brave this danger to get some of the biggest barrels you can find for bodysurfing. ■TIP→ **But keep in mind that the beach is nicknamed "Break-Neck Beach" for a reason: many neck and back injuries are sustained here each year.** Use extreme caution when swimming here, or just kick back and watch the drama unfold from the comfort of your beach chair. **Amenities:** lifeguards; showers; toilets; parking (no fee). **Best for:** surfing, walking. ⊠ *7850 Kalanianaole Hwy., makai of Kalanianaole Hwy., 2 miles east of Hanauma Bay., Hawaii Kai.*

WINDWARD OAHU

The windward side lives up to its name, with ideal spots for windsurfing and kiteboarding, or for the more intrepid, hang gliding. For the most part the waves are mellow, and the bottoms are all sand—making for nice spots to visit with younger kids. The only drawback is that this side does tend to get more rain. But the vistas are so beautiful that a little sprinkling of "pineapple juice" shouldn't dampen your experience; plus, it benefits the waterfalls that cascade down the Koolaus.

Bellows Beach. Bellows is the same beach as Waimanalo, but it's under the auspices of the military, making it friendlier for visitors—though that

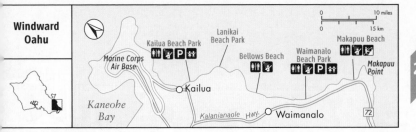

also limits public beach access to weekends. The park area is excellent for camping, and ironwood trees provide plenty of shade. ■ TIP→ **The beach is best before 2 pm. After 2, the trade winds bring clouds that get hung up on steep mountains nearby, causing overcast skies until midafternoon.** There are no food concessions, but McDonald's and other takeout fare, including *huli huli* (rotisserie) chicken on weekends, are right outside the entrance gate. **Amenities:** lifeguards; parking (no fee); showers; toilets. **Best for:** camping; solitude; swimming. ⊠ *520 Tinker Rd., Waimanalo ✛ Entrance on Kalanianaole Hwy. near Waimanalo town center.*

Kahana Bay Beach Park. Local parents often bring their children here to wade in safety in the very shallow, protected waters. This pretty beach cove, surrounded by mountains, has a long arc of sand that is great for walking and a cool, shady grove of tall ironwood and pandanus trees that is ideal for a picnic. An ancient Hawaiian fishpond, which was in use until the 1920s, is visible nearby. The water here is not generally a clear blue due to the runoff from heavy rains in the valley. **Amenities:** lifeguards; showers; toilets; parking (no fee). **Best for:** walking, swimming. ⊠ *52-201 Kamehameha Hwy., north of Kualoa Park, Kaneohe.*

Fodor's Choice
★
☼
Kailua Beach Park. A cobalt blue sea and a wide continuous arc of powdery sand make Kailua Beach Park one of the island's best beaches, illustrated by the crowds of local families who spend their weekend days here. This is like a big Lanikai Beach, but a little windier and a little wider, and a better spot for spending a full day. Kailua Beach has calm water, a line of palms and ironwoods that provide shade on the sand, and a huge park with picnic pavilions where you can escape the heat. This is the "it" spot if you're looking to try your hand at windsurfing or kiteboarding. You can rent kayaks nearby at Kailua Sailboards and Kayaks (*130 Kailua Rd.*) and take them to the Mokulua Islands for the day. Two-seaters cost $55 for four hours or $65 for a full day. *See Windsurfing and Kiteboarding.* **Amenities:** lifeguards; parking (no fee); showers; toilets; water sports. **Best for:** walking; windsurfing. ⊠ *437 Kawailoa Rd., Kailua ✛ Near Kailua town, turn right on Kailua Rd. At market, cross bridge, then turn left into beach parking lot.*

Kualoa Park. Grassy expanses border a long, narrow stretch of beach with spectacular views of Kaneohe Bay and the Koolau Mountains, making Kualoa one of the island's most beautiful picnic, camping, and beach areas. Dominating the view is an islet called Mokolii, better known as Chinaman's Hat, which rises 206 feet above the water. You can swim in the shallow areas year-round. The one drawback is that it's

For a hopping scene with everything from surfing to volleyball, head to Waikiki Beach.

usually windy here, but the wide-open spaces are ideal for kite flying. **Amenities:** lifeguards; showers; toilets. **Best for:** solitude; swimming. ⊠ *49-479 Kamehameha Hwy., north of Waiahole, Kaaawa.*

★ **Lanikai Beach Park.** Think of the beaches you see in commercials: peaceful jade green waters, powder-soft white sand, families and dogs frolicking mindlessly, offshore islands in the distance. It's an ideal spot for camping out with a book. Though the beach hides behind multimillion-dollar houses, by state law there is public access every 400 yards. You'll find street parking on Mokulua Drive for the various public-access points to the beach. ■ **TIP➜ Look for walled or fenced pathways every 400 yards, leading to the beach. Be sure not to park in the marked bike/jogging lane.** There are no shower or bathroom facilities here—they are a two-minute drive away at Kailua Beach Park. **Amenities:** None. **Best for:** walking, swimming. ⊠ *974 Mokulua Dr., past Kailua Beach Park, Kailua.*

Fodor'sChoice **Makapuu Beach.** A magnificent beach protected by Makapuu Point welcomes you to the windward side. Hang gliders circle above the beach, and the water is filled with body boarders. Just off the coast you can see Bird Island, a sanctuary for aquatic fowl, jutting out of the blue. The currents can be heavy, so check with a lifeguard if you're unsure of safety. Before you leave, take the prettiest (and coldest) outdoor shower available on the island. Being surrounded by tropical flowers and foliage while you rinse off that sand will be a memory you will cherish from this side of the rock. **Amenities:** lifeguards; showers; toilets; parking (no fee). **Best for:** swimming, walking. ⊠ *41-095 Kalanianaole Hwy, Across from Sea Life Park, 2 miles south of Waimanalo, Waimanalo.*

Waimanalo Beach Park. One of the most beautiful beaches on the island, Waimanalo is a local beach, busy with picnicking families and active sports fields. Expect a wide stretch of sand; turquoise, emerald, and deep blue seas; and gentle shore-breaking waves that are fun for all ages. Theft is an occasional problem, so lock your car. **Amenities:** lifeguards; parking (no fee); showers; toilets. **Best for:** sunrise; walking, swimming. ✉ *41-849 Kalanianaole Hwy., south of Waimanalo town center, Waimanalo.*

THE NORTH SHORE

"North Shore, where the waves are mean, just like a washing machine," sing the Kaau Crater Boys about this legendary side of the island. And in winter they are absolutely right. At times the waves overtake the road, stranding tourists and locals alike. When the surf is up, there are signs on the beach telling you how far to stay back so that you aren't swept out to sea. The most prestigious big-wave contest in the world, the Eddie Aikau, is held at Waimea Bay on waves the size of a five- or six-story building. The Triple Crown of Surfing roams across three North Shore beaches in the winter months.

All this changes come summer when this tiger turns into a kitten, with water smooth enough to water-ski on and ideal for snorkeling. The fierce Banzai Pipeline surf break becomes a great dive area, allowing you to explore the coral heads that, in winter, have claimed so many lives on the ultra-shallow but big, hollow tubes created here. Even with the monster surf subsided, this is still a time for caution: lifeguards are scarce, and currents don't subside just because the waves do.

That said, it's a place like no other on earth, and must be explored. From the turtles at Mokuleia to the tunnels at Shark's Cove, you could spend your whole trip on this side and not be disappointed.

Ehukai Beach Park. What sets Ehukai apart is the view of the famous Banzai Pipeline, where the winter waves curl into magnificent tubes, making it an experienced wave-rider's dream. It's also an inexperienced swimmer's nightmare, though spring and summer waves are more accommodating to the average swimmer, and there's good snorkeling. Except when the surf contests are going on, there's no reason to stay on the central strip. Travel in either direction from the center, and the conditions remain the same but the population thins out, leaving you with a magnificent stretch of sand all to yourself. **Amenities:** lifeguards; parking (no fee); showers; toilets. **Best for:** surfing, snorkeling. ✉ *59-406 Kamehameha Hwy., 1 mile north of Foodland at Pupukea, Haleiwa.*

Haleiwa Alii Beach Park. The winter waves are impressive here, but in summer the ocean is like a lake, ideal for family swimming. The beach itself is big and often full of locals. Its broad lawn off the highway invites volleyball and Frisbee games and groups of barbecuers. This is also the opening break for the Triple Crown of Surfing, and the grass is often filled with art festivals or carnivals. **Amenities:** lifeguards; parking (no fee); showers; toilets. **Best for:** surfing, swimming. ✉ *66-162 Haleiwa Rd., north of Haleiwa town center and past harbor, Haleiwa.*

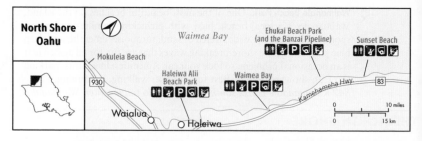

Mokuleia Beach Park. There is a reason why the producers of the TV show *Lost* chose this beach for their set. On the remote northwest point of the island, it is about 10 miles from the closest store or public restroom; you could spend a day here and not see another living soul. And that is precisely its beauty—all the joy of being stranded on a deserted island without the trauma of the plane crash. The beach is wide and white, the waters bright blue (but a little choppy) and full of sea turtles and other marine life. Mokuleia is a great secret find; just remember to pack supplies and use caution, as there are no lifeguards. **Amenities:** None. **Best for:** solitude. ⊠ 68-67 *Farrington Hwy., east of Haleiwa town center, across from Dillingham Airfield, Haleiwa.*

★ **Sunset Beach.** The beach is broad, the sand is soft, the summer waves are gentle, making for good snorkeling, and the winter surf is crashing. Many love searching this shore for the puka shells that adorn the necklaces you see everywhere. Carryout truck stands selling shave ice, plate lunches, and sodas usually line the adjacent highway. **Amenities:** food and drink; lifeguards; showers; toilets; parking (no fee). **Best for:** snorkeling, sunset. ⊠ 59 *Kamehameha Hwy., 1 mile north of Ehukai Beach Park, Haleiwa.*

Turtle Bay. Now known more for its resort (the Turtle Bay Resort) than its magnificent beach, Turtle Bay is mostly passed over on the way to the better-known beaches of Sunset and Waimea. But for the average visitor with the average swimming capabilities, this is the place to be on the North Shore. The crescent-shaped beach is protected by a huge sea wall. You can see and hear the fury of the northern swell, while blissfully floating in cool, calm waters. The convenience of this spot is also hard to pass up—there is a concession selling sandwiches and sunblock right on the beach. The resort has free parking for beach guests. **Amenities:** food and drink; parking (no fee); showers; toilets. **Best for:** swimming, sunset. ⊠ 57-20 *Kuilima Dr., 4 miles north of Kahuku, Kahuku ✛ Turn into Turtle Bay Resort, and let the guard know where you are going.*

FodorsChoice ★ **Waimea Bay.** Made popular in that old Beach Boys song "Surfin' U.S.A.," Waimea Bay is a slice of big-wave heaven, home to king-size 25- to 30-foot winter waves. Summer is the time to swim and snorkel in the calm waters. The shore break is great for novice bodysurfers. Due to its popularity, the postage-stamp parking lot is quickly filled, but everyone parks along the side of the road and walks in. **Amenities:** lifeguards; parking (no fee); showers; toilets. **Best for:** surfing (in winter), swimming and snorkeling (in summer). ⊠ 61-31 *Kamehameha Hwy., across from Waimea Valley, 3 miles north of Haleiwa, Haleiwa.*

WEST (LEEWARD) OAHU

The North Shore may be known as "Country," but the west side is truly the rural area on Oahu. There are commuters from this side to Honolulu, but many are born, live, and die on this side with scarcely a trip to town. For the most part, there's little hostility toward outsiders, but occasional problems have flared up, mostly due to drug abuse that has ravaged the fringes of the island. The problems have generally been car break-ins, not violence. So, in short, lock your car, don't bring valuables, and enjoy the amazing beaches.

The beaches on the west side are expansive and empty. Most Oahu residents and tourists don't make it to this side simply because of the drive; in traffic it can take almost 90 minutes to make it to Kaena Point from downtown Honolulu. But you'll be hard-pressed to find a better sunset anywhere.

★ **Ko Olina.** This is the best spot on the island if you have small kids. The
☺ resort commissioned a series of four man-made lagoons, but, as it has to provide public beach access, you are the winner. Huge rock walls protect the lagoons, making them into perfect spots for the kids to get their first taste of the ocean without getting bowled over. The large expanses of seashore grass and hala trees that surround the semicircle beaches are made-to-order for naptime. A 1½-mile jogging track connects the lagoons. Due to its appeal for *keiki* (children), Ko Olina is popular, and the parking lot fills up quickly when school is out and on weekends, so try to get here before 10 am. The biggest parking lot is at the farthest lagoon from the entrance. There are actually three resorts here: Aulani (the Disney resort), the J.W. Marriott Ihilani Resort & Spa, and the Ko Olina Beach Villas Resort (which has a time-share section as well). **Amenities:** food and drink; parking (no fee); showers; toilet. **Best for:** swimming; walking. ⊠ *92 Aliinui Dr., 23 miles west of Honolulu, Kapolei* ✛ *Take Ko Olina exit off H1 West and proceed to guard shack.*

Makaha Beach Park. This beach provides a slice of local life most visitors don't see. Families string up tarps for the day, fire up hibachis, set up lawn chairs, get out the fishing gear, and strum ukulele while they "talk story" (chat). Legendary waterman Buffalo Kaeulana can be found in the shade of the palms playing with his grandkids and spinning yarns of yesteryear. In these waters Buffalo not only invented some of the most outrageous methods of surfing, but also raised his world-champion son Rusty. He also made Makaha the home of the world's first international surf meet in 1954 and still hosts his Big Board Surfing Classic. With its long, slow-building waves, it's a great spot to try out longboarding. The swimming is generally decent in summer, but avoid the big winter waves. The only parking is along the highway, but it's free. **Amenities:** lifeguards; showers; toilets. **Best for:** swimming; surfing. ⊠ *84-450 Farrington Hwy., Waianae* ✛ *Go 32 miles west of Honolulu on the H1, then exit onto Farrington Hwy. The beach will be on your left.*

Continued on page 104

Imagine picking your seat for free at the Super Bowl or wandering the grounds of Augusta National at no cost during The Masters, and you glimpse the opportunity you have when attending the Vans Triple Crown of Surfing on the North Shore.

NORTH SHORE SURFING & THE TRIPLE CROWN

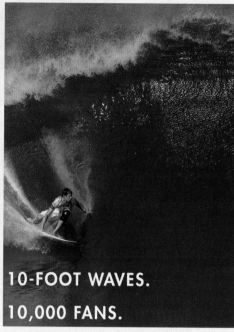

10-FOOT WAVES.
10,000 FANS.
TOP 50 SURFERS.

Long considered the best stretch of surf breaks on Earth, the North Shore surf area encompasses 6 miles of coastline on the northwestern tip of Oahu from Haleiwa to Sunset Beach. There are over 20 major breaks within these 6 miles. Winter storms in the North Pacific send huge swells southward which don't break for thousands of miles until they hit the shallow reef of Oahu's remote North Shore. This creates optimum surfing all winter long and was the inspiration for having surf competitions here each holiday season.

Every November and December the top 50 surfers in world rankings descend on "The Country" to decide who is the best all-around surfer in the world. Each of the three invitation-only contests that make up the Triple Crown has its own winner; competitors also win points based on the final standings. The surfer who excels in all three contests, racking up the most points overall, wins the Vans Triple Crown title. The first contest is held at **Haleiwa Beach,** the second at **Sunset Beach.** The season reaches its crescendo at the most famous surf break in the world, the **Banzai Pipeline.**

The best part is the cost to attend the events—nothing; your seat for the show—wherever you set down your beach towel. Just park your car, grab your stuff, and watch the best surfers in the world tame the best waves in the world.

The only surfing I understand involves the TV.

The contests were created not only to name an overall champion, but to attract the casual fan to the sport. Announcers explain each ride over the loudspeakers, discussing the nuances and values being weighed by the judges. A scoreboard displays points and standings during the four days of each event.

If this still seems incomprehensible to you, the action on the beach can also be exciting as some of the most beautiful people in the world are attracted to these contests.

For more information, see www.triplecrownofsurfing.com.

What should I bring?

Pack for a day at the Triple Crown the way you would for any day at the beach—sun block, beach towel, bottled water, and if you want something other than snacks, food.

These contests are held in rural neighborhoods (read: few stores), so pack anything you might need during the day. Also, binoculars are suggested, especially for the contest at Sunset. The pros will be riding huge outside ocean swells, and it can be hard to follow from the beach without binoculars. Haleiwa's breaks and Pipeline are considerably closer to shore, but binoculars will let you see the intensity on the contestants' faces.

Haleiwa Alii Beach Park
Vans Triple Crown Contest #1: Reef Pro Hawaii

The Triple Crown gets underway with high-performance waves (and the know-how to ride them) at Haleiwa. Though lesser known than the other two breaks of the Triple Crown, it is the perfect wave for showing off: the contest here is full of sharp cutbacks (twisting the board dramatically off the top or bottom of the wave), occasional barrel rides, and a crescendo of floaters (balancing the board on the top of the cresting wave) before the wave is destroyed on the shallow tabletop reef called the Toilet Bowl. The rider who can pull off the most tricks will win this leg, evening the playing field for the other two contests, where knowledge of the break is the key. Also, the beach park is walking distance from historic Haleiwa town, a mecca to surfers worldwide who make their pilgrimage here every winter to ride the waves. Even if you are not a fan, immersing yourself in their culture will make you one by nightfall.

Sunset Beach
Vans Triple Crown Contest #2: Vans World Cup of Surfing

At Sunset, the most guts and bravado win the day. The competition is held when the swell is at 8 to 12 feet and from the northwest. Sunset gets the heaviest surf because it is the exposed point on the northern tip of Oahu. Surfers describe the waves here as "moving mountains." The choice of waves is the key to this contest as only the perfect one will give the competitor a ride through the jigsaw-puzzle outer reef, which can kill a perfect wave instantly, all the way into the inner reef. Big bottom turns (riding all the way down the face of the wave before turning dramatically back onto the wave) and slipping into a super thick tube (slowing down to let the wave catch you and riding inside its vortex) are considered necessary to carry the day.

Banzai Pipeline
Vans Triple Crown Contest #3: Billabong Pipeline Masters

Surfing competitions are generally judged on the top three waves ridden by the competitors. In the Pipeline Masters, however, instead of accruing points through tricks and jumps, the surfers score high by dropping in the deepest and staying inside the tube the longest. The best trick at Pipeline is surviving this incredibly hollow and heavy wave, no other artistry is necessary.

How does the wave become hollow in the first place? When the deep ocean floor ascends steeply to the shore, the waves that meet it will pitch over themselves sharply, rather than rolling. This pitching causes a tube to form, and in most places in the world that tube is a mere couple of feet in diameter. In the case of Pipeline, however, its unique, extremely shallow reef causes the swells to open into 10-foot-high moving hallways that surfers can pass through. Only problem: a single slip puts them right into the raggedly sharp coral heads that caused the wave to pitch in the first place. Broken arms and boards are the rule rather than the exception for those who dare to ride and fail.

■ TIP➜ The Banzai Pipeline is a surf break, not a beach. The best place to catch a glimpse of the break is from Ehukai Beach.

When Are the Contests?

The first contests at Haleiwa begin the second week of November, and the Triple Crown finishes up right before Christmas.

Surfing, more so than any other sport, relies on Mother Nature to allow competition. Each contest in the Triple Crown requires only four days of competition, but each is given a window of twelve days. Contest officials decide by 7 AM of each day whether the contest will be held or not, and they release the information to radio stations and via a hotline (the number changes each year, unfortunately). By 7:15, you will know if it is on or not. Consult the local paper's sports section for the hotline number or listen to the radio announcement. The contests run from 8:30 to 4:30, featuring half-hour heats with four to six surfers each.

If big crowds bother you, go early on in the contests, within the first two days of each one. While the finale of the Pipeline Masters may draw about 10,000 fans, the earlier days have the same world-class surfers with fewer than a thousand fans.

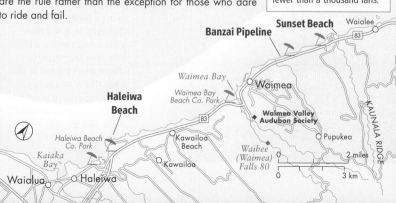

How Do I Get There?

If you hate dealing with parking and traffic, take TheBus. It will transport you from Waikiki to the contest sites in an hour for two bucks and no hassle.

If you must drive, watch the news the night before. If they are expecting big waves that night, there is a very good chance the contest will be on in the morning. Leave by 6 AM to beat the crowd. When everybody else gets the news at 7:15 AM that the show is on, you will be parking your car and taking a snooze on the beach waiting for the surfing to commence.

Parking is limited so be prepared to park alongside Kamehameha Highway and trek it in.

But I'm not coming until Valentine's Day.

There doesn't need to be a contest underway for you to enjoy these spots from a spectator's perspective. The North Shore surf season begins in October and concludes at the end of March. Only the best can survive the wave at Pipeline. You may not be watching 11-time world champ Kelly Slater ripping, but, if the waves are up, you will still see surfing that will blow your mind. Also, there are surf contests year-round on all shores of Oahu, so check the papers to see what is going on during your stay. A few other events to be on the lookout for:

Buffalo's Annual Big Board Surfing Classic

Generally held in March at legendary waterman "Buffalo" Keaulana's home beach of Makaha, this is the Harlem Globetrotters of surfing contests. You'll see tandem riding, headstands, and outrigger canoe surfing. The contest is more about making the crowds cheer than beating your competitors, which makes it very accessible for the casual fan.

Converse Hawaiian Open

During the summer months, the waves switch to the south shore, where there are surf contests of one type or another each week. The Open is one of the biggest and is a part of the US Professional Longboard Surfing Championships. The best shoot it out every August on the waves Duke Kahanamoku made famous at Queen's Beach in Waikiki.

Quiksilver in Memory of Eddie Aikau Big Wave Invitational

The granddaddy of them all is a one-day, winner-take-all contest in 25-foot surf at Waimea Bay. Because of the need for huge waves, it can be held only when there's a perfect storm. That could be at any time in the winter months, and there have been many years when it didn't happen at all. When Mother Nature does comply, however, it is not to be missed. You can hear the waves from the road, even before you can see the beach or the break.

BOARD SHAPES

Longboard: Lengthier (about 2.5–3 m/9–10.5 feet), wider, thicker, and more buoyant than the often-miniscule shortboards. Offers more flotation and speedier paddling, which makes it easier to get into waves. Great for beginners and those with relaxed surf styles. Skill level: Beginner to Intermediate.

Funboard: A little shorter than the longboard with a slightly more acute nose and blunt tail, the Funboard combines the best attributes of the longboards with some similar characteristics of the shorter boards. Good for beginners or surfers looking for a board more maneuverable and faster than a longboard. Skill level: Beginner to Intermediate.

Fishboard: A stumpy, blunt-nosed, twin-finned board that features a "V" tail (giving it a "fish" like look, hence the name) and is fast and maneuverable. Good for catching small, steep, slow waves and pulling tricks. At one point this was the world's best-selling surfboard. Skill level: Intermediate to Expert.

Shortboard: Shortboards came on the scene in 1967-70 when the average board length dropped from 9'6" to 6'6" (2.9m to 2m) and changed the wave riding styles in the surf world forever. This board is a short, light, high-performance stick that is designed for carving the wave with a high amount of maneuverability. These boards need a fast steep wave, completely different than a longboard break, which tends to be slower with shallower wave faces. Skill level: Expert.

Beginner   **Expert**

Funboards
Longboards

Fishboards
Shortboards

Shallow wave faces, easiest surfing   Steeper wave faces, difficult surfing

Fodor'sChoice   **White Plains.** Concealed from the public eye for many years as part of
★   the former Barbers Point Naval Air Station, this beach is reminiscent
☾   of Waikiki but without the condos and the crowds. It is a long, sloping
beach with numerous surf breaks, but it is also mild enough at shore
for older children to play freely. It has views of Pearl Harbor and, over
that, Diamond Head. Although the sand lives up to its name, the real
joy of this beach comes from its history as part of a military property
for the better part of a century. Expansive parking, great restroom facilities, and numerous tree-covered barbecue areas make it a great day-trip
spot. As a bonus, a Hawaiian monk seal takes up residence here several
months out of the year (seals are rare in the Islands). **Amenities:** lifeguards; parking (no fee); showers; toilets. **Best for:** swimming, surfing.
⊠ *Essex Rd. and Tripoli Rd., off H1 W., Kapolei* ✛ *Take the Makakilo
exit off H1 West, then turn left. Follow it into base gates, make a left.
Blue signs lead to beach.*

WATER SPORTS AND TOURS

Updated by
Catherine E.
Toth

From snorkeling on the North Shore to kayaking to small islands off
Kailua Beach to stand-up paddleboarding in Waikiki—when you're on
Oahu, there's always a reason to get wet. You can swim with native
fish in a protected bay, surf waves in an outrigger canoe, take to the
skies in a parasail above Diamond Head, or enjoy panoramic views of
Waikiki aboard a 45-foot catamaran. Diving into the ocean—whether
in a boat, on a board, or with your own finned feet—is a great way to
experience Oahu.

But as with any physical activity, heed the warnings. The ocean is unpredictable and unforgiving, and it can be as dangerous as it can be awe-
inspiring. But if you respect it, it can offer you the kind of memories
that last well after your vacation.

BOAT TOURS AND CHARTERS

Being on the water can be the best way to enjoy the Islands. Whether
you want to see the fish in action or experience how they taste, there
is a tour for you.

For a sailing experience in Oahu, you need go no farther than the
beach in front of your hotel in Waikiki. Strung along the sand are seven
beach catamarans that will provide you with one-hour rides during
the day and 90-minute sunset sails. Look for $23 to $25 for day sails
and $30 to $34 for sunset rides. ■TIP➜ Feel free to haggle, especially
with the smaller boats. Some provide drinks for free, some charge for
them, and some let you pack your own, so keep that in mind when
pricing the ride.

Hawaii Nautical. Catamaran cruises lead to snorkeling with dolphins,
gourmet-dinner cruises head out of beautiful Kalaeloa harbor, and sailing lessons are available on a 20-foot sailboat and a 50-foot cat. If
you're driving out from Waikiki, you may want to make a day of it, with
sailing in the morning then 18 holes on one of the five golf courses in
the area in the afternoon. Three-hour cruise rates with snacks and two

drinks begin at $109 per person. There's a second location at 91-607 Malakole Street in Kapolei. ✉ *Kewalo Basin Harbor, 1125 Ala Moana Blvd., Kapolei* ☎ *808/234–7245* ⊕ *www.hawaiinautical.com.*

Maitai **Catamaran.** Taking off from the stretch of sand between the Sheraton Waikiki and the Halekulani Hotel, this 44-foot twin-hull cat is the fastest and sleekest on the beach. If you have a need for speed and enjoy a little more upscale experience, this is the boat for you. ✉ *Waikiki Beach, between the Sheraton Waikiki and the Halekulani Hotel, Waikiki, Honolulu* ☎ *808/922–5665, 800/462–7975* ⊕ *www. maitaicatamaran.net* ✏ *$28–$45.*

Na Hoku II **Catamaran.** The boat's motto is "Free drinks, easy crew." It features thumping reggae music and includes free booze in its $25 price tag ($30 for sunset cruises). The 45-foot catamaran is tied up near Duke's Barefoot Bar and sails five times daily. ✉ *Waikiki Beach, between the Sheraton Moana Surfrider Hotel and Duke's Barefoot Bar, Honolulu* ☎ *No phone* ⊕ *www.nahokuii.com* ✏ *$25–$30.*

Red Dolphin. Despite its name, the Red Dolphin is actually a yellow, blue, and green floating platform anchored off Waikiki. It's like an 11,000-square-foot playground with diving platforms, waterslides, trampoline, and floating bar and grill. Admission is $49, with activities like snorkeling, kayaking, paddleboarding, and parasailing costing extra. The platform holds up to 400 people and is open daily. There are eight pickup points throughout Waikiki. ✉ *1025 Ala Moana Blvd., Honolulu* ☎ *808/753–9446* ⊕ *www.reddolphin.net* ✏ *$49.*

Star of Honolulu Cruises. Founded in 1957, this company recently expanded its fleet to include the 65-foot *Hoku Naia*, docked on Oahu's west coast. It offers everything from snorkeling cruises in the pristine waters off the Waianae coast to gourmet-dinner cruises with live entertainment to seasonal whale-watching sails on one of two vessels. Popuar cruises teach you how to string lei and dance hula. Two-hour whale-watching-excursion rates begin at $30 per person, while dinner cruises start at $175. The company has a second location at 85-371 Farrington Highway in Waianae. ✉ *Aloha Tower Marketplace, 1 Aloha Tower Dr., Honolulu* ☎ *808/983–7827* ⊕ *www. starofhonolulu.com* ✏ *$30–$175.*

Tradewind Charters. This company's half-day excursions feature sailing, snorkeling, and whale-watching. Traveling on these luxury yachts not only gets you away from the crowds, but also gives you the opportunity to "take the helm" if you wish. The cruise includes snorkeling at an exclusive anchorage, as well as hands-on snorkeling and sailing instruction. Charter prices are about $495 for up to six passengers. ✉ *Kewalo Basin Harbor, 1125 Ala Moana Blvd., Ala Moana, Honolulu* ☎ *800/829–4899* ⊕ *www.tradewindcharters.com.*

The windward side has many good spots for body boarding.

BODY BOARDING AND BODYSURFING

Body boarding (or sponging) has long been a popular alternative to surfing for a couple of reasons. First, the start-up cost is much less—a usable board can be purchased for $30 to $40 or can be rented on the beach for $5 an hour. Second, it's a whole lot easier to ride a body board than to tame a surfboard. All you have to do is paddle out to the waves, then turn toward the beach as the wave approaches and kick like crazy.

Most grocery and convenience stores sell body boards. Though these boards don't compare to what the pros use, beginners won't notice a difference in their handling on smaller waves. ■TIP➜ Another small investment you'll want to make is surf fins. These smaller, sturdier versions of dive fins sell for $25 to $60 at surf and dive stores, and sporting-goods stores. Most beach stands don't rent fins with the boards. Though they are not necessary for body boarding, fins do give you a tremendous advantage when you're paddling. If you plan to go out into bigger surf, we would also suggest getting a leash, which reduces the chance you'll lose your board.

Bodysurfing requires far less equipment—just a pair of swim fins with heel straps—but it can be a lot more

> ### WORD OF MOUTH
>
> "Whale-watching should be good in March—try to book a cruise. They also have glass-bottom boat rides, which I enjoyed. Parasailing, stand-up paddling, snorkeling at Hanauma Bay are all fun activities and can be arranged at your hotel or in advance."
>
> —Himom

challenging to master. Typically, surf breaks that are good for body boarding are good for bodysurfing.

If the direction of the current or dangers of the break are not readily apparent to you, don't hesitate to ask a lifeguard for advice.

BEST SPOTS

Body boarding and bodysurfing can be done anywhere there are waves, but due to the paddling advantage surfers have over spongers, it's usually more fun to go to surf breaks exclusively for body boarding.

Bellows Field Beach. On Oahu's windward side, Bellows Field Beach has shallow waters and a consistent break that makes it an ideal spot for body boarders and bodysurfers. (Surfing isn't allowed between the two lifeguard towers.) But take note: the Portuguese man-o-war, a blue jellyfish-like invertebrate that delivers painful and powerful stings, is often seen here. ⊠ *41-043 Kalanianaole Hwy., Waimanalo.*

Kuhio Beach. This beach is an easy spot for first-timers to check out the action. The Wall, a break near the large pedestrian walkway called Kapahulu Groin, is the quintessential body-boarding spot. The soft, rolling waves make it perfect for beginners. Even during summer's south swells, it's relatively tame because of the outer reefs. ⊠ *Waikiki Beach, between the Sheraton Moana Surfrider Hotel and the Kapahulu Groin, Honolulu.*

Makapuu Beach. With its extended waves, Makapuu Beach is a sponger's dream. If you're a little more timid, go to the far end of the beach to **Keiki's,** where the waves are mellowed by Makapuu Point. Although the main break at Makapuu is much less dangerous than Sandy's, check out the ocean floor—the sands are always shifting, sometimes exposing coral heads and rocks. Always check (or ask lifeguards about) the currents, which can get pretty strong. ⊠ *41-095 Kalanianaole Hwy., across from Sea Life Park.*

EQUIPMENT

There are more than 30 rental spots along Waikiki Beach, all offering basically the same prices. But if you plan to body board for more than just an hour, we would suggest buying an inexpensive board for $20 to $40 at an ABC Store—there are more than 30 in the Waikiki area—and giving it to a kid at the end of your vacation. It will be more cost-effective for you, and you'll be passing along some aloha spirit in the process.

DEEP-SEA FISHING

Fishing isn't just a sport in Hawaii, it's a way of life. A number of charter boats with experienced crews can take you on a sportfishing adventure throughout the year. Sure, the bigger yellowfin tuna (ahi) are generally caught in summer, and the coveted spearfish are more frequent in winter, but you can still hook them any day of the year. You can also find dolphinfish (mahimahi), wahoo (ono), skip jacks, and the king—Pacific blue marlin—ripe for the picking on any given day. The largest marlin ever caught, weighing in at 1,805 pounds, was reeled in along Oahu's coast.

When choosing a fishing boat in the Islands, keep in mind the immensity of the surrounding ocean. Look for veteran captains who have decades of experience. Better yet, find those who care about Hawaii's fragile marine environment. Many captains now tag and release their catches to preserve the state's fishing grounds.

The general rule for the catch is an even split with the crew. Unfortunately, there are no "freeze-and-ship" providers in the state, so unless you plan to eat the fish while you're here, you'll probably want to leave it with the boat. Most boats do offer mounting services for trophy fish; ask your captain.

Besides the gift of fish, a gratuity of 10% to 20% is standard, but use your own discretion depending on how you felt about the overall experience.

BOATS AND CHARTERS

Hawaii Fishing Charters. Based out of Ko Olina resort, Captain Jim and his crew try to bring the full Hawaiian experience to their fishing trips. While most fishing boats head straight out to the open ocean, Captain Jim trolls along the leeward coast, giving visitors a nice sense of the island while stalking the fish. The company also offers an overnighter to Molokai's Penguin Banks, reputed to be some of Hawaii's best fishing grounds, starting at $2,000. ⊠ *Ko Olina Resort and Marina, 92 Aliinui Dr., Kapolei* ☎ *808/783–9274* ⊕ *www.hawaiifishingcharters.net.*

Maggie Joe Sport Fishing. The oldest sportfishing company on Oahu also boasts landing one of the largest marlins every caught out of Kewalo Basin. With two smaller boats and the 53-foot custom *Maggie Joe* (which can hold up to 25 anglers), it has air-conditioned cabins, hot showers, and cutting-edge fishing equipment. A marine taxidermist can mount the monster you reel in. Half-day exclusive charter rates for groups of six begin at $652 on the 41-foot *Sea Hawk* or the 38-foot *Ruckus*. Charters on the *Maggie Joe* start at $890. ⊠ *Kewalo Basin, 1025 Ala Moana Blvd., Honolulu* ☎ *808/591–8888, 877/806–3474* ⊕ *www.maggiejoe.com.*

Magic Sportfishing. This 50-foot Pacifica fishing yacht, aptly named *Magic,* boasts a slew of sportfishing records, including some of the largest marlins caught in local tournaments and the most mahimahi hooked during a one-day charter. This yacht is very comfortable, with twin diesel engines that provide a smooth ride, air-conditioning, and a cozy seating area. The boat can accommodate up to six passengers. ⊠ *Kewalo Basin Harbor, 1025 Ala Moana Blvd., Honolulu* ☎ *808/596–2998, 808/286–2998* ⊕ *www.magicsportfishing.com.*

Sashimi Fun Fishing. A combination trip suits those who aren't quite ready to troll for big game in the open-ocean swells. Sashimi Fun Fishing runs a dinner cruise with fishing and music. The boat keeps close enough to shore so that while you're hooking reef fish, you can still see Oahu. The cruise includes a local barbecue dinner, and you can also cook what you catch. With hotel transportation included, the rates begin at $63 per person. ⊠ *Kewalo Basin Harbor, 1125 Ala Moana Blvd., Honolulu* ☎ *808/955–3474* ⊕ *www.808955fish.com.*

KAYAKING

Kayaking is an easy way to explore the ocean—and Oahu's natural beauty—without much effort or skill. It offers a vantage point not afforded by swimming or surfing, and a workout you won't get lounging on a catamaran. Even novices can get in a kayak and enjoy the island's scenery.

The ability to travel long distances can also get you into trouble. ⚠ Experts agree that rookies should stay on the windward side. Their reasoning is simple: if you get tired, break or lose an oar, or just plain pass out, the onshore winds will eventually blow you back to the beach. The same cannot be said for the offshore breezes of the North Shore and West Oahu.

Kayaks are specialized: some are better suited for riding waves while others are designed for traveling long distances. Your outfitter can address your needs depending on your skill level. Sharing your plans with your outfitter can lead to a more enjoyable—and safer—experience.

BEST SPOTS

Kahana River. For something a little different, try the Kahana River on the island's windward side. The river may not have the blue water of the ocean, but the majestic Koolau Mountains, with waterfalls during rainy months, make for a picturesque backdrop. It's a short jaunt, about 2 miles round-trip, but it's tranquil and packed with rain-forest foliage. Bring mosquito repellent. ⊠ *Kamehameha Hwy., 8 miles east of Kaneohe.*

Lanikai Beach. The perennial favorite of kayakers is Lanikai Beach, on the island's windward side. Tucked away in an upscale residential area, this award-winning beach has become a popular spot for amateur kayakers because of its calm waters and onshore winds. More adventurous paddlers can head to the Mokulua Islands, two islets less than 1 mile from the beach. You can land on Moku Nui, which has surf breaks and small beaches great for picnicking. Take a dip in Queen's Bath, a small saltwater swimming hole. ⊠ *Mokulua Dr., past Kailua Beach Park, Kailua.*

EQUIPMENT, LESSONS, AND TOURS

Kailua Sailboards and Kayaks. One of the best places for beginners to rent kayaks is Kailua Beach. Kailua Sailboards and Kayaks has an ideal location just across the street. More adventurous kayakers can venture to the Mokulua Islands off Lanikai. This one-stop shop also provides kayak tours starting at $69 per person. Half-day kayak rentals start at $39 for a single, $55 for a double. ⊠ *130 Kailua Rd., Kailua* ☎ *808/262–2555* ⊕ *www.kailuasailboards.com.*

Twogood Kayaks Hawaii. The outfitter offers kayak rentals, lessons, guided tours, and even weeklong camps if you want to immerse yourself in the sport. Guides are trained in the history, geology, and birds of the area. Full-day rental rates begin at $55 for single kayaks, $65 for doubles. Full-day kayak excursions are $125, including lunch, snorkeling gear, and transportation to and from Waikiki. Although the prices are slightly higher than average, this outfitter puts the boats in the water for you and gives you a crash course in ocean safety. ✉ *134B Hamakua Dr., Kailua* ☎ *808/262–5656* ⊕ *www.twogoodkayaks.com.*

SCUBA DIVING

Not all of Hawaii's beauty is above water. What lurks below can be just as magnificent.

While snorkeling and snuba (more on that later) provide adequate access to this underwater world, nothing gives you the freedom—or depth, quite literally—as scuba.

The diving on Oahu is comparable with any you might do in the tropics, but its uniqueness comes from the isolated environment of the Islands. There are literally hundreds of species of fish and marine life that you can find only in this chain. In fact, about 25% of Hawaii's marine life can be seen here only—nowhere else in the world. Adding to the singularity of diving off Oahu is the human history of the region. Military activities and tragedies of the 20th century filled the waters surrounding Oahu with wreckage that the ocean creatures have since turned into their homes.

Although instructors certified to license you in scuba are plentiful in the Islands, we suggest that you get your PADI certification before coming, as a week of classes may be a bit of a commitment on a short vacation. ■TIP→ You can go on introductory dives without the certification, but the best dives require it.

BEST SPOTS

Hanauma Bay Nature Preserve. On Oahu's southeast shore, Hanauma Bay Nature Preserve is home to more than 250 different species of fish, of which a quarter can be found nowhere else in the world. This has made this volcanic crater bay one of the most popular dive sites in the state. It's a long walk from the parking lot to the beach—even longer lugging equipment—so consider hooking up with a licensed dive-tour operator. Preservation efforts have aided the bay's delicate ecosystem, so expect to see various butterfly fish, surgeonfish, tangs, parrot fish, and endangered Hawaiian sea turtles. ✉ *7455 Kalanianaole Hwy., Honolulu* ☎ *808/396–4229.*

Mahi Waianae. Hawaii's waters are littered with shipwrecks, but one of the most intact and accessible is the *Mahi Waianae*, a 165-foot minesweeper that was sunk in 1982 off the Waianae Coast. It lays upright in about 90 feet of calm and clear water, encrusted in coral and patrolled by white spotted eagle rays and millet seed butterfly fish. The wreck serves as an artificial reef for such Hawaii aquatic residents as blue-striped snappers, puffer fish, lionfish, moray eels, and octopus. Visibility averages about 100 feet, making this one of the most popular dives on the island. ✉ *Waianae.*

Fodor's Choice
★
Shark's Cove. Oahu's best shore dive is accessible only during the summer months. Shark's Cove, on Oahu's North Shore, churns with monster surf during the winter, making this popular snorkeling and diving spot extremely dangerous. In summer, the cavernous lava tubes and tun-

nels are great for both novices and experienced divers. Some dive-tour companies offer round-trip transportation from Waikiki.

Three Tables. A short walk from Shark's Cove is Three Tables, named for a trio of flat rocks running perpendicular to shore. There are lava tubes to the right of these rocks that break the surface and then extend out about 50 feet. While this area isn't as active as Shark's Cove, you can still spot octopus, moray eels, parrot fish, green sea turtles, and the occasional shark. ⊠ *Haleiwa.*

EQUIPMENT, LESSONS, AND TOURS

Captain Bruce's Hawaii. Focusing on the island's western and eastern shores, this full-service company offers refresher and introductory dives as well as more advanced drift and night dives. Everything is provided, including transportation to and from Waikiki. Most important, the boat has hot showers. Two-tank dives begin at $115 per person. ⊠ *86-222 Moeha St., Waianae* ☎ *808/373–3590, 800/535–2487* ⊕ *www.captainbruce.com.*

Hanauma Bay Dive Tours. You can guess the specialty here. This tour operator offers introductory courses in the federally protected reserve for divers aged 12 and above, with snuba available for younger kids. The charge is $115 for a one-tank dive. ⊠ *460 Ena Rd., Honolulu* ☎ *808/256–8956, 800/505–8956* ⊕ *www.hanaumabaydivetours.com.*

Surf 'N Sea. The North Shore headquarters for all things water related is also great for diving. An interesting perk—a cameraman can shoot a video of you diving. It's hard to see facial expressions under the water, but it still might be fun for those who want to prove that they took the plunge. Two-tank boat-dive rates begin at $100 per certified diver (prices are higher for noncertified divers). ⊠ *62-595 Kamehameha Hwy., Haleiwa* ☎ *800/899–7873* ⊕ *www.surfnsea.com.*

SNORKELING

If you can swim, you can snorkel. And you don't need any formal training, either.

Snorkeling is a favorite pastime for both visitors and residents, and can be done anywhere there's enough water to stick your face in. Each spot will have its great days depending on the weather and time of year, so consult with the purveyor of your gear for tips on where the best viewing is that day. Keep in mind that the North Shore should be attempted only when the waves are calm, namely in the summertime.

■ TIP➜ **Think of buying a mask and snorkel as a prerequisite for your trip—they make any beach experience better.** Just make sure you put plenty of sunscreen on your back because once you start gazing below, your head may not come back up for hours.

BEST SPOTS

Electric Beach. Directly across from the electricity plant—hence the name—Electric Beach is a haven for tropical fish, making it a great snorkeling spot. The expulsion of hot water from the plant raises the temperature of the ocean, attracting Hawaiian green sea turtles, spotted moray eels, and spinner dolphins. Although the visibility is not always

Oahu's North Shore has the island's biggest waves as well as some of the best snorkeling.

the best, the crowds are small and the fish are guaranteed. ✉ *Farrington Hwy., 1 mile west of Ko Olina Resort, Kapolei.*

Hanauma Bay. What Waimea Bay is to surfing, Hanauma Bay in southeast Oahu is to snorkeling. Easily the most popular snorkeling spot on the island, it's home to more more than 250 different species of marine life. Due to the protection of the narrow mouth of the cove and the prodigious reef, you will be hard-pressed to find a place you will feel safer while snorkeling. ✉ *7455 Kalanianaole Hwy., Honolulu* ☎ 808/396–4229.

Fodor's Choice
★
Shark's Cove. Great shallows protected by a huge reef make Shark's Cove on the North Shore a prime spot for snorkelers, even young ones, in the summer. You'll find a plethora of critters from crabs to octopus in water that's no more than waist deep. When the winter swells come, this area can turn treacherous. ✉ *Kamehameha Hwy., across from Foodland, Haleiwa.*

EQUIPMENT AND TOURS

Hawaii Nautical. The dock in Ko Olina harbor is a little more out of the way, but this is a much more luxurious option than the town snorkel cruises. Two-hour morning and afternoon tours of the west side of Oahu are punctuated with stops for observing dolphins from the boat and to a snorkel spot well populated with fish. All gear, snacks, sandwiches, and two alcoholic beverages make for a more complete experience, but also a pricier one (starting at $109 per person). ✉ *91-607 Malakole St., Kapolei* ☎ 808/234–7245 ⊕ *www.hawaiinautical.com.*

Snorkel Bob's. This place has all the stuff you'll need—and more—to make your water adventures more enjoyable. Feel free to ask the staff about good snorkeling spots, as the best ones can vary with weather and the seasons. ✉ *700 Kapahulu Ave., Honolulu* ☎ *808/735–7944, 800/262–7725* ⊕ *www.snorkelbob.com.*

SUBMARINE TOURS

★ **Atlantis Submarines.** This is the underwater adventure for the unadventurous. Not fond of swimming, but want to see what you've been missing? Board this 64-passenger vessel for a ride past shipwrecks, turtle breeding grounds, and coral reefs. The tours, which depart from the pier at the Hilton Hawaiian Village, are available in several languages and start at $119. ✉ *Hilton Hawaiian Village Beach Resort and Spa, 2005 Kalia Rd., Honolulu* ☎ *808/973–1296, 800/548–6262* ⊕ *www. atlantisadventures.com.*

STAND-UP PADDLING

From the lakes of Wisconsin to the coast of Lima, Peru, stand-up paddling (or SUP, for short) is taking the sport of surfing to the most unexpected places. Still, the sport remains firmly rooted in the Hawaiian Islands.

Back in the 1960s, Waikiki beach boys would paddle out on their longboards using a modified canoe paddle. It was longer than a traditional paddle, enabling them to stand up and stroke. It was easier this way to survey the ocean and snap photos of tourists learning how to surf. Eventually it became a sport unto itself, with professional contests at world-class surf breaks and long-distance races across treacherous waters.

Stand-up paddling is easy to learn—though riding waves takes some practice—and most outfitters on Oahu offer lessons for all skill levels. It's also a great workout; you can burn off yesterday's dinner buffet, strengthen your core, and experience the natural beauty of the island's coastlines all at once.

If you're looking to learn, go where there's already an SUP presence. Avoid popular surf breaks, unless you're an experienced stand-up paddle surfer, and be wary of ocean and wind conditions. You'll want to find a spot with calm waters, easy access in and out of the ocean, and a friendly crowd that doesn't mind the occasional stand-up paddler.

BEST SPOTS

Ala Moana Beach Park. About a mile west of Waikiki, Ala Moana is the most SUP-friendly spot on the island. In fact, the state installed a series of buoys in the flat-water lagoon to separate stand-up paddlers and swimmers. There are no waves here, making it a great spot to learn, but beware of strong trade winds, which can push you into the reef.

Waikiki. There are a number of outfitters on Oahu's south shore that take beginners into the waters off Waikiki. **Canoes,** the surf break fronting the Duke Kahanamoku statue, and the channels between breaks are often suitable for people learning how to maneuver their boards in not-so-flat conditions. But south swells here can be deceptively menacing,

Stand-up paddling has become one of Hawaii's most popular water activities.

and ocean conditions can change quickly. Check with lifeguards before paddling out and be mindful of other surfers in the water.

EQUIPMENT AND LESSONS

Hawaiian Watersports. Paddle in the picturesque Kailua Bay or in the waters off Waikiki with Hawaiian Watersports. Two-hour lessons are $99 for groups and $179 for private sessions. If you book eight hours of lessons you get a discounted rate. Rentals start at $49 for a half day. There's also a branch in Kailua. ⊠ *415 Kapahulu Ave., Honolulu* 🕾 *808/262–5483, 808/739–5483* ⊕ *www.hawaiianwatersports.com.*

Paddle Core Fitness. Paddling is a way of life for Reid Inouye, who now shares his passion for the sport with students. (He's also the publisher of *Standup Paddle Magazine.*) His company offers introductory classes as well as fitness programs for serious paddlers. Lessons are held in the flat waters of Ala Moana Beach, where there's a designated area for paddling. Prices range from $50 for group lessons to $75 for private lessons. ⊠ *Ala Moana Beach Park, Ala Moana Blvd., Honolulu* 🕾 *808/723–5357* ⊕ *www.paddlecorefitness.com.*

SURFING

Perhaps no word is more associated with Hawaii than surfing. Every year the best of the best gather on Oahu's North Shore to compete in their version of the Super Bowl: the prestigious Vans Triple Crown of Surfing. The pros dominate the waves for a month, but the rest of the year belongs to folks just trying to have fun.

Oahu is unique because it has so many famous spots: Banzai Pipeline, Waimea Bay, Kaiser Bowls, and Sunset Beach. But the island also has miles of coastline with surf spots that are perfect for everyday surfers. But remember this surfer's credo: when in doubt, don't go out. If you're unsure about conditions, stay on the beach.

If you're nervous and don't want to run the risk of a confrontation, try some of the alternate spots listed below. They may not have the name recognition, but the waves can be just as great.

BEST SPOTS

Makaha Beach. If you like to ride waves, try Makaha Beach on Oahu's west side. It has legendary, interminable rights that allow riders to perform all manner of stunts: from six-man canoes with everyone doing headstands to bully boards (oversize body boards) with whole families along for the ride. Mainly known as a longboarding spot, it's predominantly local but respectful to outsiders. Use caution in the winter, as the surf can get huge. It's not called Makaha—which means "fierce"—for nothing. ⊠ *84-369 Farrington Hwy., Waianae.*

Ulukou Beach. In Waikiki you can paddle out to **Populars,** a break at Ulukou Beach. Nice and easy, Populars—or Pops—never breaks too hard and is friendly to both newbies and veterans. It's one of the best places to surf during pumping south swells, as this thick wave breaks in open ocean, making it more rideable. The only downside is the long paddle out to the break from Kuhio Beach, but that keeps the crowds manageable. ⊠ *Waikiki Beach, in front of the Sheraton Waikiki hotel, Honolulu.*

EQUIPMENT AND LESSONS

Aloha Beach Services. It may sound like a cliché, but there's no better way to learn to surf than from a beach boy in Waikiki. And there's no one better than Harry "Didi" Robello, a second-generation beach boy and owner of Aloha Beach Services. Learn to surf for $30 in an hour-long group lesson, $50 for a semiprivate lesson, or $80 with just you and an instructor. You can also rent a board for $15 an hour. ⊠ *2365 Kalakaua Ave., on the beach near the Moana Surfrider, Honolulu* ☎ *808/922–3111* ⊕ *www.alohabeachservices.com.*

Faith Surf School. Professional surfer Tony Moniz started his own surf school in 2000, and since then he and his wife Tammy have helped thousands of people catch their first waves in Waikiki. The 90-minute group lessons are $60 per person and include all equipment and transportation. Semiprivate lessons with up to three people are $100 per person, and private lessons are $125. For $500 per person you can book an all-day surf tour with Moniz, riding waves with him at his favorite breaks. ⊠ *Sheraton Waikiki, 2255 Kalakaua Ave., Honolulu* ☎ *808/931–6262* ⊕ *www.faithsurfschool.com.*

⟳ **Hawaiian Fire.** Learn how to surf from some of Hawaii's most knowledgeable water-safety experts at this school, owned and operated by Honolulu firefighters. Lessons include two hours of surfing time (with a lunch break) at a secluded beach near Barbers Point. Transportation is available to and from Waikiki. Two-hour group lessons begin at $109 per person, while private lessons are $189 per person. ⊠ *3318 Campbell Ave., Honolulu* ☎ *808/737–3473, 888/955–7873* ⊕ *www.hawaiianfire.com.*

★ **Surf 'N Sea.** This is a one-stop shop for water-sports enthusiasts on the North Shore. Rent a shortboard for $5 an hour or a longboard for $7 an hour ($24 and $30 for full-day rentals). Lessons start at $85 for three hours. Surf safaris, which can last between four to five hours, are $220 per person. ⊠ *62-595 Kamehameha Hwy., Haleiwa* ☎ *808/637–7973, 800/899–7873* ⊕ *www.surfnsea.com.*

WHALE-WATCHING

November is marked by the arrival of snow in much of America, but in Hawaii it marks the return of the humpback whale. These migrating behemoths move south from their North Pacific homes during the winter months for courtship and calving, and they put on quite a show. Watching males and females alike throwing themselves out of the ocean and into the sunset awes even the saltiest of sailors. Newborn calves riding gently next to their two-ton mothers will stir you to your core. These gentle giants can be seen from the shore as they make a splash, but there is nothing like having your boat rocking beneath you in the wake of a whale's breach.

★ **Wild Side Specialty Tours.** Boasting a marine-biologist crew, this company takes you to undisturbed snorkeling areas. Along the way you can view dolphins, turtles, and, in winter, migrating humpback whales. The tours depart at 7:30 am, so it's important to plan ahead. Four-hour whale-watching cruises on a 42-foot catamaran start at $115. There's a second location in Waianae. ⊠ *Kewalo Basin Harbor, 1125 Ala Moana Blvd., Honolulu* ☎ *808/306–7273* ⊕ *www.sailhawaii.com.*

WINDSURFING AND KITEBOARDING

Those who call windsurfing and kiteboarding cheating because they require no paddling have never tried hanging on to a sail or kite. It will turn your arms to spaghetti quicker than paddling ever could, and the speeds you generate earn these sports the label of "extreme."

Windsurfing was born here in the Islands. For amateurs, the windward side is best because the onshore breezes will bring you back to land even if you don't know what you're doing. The newer sport of kiteboarding is tougher but more exhilarating, as the kite will sometimes take you in the air for hundreds of feet. We suggest only those in top shape try the kites, but windsurfing is fun for all ages.

EQUIPMENT AND LESSONS

Kailua Sailboards and Kayaks. This company offers both beginner and high-performance gear. You can also take lessons, either at $129 for a four-hour group lesson or $109 for a one-hour individual lesson. ■ TIP➜ Since both options are around the same price, we suggest the one-hour individual lesson; then you have the rest of the day to practice what these instructors preach. Half-day rentals for the more experienced run from $59 for the standard board to $79 for a high-performance board. ⊠ *130 Kailua Rd., Kailua* ☎ *808/262–2555* ⊕ *www.kailuasailboards.com.*

GOLF, HIKING, AND OUTDOOR ACTIVITIES

Updated by
Michael Levine

Although much is written about the water surrounding this little rock known as Oahu, there is as much to be said for the rock itself. It's a wonder of nature, thrust from the ocean floor thousands of millennia ago by a volcanic hot spot that is still spitting out islands today. Hawaii is the most remote island chain on earth, and there are creatures and plants that can be seen here and nowhere else. And there are dozens of ways for you to check them all out.

AERIAL TOURS

Taking an aerial tour of the Islands opens up a world of perspective. Look down from the sky at the outline of the USS *Arizona* where it lies in its final resting place below the waters of Pearl Harbor, or get a glimpse of the vast carved expanse of a volcanic crater—here are views only seen by an "eye in the sky." Don't forget your camera.

Blue Hawaiian Helicopters. This company stakes its claim as Hawaii's largest 'copter company, with tours on all the major islands and more than two dozen choppers in its fleet. The Oahu tour, with six seats and narration from your friendly pilot, takes a little less than an hour and includes sweeping views of Waikiki, the beautiful windward coast, and the North Shore. If you like to see the world from above or are just pinched for time and want to get a quick overview of the whole island without renting a car, this is the way to go. Tours are $233 per person. ⊠ *99 Kaulele Pl., Honolulu* ☎ *808/831–8800* ⊕ *www.bluehawaiian.com.*

★ **Island Seaplane Service.** Harking back to the days of the earliest air visitors to Hawaii, the seaplane has always had a special spot in island lore. The only seaplane service still operating in Hawaii takes off from Keehi Lagoon. Flight options are either a half-hour south and eastern Oahu shoreline tour or an hour island circle tour. The *Pan Am Clipper* may be gone, but you can revisit the experience for $149 to $269. ⊠ *85 Lagoon Dr., Honolulu* ☎ *808/836–6273* ⊕ *www.islandseaplane.com.*

Makani Kai Helicopters. This may be the best way to see the beautiful Sacred Falls on the windward side of the island, as the park around the falls was closed to hikers after a deadly 1999 rock slide. Makani Kai dips the helicopter down to show you one of Hawaii's former favorite trails and the pristine waterfall it leads to. Half-hour tour rates begin at $155 per person, and full-hour tours are $263. Customized private

Take a helicopter tour for a unique perspective of the island.

charters are available starting at $1,750 per hour. ✉ *130 Iolana Pl., Honolulu* ☎ *808/834–5813* ⊕ *www.makanikai.com.*

★ **The Original Glider Rides.** "Mr. Bill" has been offering piloted glider (sailplane) rides over the northwest end of Oahu's North Shore since 1970. These are piloted scenic rides for one or two passengers in sleek, bubbletop, motorless aircraft. You'll get aerial views of mountains, shoreline, coral pools, windsurfing sails, and, in winter, humpback whales. Reservations are recommended; flights range from 10 to 60 minutes long and depart continuously from 10 to 5 daily. The charge for one passenger is $79–$215, depending on the length of the flight; two people fly for $128–$390. ✉ *Dillingham Airfield, 68 Farrington Hwy., Waialua* ☎ *808/677–3404* ⊕ *www.honolulusoaring.com.*

BIKING

Oahu's coastal roads are flat, well paved, and unfortunately, awash in vehicular traffic. Frankly, biking is no fun in either Waikiki or Honolulu, but things are a bit better outside the city. Your best bet is to get off the road and check out the island's bike trails.

Honolulu City and County Bike Coordinator. This office can answer all your biking questions concerning trails, permits, and state laws. ☎ *808/768–8335* ⊕ *www1.honolulu.gov/dts/bikepage.htm.*

BEST SPOTS

Fodor's Choice **Aiea Loop Trail.** Our favorite ride is in central Oahu on the Aiea Loop
★ Trail. There's a little bit of everything you expect to find in Hawaii—wild pigs crossing your path, an ancient Hawaiian *heiau* (holy ground),

2

and the remains of a World War II crashed airplane. Campsites and picnic tables are available along the way and, if you need a snack, strawberry guava trees abound. Enjoy the foliage change from bamboo to Norfolk pine in your climb along this 4½-mile track. ⊠ *End of Aiea Heights Dr., just past Keaiwa Heiau State Park, Aiea.*

EQUIPMENT AND TOURS

Blue Sky Rentals & Sports Center. Known more for motorcycles than for man-powered bikes, Blue Sky does rent bicycles for $20 for eight hours, $25 for a day, and $75 per week—no deposit is required. The prices include a bike, a helmet, and a lock. ⊠ *1920 Ala Moana Blvd., across from Hilton Hawaiian Village, Waikiki, Honolulu* ☎ 808/947–0101.

Boca Hawaii LLC. If you want to do intense riding this is your first stop. The triathlon shop, owned and operated by top athletes, has full-suspension Fuji road and mountain bikes, both for $40 a day and $175 a week. Call ahead and reserve a bike, as supplies are limited. The shop is closed Sunday. ⊠ *330 Cooke St., next to BIKEFACTORY, Kakaako, Honolulu* ☎ 808/591–9839 ⊕ *www.bocahawaii.com.*

CAMPING

For a more rugged escape from the resorts of Waikiki, consider pitching a tent on the beach or in the mountains, where you have easy access to hiking trails and the island's natural features. ■ TIP→ Camping here is not as highly organized as it is on the mainland: expect few marked sites, scarce electrical outlets, and nary a ranger station. What you find instead are unblemished spots in the woods and on the beach. With price tags ranging from free to $5, it's hard to complain about the lack of amenities.

There are four state recreation areas at which you can camp, one in the mountains and three on the beach. All state parks' campsites can now be reserved up to a year in advance online at ⊕ *www.hawaiistateparks. org.* The fee is $18 a night per campsite for up to six people. As for the county spots, there are 15 currently available and all require a permit. The good news is that the permits are free and are easy to obtain, as long as you're not trying to go on a holiday weekend. Visit ⊕ *www1. honolulu.gov/parks* for more information.

GOLF

Unlike on the Neighbor Islands, the majority of Oahu's golf courses are not associated with hotels and resorts. In fact, of the island's three-dozen-plus courses, only five are tied to lodging and none of them are in the tourist hub of Waikiki.

Municipal courses are a good choice for budget-conscious golfers. Your best bet is to call the day you want to play and inquire about walk-on availability. Greens fees are standard at city courses: walking rate, $49 for visitors; riding cart $20 for 18 holes; pull carts $4.

Greens fees listed here are the highest course rates per round on weekdays and weekends for U.S. residents. (Some courses charge non-U.S. residents higher prices.) Discounts are often available for resort guests and for those who book tee times online. Twilight fees are usually offered; call individual courses for information.

WAIKIKI

Ala Wai Municipal Golf Course. Just across the Ala Wai Canal from Waikiki, Ala Wai is said to host more rounds than any other U.S. course—up to 500 per day. Not that it's a great course, just really convenient. Although residents can obtain a city golf card that allows automated tee-time reservation over the phone, the best bet for a visitor is to show up and expect to wait at least an hour. The course itself is flat. Robin Nelson did some redesign work in the 1990s, adding mounding, trees, and a lake. The Ala Wai Canal comes into play on several holes on the back nine, including the treacherous 18th. ⊠ *404 Kapahulu Ave., Waikiki, Honolulu* ☎ *808/733–7387 starter's office, 808/738–4652 golf shop* ⊕ *www1.honolulu.gov/des/golf/alawai.htm* ⅃ *18 holes. 5861 yds. Par 70. Greens fee: $49* ↝ *Facilities: Driving range, putting green, golf carts, pull carts, rental clubs, pro shop, lessons.*

SOUTHEAST OAHU

Hawaii Kai Golf Course. The Championship Golf Course (William F. Bell, 1973) winds through a Honolulu suburb at the foot of Koko Crater. Homes (and the liability of a broken window) come into play on many holes, but they are offset by views of the nearby Pacific and a crafty routing of holes. With several lakes, lots of trees, and bunkers in all the wrong places, Hawaii Kai really is a "championship" golf course, especially when the trade winds howl. The **Executive Course** (1962), a par-55 track, is the first of only three courses in Hawaii built by Robert Trent Jones Sr. Although a few changes have been made to his original design, you can find the usual Jones attributes, including raised greens and lots of risk-reward options. ⊠ *8902 Kalanianaole Hwy., Hawaii Kai* ☎ *808/395– 2358* ⊕ *www.hawaiikaigolf.com* ⅃ *Championship Course: 18 holes. 6222 yds. Par 72. Greens fee: $100. Executive Course: 18 holes. 2223 yds. Par 55. Greens fee: $39* ↝ *Facilities: Driving range, putting green, golf carts, pull carts, rental clubs, pro shop, lessons, restaurant, bar.*

WINDWARD OAHU

Koolau Golf Club. Koolau Golf Club is marketed as the toughest golf course in Hawaii and one of the most challenging in the country. Dick Nugent and Jack Tuthill (1992) routed 10 holes over jungle ravines that require at least a 110-yard carry. The par-4 18th may be the most difficult closing hole in golf. The tee shot from the regular tees must carry 200 yards of ravine, 250 from the blue tees. The approach shot is back across the ravine, 200 yards to a well-bunkered green. Set at the Windward base of the Koolau Mountains, the course is as much beauty as beast. Kaneohe Bay is visible from most holes, orchids and yellow ginger bloom, the shama thrush (Hawaii's best singer since Don Ho) chirrups, and waterfalls flute down the sheer, green mountains above. ⊠ *45-550 Kionaole Rd., Kaneohe* ☎ *808/236–4653* ⊕ *www. koolaugolfclub.com* ⅃ *18 holes. 6406 yds. Par 72. Greens fee: $145* ↝ *Facilities: Driving range, putting green, golf carts, rental clubs, pro shop, golf academy, restaurant, bar.*

★ **Olomana Golf Links.** Bob and Robert L. Baldock are the architects of record for this layout, but so much has changed since it opened in 1969 that they would recognize little of it. A turf specialist was brought in to improve fairways and greens, tees were rebuilt, new bunkers added, and mangroves cut back to make better use of natural wetlands. But what really puts Olomana on the map is that this is where wunderkind Michelle Wie learned the game. ⊠ *41-1801 Kalanianaole Hwy., Waimanalo* ☎ *808/259–7926* ⊕ *www.olomanagolflinks.com* ⚐ *18 holes. 5896 yds. Par 72. Greens fee: $95* ☞ *Facilities: Driving range, putting green, golf carts, pull carts, rental clubs, pro shop, lessons, restaurant, bar.*

Fodor'sChoice **Royal Hawaiian Golf Club.** In the cool, lush Maunawili Valley, Pete and ★ Perry Dye created what can only be called target jungle golf. In other words, the rough is usually dense jungle, and you may not hit a driver on three of the four par-5s, or several par-4s, including the perilous 18th that plays off a cliff to a narrow green protected by a creek. Mt. Olomana's twin peaks tower over Luana Hills. ▣ TIP➔ **The back nine wanders deep into the valley, and includes an island green (par-3 11th) and perhaps the loveliest inland hole in Hawaii (par-4 12th).** ⊠ *770 Auloa Rd., Kailua* ☎ *808/262–2139* ⊕ *www.royalhawaiiangolfclub.com* ⚐ *18 holes. 5522 yds. Par 72. Greens fee: $125* ☞ *Facilities: Driving range, putting green, golf carts, rental clubs, pro shop, restaurant, bar.*

NORTH SHORE

★ **Turtle Bay Resort & Spa.** When the Lazarus of golf courses, the **Fazio Course** at Turtle Bay (George Fazio, 1971), rose from the dead in 2002, Turtle Bay on Oahu's rugged North Shore became a premier golf destination. Two holes had been plowed under when the **Palmer Course** at Turtle Bay (Arnold Palmer and Ed Seay, 1992) was built, while the other seven lay fallow, and the front nine remained open. Then new owners came along and re-created holes 13 and 14 using Fazio's original plans, and the Fazio became whole again. It's a terrific track with 90 bunkers. The gem at Turtle Bay, though, is the Palmer Course. The front nine is mostly open as it skirts Punahoolapa Marsh, a nature sanctuary, while the back nine plunges into the wetlands and winds along the coast. The short par-4 17th runs along the rocky shore, with a diabolical string of bunkers cutting diagonally across the fairway from tee to green. ⊠ *57-049 Kuilima Dr., Kahuku* ☎ *808/293–8574* ⊕ *www.turtlebaygolf.com* ⚐ *Fazio Course: 18 holes. 6535 yds. Par 72. Greens fee: $125. Palmer Course: 18 holes. 7199 yds. Par 72. Greens fee: $175* ☞ *Facilities: Driving range, putting green, golf carts, rental clubs, pro shop, lessons, restaurant, bar.*

CENTRAL OAHU

Royal Kunia Country Club. At one time the PGA Tour considered buying Royal Kunia Country Club and hosting the Sony Open there. It's that good. ▣ TIP➔ **Every hole offers fabulous views from Diamond Head to Pearl Harbor to the nearby Waianae Mountains.** Robin Nelson's eye for natural sight lines and dexterity with water features adds to the visual pleasure. ⊠ *94-1509 Anonui St., Waipahu* ☎ *808/688–9222* ⊕ *www.royalkuniacc.com* ⚐ *18 holes. 6002 yds. Par 72. Greens fee: $150* ☞ *Facilities: Driving range, putting green, golf carts, rental clubs, pro shop, restaurant.*

Waikele Country Club. Outlet stores are not the only bargain at Waikele. The adjacent golf course is a daily-fee course that offers a private club-like atmosphere and a terrific Ted Robinson (1992) layout. The target off the tee is Diamond Head, with Pearl Harbor to the right. Robinson's water features are less distinctive here, but define the short par-4 fourth hole, with a lake running down the left side of the fairway and guarding the green; and the par-3 17th, which plays across a lake. The par-4 18th is a terrific closing hole, with a lake lurking on the right side of the green. ⊠ *94-200 Paioa Pl., Waipahu* ☎ *808/676–9000* ⊕ *www.golfwaikele.com* ⌇ *18 holes. 6261 yds. Par 72. Greens fee: $130* ☞ *Facilities: Driving range, putting green, golf carts, rental clubs, pro shop, lessons, restaurant, bar.*

> **WORD OF MOUTH**
>
> "IMO, you can't beat the neighbor islands for picturesque golf courses. But on Oahu, I'd recommend the Palmer course at Turtle Bay. The pros play there a couple of times a year. Wonderful scenery and you'll enjoy the drive."
>
> —travelinandgolfin

WEST (LEEWARD) OAHU

★ **Coral Creek Golf Course.** On the Ewa Plain, 4 miles inland, Coral Creek is cut from ancient coral—left from when this area was still underwater. Robin Nelson (1999) does some of his best work in making use of the coral, and of some dynamite, blasting out portions to create dramatic lakes and tee and green sites. They could just as easily call it Coral Cliffs, because of the 30- to 40-foot cliffs Nelson created. They include the par-3 10th green's grotto and waterfall, and the vertical drop-off on the right side of the par-4 18th green. An ancient creek meanders across the course, but there's not much water, just enough to be a babbling nuisance. ⊠ *91-1111 Geiger Rd., Ewa Beach* ☎ *808/441–4653* ⊕ *www.coralcreekgolfhawaii.com* ⌇ *18 holes. 6810 yds. Par 72. Greens fee: $130* ☞ *Facilities: Driving range, putting green, golf carts, rental clubs, pro shop, lessons, restaurant, bar.*

Ko Olina Golf Club. Hawaii's golden age of golf-course architecture came to Oahu when Ko Olina Golf Club opened in 1989. Ted Robinson, king of the water features, went splash-happy here, creating nine lakes that come into play on eight holes, including the par-3 12th, where you reach the tee by driving behind a Disney-like waterfall. Tactically, though, the most dramatic is the par-4 18th, where the approach is a minimum 120 yards across a lake to a two-tiered green guarded on the left by a cascading waterfall. Today, Ko Olina, affiliated with the adjacent Ihilani Resort and Spa (guests receive discounted rates), has matured into one of Hawaii's top courses. You can niggle about routing issues—the first three holes play into the trade winds (and the morning sun), and two consecutive par-5s on the back nine play into the trades—but Robinson does enough solid design to make those of passing concern. ⊠ *92-1220 Aliinui Dr., Kapolei* ☎ *808/676–5300* ⊕ *www.koolinagolf.com* ⌇ *18 holes. 6432 yds. Par 72. Greens fee: $179* ☞ *Facilities: Driving range, putting green, golf carts, rental clubs, pro shop, golf academy, restaurant, bar.*

HIKING

The trails of Oahu cover a full spectrum of environments: desert walks through cactus, slippery paths through bamboo-filled rain forest, and scrambling rock climbs up ancient volcanic calderas. The only thing you won't find is an overnighter, as even the longest of hikes won't take you more than half a day. In addition to being short in length, many of the prime hikes are within 10 minutes of downtown Waikiki, meaning that you won't have to spend your whole day getting back to nature.

BEST SPOTS

Diamond Head Crater. Every vacation has requirements that must be fulfilled so that when your neighbors ask, you can say, "Yeah, did it." Climbing Diamond Head is high on that list of things to do on Oahu. It's a moderate hike if you're in good physical condition, due in part to the many stairs along the way; be sure to bring a water bottle because it's hot and dry. Only a mile up, a clearly marked trail with handrails scales the inside of this extinct volcano. At the top, the fabled final 99 steps take you up to the pillbox overlooking the Pacific Ocean and Honolulu. It's a breathtaking view and a lot cheaper than taking a helicopter ride for the same photo op. ⊠ *Diamond Head Rd. at 18th Ave., Honolulu✧ Enter on east side of crater; there's limited parking inside, most park on street and walk in .*

Fodor'sChoice
★
Kaena Point. This hike is a little longer (a 5-mile round-trip) and hotter than the Makapuu Lighthouse Trail, but it is right next to the beach, and there are spots where you can get in and cool off. Sea-carved cliffs give way to lava-rock beaches and sea arches. Halfway to the point, there is a double blowhole, which is a good indicator of sea conditions. If it is blowing good, stay out of the water. Though the area is hot and dry, there is still much wildlife here, as it is the only nesting ground for many rare sea birds. ■ TIP➔ **Keep a lookout for the Laysan albatrosses; these enormous birds have recently returned to the area. Don't be surprised if they come in for a closer look at you, too.** There has been a cave-in of an old lava tube, so be careful when crossing it, but enjoy the view in its enormous mouth. ⊠ *81-780 Farrington Hwy, Waianae✧ Take Farrington Hwy. to its end at Yokohamas. Hike in on the old 4WD trail.*

Fodor'sChoice
★
Manoa Falls. Travel up into the valley beyond Honolulu to make the Manoa Falls hike. Though only a mile long, this path passes through so many different ecosystems that you feel as if you're in an arboretum (the beautiful Lyon Arboretum is right near the trailhead, if you want to make another stop). Walk among the elephant ear ape plants, ruddy fir trees, and a bamboo forest straight out of China. At the top is a 150-foot falls with a small pool not quite suited for swimming but good for wading. This hike is more about the journey than the destination; make sure you bring some mosquito repellent because they grow 'em big up here. ⊠ *3998 Manoa Road, Honolulu✧ West Manoa Rd. behind Manoa Valley in Paradise Park. Take West Manoa Rd. to end, park on side of road, and follow trail signs in.*

Makapuu Lighthouse Trail. For the less adventurous hiker and anyone looking for a great view, this paved trail that runs up the side of Makapuu Point in southeast Oahu fits the bill. Early on, the trail is surrounded by

lava rock but, as you ascend, foliage—the tiny white *koa haole* flower and the cream-tinged spikes of the *kiawe*—begins taking over the barren rock. Once atop the point, you begin to understand how alone these Islands are in the Pacific. The easternmost tip of Oahu is where the island divides the sea, giving you a spectacular view of the cobalt ocean meeting the land in a cacophony of white caps. To the south are several tide pools and the lighthouse, while the eastern view looks down upon Rabbit and Kaohikaipu Islands, two bird sanctuaries just off the coast. The 2-mile round-trip hike is a great break on a circle-island trip. ⊠ *Makapuu Lighthouse Rd., Honolulu* ✛ *Take Kalanianaole Hwy. to base of Makapuu Point. Look for asphalt strip snaking up mountain.*

GOING WITH A GUIDE

Hawaii Nature Center. A good choice for families, the center in upper Makiki Valley conducts a number of programs for both adults and children. There are guided hikes into tropical settings that reveal hidden waterfalls and protected forest reserves. They don't run tours every day so it's a good idea to get advance reservations. ⊠ *2131 Makiki Heights Dr., Honolulu* ☎ *808/955–0100* ⊕ *www.hawaiinaturecenter.org.*

Oahu Nature Tours. Guides explain the native flora and fauna that are your companions on glorious sunrise, hidden-waterfall, mountain-forest, rain-forest, and volcano-walking tours. Tours include pick-up at any Waikiki hotel. ☎ *808/924–2473* ⊕ *www.oahunaturetours.com.*

HORSEBACK RIDING

A great way to see the island is atop a horse, leaving the direction to the pack while you drink in the views of mountains or the ocean. It may seem like a cliché, but there really is nothing like riding a horse down a stretch of beach to put you in a romantic state of mind.

★ **Happy Trails Hawaii.** Take a guided horseback ride above the North Shore's Waimea Bay along trails that offer panoramic views from Kaena Point to the famous surfing spots. Rates for a 90-minute trail ride begin at $80; a two-hour ride costs $99. Reservations are required. ⊠ *59-231 Pupukea Road, Pupukea* ✛ *1 mile mauka up Pupakea Rd. on right* ☎ *808/638–7433* ⊕ *happytrailshawaii.com.*

Kualoa Ranch. This ranch across from Kualoa Beach Park on the Windward side leads trail rides in the Kaaawa Valley. Rates for a one-hour trail ride begin at $65. Kualoa has other activities such as bus and Jeep tours, all-terrain-vehicle trail rides, and children's activities, which may be combined for half- or full-day package rates. ⊠ *49-560 Kamehameha Hwy., Kaaawa* ☎ *808/237–8515* ⊕ *www.kualoa.com.*

Turtle Bay Stables. This is the only spot on the island where you can take horses on the beach. The stables here are part of the North Shore resort, but can be utilized by nonguests. The sunset ride is a definite must if you are a friend of our four-legged friends. Rates for a 45-minute trail ride begin at $65. ⊠ *Turtle Bay Resort, 57-091 Kamehameha Hwy., Kahuku* ☎ *808/293–8811* ⊕ *www.turtlebayresort.com/activities/horseback.asp.*

SHOPPING

Updated
by Melissa
Chang

Eastern and Western traditions meet on Oahu, where savvy shoppers find luxury goods at high-end malls and scout tiny boutiques and galleries filled with pottery, blown glass, woodwork, and Hawaiian-print clothing by local artists.

Exploring downtown Honolulu, Kailua on the windward side, and the North Shore often yields the most original merchandise. Some of the small stores carry imported clothes and gifts from around the world—a reminder that, on this island halfway between Asia and the United States, shopping is a multicultural experience.

HONOLULU

DOWNTOWN HONOLULU

SHOPPING CENTERS

■ TIP➜ Getting to the Ala Moana shopping centers from Waikiki is quick and inexpensive thanks to TheBus and the Waikiki Trolley.

Ala Moana Shopping Center. The world's largest open-air shopping mall is five minutes from Waikiki by bus. More than 240 stores and 60 restaurants make up this 50-acre complex, which is a unique mix of national and international chains as well as smaller, locally owned shops and eateries—and everything in between. Thirty-five luxury boutiques in residence include Gucci, Louis Vuitton, Christian Dior, and Emporio Armani. All of Hawaii's major department stores are here, including the state's only Neiman Marcus and Nordstrom, plus Sears, and Macy's. To get to the mall from Waikiki, catch TheBus line 8, 19, or 20; a one-way ride is $2.50. Or hop aboard the Waikiki Trolley's Pink Line for $2 each way, which comes through the area every 12 minutes. ⊠ 1450 Ala Moana Blvd., Ala Moana, Honolulu ☎ 808/955–9517 ⊕ www. alamoanacenter.com.

Ward Centers. Heading west from Waikiki toward downtown Honolulu, you'll run into a section of town with five distinct shopping-complex areas; there are more than 80 specialty shops and 40 eateries here. The Ward Entertainment Center features 16 movie theaters, including a state-of-the-art, 3-D, big-screen auditorium. For distinctive Hawaiian gifts, such as locally made muumuu, koa wood products, and Niihau shell necklaces, visit Nohea Gallery, Martin & MacArthur, and Native Books/Na Mea Hawaii. Island Soap and Candle Works makes all of its candles and soaps on-site with Hawaiian flower scents. Take TheBus routes 19, 20, and 42; fare is $2.50 one way. Or hop on the Waikiki Trolley Red Line, which comes through the area every 40 minutes. There also are free parking nearby and a valet service. ⊠ 1050–1200 Ala Moana Blvd., Ala Moana, Honolulu ☎ 808/591–8411 ⊕ www.wardcenters.com.

BOOKS

★ **Native Books/Na Mea Hawaii.** In addition to clothing for adults and children and unusual artwork such as Niihau shell necklaces, this boutique's book selection covers Hawaiian history and language, and offers children's books set in the Islands. ⊠ Ward Warehouse, 1050 Ala Moana Blvd., Honolulu ☎ 808/596–8885 ⊕ www.nativebookshawaii.com.

CLOTHING

★ **Anne Namba Designs.** Anne Namba combines the beauty of classic kimonos with contemporary styles to make unique pieces for work and evening. In addition to women's apparel, she's also designed a men's line and a wedding couture line. ⊠ *324 Kamani St., Downtown Honolulu, Honolulu* ☎ *808/589–1135* ⊕ *www.annenamba.com.*

Hilo Hattie. Busloads of visitors pour in through the front doors of the world's largest manufacturer of Hawaiian and tropical aloha wear. Once shunned by Honolulu residents for its three-shades-too-bright tourist wear, it has become a favorite source for island gifts, macadamia nut and chocolate packages, and clothing for elegant Island functions. Free shuttle service is available from Waikiki. ⊠ *700 N. Nimitz Hwy., Iwilei, Honolulu* ☎ *808/535–6500* ⊕ *www.hilohattie.com.*

Reyn's. Reyn's is a good place to buy the aloha print fashions residents wear. Look for the limited-edition Christmas shirt, a collector's item manufactured each holiday season. Reyn's has eight locations statewide and offers styles for men, women, and children. ⊠ *Ala Moana Shopping Center, 1450 Ala Moana Blvd., Ala Moana, Honolulu* ☎ *808/949–5929* ⊕ *www.reynspooner.com* ☎ *808/737–8313.*

FOOD SPECIALTIES

Honolulu Chocolate Company. To really impress those back home, pick up a box of gourmet chocolates here. They dip the flavors of Hawaii, from Kona coffee to macadamia nuts, in fine chocolate. ⊠ *Ward Centre, 1200 Ala Moana Blvd., Ala Moana, Honolulu* ☎ *808/591–2997* ⊕ *www.honoluluchocolate.com.*

Longs Drugs. For gift items in bulk, try one of the many outposts of Longs, the perfect place to stock up on chocolate-covered macadamia nuts—at reasonable prices—to carry home. ⊠ *Ala Moana Shopping Center, 1450 Ala Moana Blvd., 2nd level, Ala Moana, Honolulu* ☎ *808/941–4433* ☎ *808/732–0784.*

GALLERIES

Jeff Chang Pottery & Fine Crafts. With locations around the island, Jeff Chang has become synonymous with excellent craftsmanship and originality in Raku pottery, blown glass, and koa wood. Gift ideas include petroglyph stoneware coasters, ceramic and glass jewelry, blown-glass penholders and business-card holders, and Japanese Aeto chimes. The owners choose work from 300 different local and national artists. ⊠ *Ward Center, 1200 Ala Moana Blvd., Honolulu* ☎ *808/591–1440.*

★ **Nohea Gallery.** These shops are really galleries representing more than 450 artists who specialize in koa furniture, bowls, and boxes, as well as art glass and ceramics. Original paintings and prints—all with an island theme—add to the selection. They also carry unique handmade Hawaiian jewelry with ti leaf, maile, and coconut-weave designs. ■ TIP➔ **The koa photo albums in these stores are easy to carry home and make wonderful gifts.** ⊠ *Ward Warehouse, 1050 Ala Moana Blvd., Ala Moana, Honolulu* ☎ *808/596–0074* ⊕ *www.noheagallery.com.*

GIFTS

Blue Hawaii Lifestyle. The Ala Moana store carries a large selection of locally made products, including soaps, honey, tea, salt, chocolates, art, and CDs. Every item, in fact, is carefully selected from various Hawaii companies, artisans, and farms, from the salt fields of Molokai to the lavender farms on Maui to the single-estate chocolate on Oahu's North Shore. ⊠ *Ala Moana Center, 1450 Ala Moana Blvd., Honolulu* ☎ *808/949–0808* ⊕ *www.bluehawaiilifestyle.com.*

HAWAIIAN ARTS AND CRAFTS

Hawaiian Quilt Collection. Traditional island comforters, wall hangings, pillows, and other Hawaiian-print quilt items are the specialty here. ⊠ *Ala Moana Center, 1450 Ala Moana Blvd., Ala Moana, Honolulu* ☎ *808/946–2233* ⊕ *www.hawaiian-quilts.com.*

Na Hoku. If you look at the wrists of *kamaaina* (local) women, you are apt to see Hawaiian heirloom bracelets fashioned in either gold or silver in a number of island-inspired designs. Na Hoku sells jewelry in designs that capture the heart of the Hawaiian lifestyle in all its elegant diversity. ⊠ *Ala Moana Center, 1450 Ala Moana Blvd., Ala Moana, Honolulu* ☎ *808/946–2100* ⊕ *www.nahoku.com.*

CHINATOWN

SHOPPING CENTERS

Aloha Tower Marketplace. Billing itself as a festival marketplace, Aloha Tower cozies up to Honolulu Harbor. Along with restaurants and entertainment venues, it has about two-dozen shops and kiosks selling mostly visitor-oriented merchandise, from sunglasses to apparel to souvenir refrigerator magnets. You can also find a nice selection of locally crafted ukuleles at The Hawaiian Ukulele Company, or music CDs if you prefer to just listen. To get there from Waikiki take the E-Transit Bus, which goes along TheBus routes every 15 minutes. ⊠ *1 Aloha Tower Dr., at Piers 8, 9, and 10, Downtown Honolulu, Honolulu* ☎ *808/566–2337* ⊕ *www.alohatower.com.*

GALLERIES

Louis Pohl Gallery. Stop in this gallery to browse modern works from some of Hawaii's finest artists. In addition to pieces by resident artists, there are monthly exhibitions from visiting artists. ⊠ *1111 Nuuanu Ave., Downtown Honolulu, Honolulu* ☎ *808/521–1812* ⊕ *www.louispohlgallery.com.*

GREATER HONOLULU

Kapahulu, like many older neighborhoods, should not be judged at first glance. It begins at the Diamond Head end of Waikiki and continues up to the H1 freeway and is full of variety; shops and restaurants are located primarily on Kapahulu Avenue. The upscale residential neighborhood of Kahala, near the slopes of Diamond Head, is 10 minutes by car from Waikiki and has a shopping mall and some gift stores.

SHOPPING CENTERS

Kahala Mall. The upscale residential neighborhood of Kahala, near the slopes of Diamond Head, is 10 minutes by car from Waikiki. The only shopping of note in the area is located at the indoor mall, which has 90 stores and restaurants, including Macy's, Gap, Reyn's Aloha Wear, and Barnes & Noble. Don't miss fashionable boutiques such as **Ohelo Road** (☎ 808/735–5525), where contemporary clothing for all occasions fills the racks. You can also browse local foods and products at Whole Foods. Eight movie theaters provide post-shopping entertainment. ✉ *4211 Waialae Ave., Kahala, Honolulu* ☎ *808/732–7736* ⊕ *www.kahalamallcenter.com.*

CLOTHING

Bailey's Antiques & Aloha Shirts. Vintage aloha shirts are the specialty at this kitschy store. Prices can start at $3.99 for the 10,000 shirts in stock, and the tight space and musty smell are part of the thrift-shop atmosphere. ■TIP→ **Antiques hunters can also buy old-fashioned post-cards, authentic military clothing, funky hats, and denim jeans from the 1950s.** ✉ *517 Kapahulu Ave., Kapahulu, Honolulu* ☎ *808/734–7628* ⊕ *alohashirts.com.*

Island Treasures. Local residents come here to shop for gifts that are both unique and within reach of almost every budget, ranging in price from $1 to $5,000. Next to Zippy's and overlooking the ocean, the store has handbags, toys, jewelry, home accessories, soaps and lotions, and locally made original artwork. Certainly the most interesting shop in Hawaii Kai's suburban-mall atmosphere, this store is also a good place to purchase CDs of some of the best Hawaiian music. ✉ *Koko Marina Center, 7192 Kalanianaole Hwy., Hawaii Kai* ☎ *808/396–8827.*

WAIKIKI

SHOPPING CENTERS

DFS Galleria Waikiki. Hermès, Cartier, Michael Kors and Marc Jacobs are among the shops on the Waikiki Luxury Walk in this enclosed mall, as well as Hawaii's largest beauty and cosmetic store. The third floor caters to duty-free shoppers only and features an exclusive Watch Shop. The Kalia Grill and Starbucks offer a respite for weary shoppers. ✉ *Kalakaua and Royal Hawaiian Aves., Waikiki* ☎ *808/931–2655* ⊕ *www. dfsgalleria.com/en/hawaii/.*

Royal Hawaiian Center. An open and inviting facade has made this three-block-long center a garden of Hawaiian shops. There are more than 100 stores and restaurants, including local gems such as Aloha Aina Boutique, Honolulu Home Collection, and Koi Boutique. Bike buffs can check out the Harley-Davidson Honolulu store, while Bob's Uku-lele may inspire musicians to learn a new instrument. Nine restaurants round out the dining options, along with the Paina Lanai Food Court and Five-O Bar & Lounge. ✉ *2201 Kalakaua Ave., Waikiki* ☎ *808/922–0588* ⊕ *www.shopwaikiki.com.*

2100 Kalakaua. Tenants of this elegant, town house–style center include Chanel, Coach, Tiffany & Co., Yves Saint Laurent, Gucci, and Tod's. ✉ *2100 Kalakaua Ave., Waikiki* ☎ *808/971–9011* ⊕ *www. 2100kalakaua.com.*

Waikiki Beach Walk. This open-air shopping center greets visitors at the west end of Waikiki's Kalakaua Avenue with 70 locally owned stores and restaurants. Get reasonably priced, fashionable resort wear for yourself at Mahina or for your pet at Planet U2; find unique pieces by local artists at Under the Koa Tree; or browse locally made gifts and treats from Coco Cove. The mall also features free local entertainment on the fountain stage at least once a week. ⊠ *226 Lewers St., Waikiki* ☎ *808/931–3591* ⊕ *www.waikikibeachwalk.com.*

CLOTHING

Newt at the Royal. Newt is known for high-quality, hand-woven Panama hats and tropical sportswear. ⊠ *The Royal Hawaiian Hotel, 2259 Kalakaua Ave., Waikiki* ☎ *808/949–4321* ⊕ *www.newtattheroyal.com.*

GIFTS

★ **Sand People.** This little shop stocks easy-to-carry gifts, such as fish-shaped Christmas ornaments, Hawaiian-style notepads, charms in the shape of flip-flops (known locally as "slippers"), soaps, and ceramic clocks. There's another branch in Kailua. ⊠ *Moana Surfrider, 2369 Kalakaua, Waikiki* ☎ *808/924–6773.*

JEWELRY

Philip Rickard. The heirloom design collection of this famed jeweler features custom Hawaiian wedding jewelry, sought by various celebrities. ⊠ *Royal Hawaiian Shopping Center, 2201 Kalakaua Ave., Waikiki* ☎ *808/924–7972.*

SURF SHOPS

Local Motion. If you plan on surfing or just want to look like a surfer, check out this outfitter's flagship store. They have it all—from surfboards to surf wear. ⊠ *2255 Kalakaua Ave., Waikiki* ☎ *808/254–7873* ⊕ *localmotionhawaii.com.*

Maui Divers Design Center. For a look into the harvesting and design of coral and black pearl jewelry, visit this shop and its adjacent factory near the Ala Moana Shopping Center. ⊠ *1520 Liona St., Moiliili* ☎ *808/946–7979* ⊕ *www.mauidivers.com.*

WINDWARD OAHU

Fodor's Choice
★ **Bookends.** The perfect place to shop for gifts, or just take a break with the family, this bookstore feels more like a small-town library, welcoming browsers to linger for hours. The large children's section is filled with toys and books to read. ⊠ *600 Kailua Rd., Kailua* ☎ *808/261–1996.*

Fodor's Choice
★ **Global Village.** Tucked into a tiny strip mall near Maui Tacos, this boutique features contemporary apparel for women, Hawaiian-style children's clothing, and unusual jewelry and gifts from all over the world. Look for Kula Cushions eye pillows (made with lavender grown on Maui), coasters in the shape of flip-flops, a wooden key holder shaped like a surfboard, and placemats made from lauhala and other natural fibers, plus accessories you won't find anywhere else. ⊠ *Kailua Village Shops, 539 Kailua Rd., Kailua* ☎ *808/262–8183* ⊕ *www.globalvillagehawaii.com.*

Fodor's Choice
★ **Under a Hula Moon.** Exclusive tabletop items and Pacific home decor, such as shell wreaths, shell night-lights, Hawaiian print kitchen towels, and Asian silk clothing, define this eclectic shop. ⊠ *Kailua Shopping Center, 600 Kailua Rd., Kailua* ☎ *808/261–4252* ⊕ *www.hulamoonhawaii.com.*

NORTH SHORE

★ **Global Creations Interiors.** Look for Hawaiian bath products, pikake perfume, locally made jewelry, and a carefully chosen selection of Hawaiian music CDs. Fun gifts include chip-and-dip plates and spreaders shaped like ukuleles. ✉ *66-079 Kamehameha Hwy., Haleiwa* ☎ *808/637–1780* ⊕ *www.globalcreationscart.com.*

★ **The Growing Keiki.** Frequent visitors return to this store year after year for a fresh supply of original, handpicked, Hawaiian-style clothing for youngsters. ✉ *66-051 Kamehameha Hwy., Haleiwa* ☎ *808/637–4544* ⊕ *www.thegrowingkeiki.com.*

Fodor's Choice   **Silver Moon Emporium.** This small boutique carries everything from Brighton accessories and fashionable T-shirts to Betsy Johnson formal wear,
★ and provides attentive yet casual personalized service. Its stock changes frequently, and there's always something wonderful on sale. No matter what your taste, you'll find something for everyday wear or special occasions. ✉ *North Shore Marketplace, 66-250 Kamehameha Hwy., Haleiwa* ☎ *808/637–7710.*

WEST (LEEWARD) OAHU

Aloha Stadium Swap Meet. This thrice-weekly outdoor bazaar attracts hundreds of vendors and even more bargain hunters. Every Hawaiian souvenir imaginable can be found here, from coral shell necklaces to bikinis, as well as a variety of ethnic wares, from Chinese brocade dresses to Japanese pottery. There are also ethnic foods, silk flowers, and luggage in aloha floral prints. Shoppers must wade through the typical sprinkling of used and stolen goods to find value. Wear comfortable shoes, use sunscreen, and bring bottled water. The flea market takes place in the Aloha Stadium parking lot Wednesday and Saturday from 8 to 3; Sunday from 6:30 to 3. Admission is $1 per person ages 12 and up.

Several shuttle companies serve Aloha Stadium for the swap meet, including VIP Shuttle (☎ *808/839–0911*); Reliable Shuttle (☎ *808/924–9292*); and Hawaii Supertransit (☎ *808/841–2928*). The average cost is $12 per person, round-trip. For a cheaper but slower ride, take TheBus (⊕ *www.thebus.org*). ✉ *99-500 Salt Lake Blvd., Aiea* ☎ *808/486–6704* ⊕ *www.alohastadiumswapmeet.net.*

Waikele Premium Outlets. Anne Klein Factory, Donna Karan Company Store, Kenneth Cole, and Saks Fifth Avenue Outlet anchor this discount destination. You can take a shuttle to the outlets, but the companies do change over frequently. One to try: **P.G. Plover** (☎ *808/744–2836*); $10 round-trip. ✉ *94-790 Lumiaina St., Waipahu, Waikele* ☎ *808/ 676–5656.*

SPAS

Updated
by Melissa
Chang

If you're getting a massage at a spa, there's a spiritual element to the *lomilomi* that calms the soul while the muscles release tension. During a hot-stone massage, smooth rocks, taken from the earth with permission from Pele, the goddess of volcanoes, are heated and placed at focal points on the body. Others are covered in oil and rubbed over tired limbs, feeling like powerful fingers. For an alternative, refresh skin with mango scrubs so fragrant they seem edible. Savor the unusual sensation of bamboo tapped against the arches of the feet. Indulge in a scalp massage that makes the entire body tingle. Day spas provide additional options to the self-indulgent services offered in almost every major hotel on the island.

HONOLULU

Ampy's European Facials and Body Spa. This 30-year-old spa has kept its prices reasonable over the years thanks to their "no frills" way of doing business. All of Ampy's facials are 75 minutes (except for teens), and the spa has become famous for custom aromatherapy treatments. Call at least a week in advance because the appointment book fills up quickly here. It's in the Ala Moana Building, adjacent to the Ala Moana Shopping Center. ⊠ *1441 Kapiolani Blvd., Suite 377, Ala Moana* ☎ *808/946–3838* ⊕ *www.ampys.com* ☞ *$95, 60-min lomilomi massage. Sauna. Services: body treatments, facials, hand and foot care, massage.*

Hoala Salon and Spa. This Aveda concept spa has everything from Vichy showers to hydrotherapy rooms to customized aromatherapy. Ladies, they'll even touch up your makeup for free before you leave. ⊠ *Ala Moana Shopping Center, 3rd fl., 1450 Ala Moana Blvd.* ☎ *808/947–6141* ⊕ *www.hoalasalonspa.com* ☞ *$160, 75-min lomilomi massage. Hair salon, eucalyptus-steam room. Services: body treatments, facials, massage, nail care, waxing.*

WAIKIKI

Mandara Spa at the Hilton Hawaiian Village Beach Resort & Spa. From its perch in the Kalia Tower, Mandara Spa, an outpost of the chain that originated in Bali, overlooks the mountains, ocean, and downtown Honolulu. Fresh Hawaiian ingredients and traditional techniques headline an array of treatments. Try an exotic upgrade, such as reflexology or an eye treatment using Asian silk protein. The delicately scented, candlelit foyer can fill up quickly with robe-clad conventioneers, so be sure to make a reservation. There are spa suites for couples, a private infinity pool, and a boutique. ⊠ *Hilton Hawaiian Village Beach Resort and Spa, 2005 Kalia Rd., Waikiki* ☎ *808/949–4321* ⊕ *www. hiltonhawaiianvillage.com* ☞ *$130, 50-min lomilomi massage. Hair salon, hot tubs (indoor and outdoor), sauna, steam room. Gym with: cardiovascular machines, free weights, weight-training equipment. Services: aromatherapy, body wraps and scrubs, facials, massage.*

Na Hoola at the Hyatt Regency Waikiki Resort & Spa. Na Hoola is the premier resort spa in Waikiki, with 16 treatment rooms sprawling across the fifth and sixth floors of the Hyatt. Arrive early for your treatment to

2

enjoy the postcard views of Waikiki Beach. Four packages identified by Hawaii's native healing plants—noni, kukui, awa, and kalo—combine various body, face, and hair treatments; they also have packages that last 3 to 6 hours. The Kele Kele body wrap employs a self-heating mud wrap to release tension and stress. The small exercise room is for use by hotel guests only. ⊠ *Hyatt Regency Waikiki Resort and Spa, 2424 Kalakaua Ave., Waikiki* ☎ *808/921–6097* ⊕ *www.waikiki.hyatt.com* ☞ *$139, 50-min lomilomi massage. Sauna. Gym with: cardiovascular machines. Services: aromatherapy, body scrubs and wraps, facials, hydrotherapy, massage.*

Fodor's Choice
★

SpaHalekulani. SpaHalekulani mines the traditions and cultures of the Pacific Islands with massages, body, and facial therapies. Try the Polynesian Nonu, which uses warm stones and healing nonu gel. The exclusive line of bath and body products is scented by maile, lavender, orchid, or coconut passion. Facilities specific to treatment but may include Japanese furo bath or steam shower. ⊠ *Halekūlani Hotel, 2199 Kalia Rd., Waikiki* ☎ *808/931–5322* ⊕ *www.halekulani.com* ☞ *$180, 55-min lomilomi massage plus 20-min pre- and post-treatment work. Services: body treatments, facials, hair salon, massage, nail care.*

The Spa at Trump Waikiki. One of the newest in Waikiki, The Spa at Trump offers private changing and showering areas for each room, creating an environment of uninterrupted relaxation. No matter what treatment you choose, it is inspired by "personal intention," such as to purify, balance, heal, revitalize, or calm, to elevate the senses throughout your time there. Don't miss the signature gemstone treatments, which feature products by Shiffa; or treat yourself to a Kate Somerville facial to emerge with younger-looking skin. The Hawaiian pineapple lime exfoliation massage is the most popular, as it is exclusive to this spa. ⊠ *Trump International Hotel Waikiki, 223 Saratoga Rd., Waikiki* ☎ *808/683–7466* ⊕ *www.trumpwaikikihotel.com* ☞ *$165, 50-min lomilomi massage. Services: aromatherapy, body scrubs and wraps, facials, hydrotherapy, lash extensions, massage, nail care, waxing.*

THE NORTH SHORE

The Spa Luana at Turtle Bay Resort. Luxuriate at the ocean's edge in this serene spa. Don't miss the tropical Pineapple Pedicure ($100 with polish; $85 without), administered outdoors overlooking the North Shore. Tired feet soak in a bamboo bowl filled with coconut milk before the pampering really begins with Hawaiian algae salt, island bee honey, kukui nut oil, and crushed pineapple. There are private spa suites, an outdoor treatment cabana that overlooks the surf, an outdoor exercise studio, and a lounge area and juice bar. ⊠ *Turtle Bay Resort, 57-091 Kamehameha Hwy., Kahuku* ☎ *808/447–6868* ⊕ *www.turtlebayresort. com* ☞ *$145, 50-min lomilomi massage. Hair salon, outdoor hot tub, steam room. Gym with: cardiovascular machines, free weights, weight-training equipment. Services: body treatments, facials, massage, waxing. Classes and programs: aerobics, Pilates, yoga.*

WEST (LEEWARD) OAHU

Fodor's Choice
★

JW Marriott Ihilani Resort & Spa. Soak in warm seawater among velvety orchid blossoms at this unique Hawaiian hydrotherapy spa. Thalassotherapy treatments combine underwater jet massage with color therapy and essential oils. Specially designed treatment rooms have a hydrotherapy tub, a Vichy-style shower, and a needle shower with 12 heads. The spa's Ohia Ai Mountain Apple line of natural aromatherapy products, which uses the essence of the mountain apple fruit in lotions, bath salts, shampoos and conditioners. ⊠ *JW Marriott Ihilani Resort, 92-1001 Olani St., Kapolei* ☎ *808/679–0079* ⊕ *www.ihilani. com* ☞ *$145, 50-min lomilomi massage. Hair salon, hot tubs (indoor and outdoor), sauna, steam room. Gym with: cardiovascular machines, free weights, weight-training equipment. Services: aromatherapy, body wraps and scrubs, facials, massage, thalassotherapy. Classes and programs: aerobics, body sculpting, dance classes, fitness analysis, guided walks, personal training, Pilates, tai chi, yoga.*

Laniwai Spa at Aulani, A Disney Resort & Spa. Every staff member at this spa, or "cast member," as they call themselves, is extensively trained in Hawaiian culture and history to ensure they are projecting the right *mana*, or energy, in their work. To begin each treatment, you select a special *pohaku* (rock) with words of intent then cast it into a reflective pool. Choose from about 150 spa therapies, and indulge in Kulu Wai, the only outdoor hydrotherapy garden on Oahu—with private vitality pools, co-ed mineral baths, six different "rain" showers, whirlpool jet spas, and more. ⊠ *Aulani, A Disney Resort & Spa, 92-1185 Aliinui Dr., Ko Olina, Kapolei* ☎ *714/520–7001* ⊕ *resorts.disney.go.com/ aulani-hawaii-resort* ☞ *$150, 50-min lomilomi massage. Hot tubs, sauna, steam room. Services: Aromatherapy, body wraps and scrubs, facials, massage, Vichy shower treatment.*

ENTERTAINMENT AND NIGHTLIFE

Updated by
Catherine E.
Toth

Many people arrive in Oahu expecting to find white-sand beaches, swaying palm trees, and the kind of picturesque scenery you'd see in postcards. If they think about nightlife at all, it's sunsets over Waikiki.

But Oahu does have an after-dark scene, ranging from torch-lit luau shows to hip bars to sleek nightclubs. Posh bars are found in many of the larger hotels, and smaller neighborhoods hide comfortable local watering holes. Every night of the week you can find musicians in venues from Kailua to Ko Olina—and everywhere in between. Or you can simply walk down Kalakaua Avenue to be entertained by Waikiki's street performers.

And if all-night dancing isn't for you, Oahu boasts a thriving arts and culture scene, with community-theater productions, stand-up comedy, outdoor concerts, film festivals, and chamber-music performances. Major Broadway shows, dance companies, rock stars, and comedians come through the Islands, too. Check local newspapers—the *Honolulu Star-Advertiser, Midweek, Honolulu Weekly*—for the latest events.

Websites like ⊕ www.nonstophonolulu.com and *www.honolulupulse. com* also have great information.

Whether you stay out all night or get up early to catch the morning surf, there's something for everyone on Oahu.

ENTERTAINMENT

DINNER CRUISES AND SHOWS

Dinner cruises depart either from the piers adjacent to the Aloha Tower Marketplace in downtown Honolulu or from Kewalo Basin, near Ala Moana Beach Park, and head along the coast toward Diamond Head. There's usually a buffet-style dinner with a local accent, dancing, drinks, and a sensational sunset. Except as noted, dinner cruises cost approximately $40 to $110, cocktail cruises $25 to $40. Most major credit cards are accepted. In all cases, reservations are essential. Check the websites for savings of up to 15%.

Alii Kai **Catamaran.** Patterned after an ancient Polynesian vessel, this 170-foot catamaran casts off from Aloha Tower with 1,000 passengers. The deluxe dinner cruise has two bars, a huge dinner, and an authentic Polynesian show with dancers, drummers, and chanters. The menu is varied, and the after-dinner show is loud and fun. Cost is $75.60 and includes round-trip transportation. Vegetarian meals are available. ⊠ *Aloha Tower Marketplace, Aloha Tower Dr.* ☎ *808/954–8652, 866/898–2519* ⊕ *www.aliikaicatamaran.com.*

★ **Atlantis Cruises.** The sleekly high-tech *Navatek*, designed to sail smoothly in rough waters, powers farther along Waikiki's coastline than its competitors, sailing past Diamond Head. Enjoy sunset dinners or moonlight cruises aboard the 300-passenger boat, feasting on roast beef tenderloin or whole Maine lobster. Rates begin at $94 for a bountiful buffet; five-course dinners, which include three drinks, start at $126. ⊠ *Aloha Tower Marketplace, 1 Aloha Tower Rd., Pier 6* ☎ *808/973–1311, 800/548–6262* ⊕ *www.atlantisadventures.com.*

Creation: A Polynesian Journey. A daring Samoan fire-knife dancer is the highlight of this show that traces Hawaii's culture and history, from its origins of discovery to statehood. The buffet dinner is priced at $95; a sit-down dinner with steak and lobster is $145. You can also choose to see the show without dinner for $55. ⊠ *Ainahau Showroom, Sheraton Princess Kaiulani Hotel, 120 Kaiulani Ave.* ☎ *808/931–4660* ⊕ *www. princess-kaiulani.com/dining/creation* ⊡ *$55–$145* ⊙ *Dinner shows Tues. and Thurs.–Sun. at 6; closed Mon. and Wed.*

★ **Magic of Polynesia.** Hawaii's top illusionist, John Hirokawa, displays mystifying sleight of hand in this highly entertaining show, which incorporates contemporary hula and island music into its acts. It's held in the Holiday Inn Waikiki's $7.5 million showroom. Reservations are required for dinner and the show, which is priced at $125.10. Walk-ups are permitted if you just want the entertainment for $49.50. ⊠ *Holiday Inn Waikiki Beachcomber Hotel, 2300 Kalakaua Ave., Waikiki* ☎ *808/971–4321, 866/898–2519* ⊕ *www.magicofpolynesia.com* ⊙ *Nightly at 8.*

🐾 **Polynesian Cultural Center.** Easily one of the best on the Islands, this show has soaring moments and an "erupting volcano." It's a long drive—about an hour from Waikiki—but you can take part in the popular Alii Luau or stay for the heralded "Ha: Breath of Life" show. General admission starts at $49.95. ✉ *55-370 Kamehameha Hwy., Laie* ☎ *808/293–3333, 800/367–7060* ⊕ *www.polynesia.com* 🕐 *Mon.–Sat. 12:30–9:30.*

Society of Seven. This lively, popular cabaret show has great staying power and, after more than 30 years, continues to put on one of the most popular shows in Waikiki. The cast sings, dances, does impersonations, plays instruments, and, above all, entertains with its contemporary sound. ✉ *Outrigger Waikiki on the Beach, 2335 Kalakaua Ave., Waikiki* ☎ *808/923–0711, 808/922–6408* ⊕ *www.outrigger.com.*

LUAU

The luau is an experience that everyone, both local and tourist, should have. Today's luau still offer traditional foods and entertainment, but there's often a fun, contemporary flair. With many, you can watch the roasted pig being carried out of its *imu*, a hole in the ground used for cooking meat with heated stones.

Luau average around $100 per person—some are cheaper, others twice that amount—and are held around the island, not just in Waikiki. Reservations—and a camera—are a must.

Fia Fia at the Ihilani. Just after sunset, on the resort's oceanfront lagoon lawn, the charismatic Chief Sielu Avea leads the Samoan-based "Fia Fia," an entertaining show that takes guests on the journey through the South Pacific. Every show is different and unscripted, but always a good look at Polynesian culture. It's the only show with eight fire-knife dancers in a blazing finale. Admission includes buffet. ✉ *JW Marriott Ihilani Resort & Spa, 92-1001 Olani St., Ko Olina, Kapolei* ☎ *808/679–0079, 888/236–2427* ⊕ *www.ihilani.com* 🕐 *Thurs. at 4:30.*

Germaine's Luau. More than 3 million visitors have come to this luau, held about 40 minutes west of Waikiki. Widely considered one of the most folksy and local, it offers a tasty, multicourse, all-you-can-eat buffet. Admission, which starts at $72, includes buffet, three drinks, and shuttle transport from Waikiki. ✉ *91-119 Olai St., Kapolei* ☎ *808/949–6626, 800/367–5655* ⊕ *www.germainesluau.com* 🕐 *Daily at 6.*

★ **Paradise Cove Luau.** One of the largest shows on Oahu, the lively Paradise Cove Luau is held in Kapolei, about 40 minutes from Waikiki. Drink in hand, you can stroll through the authentic village, learn traditional arts and crafts, and play local games. The stage show includes a fire-knife dancer, singing emcee, and both traditional and contemporary hula and other Polynesian dances. Admission includes the buffet, activities, and the show, as well as shuttle transport from Waikiki. You pay extra for table service and box seating. The stunning sunsets are free. ✉ *92-1089 Alii Nui Dr., Kapolei* ☎ *808/842–5911, 800/775–2683* ⊕ *www.paradisecove.com* 🍴 *$86–$149* 🕐 *Daily at 5:30.*

Fodor's Choice ★ **Polynesian Cultural Center Alii Luau.** This elaborate luau has the sharpest production values but no booze (it's a Mormon-owned facility). It's held amid the seven re-created villages at the Polynesian Cultural Center in

the North Shore town of Laie, about an hour's drive from Honolulu. The luau—considered one of the most authentic on Oahu—includes the "Ha: Breath of Life" show that has long been popular with both residents and visitors. Rates start at $91 and go up depending on activities and amenities (personalized tours, reserved seats, or table service, for example). Waikiki transport is available. ⊠ *Polynesian Cultural Center, 55-370 Kamehameha Hwy., Laie* ☎ *808/293–3333, 800/367–7060* ⊕ *www.polynesia.com* ◷ *Mon.–Sat. at 5.*

FILM

Hawaii International Film Festival. It may not be Cannes, but this festival is unique and exciting in its own right. During the weeklong event in the middle of October, top films from all over the world, as well as some by local filmmakers, are screened day and night to packed crowds. It's a must-see for film adventurers. ⊠ *Regal Dole Cannery Theaters, 680 Iwilei Rd.* ☎ *808/792–1577* ⊕ *www.hiff.org.*

★ **Sunset on the Beach.** It's like watching a movie at the drive-in, minus the car and the speaker box. Bring a blanket and find a spot on the sand to enjoy live entertainment, food from top local restaurants, and a movie on a 40-foot screen. Held twice a month on Queen's Surf Beach across from the Honolulu Zoo, Sunset on the Beach is a favorite event for both locals and visitors. If the weather is blustery, beware of flying sand. ⊠ *Queen's Surf Beach, Kalakaua Ave., Waikiki* ☎ *808/923–1094* ⊕ *www.waikikiimprovement.com.*

MUSIC

First Friday. Rain or shine, on the first Friday of every month, the downtown Honolulu and Chinatown districts come alive after dark with a lively street party. Art galleries and restaurants open late, and local musicians and DJs provide the soundtrack for the evening. Check the website for featured artists and musicians. ⊠ *Downtown Honolulu* ☎ *808/739–9797* ⊕ *www.firstfridayhawaii.com* ⊡ *Free.*

Hawaii Opera Theatre. Better known as "HOT," the Hawaii Opera Theatre has been known to turn the opera-challenged into opera lovers since 1960. All operas are sung in their original language with projected English translation. Tickets range from $34 to $125. ⊠ *Neal S. Blaisdell Center Concert Hall, 777 Ward Ave.* ☎ *808/596–7372, 800/836–7372* ⊕ *www.hawaiiopera.org.*

Honolulu Zoo Concerts. For two decades, the Honolulu Zoo Society has sponsored hour-long evening concerts called the "Wildest Show in Town." They're held at 6 pm on Wednesday from June to August. Listen to local legends play everything from Hawaiian to jazz to Latin music. ■TIP→ **At just $3 admission, this is one of the best deals in town.** Take a brisk walk through the zoo, or join in the family activities. This is an alcohol-free event, and there's a food for those who haven't brought their own picnic supplies. ⊠ *Honolulu Zoo, 151 Kapahulu Ave., Waikiki* ☎ *808/971–7171* ⊕ *www.honoluluzoo.org* ⊡ *$1* ◷ *Gates open at 4:30.*

Waikiki Aquarium Concerts. Every other Thursday evening in June and July, the Waikiki Aquarium holds an ocean-side concert series called "Ke Kani O Ke Kai." You can listen to top performers while enjoying food from local restaurants. The aquarium stays open throughout the night, so you can see the marine life in a new light. Bring your own beach chairs. Proceeds support the aquarium, the third oldest in the United States. ⊠ *Waikiki Aquarium, 2777 Kalakaua Ave., Waikiki* ☎ *808/923–9741* ⊕ *www.waquarium.org* ⌚ *$30.*

NIGHTLIFE

Oahu is the best of all the Islands for nightlife. The locals call it *pau hana*, but you might call it "off the clock and ready for a cocktail." (The literal translation of the Hawaiian phrase means "done with work.") On weeknights, it's likely that you'll find the working crowd, still in their casual-business attire, downing chilled beers even before the sun goes down. Those who don't have to wake up in the early morning should change into a fresh outfit and start the evening closer to 10 pm.

On the weekends, it's typical to have dinner at a restaurant before hitting the clubs around 9:30. Some bar-hoppers start as early as 7, but partygoers typically don't patronize more than two establishments a night. That's because getting from one Oahu nightspot to the next usually requires packing your friends into the car and driving.

You can find a bar in just about any area on Oahu. Most of the clubs, however, are in Waikiki, near Ala Moana, and in and around downtown Honolulu. The drinking age is 21 on Oahu and throughout Hawaii. Many bars will admit younger people but will not serve them alcohol. By law, all establishments that serve alcoholic beverages must close by 2 am. The only exceptions are those with a cabaret license, which can stay open until 4 am. ■ TIP→ Most places have a cover charge of $5 to $10, but with some establishments, getting there early means you don't have to pay.

HONOLULU

BARS

Fodor's Choice ★ **Mai Tai Bar.** After a long day of shopping, the third-floor Mai Tai Bar is a perfect spot to relax. There's live entertainment and two nightly happy hours: one for food and another strictly for drinks. There's never a cover charge and no dress code. To avoid waiting in line, get here before 9 pm. ⊠ *Ala Moana Center, 1450 Ala Moana Blvd., Ala Moana* ☎ *808/947–2900* ⊕ *www.maitaibar.com.*

Murphy's Bar & Grill. On the edge of Chinatown, this 120-year-old bar has been serving drinks to locals and visitors since Hawaii's days as a territory. The kind of Irish pub you'd find in Boston, Murphy's is a break from all the colorful drinks garnished with slices of fruit, and it's definitely the place to be on St. Patrick's Day. On Friday it serves some of the best homemade fruit pies around. They're so good, they sell out during lunch. ⊠ *2 Merchant St., Downtown Honolulu* ☎ *808/531–0422* ⊕ *www.murphyshawaii.com.*

Nocturna Lounge. This is Hawaii's first self-described NextGen lounge, a stylish and sophisticated karaoke and gaming lounge at the Waterfront Plaza. It boasts a full bar, four private suites with state-of-the-art karaoke, and video game consoles around the lounge featuring the latest in social gaming. Play "Street Fighter" in the open lounge, perfect your moves in "Dance Central" on the Xbox Kinect in a side room, or wander through the noisy club while sipping one of Nocturna's creative cocktails with names like Sonic Boomtini and Yuzu Is About to Die. The crowd isn't as young as you'd expect at a club outfitted with video game consoles. ✉ *Waterfront Plaza, 500 Ala Moana Blvd., Downtown Honolulu* ☎ *808/521–1555* ⊕ *www.nocturnalounge.com.*

thirtyninehotel. This loft and art gallery is on the cutting edge of what's hot downtown. Every three months it gets a new "art installation," where a local artist repaints and reconfigures the entire space. The bartenders and their "market-fresh" cocktails have become the stuff of local legend, using Hawaiian produce to re-create classic turn-of-the-century libations. Entertainment varies from jazz combos to DJs spinning the latest hits. ✉ *39 N. Hotel St., Downtown Honolulu* ☎ *808/599–2552* ⊕ *www.thirtyninehotel.com.*

CLUBS

The Dragon Upstairs. In the heart of Chinatown, this cool club—formerly a tattoo parlor, hence the dragon mural—serves up classic cocktails along with lounge-y jazz performances most nights of the week. You'll hear local vocalists, as well as small combos, in this unique venue upstairs from Hank's Cafe Honolulu. ✉ *1038 Nuuanu Ave., Chinatown, Honolulu* ☎ *808/526–1411* ⊕ *www.thedragonupstairs.com.*

Pearl Ultralounge. A hip after-work crowd flocks here on weekdays to unwind at happy hour. Weekends it's packed with the see-and-be-seen set. ✉ *Ala Moana Center, 1450 Ala Moana Blvd., 3rd fl., Ala Moana, Honolulu* ☎ *808/944–8000* ⊕ *www.pearlhawaii.com.*

Fodor'sChoice
★ **Rumours.** It may not be the hippest club in town, but Rumours prides itself on its theme events and its retro vibe, spinning hits from the '70s and '80s. It's got free pupu to nibble on and cages to dance inside. ✉ *Ala Moana Hotel, 410 Atkinson St., Ala Moana, Honolulu* ☎ *808/955–4811.*

WAIKIKI

BARS

★ **Duke's Waikiki.** Making the most of its spot on Waikiki Beach, Duke's presents live music every Friday, Saturday, and Sunday. Contemporary Hawaiian musicians like Henry Kapono and Maunalua have performed, as well as nationally known musicians like Jimmy Buffett. Solo Hawaiian musicians take the stage nightly, and it's not unusual for surfers to leave their boards outside to step in for a casual drink after a long day on the waves. ✉ *Outrigger Waikiki, 2335 Kalakaua Ave., Suite 116, Waikiki* ☎ *808/922–2268* ⊕ *www.dukeswaikiki.com.*

Lewers Lounge. A great spot for predinner drinks or post-sunset cocktails, Lewers Lounge offers a relaxed but chic atmosphere in the middle of Waikiki. There are classic and contemporary cocktails, many created by Dale DeGroff, the "King of Cocktails" from New York City's Rainbow Room. He's ditched the soda guns and mixes and brought back the craft of cocktails, using fresh and natural ingredients. Some standouts include the Ginger Lychee Caipirissima and the Blackberry Julep. Enjoy your libation with live jazz and tempting desserts, such as the hotel's famous coconut cake. Or just sit back and relax in the grand setting of

Experience one of Hawaii's most spectacular luau at the Polynesian Cultural Center.

the luxurious lounge, which is decked in dramatic drapes and cozy banquettes. ✉ *Halekulani Hotel, 2199 Kalia Rd., Waikiki* ☎ *808/923–2311* ⊕ *www.halekulani.com.*

Lobby Bar. It's tricky to find the Lobby Bar at the new Modern Honolulu—it's behind a huge, revolving bookcase in the lobby behind the registration desk. It's an überchic space, with intimate alcoves and oversized sofas that are both hip and inviting. The cocktails, like the Deconstructed Mai Tai, are pricey but cool. ✉ *The Modern Honolulu Hotel, 1775 Ala Moana Blvd., Waikiki* ☎ *808/943–5800.*

Lulu's Waikiki. Even if you're not a surfer, you'll love this place's retro vibe and the unobstructed second-floor view of Waikiki Beach. The open-air setting, casual dining menu, and tropical drinks are all you need to help you settle into your vacation. The venue transforms from a nice spot for lunch or dinner to a bustling, high-energy club with live music lasting into the wee hours. ✉ *Park Shore Waikiki Hotel, 2586 Kalakaua Ave., Waikiki* ☎ *808/926–5222* ⊕ *www.luluswaikiki.com.*

★ **Mai Tai Bar.** The bartenders here sure know how to mix up a killer mai tai. This is, after all, the establishment that first concocted the famous drink. The umbrella-shaded tables at the outdoor bar are front-row seating for sunsets and also have an unobstructed view of Diamond Head. Contemporary Hawaiian musicians hold jam sessions onstage. ✉ *Royal Hawaiian Hotel, 2259 Kalakaua Ave., Waikiki* ☎ *808/923–7311* ⊕ *www.royal-hawaiian.com.*

Fodor'sChoice
★ **Moana Terrace.** Three floors up from Waikiki Beach, this casual, open-air terrace is the home of the Keawe Ohana, a family comprised of some of Hawaii's finest musicians. Order a drink served in a fresh pineapple

If it's nightlife you're after, there's no better place in Hawaii than Waikiki Beach.

and watch the sun dip into the Pacific Ocean. ✉ *Waikiki Beach Marriott Resort, 2552 Kalakaua Ave., Waikiki* ☎ *808/922–6611.*

Rumfire. Locals and visitors head here for the convivial atmosphere and the million-dollar view of Waikiki Beach and Diamond Head. Come early to get a seat for happy hour, which is nightly from 4 to 6 and 9:30 to 11. If you're feeling peckish, there's a menu of Asian-influenced dishes. Rumfire also features original cocktails, signature shots, and live music. ✉ *Sheraton Waikiki, 2255 Kalakaua Ave., Waikiki* ☎ *808/922–4422* ⊕ *www.rumfirewaikiki.com.*

Tiki's Grill & Bar. Tiki torches light the way to this restaurant and bar overlooking Kuhio Beach. A mix of locals and visitors head here on the weekend to get their fill of kitschy cool. There's nightly entertainment featuring contemporary Hawaiian musicians. Don't leave without sipping on the Lava Flow, served in a whole coconut, or noshing on the famous coconut shrimp. ✉ *Aston Waikiki Beach Hotel, 2570 Kalakaua Ave.* ☎ *808/923–8454* ⊕ *www.tikisgrill.com.*

The Veranda. The Veranda at the Moana Surfrider—Waikiki's first hotel—has its own interesting history. From this location, the radio program *Hawaii Calls* first broadcast the sounds of Hawaiian music to a U.S. mainland audience in 1935. Hawaiian entertainers continue to provide the perfect accompaniment to the sounds of the waves. There's a small bar in the dining area—this space turns into the Beach House at the Moana for dinner—or mosey to The Beach Bar below and enjoy live Hawaiian music nightly. ✉ *Moana Surfrider, 2365 Kalakaua Ave., Waikiki* ☎ *808/922–3111, 808/921–4600* ⊕ *www.moana-surfrider.com.*

CLUBS

Addiction Nightclub. This new nightclub at The Modern Honolulu was launched by the hotel's director of nightlife, Matt Bendik, who also manages and owns nightlife concepts in Los Angeles and Hollywood. Traditional banquettes offer intimate seating for VIP tables, and bottle service lends a New York City feel. Red-velvet ropes guide you in the entrance; once inside you can dance to house and hip-hop music under a stunning ceiling installation of 40,000 round lights. But Addiction comes with a price—there's a $20 cover and drinks aren't cheap. ⊠ *The Modern Honolulu, 1775 Ala Moana Blvd., Waikiki* ☎ *808/943–5800* ⊕ *www.addictionnightclub.com.*

Apartment 3. Tucked away on the third floor of an office building on the edge of Waikiki, this cool club is a favorite among cosmopolitan locals and the occasional celebrity—Johnny Depp has been spotted here. There's something going on every night of the week, except Sunday. The food—traditional comfort eats with a modern twist—is great, too. ⊠ *Century Center, 1750 Kalakaua Ave., Waikiki* ☎ *808/955–9300* ⊕ *www.apartmentthree.com.*

Hula's Bar and Lei Stand. Hawaii's oldest and best-known gay-friendly nightspot offers panoramic views of Diamond Head by day and high-energy club music by night. Check out the soundproof, glassed-in dance floor. Patrons have included Elton John, Adam Lambert, and Dolly Parton. ⊠ *Waikiki Grand Hotel, 134 Kapahulu Ave., 2nd fl., Waikiki* ☎ *808/923–0669* ⊕ *www.hulas.com.*

Nashville Waikiki. Country music in the tropics? You bet! Dress up like a *paniolo* (Hawaiian cowboy) and mosey on out to the giant dance floor at Nashville Waikiki. There's line dancing and free dance lessons five nights a week. Look for wall-to-wall crowds on the weekend. Pool tables, dartboards, and Wii consoles keep them occupied. ⊠ *Ohana Waikiki West Hotel, 2330 Kuhio Ave., Waikiki* ☎ *808/926–7911* ⊕ *www.nashvillewaikiki.com.*

Zanzabar. Traverse the winding staircase to make a grand entrance at Zanzabar, where DJs spin everything from hip-hop and soul to techno and trance. With three bars, it's easy to find a drink at this high-energy nightspot. Not sure how to get your groove on? Zanzabar offers free Latin dance lessons every Tuesday night. ⊠ *Waikiki Trade Center, 2255 Kuhio Ave., Waikiki* ☎ *808/924–3939* ⊕ *www.zanzabarhawaii.com.*

SOUTHEAST OAHU

The Shack. This sports bar and restaurant is about the only late-night spot you can find in Southeast Oahu. After a day of snorkeling at Hanauma Bay, stop by to kick back, have a beer, eat a burger, or play a game of pool. ⊠ *Hawaii Kai Shopping Center, 377 Keahole St., Hawaii Kai* ☎ *808/396–1919* ⊕ *www.shackhawaiikai.com.*

WINDWARD OAHU

Boardrider's Bar & Grill. Tucked away in Kailua Town, Boardrider's has long been the place for local bands to strut their stuff. Look for live music—reggae to rock and roll—every Friday and Saturday night. The spruced-up space includes pool tables, dartboards, and eight TVs for watching the game. ✉ *201-A Hamakua Dr., Kailua* ☎ *808/261–4600.*

THE NORTH SHORE

Breaker's Restaurant. Just about every surf competition post-party is celebrated at this family-owned establishment. (The owner's son, Benji Weatherly, is a pro surfer.) Surfing memorabilia, including longboards hanging from the ceiling, fill the space. A tasty late-night menu is available until midnight. There's live music on Saturday. ✉ *Marketplace Shopping Center, 66-250 Kamehameha Hwy., Haleiwa* ☎ *808/ 637–9898.*

WHERE TO EAT

Updated by Melissa Chang

Oahu, where the majority of the Islands' 2,000-plus restaurants are located, offers the best of all worlds: it has the exoticness and excitement of Asia and Polynesia, but when the kids need McDonald's, or when you just have to have a Starbucks latte, they're here, too.

Budget for a pricey dining experience at the very top of the restaurant food chain, where chefs Alan Wong, Roy Yamaguchi, George Mavrothalassitis, and others you've seen on the Food Network and Travel Channel put a sophisticated and unforgettable spin on local foods and flavors. Savor seared ahi tuna in sea urchin beurre blanc or steak marinated in Korean kimchee sauce.

Spend the rest of your food dollars where budget-conscious locals do: in plate-lunch places and small ethnic eateries, at roadside stands and lunch wagons, or at window-in-the-wall delis. Snack on a *musubi* (a handheld rice ball wrapped with seaweed and often topped with Spam), slurp shave ice with red-bean paste, or order up Filipino pork adobo with two scoops of rice and macaroni salad.

In Waikiki, where most visitors stay, you can find choices from gracious rooms with a view to surprisingly authentic Japanese noodle shops. But hop in the car, or on the trolley or bus, and travel just a few miles in any direction, and you can save your money and get in touch with the real food of Hawaii.

Kaimuki's Waialae Avenue, for example, offers one of the city's best espresso bars, a hugely popular Chinese bakery, a highly recommended patisserie, an exceptional Italian bistro, a dim-sum restaurant, Mexican food (rare here), and a Hawaii regional cuisine standout, 3660 on the Rise—all in three blocks, and 10 minutes from Waikiki. Chinatown, 10 minutes in the other direction and easily reached by the Waikiki Trolley, is another dining (and shopping) treasure, not only for Chinese but also Vietnamese, Filipino, Malaysian, and Indian food, and with even a chic little tea shop.

Prices in the reviews are the average cost of a main course at dinner or, if dinner is not served, at lunch.

HONOLULU

DOWNTOWN HONOLULU

$ JAPANESE 🍴 **Akasaka.** Step inside this tiny sushi bar tucked behind the Ala Moana Hotel, and you'll swear you're in an out-of-the-way Edo neighborhood in some indeterminate time. Don't be deterred by its location between strip clubs or its reputation for inconsistent service. Greeted with a cheerful "*Iraishaimase!*" (Welcome!), sink down at a diminutive table or perch at the handful of seats at the sushi bar. It's safe to let the sushi chefs here decide (*omakase*-style) or you can go for the delicious grilled specialties, such as scallop *battayaki* (grilled in butter). [$] *Average main: $17* ✉ *1646 B Kona St., Ala Moana* ☎ *808/942–4466* 🌐 *www.akasakahawaii.com/home.html* 🕒 *No lunch Sun.*

$ VIETNAMESE 🍴 **Bac Nam.** Tam and Kimmy Huynh's menu is much more extensive than most, ranging far beyond the usual *pho* (beef noodle soup) and *bun* (cold noodle dishes). Coconut milk curries, an extraordinary crab noodle soup, and other dishes hail from both North and South Vietnam. The atmosphere is welcoming and relaxed, and they'll work with you to make choices. Reservations are not accepted for groups fewer than six. [$] *Average main: $12* ✉ *1117 S. King St., Downtown Honolulu* ☎ *808/597–8201.*

$ AMERICAN 🍴 **Big City Diner.** Part of a chain of unfussy retro diners, Big City offers a short course in local-style breakfasts—rice instead of potatoes, option of fish or Portuguese sausage instead of bacon, roasted-macadamia-nut pancakes smothered in haupia (coconut) sauce—with generous portions, low prices, and pronounced flavors. Lunch and dinner focus on local-style comfort food—baby back ribs, kimchee fried rice—and burgers. There are always daily specials. [$] *Average main: $12* ✉ *Ward Entertainment Center, 1060 Auahi St., Ala Moana* ☎ *808/591–8891* 🌐 *www.bigcitydinerhawaii.com.*

$$$ ECLECTIC 🍴 **Chai's Island Bistro.** Chai Chaowasaree's stylish, light-bathed, and orchid-draped lunch and dinner restaurant expresses the sophisticated side of this Thai-born immigrant. He plays East against West on the plate in signature dishes such as *kataifi* (baked and shredded phyllo), macadamia-crusted prawns, ahi *katsu* (tuna steaks dredged with crisp Japanese bread crumbs and quickly deep-fried), crispy duck confetti spring rolls, and Japanese eggplant zucchini soufflé. Some of Hawaii's best-known contemporary Hawaiian musicians play brief dinner shows here every night. [$] *Average main: $35* ✉ *Aloha Tower Marketplace, 1 Aloha Tower Dr., Downtown Honolulu* ☎ *808/585–0011* 🌐 *www.chaisislandbistro.com* 🕒 *No lunch.*

$$ ASIAN 🍴 **Hiroshi Eurasion Tapas.** Built around chef Hiroshi Fukui's signature style of "West & Japan" cuisine, this sleek dinner house focuses on small plates to share (enough for two servings each), with an exceptional choice of hard-to-find wines by the glass and in flights. Do not miss Hiroshi's braised veal cheeks (he was doing them before everyone else), the locally raised *kampachi* fish carpaccio, or the best *misoyaki* (marinated in a rich miso-soy blend, then grilled) butterfish ever. For a decadent treat, try the foie gras *nigiri*. You can also order off the menu from Vino, next door, as they share a kitchen. [$] *Average main: $26* ✉ *Restaurant Row, 500 Ala Moana Blvd., Ala Moana* ☎ *808/533–4476* 🌐 *www.hiroshihawaii.com* 🕒 *No lunch.*

BEST BETS FOR OAHU DINING

Fodor's Choice ★

Alan Wong's, $$$$, p. 151

Buzz's Original Steakhouse, $$, p. 160

Chef Mavro, $$$$, p. 152

Little Village Noodle House, $, p. 151

Ola at Turtle Bay Resort, $$$$, p. 162

By Price

$

Bac Nam, p. 145

Little Village Noodle House, p. 151

Kakaako Kitchen, p. 146

Keo's in Waikiki, p. 155

Ono Hawaiian Foods, p. 153

Pah Ke's Chinese Restaurant, p. 161

To Chau, p. 149

Wailana Coffee House, p. 158

$$

Buzz's Original Steakhouse, p. 160

Roy's, p. 159

$$$

3660 on the Rise, p. 151

Sam Choy's Breakfast Lunch & Crab and Big Aloha Brewery, p. 153

$$$$

Alan Wong's, p. 151

Chef Mavro, p. 152

Hoku's at the Kahala, p. 152

Nobu, p. 157

Ola at Turtle Bay Resort, p. 162

By Cuisine

HAWAIIAN

Alan Wong's, $$$$, p. 151

Chef Mavro, $$$$, p. 152

Hoku's at the Kahala, $$$$, p. 152

Roy's, $$, p. 159

PLATE LUNCH

Ono Hawaiian Foods, $, p. 153

Ted's Bakery, $, p. 162

SUSHI

Nobu, $$$$, p. 157

Sushi Sasabune, $$$$, p. 154

Yanagi Sushi, $$, p. 150

$
AMERICAN
✕ **Honolulu Museum of Art Cafe.** The cool courtyards and varied galleries of the Honolulu Museum of Art are well worth a visit and, afterward, so is Mike Nevin's popular lunch restaurant. The café overflows onto a lanai from which you can ponder Asian statuary and a burbling water feature while you wait for your salade niçoise or signature Piadina sandwich (fresh-baked flatbread rounds stuffed with arugula, tomatoes, basil, and cheese). $ *Average main: $15* ⊠ *Honolulu Museum of Art, 900 S. Beretania St., Downtown Honolulu* ☎ *808/532–8734* ⊕ *www.honolulumuseum.org* ⌖ *Reservations essential.*

$
MODERN
HAWAIIAN
☕
✕ **Kakaako Kitchen.** Russell Siu was the first of the local-boy fine dining chefs to open a place of the sort he enjoys when he's off-duty, serving high-quality plate lunches (house-made sauce instead of from-a-mix brown gravy, for example). Here you can get your two scoops of either brown or white rice, green salad instead of the usual macaroni salad, grilled fresh fish specials, and vegetarian fare. Breakfast is especially good, with combos like corned-beef hash and eggs, and exceptional baked goods. $ *Average main: $12* ⊠ *Ward Centre, 1200 Ala Moana Blvd., Kakaako* ☎ *808/596–7488* ⊕ *kakaakokitchen.com* ⌖ *Reservations not accepted.*

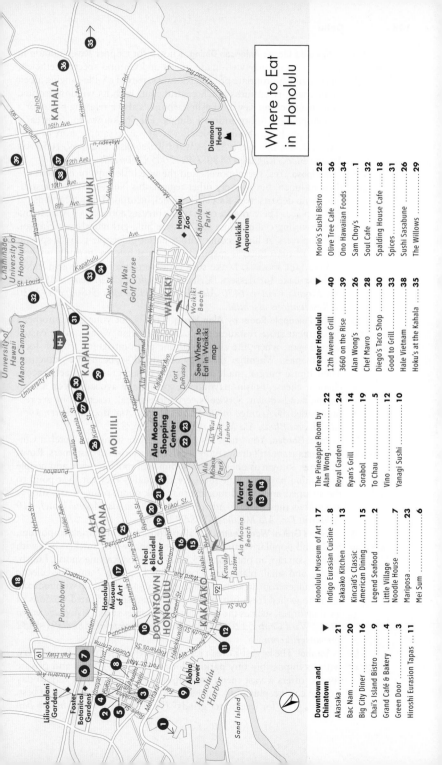

Where to Eat in Honolulu

$$$ AMERICAN 👍 🍴 **Kincaid's Classic American Dining.** Known for Copper River salmon in season, consistently well-made salads and seafood specials, efficient service, and appropriate pricing, Kincaid's, part of a wide-ranging albeit small chain, is business-lunch central. But, with its window-fronted room overlooking Kewalo Basin harbor, it's also a relaxing place for a postshopping drink or intimate dinner. They're known for their early or late night happy hours, which is a great way to sample more of their dishes. [$] *Average main: $27* ✉ *Ward Warehouse, 2nd level, 1050 Ala Moana Blvd., Kakaako* ☎ *808/591–2005* 🌐 *kincaids.com.*

$$$ ASIAN 🍴 **Mariposa.** Yes, the popovers and the wee little cups of bouillon are there at lunch, but in every other regard, this Neiman Marcus restaurant menu departs from the classic model, incorporating a clear sense of Pacific place. The veranda, open to the breezes and view of Ala Moana Park, twirling ceiling fans, and life-size hula-girl murals say Hawaii. The popovers at lunch come with a butter-pineapple-papaya spread; the oxtail osso buco is inspired, and local fish are featured nightly in luxuriant specials. Make sure to leave room for the warm lilikoi pudding cake for dessert. [$] *Average main: $35* ✉ *Nieman Marcus, Ala Moana Center, 1450 Ala Moana, Ala Moana* ☎ *808/951–3420* ✍ *Reservations essential.*

$$ MODERN HAWAIIAN 🍴 **The Pineapple Room by Alan Wong.** This is not your grandmother's department store restaurant. It's überchef Alan Wong's more casual second spot, where the chef de cuisine plays intriguing riffs on local food themes. Warning: the spicy chili-fried soybeans are addicting. Their house burger, made with locally raised grass-fed beef, bacon, cheddar cheese, hoisin-mayonnaise spread, and avocado, won a local tasting hands-down. Service is very professional; reservations are recommended. [$] *Average main: $22* ✉ *Macy's, Ala Moana Center, 1450 Ala Moana Blvd., Ala Moana* ☎ *808/945–6573.*

$$ CHINESE 🍴 **Royal Garden.** You know it's good if, despite being in a hotel, a Chinese restaurant still draws more locals than tourists as customers. Royal Garden is known as one of the best dim sum spots in town, and people don't mind paying a little more for the quality they get. Just point to the steamed and baked morsels that look good; chances are, they're as good as they look. [$] *Average main: $20* ✉ *Ala Moana Hotel, 410 Atkinson Dr., Ala Moana* ☎ *808/942–7788.*

$ AMERICAN 🍴 **Ryan's Grill at Ward Centre.** An all-purpose food and drink emporium, lively and popular Ryan's has an exceptionally well-stocked bar, with 20 beers on tap, an outdoor deck, and TVs broadcasting sports. Lunch, dinner, and small plates are served from 11 am to 2 am. The eclectic menu ranges from an addictive hot crab-and-artichoke dip with focaccia bread to grilled fresh fish, pasta, salads, and sophisticated versions of local favorites, such as the Kobe beef hamburger steak. [$] *Average main: $16* ✉ *Ward Centre, 1200 Ala Moana Blvd., Kakaako* ☎ *808/591–9132* 🌐 *ryansgrill.com.*

$$ KOREAN 🍴 **Sorabol.** The largest Korean restaurant in the city, this 24-hour eatery, with its impossibly tiny parking lot and maze of booths and private rooms, offers a vast menu encompassing the entirety of day-to-day Korean cuisine, plus sushi. English menu translations are cryptic at best. Still, it's great for wee hour "grinds" (local slang for food): *bi bim bap*

Authentic Asian food can be found all over Hawaii and some of the best is in Chinatown in downtown Honolulu.

(veggies, meats, and eggs on steamed rice), *kal bi* and *bulgogi* (barbecued meats), meat or fish *jun* (thin fillets fried in batter), and kimchi pancakes. $ *Average main: $19* ⊠ *805 Keeaumoku St., Ala Moana* ☎ *808/947–3113* ⊕ *sorabolhawaii.com.*

$ ✕ **Spalding House Cafe.** This tasteful lunch spot in the Spalding Horse
AMERICAN offers light and healthful food from a short but well-selected menu of housemade soups, crostini of the day, innovative sandwiches garnished with fruit, and a hummus plate with fresh pita. In the exclusive Makiki Heights neighborhood above the city, the restaurant spills out of the ground floor of the museum onto the lawn. The cafe now offers a "Lauhala and Lunch" picnic lunch for two, priced at $30, which includes a choice of sandwich or salad for each person, dessert bars, and choice of beverages all packed in a pretty picnic basket. $ *Average main: $11* ⊠ *The Contemporary Museum, 2411 Makiki Heights Dr., Makiki* ☎ *808/523–3362* ⚇ *Reservations not accepted* ⛾ *$5 corkage* ☺ *No dinner. Closed Mon.*

$ ✕ **To Chau.** If you need proof that To Chau is highly regarded for its
VIETNAMESE authentic *pho* (Vietnamese beef noodle soup), just check the lines that form in front every morning of the week. It's said that the broth is the key, and it won't break the bank for you to find out, as the average check is less than $10. The restaurant is open only until 2:30 pm, but you may be turned away if the food runs out earlier. $ *Average main: $8* ⊠ *1007 River St., Chinatown* ☎ *808/533–4549* ⚇ *Reservations not accepted* ⊟ *No credit cards* ☺ *No dinner.*

$$ ✕ **Vino.** Small plates of Italian-inspired appetizers, a wine list selected
ITALIAN by the state's first Master Sommelier, a relaxed atmosphere, and periodic special tastings are the formula for success at this wine bar. You

can order items from the adjacent Hiroshi's Eurasion Tapas, as they share a kitchen. ■TIP→**Vino is well situated for stopping off between downtown sightseeing and a return to your Waikiki hotel.** $ *Average main: $25* ✉ *Restaurant Row, 500 Ala Moana Blvd., Downtown Honolulu* ☎ *808/524–8466* ⊕ *vinohawaii.com* ⌂ *Reservations essential* ⊘ *Closed Sun.–Tues.*

$$ ✕**Yanagi Sushi.** One of relatively
JAPANESE few restaurants to serve the complete menu until 2 am (Sunday only until 10 pm), Yanagi is a full-service Japanese restaurant offering not only sushi and sashimi around a small bar, but also *teishoku* (combination menus), tempura, stews, and grill-it-yourself shabu-shabu. The fish here can be depended on for freshness and variety. $ *Average main: $20* ✉ *762 Kapiolani Blvd., Downtown Honolulu* ☎ *808/597–1525* ⊕ *yanagisushi-hawaii.com.*

CHINATOWN

$ ✕**Grand Café & Bakery.** This well-scrubbed, pleasantly furnished
AMERICAN breakfast, brunch, and lunch spot is ideal for taking a break before
☺ or after a trek around Chinatown. Its period feel comes from the fact that chef Anthony Vierra's great-grandfather had a restaurant of this name in Chinatown nearly 100 years ago. The delicious and well-presented food ranges from retro diner dishes (chicken pot pie) to contemporary creations such as beet-and-goat-cheese-salad. $ *Average main: $15* ✉ *31 N. Pauahi, Chinatown* ☎ *808/531–0001* ⊕ *www.grandcafeandbakery.com* ⌂ *Reservations essential* ⊘ *Closed Mon. No dinner Tues.–Thurs. and Sun.*

$ ✕**Green Door.** Closet-size and fronted by a green door and a row of wel-
ASIAN coming Chinese lanterns, this Chinatown café has introduced Honolulu to budget- and taste bud–friendly Malaysian and Singaporean foods, redolent of spices and crunchy with fresh vegetables. The restaurant's owner gets mixed reviews, as she may be rude to customers who question her cooking. Just order from the flavorful menu of fewer than 10 dishes, and you'll do fine. $ *Average main: $10* ✉ *1110 Nuuanu Ave., Chinatown* ☎ *808/533–0606* ⌂ *Reservations not accepted* ▭ *No credit cards* ⊘ *Closed Mon.*

$$ ✕**Indigo Eurasian Cuisine.** Indigo sets the right mood for an evening out
ECLECTIC on the town: the walls are redbrick, the ceilings are high, and from the restaurant's lounge next door comes the sultry sound of late-night jazz. Take a bite of goat cheese wontons with four-fruit sauce followed by rich Mongolian lamb chops. After dinner, duck into the hip Green Room lounge for a nightcap. If you're touring downtown at lunchtime, the Eurasian buffet with trio of dim sum is an especially good deal at around $16 per person. $ *Average main: $25* ✉ *1121 Nuuanu Ave., Chinatown* ☎ *808/521–2900* ⊕ *www.indigo-hawaii.com.*

$ ✕**Legend Seafood Restaurant.** Do as the locals do: start your visit to
CHINESE Chinatown with breakfast dim sum at Legend. If you want to be able

to hear yourself think, get there before 9 am, especially on weekends. And don't be shy: use your best cab-hailing technique and sign language to make the cart ladies stop at your table and show you their wares. The pork-filled steamed buns, hearty spare ribs, prawn dumplings, and still-warm custard tarts are excellent preshopping fortification. $ *Average main: $13 ⊠ Chinese Cultural Plaza, 100 N. Beretania St., Chinatown* ☎ *808/532–1868* ⊕ *www.legendseafoodhonolulu.com* ⌲ *Reservations essential.*

$ ✕ **Little Village Noodle House.** Unassuming and budget-friendly, Little Village sets a standard of friendly and attentive service to which every Chinese restaurant should aspire. We have roamed the large, pan-China menu and found a new favorite in everything we've tried: shredded beef, spinach with garlic, Shanghai noodles, honey-walnut shrimp, orange chicken, dried green beans. Two words: go there. Reservations are accepted for parties of five or more. ∎ **TIP→ Two hours of free parking is available next door.** $ *Average main: $15 ⊠ 1113 Smith St., Chinatown* ☎ *808/545–3008* ⊕ *littlevillagehawaii.com.*

CHINESE
Fodor's Choice
★

$ ✕ **Mei Sum Chinese Dim Sum Restaurant.** In contrast to the sprawling and noisy halls in which dim sum is generally served, Mei Sum is compact and shiny bright. It's open daily, one of the few places that serves dim sum from 7:45 am all the way to 8:45 pm. Be ready to guess and point at the color photos of dim sum favorites as not much English is spoken, but the delicate buns and tasty bits are exceptionally well prepared and worth the charades. Other menu items and specials are also served. $ *Average main: $10 ⊠ 1170 Nuuanu Ave., Chinatown* ☎ *808/531–3268* ⊟ *No credit cards.*

CHINESE

GREATER HONOLULU

$$ ✕ **12th Avenue Grill.** At this clean, well-lighted place on a backstreet, chef Jason Schoonover dishes up diner chic, including macaroni-and-cheese glazed with house-smoked Parmesan and topped with savory breadcrumbs. The kimchi steak, a sort of teriyaki with kick, is a winner. Go early (5 pm) or late (8:30 pm). Enjoy wonderful, homey desserts. There's a small, exquisitely selected wine list. $ *Average main: $20 ⊠ 1145C 12th Ave., Kaimuki* ☎ *808/732–9469* ⊕ *12thavegrill.com* ⊗ *Closed Sun. No lunch.*

MODERN
HAWAIIAN

$$$ ✕ **3660 on the Rise.** This casually stylish eatery is a 10-minute drive from Waikiki in the culinary mecca of Kaimuki. Sample Chef Russell Siu's New York Steak Alae (steak grilled with Hawaiian clay salt), the crab cakes, or the signature ahi katsu wrapped in nori and deep-fried with a wasabi-ginger butter sauce. Siu combines a deep understanding of local flavors with a sophisticated palate, making this place especially popular with homegrown gourmands. The dining room can feel a bit snug when it's full (as it usually is); go early or later. $ *Average main: $31 ⊠ 3660 Waialae Ave., Kaimuki* ☎ *808/737–1177* ⊕ *3660.com.*

MODERN
HAWAIIAN

$$$$ ✕ **Alan Wong's Restaurant Honolulu.** This not-to-be-missed restaurant is like that very rare shell you stumble upon on a perfect day at the beach—well polished and without a flaw. We've never had a bad experience here, and we've never heard of anyone else having one either. The "Wong Way," as it's not-so-jokingly called by his staff, includes an ingrained understanding of the aloha spirit, evident in the skilled but

MODERN
HAWAIIAN
Fodor's Choice
★

unstarched service, and creative and playful interpretations of Island cuisine. Try Da Bag (seafood steamed in an aluminum pouch), Chinatown Roast Duck Nachos, and ginger crusted *onaga* (snapper). With warm tones of koa wood, and *lauhala* grass weaving, you forget you're on the third floor of an office building. [$] *Average main: $38* ✉ *McCully Court, 1857 S. King St., 3rd fl., Moiliili* ☎ *808/949–2526* 🌐 *www.alanwongs.com* ✍ *Reservations essential* ⏰ *No lunch.*

$$$$ MODERN HAWAIIAN Fodor's Choice ★ 🍴 **Chef Mavro.** George Mavrothalassitis, who took two hotel restaurants to the top of the ranks before founding this James Beard Award–winning restaurant, admits he's crazy. Crazy because of the care he takes to draw out the truest and most concentrated flavors, to track down the freshest fish, to create one-of-a-kind wine pairings that might strike others as mad. But for this passionate Provençal transplant, there's no other way. The menu changes quarterly, every dish (including dessert) matched with a select wine. Several options (three to six courses, including a vegetarian option) are offered at various price levels, with a supplement for wine pairings at each level. Etched-glass windows screen the busy street-corner scene and all within is mellow and serene with starched white tablecloths, fresh flowers, wood floors, and contemporary island art. [$] *Average main: $75* ✉ *1969 S. King St., Moiliili* ☎ *808/944–4714* 🌐 *www.chefmavro.com* ✍ *Reservations essential* ⏰ *No lunch.*

$ MEXICAN 🍴 **Diego's Taco Shop.** Diego's is a no-frills, simple joint where the smell of masa cooking permeates the air, salsa comes in mini plastic containers, and the food is filling and reasonable. The ambience, if you can call it that, is laid-back with college students shuffling in after the beach and "grinding" (eating) at the drive-in style tables. Carne asada is the top pick for taco and burrito filling and the flavor is San Diego Mexican. [$] *Average main: $7* ✉ *2239 S. King St., McCully* ☎ *808/949–2239* ✍ *Reservations not accepted* 💳 *No credit cards.*

$ AMERICAN 🍴 **Good to Grill.** Specializing in grilled meats, this casual restaurant is a good choice for a full, quality meal at reasonable prices. From prime rib to melt-in-your-mouth short ribs to garlic shrimp pasta, you can count on a consistently good experience every time. It's modest but tasty and well-prepared food. The reasonable breakfasts on weekends and BYOB policy are definite pluses. No wonder Scott Caan of *Hawaii Five-0* is a repeat customer. [$] *Average main: $13* ✉ *Safeway Center Kapahulu, 888 Kapahulu Ave., Kapahulu* ☎ *808/734–7345* 🌐 *goodtogrill.com* ✍ *Reservations not accepted* 🍷 *BYOB.*

$ ASIAN 🍴 **Hale Vietnam.** One of Oahu's first Vietnamese restaurants, this popular neighborhood spot expresses its friendly character with its name: *hale* (hah-lay) is the Hawaiian word for house or home. If you're not sure what to order, just ask. The staff is known for their willingness to help those who don't know much about Vietnamese food. Be sure to try the piquant and crunchy green-papaya salad. Reservations are taken for groups only. [$] *Average main: $12* ✉ *1140 12th Ave., Kaimuki* ☎ *808/735–7581.*

$$$$ MODERN HAWAIIAN 🍴 **Hoku's at the Kahala.** Everything about this room speaks of quality and sophistication: the wall of windows with their beach views, the avant-garde cutlery and dinnerware, the solicitous staff, and border-busting

Pacific Rim cuisine. The menu constantly changes, but you can count on Chef Wayne Hirabayashi to use fresh, local ingredients when possible in his innovative fusion flair. An excellent choice for special occasions. The dress code is collared shirts, no beachwear. [$] *Average main: $55* ✉ *The Kahala Hotel & Resort, 5000 Kahala Ave., Kahala* ☎ *808/739–8888* ✍ *Reservations essential* ⏲ *No lunch Sat.*

$$$ SUSHI 🍴 **Morio's Sushi Bistro.** This small sushi bar is a favorite of locals, offering amazingly fresh sashimi and interesting cooked dishes at reasonable prices. But more important, it's BYOB here, so you can bond with the gregarious owner-chef, Morio, by sharing what you're drinking. If you're able to get a reservation here, then count yourself lucky; most seats at the bar require a month's notice, but you may be able to get table seating. For a special treat, order the *omakase* (chef's choice) 24 hours in advance. [$] *Average main: $35* ✉ *1160-A S. King St., McCully* ☎ *808/741–5121* 🌐 *www.moriosushibistro.com* ✍ *Reservations essential* 🍷 *BYOB* ⏲ *Closed Sun. No lunch.*

$$ MEDITERRANEAN 🍴 **Olive Tree Cafe.** Mediterranean food is scarce in the Islands, so Olive Tree keeps insanely busy; expect a wait for your hummus, fish souvlaki, Greek egg-and-lemon soup, and other specialties at this small spot behind Kahala Mall. It's worth the wait—it's probably the best Greek food in these Islands. [$] *Average main: $20* ✉ *4614 Kiauea Ave., Kahala* ☎ *808/737–0303* ✍ *Reservations not accepted* 💳 *No credit cards* 🍷 *BYOB* ⏲ *No lunch.*

$ HAWAIIAN 🍴 **Ono Hawaiian Foods.** The adventurous in search of a real local food experience should head to this no-frills hangout. You know it has to be good if residents are waiting in line to get in. Here you can sample *poi* (a paste made from pounded taro root), *lomilomi* salmon (salmon massaged until tender and served with minced onions and tomatoes), laulau, *kalua* pork (roasted in an underground oven), and *haupia* (a gelatinlike dessert made from coconut milk). Appropriately enough, the Hawaiian word *ono* means "delicious." [$] *Average main: $13* ✉ *726 Kapahulu Ave., Kapahulu* ☎ *808/737–2275* ✍ *Reservations not accepted* 💳 *No credit cards* ⏲ *Closed Sun.*

$$$ SEAFOOD 👶 🍴 **Sam Choy's Breakfast, Lunch & Crab and Big Aloha Brewery.** In this casual, family-friendly setting, diners can down crab and lobster—but since these come from elsewhere, we recommend the catch of the day, the *char siu* (Chinese barbecue), baby back ribs, Sam's special fried *poke* (flash-fried tuna), or Papa Choy's beef stew omelet. This eatery's warehouse size sets the tone for its *bambucha* (huge) portions. An on-site microbrewery brews five varieties of Big Aloha beer. Sam Choy's is in Iwilei past downtown Honolulu on the highway heading to Honolulu International Airport, making it convenient for long layovers. [$] *Average main: $28* ✉ *580 Nimitz Hwy., Iwilei* ☎ *808/545–7979* 🌐 *samchoyhawaii.com* ⏲ *No dinner Mon.*

$ SOUTHERN 🍴 **Soul Cafe.** If you have a hankering for down-home southern fare with a gourmet twist and Pacific flair, chef Sean Priester has it all. Must-tries include shrimp and cheesy grits with bacon gravy, crab cake on spring greens with an Asian black bean dressing, and the best fried chicken in town. Be prepared to order extra cornbread. It's that good.

$ *Average main: $12* ⊠ *3040 Waialae Ave., Kaimuki* ☎ *808/947–3113* ⊕ *pacificsoulhawaii.com.*

$ ✕**Spices.** Created by a trio of well-traveled friends who enjoy the foods
MODERN ASIAN   of Southeast Asia, Spices is alluringly decorated in spicelike oranges
and reds and offers a lunch and dinner menu far from the beaten path,
even in a city rich in the cuisine of this region. Leave room for dessert,
as their exotic ice cream is to die for. They claim inspiration but not
authenticity and use island ingredients to everyone's advantage. The
menu is vegetarian-friendly. $ *Average main: $13* ⊠ *2671 S. King St.,
Moiliili* ☎ *808/949–2679* ⊕ *spiceshawaii.com* ⌒ *Reservations essential*
⊙ *Closed Mon.*

$$$$ ✕**Sushi Sasabune.** Meals here are unforgettable, though you may find the
JAPANESE   restaurant's approach exasperating and a little condescending. It's possible to order from the menu, but you're strongly encouraged to order
omakase-style (oh-*mah*-ka-*say*, roughly, "trust me"), letting the chef
send out his choices for the night. The waiters keep up a steady mantra
to instruct patrons in the proper way to eat their delicacies: "Please,
no shoyu on this one." "One piece, one bite." But any trace of annoy-
ance vanishes with the first bite of California baby squid stuffed with
Louisiana crab, or unctuous *toro* (ahi belly) smeared with a light soy
reduction, washed down with a glass of the smoothest sake you've ever
tasted. A caution: the courses come very rapidly—ask the server to slow
down the pace a bit. An even bigger caution: the courses, generally two
pieces of sushi or six to eight slices of sashimi, add up fast. $ *Average
main: $60* ⊠ *1419 S. King St., Moiliili* ☎ *808/947–3800* ⌒ *Reservations
essential* ⊙ *Closed Sun. No lunch Sat. and Mon.*

$$$ ✕**The Willows.** An island dream, this buffet restaurant is made up of
HAWAIIAN   pavilions overlooking a network of ponds (once natural streams flow-
ing from mountain to sea). The island-style comfort food includes the
trademark Willows curry along with Hawaiian dishes such as *laulau*
(a steamed bundle of ti leaves containing pork, butterfish, and taro
tops) and local favorites such as Korean barbecue ribs. $ *Average main:
$35* ⊠ *901 Hausten St., Moiliili* ☎ *808/952–9200* ⊕ *willowshawaii.com*
⌒ *Reservations essential.*

WAIKIKI

$$$$ ✕**dk Steakhouse.** Around the country, the steak house has returned to
STEAKHOUSE   prominence as chefs rediscover the art of dry-aging beef and of prepar-
ing the perfect béarnaise sauce. D.K. Kodama's chic second-floor res-
taurant characterizes this trend with such presentations as a 22-ounce
"Paniolo" (cowboy) rib-eye steak, dry-aged 30 days on the bone with
house-made rub, grilled local onions, and creamed corn. The restaurant
shares space, but not a menu, with Kodama's Sansei Seafood Restau-
rant & Sushi Bar; sit at the bar perched between the two and you can
order from either menu. $ *Average main: $45* ⊠ *Waikiki Beach Mar-
riott Resort and Spa, 2552 Kalakaua Ave., Waikiki* ☎ *808/931–6280*
⊕ *www.dksteakhouse.com* ⊙ *No lunch.*

$$ ✕**Duke's Canoe Club.** Named for the father of modern surfing, and out-
AMERICAN   fitted with much Duke Kahanamoku memorabilia, Duke's is both an
open-air bar and a very popular steak-and-seafood grill. It's known

2

for its slow-roasted prime rib, *huli huli* (rotisserie) chicken, and grilled catch of the day, as well as for a simple and economical Sunday brunch. Their cocktails are probably the best in Waikiki. A drawback is that it's often loud and crowded, and the live contemporary Hawaiian music often stymies conversation. $ *Average main: $24* ✉ *Outrigger Waikiki on the Beach, 2335 Kalakaua Ave., Waikiki* ☎ *808/922–2268* ⊕ *www. dukeswaikiki.com* ⚓ *Reservations essential.*

$$$$ ✕ **Hau Tree Lanai.** The vine-like *hau* tree is ideal for sitting under, and
SEAFOOD   it's said that the one that spreads itself over this beachside courtyard is the very one that shaded Robert Louis Stevenson as he mused and wrote about Hawaii. In any case, diners are still enjoying the shade and the island-casual food, but we like the place for late-afternoon or early-evening drinks, pupu, and people-watching. The poi pancakes at breakfast, papaya chicken salad at lunch, and fresh fish selection at dinner are all favorites. $ *Average main: $41* ✉ *New Otani Kaimana Beach Hotel, 2863 Kalakaua Ave., Waikiki* ☎ *808/921–7066* ⊕ *www. kaimana.com* ⚓ *Reservations essential.*

$ ✕ **Keo's in Waikiki.** Many Islanders—and many Hollywood stars—got
THAI   their first taste of pad thai noodles, lemongrass, and coconut milk curry at one of Keo Sananikone's restaurants. This one, perched right at the entrance to Waikiki, characterizes his formula: a bright, clean space awash in flowers with intriguing menu titles and reasonable prices. Evil Jungle Prince, a stir-fry redolent of Thai basil, flecked with chilis and rich with coconut milk, is a classic; also try the apple bananas (smaller, sweeter variety of banana) in coconut milk. The Eastern and Western breakfasts are popular. $ *Average main: $16* ✉ *2028 Kuhio Ave., Waikiki* ☎ *808/951–9355* ⊕ *keosthaicuisine.com.*

$$$$ ✕ **La Mer.** Like the hotel in which it's housed (Halekulani, "house befit-
FRENCH   ting heaven"), La Mer is pretty much heavenly: a softly lighted, low-ceiling room has its windows open to the breeze, a perfectly framed vista of Diamond Head, and the faint sound of music from a courtyard below. The food captures the rich and yet sunny flavors of the south of France in one tiny, exquisite course after another. Four prix-fixe options are offered (from three to five or more courses), as well as several rather expensive supplements. We recommend the degustation menu; place yourself in the sommelier's hands for wine choices from the hotel's exceptional cellar. $ *Average main: $130* ✉ *Halekulani, 2199 Kalia Rd., Waikiki* ☎ *808/923–2311* ⚓ *Reservations essential* ⌂ *Jacket required* ☾ *No lunch.*

$$$$ ✕ **Michel's at the Colony Surf.** With its wide-open windows so close to the
FRENCH   water that you literally feel the soft mist at high tide, this is arguably the most romantic spot in Waikiki for a sunset dinner for two. Venerable Michel's is synonymous with fine dining in the minds of Oahuans who have been coming here for more than 40 years. The menu is très, très French with both classic choices (escargot, foie gras) and contemporary items (Hardy's Hawaiian Bouillabaisse—named after the chef who created a Hawaiian twist on a French classic). There's dinner nightly and Sunday brunch. $ *Average main: $53* ✉ *Colony Surf, 2895 Kalakaua Ave., Waikiki* ☎ *808/923–6552* ⊕ *michelshawaii.com* ⚓ *Reservations essential* ☾ *No lunch.*

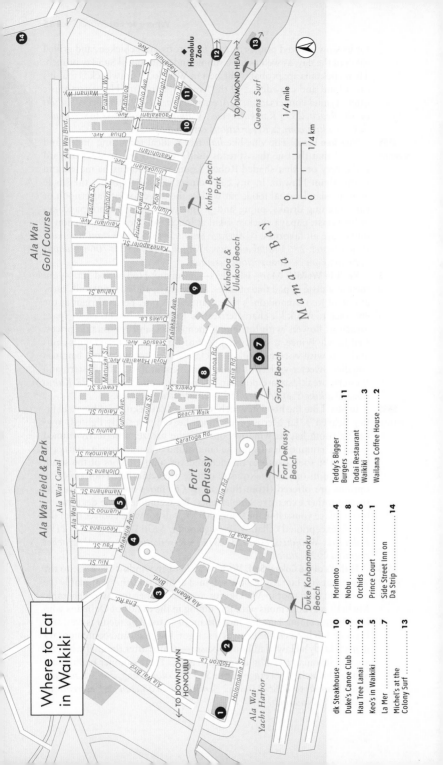

Where to Eat in Waikiki

dk Steakhouse **10**
Duke's Canoe Club **9**
Hau Tree Lanai **12**
Keo's in Waikiki **5**
La Mer **7**
Michel's at the
Colony Surf **13**

Morimoto **4**
Nobu **8**
Orchids **6**
Prince Court **1**
Side Street Inn on
Da Strip **14**

Teddy's Bigger
Burgers **11**
Todai Restaurant
Waikiki **3**
Wailana Coffee House **2**

Ala Wai Golf Course

Ala Wai Field & Park

Ala Wai Canal

TO DOWNTOWN HONOLULU

Ala Wai Yacht Harbor

Fort DeRussy

Duke Kahanamoku Beach

Fort DeRussy Beach

Grays Beach

Kahaloa &
Ulukou Beach

Kuhio Beach Park

Queens Surf

TO DIAMOND HEAD →

Honolulu Zoo

Mamala Bay

Ala Wai Blvd.
Ala Moana Blvd.
Ena Rd.
Holomoana St.
Hobron La.
Kalia Rd.
Paoa Pl.
Saratoga Rd.
Beach Walk
Kalakaua Ave.
Royal Hawaiian Ave.
Lewers St.
Seaside Ave.
Dukes La.
Helumoa Rd.
Kaiulani Ave.
Koa Ave.
Prince Edward St.
Liliuokalani Ave.
Kealohilani Ave.
Ohua Ave.
Paokalani Ave.
Lemon Rd.
Cartwright Rd.
Kapahulu Ave.
Kanekapolii St.
Uluniu St.
Kaiulani Ave.
Kanekoa
Kuhio Ave.
Wainani Wy.
Paiaina Wy.

Kuamoo St.
Keoniana St.
Kalakaua Ave.
Niu St.
Pau St.
Namahana St.
Olohana St.
Kalaimoku St.
Launiu St.
Kaioli St.
Kuhio Ave.
Lauula St.
Manuka St.
Aloha Drive
Lewers St.
Nahua St.
Tusitala St.
Cleghorn St.
Walina St.

1/4 mile
1/4 km
0

$$$$ JAPANESE 🍴 **Morimoto.** Iron Chef Morimoto of Food Network fame is a big part of the dining scene in Honolulu. The menu is made up primarily of sushi and cooked seafood, with a couple of expensive cuts of steak thrown in as well as a wide selection of appetizers, all heavily weighted toward seafood. If you're adventurous, try the *omakase* (chef's choice) menu, which changes daily. You can choose to sit at the sushi bar, the regular bar, or at a table, but try to get a seat outside, as the room gets pretty noisy. This has become a popular spot for brunch, as well, with a view overlooking the yacht harbor. [$] *Average main: $39* ✉ *The Modern, 1775 Ala Moana Blvd., Waikiki* ☎ *808/943–5900* 🌐 *morimotowaikiki.com.*

$$$$ JAPANESE 🍴 **Nobu.** Famed chef Nobu Matsuhisa is the master of innovative Japanese cuisine, and his Hawaiian outpost is definitely a Waikiki hot spot. Fish is the obvious centerpiece, with entrees such as Tasmanian ocean trout with crispy spinach and yuzu soy, seafood harumaki with caviar and Maui onion salsa, and even Nobu's version of fish-and-chips. Cold dishes include tuna *tataki* (seared raw fish slices) with ponzu, yellowtail sashimi with jalapeño, and whitefish sashimi with dried miso. The warm decor and sexy lighting means there isn't a bad seat in the house. [$] *Average main: $38* ✉ *Waikiki Parc Hotel, 2233 Helumoa Rd., Waikiki* ☎ *808/237–6999* 🌐 *www.noburestaurants.com.*

$$$$ SEAFOOD 🍴 **Orchids.** Perched along the seawall at historic Gray's Beach, Orchids is beloved by power breakfasters, ladies who lunch, and family groups celebrating at the elaborate Sunday brunch. La Mer, upstairs, is better known for the evening, but we have found dinner at Orchids equally enjoyable. The louvered walls are open to the breezes, the orchids add splashes of color, the seafood is perfectly prepared, and the wine list is intriguing. Plus, it is more casual and a bit less expensive than La Mer. Whatever meal you have here, finish with the hotel's signature coconut layer cake. [$] *Average main: $40* ✉ *Halekulani, 2199 Kalia Rd., Waikiki* ☎ *808/923–2311* 🌐 *www.halekulani.com/dining/orchids/* ✍ *Reservations essential.*

$$$$ ECLECTIC 🍴 **Prince Court.** This restaurant overlooking Ala Wai Yacht Harbor is a multifaceted success, with exceptional high-end lunches and dinners, daily breakfast buffets, weekly dinner seafood buffets, and sold-out weekend brunches. With a truly global mix of offerings, the overall style is Eurasian. Their ever-changing prix-fixe menu includes offerings such as Australian rack of lamb, Kahuku prawns, and medallions of New York Angus beef. [$] *Average main: $45* ✉ *Hawaii Prince Hotel, 100 Holomoana St., Waikiki* ☎ *808/944–4494* 🌐 *www.princeresortshawaii.com/hawaii-prince-court.php* ✍ *Reservations essential.*

$ HAWAIIAN 🍴 **Side Street Inn on Da Strip.** The original Hopaka Street pub is famous as the place where celebrity chefs gather after hours; this second location, also run by local boy Colin Nishida, is on the bustling Kapahulu Avenue, closer to Waikiki. Local-style bar food comes in huge, share-plate portions, and Nishida's famous pork chops, fried rice, and lilikoi ribs make it worth the trip. This is a place to dress any way you like, nosh all night, and watch sports on TV. Pupu (in portions so large as to be dinner) are served from 4 pm to 12:30 am daily. [$] *Average main: $16* ✉ *614 Kapahulu Ave., Waikiki* ☎ *808/739–3939* 🌐 *www.sidestreetinn.com* ✍ *Reservations essential* ⏲ *No lunch weekends.*

A typical Hawaiian "plate lunch" usually includes meat along with one scoop of rice and another of macaroni salad.

$
AMERICAN
✕ **Teddy's Bigger Burgers.** Though the focus at Teddy's is on the burgers, fries, and shakes, their success has inspired them to add a chicken, veggie, and fish sandwich to their menu. But, for those who like a classic, the burgers are beefy, the fries crisply perfect, the shakes rich and sweet. The original location in Waikiki combines burger shack simplicity with surf-boy cool—there's even a place to store your surfboard while you have your burger. This popular location has given birth to several others around the state. $ *Average main: $10* ⊠ *134 Kapahulu Ave., Waikiki* ☎ *808/926-3444.*

$$$
SEAFOOD
✕ **Todai Restaurant Waikiki.** Bountiful buffets and menus that feature seafood are popular with Islanders, so this Japan-based restaurant is a local favorite. It's popular with budget-conscious travelers as well, for the wide range of hot dishes, sushi, and the 160-foot seafood spread. The emphasis here is more on quantity than quality. $ *Average main: $32* ⊠ *1910 Ala Moana Blvd., Waikiki* ☎ *808/947–1000* ⚐ *Reservations essential.*

$
AMERICAN
✕ **Wailana Coffee House.** Despite the notoriously inattentive waitstaff, budget-conscious snowbirds, night owls with a yen for karaoke, all-day drinkers of both coffee and the stronger stuff, hearty eaters, and lovers of local-style plate lunches contentedly rub shoulders at this venerable diner and cocktail lounge at the edge of Waikiki. Most checks are under $9, and there's a $2.50 children's menu. It's open 24 hours a day, seven days a week, 365 days a year (except Tuesday, when the restaurant closes from midnight to 6 am), but the place fills up and a line forms around the corner at breakfast time, so arrive early or late. $ *Average main: $9* ⊠ *Wailana Condominium, 1860 Ala Moana Blvd., corner of*

Oahu Food Trucks

Lunch wagons, or food trucks, as they are now known around the country, have been a staple for plate lunches around Hawaii for decades, even before they were trendy. But now, with the taco-truck craze and the emergence of social media, more food trucks are popping up, serving an amazing variety of local flavors.

You can check the trucks' locations and daily menus on Twitter, or try a sampling from more than two-dozen vendors at the monthly Eat the Street food-truck rally or the weekly Tacoako Tuesdays. Visit ⊕ *www.Streetgrindz.com* for details.

Here are some of our favorite lunch wagons:

Camille's on Wheels (⊕ *Twitter.com/Camillesonwheel*) combines Mexican, American, and Asian flavors in tacos and other dishes. Check out the shoyu chicken tacos, homemade salsas, and any of the homemade desserts. Camille's uses local ingredients whenever possible.

Elena's (⊕ *Twitter.com/ElenasFilipino*) is an extension of the popular, family-run Filipino restaurant in Waipahu.

There are three trucks, in Campbell, Mililani, and the airport area. Try the AFRO, an adobo–fried rice omelet, or the famous *lechón* (roast pork with onions and tomatoes) special.

Ono To Go (⊕ *Twitter.com/Onotogo*) has a regular spot on Sheridan Street off King Street. It's open Monday through Saturday from 11 am until the food sells out—which is often, as the plate lunches are restaurant quality at lower prices. Best sellers are pork chops, teriyaki-citrus salmon, *pulehu* (fire-broiled) short ribs, poke, and roast turkey. Park on the street or at the car-repair shop next door.

Shogunai Tacos (⊕ *Twitter.com/Shogunai_tacos*) serves up hearty tacos with unique fillings that have Greek, Korean, Italian, Indian, Mexican, Thai, and Japanese flavors. The most popular item is the Osaka Jo taco, which is brimming with pork marinated in ginger, shoyu, garlic, lemon, a special sauce, sprouts, and then sprinkled with *furikake* (shredded dried seaweed). Make it a meal with the Moroccan-inspired French fries.

Ena Rd. and Ala Moana, Waikiki ☎ *808/955–1674* ⌖ *Reservations not accepted.*

SOUTHEAST OAHU

$$ ✕ **BluWater Grill.** Time your drive through East Honolulu to allow for a
ECLECTIC stop at this relaxed restaurant on Kuapa Pond. The savvy chef-manager team left a popular chain restaurant to found this "American eclectic" eatery, serving wok-seared moi fish, mango and guava ribs, and lots of other interesting small dishes. They're open until 10 pm Sunday through Thursday, and until 11 pm Friday and Saturday. $ *Average main: $20* ✉ *Hawaii Kai Shopping Center, 377 Keahole St.* ☎ *808/395–6224* ⊕ *bluwatergrill.com.*

$$ ✕ **Roy's.** Roy Yamaguchi's flagship restaurant across the highway from
ASIAN Maunalua Bay attracts food-savvy visitors as the North Shore attracts

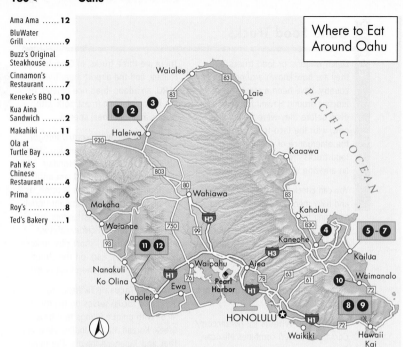

Where to Eat
Around Oahu

surfers. But it also has a strong following among well-heeled Oahuans from surrounding neighborhoods, who consider the place an extension of their homes and Roy's team their personal chefs. For this reason, Roy's is always busy and sometimes overly noisy. It's best to visit later in the evening if you're sensitive to pressure to turn the table, or very early to catch the sunset. The wide-ranging and ever-interesting Hawaiian fusion menu changes daily except for signature dishes like Szechuan spiced barbecue baby back ribs, Roy's Original blackened ahi with soy mustard butter sauce, and a legendary meat loaf. There's an exceptional wine list. $ *Average main: $25* ⊠ *Hawaii Kai Corporate Plaza, 6600 Kalanianaole Hwy., Hawaii Kai, Honolulu* ☎ *808/396–7697* ⊕ *www. roysrestaurant.com* ⌂ *Reservations essential.*

WINDWARD OAHU

$$ ✕ **Buzz's Original Steakhouse.** Virtually unchanged since it opened in
STEAKHOUSE   1967, this cozy maze of rooms opposite Kailua Beach Park is filled
Fodor's Choice   with the enticing aroma of grilling steaks. It doesn't matter if you're a
★   bit sandy (but bare feet are not allowed). Stop at the salad bar, order
up a steak, a burger, teri chicken, or the fresh fish special. If you sit
at the bar, expect to make friends. And remember that this place is

cash only. $ *Average main: $25* ✉ *413 Kawailoa Rd.* ☎ *808/261–4661* ⊕ *buzzssteakhouse.com* ▭ *No credit cards.*

$ ✗ **Cinnamon's Restaurant.** Known for uncommon variations on common
AMERICAN breakfast themes (pancakes, eggs Benedict, French toast, home fries, and eggs), this neighborhood favorite is tucked into a hard-to-find Kailua office park; call for directions. Lunch and dinner feature local-style plate lunch and a diner-style menu (meat loaf, baked beans) which are good, but the main attraction is breakfast. Don't miss the guava chiffon pancakes. $ *Average main: $11* ✉ *315 Uluniu* ☎ *808/261–8724* ⊕ *www.cinnamonsrestaurant.com* ☾ *No dinner Sun.–Wed.*

$ ✗ **Keneke's Plate Lunch & BBQ.** When you're sightseeing between Hanauma
HAWAIIAN Bay and Makapuu, the food pickings are slim. But every day, 365 days a year, there's Keneke's in Waimanalo town. It's the home of inexpensive plate lunches, shave ice, and scriptural graffiti on the walls (Keith "Keneke" Ward, the burly, weight-lifting, second-generation owner of the place, is a born-again Christian). The food is diet busting, piled high, and mostly pretty good, particularly the Asian-style barbecue (including teriyaki chicken or beef and Korean *kal bi* (barbecue), and Filipino *guisantes* (pork and peas in tomato gravy) and adobo (piquant pork stew). If you want a treat, try the shave ice with ice cream. $ *Average main: $6* ✉ *41-855 Kalanianaole Hwy., Waimanalo* ☎ *808/259–9800* ⊕ *www.kenekes.net.*

$ ✗ **Pah Ke's Chinese Restaurant.** Chinese restaurants tend to be interchange-
CHINESE able, but this one—named for the local Pidgin term for Chinese (literally translated this is Chinese's Chinese Restaurant)—is worth the drive from Honolulu for its focus on healthier cooking techniques and use of local ingredients, its seasonal specials such as cold soups and salads made from locally raised produce, and its exceptional East–West desserts. The menu offers all the usual suspects, but ask the owner and chef Raymond Siu, a former hotel pastry chef, if he's got anything different and interesting in the kitchen, or call ahead to ask for a special menu. $ *Average main: $15* ✉ *46-018 Kamehameha Hwy., Kaneohe* ☎ *808/235–4505* ⛔ *BYOB.*

$$$ ✗ **Prima.** Owned by two of Hawaii's rising stars in the culinary indus-
MODERN ITALIAN try—Aker Briceno and Lindsey Ozawa—Prima offers locavore dishes with Italian and Japanese twists. Our favorites include the savory fennel panna cotta, curry Bolognese on pappardelle with fried curry leaves, and any of the signature pizzas. Save room for Aker's homemade gelatos in an array of unique flavors. $ *Average main: $35* ✉ *Kailua Shopping Center, 108 Hekili St., Kailua, Honolulu* ☎ *808/888–8933* ⊕ *primahawaii.com* ⌕ *Reservations essential* ☾ *Closed Sun. and Mon.*

THE NORTH SHORE

$ ✗ **Kua Aina Sandwich.** A must-stop spot during a drive around the island,
AMERICAN this North Shore eatery specializes in large, hand-formed burgers heaped with bacon, cheese, salsa, and pineapple; or try the grilled mahimahi sandwich. The crispy shoestring fries alone are worth the trip. Kua Aina also has a south-shore location in the Ward Centre in Honolulu. $ *Average main: $11* ✉ *66-160 Kamehameha Hwy.* ☎ *808/637–6067* ⌕ *Reservations not accepted.*

$$$$
MODERN
HAWAIIAN
Fodor's Choice
★

✕ **Ola at Turtle Bay Resort.** In a pavilion literally on the sand, this casual but refined restaurant wowed critics from the moment it opened, both with its idyllic location on Kuilima Cove and with chef Fred DeAngelo's reliably wonderful food. Ola means "life, living, healthy," an apt name for a place that combines a commitment to freshness and wholesomeness with a discriminating and innovative palate in such dishes as a vegan risotto made with local mushrooms and orzo pasta, slow-poached salmon with caramelized cane sugar and Okinawan sweet potatoes. It is absolutely worth the drive. $ *Average main: $37* ⊠ *57-091 Kamehameha Hwy., Kahuku* ☎ *808/293–0801* ⊕ *olaislife.com.*

$
AMERICAN

✕ **Ted's Bakery.** Across from Sunset Beach and famous for its chocolate *haupia* pie (layered coconut and chocolate puddings topped with whipped cream), Ted's Bakery is also favored by surfers and area residents for quick breakfasts, sandwiches, or plate lunches, to-go or eaten at the handful of umbrella-shaded tables outside. $ *Average main: $8* ⊠ *59-024 Kamehameha Hwy.* ☎ *808/638–8207* ⊕ *www.tedsbakery. com* ⋨ *Reservations not accepted.*

WEST (LEEWARD) OAHU

$$$$
MODERN
HAWAIIAN

✕ **Ama Ama.** It's not enough that this restaurant looks out upon the Ko Olina lagoons and the vast Pacific Ocean—the food is wonderful, too. Thanks to renowned local chef Kevin Chong, you can enjoy modern as well as classic menu items made from local ingredients. Even the Kahuku corn chowder tastes great on a warm day; other favorites include the light and colorful goat cheese ravioli, firecracker chicken, and nori-wrapped ahi tuna. Save room for dessert: the Hawaiian Chocolate Cake is an amazing treat. If you're on a budget, skip dinner—breakfast and lunch entrées are half the price (although menu offerings vary). Make your reservations online at the Disney Resorts website. $ *Average main: $40* ⊠ *Aulani, a Disney Resort & Spa, 92-1185 Aliinui Dr., Ko Olina, Kapolei* ☎ *714/520–7001* ⊕ *disneyparks.disney. go.com* ⋨ *Reservations essential.*

$$$$
HAWAIIAN

✕ **Makahiki—The Bounty of the Islands.** The buffet restaurant at Disney's Aulani resort offers a wide variety of locally produced items, as well as familiar dishes from stateside and the rest of the world. A chef walking the line can explain the various dishes, which always include sustainable Hawaiian seafood and Asian selections. You'll also always find famliar grilled meats and vegetables, in addition to a kids' menu. If you have children, plan months in advance to get a reservation for the Character Breakfast, as it's only offered on select days and is always sold out. ■TIP➔ Arrive early for dinner and have a drink at the adjacent Olelo Room, where the staff are fluent in Hawaiian; you can get a language lesson along with your libation. $ *Average main: $43* ⊠ *Aulani, a Disney Resort & Spa, 92-1185 Aliinui Dr., Ko Olina, Kapolei* ☎ *714/520–7001* ⋨ *Reservations essential* ⊘ *No lunch.*

WHERE TO STAY

Updated by
Catherine E.
Toth

As in real estate, location matters. And though Oahu is just 44 miles long and 30 miles wide—meaning you can circle the entire island before lunch—it boasts neighborhoods and lodgings with very different vibes and personalities. If you like the action and choices of big cities, consider Waikiki, a 24-hour playground with everything from surf to karaoke bars. Those who want an escape from urban life look to the island's leeward or windward sides, or the North Shore, whose surf culture creates a laid-back atmosphere.

Most of the island's major hotels and resorts are in Waikiki, which has a lot to offer within a small area, namely shopping, restaurants, nightlife, and nearly 3 miles of sandy beach. You don't need a car in Waikiki; everything is nearby, from the Honolulu Zoo and Waikiki Aquarium, the 300-acre Kapiolani Park, running and biking paths, grocery stores, and access to public transportation that can take you to museums, shopping centers, and historic landmarks around the island.

You'll find places to stay along the entire stretch of Kalakaua Avenue, with smaller and quieter hotels and condos at the eastern end, and more business-centric accommodations on the western edge of Waikiki, near the Hawaii Convention Center, Ala Moana Center, and downtown Honolulu.

The majority of tourists who come to Oahu stay in Waikiki, but choosing accommodations in downtown Honolulu affords you the opportunity to be close to shopping and restaurants at Ala Moana Center, the largest shopping mall in the state. It also provides easy access to the airport.

If you want to get away from the bustle of the city, consider a stay on Oahu's leeward coast—namely, at the Ko Olina resort area, about 20 minutes from the Honolulu International Airport and 40 minutes from Waikiki. Here, there are great golf courses and quiet beaches and coves that make for a relaxing getaway. But you'll need a car to get off the property if you want to explore the rest of the island.

Other more low-key options are on Windward Oahu or the North Shore. Both regions are rustic and charming, with quaint eateries and coffee shops, unique shops, and some of the island's best beaches—plus one of the top resorts, Turtle Bay, on the North Shore. *Prices shown in reviews are the lowest price of a standard double room in high season. Prices for rentals are the lowest per-night cost for a one-bedroom unit in high season.*

For expanded hotel reviews, visit Fodors.com.

HONOLULU

$$
HOTEL

Ala Moana Hotel. Shoppers might wear out their Manolos here: this renovated condo-hotel is connected to Oahu's largest mall, the Ala Moana Center, by a pedestrian ramp, and it's a four-block stroll away from the eclectic shopping at Ward Centers. **Pros:** adjacent to Ala Moana Center and all of its shops and restaurants; rooms nicely appointed; quick walk to the beach. **Cons:** outside the heartbeat of

BEST BETS FOR OAHU LODGING

Fodor's Choice★

Halekulani, p. 167

The Kahala Hotel & Resort, p. 164

The Turtle Bay Resort, p. 175

By Price

$

The Breakers, p. 165

The Equus Hotel and Marina Tower, p. 167

Royal Grove Hotel, p. 172

$$

Ala Moana Hotel, p. 163

Hilton Hawaiian Village Beach Resort and Spa, p. 168

Waikiki Parc, p. 173

$$$$

Halekulani, p. 167

JW Marriott Ihilani Resort & Spa, p. 175

The Kahala Hotel & Resort, p. 164

Marriott Ko Olina Beach Vacation Club, p. 176

Moana Surfrider, p. 171

Outrigger Reef on the Beach, p. 171

The Royal Hawaiian, p. 172

By Experience

BEST FOR ROMANCE

Halekulani, $$$$, p. 167

JW Marriott Ihilani Resort & Spa, $$$$, p. 175

The Kahala Hotel & Resort, $$$$, p. 164

Moana Surfrider, $$$$, p. 171

The Royal Hawaiian, $$$$, p. 172

BEST BEACH

JW Marriott Ihilani Resort and Spa, $$$$, p. 175

The Kahala Hotel & Resort, $$$$, p. 164

Marriott Ko Olina Beach Vacation Club, $$$$, p. 176

Moana Surfrider, $$$$, p. 171

The Turtle Bay Resort, $$$$, p. 175

Waikiki; can feel a bit distant from the action; not right on the beach. **TripAdvisor:** "good location," "a shopper's dream," "great room view." $ *Rooms from: $249* ⊠ *410 Atkinson Dr., Ala Moana, Honolulu* ☎ *808/955–4811, 888/367–4811* ⊕ *www.alamoanahotel.com* ↩ *1,150 studios, 67 suites* ⫶⊙⫶ *No meals.*

$$$$
HOTEL
Fodor's Choice
★
The Kahala Hotel & Resort. Hidden away in the upscale residential neighborhood of Kahala (on the other side of Diamond Head from Waikiki), this elegant oceanfront hotel has played host to both presidents and princesses as one of Hawaii's very first luxury resorts. **Pros:** away from hectic Waikiki; beautiful rooms and public spaces; heavenly spa; pet-friendly. **Cons:** Waikiki is a drive away. **TripAdvisor:** "a week in paradise," "great staff," "loved the dolphins." $ *Rooms from: $605* ⊠ *5000 Kahala Ave., Kahala, Honolulu* ☎ *808/739–8888, 800/367–2525* ✎ *reservations@kahalaresorts.com* ⊕ *www.kahalaresort.com* ↩ *345 rooms, 33 suites* ⫶⊙⫶ *No meals.*

WAIKIKI

$$
RENTAL
☾
Aston at the Waikiki Banyan. The recreation deck at this family-oriented property has outdoor grills, a heated swimming pool, two hot tubs, a children's playground, a mini putting green, and volleyball, basketball

and tennis courts. **Pros:** many rooms have great views; walking distance to shops and restaurants. **Cons:** trekking to the beach (a block away) with all of your gear; no on-site restaurant. **TripAdvisor:** "great service," "best value for family vacation," "a lovely apartment hotel." [$] *Rooms from: $229* ✉ *201 Ohua Ave., Waikiki* ☎ *808/922–0555, 877/997–6667* 🌐 *www.astonhotels.com* ⇨ *876 units* 🍴 *No meals.*

2

$ RENTAL 🏨 **Aston Waikiki Beach Tower.** You'll find the elegance of a luxury all-suites condominium combined with the intimacy and service of a boutique hotel at this Kalakaua Avenue address. **Pros:** *very* large rooms—big enough to move into. **Cons:** no on-site restaurants; you must cross a busy street to the beach. **TripAdvisor:** "great service," "it's all about the view," "the perfect Waikiki condo." [$] *Rooms from: $165* ✉ *2470 Kalakaua Ave., Waikiki* ☎ *808/926–6400, 877/997–6667* 🌐 *www.astonhotels.com* ⇨ *140 units* 🍴 *No meals.*

$ RENTAL 🏨 **The Breakers.** Despite an explosion of high-rise construction all around it, the low-rise Breakers continues to offer a taste of '60s Hawaii in this small complex a mere half block from Waikiki Beach. **Pros:** intimate atmosphere; great location. **Cons:** parking space is limited. **TripAdvisor:** "charming," "Waikiki Hideaway," "traditional." [$] *Rooms from: $130* ✉ *250 Beach Walk, Waikiki* ☎ *808/923–3181, 800/426–0494* 🌐 *www.breakers-hawaii.com* ⇨ *64 units* 🍴 *No meals.*

$$$ RENTAL 🏨 **Castle Waikiki Shore.** Nestled between Fort DeRussy Beach Park and the Outrigger Reef on the Beach, this is the only condo situated right on Waikiki Beach. **Pros:** great security; great views; great management; free high-speed Internet access. **Cons:** beach out front is kind of thin; two-night stay minimum. **TripAdvisor:** "brilliant accommodations," "a lovely condo on the beach," "great location." [$] *Rooms from: $270* ✉ *2161 Kalia Rd., Waikiki* ☎ *808/952–4500, 800/367–5004* 🌐 *www.castleresorts.com* ⇨ *168 units.*

$$ HOTEL 👶 🏨 **Doubletree Alana Waikiki.** The location (a 10-minute walk from the Hawaii Convention Center), three phones in each room, and the 24-hour business center and gym meet the requirements of the Doubletree's global business clientele, which also appeals to vacationers. **Pros:** professional staff; pleasant public spaces; pet-friendly; walk-in glass showers with oversized rain showerheads. **Cons:** beach is a bit of a walk. **TripAdvisor:** "friendly staff made this place shine," "pleasant stay," "away from the major crowd crunch." [$] *Rooms from: $209* ✉ *1956 Ala Moana Blvd., Waikiki* ☎ *808/941–7275, 800/222–8733* 🌐 *www.alana-doubletree.com* ⇨ *317 rooms, 385 suites* 🍴 *No meals.*

$$$ HOTEL 👶 🏨 **Embassy Suites Waikiki Beach Walk.** In a place where space is at a premium, the only all-suites resort in Hawaii offers families and groups traveling together a bit more room to move about, with two 21-story towers housing one- and two-bedroom suites. **Pros:** great location next to Waikiki Beach Walk and all of its shops and restaurants; great vibe; nice pool deck; complimentary hot breakfast served daily. **Cons:** no direct beach access. **TripAdvisor:** "fantastic breakfast," "ideal for family or couples," "wonderful friendly staff." [$] *Rooms from: $269* ✉ *201 Beachwalk St., Waikiki* ☎ *800/362–2779, 808/921–2345* 🌐 *www.embassysuiteswaikiki.com* ⇨ *353 1-bedroom suites, 68 2-bedroom suites* 🍴 *Breakfast.*

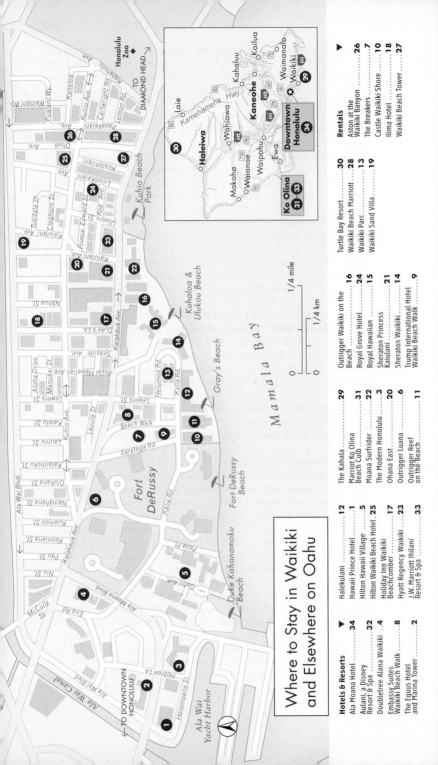

Where to Stay in Waikiki and Elsewhere on Oahu

Hotels & Resorts ▶

Ala Moana Hotel	34
Aulani, a Disney Resort & Spa	32
Doubletree Alana Waikiki	4
Embassy Suites Waikiki Beach Walk	8
The Equus Hotel and Marina Tower	2
Halekulani	12
Hawaii Prince Hotel	1
Hilton Hawaii Village	5
Hilton Waikiki Beach Hotel	25
Holiday Inn Waikiki Beachcomber	17
Hyatt Regency Waikiki	23
J.W. Marriott Ihilani Resort & Spa	33
The Kahala	29
Marriot Ko Olina Beach Culb	31
Moana Surfrider	22
The Modern Honolulu	3
Ohana East	20
Outrigger Luana	6
Outrigger Reef on the Beach	11
Outrigger Waikiki on the Beach	16
Royal Grove Hotel	24
Royal Hawaiian	15
Sheraton Princess Kaiulani	21
Sheraton Waikiki	14
Trump International Hotel Waikiki Beach Walk	9
Turtle Bay Resort	30
Waikiki Beach Marriott	28
Waikiki Parc	13
Waikiki Sand Villa	19

Rentals ▶

Aston at the Waikiki Banyon	26
The Breakers	7
Castle Waikiki Shore	10
Ilima Hotel	18
Waikiki Beach Tower	27

2

WHERE TO STAY ON OAHU

	Local Vibe	Pros	Cons
Honolulu	Lodging options are limited in downtown Honolulu, but if you want an urban feel or to be near Chinatown, look no farther.	Access to a wide selection of art galleries, boutiques, and new restaurants as well as Chinatown.	No beaches within walking distance. If you're looking to get away from it all, this is not the place.
Waikiki	Lodgings abound in Waikiki, from youth hostels to five-star accommodations. The area is always abuzz with activity and anything you desire is within walking distance.	You can surf in front of the hotels, wander miles of beach, and explore hundreds of restaurants and bars.	This is tourist central. Prices are high, and you are not going to get the true Hawaii experience.
North Shore	This is true country living, with one luxurious resort exception. It's bustling in the winter (when the surf is up) but pretty slow-paced in the summer.	Amazing surf and long stretches of sand truly epitomize the beach culture in Hawaii. Historic Haleiwa has enough stores to keep shopaholics busy.	There is no middle ground for accommodations; you're either in backpacker cabanas or $300-a-night suites. There is also zero nightlife, and traffic can get heavy during winter months.
West (Leeward) Oahu	This is the resort side of the rock; there is little outside of these resorts, but plenty on the grounds to keep you occupied for a week.	Ko Olina's lagoons offer the most kid-friendly swimming on the island, and the golf courses on this side are magnificent. Rare is the rainy day out here.	You are isolated from the rest of Oahu, with little in the way of shopping or jungle hikes.

$ HOTEL **The Equus Hotel and Marina Tower.** Formerly the Hawaii Polo Inn, this small hotel has been completely renovated with a Hawaiian country theme that pays tribute to Hawaii's polo-playing history. **Pros:** casual; fun atmosphere; attentive staff; nicely furnished rooms. **Cons:** on a very busy road you must cross to get to the beach. **TripAdvisor:** "affordable accommodations with Hawaiian grace," "friendly staff and comfortable beds," "good budget hotel." [$] *Rooms from: $149* ✉ *1696 Ala Moana Blvd., Waikiki* ☎ *808/949–0061, 800/669–7719* 🌐 *www.equushotel.com* 🛏 *70 rooms* 🍴 *Breakfast.*

$$$$ RESORT Fodor's Choice ★ **Halekulani.** The luxurious Halekulani exemplifies the translation of its name—the "house befitting heaven"—and from the moment you step inside the lobby, the attention to detail and impeccable service wraps you in privilege. **Pros:** heavenly interior spaces and wonderful dining opportunities in-house; world-class service. **Cons:** might feel a bit formal for Waikiki; pricey. **TripAdvisor:** "service and luxury," "the best of the best," "relaxation and romance." [$] *Rooms from: $500* ✉ *2199 Kalia Rd., Waikiki* ☎ *808/923–2311, 800/367–2343* 🌐 *www.halekulani.com* 🛏 *412 rooms, 43 suites* 🍴 *No meals.*

$$ HOTEL 🏨 **Hawaii Prince Hotel & Golf Club Waikiki.** This slim high-rise with 521 oceanfront rooms and 57 luxury suites fronts Ala Wai Yacht Harbor at the *ewa* (west) edge of Waikiki. **Pros:** fantastic views; all very elegant; easy exit from complicated-to-maneuver Waikiki. **Cons:** can feel a bit stuffy as it caters more to business travelers. **TripAdvisor:** "excellent hotel and service," "great views," "fabulously beautiful location." [$] *Rooms from: $189* ✉ *100 Holomoana St., Waikiki* ☎ *808/956–1111, 888/977–4623* 🌐 *www.hawaiiprincehotel.com* 🛏 *521 rooms, 57 suites* 🍴 *No meals.*

$$ RESORT 🏨 **Hilton Hawaiian Village Beach Resort and Spa.** Location, location, location: this megaresort and convention destination sprawls over 22 acres on Waikiki's widest stretch of beach, with the green lawns of neighboring Fort DeRussy creating a buffer zone to the high-rise lineup of central Waikiki. **Pros:** activities and amenities can keep you busy for weeks. **Cons:** temptation to stay on-site and not venture out; frequent renovations and construction; size of property can be overwhelming. **TripAdvisor:** "amazing vacation spot," "wonderful view," "beautiful hotel." [$] *Rooms from: $219* ✉ *2005 Kalia Rd., Waikiki* ☎ *808/949-4321, 800/445-8667* 🌐 *www.hiltonhawaiianvillage.com* 🛏 *3,432 rooms, 365 suites, 264 condominiums* 🍴 *No meals.*

$$ HOTEL 🏨 **Hilton Waikiki Beach Hotel.** You enter through a lobby of rich wood detailing, contemporary fabrics, and magnificent tropical floral displays whose colors match the hibiscus reds of the carpeting. **Pros:** good value; central location; pleasant, comfortable public spaces. **Cons:** a bit of a distance to the beach; very few rooms with views. **TripAdvisor:** "close to everything," "perfection," "friendly service." [$] *Rooms from: $209* ✉ *2500 Kuhio Ave., Waikiki* ☎ *808/922–0811, 888/370–0980* 🌐 *www.hilton.com* 🛏 *601 rooms* 🍴 *No meals.*

$ HOTEL 👶 🏨 **Holiday Inn Waikiki Beachcomber Resort.** The property is almost directly across from the upgraded Royal Hawaiian Center, next door to the International Marketplace, and 300 steps to the beach. **Pros:** lots of freebies; in the thick of Waikiki action. **Cons:** very busy area; no direct beach access; no on-site cultural activities. **TripAdvisor:** "great location," "clean," "well maintained." [$] *Rooms from: $155* ✉ *2300 Kalakaua Ave., Waikiki* ☎ *808/922–4646, 877/317–5756* 🌐 *www.waikikibeachcomberresort.com* 🛏 *500 rooms, 7 suites* 🍴 *No meals.*

$$$ RESORT 👶 🏨 **Hyatt Regency Waikiki Resort and Spa.** Though it's across the street from Kuhio Beach, the recently renewed Hyatt is actually considered oceanfront, as there's no resort between it and the Pacific Ocean. **Pros:** public spaces are open; great little coffee shop, Kimo Bean, in the lobby; kid-friendly. **Cons:** in a very busy and crowded part of Waikiki; parking and ballrooms are across the street. **TripAdvisor:** "in the middle of everything," "priceless view of Waikiki beach," "great service and friendly people." [$] *Rooms from: $324* ✉ *2424 Kalakaua Ave., Waikiki* ☎ *808/923–1234, 800/633–7313* 🌐 *www.hyattregencywaikiki.com* 🛏 *1,230 rooms, 18 suites* 🍴 *No meals.*

$$ RENTAL 🏨 **Ilima Hotel.** Tucked away on a residential side street near Waikiki's Ala Wai Canal, this locally owned 17-story condominium-style hotel is a gem. **Pros:** big rooms are great for families; free parking in Waikiki is a rarity; on-site coin-operated laundry facilities; smoking rooms available.

Fodor's Choice ★

The Kahala

Halekulani

Cons: limited hotel parking, and street parking can be difficult to find; not the most luxurious accommodations. **TripAdvisor:** "lovely staff," "nice location," "great condo." [$] *Rooms from: $188* ✉ *445 Nohonani St., Waikiki* ☎ *808/923–1877, 800/684–2140* 🌐 *www.ilima.com* 🔑 *99 units* 🍴 *No meals.*

$$$$ RESORT 🏨 **Moana Surfrider, A Westin Resort & Spa.** Outrageous rates of $1.50 per night were the talk of the town when the "First Lady of Waikiki" opened her doors in 1901; today, this historic beauty—the oldest hotel in Waikiki—is still a wedding and honeymoon favorite with a sweeping main staircase and period furnishings in its historic main wing, the Moana. **Pros:** elegant; historic property; best place on Waikiki Beach to watch hula and have a drink; can't beat the location. **Cons:** you'll likely dodge bridal parties in the lobby. **TripAdvisor:** "best Mai Tai on the islands," "excellent service," "a charming place." [$] *Rooms from: $499* ✉ *2365 Kalakaua Ave., Waikiki* ☎ *808/922–3111, 888/488–3535, 866/500–8313* 🌐 *www.moana-surfrider.com* 🔑 *793 rooms, 46 suites* 🍴 *No meals.*

$$$$ HOTEL 🏨 **The Modern Honolulu.** It's a long story: formerly an annex of the iconic Ilikai Hotel, this first incarnation of Marriott International's boutique Edition chain was quickly converted into an Aqua property, but the modern touches of the former owner remain. **Pros:** newly refurbished; great bars and restaurants. **Cons:** not kid-friendly; on the outer edge of Waikiki; no direct beach access. **TripAdvisor:** "nice design," "a refined chic atmosphere," "real nightlife in Waikiki." [$] *Rooms from: $500* ✉ *1775 Ala Moana Blvd., Waikiki* ☎ *808/943–5800, 866/970–4161* 🌐 *www.themodernhonolulu.com* 🔑 *353 rooms* 🍴 *No meals.*

$$$ HOTEL 🏨 **Ohana East.** If you want to be in central Waikiki and don't want to pay beachfront lodging prices, consider the flagship property for Ohana Hotels in Waikiki. **Pros:** close to the beach and reasonable rates; decent on-site eateries, including a piano bar. **Cons:** no lanai and very basic public spaces. **TripAdvisor:** "good location," "felt at home," "family friendly." [$] *Rooms from: $279* ✉ *150 Kaiulani Ave., Waikiki* ☎ *808/922–5353, 866/956–4262* 🌐 *www.ohanahotels.com* 🔑 *420 rooms, 20 suites* 🍴 *No meals.*

$$ HOTEL 🏨 **Outrigger Luana.** At the entrance to Waikiki near Fort DeRussy is this welcoming hotel offering both rooms and condominium units. **Pros:** two lanai in suites; barbecue area (rare for Waikiki); walking distance to shops and restaurants. **Cons:** no direct beach access. **TripAdvisor:** "kind and helpful staff," "the best smaller hotel in Waikiki," "great location." [$] *Rooms from: $209* ✉ *2045 Kalakaua Ave., Waikiki* ☎ *808/955–6000, 866/956–4262* 🌐 *www.outrigger.com* 🔑 *218 units* 🍴 *No meals.*

$$$$ HOTEL 🏨 **Outrigger Reef on the Beach.** Recent renovations have drastically updated this beachfront property, adding a new entrance that incorporates a Hawaiian voyaging design theme; expanded guest rooms; larger and more contemporary bathrooms; and a new signature restaurant—the poolside Kani Ka Pila Grille, with nightly live music by legendary Hawaiian entertainers—though the Shore Bird Restaurant & Beach Bar and Ocean House Restaurant also remain. **Pros:** on beach; direct access to Waikiki Beach Walk. **Cons:** views from non-oceanfront rooms

are uninspiring; can be pricey. **TripAdvisor:** "fantastic hotel on the beach," "great view," "on the quiet end." [$] *Rooms from: $489* ✉ *2169 Kalia Rd., Waikiki* ☎ *808/923–3111, 866/956–4262* 🌐 *www.outrigger.com* 🛏 *631 rooms, 44 suites* 🍴 *No meals.*

ASK FOR A LANAI

Islanders love their porches, balconies, and verandas—all wrapped up in a single Hawaiian word: *lanai.* You may not want to look at a parking lot, so when booking, ask about the lanai and be sure to specify the view (understanding that top views command top dollars). Also, check that the lanai is not merely a step-out or Juliet balcony, with just enough room to lean against a railing—you want a lanai that is big enough for patio seating.

$$$$ RESORT **Outrigger Waikiki on the Beach.** This star of Outrigger Hotels & Resorts sits on one of the finest strands of Waikiki Beach. **Pros:** the best bar on the beach is downstairs; free Wi-Fi in lobby. **Cons:** the lobby feels a bit like an airport with so many people using it as a throughway to the beach. **TripAdvisor:** "excellent location," "great restaurants," "paradise." [$] *Rooms from: $489* ✉ *2335 Kalakaua Ave., Waikiki* ☎ *808/923–0711, 808/956–4262* 🌐 *www.outrigger.com* 🛏 *524 rooms, 30 suites* 🍴 *No meals.*

$ HOTEL **Royal Grove Hotel.** Two generations of the Fong family have put their heart and soul into the operation of this tiny (by Waikiki standards), six-story hotel that feels like a throwback to the days of boarding houses, where rooms were outfitted for function, not style, and served up with a wealth of home-style hospitality at a price that didn't break the bank. **Pros:** very economical Waikiki option; lots of character. **Cons:** no a/c in some rooms; rooms are dated. **TripAdvisor:** "over 40 years of fun," "welcoming and friendly," "close to the beach." [$] *Rooms from: $67* ✉ *151 Uluniu Ave., Waikiki* ☎ *808/923–7691* 🌐 *www.royalgrovehotel.com* 🛏 *78 rooms, 7 suites* 🍴 *No meals.*

$$$$ HOTEL **The Royal Hawaiian, a Luxury Collection Resort.** There's nothing like the legendary Pink Palace of the Pacific, and after a recent $85 million face-lift—which included removing the storefronts that clogged the lobby and opening up the public spaces—the iconic hotel on Waikiki Beach is a unique blend of luxury and tradition. **Pros:** can't be beat for history; mai tais and sunsets are amazing; there's a doctors-on-call service. **Cons:** history is not cheap; you'd better like pink. **TripAdvisor:** "truly magical," "tranquility and quality," "a Hawaiian classic." [$] *Rooms from: $630* ✉ *2259 Kalakaua Ave., Waikiki* ☎ *888/488–3535, 808/923–7311, 866/500–8313* 🌐 *www.royal-hawaiian.com* 🛏 *528 rooms, 53 suites* 🍴 *No meals.*

$$$ HOTEL **Sheraton Princess Kaiulani.** This hotel sits across the street from its upscale sister property, the Moana Surfrider. **Pros:** in the heart of everything in Waikiki; on-site surfboard storage (for a fee). **Cons:** no direct beach access; kids' activities off-site; pool closes early; no spa. **TripAdvisor:** "excellent location," "impeccable service," "beautiful facility." [$] *Rooms from: $270* ✉ *120 Kaiulani Ave., Waikiki* ☎ *808/922–5811, 866/716–8109, 800/325–3535* 🌐 *www.princess-kaiulani.com* 🛏 *1,142 rooms, 14 suites* 🍴 *No meals.*

$$$$ HOTEL 🏨 **Sheraton Waikiki.** If you don't mind crowds, this could be the place for you: towering over its neighbors on the prow of Waikiki's famous sands, the Sheraton is center stage on Waikiki Beach. **Pros:** location in the heart of everything. **Cons:** busy atmosphere clashes with laid-back Hawaiian style. **TripAdvisor:** "everything about this place was perfect," "excellent amenities," "modern rooms." [$] *Rooms from: $450* ✉ *2255 Kalakaua Ave., Waikiki* ☎ *808/922–4422, 866/716–8109* 🌐 *www.sheraton-waikiki.com* 🛏 *1,695 rooms, 128 suites* 🍴 *No meals.*

$$$$ HOTEL 🏨 **Trump International Hotel Waikiki Beach Walk.** One of the chicest hotels on the Waikiki scene, Trump has been drawing rave reviews since its opening in November 2009. **Pros:** beautifully appointed rooms; on the edge of Waikiki so a bit quieter; great views of Friday fireworks. **Cons:** must cross street to reach the beach; pricey. **TripAdvisor:** "excellent service," "very comfortable," "beautiful rooms." [$] *Rooms from: $425* ✉ *223 Saratoga Rd., Waikiki* ☎ *808/683–7777, 877/683–7401* 🌐 *www.trumphotelcollection.com/waikiki* 🛏 *1,462 rooms* 🍴 *No meals.*

$$$ RESORT 🏨 **Waikiki Beach Marriott Resort & Spa.** On the eastern edge of Waikiki, this flagship Marriott sits across from Kuhio Beach and close to Kapiolani Park, the Honolulu Zoo, and Waikiki Aquarium. **Pros:** stunning views of Waikiki; professional service; airy tropical public spaces. **Cons:** noise from Kalakaua Avenue can drown out surf below. **TripAdvisor:** "friendly staff," "great view," "upscale hotel with convenient location." [$] *Rooms from: $289* ✉ *2552 Kalakaua Ave., Waikiki* ☎ *808/922–6611, 800/848–8110* 🌐 *www.marriottwaikiki.com* 🛏 *1,310 rooms, 13 suites* 🍴 *No meals.*

$$ HOTEL 🏨 **Waikiki Parc.** In contrast to the stately vintage-Hawaiian elegance of her sister hotel, the Halekulani, the Waikiki Parc makes a chic and contemporary statement to its Gen-X clientele, offering the same attention to detail in service and architectural design but lacking the beachfront location and higher prices. **Pros:** stunningly modern; high-design rooms; great access to Waikiki Beach Walk. **Cons:** no direct beach access. **TripAdvisor:** "friendly and convenient," "quiet," "attentive staff with integrity." [$] *Rooms from: $190* ✉ *2233 Helumoa Rd., Waikiki* ☎ *808/921–7272, 800/422–0450* 🌐 *www.waikikiparc.com* 🛏 *297 rooms* 🍴 *No meals.*

$ HOTEL 🏨 **Waikiki Sand Villa.** Families and others looking for an economical rate without sacrificing proximity to Waikiki's beaches, dining, and

HOTELS' CULTURAL PROGRAMS

Hotels, especially in Waikiki, are fueling a resurgence in Hawaiian culture, thanks to repeat visitors who want a more authentic island experience. In addition to lei-making and hula-dancing lessons, you can learn how to strum a ukulele, listen to Grammy Award–winning Hawaiian musicians, watch a revered master *kumu* (teacher) share the art of ancient hula and chant, chat with a marine biologist about Hawaii's endangered species, or get a lesson in the art of canoe making. Check with the concierge for daily Hawaiian activities at the hotel or nearby.

Turtle Bay Resort

shopping return to the Waikiki Sand Villa year after year. **Pros:** fun bar; economical choice. **Cons:** the noise from the bar might annoy some; 10-minute walk to the beach. **TripAdvisor:** "a nice clean place to sleep," "enjoyable getaway," "good location." *Rooms from: $165 ⌨ 2375 Ala Wai Blvd., Waikiki* ☎ *808/922–4744, 800/247–1903* ⊕ *www. sandvillahotel.com* ⤴ *214 rooms* ⦿ *Breakfast.*

2

NORTH SHORE

$$$$
RESORT
Fodor'sChoice
★

The Turtle Bay Resort. Sprawling over 880 acres of natural landscape on the edge of Kuilima Point in Kahuku, the luxe Turtle Bay Resort boasts spacious guest rooms averaging nearly 500 square feet, with lanai that showcase stunning peninsula views. **Pros:** great open, public spaces in a secluded area of Oahu; world-class spa. **Cons:** very far from anything else—even Haleiwa is a 20-minute drive; hotel charges a $25 per night resort fee. **TripAdvisor:** "relaxing," "amazing destination," "great getaway." *Rooms from: $450 ⌨ 57-091 Kamehameha Hwy., Box 187, Kahuku* ☎ *808/293–8811, 800/203–3650* ⊕ *www. turtlebayresort.com* ⤴ *373 rooms, 40 suites, 42 beach cottages, 56 ocean villas* ⦿ *No meals.*

WEST (LEEWARD) OAHU

$$$$
RESORT
☾

Aulani, A Disney Resort & Spa. In September 2011, Disney opened its first hotel and time-share develoment not connected to a theme park, and first property in Hawaii, in the resort area of Ko Olina, about a 40-minute drive from Waikiki on Oahu's leeward side. **Pros:** tons to do on premises; very kid-friendly; a 1,500-square-foot teens-only spa with a private entrance, yogurt bar, and teen-specific treatments. **Cons:** a long way from Waikiki; "character breakfasts" are often sold out; resort still under construction. **TripAdvisor:** "kids dreams come true," "a magical stay," "Hawaiian paradise with Disney magic." *Rooms from: $474 ⌨ 92-1185 Aliinui Dr., Ko Olina, Kapolei* ☎ *714/520–7001, 808/674–6200, 866/443–4763* ⊕ *resorts.disney. go.com/aulani-hawaii-resort* ⤴ *359 rooms, 481 villas* ⦿ *No meals.*

$$$$
RESORT
☾

JW Marriott Ihilani Resort & Spa. Forty-five minutes and a world away from the bustle of Waikiki, this sleek, 17-story resort anchors the still-developing Ko Olina Resort and Marina on Oahu's leeward coastline. **Pros:** beautiful property; impeccable service; pool is stunning at night. **Cons:** a bit of a drive from Honolulu; rental car

---

CONDO COMFORTS

The local **Foodland** (⌨ *Market City, 2939 Harding Ave., near intersection with Kapahulu Ave. and highway overpass, Kaimuki* ☎ *808/734–6303* ⌨ *Ala Moana Center, 1450 Ala Moana Blvd., ground level, Ala Moana* ☎ *808/949–5044*) grocery-store chain has two locations near Waikiki. A smaller version of larger Foodland, **Food Pantry** (⌨ *2370 Kuhio Ave., across from Miramar hotel, Waikiki* ☎ *808/923–9831* ⌨ *2370 Kuhio Ave., across from Miramar hotel, Waikiki* ☎ *808/923–9831*) also has apparel, beach stuff, and tourist-oriented items.

a must. **TripAdvisor:** "incredible location," "great room," "quiet and beautiful." [$] *Rooms from: $545* ✉ *92-1001 Olani St., Ko Olina, Kapolei* ☎ *808/679–0079, 800/626–4446* 🌐 *www.ihilani.com* 🛏 *387 rooms, 36 suites* 🍴 *No meals.*

$$$$ HOTEL **Marriott Ko Olina Beach Vacation Club.** If you have your heart set on getting away to Oahu's western shores, check out the Marriott, which is primarily a vacation-ownership property, though it also offers nightly rental rates for its rooms, which range from hotel-style standard guest rooms to expansive and elegantly appointed one- or two-bedroom guest villa apartments. **Pros:** suites are beautifully decorated and have ample space for families; full kitchens; nice views; fairly private lagoon; on-site luau and dinner show. **Cons:** at least a half-hour drive to Honolulu; ongoing construction at other properties nearby. **TripAdvisor:** "away from the hustle and bustle," "well maintained," "outstanding tropical lagoons." [$] *Rooms from: $401* ✉ *92-161 Waipahe Pl., Ko Olina, Kapolei* ☎ *808/679–4900, 877/229–4484* 🌐 *www.marriottvacationclub.com* 🛏 *200 units* 🍴 *No meals.*

Maui

WORD OF MOUTH

"I think the Road to Hana is definitely worthwhile. Get an early start and make plenty of stops along the way. You must take the side road down to the Keanae area and linger for a while. Also be sure to stop at Waianapanapa State Park and relax on the black sand beach, or hike along the coast on a lava bed under coconut trees."

—gatormillson

WELCOME TO MAUI

TOP REASONS TO GO

★ **The Road to Hana:** Each curve of this legendary cliff-side road pulls you deeper into the lush green rain forest of Maui's eastern shore.

★ **Haleakala National Park:** Explore the lava bombs, cinder cones, and silverswords at the gasp-inducing, volcanic summit of Haleakala, the House of the Sun.

★ **Hookipa Beach:** On Maui's North Shore, the world's top windsurfers will dazzle you as they maneuver above the waves like butterflies shot from cannons.

★ **Waianapanapa State Park:** Head to East Maui and take a dip at the stunning black-sand beach or in the cave pool where an ancient princess once hid.

★ **Resorts, Resorts, Resorts:** Opulent gardens, pools, restaurants, and golf courses make Maui's resorts some of the best in the Islands.

1 West Maui. This leeward, sunny area is ringed by resorts and condominiums in areas such as Kaanapali and Kapalua. Also on the coast is the busy, tourist-oriented town of Lahaina, a former whaling center.

2 South Shore. The leeward side of Maui's eastern half is what most people mean when they say South Shore. This popular area is sunny and warm year-round and is home to Wailea, an upscale resort area.

3 Central Maui. Between Maui's two mountain areas is Central Maui, the location of the county seat of Wailuku and the commercial center of Kahului. Kahului Airport is here.

4 Upcountry. Island residents affectionately call the regions climbing up the slope of Haleakala Crater Upcountry. This is farm and ranch country.

5 North Shore. The North Shore has no large resorts, just plenty of picturesque small towns like Paia and Haiku—and great surfing action at Hookipa Beach.

6 Road to Hana. The island's northeastern, windward side is largely one great rain forest, traversed by the stunning Road to Hana. The town of Hana preserves the slow pace of the past.

GETTING ORIENTED

Maui, the second-largest island in the Hawaiian chain, is made up of two distinct circular landmasses. The smaller, on the western part of the island, consists of 5,788-foot Puu Kukui and the rain-chiseled West Maui Mountains. The large landmass composing the eastern half of Maui is Haleakala, with its cloud-wreathed volcanic peak. Maui has very different areas, from the resorts of sunny West Maui and the South Shore to the ranches of Upcountry and the remote village of Hana in unspoiled East Maui.

3

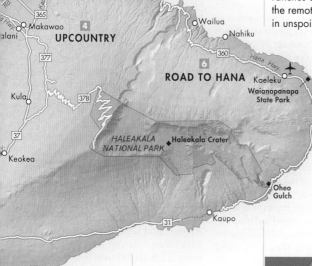

Hookipa Beach

Hwy 36

Haiku Ulumalu Huelo
Kailua

NORTH SHORE **5**

Kawaakaloa Rd

Road to Hana

Haleakala Hwy 365

Makawao **4**
alani UPCOUNTRY

377

Wailua
Nahiku

360 Hana Hwy

6
ROAD TO HANA Kaeleku

Waianapanapa State Park

Kula 378 Hana

37

HALEAKALA NATIONAL PARK Haleakala Crater

Keokea

Oheo Gulch

31 Kaupo

GREAT ITINERARIES

Maui's landscape is incredibly diverse, offering everything from underwater encounters with eagle rays to treks across moonlike terrain. Although daydreaming at the pool or on the beach may fulfill your initial island fantasy, Maui has much more to offer. The following one-day itineraries will take you to our favorite spots on the island.

Beach Day in West Maui

West Maui has some of the island's most beautiful beaches, though many of them are hidden by megaresorts. If you get an early start, you can begin your day snorkeling at Slaughterhouse Beach (in winter, D.T. Fleming Beach is a better option as it's less rough). Then spend the day beach hopping through Kapalua, Napili, and Kaanapali as you make your way south. You'll want to get to Lahaina before dark so you can spend some time exploring the historic whaling town before choosing a restaurant for a sunset dinner.

Focus on Marine Life on the South Shore

Start your South Shore trip early in the morning, and head out past Makena into the rough lava fields of rugged La Pérouse Bay. At the road's end, there are areas of the Ahihi-Kinau Marine Preserve open to the public (others are closed indefinitely) that offer good snorkeling. If that's a bit too far afield for you, there's excellent snorkeling at Polo Beach. Head to the right (your right while facing the ocean) for plenty of fish and beautiful coral. Head back north to Kihei for lunch, and then enjoy the afternoon learning more about Maui's marine life at the outstanding Maui Ocean Center at Maalaea.

The Road to Hana

This cliff-side driving tour through rainforest canopy reveals Maui's most lush and tropical terrain. It will take a full day, especially if you plan to make it all the way to Oheo Gulch. You'll pass through communities where Old Hawaii still thrives, and where the forest runs unchecked from the sea to the summit. You'll want to make frequent exploratory stops. To really soak in the magic of this place, consider staying overnight in Hana town. That way you can spend a full day winding toward Hana, hiking and exploring along the way, and the next day traveling leisurely back to civilization.

Haleakala National Park, Upcountry, and the North Shore

If you don't plan to spend an entire day hiking in the crater at Haleakala National Park, this itinerary will at least allow you to take a peek at it. Get up early and head straight for the summit of Haleakala (if you're jet-lagged and waking up in the middle of the night, you may want to get there in time for sunrise). Bring water, sunscreen, and warm clothing; it's freezing at sunrise. Plan to spend a couple of hours exploring the various lookout points in the park. On your way down the mountain, turn right on Makawao Avenue, and head into the little town of Makawao. You can have lunch here, or make a left on Baldwin Avenue and head downhill to the town of Paia where there are a number of great lunch spots and shops to explore. Spend the rest of your afternoon at Paia's main strip of sand, Hookipa Beach.

3

"Maui no ka oi" is what locals say—it's the best, the most, the top of the heap. To those who know Maui well, there's good reason for the superlatives. The island's miles of perfect-tan beaches, lush green valleys, historic villages, top-notch windsurfing and diving, stellar restaurants and high-end hotels, and variety of art and cultural activities have made it an international favorite.

At 729 square miles, Maui is the second-largest Hawaiian Island, but offers more miles of swimmable beaches than any of the other Islands. The island draws more than 2 million visitors each year, and some decide to return for good. Despite growth over the past few decades, the local population is still fairly small, totaling only 155,000.

GEOLOGY

Maui is made up of two volcanoes, one now extinct and the other dormant, that erupted long ago and joined into one island. The resulting depression between the two is what gives the island its nickname, the Valley Isle. West Maui's 5,788-foot Puu Kukui was the first volcano to form, a distinction that gives that area's mountainous topography a more weathered look. Rainbows seem to grow wild over this terrain as gentle mists fill the deeply eroded canyons. The Valley Isle's second volcano is the 10,023-foot Haleakala, where desertlike terrain butts up against tropical forests.

FLORA AND FAUNA

Haleakala is one of few homes to the rare *ahinahina* (silversword plant). The plant's brilliant silver leaves are stunning against the red lava rock that blankets the walls of Haleakala's caldera—particularly during blooming season from July to September. A distant cousin of the sunflower, the silversword blooms just once before it dies—producing a single towering stalk awash in tiny fragrant blossoms. Also calling Haleakala home are a few hundred *nene*—the Hawaiian state bird (related to the Canada goose), currently fighting its way back from near extinction. Maui is one of the better Islands for whale watching, and migrating humpbacks can be seen off the island's coast from December to April, and sometimes into May.

HISTORY

Maui's history is full of firsts—Lahaina was the first capital of Hawaii and the first destination of the whaling industry (early 1800s), which explains why the town still has that fishing-village vibe; Lahaina was also the first stop for missionaries (1823). Although they suppressed aspects of Hawaiian culture, the missionaries did help invent the Hawaiian alphabet and built a printing press in Lahaina (the first west of the Rockies), which rolled out the news in Hawaiian. Maui also boasts the first sugar plantation in Hawaii (1849) and the first Hawaiian luxury resort (Hotel Hana-Maui, 1946: now the Travaasa Hana).

ON MAUI TODAY

In the mid-1970s, savvy marketers saw a way to improve Maui's economy by promoting the Valley Isle to golfers and luxury travelers. The ploy worked all too well; Maui's visitor count continues to swell. Impatient traffic now threatens to overtake the ubiquitous aloha spirit, development encroaches on agricultural lands, and county planners struggle to meet the needs of a burgeoning population. But Maui is still carpeted with an eyeful of green, and for every tailgater, there's a carefree local on "Maui time" who stops for each pedestrian, whale spout, and sunset.

MAUI PLANNER

GETTING HERE AND AROUND

AIR TRAVEL

Most visitors arrive at Kahului Airport in Central Maui. A rental car is the best way to get from the airport to your destination. The major car-rental companies have desks at the airport and can provide a map and directions to your hotel. ■ TIP→ Flights in Maui tend to land around the same time, leading to long lines at car-rental windows. If possible, send one person to pick up the car while the others wait for the baggage.

CAR TRAVEL

A rental car is a must on Maui. It's also one of your biggest trip expenses, especially given the price of gasoline—higher on Maui than on Oahu or the mainland. If you need to ask for directions, try your best to pronounce the multivowel road names. Locals don't use (or know) highway route numbers and will respond with looks as lost as yours. Also, they will give you directions by the time it takes to get somewhere instead of by the mileage.

Kahului is the transportation hub—the main airport and largest harbor are here. Traffic on Maui's roads can be heavy, especially during the rush hours of 6 am to 8:30 am and 3:30 pm to 6:30 pm.

See Travel Smart Hawaii for more information on renting a car and driving.

ISLAND DRIVING TIMES   Driving from one point on Maui to another can take longer than the mileage indicates. It's 52 miles from Kahului Airport to Hana, but the drive will take you about three hours. As for driving to Haleakala, the 38-mile drive from sea level to the summit will take you about two hours. The roads are narrow and winding; you must go at a slow pace. Here are average driving times.

DRIVING TIMES	
Kahului to Wailea	17 miles/30 mins
Kahului to Kaanapali	25 miles/45 mins
Kahului to Kapalua	36 miles/1 hr, 15 mins
Kahului to Makawao	13 miles/25 mins
Kapalua to Haleakala	73 miles/3 hrs
Kaanapali to Haleakala	62 miles/2 hrs, 30 mins
Wailea to Haleakala	54 miles/2 hrs, 30 mins
Kapalua to Hana	88 miles/5 hrs
Kaanapali to Hana	77 miles/5 hrs
Wailea to Hana	69 miles/4 hrs, 30 mins
Wailea to Lahaina	20 miles/45 mins
Kaanapali to Lahaina	4 miles/15 mins
Kapalua to Lahaina	12 miles/25 mins

RESTAURANTS

There's a lot going on for a place the size of Maui, from ethnic holes-in-the-wall to fancy oceanfront fish houses. Much of it is excellent, but some of it is overpriced and touristy. Choose menu items made with products that are abundant on the island, including local fish. Local cuisine is a mix of foods brought by ethnic groups since the late 1700s, blended with the foods Native Hawaiians have enjoyed for centuries. For a food adventure, take a drive into Central Maui and eat at one of the "local" spots recommended here. *Prices in the reviews are the average cost of a main course at dinner or, if dinner is not served, at lunch.*

HOTELS

Maui is well known for its lovely resorts, some of them very luxurious; many cater to families. But there are other options, including abundant and convenient apartment and condo rentals for all budgets. The resorts and rentals cluster largely on Maui's sunny coasts, in West Maui and the South Shore. For a different, more local experience, you might spend part of your time at a small bed-and-breakfast. Check Internet sites and ask about discounts and packages. *Prices in the reviews are the lowest cost of a standard double room in high season or, for rentals, the lowest per-night cost for a one-bedroom unit in high season.*

VISITOR INFORMATION

The Hawaii Visitors & Convention Bureau (HVCB) has plenty of general and vacation-planning information for Maui and all the Islands, and offers a free official vacation planner. The Maui Visitors Bureau website includes information on accommodations, sights, events, and suggested itineraries for some of the most popular destinations and activities.

Information Hawaii Visitors & Convention Bureau ✉ *2270 Kalakaua Ave., Suite 801, Honolulu* ☎ *808/923–1811, 800/464–2924 to order free visitor guide* ⊕ *www.gohawaii.com.* **Maui Visitors Bureau** ☎ *808/244–3530, 800/525–6284* ⊕ *www.visitmaui.com.*

EXPLORING

Updated by Bonnie Friedman

Maui is more than a sandy beach with palm trees. The natural bounty of this place is impressive. Puu Kukui, the 5,788-foot interior of the West Maui Mountains, is one of the earth's wettest spots—annual rainfall of 400 inches has sculpted the land into impassable gorges and razor-sharp ridges. On the opposite side of the island, the blistering lava fields at Ahihi-Kinau receive scant rain. And just above this desert, *paniolo* (Hawaiian cowboys) herd cattle on rolling, fertile ranchlands reminiscent of northern California. On the island's rugged east side is the lush, tropical Hawaii of travel posters.

Nature isn't all Maui has to offer—it's also home to a rich and vivid culture. In small towns like Paia and Hana you can see remnants of the past mingling with modern-day life. Ancient *heiau* (Hawaiian stone platforms once used as places of worship) line busy roadways. Old coral and brick missionary homes now house broadcasting networks. The antique smokestacks of sugar mills tower above communities where the children blend English, Hawaiian, Japanese, Chinese, Portuguese, Filipino, and more into one colorful language. Hawaii is a melting pot like no other. Visiting an eclectic mom-and-pop shop (like Komoda Store & Bakery) can feel like stepping into another country, or back in time. The more you look here, the more you will find.

WEST MAUI

Separated from the remainder of the island by steep *pali* (cliffs), West Maui has a reputation for attitude and action. Once upon a time, this was the haunt of whalers, missionaries, and the kings and queens of Hawaii; now it's one of Maui's main resort areas. Lahaina Town was not only once the kingdom's capital but also the *alii's* (royalty's) playground. Today the main drag, Front Street, is crowded with T-shirt and trinket shops, art exhibits, and restaurants. Farther north is Kaanapali, Maui's first planned resort area. Its first hotel, the Sheraton, was opened in 1963. Since then, resorts, luxury condominiums, and a shopping center have sprung up along the white-sand beaches, with championship golf courses across the road. A few miles farther up the coast is the ultimate in West Maui luxury, the resort area of Kapalua. In between, dozens of condominiums and strip malls line both the *makai* (toward the sea) and *mauka* (toward the mountains) sides of the highway. There are gems here, too, like Napili Bay and its crescent of sand.

LAHAINA

27 miles west of Kahului; 4 miles south of Kaanapali.

Today Lahaina may best be described as either charming or tacky, depending on your point of view—and opinions do differ. Too many

Old Lahaina Luau: "A beautiful picture while waiting for the best luau in Hawaii." –Tammy Davis, Fodors.com photo contest participant.

T-shirt shops have supplanted ethnic mom-and-pops, but there are some excellent restaurants and interesting galleries. Sunset cruises and other excursions depart from Lahaina Harbor. Happily, at the far south end of town an important ancient site—Mokuula—is being excavated and restored. ■ TIP➜ If you arrange to spend a Friday afternoon exploring Front Street, you can dine in town and hang around for Art Night, when the galleries stay open into the evening and entertainment fills the streets.

GETTING HERE AND AROUND

It's about a 45-minute drive from Kahului Airport to Lahaina (take Route 380 to Route 30) depending on the traffic on this heavily traveled route. Traffic can be slow around Lahaina, especially between 4 and 6 pm. Shuttles and taxis are available from Kahului Airport. The Maui Bus Lahaina Islander route runs from Queen Kaahumanu Center in Kahului to the Wharf Cinema Center on Front Street, Lahaina's main thoroughfare.

TOP ATTRACTIONS

★ **Baldwin Home Museum.** If you want some insight into 19th-century life in Hawaii, this informative museum is an excellent place to start. Begun in 1834 and completed the following year, the coral and stone house was originally home to missionary Dr. Dwight Baldwin and his family. The building has been carefully restored to reflect the period; many of the original furnishings remain. You can view the family's grand piano, carved four-poster bed, and most interesting, Dr. Baldwin's dispensary. During a brief tour conducted by Lahaina Restoration Foundation volunteers, you'll be shown the "thunderpot" and told how the doctor single-handedly inoculated 10,000 Maui residents against smallpox.

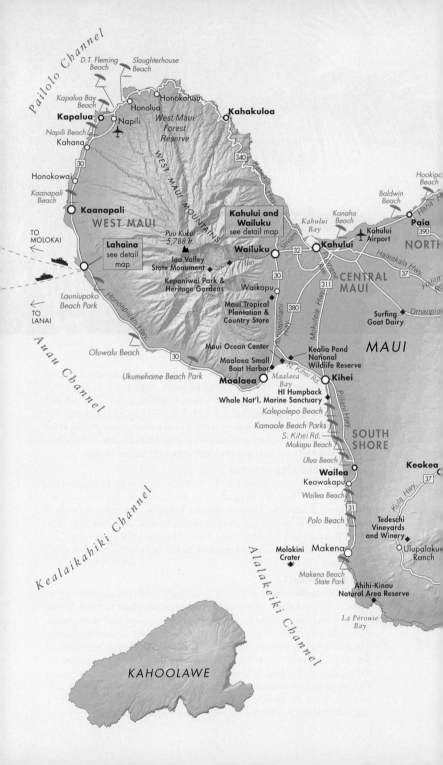

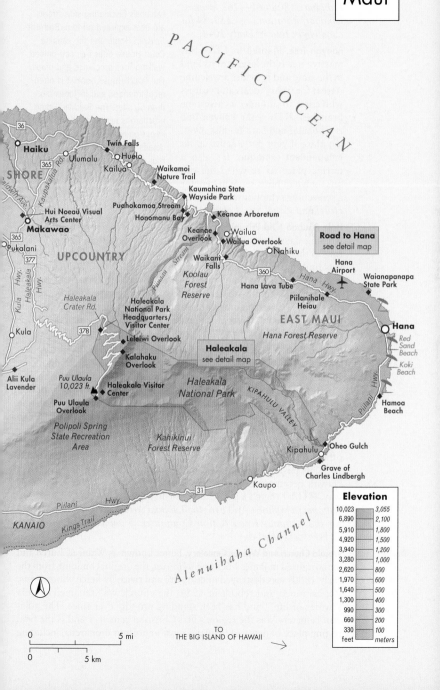

Maui

PACIFIC OCEAN

36
Haiku
365
Ulumalu
Kailua
Huelo
Twin Falls
Waikamoi Nature Trail
NORTH SHORE
Baldwin Ave.
Kaupakalua Rd.
Puahokamoa Stream
Kaumahina State Wayside Park
Hui Noeau Visual Arts Center
Makawao
Honomanu Bay
Keanae Arboretum
Keanae Overlook
365
Wailua
Wailua Overlook
377
Pukalani
UPCOUNTRY
Kula Hwy.
Haleakala Hwy.
Nahiku
Waikani Falls
Koolau Forest Reserve
Road to Hana
see detail map
Hana Airport
Waianapanapa State Park
Hana Lava Tube
Piilanihale Heiau
360
Hana Hwy.
Haleakala Crater Rd.
Haleakala National Park Headquarters/ Visitor Center
Leleiwi Overlook
Kula
378
Kalahaku Overlook
EAST MAUI
Hana Forest Reserve
Hana
Red Sand Beach
Koki Beach
Haleakala
see detail map
Alii Kula Lavender
Puu Ulaula 10,023 ft.
Haleakala Visitor Center
Haleakala National Park
KIPAHULU VALLEY
Pinunt Stream
Puu Ulaula Overlook
Polipoli Spring State Recreation Area
Kahikinui Forest Reserve
Hamoa Beach
Kipahulu
Oheo Gulch
Grave of Charles Lindbergh
31
Kaupo
Piilani Hwy.
KANAIO
Kings Trail
Piilani Hwy.
Alenuihaha Channel

N

0   5 mi
0   5 km

TO THE BIG ISLAND OF HAWAII →

Elevation

feet	meters
10,023	3,055
6,890	2,100
5,910	1,800
4,920	1,500
3,940	1,200
3,280	1,000
2,620	800
1,970	600
1,640	500
1,300	400
990	300
660	200
330	100
feet	meters

Friday at 6:30 pm are special candlelight tours. ✉ 696 Front St.,
Lahaina ☎ 808/661–3262 ⊕ www.
lahainarestoration.org ✆ $3, $4 for
candlelight tour ⊙ Daily 10–4.

Banyan Tree. Planted in 1873, this
massive tree is the largest of its kind
in the state and provides a welcome
retreat for weary locals and visitors
who come to sit under its awesome
branches. ■TIP➜ The Banyan Tree
is a popular and hard-to-miss meeting place if your party splits up for
independent exploring. It's also a
terrific place to be when the sun
sets—mynah birds settle in here for

a screeching symphony, which is an event in itself. ✉ Front St., between
Hotel and Canal Sts., Lahaina.

Hale Paahao (Old Prison). Lahaina's jailhouse is a reminder of rowdy
whaling days. Its name literally means "stuck-in-irons house," refer-
ring to the wall shackles and ball-and-chain restraints. The compound
was built in the 1850s by convict laborers out of blocks of coral that
had been salvaged from the demolished waterfront fort. Most prisoners were sent here for desertion, drunkenness, or reckless horse riding. Today, a wax figure representing an imprisoned old sailor tells
his recorded tale of woe. ✉ Wainee and Prison Sts., Lahaina ✆ Free
⊙ Weekdays 10–4.

Lahaina Court House. The Lahaina Arts Society and the Lahaina Heritage Museum occupy this charming old government building in the
center of town. Wander among the terrific displays, pump the knowledgeable museum staff for interesting trivia, and ask for the walking-
tour brochure covering historic Lahaina sites. The nonprofit Lahaina
Town Action Committee, which oversees Lahaina's attractions, can
also be found here. Erected in 1859 and restored in 1999, the building has served as a customs and court house, governor's office, post
office, vault and collector's office, and police court. On August 12,
1898, its postmaster witnessed the lowering of the Hawaiian flag when
Hawaii became a U.S. territory. The flag now hangs above the stair-
way. ■TIP➜ There's a public restroom in the building. ✉ 648 Wharf St.,
Lahaina ☎ 808/661–0111 for the Lahaina Arts Society, 808/667–9175
for the Lahaina Town Action Committee ⊕ www.lahaina-arts.com
✆ Free ⊙ Daily 9–5.

Fodor'sChoice **Waiola Church and Wainee Cemetery.** Better known as Wainee Church and
★ immortalized in James Michener's Hawaii, the original building from the
early 1800s was destroyed once by fire and twice by fierce windstorms.
Repositioned and rebuilt in 1954, the church was renamed Waiola
("water of life") and has been standing proudly ever since. The adjacent cemetery was the region's first Christian cemetery and is the final
resting place of many of Hawaii's most important monarchs, including

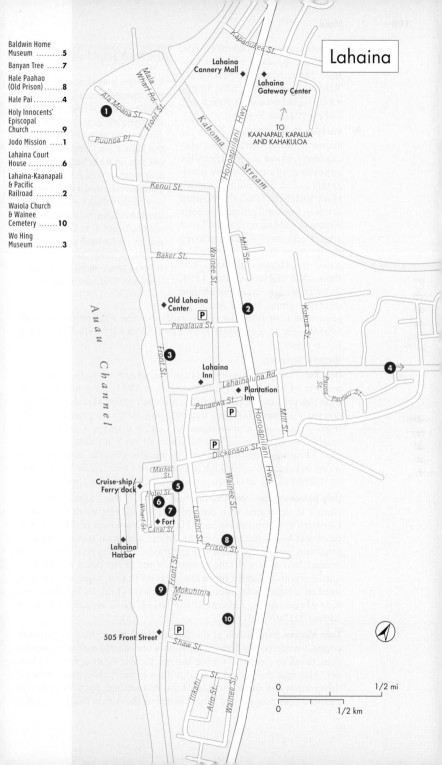

Lahaina

Lahaina
Cannery Mall

Lahaina
Gateway Center

TO
KAANAPALI, KAPALUA
AND KAHAKULOA

Kapanukea St.

Mala Wharf Rd.

Ala Moana St.

Front St.

Puunoa Pl.

Kahoma Stream

Honoapiilani Hwy.

Kenui St.

Wainee St.

Mill St.

Baker St.

Old Lahaina
Center

Papalaua St.

Front St.

Lahaina
Inn

Lahainaluna Rd.

Plantation
Inn

Panaewa St.

Kukua St.

Pauoa St.

Paunau St.

Honoapiilani Hwy.

Mill St.

Dickenson St.

Wainee St.

Market
St.

Cruise-ship/
Ferry dock

Hotel St.

Wharf St.

Fort

Canal St.

Luakini St.

Prison St.

Lahaina Harbor

Front St.

Mokuhinia
St.

505 Front Street

Shaw St.

Ilikahi St.

Aho St.

Wainee St.

A n a u

C h a n n e l

0   1/2 mi

0   1/2 km

Kamehameha the Great's wife, Queen Keopuolani, who was baptized during her final illness. ⊠ 535 Wainee St., Lahaina 🕾 808/661–4349 ⊕ www.waiolachurch.org. 🖾 Free ⊗ Daily 9–4.

ISLAND HOPPING

If you have a week or more on Maui, consider taking a day or two for a trip to Molokai or Lanai. Tour operators such as Trilogy offer day-trip packages to Lanai that include snorkeling and a van tour. Ferries to both Islands have room for your golf clubs and mountain bike. (Avoid ferry travel on a blustery day.) If you prefer to travel to Molokai or Lanai by air and don't mind 4- to 12-seaters, you can take a small air taxi. Book with Pacific Wings (see Air Travel in Travel Smart Hawaii). See Chapters 6 and 7 for more information.

★ **Wo Hing Museum.** Smack-dab in the center of Front Street, this eye-catching Chinese temple reflects the importance of early Chinese immigrants to Lahaina. Built by the Wo Hing Society in 1912, the museum contains beautiful artifacts, historic photos of old Lahaina, and a Taoist altar. Don't miss the films playing in the rustic theater next door—some of Thomas Edison's first films, shot in Hawaii circa 1898, show Hawaiian wranglers herding steer onto ships. Ask the docent for some star fruit from the tree outside, for the altar or for yourself. ⊠ 858 Front St., Lahaina 🕾 808/661–5553 🖾 $2 ⊗ Sat.–Thurs. 10–4, Fri. 1–8 pm.

WORTH NOTING

Hale Pai. Protestant missionaries established Lahainaluna Seminary as a center of learning and enlightenment in 1831. Six years later, they built this printing shop, where they and their young Hawaiian scholars created a written Hawaiian language and used it to produce a Bible, history texts, and a newspaper. An exhibit displays a replica of the original Rampage press and facsimiles of early printing. The oldest U.S. educational institution west of the Rockies, the seminary now serves as Lahaina's public high school. ⊠ 980 Lahainaluna Rd., Lahaina 🕾 808/661–3262 🖾 Donations accepted ⊗ Weekdays 10–4.

Holy Innocents' Episcopal Church. Built in 1927, this beautiful open-air church is decorated with paintings depicting Hawaiian versions of Christian symbols (including a Hawaiian Madonna and child), rare or extinct birds, and native plants. At the afternoon services, the congregation is typically dressed in traditional clothing from Samoa and Tonga. Anyone is welcome to slip into one of the pews, carved from native woods. Queen Liliuokalani, Hawaii's last reigning monarch, lived in a large grass house on this site as a child. ⊠ 561 Front St., near Mokuhina St., Lahaina 🕾 808/661–4202 ⊕ www.holyimaui.org 🖾 Free ⊗ Daily 8–5.

Jodo Mission. Established at the turn of the 20th century by Japanese contract workers, this Buddhist mission is one of Lahaina's most popular sites, thanks to its idyllic setting and spectacular views across the channel. Although the buildings are not open to the public, you can stroll the grounds and enjoy glimpses of the 90-foot-high pagoda, as well as a great 3.5-ton copper and bronze statue of the Amida Buddha (erected in 1968). If you're nearby at 8 any evening, listen for the temple bell to toll 11 times; each peal has a specific significance. ⊠ *12 Ala Moana St., near Lahaina Cannery Mall, Lahaina* ☎ *808/661–4304* ⛝ *Free.*

Lahaina Harbor. For centuries, Lahaina has drawn ships of all sizes to its calm harbor: King Kamehameha's conquering fleet of 800 carved *koa* canoes gave way to Chinese trading ships, Boston Whalers, United States Navy frigates, and, finally, a slew of pleasure craft. The picturesque harbor is the departure point for ferries headed to nearby Islands, sailing charters, deep-sea fishing trips, and snorkeling excursions. ⊠ *Wharf St., Lahaina* ⛝ *Free.*

☼ **Lahaina–Kaanapali and Pacific Railroad.** Affectionately called the Sugar Cane Train, Maui's only passenger train is an 1890s-vintage railway that once shuttled crops but now moves sightseers between Kaanapali and Lahaina. This quaint little attraction with its singing conductor is a big deal for Hawaii but probably not much of a thrill for those more accustomed to trains (though children like it no matter where they grew up). ⊠ *Honoapiilani Hwy. at Hinau St., 1½ blocks north of Lahainaluna Rd. stoplight, Lahaina* ☎ *808/661–0080,* ⊕ *www.sugarcanetrain.com* ⛝ *$22.95* ☼ *Weekdays 10:15–4.*

KAANAPALI AND VICINITY
Kaanapali is 4 miles north of Lahaina.

As you drive north from Lahaina, the first resort community you come to is Kaanapali, a substantial cluster of high-rise hotels framing a beautiful white-sand beach. This is part of West Maui's famous resort strip. A little farther up the road lie the condo-filled beach towns of Honokowai, Kahana, and Napili, followed by Kapalua.

GETTING HERE AND AROUND
Shuttles and taxis are available from Kahului and West Maui airports. Resorts offer free shuttles between properties and some hotels also provide free shuttles into Lahaina. In the Maui Bus system, the Napili Islander begins and ends at Whalers Village in Kaanapali and stops at most condos along the coastal road as far north as Napili Bay.

EXPLORING
Kaanapali. The theatrical look of Hawaii tourism—planned resort communities where luxury homes mix with high-rise hotels, fantasy swimming pools, and a theme-park landscape—all began right here in the 1960s, when clever marketers built this sunny shoreline into a playground for the world's vacationers. Three miles of uninterrupted white-sand beach and placid water form the front yard for this artificial utopia, with its 40 tennis courts and two championship golf courses.

In ancient times, this area was known for its bountiful fishing (especially lobster) and its seaside cliffs. Puu Kekaa, today incorrectly referred to as "Black Rock," was a *lele*, a place in ancient Hawaii from which souls leaped into the afterlife. (Today this site is near the Sheraton Maui.) But times changed and the sleepy fishing village was washed away by the wave of Hawaii's new economy: tourism. ⊠ *Kaanapali.*

Whalers Village. While the kids hit Honolua Surf Company, Mom can peruse shops such as Louis Vuitton, Sephora, and Coach, as well as art

MAUI SIGHTSEEING TOURS

Maui is really too big to see all in one day, so tour companies offer specialized tours, visiting either Haleakala or Hana and its environs. A tour of Haleakala and Upcountry is usually a half-day excursion and is offered in several versions by different companies for $60 and up. The trip often includes stops at Tedeschi Vineyards, Maui's only winery.

A Haleakala sunrise tour starts before dawn so that you can get to the top of the dormant volcano before the sun peeks over the horizon. Because trips offer hotel pickup around the island, many sunrise trips leave around 2:30 am.

A tour of Hana is almost always done in a van, since the winding Road to Hana just isn't built for bigger buses. Guides decide where you stop for photos. Tours run from $80 to $120.

The key is to ask how many stops you get and how many other passengers will be on board—otherwise you could end up on a packed bus, sightseeing through a window.

Most of the tour guides have been in the business for years, and some have taken classes to learn more about the culture and lore. They expect a tip ($1 per person at least), but they're just as cordial without one.

Polynesian Adventure Tours. This company uses large buses with floor-to-ceiling windows. The drivers are fun and, because they have extensive training, really know the island. Some Haleakala tours also include visits to Iao Valley and Lahaina. ☎ 808/877–4242, 800/622–3011 ⊕ www.polyad.com.

Roberts Hawaii Tours. This is one of the state's largest tour companies, and its staff can arrange tours with bilingual guides if requested ahead of time. Eleven-hour trips venture out to Kaupo, the wild area past Hana. ☎ 808/871–6226, 866/898–2519 ⊕ www.robertshawaii.com.

Temptation Tours. An affluent older crowd is the market for this company. Tours in plush eight-passenger limo-vans explore Haleakala and Hana, and range from $210 to $360 per person. The "Hana Sky-Trek" includes a return trip via helicopter. ☎ 808/877–8888, 800/817–1234 ⊕ www.temptationtours.com.

Tour da Food Maui. Maui resident Bonnie Friedman (a Fodor's contributor) guides small, customized ethnic food tours in Wailuku and Upcountry that include a couple of holes-in-the-wall some locals don't even know about. Tours leave Tuesday, Wednesday, and Thursday mornings and cost $140–$180 per person. ☎ 808/242–8383 ⊕ www.tourdafoodmaui.com.

galleries and several fine jewelry stores, at this casual, classy mall fronting Kaanapali Beach. Pizza and Häagen-Dazs ice cream are available in the center courtyard. At the beach entrance is a wonderful restaurant, Hula Grill. ⊠ 2435 Kaanapali Pkwy., Kaanapali ☎ 808/661–4567 ⊕ www.whalersvillage.com.

🕲 **Whalers Village Museum.** The skeleton of a massive whale leads the way to the Whale Center of the Pacific on the second floor of Whalers Village. Here you can learn about the hard life of whalers during the 19th-century Moby-Dick era. A replica of their living quarters, their tools and equipment, their letters and business papers, and other artifacts are on display. Many historical photos illustrate how the whalers chased and captured these giants of the deep and how they processsed their catch while out at sea. Several short films run continuously, including one about Hawaiian turtles and the folklore surrounding them. ⊠ *2435 Kaanapali Pkwy., Suite H16, Kaanapali* ☎ *808/661–5992* ⊕ *www. whalersvillage.com/museum.htm* 🖾 *Free* ⊙ *Daily 10–6.*

KAPALUA AND KAHAKULOA

Kapalua is 10 miles north of Kaanapali and 36 miles west of Kahului.

Upscale Kapalua is north of the Kaanapali resorts, past Napili. At the end of the Honoapiilani Highway, you'll find the remote village of Kahakuloa—quite a contrast to Kapalua.

GETTING HERE AND AROUND

Shuttles and taxis are available from Kahului and West Maui airports. The Ritz-Carlton, Kapalua, has a resort shuttle within the Kapalua Resort.

EXPLORING

Kahakuloa. The wild side of West Maui and untouched by progress, this tiny village at the north end of Honoapiilani Highway is a relic of pre-jet-travel Maui. Remote villages similar to Kahakuloa were once tucked away in several valleys in this area. Many residents still grow taro and live in the Old Hawaiian way. Driving this route is not for the faint of heart: the unimproved road weaves along coastal cliffs, and there are lots of blind curves; it's not wide enough for two cars to pass in places. Watch out for stray cattle, roosters, and falling rocks. True adventurers will find terrific snorkeling and swimming along this drive, as well as some good hiking trails. ⊠ *Kahakuloa.*

Kapalua. Beautiful and secluded, Kapalua is West Maui's northernmost, most exclusive resort community. First developed in the late 1970s, the resort now includes the Ritz-Carlton, posh residential complexes, two golf courses, and the surrounding fields of pineapple. The area's distinctive shops and freestanding restaurants cater to dedicated golfers, celebrities who want to be left alone, and some of the world's richest folks. In addition to golf, recreational activities include hiking and snorkeling. Mists regularly envelop the landscape of tall Cook pines and rolling fairways in Kapalua, which is cooler and quieter than its southern neighbors. The beaches here, including Kapalua and D.T. Fleming, are among Maui's finest. ⊠ *Kapalua.*

NEED A BREAK?

Honolua Store. In contrast to Kapalua's many high-end retailers, the old Honolua Store still plies the groceries, household wares, and fishing nets it did in plantation times. Hefty plates of *ono* (delicious) local foods are served at the deli until 3 pm. The plate lunches are the quintessential local meal and very popular. ⊠ *502 Office Rd., Kapalua* ☎ *808/665–9105.*

Ideal for snorkeling and swimming, sheltered Kapalua Bay Beach borders the luxurious Kapalua Resort.

THE SOUTH SHORE

Blessed by more than its fair share of sun, the southern shore of Haleakala was an undeveloped wilderness until the 1970s. Then the sun worshippers found it; now restaurants, condos, and luxury resorts line the coast from the world-class aquarium at Maalaea Harbor, through working-class Kihei, to upscale Wailea, a resort community rivaling those on West Maui. Farther south, the road disappears and unspoiled wilderness still has its way.

Because the South Shore includes so many fine beach choices, a trip here (if you're staying elsewhere on the island) is an all-day excursion—especially if you include a visit to the aquarium. Get active in the morning with exploring and snorkeling, then shower in a beach park, dress up a little, and enjoy the cool luxury of the Wailea resorts. At sunset, settle in for dinner at one of the area's many fine restaurants.

MAALAEA

13 miles south of Kahului; 6 miles west of Kihei; 14 miles southeast of Lahaina.

Maalaea, pronounced Mah-*ah*-lye-*ah*, is not much more than a few condos, an aquarium, and a wind-blasted harbor—but that's more than enough for some visitors. Humpback whales seem to think Maalaea is tops for meeting mates. Green sea turtles treat it like their own personal spa, regularly seeking appointments with cleaner wrasses in the harbor. Surfers revere this spot for "Freight Train," reportedly the world's fastest wave.

GETTING HERE AND AROUND

To reach Maalaea from Kahului Airport, take Route 380 to Route 30. The town is also a transfer point for many Maui Bus routes.

EXPLORING

Maalaea Small Boat Harbor. With only 89 slips and so many good reasons to take people out on the water, this active little harbor needs to be expanded. There was a plan to do so, but surfers argued that would have destroyed their surf breaks. In fact, the surf here is world-renowned. The elusive spot to the left of the harbor called Freight _rain rarely breaks, but when it does, it's said to be the fastest anywhere. ✉ *101 Maalaea Boat Harbor Rd., off Honoapiilani Hwy.*

Fodor's Choice
★
☻
Maui Ocean Center. You'll feel as though you're walking from the seashore down to the bottom of the reef at this aquarium, which focuses on creatures of the Pacific. Vibrant exhibits get you up close with turtles, rays, sharks, and the unusual creatures of the tide pools; allow two hours or so to explore it all. It's not an enormous facility, but it does provide an excellent (though pricey) introduction to the sea life that makes Hawaii special. The center is part of a complex of retail shops and restaurants overlooking the harbor. Enter from Honoapiilani Highway as it curves past Maalaea Harbor. ✉ *192 Maalaea Rd., off Honoapiilani Hwy.* ☎ *808/270–7000* ⊕ *www.mauioceancenter.com* ✆ *$25.50* ⊙ *Sept.–June, daily 9–5; July and Aug., daily 9–6.*

KIHEI

9 miles south of Kahului; 20 miles east of Lahaina.

Traffic lights and minimalls may not fit your notion of paradise, but Kihei offers dependably warm sun, excellent beaches, and a front-row seat to marine life of all sorts. Besides all the sun and sand, the town's relatively inexpensive condos and excellent restaurants make this a home base for many Maui visitors.

The county beach parks such as Kamaole I, II, and III have lawns, showers, and picnic tables. ■TIP→ Remember: Beach park or no beach park, the public has a right to the entire coastal strand but not to cross private property to get to it.

GETTING HERE AND AROUND

Kihei is a 20-minute ride from Kahului once you're past the heavy traffic on Dairy Road and get on the four-lane Mokulele Highway (Route 311).

EXPLORING

★
☻
Hawaiian Islands Humpback Whale National Marine Sanctuary. This nature center sits in prime humpback-viewing territory beside a restored ancient Hawaiian fishpond. Whether the whales are here or not, the education center is a great stop for youngsters curious to know more about underwater life. Interactive displays and informative naturalists will explain it all. Throughout the year, the center hosts intriguing activities including "Forty-Five-Ton Talks." The sanctuary itself includes virtually all the waters surrounding the archipelago. ✉ *726 S. Kihei Rd.* ☎ *808/879–2818, 800/831–4888* ⊕ *www.hawaiihumpbackwhale. noaa.gov* ✆ *Free* ⊙ *Weekdays 10–3.*

MAUI'S BEST FARMERS' MARKETS

Join the locals seeking out Maui-grown fresh produce and flowers.

Farmers' Market of Maui–Hono-kowai. From pineapples to corn, the produce at this West Maui open-air market is local and flavorful. Prices are good, too. Colorful tropical flowers and handcrafted items are also available. ⊠ *Honoapiilani Hwy., across from Honokowai Park, Hono-kowai* ☎ *808/669–7004* ⊙ *Mon., Wed., and Fri. 7 am–11 am.*

Farmers' Market of Maui–Kihei. Tropical flowers, tempting produce, and locally made preserves, baked goods, and crafts are among the bargains at this South Shore market. It's in the west end of Kihei, next to the ABC Store. ⊠ *61 S. Kihei Rd., Kihei* ☎ *808/875–0949* ⊙ *Weekdays 8 am–4 pm.*

Green Dragon Farmers' Market. In Central Maui, the island's only indoor farmers' market offers fresh flowers, organic produce, and Hawaiian arts and crafts. There's live entertainment and also food vendors selling baked goods, aromatic coffee, and even plate lunches. ⊠ *200 Waiehu Beach Rd., Wailuku* ☎ *808/333–2478* ⊙ *7 am–7 pm.*

Maui's Fresh Produce Farmers' Market. Local purveyors showcase their fruits, vegetables, orchids, and crafts in the central courtyard at the Queen Kaahumanu Shopping Center. ⊠ *Queen Kaahumanu Shopping Center, 275 W. Kaahumanu Ave., Kahului* ☎ *808/877–4325* ⊙ *Tues., Wed., Fri. 7 am–4 pm.*

Maui Swap Meet. Even locals get up early to go to the Maui Swap Meet for fresh produce and floral bouquets. Hundreds of stalls sell everything from quilts to didgeri-doos. Enter the parking lot from the traffic light at Kahului Beach Road. ⊠ *University of Hawaii, 310 Kaahu-manu Ave., Kahului* ☎ *808/244–3100* ⊕ *www.mauiexposition.com* ⊙ *Sat. 7 am–1 pm.*

Ono Organic Farms Farmers' Market. The family-owned Ono Farms offers certified organic produce at this roadside market at an old gas station. You may find such unusual delicacies as *rambutan* (resembling grapes), jackfruit (taste like bananas), and *lilikoi* (passion fruit). ⊠ *Hana Hwy., near Hasegawa General Store, Hana* ☎ *808/248–7779* ⊕ *www.onofarms.com* ⊙ *Daily 10–6.*

Upcountry Farmers' Market. Most of Maui's produce is grown Upcountry, which is why everything is fresh at this outdoor market at the football field parking lot in Kulamalu Town Center. Farmers offer fruits, vegetables, and flowers, as well as jellies and breads. Go early, as nearly everything sells out. ⊠ *Rte. 37, near Longs Drugs, Kula* ⊕ *www.upcountryfamersmarket.com* ⊙ *Sat. 7 am–10:30 am.*

★ **Kealia Pond National Wildlife Reserve.** Natural wetlands have become rare in the Islands, and the 700 acres of this reserve attract migratory birds and other wildlife. Long-legged stilts casually dip their beaks into the shallow waters as traffic shuttles by. Sharp-eyed birders may catch sight of migratory visitors such as osprey. Interpretive signs on the board-walk explain how the endangered hawksbill turtles return to the sandy dunes year after year. The boardwalk stretches along the coast by North Kihei Road; the main entrance to the reserve is on Mokulele Highway.

A visitor center with the reserve headquarters and exhibits provides an introduction to the area. ⊠ *Mokulele Hwy., mile marker 6* ☎ *808/875–1582* ⊕ *www.fws.gov/kealiapond* ⤴ *Free* ☉ *Weekdays 7:30–4.*

WAILEA AND FARTHER SOUTH

15 miles south of Kahului; at the southern border of Kihei.

Wailea, the South Shore's resort community, is slightly quieter and drier than its West Maui sister, Kaanapali. Many visitors cannot pick a favorite, so they stay at both. The luxury of the resorts (edging on the excessive) and the simple grandeur of the coastal views make the otherwise stark landscape an outstanding destination; take time to stroll the coastal beach path. A handful of perfect little beaches, all with public access, front the resorts.

The first two resorts were built here in the late 1970s. Soon a cluster of upscale properties sprung up, including the Four Seasons and the Fairmont Kea Lani. Check out the Grand Wailea Resort's chapel, which tells a Hawaiian love story in stained glass.

GETTING HERE AND AROUND

From Kahului Airport, take Route 311 (Mokulele Highway) to Route 31 (Piilani Highway) until it ends in Wailea. Shuttles and taxis are available at the airport. By bus, transfer at Maalaea to the Kihei Islander route of the Maui Bus to reach the Shops at Wailea. There's a resort shuttle, and a paved shore path goes between the hotels.

EXPLORING

Ahihi-Kinau Natural Area Reserve. South of Makena Beach, the road fades away into a vast territory of black-lava flows, the result of Haleakala's last eruption and now a place for exploration on land and below the water. Before it ends, the road passes through the Ahihi-Kinau Natural Area Reserve, an excellent place for morning snorkel adventures (*see Water Sports and Tours*). The area was so popular that it had to be temporarily closed in 2008. At this writing it was scheduled to reopen on August 1, 2012. Parts that remain open include the coastal area along Ahihi Bay, including the "Dumps" surf break. This area is the start of the Hoapili Trail, where you can hike through the remains of one of Maui's ancient villages. ■ TIP→ Bring water and a hat, as there are no public facilities and little shade, and tread carefully over this culturally important landscape. ⊠ *Just before end of Makena Alanui Rd.* ⊕ *hawaii.gov/dlnr.*

★ **Coastal Nature Trail.** A 1.5-mile-long paved beach walk allows you to stroll among Wailea's prettiest properties, restaurants, and rocky coves. The trail teems with joggers in the morning hours. The *makai*, or ocean side, is landscaped with exceptionally rare native plants. Look for the silvery *hinahina*, named after the Hawaiian moon goddess because of its color. In winter this is a great place to watch whales. The trail is also accessible from Polo Beach. ⊠ *Wailea Beach, Wailea Alanui Dr., south of Grand Wailea Resort entrance.*

Fodor'sChoice **Makena Beach State Park.** Although it's commonly known as Big Beach,
★ this part of the shoreline is correctly called Oneloa, meaning "long sand." That's exactly what it is—a huge stretch of heavenly golden powder without a house or hotel in sight. More than a decade ago, Maui citizens campaigned successfully to preserve this beloved beach

from development. It's still wild, lacking in modern amenities (such as plumbing) but frequented by dolphins and turtles; sunsets are glorious. At the end of the beach farthest from Wailea, skim boarders catch air. On the opposite end rises the beautiful hill called Puu Olai, a perfect cinder cone. A climb over the steep rocks at this end leads to Little Beach, which, although technically illegal, is clothing-optional. On Sunday, it's a mecca for drummers and island gypsies. On any day of the week watch out for the mean shore break—those crisp, aquamarine waves are responsible for more than one broken arm. ⊠ *End of Wailea Alanui Dr.* ⊕ *www.hawaiistateparks.org* ⬚ *Free* ☉ *Weekdays 6–6.*

The Shops at Wailea. Louis Vuitton, Tiffany & Co., and the sumptuous Cos Bar lure shoppers to this elegant mall with more than 50 shops. Honolulu Coffee brews perfect shots of espresso to fuel those "shop-'til-you-drop" types. The kids can buy island-themed T-shirts while their parents ponder vacation ownership upstairs. Tommy Bahama's, Ruth's Chris, and Longhi's are all good dining options. ⊠ *3750 Wailea Alanui Dr.* ☎ *808/891–6770* ⊕ *www.shopsatwailea.com.*

CENTRAL MAUI

Kahului, where you most likely landed when you arrived on Maui, is the industrial and commercial center of the island. West of Kahului is Wailuku, the county seat since 1950. It's the most charming town in Central Maui, with some good, inexpensive restaurants. Outside of these towns are attractions from museums and historic sites to gardens.

You can combine sightseeing in Central Maui with some shopping at the Queen Kaahumanu Center, Maui Mall, and Maui Marketplace. This is one of the best areas on the island to stock up on groceries and supplies, thanks to major retailers including Walmart, Kmart, and Costco. Grocery prices are much higher than on the mainland.

KAHULUI AND WAILUKU

3 miles west of Kahului Airport; 9 miles north of Kihei; 31 miles east of Kaanapali; 51 miles west of Hana.

The area around Kahului, now Maui's commercial hub, was developed in the early 1950s to meet the housing needs of the large sugarcane interests here, specifically those of Alexander & Baldwin. The company was tired of playing landlord to its many plantation workers and sold land to a developer who promised to create affordable housing. The scheme worked, and "Dream City," the first planned city in Hawaii, was born.

Wailuku is peaceful now—though it wasn't always so. Its name means "Water of Destruction," after the fateful battle in Iao Valley that pitted King Kamehameha the Great against Maui warriors. Wailuku was a politically important town until the sugar industry began to decline in the 1960s and tourism took hold. Businesses left the cradle of the West Maui Mountains and followed the new market (and tourists) to the shore. Wailuku houses the county government but has the feel of a town that's been asleep for several decades. The shops and offices now inhabiting Main Street's plantation-style buildings serve as reminders

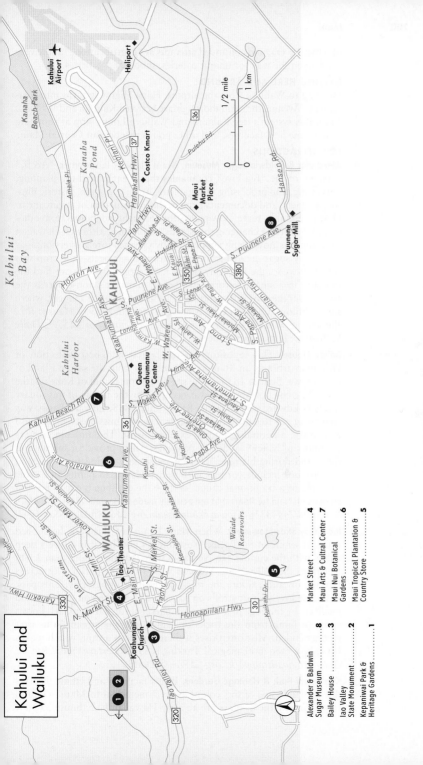

Kahului and Wailuku

Kahului Airport

Heliport

Kahana Beach Park

Kanaha Pond

Kahului Bay

Kahului Harbor

KAHULUI

WAILUKU

Queen Ka'ahumanu Center

Maui Market Place

Costco Kmart

Puunene Sugar Mill 8

Iao Theater 4

Ka'ahumanu Church 3

Waiale Reservoirs

Iao Stream

7

6

5

Amala Pl.

Hobron Ave.

Keolani Pl.

Haleakala Hwy.

Hana Hwy.

Dairy Rd.

Pulehu Rd.

Hansen Rd.

Ka'ahumanu Ave.

Kahului Beach Rd.

S. Wakea Ave.

Kanaloa Ave.

Ka'ahumanu Ave.

S. Puunene Ave.

S. Puunene Ave.

S. Kamehameha Ave.

Hina Ave.

Kaohu St.

Kaahu St.

Mahalani St.

Keonaloa St.

Kuikahi Dr.

Honoapiilani Hwy.

Kahekili Hwy.

Lower Main St.

N. Market St.

S. Market St.

E. Main St.

Mill St.

Elua St.

Liholio St.

Iao Valley Rd.

Vineyard Ave.

Wells St.

E. Wakea Ave.

Alamaha St.

Iao Pl.

Laie Pl.

E. Papa Pl.

Hukilike St.

Alani St.

E. Kauai St.

S. Lanai St.

Mlokai Ave.

S. Lono Ave.

W. Papa Ave.

Makaani St.

S. Papa Ave.

Kui Helani Hwy.

Mololikau Pl.

W. Kamehameha

Lonohana Ave.

W. Wakea Ave.

W. Kaahumanu Ave.

W. Lani Ave.

Oahu St.

Onehee Ave.

Kea St.

Waiaka St.

Dohi St.

Kaulana St.

Kuihi Ln.

Kukui Pl.

Olea St.

36

37

36

380

350

320

330

30

1/2 mile

1 km

of a bygone era, and continued attempts at "gentrification," at the very least, open the way for unique eateries, shops, and galleries.

GETTING HERE AND AROUND

Heading to Wailuku from the airport, Hana Highway turns into Kaahumanu Avenue, the main thoroughfare between Kahului and Wailuku. Maui Bus system's free Kahului and Wailuku Loops stop at shopping centers, medical facilities, and other points throughout Central Maui.

TOP ATTRACTIONS

★ **Alexander & Baldwin Sugar Museum.** Maui's largest landowner, "A&B," was one of the "Big Five" companies that spearheaded the planting, harvesting, and processing of sugarcane. At this museum, historic photos, artifacts, and documents explain the introduction of sugarcane to Hawaii. Exhibits reveal how plantations brought in laborers from other countries, forever changing the Islands' ethnic mix. Although Hawaiian cane sugar is now being supplanted by cheaper foreign versions—as well as by sugar derived from inexpensive sugar beets—the crop was for many years the mainstay of the local economy. You can find the museum in a small, restored plantation manager's house across the street from the post office and the still-operating sugar refinery, where smoke billows up when cane is being processed. ⊠ *3957 Hansen Rd., Puunene* ☎ *808/871–8058* ⊕ *www.sugarmuseum.com* ⊡ *$7* ☉ *Daily 9:30–4:30; last admission at 4.*

Fodor's Choice **Bailey House.** This repository of the largest and best collection of
★ Hawaiian artifacts on Maui includes objects from the sacred island of Kahoolawe. Built in 1833 on the site of the compound of Kahekili (the last ruling chief of Maui), it was occupied by the family of missionary teachers Edward and Caroline Bailey until 1888. Edward Bailey was something of a Renaissance man: beyond being a missionary, he was also a surveyor, a naturalist, and an excellent artist. The museum displays a number of Bailey's landscape paintings, which provide a snapshot of the island during his time. There is missionary-period furniture, and the grounds include gardens with native Hawaiian plants and a fine example of a traditional canoe. ■TIP→ The gift shop is one of the best sources on Maui for items that are actually made in Hawaii. ⊠ *2375A Main St.* ☎ *808/244–3326* ⊕ *www.mauimuseum.org* ⊡ *$7* ☉ *Mon.–Sat. 10–4.*

Fodor's Choice **Iao Valley State Monument.** When Mark Twain saw this park, he dubbed
★ it the Yosemite of the Pacific. Yosemite it's not, but it is a lovely deep valley with the curious **Iao Needle**, a spire that rises more than 2,000 feet from the valley floor. You can walk from the parking lot across Iao Stream and explore the thick, junglelike topography. This park has some lovely short strolls on paved paths, where you can stop and meditate by the edge of a stream or marvel at the native plants. Locals come to jump from the rocks or bridge into the stream—this isn't recommended. Mist often rises if there has been a rain, which makes being here even more magical. Parking is $5. ⊠ *Western end of Rte. 32* ⊕ *www.hawaiistateparks.org* ⊡ *Free* ☉ *Daily 7–7.*

☾ **Kepaniwai Park & Heritage Gardens.** Picnic facilities and ethnic displays dot the landscape of this county park, a memorial to Maui's cultural roots. Among the displays are an early-Hawaiian *hale* (house), a New

England–style saltbox, a Portuguese-style villa with gardens, and dwellings from such other cultures as China and the Philippines. Next door, the **Hawaii Nature Center** has excellent interactive exhibits and hikes easy enough for children.

The peacefulness here belies the history of the area. In 1790, King Kamehameha the Great from the Island of Hawaii waged a successful and bloody battle against Kahekili, the son of Maui's chief. An earlier battle at the site had pitted Kahekili himself against an older Hawaii Island chief, Kalaniopuu. Kahekili prevailed, but the carnage was so great that the nearby stream became known as Wailuku (water of destruction), and the place where fallen warriors choked the stream's flow was called Kepaniwai (damming of the waters). ⊠ *870 Iao Valley Rd.* ⊟ *Free* ⊘ *Daily 7–7.*

Market Street. An idiosyncratic assortment of shops makes Wailuku's Market Street a delightful place for a stroll. Brown-Kobayashi and the Bird of Paradise Unique Antiques are the best shops for interesting collectibles and furnishings. Wailuku Coffee Company houses works by local artists and occasionally offers live entertainment in the evening. On the first Friday of every month Market Street closes to traffic from 5:30 to 9 for Wailuku's First Friday celebration. The fun includes street vendors, live entertainment, and food. ⊠ *Wailuku.*

★ **Maui Arts & Cultural Center (MACC).** This hub of all highbrow arts features everything from hip-hop and reggae performances to Hawaiian slack-key guitar shows to international dance and circus troupes—you name it. On selected evenings, the MACC hosts movie selections from the Maui Film Festival. The complex includes the 350-seat McCoy Theater, the 1,200-seat Castle Theater, a 4,000-seat amphitheater for outdoor concerts, and a courtyard café for preshow dining and drinks. For upcoming events, check the *Maui News.* ⊠ *1 Cameron Way, Kahului* ☎ *808/242–7469* ⊕ *www.mauiarts.org.*

WORTH NOTING

☺ **Maui Nui Botanical Gardens.** Polynesian species are cultivated at this fascinating 7-acre garden, including Hawaiian bananas, local varieties of sweet potatoes and sugarcane, native poppies, hibiscus, and *anapanapa,* a plant that makes a natural shampoo when rubbed between your hands. Reserve ahead for the ethnobotany tours that are offered twice a week. Self-guided tour booklets cost $4. ⊠ *150 Kanaloa Ave., Kahului* ☎ *808/249–2798* ⊕ *www.mnbg.org* ⊟ *Free* ⊘ *Mon.–Sat. 8–4.*

☺ **Maui Tropical Plantation & Country Store.** When Maui's cash crop declined in importance, a group of visionaries opened an agricultural theme park on the site of this former sugarcane field. The 60-acre preserve offers a 30-minute tram ride with an informative narration covering the growing process and plant types. Children will enjoy such hands-on activities as coconut husking. Also here are an art gallery, a restaurant, and a store specializing in "Made in Maui" products. ⊠ *1670 Honoapiilani Hwy., Waikapu* ☎ *808/244–7643* ⊕ *www.mauitropicalplantation.com* ⊟ *Free; $15 for tram ride* ⊘ *Daily 9–5.*

Hawaiian Aquarium at the Maui Ocean Center: "We sat and just watched this sight. It was so calming."
–Kevin J. Klitzke, Fodors.com photo contest participant.

UPCOUNTRY MAUI

The west-facing upper slopes of Haleakala are locally called "Upcountry." This region is responsible for much of Hawaii's produce—lettuce, tomatoes, strawberries, sweet Maui onions, and much, much more. You'll notice cactus thickets mingled with purple jacaranda, wild hibiscus, and towering eucalyptus trees. Keep an eye out for *pueo,* Hawaii's native owl, which hunts these fields during daylight hours.

Upcountry is also fertile ranch land; cowboys still work the fields of the historic 20,000-acre Ulupalakua Ranch and the 32,000-acre Haleakala Ranch. ■TIP→ This is a great area in which to take an agricultural tour and learn more about the island's bounty. Lavender, vegetables, cheese, and wine are among your choices.

A drive to Upcountry Maui from Wailea (South Shore) or Kaanapali (West Maui) can be an all-day outing if you take the time to visit Tedeschi Vineyards and the tiny but entertaining town of Makawao. You may want to cut these side trips short and combine your Upcountry tour with a visit to Haleakala National Park. It's a Maui must-see. If you leave early enough to catch the sunrise from the summit of Haleakala, you'll have plenty of time to explore the mountain, have lunch in Kula or at Ulupalakua Ranch, and end your day with dinner in Makawao.

THE KULA HIGHWAY

15 miles east of Kahului; 44 miles east of Kaanapali; 28 miles east of Wailea.

Kula: Most Mauians say it with a hint of a sigh. Why? It's just that much closer to heaven. Explore it for yourself on some of the area's agricultural tours.

On the broad shoulder of Haleakala, this is blessed country. From the Kula Highway most of Central Maui is visible—from the lava-scarred plains of Kenaio to the cruise-ship-lighted waters of Kahului Harbor. Beyond the central valley's sugarcane fields, the plunging profile of the West Maui Mountains can be seen in its entirety, wreathed in ethereal mist. If this sounds too dramatic a description, you haven't been here yet. These views, coveted by many, continue to drive real-estate prices further skyward. Luckily, you can still have them for free—just pull over on the roadside and drink them in.

GETTING HERE AND AROUND

From Kahului, take Route 37 (Haleakala Highway), which runs into Route 377 (Kula Highway). Upper and Lower Kula Highways are both numbered 377 but join each other at two points.

EXPLORING

★ **Alii Kula Lavender.** Reserve a spot for tea or lunch at this lavender farm with a falcon's view: It's *the* relaxing remedy for those suffering from too much sun, shopping, or golf. Knowledgeable guides lead tours through winding paths of therapeutic lavender varieties, protea, succulents, and rare Maui wormwood. The gift shop abounds with many locally made lavender products such as brownies, moisturizing lotions, and fragrant sachets. ⊠ *1100 Waipoli Rd.* ☎ *808/878–3004* ⊕ *www.aklmaui.com* ☑ *Free; $12 for walking tours* ☉ *Daily 9–4.*

Fodor'sChoice **Haleakala National Park.** *See Golf, Hiking, and Outdoor Activities for*
★ *information about this park, one of Maui's top attractions.*

Keokea. More of a friendly gesture than a town, this tiny outpost is the last bit of civilization before Kula Highway becomes a winding backside road. A coffee tree pushes through the sunny deck at Grandma's Coffee Shop, the morning watering hole for Maui's cowboys who work at Ulupalakua or Kaupo ranch. Keokea Gallery next door sells some of the most original artwork on the island. ■ TIP→ **The only restroom for miles is across the street at the public park, and the view makes stretching your legs worth it.**

Ⓒ **Surfing Goat Dairy.** It takes goats to make goat cheese, and they've got plenty of both at this 42-acre farm. Tours range from "casual" to "grand," and any of them delight children. If you have the time, the "Evening Chores and Milking Tour" is educational and fun. The owners make more than two dozen kinds of goat cheese, from the plain, creamy "Udderly Delicious" to more exotic varieties that include other, sometimes tropical, ingredients. All are available in the dairy store, along with gift baskets and even goat-milk soaps. ⊠ *3651 Omaopio Rd.* ☎ *808/878–2870* ⊕ *www.surfinggoatdairy.com* ☑ *$10* ☉ *Mon.–Sat. 9–5, Sun. 9–2.*

Tedeschi Vineyards and Winery. You can tour Maui's only winery and its historic grounds, the former Rose Ranch, and sample such wines as Rose Ranch Cuvee, Ulupalakua Red, and a pleasant white wine called Upcountry Gold. The top seller, naturally, is the pineapple wine, Maui Blanc. The tasting room is a cottage built in the late 1800s for the frequent visits of King Kalakaua. The cottage also contains the **Ulupalakua Ranch History Room**, which tells colorful stories of the ranch's owners, the *paniolo* (Hawaiian cowboy) tradition that developed here, and Maui's polo teams. The old Ranch Store may look like a museum, but in fact it's an excellent pit stop. ■ TIP➔ The elk burgers are fantastic. ✉ *Kula Hwy.* ☎ *808/878–6058* ⊕ *www.mauiwine.com* ⊠ *Free* ☼ *Daily 10–5; tours at 10:30 and 1:30.*

MAKAWAO
10 miles east of Kahului; 7 miles southeast of Paia.

At the intersection of Baldwin and Makawao avenues, this once-tiny town has managed to hang on to its country charm (and eccentricity) as it has grown in popularity. Its good selection of specialized shops makes Makawao a fun place to spend some time.

The district was originally settled by Portuguese and Japanese immigrants who came to Maui to work the sugar plantations and then moved Upcountry to establish small farms, ranches, and stores. Descendants now work the neighboring Haleakala and Ulupalakua ranches. Every July 4 the *paniolo* set comes out in force for the Makawao Rodeo.

The crossroads of town—lined with shops and down-home eateries—reflects a growing population of people who came here just because they liked it. For those seeking greenery rather than beachside accommodations, there are secluded B&Bs around the town.

GETTING HERE AND AROUND
To get to Makawao by car, take Route 37 (Haleakala Highway) to Pukalanai, then turn left on Makawao Avenue. You can also take Route 36 (Hana Highway) to Paia and make a right onto Baldwin Avenue. Either way, you'll arrive in the heart of Makawao.

EXPLORING
Hui Noeau Visual Arts Center. "The Hui" is the grande dame of Maui's visual arts scene, and its exhibits are always satisfying. The lovely grounds might as well be a botanical garden, and the main building, just outside the town of Makawao on the old Baldwin estate, is an elegant two-story Mediterranean-style villa designed in the 1920s by the defining Hawaii architect C.W. Dickey. ✉ *2841 Baldwin Ave.* ☎ *808/572–6560* ⊕ *www.huinoeau.com* ⊠ *Free* ☼ *Mon.–Sat. 10–4.*

QUICK BITES

Komoda Store and Bakery. One of Makawao's most famous landmarks is Komoda Store and Bakery, a classic mom-and-pop shop that has changed little in three-quarters of a century. You can get a delicious cream puff if you arrive early enough. They make hundreds but sell out each day. ✉ *3674 Baldwin Ave.* ☎ *808/572–7261.*

Continued on page 214

ROAD TO HANA

As you round the impossibly tight turn, a one-lane bridge comes into view. Beneath its worn surface, a lush forested gulch plummets toward the coast. The sound of rushing water fills the air, compelling you to search the over-grown hillside for waterfalls. This is the Road to Hana, a 55-mile journey into the unspoiled heart of Maui. Tracing a centuries-old path, the road begins as a well-paved highway in Kahului and ends in the tiny town of Hana on the island's rain-gouged windward side.

★ Fodor's Choice Despite the twists and turns, the road to Hana is not as frightening as it may sound. You're bound to be a little nervous approaching it the first time; but afterwards you'll wonder if somebody out there is making it sound tough just to keep out the hordes. The challenging part of the road takes only an hour and a half, but you'll want to stop often and let the driver enjoy the view, too. Don't expect a booming city when you get to Hana. Its lure is its quiet timelessness. As the adage says, the journey *is* the destination.

During high season, the road to Hana tends to clog—well, not clog exactly, but develop little choo-choo trains of cars, with everyone in a line of six or a dozen driving as slowly as the first car. The solution: leave early (dawn) and return late (dusk). And if you find yourself playing the role of locomotive, pull over and let the other drivers pass. You can also let someone else take the turns for you—several companies offer van tours, which make stops all along the way (*see Maui Sightseeing Tours box in this chapter*).

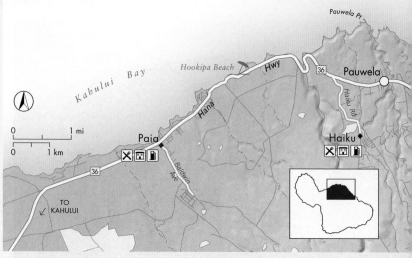

DRIVING THE ROAD TO HANA

Begin your journey in Paia, the little town on Maui's North Shore. Be sure to fill up your gas tank here. There are no gas stations along Hana Highway, and the station in Hana closes by 6 PM. You should also pick up a picnic lunch. Lunch and snack choices along the way are limited to rustic fruit stands.

About 10 miles past Paia, at the bottom of Kaupakalua Road, the roadside mileposts begin measuring the 36 miles to Hana town. The road's trademark noodling starts about 3 miles after that. Once the road gets twisty, remember that many residents make this trip frequently. You'll recognize them because they're the ones zipping around every curve. They've seen this so many times before they don't care to linger. Pull over to let them pass.

All along this stretch of road, waterfalls are abundant. Roll down your windows. Breathe in the scent of guava and ginger. You can almost hear the bamboo growing. There are plenty of places to pull completely off the road and park safely. Do this often, since the road's curves make driving without a break difficult. ■TIP➔ If you're prone to carsickness, be sure to take medication before you start this drive. You may also want to stop periodically.

❶ **Twin Falls.** Keep an eye out for the fruit stand just after mile marker 2. Stop here and treat yourself to some fresh sugarcane juice. If you're feeling adventurous, follow the path beyond the stand to the paradisiacal waterfalls known as Twin Falls. Once a rough trail plastered with "no trespassing" signs, this treasured spot is now easily accessible. In fact, there's usually a mass of cars surrounding the fruit stand at the trail head. Several deep, emerald pools sparkle beneath waterfalls and offer excellent swimming and photo opportunities.

While this is still private property, the "no trespassing" signs have been replaced by colorfully painted arrows pointing away from residences and toward the falls. ■TIP➔ Bring water shoes for crossing streams along the way. Swim at your own risk and beware: flash floods here and in all East Maui stream areas can be sudden and deadly. Check the weather before you go.

❷ **Huelo and Kailua.** Dry off and drive on past the sleepy country villages of Huelo (near mile marker 5) and Kailua (near mile marker 6). The little farm town of Huelo has two quaint churches. If you linger awhile, you could meet local residents and learn about a rural lifestyle you might not expect to find on the Islands.

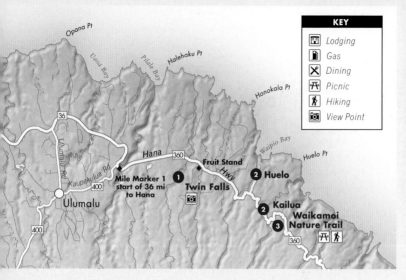

KEY

🏨	Lodging
⛽	Gas
✗	Dining
⛱	Picnic
🚶	Hiking
📷	View Point

Opana Pt

Uaoa Bay

Pilale Bay

Halehaku Pt

Honokala Pt

Waipio Bay

Huelo Pt

36

Uhumalu Rd

Kaupakulua Rd

400

Ulumalu

400

Hana 360

Fruit Stand

Mile Marker 1 start of 36 mi to Hana

1 Twin Falls

Hwy

2 Huelo

2 Kailua

Waikamoi Nature Trail

3 ⛱ 🚶

360

The same can be said for nearby Kailua, home to Alexander & Baldwin's irrigation employees.

3 Waikamoi Nature Trail. Between mile markers 9 and 10, the Waikamoi Nature Trail sign beckons you to stretch your car-weary limbs. A short (if muddy) trail leads through tall eucalyptus trees to a coastal vantage point with a picnic table and barbecue. Signage reminds visitors QUIET, TREES AT WORK and BAMBOO PICKING PERMIT REQUIRED. Awapuhi, or Hawaiian shampoo ginger, sends up fragrant shoots along the trail.

4 Puohokamoa Stream. About a mile farther, near mile marker 11, you can stop at the bridge over Puohokamoa Stream. This is one of many bridges you cross en route from Paia to Hana. It spans pools and waterfalls. Picnic tables are available, but there are no restrooms.

5 Kaumahina State Wayside Park. If you'd rather stretch your legs and use a flush toilet, continue another mile to Kaumahina State Wayside Park (at mile marker 12). The park has a picnic area, restrooms, and a lovely overlook to the Keanae Peninsula. The park is open from 6 AM to 6 PM and admission is free. ☎ 808/984–8109.

🕐 **TIMING TIPS**

With short stops, the drive from Paia to Hana should take you between two and three hours one-way. Lunching in Hana, hiking, and swimming can easily turn the round-trip into a full-day outing, especially if you continue past Hana to Oheo Gulch and Kipahulu. If you go that far, you might consider continuing around the "back side" for the return trip. The scenery is completely different and you'll end up in beautiful Upcountry Maui. Since there's so much scenery to take in, we recommend staying overnight in Hana. It's worth taking time to enjoy the waterfalls and beaches without being in a hurry. Try to plan your trip for a day that promises fair, sunny weather—though the drive can be even more beautiful when it's raining.

Keanae Peninsula

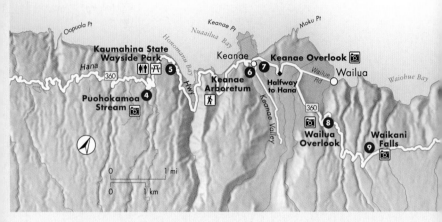

Near mile marker 14, before Keanae, you find yourself driving along a cliff side down into deep, lush Honomanu Bay, an enormous valley, with a rocky black-sand beach.

The Honomanu Valley was carved by erosion during Haleakala's first dormant period. At the canyon's head there are 3,000-foot cliffs and a 1,000-foot waterfall, but don't try to reach them. There's not much of a trail, and what does exist is practically impassable.

❻ Keanae Arboretum. Another 4 miles brings you to mile marker 17 and the Keanae Arboretum where you can add to your botanical education or enjoy a challenging hike into a forest. Signs help you learn the names of the many plants and trees now considered native to Hawaii. The meandering Piinaau Stream adds a graceful touch to the arboretum and provides a swimming pond.

You can take a fairly rigorous hike from the arboretum if you can find the trail at one side of the large taro patch. Be careful not to lose the trail once you're on it. A lovely forest waits at the end of the 25-minute hike. Access to the arboretum is free.

You can explore the lovely Keanae Peninsula by driving on the unmarked road shortly past the arboretum. It will take you to a small settlement that is a piece of traditional

Hawaii, and beyond that to a beach park with crashing surf.

❼ Keanae Overlook. A half mile farther down Hana Highway you can stop at the Keanae Overlook. From this observation point, you can take in the quilt-like effect the taro patches create below. The people of Keanae are working hard to revive this Hawaiian agricultural art and the traditional cultural values that the crop represents. The ocean provides a dramatic backdrop for the patches. In the other direction there are awesome views of Haleakala through the foliage.

■ TIP→ **Coming up is the halfway mark to Hana. If you've had enough scenery, this is as good a time as any to turn around and head back to civilization.**

Taro patch viewed from Hana Highway

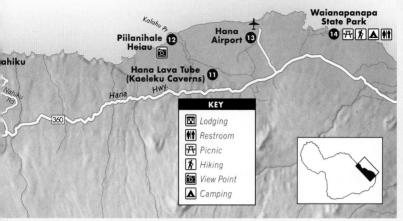

8 Wailua Overlook. Shortly before mile marker 19, on the mountain side, you find Wailua Overlook. From the parking lot you can see Wailua Canyon, but you have to walk up steps to get a view of Wailua Village. The landmark in Wailua Village is a church made of coral, built in 1860. Once called St. Gabriel's Catholic Church, the current Our Lady of Fatima Shrine has an interesting legend surrounding it. As the story goes, a storm washed enough coral up onto shore to build the church and then took any extra coral back to sea.

Just after mile marker 19, there is another overlook on the ocean side.

9 Waikani Falls. Past mile marker 21, you hit the best falls on the entire drive to Hana, Waikani Falls. Though not necessarily bigger or taller than the other falls, these are the most dramatic falls you'll find in East Maui. That's partly because the water is not diverted for sugar irrigation; the taro farmers in Wailua need all the runoff. This is a particularly good spot for photos.

10 Nahiku. At about mile marker 25 you see a road that heads down toward the ocean and the village of Nahiku. In ancient times this was a busy settlement with hundreds of residents. Now only about 80 people live in Nahiku, mostly native Hawaiians

and some back-to-the-land types. A rubber grower planted trees here in the early 1900s, but the experiment didn't work out, and Nahiku was essentially abandoned. The road ends at the sea in a pretty landing. This is the rainiest, densest part of the East Maui rain forest.

Coffee Break. Back on the Hana Highway, about 10 minutes before Hana town, you can stop for—of all things—espresso. The tiny, colorful **Nahiku Ti Gallery and Coffee Shop** (between mile markers 27 and 28) sells local coffee, dried fruits and candies, and delicious (if pricey) banana bread. Sometimes the barbecue is fired up and you can try baked breadfruit (an island favorite nearly impossible to find elsewhere). The Ti Gallery sells Hawaiian crafts.

11 Hana Lava Tube (Kaeleku Caverns). If you're interested in exploring underground, turn left onto Ulaino Road, just after mile marker 31, and follow the signs to the Hana Lava Tube. Visitors get a brief orientation before heading into Maui's largest lava tube, which is accentuated with colorful underworld formations.

You can take a self-guided, 30- to 40-minute tour daily, from 10:30 to 4 PM, for $11.95 per person. LED flashlights are provided. Children under five are free with a paid adult. ☎ 808/248–7308 ⊕ *www.mauicave.com*

Hana

TO KAHULUI &
HANA AIRPORT

360

Waikoloa

Rd

Kings Road Trail

Nanualele Point

Ukkea Rd

Waikaloa Beach

Kauiki St

Hana Hwy

Alau Pl

Keanini Dr

Hana Bay

Hana Cultural
Center Museum
🔄 16

Keawa Pl

*Popolana &
Pokuolae Rocks*

**Travaasa
Hana Hotel** 17

Ukea Rd

Hauoli Rd

*Kauiki
Head*

Fagan
Memorial Cross ◆

Hasegawa
General Store ◆

360

TO
OHEO GULCH

Red Sand Beach ☂

0   .4 mi

0   .4 km

★ **⑫ Piilanihale Heiau.** Continue on Ulaino Road, which doubles back for a mile, loses its pavement, and even crosses a stream before reaching Kahanu Garden and Piilanihale Heiau, the largest pre-contact monument in Hawaii. This temple platform was built for a great 16th-century Maui king named Piilani and his heirs. This king also supervised the construction of a 10-foot-wide road that completely encircled the island. (That's why his name is part of most of Maui's highway titles.)

Hawaiian families continue to maintain and protect this sacred site as they have for centuries, and they have not been eager to turn it into a tourist attraction. However, they now offer a brochure so you can tour the property yourself for $10 per person. Tours include the 122-acre **Kahanu Garden**, a federally funded research center focusing on the ethno-botany of the Pacific (best for those seriously interested in plants). The heiau and garden are open weekdays from 10 AM to 2 PM. For a guided tour on Saturday, reserve through www.ntbg.org. ☎ *808/248–8912*

⑬ Hana Airport. Back on the Hana Highway, and less than ½ miles farther, is the turnoff for the Hana Airport. Think of Amelia Earhart. Think of Waldo Pepper.

If these picket-fence runways don't turn your thoughts to the derring-do of barnstorming pilots, you haven't seen enough old movies. Only the smallest planes can land and depart here, and when none of them happens to be around, the lonely wind sock is the only evidence that this is a working airfield. ☎ *808/248–8471*

★ **⑭ Waianapanapa State Park.** Just beyond mile marker 32 you reach Waianapanapa State Park, home to one of Maui's only volcanic-sand beaches and some freshwater caves for adventurous swimmers to explore. The park is right on the ocean, and it's a lovely spot in which to picnic, camp, hike, or swim. To the left you'll find the black-sand beach, picnic tables, and cave pools. To the right you'll find cabins and an ancient trail which snakes along the ocean past blowholes, sea arches, and archaeological sites.

The tide pools here turn red several times a year. Scientists say it's explained by the arrival of small shrimp, but legend claims the color represents the blood of Popoalaea, a princess said to have been murdered in one of the caves by her husband, Chief Kaakea. Whichever you choose to believe, the drama of the landscape itself—black sand, green beach vines, azure water—is bound to leave a lasting impression.

With a permit you can stay in state-run cabins here for less than $99 a night—the price varies depending on the number of people—but reserve early online. They often book up a year in advance. ☎ *808/984–8109* ⊕ *www.hawaiistateparks.org*

🕙 **Hana.** By now the relaxed pace of life that Hana residents enjoy should have you in its grasp, so you won't be discouraged to learn that "town" is little more than a gas station, a post office, a grocery, and the Hasegawa General Store (stuffed with all kinds of oddities and practical items).

Hana, in many ways, is the heart of Maui. It's one of the few places where the slow pulse of island life is still strong. The town centers on its lovely circular bay, dominated on the right-hand shore by a puu called Kauiki. A short trail here leads to a cave, the birthplace of Queen Kaahumanu. This area is rich in Hawaiian history and legend. Two miles beyond town another puu presides over a loop road that passes two of Hana's best beaches—Koki and Hamoa. The hill is called Ka Iwi O Pele (Pele's Bone). Offshore here, at tiny Alau Island, the demigod Maui supposedly fished up the Hawaiian islands.

Sugar was once the mainstay of Hana's economy; the last plantation shut down in the '40s. In 1946 rancher Paul Fagan built the **Hotel Hana-Maui (now Travaasa Hana)** and stocked the surrounding pastureland with cattle. The cross you see on the hill above the hotel was put there in memory of Fagan. Now it's the ranch and hotel that put food on most tables, though many families still farm, fish, and hunt as in the old days. Houses around town are decorated with glass balls and nets, which indicate a fisherman's lodging.

🕡 **Hana Cultural Center Museum.** If you're determined to spend some time and money in Hana after the long drive, a single turn off the highway onto Uakea Street, in the center of town, will take you to the Hana Cultural Center Museum. Besides operating a well-stocked gift shop, it displays artifacts, quilts, a replica of an authentic *kauhale* (an ancient Hawaiian living complex, with thatch huts and food gardens), and other Hawaiiana. The knowledgeable staff can explain it all to you. The center is open weekdays 10 to 4. ✉ *4974 Uakea Rd.* ☎ *808/248–8622* ✉ *$3* ⊕ *www. hanaculturalcenter.org*

🕖 **Travaasa Hana Hotel.** With its surrounding ranch, the upscale hotel is the mainstay around this beautifully rustic property. The library houses interesting, authentic local Hawaiian artifacts. In the evening, while local musicians play in the lobby bar their

Hala Trees, Waianapanapa State Park

Hāna

friends jump up to dance hula. The Sea Ranch cottages across the road, built to look like authentic plantation housing from the outside, are also part of the hotel. *See Where to Stay for more information.*

Don't be suprised if the mile markers suddenly start descending as you head past Hana. Technically, Hana Highway (Route 360) ends at the Hana Bay. The road that continues south is Piilani Highway (Route 31)—though everyone still refers to it as the Hana Highway.

18 Hamoa Beach. Just outside Hana, take a left on Haneoo Loop to explore lovely Hamoa. Indulge in swimming or body-surfing at this beautiful salt-and-pepper beach. Picnic tables, restrooms, and showers beneath the idyllic shade of coconut trees offer a more than comfortable rest stop.

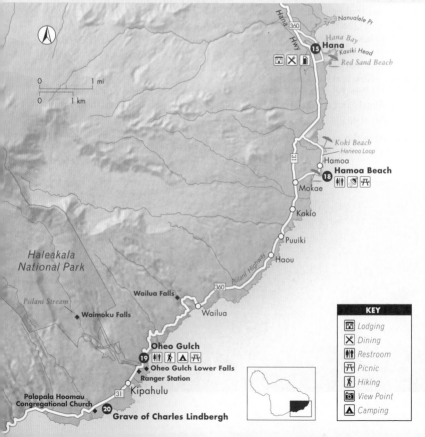

The road leading to Hamoa also takes you to **Koki Beach**, where you can watch the Hana surfers mastering the swells and strong currents, and the seabirds darting over **Alau**, the palm-fringed islet off the coast. The swimming is safer at Hamoa.

★ ⑲ **Oheo Gulch.** Ten miles past town, at mile marker 42, you'll find the pools at Oheo Gulch. One branch of Haleakala National Park runs down the mountain from the crater and reaches the sea here, where a basalt-lined stream cascades from one pool to the next. Some tour guides still call this area Seven Sacred Pools, but in truth there are more than seven, and they've never been considered sacred. You can park here—for a $10 fee—and walk to the lowest pools for a cool swim. The place gets crowded, since most people who drive the Hana Highway make this their last stop.

If you enjoy hiking, go up the stream on the 2-mile hike to **Waimoku Falls.** The trail crosses a spectacular gorge, then turns into a boardwalk that takes you through an amazing bamboo forest. You can pitch a tent in the grassy campground down by the sea. *See Hiking in Golf, Hiking, and Outdoor Activities.*

⑳ **Grave of Charles Lindbergh.** Many people travel the mile past Oheo Gulch to see the Grave of Charles Lindbergh. You see a ruined sugar mill with a big chimney on the right side of the road and then, on the left, a rutted track leading to Palapala Hoomau Congregational Church. The simple one-room church sits on a bluff over the sea, with the small graveyard on the ocean side. The world-renowned aviator chose to be buried here because he and his wife, writer Anne Morrow Lindbergh, spent a lot of time living in the area. He was buried here in 1974. Since this is a churchyard, be considerate and leave everything exactly as you found it. Next to the churchyard on the ocean side is a small county park, good for a picnic.

Kaupo Road. The road to Hana continues all the way around Haleakala's "back side" through Ulupalakua Ranch and into

TROPICAL DELIGHTS

The drive to Hana wouldn't be as enchanting without a stop or two at one of the countless fruit (and banana bread) and flower stands by the highway. Every 1/2 mile or so a thatched hut tempts passersby with apple bananas (a smaller firmer variety), lilikoi (passion fruit), avocados, or starfruit just plucked from the tree. Leave a few dollars in the can for the folks who live off the land. Huge bouquets of tropical flowers are available for a handful of change, and some farms will ship.

Kula. The desert-like topography, with its grand vistas, is unlike anything else on the island, but the road itself is bad, sometimes impassable in winter, and parts of it are unpaved. Car-rental agencies call it off-limits to their passenger cars and there is no emergency assistance available. The danger and dust from increasing numbers of speeding jeep drivers are making life tough for the residents, especially in Kaupo, with its 4 miles of unpaved road. The small communities around East Maui cling tenuously to the old ways. Please keep that in mind if you do pass this way. If you can't resist the adventure, try to make the drive just before sunset. The light slanting across the mountain is incredible. At night, giant potholes, owls, and loose cattle can make for some difficult driving.

In the past few years bridges and parts of the road have been upgraded. Please note, however, that the road remains rough.

THE NORTH SHORE

Blasted by winter swells and wind, Maui's North Shore draws water-sports thrill seekers from around the world. But there's much more to this area of Maui than coastline. Inland, a lush, waterfall-fed Garden of Eden beckons. In forested pockets, wealthy hermits have carved out a little piece of paradise for themselves.

North Shore action centers around the colorful town of Paia and the windsurfing mecca, Hookipa Beach. It's a far cry from the more developed resort areas of West Maui and the South Shore. Paia is also a starting point for one of the most popular excursions in Maui, the Road to Hana *(see Road to Hana)*. Waterfalls, phenomenal views of the coast and ocean, and lush rain forest are all part of the spectacular 55-mile drive into East Maui.

PAIA

9 miles east of Kahului; 4 miles west of Haiku.

★ At the intersection of Hana Highway and Baldwin Avenue, Paia has eclectic boutiques that supply everything from high fashion to hemp-oil candles. Some of Maui's best shops for surf trunks, Brazilian bikinis, and other beachwear are here. Restaurants provide excellent people-watching and an array of dining and takeout options from a sushi bar to a fish market. The abundance is helpful because Paia is the last place to snack before the pilgrimage to Hana and the first stop for the famished on the return trip.

This little town on Maui's North Shore was once a sugarcane enclave, with a mill, plantation camps, and shops. The old sugar mill finally closed, but the town continues to thrive. In the 1970s, Paia became a hippie town as dropouts headed for Maui to open boutiques, galleries, and unusual eateries. In the 1980s windsurfers—many of them European—discovered nearby Hookipa Beach and brought an international flavor to Paia. Today, this historic town is hip and happening.

GETTING HERE AND AROUND

Route 36 (Hana Highway) runs directly though Paia; 4 miles later follow the sign to Haiku, a short detour off the highway. You can take the Maui Bus from the airport and Queen Kaahumanu Shopping Center in Kahului to Paia and on to Haiku.

EXPLORING

Fodor's Choice
★ **Hookipa Beach.** There's no better place on this or any other island to watch the world's finest windsurfers in action. The surfers know the five different surf breaks here by name. Unless it's a rare day without wind or waves, you're sure to get a show. ■TIP→ It's not safe to park on the shoulder. Use the ample parking lot at the county park entrance. ⊠ *Rte. 36.*

QUICK BITES

Charley's Restaurant. Charley's Restaurant is an easygoing saloon-type hangout where locals gather in the bar to watch football games on big-screen TVs. Breakfasts are big and delicious. ⊠ *142 Hana Hwy.* ☎ *808/579-9453* ⊕ *www.charleysmaui.com.*

Mana Foods. The North Shore's natural-foods store, Mana Foods has an inspired deli with wholesome hot and cold items. ⌧ *49 Baldwin Ave.* ☎ *808/579–8078* ⊕ *www.manafoodsmaui.com.*

Paia Fishmarket Restaurant. The long line at Paia Fishmarket Restaurant attests to the popularity of the tasty fresh-fish sandwiches, plates, and tacos. ⌧ *2A Baldwin Ave.* ☎ *808/579–8030* ⊕ *www.paiafishmarket.com.*

HAIKU

13 miles east of Kahului; 4 miles east of Paia.

At one time this area vibrated around a couple of enormous pineapple canneries. Both have been transformed into rustic warehouse malls. Because of the post office next door, Old Haiku Cannery earned the title of town center. Here you can try eateries offering everything from plate lunches to vegetarian dishes to juicy burgers and full dinners. Follow windy Haiku Road to Pauwela Cannery, the other defunct factory-turned-hangout. Don't fret if you get lost. This jungle hillside is a maze of flower-decked roads that seem to double back upon themselves. Up Kokomo Road is a large *puu* (volcanic cinder cone) capped with a grove of columnar pines, and the 4th Marine Division Memorial Park. During World War II, American GIs trained here for battles on Iwo Jima and Saipan. Locals nicknamed the cinder cone "Giggle Hill" because it was a popular hangout for Maui women and their favorite servicemen.

GETTING HERE AND AROUND

Haiku is a short detour off Hana Highway (Route 36) just past Hookipa Beach Park on the way to Hana. Haiku Road turns into Kokomo Road at the post office.

BEACHES

Updated by Heidi Pool

Of all the beaches in the Hawaiian Islands, Maui's are some of the most diverse. You can find the pristine, palm-lined shores you expect with waters as clear and inviting as sea green glass, but you'll also discover rich red- and black-sand beaches, craggy cliffs with surging whitecaps, and year-round sunsets that quiet the soul. As on the other Islands, all Maui's beaches are public—but that doesn't mean it's not possible to find a secluded cove where you can truly get away from the world.

The island's leeward shores (the South Shore and West Maui) have the calmest, sunniest beaches. Hit the beach early, when the aquamarine waters are as accommodating as bathwater. In summer, afternoon winds can be a sandblasting force, which can chase even the most dedicated sun worshippers away. From November through May, the South and West beaches are also great spots to watch the parade of whales that spend the winter and early spring in Maui's waters.

Windward shores (the North Shore and East Maui) are for the more adventurous. Beaches face the open ocean (rather than other Islands) and tend to be rockier and more prone to powerful swells. This is

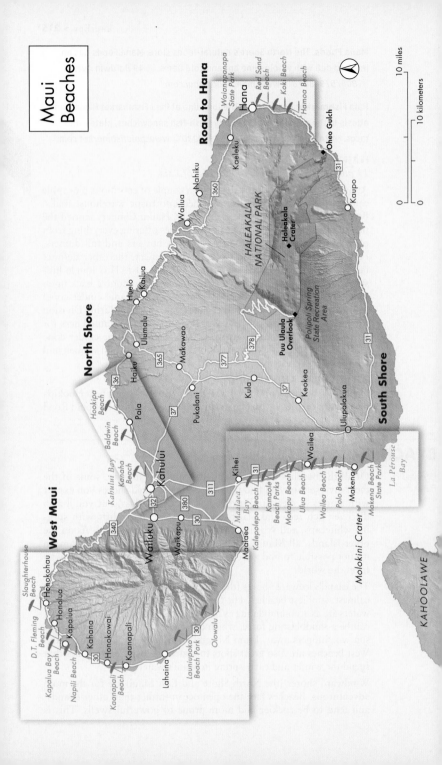

Maui Beaches

Road to Hana

North Shore

West Maui

South Shore

HALEAKALA NATIONAL PARK

KAHOOLAWE

Haleakala Crater

Polipoli Spring State Recreation Area

Puu Ulaula Overlook

Molokini Crater

10 miles

10 kilometers

Hana

Waianapanapa State Park
Red Sand Beach
Koki Beach
Hamoa Beach
Oheo Gulch

Kaeleku

Nahiku

Wailua

Kaupo

Huelo
Kailua
Ulumalu
Makawao
Haiku
Paia
Makena

Hookipa Beach
Baldwin Beach
Kanaha Beach

Kahului
Kahului Bay

Kula
Keokea
Ulupalakua

Pukalani

Wailuku
Waikapu
Waiehu

Kihei
Maalaea Bay
Maalaea

Wailea

La Pérouse Bay

Kalepolepo Beach
Kamaole Beach Parks
Mokapu Beach
Ulua Beach
Wailea Beach
Polo Beach
Makena Beach
Makena Beach State Park

Slaughterhouse Beach
D.T. Fleming Beach
Honokohau
Honolua
Kapalua
Kapalua Bay Beach
Napili Beach
Kahana
Honokowai
Kaanapali
Kaanapali Beach
Lahaina
Launiupoko Beach Park
Olowalu

30
31
32
36
37
340
360
365
377
378
380
311

particularly true in winter, when the North Shore becomes a playground for experienced big-wave riders and windsurfers. Don't let this keep you away completely, however. Some of the island's best beaches are those remote slivers of volcanic sand found on the wild windward shore.

WEST MAUI

West Maui beaches are legendary for their glittering aquamarine waters banked by long stretches of golden sand. Reef fronts much of the western shore, making the underwater panorama something to behold. Parking can be challenging in resort areas. Look for the blue "Shoreline Access" signs to find limited parking and a public path to the beach. Watch out for kiawe thorns when you park off-road: they can puncture tires—and feet.

There are a dozen roadside beaches to choose from on Route 30; these are the ones we like best.

> **DON'T FORGET**
>
> All of the island's beaches are free and open to the public—even those that grace the front yards of fancy hotels—so you can make yourself at home on any one of them. Some of the prettiest beaches are often hidden by buildings; look for the blue "Beach Access" signs that indicate public rights-of-way through condominiums, resorts, and other private properties.

The beaches listed here start in the north at Kapalua and head south past Kaanapali and Lahaina.

"Slaughterhouse" (Mokuleia) Beach. The island's northernmost beach is part of the Honolua-Mokuleia Marine Life Conservation District. "Slaughterhouse" is the surfers' nickname for what is officially Mokuleia. Weather permitting, this is a great place for bodysurfing and sunbathing. Concrete steps and a green railing help you get down the cliff to the sand. The next bay over, Honolua, has no beach but offers one of the best surf breaks in Hawaii. Competitions are often held there; telltale signs are cars pulled off the road and parked in the pineapple field. **Amenities:** none. **Best for:** sunset; surfing. ⊠ *Rte. 30, mile marker 32 past Kapalua, Kapalua.*

D.T. Fleming Beach. Because the current can be quite strong, this charming, mile-long sandy cove is better for sunbathing than for swimming or water sports. Still, it's one of the island's most popular beaches. It's a perfect spot to watch the spectacular Maui sunsets, and there are picnic tables and grills. Part of the beach runs along the front of the Ritz-Carlton Kapalua—a good place to grab a cocktail and enjoy the view. **Amenities:** lifeguard, parking (no fee), showers, toilets. **Best for:** sunset; walking. ⊠ *Rte. 30, 1 mile north of Kapalua, Kapalua.*

Kapalua Bay Beach. Over the years Kapalua has been recognized as one of the world's best beaches, and for good reason: it fronts a pristine bay good for snorkeling, swimming, and general lazing. Just north of Napili Bay, this lovely, sheltered shore often remains calm late into the afternoon, although currents may be strong offshore. Snorkeling is easy here and there are lots of colorful reef fish. This area is quite popular and is bordered by the Kapalua Resort, so don't expect to have the beach to yourself. Walk

through the tunnel from the parking lot at the end of Kapalua Place to get here. **Amenities:** parking (no fee); showers; toilets. **Best for:** snorkeling; sunset; swimming. ⊠ *Rte. 30, turn onto Kapalua Pl., Kapalua.*

BEACHES KEY

🕴	*Restroom*
🚿	*Showers*
🏄	*Surfing*
◎	*Snorkel/Scuba*
👫	*Good for kids*
Ⓟ	*Parking*

Fodor's Choice
★
☺

Napili Beach. Surrounded by sleepy condos, this round bay is a turtle-filled pool lined with a sparkling white crescent of sand. Sunbathers love this beach, which is also a terrific sunset spot. The shore break is steep but gentle, so it's great for body boarding and bodysurfing. It's easy to keep an eye on kids here as the entire bay is visible from any point in the water. The beach is right outside the Napili Kai Beach Club, a popular little resort for honeymooners, only a few miles south of Kapalua. **Amenities:** showers; toilets. **Best for:** sunset; surfing; swimming. ⊠ *5900 Lower Honoapiilani Hwy., look for Napili Pl. or Hui Dr., Napili.*

★
☺

Kaanapali Beach. Stretching from the Sheraton Maui at its northernmost end to the Hyatt Regency Maui at its southern tip, Kaanapali Beach is lined with resorts, condominiums, restaurants, and shops. If you're looking for quiet and seclusion, this is not the beach for you. But if you want lots of action, spread out your towel here. The center section in front of Whalers Village, also called "Dig Me Beach," is one of Maui's best people-watching spots: folks in catamarans, windsurfers, and stand-up paddleboarders head out from here while the beautiful people take in the scenery. A cement pathway weaves along the length of this 3-mile-long beach, leading from one astounding resort to the next.

The drop-off from Kaanapali's soft, sugary sand is steep, but waves hit the shore with barely a rippling slap. The area at the northernmost end (in front of the Sheraton Maui), known as Kekaa, was, in ancient Hawaii, a *lele,* or jumping-off place for spirits. It's easy to get into the water from the beach to enjoy the prime snorkeling among the lava rock outcroppings.

Throughout the resort, blue Shoreline Access signs point the way to a few free-parking stalls and public rights-of-way to the beach. Kaanapali Resort public beach parking can be found between the Hyatt and the Marriott, between the Marriott and the Kaanapali Alii, next to Whalers Village, and at the Sheraton. You can park for a fee at most of the large hotels and at Whalers Village. The merchants in the shopping village will validate your parking ticket if you make a purchase. **Amenities:** parking (no fee); showers; toilets. **Best for:** snorkeling; sunset; swimming; walking. ⊠ *Honoapiilani Hwy., follow any of 3 Kaanapali exits, Kaanapali.*

The sandy crescent of Napili Beach on West Maui is a lovely place to wait for sunset.

Launiupoko Beach Park. Launiupoko is the beach park of all beach parks: both a surf break and a beach, it offers a little something for everyone with its inviting stretch of lawn, soft white sand, and gentle waves. The shoreline reef creates a protected wading pool, perfect for small children. Outside the reef, beginner surfers will find good longboard rides. From the long sliver of beach (good for walking), you can enjoy superb views of Neighbor Islands, and, landside, of deep valleys cutting through the West Maui Mountains. Because of its endless sunshine and serenity—not to mention amenities including picnic tables and grills—Launiupoko draws a crowd on the weekends, but there's space for everyone (and overflow parking across the street). **Amenities:** parking (no fee); showers; toilets. **Best for:** sunset; surfing; swimming; walking. ⊠ *Rte. 30, just south of Lahaina at mile marker 18, Lahaina.*

Olowalu. More an offshore snorkel spot than a beach, Olowalu is also a great place to watch for turtles and whales in season. The beach is literally a pullover from the road, which can make for some unwelcome noise if you're looking for quiet. The entrance can be rocky (reef shoes help), but if you've got your snorkel gear it's a 200-yard swim to an extensive and diverse reef. Shoreline visibility can vary depending on the swell and time of day; late morning is best. Except for during a south swell, the waters are usually calm. A half mile north of mile marker 14 you can find the rocky surf break, also called Olowalu. Snorkeling here is along pathways that wind among coral heads. Note: This is a local hangout and can be unfriendly at times. **Amenities:** None. **Best for:** snorkeling. ⊠ *Rte. 30, south of Olowalu General Store at mile marker 14, Olowalu.*

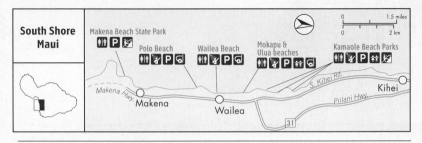

THE SOUTH SHORE

Sandy beach fronts nearly the entire southern coastline of Maui, from Kihei at the northern end to Makena at the southern tip. The farther south, the better the beaches get. Kihei has excellent beach parks in town, with white sand, showers, restrooms, picnic tables, barbecues, and paved parking lots. Good snorkeling can be found along the beaches' rocky borders. As good as Kihei is, Wailea is better. Wailea's beaches are cleaner, the views more impressive; the area's resorts line the beachfront here. You can take a mile-long walk on a shore path from Ulua to near Polo Beach. Look for blue "Public Shoreline Access" signs for parking along the main thoroughfare, Wailea Alanui. ⚠ **Break-ins have been reported at many beach lots, so don't take valuables.** As you head to Makena, the terrain gets wilder; bring lunch, water, and sunscreen.

The following South Shore beaches are listed from North Kihei southeast to Makena.

Kalama Park. This 36-acre beach park with plenty of shade is great for families and sports lovers. With its extensive lawns and sports fields, the park welcomes volleyball, baseball, and tennis players, and even has a playground and skateboard park and a roller hockey rink. Stocked with grills and picnic pavilions, it's a recreational mecca. The beach itself is all but nonexistent, but swimming is fair—though you must brave the rocky steps down to the water. If you aren't completely comfortable with this entrance, stick to the burgers and bocce ball. **Amenities:** parking (no fee); showers; toilets. **Best for:** partiers. ⊠ *S. Kihei Rd., across from Kihei Kalama Village, Kihei.*

☺ **Kamaole I, II, and III.** Three steps from South Kihei Road are three golden stretches of sand separated by outcroppings of dark, jagged, lava rocks. You can walk the length of all three beaches if you're willing to get your feet wet. The northernmost of the trio, Kamaole I (across from the ABC Store, in case you forget your sunscreen), offers perfect swimming with a sandy bottom a long way out and an active volleyball court. If you're one of those people who like your beach sans sand, there's also a great lawn for you to spread out on at the south end of the beach. Kamaole II is nearly identical, minus the lawn, and there is no parking lot here. The last beach, the one with all the people on it, is Kamaole III, perfect for throwing a disk or throwing down a blanket. This is a great family beach, complete with a playground, barbecues, kite flying, and, frequently, rented inflatable castles—a must at birthday parties for cool kids.

Locally—and quite disrespectfully, according to native Hawaiians—known as "Kam" I, II, and III, all three beaches have great swimming and lifeguards. In the morning the water can be as still as a lap pool. Kamaole III offers terrific breaks for beginning bodysurfers. **Amenities:** lifeguards; parking (no fee); showers; toilets. **Best for:** surfing; swimming; walking. ⊠ *S. Kihei Rd., between Alii Ke Alanui and the Hale Kamaole Condominums, Kihei.*

Keawakapu Beach. Who wouldn't love Keawakapu, with its long stretch of golden sand, near-perfect swimming, and views of Puu Olai cinder cone and Kahoolawe? It's great fun to walk or jog this beach south into Wailea, as it's lined with over-the-top residences. It's best here in the morning—the winds pick up in the afternoon (beware of sandstorms). Keawakapu has three entrances: one is at the Mana Kai Maui resort (look for the blue "Shoreline Access" sign); the second is directly across from the parking lot on Kilohana Street (the entrance is unmarked); and the third is at the dead end of Kihei Road. Toilets are portable. **Amenities:** parking (no fee); showers; toilets. **Best for:** sunset; swimming; walking. ⊠ *S. Kihei Rd., near Kilohana St., Kihei.*

Mokapu and Ulua. Look for a little road and public parking lot near the Wailea Marriott if you are heading to Mokapu and Ulua beaches. Though there are no lifeguards, families love this place. Reef formations create tons of tide pools for kids to explore, and the beaches are protected from major swells. Snorkeling is excellent at Ulua, the beach to the left of the entrance. Mokapu, to the right, tends to be less crowded. The Renaissance Wailea fronting this beach is closed, and construction of a new property (an Andaz resort, from Hyatt), is currently underway. **Amenities:** parking (free); showers; toilets. **Best for:** snorkeling; swimming. ⊠ *Wailea Alanui Dr., north of Wailea Marriott resort, Wailea.*

Wailea Beach. A road just after the Grand Wailea Resort takes you to Wailea Beach, a wide, sandy stretch with snorkeling, swimming, and, if you're a guest of the Four Seasons Resort, Evian spritzes. If you're not a guest at the Grand Wailea or Four Seasons, the private umbrellas and chaise lounges can be a little annoying, but any complaint is more than made up for by the calm, unclouded waters and soft, white sand. From the parking lot, walk to the right to get to the main beach; to the left is another, smaller section that fronts the Four Seasons. There are picnic tables and grills away from the beach. **Amenities:** parking (no fee); showers; toilets. **Best for:** snorkeling; swimming. ⊠ *Wailea Alanui Dr., south of Grand Wailea Resort entrance, Wailea.*

Polo Beach. Small and secluded, this crescent fronts the Fairmont Kea Lani resort. Swimming and snorkeling are great here, and it's a good place to whale-watch. As at Wailea Beach, private umbrellas and chaise lounges occupy prime sandy real estate, but there's plenty of room for you and your towel, and even a nice grass picnic area (it's a considerable distance from the beach itself). The pathway connecting the two beaches is a great spot to jog or to leisurely take in awesome views of nearby Molokini and Kahoolawe. Rare native plants grow along the ocean, or *makai*, side of the path; the honey-sweet-smelling one is *naio,*

BEST BEACHES

Ah, Maui's beaches: it's hard to single out just a few because the island's strands are so varied. Here are some favorites for different interests from around the island.

BEST FOR FAMILIES
Baldwin Beach, the North Shore. The long, shallow, calm end closest to Kahului is safe even for toddlers—with adult supervision, of course.

Kamaole III, the South Shore. Sand, gentle surf, a playground, volleyball net, and barbecues all add up to great family fun.

Napili Beach, West Maui. Kids will love the turtles that nosh on the *limu* (seaweed) growing on the lava rocks. This intimate, crescent-shape beach offers sunbathing, snorkeling, swimming, bodysurfing, and startling sunsets.

BEST OFFSHORE SNORKELING
Olowalu, West Maui. The water remains shallow far offshore, and there's plenty to see.

Ulua, the South Shore. It's beautiful, and the kids can enjoy the tide pools while the adults experience the excellent snorkeling.

BEST SURFING
Hookipa, the North Shore. This is the place to see great surfers and windsurfers: it's not for beginners or for swimmers, but Hookipa is great for experienced wave riders and also for anyone who wants to take in the North Shore scene.

Honolua Bay, West Maui. One bay over from Slaughterhouse (Mokuleia) Beach north of Kapalua, you can find one of the best surf breaks in Hawaii.

BEST SUNSETS
Kapalua Bay, West Maui. The atmosphere here is as stunning as the sunset.

Keawakapu, the South Shore. Most active beachgoers enjoy this gorgeous spot before midafternoon when the wind picks up, so it's never crowded at sunset.

BEST FOR SEEING AND BEING SEEN
Kaanapali Beach, West Maui. Backed by resorts, condos, and restaurants, this is not the beach for solitude. But the sand is soft, the waters are gentle, and the action varies from good snorkeling at Black Rock (Kekaa) to people-watching in front of Whalers Village—not for nothing is this section called "Dig Me Beach."

Wailea Beach, the South Shore. At this beach fronting the ultra-luxurious Four Seasons and Grand Wailea resorts, you never know who might be "hiding" in that private cabana.

BEST SETTING
Makena Beach State Park (Big Beach), South Shore. Don't forget the camera for this beauty, a state park away from the Wailea resorts. Finding it is worth the effort—a long, wide stretch of golden sand, and translucent offshore water. Use caution for swimming because the steep, onshore break can get big.

Waianapanapa State Park, East Maui. This rustic black-sand beach will capture your heart—it's framed by lava cliffs and backed by bright green beach *naupaka* bushes. Ocean currents can be strong, so enjoy the views and cool off in one of two freshwater pools.

or false sandalwood. **Amenities:** parking (no fee); showers; toilets. **Best for:** snorkeling; swimming. ⊠ *Kaukahi St., south of Fairmont Kea Lani resort entrance, Wailea.*

Fodor'sChoice ★ **Makena Beach State Park (Big Beach).** Locals successfully fought to give Makena—one of Hawaii's most breathtaking beaches—state-park protection; this stretch of deep golden sand abutting sparkling aqua water is 3,000 feet long and 100 feet wide. It's often mistakenly referred to as "Big Beach," but natives prefer its Hawaiian name, Oneloa. Makena is never crowded, no matter how many cars cram into the lots. The water is fine for swimming, but use caution. ■TIP→ **The shore drop-off is steep, and swells can get deceptively big.** Despite the infamous "Makena cloud," a blanket that rolls in during the early afternoon and obscures the sun, it rarely rains here. For a dramatic view of the beach, climb Puu Olai, the steep cinder cone near the first entrance you pass if you're driving south. Continue over the cinder cone's side to discover "Little Beach"—clothing optional by popular practice, although this is technically illegal. On Sunday, free spirits of all kinds crowd Little Beach's tiny shoreline for a drumming circle and bonfire. Little Beach has the island's best bodysurfing (no pun intended). Skim boarders catch air at Makena's third entrance, which is a little tricky to find (it's just a dirt path with street parking only). There are picnic tables and portable toilets. **Amenities:** lifeguards; parking (no fee); toilets. **Best for:** surfing; swimming; walking. ⊠ *Off Wailea Alanui Dr., Makena.*

THE NORTH SHORE

Many of the folks you see jaywalking in Paia sold everything they owned to come to Maui and live a beach bum's life. Beach culture abounds on the North Shore. But these folks aren't sunbathers; they're big-wave riders, windsurfers, or kiteboarders. The North Shore is their challenging sports arena. Beaches here face the open ocean and tend to be rougher and windier than beaches elsewhere on Maui—but don't let that scare you off. On calm days, the reef-speckled waters are truly beautiful and offer a quieter and less commercial beachgoing experience than the leeward shore.

Beaches below are listed from Kahului (near the airport) eastward to Hookipa.

Kanaha Beach. Windsurfers, kiteboarders, joggers, and picnicking families like this long, golden strip of sand bordered by a wide grassy area with lots of shade. The winds pick up in the early afternoon, making for the best kiteboarding and windsurfing conditions—if you know what you're doing, that is. The best spot for watching kiteboarders is at the far left end of the beach. Drive through Kahului Airport and make a right onto the car-rental road (Koeheke); turn right onto Amala Place and take any left (there are three entrances) into Kanaha. **Amenities:** lifeguard; parking (free); showers; toilets. **Best for:** walking; windsurfing. ⊠ *Amala Pl., Kahului.*

★ ☺ **Baldwin Beach.** A local favorite, right off the highway and just west of Paia town, Baldwin Beach is a big stretch of comfortable white sand. It's a good place to stretch out, jog, or swim, though the waves can sometimes be choppy and the undertow strong. Don't be afraid of those

DID YOU KNOW?

Maui's beaches are famous for their variety. Those on the North Shore are generally rockier and get larger swells than beaches in other areas, making them great for wind-surfing. When the water is calm, the reef-dotted waters are lovely. Beachgoing is often quieter here than in the busy resort areas.

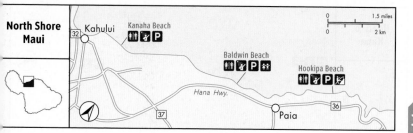

3

big brown blobs floating beneath the surface; they're just pieces of seaweed awash in the surf. You can find shade along the beach beneath the ironwood trees, or in the large pavilion, a spot regularly used for local parties and community events. There are picnic tables and grills at the beach as well.

The long, shallow pool at the Kahului end of the beach is known as "Baby Beach." Separated from the surf by a flat reef wall, this is where ocean-loving families bring their kids (and sometimes puppies) to practice a few laps. Take a relaxing stroll along the water's edge from one end of Baldwin Beach to Baby Beach and enjoy the scenery. The view of the West Maui Mountains is hauntingly beautiful from here. **Amenities:** lifeguard; parking (free); showers; toilets. **Best for:** swimming; walking. ⊠ *Hana Hwy., 1 mile west of Baldwin Ave., Paia.*

★ **Hookipa Beach.** If you want to see some of the world's finest windsurfers in action, hit this beach along the Hana Highway. The sport was largely developed right at Hookipa and has become an art to many and a career to some. This beach is also one of Maui's hottest surfing spots, with waves that can be as high as 20 feet. Hookipa is not a good swimming beach, nor the place to learn windsurfing, but it's great for hanging out and watching the pros. There are picnic tables and grills. Bust out your telephoto lens at the cliff-side lookout to capture the aerial acrobatics of board sailors and kiteboarders. **Amenities:** lifeguard; showers; parking (free). **Best for:** surfing; windsurfing. ⊠ *Rte. 36, 2 miles east of Paia, Paia.*

ROAD TO HANA

East Maui's and Hana's beaches will literally stop you in your tracks—they're that beautiful. Black and red sands stand out against pewter skies and lush tropical foliage creating picture-perfect scenes, which seem too breathtaking to be real. Rough conditions often preclude swimming, but that doesn't mean you can't explore the shoreline.

Beaches below are listed in order from the west end of Hana town eastward.

Fodor's Choice **Waianapanapa State Park.** Small but rarely crowded, this beach will
★ remain in your memory long after visiting. Fingers of white foam rush onto a black volcanic-pebble beach fringed with green beach vines and palms. Swimming here is both relaxing and invigorating: Strong currents bump smooth stones up against your ankles while seabirds flit

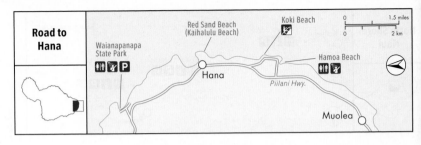

above a black, jagged sea arch draped with vines. There are picnic tables and grills. At the edge of the parking lot, a sign tells you the sad story of a doomed Hawaiian princess. Stairs lead through a tunnel of interlocking Polynesian *hau* (a native tree) branches to an icy cave pool—the secret hiding place of the ancient princess. ■ TIP→ **You can swim in this pool, but be wary of mosquitoes.** In the other direction, a dramatic 3-mile coastal path continues beyond the campground, past sea arches, blowholes, and cultural sites all the way to Hana town. Grassy tent sites and rustic cabins that accommodate up to six people are available by reservation only; call ahead for information. **Amenities:** parking (free); showers; toilets. **Best for:** walking. ⊠ *Hana Hwy., near mile marker 32* ☎ *808/984–8109.*

★ **Red Sand Beach (Kaihalulu Beach).** Kaihalulu Beach, better known as "Red Sand Beach," is unmatched in its raw and remote beauty. It's not simple to find, but when you round the last corner of the trail and are confronted with the sight of it, your jaw is bound to drop. Earthy red cliffs tower above the deep maroon–sand beach, and swimmers bob about in a turquoise blue lagoon formed by volcanic boulders just offshore. The experience is like floating in a giant natural bathtub. It's worth spending a night in Hana to make sure you can get here early and have time to enjoy it before anyone else shows up.

Keep in mind that getting here is not easy, and you have to pass through private property along the way—do so at your own risk. You need to tread carefully up and around Kauiki (the red-cinder hill); the cliff-side cinder path is slippery and constantly eroding. Hiking is not recommended in shoes without traction, or in bad weather. By popular practice, clothing on the beach is optional. The beach is at the end of Uakea Road past the baseball field. Park near the community center and walk through the grass lot to the trail below the cemetery. **Amenities:** None. **Best for:** swimming. ⊠ *Uakea Rd.*

Koki Beach. You can tell from the trucks parked alongside the road that this is a favorite local surf spot. ■ TIP→ **Watch conditions before swimming or bodysurfing; riptides can be mean.** Look for awesome views of the rugged coastline and a sea arch on the left end. *Iwa,* or white-throated frigate birds, dart like pterodactyls over Alau islet offshore. **Amenities:** None. **Best for:** surfing. ⊠ *Haneoo Loop Rd., 2 miles south of Hana town.*

Hamoa Beach. Why did James Michener describe this stretch of salt-and-pepper sand as the most "South Pacific" beach he'd come across, even though it's in the North Pacific? Maybe it was the perfect half-moon shape, speckled with the shade of palm trees. Perhaps he was intrigued by the jutting black coastline, often outlined by rain showers out at sea, or the pervasive lack of hurry he felt once settled in here. Whatever it was, many still feel the lure. The beach can be crowded but nonetheless relaxing. Expect to see a few chaise lounges and a guest-only picnic area set up by the Travaasa Hana hotel. Early mornings and late afternoons are best for swimming. At times, the churning surf might intimidate beginning swimmers, but bodysurfing can be great here. Hamoa is half a mile past Koki Beach on Haneoo Loop Road, 2 miles south of Hana town. **Amenities:** showers; toilets. **Best for:** surfing; swimming. ⊠ *Haneoo Loop Rd.*

WATER SPORTS AND TOURS

Updated by
Eliza Escaño-
Vasquez

Getting into (or onto) the water will be the highlight of your Maui trip. At Lahaina and Maalaea harbors, you can board boats for snorkeling, scuba diving, deep-sea fishing, parasailing, and sunset cocktail adventures. You can learn to surf, catch a ferry to Lanai, or grab a seat on a fast inflatable raft. From December into May, whale-watching adventures become a top attraction as humpbacks escaping Alaska's frigid winter arrive in Maui's warm waters to frolic, mate, and birth. Along the leeward coastline, from Kaanapali on the West Shore all the way down to Waiala Cove on the South Shore, you can discover great snorkeling and swimming. If you're a thrill seeker, head out to the North Shore and Hookipa, where surfers, kiteboarders, and windsurfers catch big waves and big air.

BODY BOARDING AND BODYSURFING

Bodysurfing and "sponging" (as body boarding is called by the regulars; boogie boarding is another variation) are great ways to catch some waves without having to master surfing—and there's no balance or coordination required. A boogie board (or "sponge") is softer than a hard, fiberglass surfboard, which means you can ride safely in the rough-and-tumble surf zone. If you get tossed around (which is half the fun), you don't have a heavy surfboard nearby to bang your head on, but you do have something to hang onto. Serious spongers invest in a single short-clipped fin to help propel them into the wave.

BEST SPOTS
D.T. Fleming Beach. In West Maui, D.T. Fleming Beach offers great surf almost daily along with some nice amenities: ample parking, restrooms, a shower, grills, picnic tables, and a daily lifeguard. Caution is advised, especially during winter months when the current and undertow can get rough. ⊠ *Honoapiilani Hwy., below the Ritz-Carlton, Kapalua.*

Kamaole III. Between Kihei and Wailea on the South Shore, Kamaole III is a good spot for bodysurfing and body boarding. It has a sandy floor, with 1- to 3-foot waves breaking not too far out. It's often crowded late in the day, especially on weekends when local kids are out of school. Don't let that chase you away; the waves are wide enough for everyone. ⊠ *S. Kihei Rd., south of Keonaekai Rd., Kihei.*

Paia Bay. On the North Shore, Paia Bay has waves suitable for spongers and bodysurfers. The beach is just before Paia town, beyond the large community building and grass field. ■**TIP**→ **Park in the public lot across the street and leave your valuables at home, as this beach is known for break-ins.** ✉ *Off Rte. 36.*

EQUIPMENT

Most condos and hotels have body boards available to guests—some in better condition than others (but beat-up body boards work just as well for beginners). You can also pick up a body board from any discount shop, such as Kmart or Longs Drugs, for upward of $30.

Auntie Snorkel. You can rent decent body boards here for $6 a day or $18 a week. ✉ *2439 S. Kihei Rd., Kihei* ☎ *808/879–6263* ⊕ *www.auntiesnorkel.com.*

West Maui Sports and Fishing Supply. This old country store has been around since 1987 and has some of the best prices on the west side. Body boards go for $2.50 a day or $15 a week. ✉ *1287 Front St., Lahaina* ☎ *808/661–6252* ⊕ *www.westmauisports.com.*

> **OUTRIGGER-CANOE RACES**
>
> Polynesians first traveled to Hawaii by outrigger canoe, and racing the traditional craft is a favorite pastime on the Islands. Canoes were revered in Old Hawaii, and no voyage could begin without a blessing, ceremonial chanting, and a hula performance to ensure a safe journey.

DEEP-SEA FISHING

If fishing is your sport, Maui is your island. In these waters you'll find ahi, *aku* (skipjack tuna), barracuda, bonefish, *kawakawa* (bonito), mahimahi, Pacific blue marlin, ono, and *ulua* (jack crevalle). You can fish year-round and you don't need a license. ■**TIP**→ **Because boats fill up fast during busy seasons (Christmas, spring break, tournament weeks), consider making reservations before coming to Maui.**

Plenty of fishing boats run out of Lahaina and Maalaea harbors. If you charter a private boat, expect to spend in the neighborhood of $700 to $1,000 for a thrilling half day in the swivel seat. You can share a boat for much less if you don't mind close quarters with a stranger who may get seasick, drunk, or worse—lucky! Before you sign up, you should know that some boats keep the catch. They will, however, fillet a nice piece for you to take home. And if you catch a real beauty, you might even be able to have it professionally mounted.

You're expected to bring your own lunch and nonglass beverages. (Shop the night before; it's hard to find snacks at 6 am.) Boats supply coolers, ice, and bait. Ten-to-twenty percent tips are suggested.

BOATS AND CHARTERS

★ **Finest Kind Sportfishing.** A 1,118-pound blue marlin was reeled in by the crew aboard *Finest Kind,* a lovely 37-foot Merritt kept so clean you'd never guess the action it's seen. Captain Dave has been around these waters long enough to befriend other expert fishers. This family-run company operates four boats and specializes in live bait. Shared charters start at $150 for four hours and go up to $195 for a full day. Private trips go from $500 to $1,100. No bananas on board, please; the captain thinks they're bad luck for fishing. ✉ *Lahaina Harbor, Slip 7, Lahaina* ☏ *808/661–0338* ⊕ *www.finestkindsportfishing.com.*

Kai Palena Sportfishing. Captain Fuzzy Alboro runs a highly recommended operation on the 33-foot *Die Hard*. Check-in is at 2:15 am, and he takes a maximum of six people. The cost is from $200 for a shared boat to $1,100 for a private charter. ✉ *Lahaina Harbor, Slip 10, Lahaina* ☏ *808/878–2362* ⊕ *www.diehardsportfishing.com.*

Start Me Up Sportfishing. With more than 20 years in business, Start Me Up has a fleet of seven boats, all impeccably maintained. These 42-foot Bertram Sportfishers offer some of the most comfortable fishing trips around and come complete with all the amenities: VCRs, microwaves, and ice chests. The company provides tackle and equipment. A two-hour shared boat is $99 per person, while a private charter runs from $299 for two hours to $999 for eight hours. There's a six-person maximum. ✉ *Lahaina Harbor, Slip 12, Lahaina* ☏ *808/667–2774* ⊕ *www. sportfishingmaui.com.*

KAYAKING

Kayaking is a fantastic and eco-friendly way to experience Maui's coast up close. Floating aboard a "plastic popsicle stick" is easier than you might think, and allows you to cruise out to vibrant, living coral reefs and waters where dolphins and even whales roam. Kayaking can be a leisurely paddle or a challenge of heroic proportion, depending on your ability, the location, and the weather. ■ TIP➔ Though you can rent kayaks independently, we recommend taking a guide. An apparently calm surface can hide extremely strong ocean currents—and you don't *really* want to take an unplanned trip to Tahiti! Most guides are naturalists who will steer you away from surging surf, lead you to pristine reefs, and point out camouflaged fish, like the stalking hawkfish. Not having to schlep your gear on top of your rental car is a bonus. A half-day tour runs around $75. Custom tours can be arranged.

If you decide to strike out on your own, tour companies will rent kayaks for the day with paddles, life vests, and roof racks, and many will meet you near your chosen location. Ask for a map of good entries and plan to avoid paddling back to shore against the wind (schedule extra time for the return trip regardless). For beginners, get there early before the trade wind kicks in, and try sticking close to the shore. When you're ready to snorkel, secure your belongings in a dry pack on board and drag your boat by its bowline behind you. (This isn't as bad as it sounds).

BEST SPOTS

Makena Landing. This is an excellent starting point for a South Shore adventure. Enter from the paved parking lot or the small sandy beach a little south. The bay itself is virtually empty, but the right edge is flanked with brilliant coral heads and juvenile turtles. If you round the point on the right, you come across Five Caves, a system of enticing underwater arches. In the morning you may see dolphins, and the arches are havens for lobsters, eels, and spectacularly hued butterfly fish. Check out the million-dollar mansions lining the shoreline and guess which celebrity lives where. ⊠ *Off Makena Rd., Wailea.*

Ukumehame Beach. In West Maui, past the steep cliffs on the Honoapi-ilani Highway, there's a long stretch of inviting coastline that includes Ukumehame Beach. This is a good spot for beginners; entry is easy and there's much to see in every direction. If you want to snorkel, the best visibility is farther out at Olowalu Beach. ■ TIP→ Watch for sharp kiawe thorns buried in the sand on the way into the water. ⊠ *Rte. 30, near mile marker 12, Lahaina.*

EQUIPMENT AND TOURS

Kelii's Kayak Tours. One of the highest-rated kayak outfitters on the island, Kelii's offers kayaking trips and combo adventures where you can also surf, snorkel, or hike to a waterfall. Leading groups of up to eight people, the guides show what makes each reef unique. Trips are available on the island's north, south, and west shores, and range from $54 to $155. ⊠ *Kihei* ☎ *888/874–7652, 808/874–7652* ⊕ *www. keliiskayak.com.*

Fodor's Choice ★ **South Pacific Kayaks.** These guys pioneered recreational kayaking on Maui, so they know their stuff. Guides are friendly, informative, and eager to help you get the most out of your experience; we're talking true, fun-loving, kayak geeks. South Pacific stands out as adventurous *and* environmentally responsible. They offer a variety of trips leaving from both West Maui and South Shore locations. Trips range from $54 to $99. ☎ *800/776–2326, 808/875–4848* ⊕ *www. southpacifickayaks.com.*

KITEBOARDING

Catapulting up to 40 feet in the air above the breaking surf, kiteboarders hardly seem of this world. Silken kites hold the athletes aloft for precious seconds—long enough for the execution of mind-boggling tricks—then deposit them back in the sea. This new sport is not for the weak-kneed. No matter what people might tell you, it's harder to learn than windsurfing. The unskilled (or unlucky) can be caught in an upwind and carried far out in the ocean, or worse—dropped smack on the shore. Because of insurance (or the lack thereof), companies are not allowed to rent equipment. Beginners must take lessons, and then purchase their own gear. Devotees swear that after your first few lessons, committing to buying your kite is easy.

LESSONS

Aqua Sports Maui. "To air is human" or so they say at Aqua Sports, which calls itself the local favorite of kiteboarding schools. It's in a great location (right near Kite Beach, at the west end of Kanaha Beach), and offers basic to advanced kiteboarding lessons. Rates start at $240 for a three-hour basics course taught by certified instructors. ⊠ *Amala Pl., near Kite Beach, Kahului* ☎ *808/242–8015* ⊕ *www. mauikiteboardinglessons.com.*

★ **Hawaiian Sailboarding Techniques.** Pro kiteboarder and legendary wind-surfer Alan Cadiz will have you safely ripping in no time at lower Kanaha Beach Park. A "Learn to Kitesurf" package starts at $225 for a three-hour private lesson, equipment included. Instead of observing from the shore, instructors paddle after students on a chaseboard to give immediate feedback. The company is part of Hi-Tech Surf Sports, in the Triangle Square shopping center. ⊠ *Triangle Square, 425 Koloa St., Kahului* ☎ *808/871–5423, 800/968–5423* ⊕ *www.hstwindsurfing.com.*

PARASAILING

Parasailing is an easy, exhilarating way to earn your wings: just strap on a harness attached to a parachute, and a powerboat pulls you up and over the ocean from a launching dock or a boat's platform. ■TIP➔ Keep in mind, parasailing is limited to West Maui, and "thrill craft"—including parasails—are prohibited in Maui waters during humpback whale–calving season, December 15 to May 15.

LESSONS AND TOURS

★ **West Maui Parasail.** Soar at 800 feet above the ocean for a bird's-eye view of Lahaina, or be daring at 1,200 feet for smoother rides and even better views. The captain will be glad to let you experience a "toe dip" or "freefall" if you request it. Hour-long trips departing from Lahaina Harbor and Kaanapali Beach include 8- to 10-minute flights and run from $65 for the 800-foot ride to $75 for the 1,200-foot ride. Observers pay $35 each. ☎ *808/661–4060* ⊕ *www.westmauiparasail.com.*

RAFTING

The high-speed, inflatable rafts you find on Maui are nothing like the raft that Huck Finn used to drift down the Mississippi. While passengers grip straps, these rafts fly, skimming and bouncing across the sea. Because they're so maneuverable, they go where the big boats can't—secret coves, sea caves, and remote beaches. Two-hour trips run around $50, half-day trips upward of $100. ■TIP➔ Although safe, these trips are not for the faint of heart. If you have back or neck problems or are pregnant, you should reconsider this activity.

TOURS

Blue Water Rafting. One of the few ways to get to the stunning Kanaio Coast (the roadless southern coastline beyond Ahihi-Kinau), this rafting tour begins trips conveniently at the Kihei boat ramp on the South Shore. Dolphins, turtles, and other marine life are the highlight of this adventure, along with sea caves, lava arches, and views of Haleakala. Two-hour trips to Molokini start at $50; longer trips cost $100 to $125 and include a deli lunch. ⊠ *Kihei Boat Ramp, S. Kihei Rd., Kihei* ☎ *808/879–7238* ⊕ *www.bluewaterrafting.com.*

Ocean Riders. Start the day with a spectacular view of the sun rising above the West Maui Mountains, then cross the Au Au Channel to Lanai's Shipwreck Beach. From there, this tour circles Lanai, allowing you to view the island's 70 miles of remote coast. The "backside" of Lanai is one of Hawaii's unsung marvels, and you can expect to stop at three protected coves for snorkeling; you might chance upon sea turtles, monk seals, and a friendly reef shark. Guides slow down long enough for you to marvel at sacred burial caves and interesting rock formations and to take a short swim at a secluded beach. Tours cost $139 per person and include snorkel gear, a fruit breakfast, and a deli lunch. ⊠ *Mala Wharf, Front St., Lahaina* ☎ *808/661–3586* ⊕ *www.mauioceanriders.com.*

SAILING

With the Islands of Molokai, Lanai, Kahoolawe, and Molokini a stone's throw away, Maui waters offer visually arresting backdrops for sailing adventures. Sailing conditions can be fickle, so some operations throw in snorkeling or whale-watching, and others offer sunset cruises. Winds are consistent in summer but variable in winter, and afternoons are generally windier all throughout the year. Prices range from around $40 for two-hour trips to $80 for half-day excursions. ■TIP→ You won't be sheltered from the elements on the trim racing boats, so be sure to bring a hat (one that won't blow away), a light jacket or cover-up, sunglasses, and extra sunscreen.

BOATS AND CHARTERS

America II. This onetime America's Cup contender offers an exciting, intimate alternative to crowded catamarans. For fast action, try a morning trade-wind sail. All sails are two hours and cost $44.95. Plan to bring a change of clothes, because you will get wet. Snacks and beverages are provided. No one under five years old is permitted. ⊠ *Lahaina Harbor, Slip 6, Lahaina* ☎ *808/667–2195* ⊕ *www.sailingonmaui.com.*

Paragon. If you want to snorkel and sail, this is your boat. Many snorkel cruises claim to sail but actually motor most of the way; *Paragon* is an exception. Both *Paragon* vessels (one catamaran in Lahaina, the other in Maalaea) are ship-shape, and crews are accommodating and friendly. The mooring in Molokini Crater is particularly good, and tours will often stay after the masses have left. The Lanai trip includes a picnic lunch on Manele Bay, snorkeling, and a quick afternoon blue-water swim. Extras on the trips to Lanai include mai tais and sodas, brownies, and champagne. Hot and cold appetizers come with the sunset sail, which departs from Lahaina Harbor every Monday, Wednesday, and Friday. ⊠ *Maalaea Harbor, Maalaea* ☎ *808/244–2087, 800/441–2087* ⊕ *www.sailmaui.com.*

Trilogy Excursions. With more than 35 years of experience and a commitment to preserving the ecosystem with monthly reef-cleaning campaigns, Trilogy has a great reputation in the community. It's one of only two companies that sail, rather than motor, to Molokini Crater. A two-hour sail starts at $69. The sunset trip includes appetizers, beer, wine, champagne, margaritas, and mai tais. Boarding the catamaran from shore can be tricky—timing is everything and getting wet is inevitable, but after that it's smooth sailing. Tours depart from Lahaina Harbor, Maalaea Harbor, and, in West Maui, in front of the Kaanapali Beach Hotel. ⊠ *180 Lahainaluna Rd., Lahaina* ☎ *808/874–5649, 888/225–6284* ⊕ *www.sailtrilogy.com.*

SCUBA DIVING

Maui, just as scenic underwater as it is on dry land, has been rated one of the top 10 dive spots in the United States and the Caribbean. It's common to see huge sea turtles, eagle rays, and small reef sharks, not to mention many varieties of angelfish, parrot fish, eels, and octopi. Unlike other popular dive destinations, most of the species are unique to this area. For example, of Maui's 450 species of reef fish, 25% are endemic to the island. Dives are best in the morning, when visibility can hold a steady 100 feet. If you're a certified diver, you can rent gear at any Maui dive shop simply by showing your PADI or NAUI card. Unless you're familiar with the area, however, it's probably best to hook up with a dive shop for an underwater tour. Tours include tanks and weights and start around $130. Wet suits and BCs (buoyancy compensators) are rented separately, for an additional $15 to $30. Shops also offer introductory dives ($100 to $160) for those who aren't certified.

■TIP➔ Before signing on with any of these outfitters, it's a good idea to ask a few pointed questions about your guide's experience, the weather outlook, and the condition of the equipment.

BEST SPOTS

Ahihi Bay. Some of the southern coast's best diving is at Ahihi Bay, part of the Ahihi-Kinau Natural Area Reserve. The area was closed for several years to allow the coral to recover from overuse. At the time of this writing, it was scheduled to reopen on August 1, 2012. The reserve is best known for its "Fishbowl," a small cove right beside the road, next to a hexagonal house. Here you can find excellent underwater scenery, with many types of fish and coral. ■TIP➔ Be careful of the rocky-bottom entry (wear reef shoes if you have them). The Fishbowl can get crowded, especially in high season. If you want to steer clear of the crowds, look for a second entry ½ mile farther down the road—a gravel parking lot at the surf spot called "Dumps." Entry into the bay here is trickier, as the coastline is all lava. ⊠ *Makena Rd., south of Makena State Park, Wailea-Makena.*

Honolua Bay. This marine preserve in West Maui is alive with many varieties of coral and tame tropical fish, including large *ulua* (jack crevalle), *kahala*, barracuda, and manta rays. With depths of 20 to 50 feet, this is a popular summer dive spot, good for all levels. ■TIP➔ High surf often prohibits winter dives. ⊠ *Rte. 30, between mile markers 32 and 33, Kapalua.*

La Pérouse Bay. Formed from the last lava flow two centuries ago, La Pérouse Bay brings you the best variety of fish—more than any other site. The lava rock provides a protective habitat, and all four types of Hawaii's angelfish can be found here. To dive the spot called "Pinnacles," enter anywhere along the shore, just past the private entrance to the beach. Wear your reef shoes, as entry is sharp. To the right, you'll be in the Ahihi-Kinau Natural Area Reserve; to the left, you're outside. Look for the white, sandy bottom with massive coral heads. Pinnacles is for experienced divers only. ⊠ *Makena Rd., south of Makena State Park, Wailea.*

DIVING 101

If you've always wanted gills, Hawaii is a good place to get them. Although the bulky, heavy equipment seems freakish on shore, underwater it allows you to move about freely, almost weightlessly. As you descend into another world, you slowly grow used to the sound of your own breathing and the strangeness of being able to do so 30-plus feet down.

Most resorts offer introductory dive lessons in their pools, which allow you to acclimate to the awkward breathing apparatus before venturing out into the great blue. If you aren't starting from a resort pool, no worries. Most intro dives take off from calm, sandy beaches, such as Ulua or Kaanapali. If you're bitten by the deep-sea bug and want to continue diving, you should get certified. Only

certified divers can rent equipment or go on more adventurous dives, such as night dives, open-ocean dives, and cave dives.

There are several certification companies, including PADI, NAUI, and SSI. PADI, the largest, is the most comprehensive. A child must be at least 10 to be certified. Once you begin your certification process, stick with the same company. The dives you log will not apply to another company's certification. (Dives with a PADI instructor, for instance, will not count toward SSI certification.) Remember that you will not be able to fly or go to the airy summit of Haleakala within 24 hours of diving. Open-water certification will take three to four days and cost around $350. From that point on, the sky—or rather, the sea—is the limit!

Makena Landing. On the South Shore, one of the most popular dive spots is Makena Landing (also called "Five Graves" or "Five Caves"). You can revel in underwater delights—caves, ledges, coral heads, and an outer reef home to a large green-sea-turtle colony called "Turtle Town." ■TIP→ Entry is rocky lava, so be careful where you step. This area is for more experienced divers. ⊠ *Makena Rd., Wailea-Makena.*

Molokini Crater. Three miles offshore from Wailea on the South Shore, Molokini Crater is world renowned for its deep, crystal clear, fish-filled waters. A crescent-shape islet formed by the eroding top of a volcano, the crater is a marine preserve ranging from 10 to 80 feet deep. The numerous tame fish and brilliant coral within the crater make it a popular introductory dive site. On calm days, the backside of Molokini Crater (called Back Wall) can be a dramatic sight for advanced divers, with visibility of up to 150 feet. The enormous drop-off into the Alalakeiki Channel offers awesome seascapes, black coral, and chance sightings of larger fish and sharks.

EQUIPMENT, LESSONS, AND TOURS

★ **Ed Robinson's Diving Adventures.** Ed Robinson wrote the book, literally, on Molokini. Because he knows so much, he includes a "Biology 101" talk with every dive. An expert marine photographer, he offers diving instruction and boat charters to South Maui and the backside of Molokini Crater. Night dives are available, and there's a discount if you book ahead. Dives start at $129.95, plus $20 for the gear. ⊠ *1819 S. Kihei Rd., Kihei* ☎ *808/879–3584, 800/635–1273* ⊕ *www.mauiscuba.com.*

Snorkelers can see adorable green sea turtles around Maui.

Maui Dive Shop. With seven locations island-wide, the well-regarded Maui Dive Shop offers scuba charters, diving instruction, and equipment rental. Excursions that offer awe-inspiring beach and boat dives go to Coral Gardens, Shipwreck Beach, and Cathedrals on Lanai. The manta ray dives off of Molokini Crater have a 70% success rate. Night dives and customized trips are available, as are full SSI and PADI certificate programs. ⊠ *1455 S. Kihei Rd., Kihei* ☎ *808/879–3388, 800/542–3483* ⊕ *www.mauidiveshop.com.*

Shaka Divers. Since 1983, owner Doug Corbin has led personalized dives, including great four-hour intro dives ($99), refresher courses ($89), scuba certifications ($399), and shore dives ($69) to Ulua, Turtle Town, and Bubble Cave. Typical dives last about an hour. Dives can be booked on short notice, with afternoon tours available (hard to find on Maui). Shaka also offers night dives and torpedo-scooter dives. The twilight two-tank dive is nice for day divers who want to ease into night diving. ⊠ *24 Hakoi Pl., Kihei* ☎ *808/250–1234* ⊕ *www.shakadivers.com.*

SNORKELING

No one should leave Maui without ducking underwater to meet a sea turtle, moray eel, or *humuhumunukunukuapuaa*—the state fish. ■ TIP→ **Visibility is best in the morning, before the wind picks up.**

There are two ways to approach snorkeling—by land or by sea. Daily around 7 am, a parade of boats heads out to Lanai or Molokini Crater, that ancient cone of volcanic cinder off the coast of Wailea. Boat trips offer some advantages—deeper water, seasonal whale-watching, crew assistance, lunch, and gear. But you don't need a boat; much of Maui's best snorkeling is found just steps from the road. Nearly the entire leeward coastline from Kapalua south to Ahihi-Kinau offers prime opportunities to ogle fish and turtles. If you're patient and sharp-eyed, you may glimpse eels, octopuses, lobsters, eagle rays, and even a rare shark or monk seal.

BEST SPOTS

Snorkel sites here are listed from north to south, starting at the northwest corner of the island.

3

Fodor'sChoice **Honolua Bay.** Just north of Kapalua, the Honolua Bay Marine Life Conservation District has a superb reef for snorkeling. ■TIP→ **Bring a fish key with you, as you're sure to see many species of triggerfish, filefish, and wrasses.** The coral formations on the right side of the bay are particularly dramatic, with pink, aqua, and orange varieties. On a lucky day, you might even be snorkeling with a pod of dolphins nearby. Take care entering the water; there's no beach and the rocks and concrete ramp can be slippery.

The northeast corner of this windward-facing bay periodically gets hammered by big waves in winter. Avoid the bay then, as well as after heavy rains. ✉ *Rte. 30, between mile markers 32 and 33, Kapalua.*

★ **Black Rock.** We think Black Rock, in front of the Sheraton Maui Resort & Spa at the northernmost tip of Kaanapali Beach, is great for snorkelers of any skill level. The entry couldn't be easier—dump your towel on the sand and in you go. Beginners can stick close to shore and still see lots of action. Advanced snorkelers can swim to the tip of Black Rock to see larger fish and eagle rays. One of the underwater residents here is a turtle whose hefty size earned him the name "Volkswagen." He sits very still, so you have to look closely. Equipment can be rented on-site. Parking, in a small lot adjoining the hotel, is the only hassle. ✉ *Sheraton Maui Resort & Spa, 2605 Kaanapali Pkwy., Lahaina.*

Hanakaoo Beach Park. Along Honoapiilani Highway there are several favorite snorkel sites, including the area just out from the cemetery at Hanakaoo Beach Park. At depths of 5 and 10 feet, you can see a variety of corals, especially as you head south toward Wahikuli Wayside Park. ✉ *Rte. 30, near mile marker 23.*

Olowalu. South of Olowalu General Store, the shallow coral reef at Olowalu is good for a quick underwater tour, but if you're willing to venture out about 50 yards you'll have easy access to an expansive coral reef with abundant turtles and fish—no boat required. Swim offshore toward the pole sticking out of the reef. Except for during a south swell, this area is calm and good for families with small children. Boats sometimes stop here (they refer to this site as "Coral Gardens") when conditions in Honolua Bay are not ideal. During low tide, be extra cautious when hovering above the razor-sharp coral. ✉ *Rte. 30, at mile marker 14, Lahaina.*

Wailea. Excellent snorkeling is found down the coastline between Kihei and Makena on the South Shore. ■TIP→ **The best spots are along the rocky fringes of Wailea's beaches—Mokapu, Ulua, Wailea, and Polo—off Wailea Alanui Drive.** Find one of the public parking lots sandwiched between Wailea's luxury resorts (look for a blue sign that says

"Shoreline Access" with an arrow pointing to the lot), and enjoy the sandy entries, calm waters with relatively good visibility, and variety of fish. Of the four beaches, Ulua has the best reef. You may listen to snapping shrimp and parrot fish nibbling on coral. ✉ *Wailea Alanui Dr., Wailea-Makena.*

★ **Molokini Crater.** Between Maui and neighboring Kahoolawe you'll find the world-famous Molokini Crater. Its crescent-shape rim acts as a protective cove from the wind and provides a sanctuary for birds and colorful marine life. Most snorkeling tour operators offer a Molokini trip, and it's not unusual for your charter to share this dormant volcano with five or six other boats. The journey to this sunken crater takes more than 90 minutes from Lahaina, an hour from Maalaea, and less than half an hour from the South Shore.

Ahihi-Kinau Natural Area Reserve. In South Maui, the end of the paved section of Makena Road is where you'll find the Ahihi-Kinau Natural Area Reserve. Despite its lava-scorched landscape, the area was so popular that it had to be temporarily closed in 2008. At this writing it was scheduled to reopen on August 1, 2012. It's difficult terrain and the area did sometimes get crowded, but it's worth a visit to experience some of the reserve's outstanding treasures, such as the sheltered cove known as the "Fish Bowl." ■TIP➜ Be sure to bring water: this is a hot and unforgiving wilderness. ✉ *Just before end of Makena Alanui Rd., Wailea.*

EQUIPMENT

Most hotels and vacation rentals offer free use of snorkel gear. Beachside stands fronting the major resort areas rent equipment by the hour or day. ■TIP➜ Don't shy away from asking for instructions—a snug fit makes all the difference in the world. A mask fits if it sticks to your face when you inhale deeply through your nose. Fins should cover your entire foot (unlike diving fins, which strap around your heel). If you're squeamish about using someone else's gear (or need a prescription lens), pick up your own at any discount shop. Costco and Longs Drugs have better prices than ABC stores; dive shops have superior equipment.

Maui Dive Shop. You can rent pro gear (including optical masks, body boards, and wet suits) from seven locations islandwide. Pump these guys for weather info before heading out—they'll know better than last night's news forecaster, and they'll give you the real deal on conditions. ✉ *1455 S. Kihei Rd., Kihei* ☎ *808/873–3388* ⊕ *www.mauidiveshop.com.*

Snorkel Bob's. Here you can rent fins, masks, and snorkels, and Snorkel Bob's will throw in a carrying bag, map, and snorkel tips for as little as $9 per week. Avoid the circle masks and go for the split-level ($26 per week); it's worth the extra. There are also locations in Lahaina and Kihei. ✉ *Napili Village Hotel, 5425 Lower Honoapiilani Hwy., Napili* ☎ *808/669–9603* ⊕ *www.snorkelbob.com* ✉ *1217 Front St., Lahaina* ☎ *808/662–0104* ✉ *1279 S. Kihei Rd., No. 310, Kihei* ☎ *808/875–6188* ✉ *Kamaole Beach Center, 2411 S. Kihei Rd., Kihei* ☎ *808/879–7449.*

TOURS

Molokini Crater, a crescent about 3 miles off the shore of Wailea, is the most popular snorkel cruise destination. You can spend half a day floating above the fish-filled crater for about $80. Some say it's not as good as it's made out to be, and that it's too crowded, but others consider it to be one of the best spots in Hawaii. Visibility is generally outstanding and fish are incredibly tame. Your second stop will be somewhere along the leeward coast, either Turtle Town near Makena or Coral Gardens toward Lahaina.

■TIP➜ On blustery mornings, there's a good chance the waters will be too rough to moor in Molokini and you'll end up snorkeling some place off the shore, which you could have driven to for free. For the safety of everyone on the boat, it's the captain's prerogative to choose the best spot for the day.

Snorkel cruises vary slightly—some serve mai tais and steaks whereas others offer beer and cold cuts. You might prefer a large ferryboat to a smaller sailboat, or vice versa. Whatever trip you choose, be sure you know where to go to board your vessel; getting lost in the harbor at 6 am is a lousy start to a good day. ■TIP➜ Bring sunscreen, an underwater camera (they're double the price on board), a towel, and a cover-up for the windy return trip. Even tropical waters get chilly after hours of swimming, so consider wearing a rash guard. Wet suits can usually be rented for a fee. Hats without straps will blow away, and valuables should be left at home.

★ **Ali'i Nui Maui.** Come as you are (with a bathing suit, of course); towels, sunblock, and all your gear are provided on this 65-foot luxury catamaran. Since the owners also operate Maui Dive Shop, snorkel and dive equipment are top of the line. Wetsuit tops are available to use for stronger sun protection or to keep extra warm in the water. The boat, which holds a maximum of 60 people, is nicely appointed and is often recommended by the island's upscale resorts. A morning snorkel sail (there's a diving option, too) heads to Turtle Town or Molokini Crater and includes a Continental breakfast, lunch, and post-snorkel alcoholic drinks. The trip is $139 per person and includes transportation from your hotel. Videography is available for a fee. ✉ *Maalaea Harbor, Slip 56, Maalaea* ☎ *800/542–3483, 808/875–0333* ⊕ *www.aliinuimaui.com.*

☾ **Maui Classic Charters.** Hop aboard the *Four Winds II*, a 55-foot, glass-bottom catamaran (great fun for kids), for one of the most dependable snorkel trips around. You'll spend more time than the other charter boats do at Molokini Crater and enjoy turtle-watching on the way home. The trip includes optional snuba ($49 extra), Continental breakfast, barbecue lunch, beer, wine, and soda. The price is $89 per person. Or try the *Maui Magic*, Maalaea's fastest power cat. This boat holds fewer people than some of the larger vessels, and trips start at

$112. ⊠ *Maalaea Harbor, Slips 55 and 80, Maalaea* ☎ *808/879–8188, 800/736–5740* ⊕ *www.mauicharters.com.*

Teralani Sailing Charters. Choose between a regular snorkeling trip with a deli lunch or a top-of-the-line excursion that's an hour longer and includes two snorkel sites and a barbecue-style lunch. The company's cats could hold well over 100 people, but 49 is the maximum per trip. Freshwater showers are available, and so is an open bar after the second snorkel stop. A friendly crew provides all your gear, a flotation device, and a crash course in snorkeling. Boarding is right off Dig Me Beach at Whalers Village in West Maui. ⊠ *Whalers Village, 2435 Kaanapali Pkwy., Kaanapali* ☎ *808/661–1230* ⊕ *www.teralani.net.*

★ **Trilogy Excursions.** Many people consider a trip with Trilogy Excursions
ⓒ to be a highlight of their vacation. Maui's longest-running operation has comprehensive offerings, with seven beautiful multihull 50- to 64-foot sailing vessels at three departure sites. All excursions are staffed by energetic crews who will keep you well-fed and entertained with local stories and corny jokes. A full-day catamaran cruise to Lanai includes a Continental breakfast and barbecue lunch, a guided tour of the island, a "Snorkeling 101" class, and time to snorkel in the waters of Lanai's Hulopoe Marine Preserve (Trilogy Excursions has exclusive commercial access). The company also offers a Molokini Crater and Honolua Bay snorkel cruise that is top-notch. Tours depart from Lahaina Harbor; Maalaea Harbor; and, in West Maui, in front of the Kaanapali Beach Hotel. ⊠ *180 Lahainaluna Rd., Lahaina* ☎ *808/874–5649, 888/225–6284* ⊕ *www.sailtrilogy.com.*

STAND-UP PADDLING

Stand-up paddling (also called stand-up paddle surfing or paddleboarding), where you stand on a longboard and paddle out with a canoe oar, is the new "comeback kid" of surf sports. While paddleboarding requires even more balance and coordination than regular surfing, it is still accessible to just about every skill level and most surf schools now offer stand-up paddle lessons. There used to be a lone paddler amid a pack of surfers, but the sport has gained such popularity in recent years that stand-up paddlers seem to have proliferated in the water (sometimes to the dismay of avid surfers). The fun thing about stand-up paddleboarding is that you can enjoy it whether the surf is good or the water is flat. ■TIP➔ Because of the size and speed of a longboard, stand-up paddling can be dangerous to you and those around you, so lessons are highly recommended.

LESSONS

Stand-Up Paddle Surf School. Maui's first school devoted solely to stand-up paddleboarding was founded by the legendary Maria Souza, the first woman to surf the treacherous waves of "Jaws" on Maui's North Shore. While most surf schools offer stand-up paddling, Maria's classes are in a league of their own. They include a proper warm-up with a hula-hoop and balance ball and a cool-down with some yoga. The cost is $159 for a private session. Locations vary depending on conditions. ☎ *808/579–9231* ⊕ *www.standuppaddlesurfschool.com.*

SURFING

Maui's coastline has surf for every level of waterman or -woman. Waves on leeward-facing shores (West and South Maui) tend to break in gentle sets all summer long. Surf instructors in Kihei and Lahaina can rent you boards, give you onshore instruction, and then lead you out through the channel, where it's safe to enter the surf. They'll shout encouragement while you paddle like mad for the thrill of standing on water—some will even give you a helpful shove. These areas are great for beginners, the only danger is whacking a stranger with your board or stubbing your toe against the reef.

The North Shore is another story. Winter waves pound the windward coast, attracting water champions from every corner of the world. Adrenaline addicts are towed in by Jet Ski to a legendary, deep-sea break called "Jaws." Waves here periodically tower upward of 40 feet, dwarfing the helicopters seeking to capture unbelievable photos. The only spot for viewing this phenomenon (which happens just a few times a year) is on private property. So, if you hear the surfers next to you crowing about Jaws "going off," cozy up and get them to take you with them.

Whatever your skill, there's a board, a break, and even a surf guru to accommodate you. A two-hour lesson is a good intro to surf culture.

You can get the wave report each day by checking page two of the *Maui News,* logging onto the Glenn James weather site at ⊕ *www. hawaiiweathertoday.com,* or calling ☎ *808/871–5054* (for the weather forecast) or ☎ *808/877–3611* (for the surf report).

BEST SPOTS

Cove Park. On the South Shore, beginners can hang 10 at Kihei's Cove Park, a sometimes crowded but reliable 1- to 2-foot break. Boards can easily be rented across the street, or in neighboring Kalama Park parking lot. The only bummer is having to balance the 9-plus-foot board on your head while crossing busy South Kihei Road. ⊠ *S. Kihei Rd., Kihei.*

Hookipa Beach Park. For advanced wave riders, Hookipa Beach Park on the North Shore boasts several well-loved breaks, including "Pavilions," "Lanes," "the Point," and "Middles." Surfers have priority until 11 am, when windsurfers move in on the action. ■ TIP→ Competition is stiff here. If you don't know what you're doing, consider watching. ⊠ *Hana Hwy., 2 miles past Paia, Paia.*

Launiupoko State Wayside. Long- or shortboarders in West Maui can paddle out at Launiupoko State Wayside. The east end of the park has an easy break, good for beginners. ⊠ *Honoapiilani Hwy., near mile marker 18, Wailuku.*

Ukumehame. Also called "Thousand Peaks," Ukumehame is one of the better beginner spots in West Maui. You'll soon see how the spot got its name—the waves here break again and again in wide and consistent rows, giving lots of room for beginning and intermediate surfers. ⊠ *Honoapiilani Hwy., near mile marker 12.*

West Maui. Good surf spots in West Maui include "Grandma's" at **Papalaua Park,** just after the *pali* (cliff)—where waves are so easy a grandma could ride 'em; **Puamana Beach Park** for a mellow longboard day; and

Lahaina Harbor, which offers an excellent inside wave for beginners (called "Breakwall"), as well as the more advanced outside (a great lift if there's a big south swell).

EQUIPMENT AND LESSONS

Surf camps are becoming increasingly popular, especially with women. One- or two-week camps offer a terrific way to build muscle and self-esteem simultaneously.

Big Kahuna Adventures. Rent soft-top longboards here for $20 for two hours, or $30 for the day. The shop also offers surf lessons and rents kayaks and snorkel gear. Across from Cove Park, the company has been around for years. ⊠ *1913-C S. Kihei Rd., Kihei* ☎ *808/875–6395* ⊕ *www.bigkahunaadventures.com.*

★ **Goofy Foot.** Surfing "goofy foot" means putting your right foot forward. They might be goofy, but we like the right-footed gurus here. This shop is just plain cool and only steps away from "Breakwall," a great beginner's spot in Lahaina. A two-hour class with five or fewer students is $65, and you're guaranteed to be standing by the end or it's free. Owner and "stoke broker" Tim Sherer offers private lessons for $250 and will sometimes ride alongside to record video clips and give more thorough feedback. ⊠ *505 Front St., Suite 123, Lahaina* ☎ *808/244–9283* ⊕ *www.goofyfootsurfschool.com.*

Hi-Tech Surf Sports. Locals hold Hi-Tech in the highest regard. It has some of the best boards, advice, and attitude around. It rents even its best surfboards—choose from longboards, shortboards, and hybrids—starting at $25 per day. All rentals come with board bags, roof racks, and wax. ⊠ *425 Koloa St., Kahului* ☎ *808/877–2111* ⊕ *www.htmaui.com.*

Maui Surfer Girls. This company immerses adventurous young women in wave-riding wisdom during overnight, one- and two-week camps. ⊕ *www.mauisurfergirls.com.*

Fodor's Choice ★ **Nancy Emerson School of Surfing.** Nancy's motto is "If my dog can surf, so can you." Instructors here will get even the shakiest novice riding with the school's "Learn to Surf in One Lesson" program. A two-hour group lesson (up to five students) is $78. Private lessons with the patient and meticulous instructors are $165 for two hours. The company provides boards, rash guards, and water shoes, all in impeccable condition—and it's tops in the customer-service department. ⊠ *505 Front St., Suite 201, Lahaina* ☎ *808/244–7873* ⊕ *www.mauisurfclinics.com.*

WHALE-WATCHING

From December through May, whale-watching becomes one of the most popular activities on Maui. During the season, all outfitters offer whale-watching in addition to their regular activities, and most do an excellent job. Boats leave the wharves at Lahaina and Maalaea in search of humpbacks, allowing you to enjoy the awe-inspiring size of these creatures in closer proximity.

As it's almost impossible *not* to see whales in winter on Maui, you'll want to prioritize: is adventure or comfort your aim? If close encounters with the giants of the deep are your desire, pick a smaller boat that

Humpback whale calves are plentiful in winter; this one is breaching off West Maui.

promises sightings. Those who think "green" usually prefer the smaller, quieter vessels that produce the least amount of negative impact to the whales' natural environment. If an impromptu marine-biology lesson sounds fun, go with the Pacific Whale Foundation. For those wanting to sip mai tais as whales cruise calmly by, stick with a sunset cruise on a boat with an open bar and pupu ($40 and up). ■ TIP➜ Afternoon trips are generally rougher because the wind picks up, but some say this is when the most surface action occurs.

Every captain aims to please during whale season, getting as close as legally possible (100 yards). Crew members know when a whale is about to dive (after several waves of its heart-shaped tail) but rarely can predict breaches (when the whale hurls itself up and almost entirely out of the water). Prime-viewing space (on the upper and lower decks, around the railings) is limited, so boats can feel crowded even when half full. If you don't want to squeeze in beside strangers, opt for a smaller boat with fewer bookings. Don't forget to bring sunscreen, sunglasses, light long sleeves, and a hat you can secure. Winter weather is less predictable and at times can be extreme, especially as the wind picks up. Arrive early to find parking.

BEST SPOTS

Keawakapu Beach. The northern end of Keawakapu Beach on the South Shore seems to be a whale magnet. Situate yourself on the sand or at the nearby restaurant and watch mamas and calves. ⊠ *S. Kihei Rd., near Kilohana Dr., Kihei.*

Papawai Point Lookout. From December 15 to May 1, the Pacific Whale Foundation has naturalists in two places—on the rooftop of its

The Humpback's Winter Home

The humpback whales' attraction to Maui is legendary, and seeing them between December and May is a highlight for many visitors. More than half the Pacific's humpback population winters in Hawaii, especially in the waters around the Valley Isle, where mothers can be seen just a few hundred feet offshore training their young calves in the fine points of whale etiquette. Watching from shore it's easy to catch sight of whales spouting, or even breaching—when they leap almost entirely out of the sea, slapping back onto the water with a huge splash.

At one time there were thousands of the huge mammals, but a history of overhunting and marine pollution dwindled the world population to about 1,500. In 1966 humpbacks were put on the endangered-species list. Hunting or harassing whales is illegal in the waters of most nations, and in the United States boats and airplanes are restricted from getting too close. The word is still out, however, on the effects military sonar testing has on the marine mammals.

Marine biologists believe the humpbacks (much like humans) keep returning to Hawaii because of its warmth. Having fattened themselves in subarctic waters all summer, the whales migrate south in the winter to breed, and a rebounding population of thousands cruise Maui waters. Winter is calving time, and the young whales probably couldn't survive in the frigid Alaskan waters. No one has ever seen a whale give birth here, but experts know that calving is their main winter activity, since the 1- and 2-ton youngsters suddenly appear while the whales are in residence.

The first sighting of a humpback-whale spout each season is exciting for locals on Maui. A collective sigh of relief can be heard, "Ah, they've returned." In the not-so-far distance, flukes and flippers can be seen rising above the ocean's surface. It's hard not to anthropomorphize the tail waving; it looks like such an amiable gesture. Each fluke is uniquely patterned, like a human's fingerprint, and is used to identify the giants as they travel halfway around the globe and back.

headquarters and at the scenic viewpoint at Papawai Point Lookout. Like the commuting traffic, whales cruise along the *pali*, or cliff side, of West Maui's Honoapiilani Highway all day long. ⚠ **Make sure to park safely before craning your neck out to see them.** ⊠ *Rte. 30, 3 miles west of Maalaea Harbor, Maalaea.*

BOATS AND CHARTERS

★ **Pacific Whale Foundation.** With a fleet of seven boats, this nonprofit organization pioneered whale-watching back in 1979. The crew (including a certified marine biologist) offers insights into whale behavior and suggests ways for you to help save marine life worldwide. One of the best things about these trips is the underwater hydrophone that allows you to listen to the whales sing. Trips meet at the organization's store, which sells whale paraphernalia. You'll be sharing the boat with about 100 people in stadium-style seating, but once you catch sight of the wildlife up close, you can't help but be thrilled. ⊠ *612 Front St., Lahaina* ☎ *808/249–8811* ⊕ *www.pacificwhale.org.*

★ **Trilogy Excursions.** Whale-watching trips with Trilogy Excursions consist of smaller groups of about 20 to 36 passengers and include beverages and snacks, an onboard marine naturalist, and hydrophones that detect underwater sound waves. Trips are $39, and you load at West Maui's Kaanapali Beach Hotel. ⊠ *Kaanapali Beach Hotel, 2525 Kaanapali Pkwy., Lahaina* ☎ *808/874–5649, 888/225–6284* ⊕ *www.sailtrilogy.com.*

WINDSURFING

Something about Maui's wind and water stirs the spirit of innovation. Windsurfing, invented in the 1950s, found its true home at Hookipa in 1980. Seemingly overnight, windsurfing pros from around the world flooded Maui's North Shore. Equipment evolved, amazing film footage was captured, and a new sport was born.

If you're new to the action, you can get lessons from the experts islandwide. For a beginner, the best thing about windsurfing is (unlike surfing) you don't have to paddle. Instead, you have to hold on like heck to a flapping sail, as it whisks you into the wind. Needless to say, you're going to need a little coordination and balance to pull this off. Instructors start you on a beach at Kanaha, where the big boys go. Lessons range from two-hour introductory classes to five-day advanced "flight school." If you're an old salt, pick up tips and equipment from the companies below.

BEST SPOTS

Hookipa Bay. After Hookipa Bay was discovered by windsurfers three decades ago, this windy North Shore beach 10 miles east of Kahului gained an international reputation. The spot is blessed with optimal wave-sailing wind and sea conditions, and offers the ultimate aerial experience. ⊠ *Hana Hwy., 2 miles past Paia, Paia.*

Kalepolepo Beach. In summer the windsurfing crowd heads to Kalepolepo Beach on the South Shore. Trade winds build in strength, and by afternoon a swarm of dragonfly-sails can be seen skimming the whitecaps, with the West Maui Mountains as a backdrop. ⊠ *S. Kihei Rd., near Ohukai St., Kihei.*

Kanaha Beach Park. A great site for speed, Kanaha Beach Park is dedicated to beginners in the morning hours, before the waves and wind really get roaring. After 11 am, the professionals choose from their quiver of sails the size and shape best suited for the day's demands. This beach tends to have smaller waves and forceful winds—sometimes sending sailors flying at 40 knots. ■TIP➔ If you aren't ready to go pro, this is a great place for a

The world's best windsurfers love the action on Maui; it's fun to watch, too.

picnic while you watch from the beach. To get here, use any of the three entrances on Amala Place, which runs along the shore just north of Kahului Airport. ✉ *Amala Pl., Kahului.*

EQUIPMENT AND LESSONS

Action Sports Maui. The quirky, friendly professionals here will meet you at Kanaha Beach Park on the North Shore, outfit you with your sail and board, and guide you through your first "jibe" or turn. They promise your learning time will be cut in half. Lessons begin at 9 am every day except Sunday and cost $89 for a 2½-hour class. Three- and five-day courses cost $240 and $395. ✉ *96 Amala Pl., Kahului* ☎ *808/871–5857* ⊕ *www. actionsportsmaui.com.*

★ **Hawaiian Sailboarding Techniques.** Considered Maui's finest windsurfing school, Hawaiian Sailboarding Techniques brings you quality instruction by skilled sailors. Founded by Alan Cadiz, an accomplished World Cup Pro, the school sets high standards for a safe, quality windsurfing experience. Intro classes start at $79 for 2½ hours, gear included. The company is inside Hi-Tech Surf Sports, which offers excellent equipment rentals. ✉ *Hi-Tech Surf Sports, 425 Koloa St., Kahului* ☎ *808/877–2111* ⊕ *www.hstwindsurfing.com.*

Second Wind. Located in Kahului, this company rents boards with two sails for $49 per day. Additional sails are $5 each. Intro classes start at $79. ✉ *111 Hana Hwy., Kahului* ☎ *808/877–7467* ⊕ *www. secondwindmaui.com.*

GOLF, HIKING, AND OUTDOOR ACTIVITIES

Updated by
Heidi Pool

You may come to Maui to sprawl out on the sand, but you'll soon realize there's much more here than the beach. For a relatively small island, Maui's interior landscapes vary wildly, from the moonlike surface of Haleakala Crater to the green rain forest of Iao Valley State Monument. Whether you're exploring waterfalls on a day hike, riding horseback through ranchlands, soaring on a zipline, taking an exhilarating bicycle ride down Haleakala, or teeing off on a world-class golf course, Maui has plenty to keep you busy. Some activities are free, while organized activities vary widely in price; but there's something for every outdoor enthusiast, regardless of age, interest, or fitness level.

AERIAL TOURS

Helicopter flight-seeing excursions can take you over the West Maui Mountains, Hana, Haleakala Crater, even the Big Island lava flow, or the Islands of Lanai and Molokai. This is a beautiful, exciting way to see the island, and the only way to see some of its most dramatic areas and waterfalls. Tour prices usually include a DVD of your trip so you can relive the experience at home. Prices run from about $150 for a half-hour rain-forest tour to more than $400 for a 90-minute mega-experience that includes a champagne toast on landing. Generally the 45- to 50-minute flights are the best value, discounts may be available online or, if you're willing to chance it, by calling at the last minute.

Air Maui Helicopters. Air Maui prides itself on a perfect safety record, and provides 30- to 65-minute flights covering the waterfalls of the West Maui Mountains, Haleakala Crater, Hana, and the spectacular sea cliffs of Molokai. Prices range from $188 to $338, with considerable discounts available online. Charter flights are also available. ⊠ *Kahului Heliport, Hangar 110, Kahului Airport Rd. and Keolani Blvd., Kahului* ☎ *877/238–4942, 808/877–7005* ⊕ *www.airmaui.com.*

Sunshine Helicopters. Sunshine offers tours of Maui in its *Black Beauty* FXStar or WhisperStar aircraft. A pilot-narrated DVD of your actual flight is available for purchase. Prices start at $190 for 30 to 65 minutes, with discounts available online. First-class seating is available for an additional fee. Charter flights can be arranged. ⊠ *Kahului Heliport, Hangar 107, Kahului Airport Rd. and Keolani Blvd., Kahului* ☎ *808/270–3999, 866/501–7738* ⊕ *www.sunshinehelicopters.com.*

BIKING

Maui County biking is safer and more convenient than in the past, but long distances and mountainous terrain keep it from being a practical mode of travel. Still, painted bike lanes enable cyclists to travel all the way from Makena to Kapalua, and you'll see hardy souls battling the trade winds under the hot Maui sun.

Several companies offer guided downhill bike tours down Haleakala. This activity is a great way to see the summit of the world's largest dormant volcano and enjoy an easy, gravity-induced bike ride, but isn't for those not confident in their ability to handle a bike. The ride is inherently dangerous due to the slope, sharp turns, and the fact that you're riding down an actual road with cars on it. That said, the guided-tour bike companies do take every safety precaution. A few companies are now offering unguided (or as they like to say "self-guided") tours where they provide you with the bike and transportation to the top and then you're free to descend at your own pace. Sunrise is downright brisk at the summit, so dress in layers.

■ **TIP**→ Haleakala National Park no longer allows commercial downhill bicycle rides within the park's boundaries. As a result, tour amenities and routes vary by company. Be sure to ask about sunrise viewing from the Haleakala summit, if this is an important feature for you.

BEST SPOTS

At present there are few truly good spots to ride on Maui, though this is changing.

Thompson Road. Street bikers will want to head out to scenic Thompson Road. It's quiet, gently curvy, and flanked by gorgeous views on both sides. Plus, because it's at a higher elevation, the air temperature is cooler and the wind lighter. The coast back down toward Kahului on the Kula Highway is worth the ride up. ⊠ *Kula Hwy., off Rte. 37, Keokea.*

EQUIPMENT AND TOURS

Fodor'sChoice
★
Cruiser Phil's Volcano Riders. Known as "Cruiser Phil," owner Phil Feliciano has been in the downhill bicycle industry since 1983. He offers sunrise tours ($150) and morning tours ($135) that include hotel pickup and drop-off, Continental breakfast, a van tour of the summit, and a guided 28-mile ride down the mountain. Participants should be between 15 and 65, weigh less than 250 pounds, and have ridden a bicycle in the past year. Feliciano also offers structured independent tours ($99) and van tours for $125 (no biking). Discounts are available for online bookings. ⊠ *58-A Amala Pl., Kahului* ☎ *808/893–2332, 877/764–2453* ⊕ *www.cruiserphil.com.*

Haleakala Bike Company. If you're thinking about an unguided Haleakala bike trip, consider this company. Meet at the Old Haiku Cannery and take their van shuttle to the summit. Along the way you can learn about the history of the island, the volcano, and other Hawaiiana. Food is not included, but there are several spots along the way down to stop, rest, and eat. The simple, mostly downhill route takes you right back to the cannery where you started. HBC also offers bike sales, rentals, and services, as well as van tours. Tour prices range from $65 to $115, with discounts available for online bookings. ⊠ *810 Haiku Rd., Suite 120, Haiku* ☎ *808/575–9575, 888/922–2453* ⊕ *www.bikemaui.com.*

Island Biker. Maui's premier bike shop for rentals, sales, and service, Island Biker offers standard front-shock bikes, road bikes, and full-suspension mountain bikes. Daily rental rates range from $50 to $75 and weekly rates are $200; the price includes a helmet, pump, water bottle, cages, flat-repair kit, and spare tube. Car racks are $5 per day (free with weekly rentals). The staff can suggest routes appropriate for mountain or road biking. ⊠ *415 Dairy Rd., Kahului* ☎ *808/877–7744* ⊕ *www.islandbikermaui.com.*

West Maui Cycles. Servicing the west side of the island, West Maui Cycles offers cruisers for $15 per day ($60 per week), hybrids for $35 per day ($140 per week), and performance road bikes for $60 per day ($220 per week). Tandems start at $30 per day ($120 per week). The shop also has baby joggers and car racks for rent. Sales and service are available. ⊠ *1087 Limahana Pl., No. 6, Lahaina* ☎ *808/661–9005* ⊕ *www. westmauicycles.com.*

GOLF

3

Maui's natural beauty and surroundings offer some of the most jaw-dropping vistas imaginable on a golf course. Holes run across small bays, past craggy lava outcrops, and up into cool, forested mountains. Most courses feature mesmerizing ocean views, some close enough to feel the salt in the air. And although many of the courses are affiliated with resorts (and therefore a little pricier), the public courses are no less impressive. Greens fees listed here are the highest course rates per round on weekdays and weekends for U.S. residents. (Some courses charge non–U.S. residents higher prices.) Discounts are often available for resort guests and for those who book tee times on the Web. Rental clubs may or may not be included with greens fees. ■ **TIP→ Cheaper twilight fees are usually offered; call individual courses for information.**

Fodor'sChoice
★
The Dunes at Maui Lani. Robin Nelson is at his minimalist best here, creating a bit of British links in the middle of the Pacific. Holes run through ancient, lightly wooded sand dunes, 5 miles inland from Kahului Harbor. Thanks to the natural humps and slopes of the dunes, Nelson had to move very little dirt and created a natural beauty. During the design phase he visited Ireland, and not so coincidentally the par-3 third looks a lot like the Dell at Lahinch: a white dune on the right sloping down into a deep bunker and partially obscuring the right side of the green—just one of several blind to semiblind shots here. Popular with residents, this course (1999) has won several awards including "Five Best Kept Secret Golf Courses in America" by *Golf Digest.* ⊠ *1333 Maui Lani Pkwy., Kahului* ☎ *808/873–0422* ⊕ *www.dunesatmauilani.com* ⚐ *18 holes. 6841 yds. Par 72. Slope 136. Greens fee: $112* ☞ *Facilities: Driving range, putting green, golf carts, rental clubs, pro shop, golf academy/lessons, restaurant, bar.*

★ **Kaanapali Golf Resort.** The Royal Kaanapali (North) Course (1962) is one of three in Hawaii designed by Robert Trent Jones Sr., the godfather of modern golf architecture. The greens average a whopping 10,000 square feet, necessary because of the often-severe undulation. The par-4 18th hole (into the prevailing trade breezes, with out-of-bounds on the left, and a lake on the right) is notoriously tough. Designed by Arthur Jack Snyder, the Kaanapali Kai (South) Course (1976) shares similar seaside-into-the-hills terrain, but is rated a couple of strokes easier, mostly because putts are less treacherous. ⊠ *2290 Kaanapali Pkwy., Lahaina* ☎ *808/661–3691, 866/454–4653* ⊕ *www.kaanapali-golf.com* ⚐ *North Course: 18 holes. 6500 yds. Par 71. Slope 126. Greens Fee: $235. South Course: 18 holes. 6400 yds. Par 70. Slope 124. Greens fee: $195* ☞ *Facilities: Driving range, putting green, golf carts, rental clubs, lessons, restaurant, bar.*

Sunset views are lovely from many hotel rooms near West Maui's Kaanapali Beach.

Fodor's Choice **Kapalua Resort.** Perhaps Hawaii's best-known golf resort and the crown
★ jewel of golf on Maui, Kapalua hosts the PGA Tour's first event each
January: the Hyundai Tournament of Champions at the Plantation
Course at Kapalua. Ben Crenshaw and Bill Coore (1991) tried to
incorporate traditional shot values in a nontraditional site, taking into
account slope, gravity, and the prevailing trade winds. The par-5 18th
hole, for instance, plays 663 yards from the back tees (600 yards from
the resort tees). The hole drops 170 feet in elevation, narrowing as it
goes to a partially guarded green, and plays downwind and down-grain.
Despite the longer-than-usual distance, the slope is great enough and
the wind at your back usually brisk enough to reach the green with
two well-struck shots—a truly unbelievable finish to a course that will
challenge, frustrate, and reward the patient golfer.

The Bay Course (Arnold Palmer and Francis Duane, 1975) is the more
traditional of Kapalua's courses, with gentle rolling fairways and generous greens. The most memorable hole is the par-3 fifth hole, with a
tee shot that must carry a turquoise finger of Onelua Bay. Each of the
courses has a separate clubhouse.

Kapalua Golf Academy. The Kapalua Golf Academy offers 23 acres of
practice turf and 11 teeing areas, an 18-hole putting course, and 3-hole
walking course, as well as an instructional bay with video analysis.
⊠ *1000 Office Rd., Kapalua* ☎ *808/665–5455, 877/527–2582.*

Bay Course. The Bay Course ⊠ *300 Kapalua Dr., Kapalua* ☎ *808/669–
8044, 877/527–2582* ⊕ *www.kapalua.com/hawaii-golf* ⅃ *18 holes.
6600 yds. Par 72. Slope 133. Greens fee: $208* ☞ *Facilities: Driving
range, putting green, rental clubs, pro shop, lessons, restaurant, bar..*

BEFORE YOU HIT THE FIRST TEE . . .

Golf is golf, and Hawaii is part of the United States, but island golf nevertheless has its own quirks. Here are a few tips to make your golf experience in the Islands more pleasant.

■ All resort courses and many daily fee courses provide rental clubs. In many cases, they're the latest lines from top manufacturers. This is true for both men and women, as well as left-handers, which means you don't have to schlep clubs across the Pacific.

■ Come spikeless—very few Hawaii courses still permit metal spikes. And most of the resort courses require a collared shirt.

■ Maui is notorious for its trade winds. Consider playing early if you want to avoid the wind, and remember that while it'll frustrate you at times and make club selection difficult, you may very well see some of your longest drives ever.

■ In theory you can play golf in Hawaii 365 days a year, but there's a reason the Hawaiian Islands are so green. An umbrella and light jacket can come in handy.

■ Unless you play a muni or certain daily-fee courses, plan on taking a cart. Riding carts are mandatory at most courses and are included in the greens fees.

Plantation Course. The Plantation Course ⊠ *2000 Plantation Club Dr., Kapalua* ☎ *808/669–8044, 877/527–2582* ⊕ *www.kapalua.com/ hawaii-golf* ⅃ *18 holes. 7411 yds. Par 73. Slope 135. Greens fee: $268* ☞ *Facilities: Driving range, putting green, golf carts, pull carts, rental clubs, pro shop, golf academy/lessons, restaurant, bar.*

Fodor'sChoice
★

Makena Beach & Golf Resort. Robert Trent Jones Jr. designed Makena Golf Course (1994) in harmony with the existing landscape: Hawaiian rock walls still stand in their original locations, and natural gullies and stream beds were left in their natural states. Sculpted from the lava flows on the western flank of Haleakala, Makena offers quick greens with lots of breaks and plenty of scenic distractions. The fourth hole is one of the most picturesque inland par 3s in Hawaii, with the green guarded on the right by a duck pond. The sixth is an excellent example of option golf: The fairway is sliced up the middle by a gaping ravine, which must sooner or later be crossed to reach the green. The last three holes are relatively short par 4s, but keen accuracy is required, as the tees wind through kiawe trees. ⊠ *5415 Makena Alanui, Makena* ☎ *808/891–4000* ⊕ *www.makenagolf.com* ⅃ *18 holes. 6567 yds. Par 72. Slope 135. Greens fee: $179.* ☞ *Facilities: Driving range, putting green, golf carts, rental clubs, pro shop, golf academy/lessons, restaurant, bar.*

Pukalani Golf Course. At 1,110 feet above sea level, Pukalani (Bob E. Baldock and Robert L. Baldock, 1970) provides one of the finest vistas in all Hawaii. Holes run up, down, and across the slopes of Haleakala. The trade winds tend to come up in the late morning and afternoon. This, combined with frequent elevation change, makes club selection a test. The fairways tend to be wide, but greens are undulating and quick. ⊠ *360 Pukalani St., Pukalani* ☎ *808/572–1314* ⊕ *www.pukalanigolf.*

com ✦ *18 holes. 6962 yds. Par 72. Slope 127. Greens fee: $88* ☞ *Facilities: Driving range, putting green, golf carts, rental clubs, pro shop, restaurant, bar.*

Fodor'sChoice   **Wailea.** This is the only Hawaii resort to offer three different courses:
★   Gold, Emerald, and Old Blue. Designed by Robert Trent Jones Jr. (Gold and Emerald) and Arthur Jack Snyder (Old Blue), these courses share similar terrain, carved into the leeward slopes of Haleakala. Although the ocean does not come into play, its beauty is visible on almost every hole. ■TIP➔ Remember, putts break dramatically toward the ocean.

Jones refers to the Gold Course at Wailea (1993) as the "masculine" course. It's all trees and lava, and regarded as the hardest of the three courses. The trick here is to note even subtle changes in elevation. The par-3 8th, for example, plays from an elevated tee across a lava ravine to a large, well-bunkered green framed by palm trees, the blue sea, and tiny Molokini. The course demands strategy and careful club selection. The Emerald Course (1994) is the "feminine" layout with lots of flowers and bunkering away from greens. Although this may seem to render the bunker benign, the opposite is true. A bunker well in front of a green disguises the distance to the hole. Likewise, the Emerald's extensive flower beds are dangerous distractions because of their beauty. The Gold and Emerald share a clubhouse, practice facility, and 19th hole.

At Wailea's first course, the Old Blue Course (1971), judging elevation change is also key. Fairways and greens tend to be wider and more forgiving than on the Gold or Emerald, and run through colorful flora that includes hibiscus, wiliwili, bougainvillea, and plumeria.

   Old Blue Course. Old Blue Course: ⊠ *100 Wailea Golf Club Dr., Wailea* ☎ *808/875–7450, 888/328–6284* ⊕ *www.waileagolf.com* ✦ *18 holes. 6765 yds. Par 72. Slope 129. Greens fee: $190.* ☞ *Facilities: Driving range, putting green, golf carts, rental clubs, pro shop, golf academy/lessons, restaurant, bar..*

   Gold and Emerald Courses. Gold and Emerald Courses: ⊠ *100 Wailea Golf Club Dr., Wailea* ☎ *808/875–7450, 888/328–6284* ⊕ *www.waileagolf.com* ✦ *Gold Course: 18 holes. 6653 yds. Par 72. Slope 132. Greens fee: $225. Emerald Course: 18 holes. 6407 yds. Par 72. Slope 130. Greens fee: $225.* ☞ *Facilities: Driving range, putting green, golf carts, rental clubs, pro shop, golf academy/lessons, restaurant, bar.*

HANG GLIDING AND PARAGLIDING

If you've always wanted to know what it feels like to fly, hang gliding or paragliding might be your perfect Maui adventure. You'll get open-air, bird's-eye views of the Valley Isle that you'll likely never forget. And you don't need to be a daredevil to participate.

LESSONS AND TOURS

Hang Gliding Maui. Armin Engert will take you on an instructional powered hang-gliding trip out of Hana Airport in East Maui. With more than 13,000 hours in flight and a perfect safety record, Armin flies you 1,000 feet over Maui's most beautiful coast. A 30-minute flight lesson costs $150, a 45-minute lesson costs $200, and a 60-minute lesson is $250. Snapshots of your flight from a wing-mounted camera cost an additional $30, and a 34-minute DVD of the flight is available for $70. Reservations are required. ✉ *Hana Airport, Alalele Pl., off Hana Hwy., Hana* 🕾 *808/572–6557* ⊕ *www.hangglidingmaui.com.*

Proflyght Paragliding. Proflyght is the only paragliding outfit on Maui to offer solo, tandem, and instruction at Polipoli Spring State Recreation Area. The leeward slope of Haleakala lends itself to paragliding with breathtaking scenery and Upcountry air currents that increase and rise during the day. Polipoli creates tremendous thermals that allow you to peacefully descend 3,000 feet to land. Prices start at $95, with full certification available. ✉ *Polipoli Spring State Recreation Area, Waipoli Rd., Kula* 🕾 *808/874–5433* ⊕ *www.paraglidemaui.com.*

HIKING

Hikes on Maui range from coastal seashore to verdant rain forest to alpine desert. Orchids, hibiscus, ginger, heliconia, and anthuriums grow wild on many trails, and exotic fruits like mountain apple, *lilikoi* (passion fruit), thimbleberry, and strawberry guava provide refreshing snacks for hikers. Ironically, much of what you see in lower altitude forests is alien, brought to Hawaii at one time or another by someone hoping to improve upon nature. Plants like strawberry guava and ginger may be tasty, but they grow over native forest plants and have become serious, problematic weeds.

The best hikes get you out of the imported landscaping and into the truly exotic wilderness. Hawaii possesses some of the world's rarest plants, insects, and birds. Pocket field guides are available at most grocery or drug stores and can really illuminate your walk. Before you know it, you'll be nudging your companion and pointing out trees that look like something out of a Dr. Suess book. If you watch the right branches quietly, you can spot the same honeycreepers or happy-face spiders scientists have spent their lives studying.

BEST SPOTS

Fodor's Choice ★ **Haleakala Crater.** Undoubtedly the best hiking on the island is at Haleakala Crater, with 30 miles of trails, two camping areas, and three cabins. If you're in shape, do a day hike descending from the summit along **Keoneheehee Trail** (also known as Sliding Sands Trail) to the crater floor. If you're in shape and have time, consider spending several days here amid the cinder cones, lava flows, and all that loud silence. Going into the crater is like going to a different planet. In the early 1960s NASA actually brought moon-suited astronauts here to practice what it would be like to "walk on the moon." Today, on one of the many hikes—most moderate to strenuous—you can traverse black sand and wild lava formations, follow the trail of blooming *ahinahina* (silverswords), and witness tremendous views of big sky and burned-red cliffs.

The best time to go into the crater is in the summer months, when the conditions are generally more predictable. Be sure to bring layered clothing—and plenty of warm clothes if you're staying overnight. It may be scorching hot during the day, but it gets mighty chilly after dark. Bring your own drinking water, as it is only available at the two visitor centers. Water inside the crater is nonpotable. Note that overnight visitors must get a permit at park headquarters before entering the crater; day-use visitors do not need a permit.

Cabins are $75 per night for reservations made 21 or more days in advance ($60 per night within 21 days, nonrefundable), and accommodate 12 people. You can book up to three consecutive nights. Online cabin reservations may be made through **Friends of Haleakala National Park** (⊕ www.fhnp.org). *For detailed information on hikes in the crater, see Haleakala National Park in Exploring Maui.* ⊠ *Haleakala Crater Rd.* ☎ *808/572–4400* ⊕ *www.nps.gov/hale.*

A branch of Haleakala National Park, Oheo Gulch is famous for its pools (the area is sometimes called the "Seven Sacred Pools"). Truth is, there are more than seven pools, and there's nothing sacred about them. The former owner of the Hotel Hana-Maui started calling the area Seven Sacred Pools to attract the masses to sleepy old Hana. His plan worked and the name stuck, much to the chagrin of most Mauians.

The best time to visit the pools is in the morning, before the crowds and tour buses arrive. Start your day with a vigorous hike. Oheo has some fantastic trails to choose from, including our favorite, the Pipiwai Trail. When you're done, nothing could be better than going to the pools, lounging on the rocks, and cooling off in the freshwater reserves. (Keep in mind, however, that the park periodically closes the pools to swimming when the potential for flash flooding exists.)

You can find Oheo Gulch on Route 31, 10 miles past Hana town. All visitors must pay a $10 national park fee (per car not per person), which is valid for three days and can be used at Haleakala's summit as well. Be sure to visit Haleakala National Park's Kipahulu Visitor Center, 10 miles past Hana, for information about scheduled orientations and cultural demonstrations. Note that there is no drinking water here.

Hoapili Trail. A challenging hike through eye-popping scenery in southwestern Maui is this 5.5-mile coastal trail beyond the Ahihi-Kinau Natural Area Reserve. Named after a bygone Hawaiian king, it follows the shoreline, threading through the remains of ancient Hawaiian villages. King Hoapili created an islandwide road, and this wide path of stacked lava rocks is a marvel to look at and walk on. (It's not the easiest surface for the ankles and feet, so wear sturdy shoes.) This is brutal territory with little shade and no facilities, and extra water is a must. To get here, follow Makena Road to La Pérouse Bay. The trail begins just around the corner. ⊠ *Trailhead: La Pérouse Bay, Makena Rd..*

Iao Valley Trail. Anyone (including your grandparents) can take this easy, short walk from the parking lot at Iao Valley State Monument. On your choice of two paved walkways, you can cross the Iao Stream and explore the junglelike area. Ascend the stairs up to the **Iao Needle** for spectacular views of Central Maui, or pause in the garden of Hawaiian heritage plants and watch local youngsters hurling themselves from the bridge into the chilly pools below. ⊠ *Trailhead: Iao Valley State Monument parking lot, Rte. 32, Wailuku* ⏱ *30 min, 0.5 miles round-trip.*

Continued on page 261

HALEAKALA NATIONAL PARK

HALEAKALA CRATER

From the Tropics to the Moon! Two hours, 38 miles, 10,023 feet—those are the unlikely numbers involved in reaching Maui's highest point, the summit of the volcano Haleakala. Nowhere else on earth can you drive from sea level (Kahului) to 10,023 feet (the summit) in only 38 miles. And what's more shocking—in that short vertical ascent, you'll journey from lush, tropical-island landscape to the stark, moonlike basin of the volcano's enormous, otherworldly crater.

Established in 1916, Haleakala National Park covers an astonishing 27,284 acres. Haleakala "Crater" is the centerpiece of the park though it's not actually a crater. Technically, it's an erosional valley, flushed out by water pouring from the summit through two enormous gaps. The mountain has terrific camping and hiking, including a trail that loops through the crater, but the chance to witness this unearthly landscape is reason enough for a visit.

THE CLIMB TO THE SUMMIT

To reach Haleakala National Park and the mountain's breathtaking summit, take Route 36 east of Kahului to the Haleakala Highway (Route 37). Head east, up the mountain to the unlikely intersection of Haleakala Highway and Haleakala Highway. If you continue straight the road's name changes to Kula Highway (still Route 37). Instead, turn left onto Haleakala Highway—this is now Route 377. After about 6 mi, make a left onto

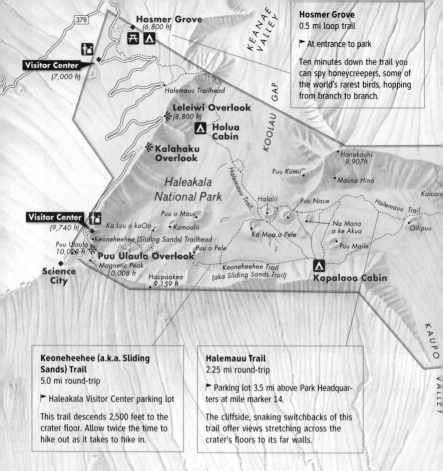

Hosmer Grove (6,800 ft)

Hosmer Grove
0.5 mi loop trail

► At entrance to park

Ten minutes down the trail you can spy honeycreepers, some of the world's rarest birds, hopping from branch to branch.

KEANAE VALLEY

378

Visitor Center (7,000 ft)

Halemauu Trailhead

Leleiwi Overlook (8,800 ft)

Holua Cabin

KOOLAU GAP

Kalahaku Overlook

Haleakala National Park

Halalii

Puu Kumu

Hanakauhi 8,907 ft

Mauna Hina

Puu o Maui

Ka Luu o kaOo

Kamoalii

Puu Naue

Na Mana o ke Akua

Halemauu Trail

Kaluai

Keoneheehee (Sliding Sands) Trailhead

Ka Moa o Pele

Puu Maile

Oilipuu

Visitor Center (9,740 ft)

Puu Ulaula 10,028 ft

Puu Ulaula Overlook

Puu o Pele

Science City

Magnetic Peak 10,008 ft

Haupaakea 9,159 ft

Keoneheehee Trail (aka Sliding Sands Trail)

Kapalaoa Cabin

KAUPO VALLEY

Keoneheehee (a.k.a. Sliding Sands) Trail
5.0 mi round-trip

► Haleakala Visitor Center parking lot

This trail descends 2,500 feet to the crater floor. Allow twice the time to hike out as it takes to hike in.

Halemauu Trail
2.25 mi round-trip

► Parking lot 3.5 mi above Park Headquarters at mile marker 14.

The cliffside, snaking switchbacks of this trail offer views stretching across the crater's floors to its far walls.

Crater Road (Route 378). After several long switchbacks (look out for downhill bikers!) you'll come to the park entrance.

■TIP→ Before you head up Haleakala, call for the latest park weather conditions (☎ 866/944-5025). Extreme gusty winds, heavy rain, and even snow in winter are not uncommon. Because of the high altitude, the mountaintop temperature is often as much as 30 degrees cooler than that at sea level. Be sure to bring a jacket. Also make sure you have a full tank of gas. No service stations exist beyond Kula.

There's a $10 per car fee to enter the park; but it's good for three days and can be used at Oheo Gulch (Kipahulu), so save your receipt.

6,800 feet, Hosmer Grove. Just as you enter the park, Hosmer Grove has campsites and interpretive trails (*see* Hiking & Camping *on the following pages*). Park rangers maintain a changing schedule of talks and hikes both here and at the top of the mountain. Call the park for current schedules.

7,000 feet, Park Headquarters/Visitor Center. Not far from Hosmer Grove, the Park Headquarters/Visitor Center (open daily from 6:30 AM to 3:45) has trail maps and displays about the vol-

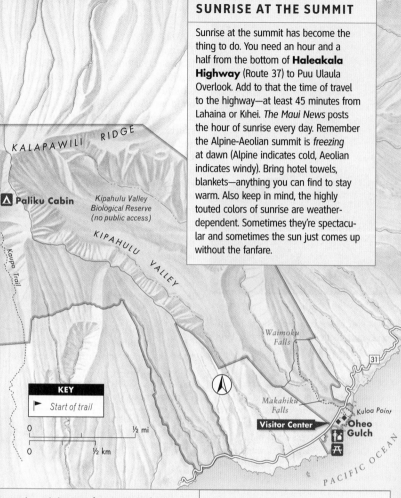

KALAPAWILI RIDGE

🏕 **Paliku Cabin**

Kipahulu Valley Biological Reserve (no public access)

Kaupo Trail

KIPAHULU VALLEY

Waimoku Falls

31

Makahiku Falls

Visitor Center

◆ **Oheo Gulch**

Kuloa Point

KEY

▶ Start of trail

0   ½ mi

0   ½ km

PACIFIC OCEAN

SUNRISE AT THE SUMMIT

Sunrise at the summit has become the thing to do. You need an hour and a half from the bottom of **Haleakala Highway** (Route 37) to Puu Ulaula Overlook. Add to that the time of travel to the highway—at least 45 minutes from Lahaina or Kihei. *The Maui News* posts the hour of sunrise every day. Remember the Alpine-Aeolian summit is *freezing* at dawn (Alpine indicates cold, Aeolian indicates windy). Bring hotel towels, blankets—anything you can find to stay warm. Also keep in mind, the highly touted colors of sunrise are weather-dependent. Sometimes they're spectacular and sometimes the sun just comes up without the fanfare.

cano's origins and eruption history. Hikers and campers should check-in here before heading up the mountain. Maps, posters, and other memorabilia are available at the gift shop.

8,800 feet, Leleiwi Overlook. Continuing up the mountain, you come to Leleiwi Overlook. A short walk to the end of the parking lot reveals your first awe-inspiring view of the crater. The small hills in the basin are volcanic cinder cones (called *puu* in Hawaiian), each with a small crater at its top, and each the site of a former eruption.

WHERE TO EAT

KULA LODGE (✉ Haleakala Hwy., Kula ☎ 808/878–2517) serves hearty breakfasts from 7 to 11 AM, a favorite with hikers coming down from a sunrise visit to Haleakala's summit, as well as those on their way up for a late-morning tramp in the crater. Spectacular ocean views fill the windows of this mountainside lodge.

If you're here in the late afternoon, it's possible you'll experience a phenomenon called the Brocken Specter. Named after a similar occurrence in East Germany's Harz Mountains, the "specter"

10,023 feet, Puu Ulaula Overlook. The highest point on Maui is the Puu Ulaula Overlook, at the 10,023-foot summit. Here you find a glass-enclosed lookout with a 360-degree view. The building is open 24 hours a day, and this is where visitors gather for the best sunrise view. Dawn begins between 5:45 and 7, depending on the time of year. On a clear day you can see the islands of Molokai, Lanai, Kahoolawe, and Hawaii (the Big Island). On a *really* clear day you can even spot Oahu glimmering in the distance.

■TIP→ The air is very thin at 10,000 feet. Don't be surprised if you feel a little breathless while walking around the summit. Take it easy and drink lots of water. Anyone who has been scuba diving within the last 24 hours should not make the trip up Haleakala.

On a small hill nearby, you can see **Science City**, an off-limits research and communications center straight out of an espionage thriller. The University of Hawaii maintains an observatory here, and the Department of Defense tracks satellites.

For more information about Haleakala National Park, contact the **National Park Service** (☎ 808/572–4400,⊕ www.nps.gov/hale).

HIKING AND CAMPING

Exploring Haleakala Crater is one of the best hiking experiences on Maui. The volcanic terrain offers an impressive diversity of colors, textures, and shapes—almost as if the lava has been artfully sculpted. The barren landscape is home to many plants, insects, and birds that exist nowhere else on earth and have developed intriguing survival mechanisms, such as the sun-reflecting, hairy leaves of the silversword, which allow it to survive the intense climate.

Stop at park headquarters to register and pick up trail maps on your way into the park.

allows you to see yourself reflected on the clouds and encircled by a rainbow. Don't wait all day for this because it's not a daily occurrence.

9,000 feet, Kalahaku Overlook. The next stopping point is Kalahaku Overlook. The view here offers a different perspective of the crater, and at this elevation the famous silversword plant grows amid the cinders. This odd, endangered beauty grows only here and at the same elevation on the Big Island's two peaks. It begins life as a silver, spiny-leaf rosette and is the sole home of a variety of native insects (it's the only shelter around). The silversword reaches maturity between 7 and 17 years, when it sends forth a 3- to 8-foot-tall stalk with several hundred tiny sunflowers. It blooms once, then dies.

9,740 feet, Haleakala Visitor Center. Another mile up is the Haleakala Visitor Center, open daily from sunrise to 3 PM except Christmas and New Year's. There are exhibits inside, and a trail from here leads to White Hill—a short easy walk that will give you an even better view of the valley.

1-Hour Hike. Just as you enter Haleakala National Park, **Hosmer Grove** offers a short 10-minute hike and an hour-long, ¹/₂-mile loop trail that will give you insight into Hawaii's fragile ecology. Anyone can go on these hikes, whereas a longer trail through the Waikamoi Cloud Forest is accessible only with park ranger–guided hikes. Call park headquarters for the schedule. Facilities here include six campsites (no permit needed, available on a first-come, first-served basis), pit toilets, drinking water, and cooking shelters.

4-Hour Hikes. Two half-day hikes involve descending into the crater and returning the way you came. The first, **Halemauu Trail** (trailhead is between mile markers 14 and 15), is 2.25 miles round-trip. The cliffside, snaking switchbacks of this trail offer views stretching across the crater's puu-speckled floor to its far walls. On clear days you can peer through the Koolau Gap to Hana. Native flowers and shrubs grow along the trail, which is typically misty and cool (though still exposed to the sun). When you reach the gate at the bottom, head back up.

The other hike, which is 5 miles round-trip, descends down **Keoneheehee (a.k.a. Sliding Sands) Trail** (trailhead is at the Haleakala Visitor Center) into an alien landscape of reddish black cinders, lava bombs, and silverswords. It's easy to imagine life before humans in the solitude and silence of this place. Turn back when you hit the crater floor.

■TIP→ **Bring water, sunscreen, and a reliable jacket. These are demanding hikes. Take it slowly to acclimate, and allow additional time for the uphill return trip.**

8-Hour Hike. The recommended way to explore the crater in a single, but full day is to go in two cars and ferry yourselves back and forth between the head of **Halemauu Trail** and the summit. This way, you can hike from the summit down **Keoneheehee Trail**, cross the crater's floor, investigate the **Bottomless Pit** and **Pele's Paint Pot**, then climb out on the switchback trail (**Halemauu**). When you emerge, the shelter of your waiting car will be very welcome (this is an 11.2-mile hike). If you don't have two cars, hitching a ride from Halemauu back to the summit should be relatively safe and easy.

■ TIP➜ Take a backpack with lunch, water, sunscreen, and a reliable jacket for the beginning and end of the 8-hour hike. This is a demanding trip, but you will never regret or forget it.

Overnight Hike. Staying overnight in one of Haleakala's three cabins or two wilderness campgrounds is an experience like no other. You'll feel like the only person on earth when you wake up inside this enchanted, strange landscape. The cabins, each tucked in a different corner of the crater's floor, are equipped with 12 bunk beds, wood-burning stoves, fake logs, and kitchen gear.

Holua cabin is the shortest hike, less than 4 hours (3.7 miles) from Halemauau Trail. **Kapalaoa** is about 5 hours (5.5 miles) down Keoneheehee Trail. The most cherished cabin is **Paliku**, an eight-hour (9.3-miles) hike starting from either trail. It's nestled against the cliffs above Kaupo Gap. Cabin reservations can be made up to 90 days in advance through the Friends of Haleakala National Park's Web site (⊕ fhnp. org/wcr) or by calling the National Park Service (☎808/572-4400) between 1 and 3 PM HST. Tent campsites at Holua

and Paliku are free and easy to reserve on a first-come, first-served basis.

■ TIP➜ Toilets and nonpotable water are available—bring iodine tablets to purify the water. Open fires are not allowed and packing out your trash is mandatory.

For more information on hiking or camping, contact the National Park Service (⊠ Box 369, Makawao 96768 ☎808/572-4459 ⊕ www.nps.gov/hale).

OPTIONS FOR EXPLORING

If you're short on time you can drive to the summit, take a peek inside, and drive back down. But the "House of the Sun" is really worth a day, whether you explore by foot, horseback, or helicopter.

BIKING
At this writing, all guided bike tours inside park boundaries were suspended indefinitely. However, the tours continue but now start outside the boundary of the park. These can provide a speedy, satisfying downhill trip. The park is still open to individual bikes for a $5 fee. There are no bike paths, however—just the same road that is used by vehicular traffic. Whether you're on your own or with a tour, be careful!

HELICOPTER TOURS
Viewing Haleakala from above can be a mind-altering experience, if you don't mind dropping $200+ per person for a few blissful moments above the crater. Most tours buzz Haleakala, where airspace is regulated, then head over to Hana in search of waterfalls.

HORSEBACK RIDING
Several companies offer half-day, full-day, and even overnight rides into the crater. On one half-day ride you descend into the crater on Keoneheehee Trail and have lunch before you head back.

For complete information on any of these activities, ⇨ see Golf, Hiking and Outdoor Activities.

Kapalua Resort. The resort offers free access to 100 miles of hiking trails to guests and visitors as a self-guided experience. Trail information and maps are available at the Kapalua Adventure Center. Access to most trails is via a complimentary resort shuttle, which must be reserved in advance. Guided hiking tours are also available. ⊠ *2000 Village Rd., corner of Office Rd., Kapalua* ☎ *808/665–4386, 877/665–4386* ⊕ *www.kapalua.com.*

KEEP IN MIND

Wear sturdy shoes while hiking; you'll want to spare your ankles from a crash course in loose lava rock. When hiking near streams or waterfalls, be extremely cautious—flash floods can occur at any time. Do not drink stream water or swim in streams if you have open cuts; bacteria and parasites are not the souvenir you want to take home with you. Wear sunscreen, a hat, and layered clothing, and be sure to drink plenty of water (even if you don't feel thirsty). At upper elevations, the weather is guaranteed to be extreme—alternately chilly or blazing.

Fodor'sChoice ★ **Pipiwai Trail.** This moderate 2-mile trek upstream leads to the 400-foot Waimoku Falls, pounding down in all its power and glory. Following signs from the parking lot, head across the road and uphill into the forest. The trail borders a sensational gorge and passes onto a boardwalk through a mystifying forest of giant bamboo. This stomp through muddy and rocky terrain includes two stream crossings and takes around three hours to fully enjoy. Although this trail is never truly crowded, it's best done early in the morning before the tours arrive. Be sure to bring mosquito repellent. ⊠ *Trailhead: Hana Hwy., near mile marker 42* ☾ *3 hrs, 4.0 miles round-trip.*

GOING WITH A GUIDE

Fodor'sChoice ★ **Friends of Haleakala National Park.** This nonprofit offers day and overnight trips into the volcanic crater. The purpose of your trip, the service work itself, isn't too much—mostly native planting, removing invasive plants, and light cabin maintenance. An interpretive park ranger accompanies each trip, taking you to places you'd otherwise miss and teaching you about the native flora and fauna. ☎ *808/876–1673* ⊕ *www.fhnp.org.*

Fodor'sChoice ★ **Hike Maui.** Started in 1983, the area's oldest hiking company remains extremely well regarded for waterfall, rain forest, and crater hikes led by enthusiastic, highly trained guides who weave botany, geology, ethnobotany, culture, and history into the outdoor experience. Prices range from $80 to $165 for excursions lasting 3 to 11 hours (discounts are available for booking online). Private tours are also available. Hike Maui supplies day packs, rain gear, mosquito repellent, first-aid supplies, bottled water, snacks, lunch for the longer trips, and transportation to and from the site. ☎ *808/879–5270, 866/324–6284* ⊕ *www. hikemaui.com.*

★ **Sierra Club.** One great avenue into the island's untrammeled wilderness is Maui's chapter of the Sierra Club. Join one of the club's hikes into pristine forests, along ancient coastal paths, to historic sites, and to Haleakala Crater. Some outings require volunteer service, but most are just for fun. Bring your own food and water, rain gear, sunscreen, sturdy shoes, and a suggested donation of $5 for hikers over age 14. This is a true bargain. ☎ *808/573–4147* ⊕ *www.hi.sierraclub.org/maui.*

HORSEBACK RIDING

Several companies on Maui offer horseback riding that's far more appealing than the typical hour-long trudge over a dull trail with 50 other horses.

GOING WITH A GUIDE

Fodor's Choice ★ **Maui Stables.** Hawaiian-owned and operated, this company provides a trip back in time to an era when life moved more slowly and reverently. Tours begin at the stable in remote Kipahulu and pass through several historic Hawaiian sites. Before heading up into the forest, your guide intones the words to a traditional *oli,* or chant, asking for permission to enter. Along the way, you can learn about the principles of Hawaiian culture, including a deep respect for the *aina* (land). By the time you reach the mountain pasture overlooking several waterfalls, including the 400-foot Waimoku Falls, you'll feel lucky to have been a part of the tradition. Rides begin at 10 am daily and cost $150 per rider—definitely well worth it. Maui Stables provides refreshments and bottled water only; bring a picnic lunch if you're a hearty eater. ✉ *Hwy. 37, between mile markers 40 and 41, Hana* ☎ *808/248–7799* ⊕ *www.mauistables.com.*

Mendes Ranch. Family-owned and run, Mendes operates out of the beautiful ranchland of Kahakuloa on the windward slopes of the West Maui Mountains. Two-hour morning and afternoon trail rides ($99) are available. Cowboys will take you cantering up rolling pastures into the lush rain forest, and then you'll descend all the way down to the ocean for a photo op with a dramatic backdrop. Don't expect a Hawaiian cultural experience here—it's all about the horses and the ride. Skip the optional barbecue lunch ($20); you'll do better in town. ✉ *3530 Kahekili Hwy., Wailuku* ☎ *808/244–7320, 800/871–5222* ⊕ *www.mendesranch.com.*

Pony Express Tours. This outfit offers trips on horseback into Haleakala Crater. The half-day ride goes down to the crater floor for a picnic lunch, and is a great way to experience the majesty of the volcano without having to hike. Prior riding experience is highly recommended, as you're on horseback for at least 4 hours. The company also offers 1½- and 2-hour rides on the slopes of the Haleakala Ranch. Prices range from $95 to $182. ☎ *808/667–2200* ⊕ *www.ponyexpresstours.com.*

TENNIS

Most courts charge by the hour but will let players continue after their initial hour for free, provided no one is waiting. In addition to the facilities listed below, many hotels and condos have courts open to nonguests for a fee.

Kapalua Tennis Garden. Home to the Kapalua Tennis Club, this complex serves the Kapalua Resort with 10 courts (four lighted for night play) and a pro shop. The fee is $10 per person per day. Each month the

Kapalua Tennis Garden plays host to a special theme tournament for resort guests and residents. ⊠ *100 Kapalua Dr., Kapalua* ☎ *808/662–7730* ⊕ *www.kapalua.com.*

Lahaina Civic Center. The best free courts are the five at the Lahaina Civic Center, near Wahikuli State Park. They all have overhead lighting for night play, and are available on a first-come, first-served basis. ⊠ *1840 Honoapiilani Hwy., Lahaina* ☎ *808/661–4685.*

Wailea Tennis Club. Featuring 11 Plexipave courts (two lighted for night play), this club also offers lessons, rentals, and ball machines. Daily clinics help you improve ground strokes, serve, volley, or doubles strategy. Rates are $15 per player. ⊠ *131 Wailea Ike Pl., Wailea* ☎ *808/879–1958* ⊕ *www.waileatennis.com.*

ZIPLINE TOURS

Ziplining lets you satisfy your inner Tarzan by soaring high above deep gulches and canyons—for a price that can seem steep. A harness keeps you fully supported on each ride. There are now multiple zipline courses on Maui to choose from. Each has its own age minimums and weight restrictions but, generally, you must be at least 10 years old and weigh a minimum of 60–80 pounds and a maximum of 250–275 pounds. You should wear closed-toe athletic-type shoes and expect to get dirty. ■ **TIP→** Although zipline tours are completely safe, you may want to reconsider this activity if you are pregnant, uncomfortable with heights, or have serious back or joint problems.

FodorsChoice
★
Flyin' Hawaiian Zipline. These guys have the longest line in the state (a staggering 3,600 feet), as well as the most unique course layout. You build confidence on the first line, then board a four-wheel-drive vehicle that takes you 1,500 feet above the town of Waikapu to seven more lines that carry you over 11 ridges and nine valleys. The total distance covered is more than 2½ miles, and the views are astonishing. The price of $185 includes water and snacks. You must be able to hike over steep, sometimes slippery terrain while carrying a 10-pound metal trolley. ☎ *808/463–5786* ⊕ *www.flyinhawaiianzipline.com.*

Kapalua Adventures Ziplines. This zipline course has almost 2 miles of parallel lines, enabling two riders to zip side by side. At 2,300 feet, line 3 is the longest. A "zipper lifter" (like a chair lift) takes you to the upper lines, but you must still be able to hike 1 mile over sometimes-steep terrain while carrying a 15-pound trolley. Prices range from $154 to $249. Kapalua Adventures also has a high-ropes challenge course and the Giant Swing, an exhilarating 40-foot-high tandem experience that's as thrilling as any amusement park ride. ⊠ *2000 Village Rd., Kapalua* ☎ *808/665–3753,* ⊕ *www.gozipmaui.com.*

FodorsChoice
★
Piiholo Ranch Zipline. This complex, on a gorgeous 900-acre family ranch, has six ziplines—five parallel lines and one quadruple—plus a 12-person climbing tower. Access to the fifth and longest line is via a four-wheel-drive vehicle to the top of Piiholo Hill, where you are treated to stunning bicoastal views. Guides do a good job of weaving Hawaiian culture into the adventure. You must be able to climb three steep suspension bridges

while hefting a 12-pound trolley over your shoulder. Prices range from $140 for four lines to $190 for five. The new canopy tour keeps you in the trees the entire time ($90 to $165). Bring a lightweight jacket. ⊠ *Piiholo Rd., Makawao* ☎ *808/572–1717* ⊕ *www.piiholozipline.com.*

SHOPPING

Updated by
Eliza Escaño-
Vasquez

Whether you're searching for a dashboard hula dancer or an original Curtis Wilson Cost painting, you can find it on Front Street in Lahaina or at the Shops at Wailea. Art sales are huge in the resort areas, where artists regularly show up to promote their work. Alongside the flashy galleries are standards like Quicksilver and ABC store, where you can stock up on swim trunks, sunscreen, and flip-flops.

Don't miss the great boutiques lining the streets of small towns like Paia and Makawao. You can purchase boutique fashions and art while strolling through these charming, quieter communities. Notably, several local designers—Tamara Catz, Letarte, and Maui Girl—all produce top-quality island fashions. In the neighboring galleries, local artisans turn out gorgeous work in a range of prices. Special souvenirs include rare hardwood bowls and boxes, prints of sea life, Hawaiian quilts, and blown glass.

Specialty food products—pineapples, coconuts, or Maui onions—and "Made in Maui" jams and jellies make great, less-expensive souvenirs. Cook Kwee's Maui Cookies have gained a following, as have Maui Potato Chips. Coffee sellers now offer Maui-grown-and-roasted beans alongside the better-known Kona varieties. Remember that fresh fruit must be inspected by the U.S. Department of Agriculture before it can leave the state, so it's safest to buy a box that has already passed inspection.

Business hours for individual shops on the island are usually 9 to 5, seven days a week. Shops on Front Street and in shopping centers tend to stay open later (until 9 or 10 on weekends).

WEST MAUI

SHOPPING CENTERS

Lahaina Cannery Mall. In a building reminiscent of an old pineapple cannery are 50 shops. The mall hosts fabulous free events year-round like the Keiki Hula Festival and an annual ice-sculpting competition. Free ukulele lessons are available on Tuesday afternoons. Recommended stops include Na Hoku, purveyor of striking Hawaiian heirloom-quality jewelry and pearls, and Banana Wind, which carries island-inspired home decor. ⊠ *1221 Honoapiilani Hwy., Lahaina* ☎ *808/661–5304* ⊕ *www.lahainacannerymall.com.*

Lahaina Center. Island department store Hilo Hattie Fashion Center anchors the complex and puts on a free hula show at 2:30 pm every Wednesday. In addition to the Hard Rock Cafe, Warren & Annabelle's magic show, and a four-screen cinema, you can find a replica of an ancient Hawaiian village complete with three full-size thatch huts built with 10,000 feet of Big Island *ohia* wood, 20 tons of *pili* grass, and more than 4 miles of handwoven coconut *senit* (twine). There's all that *and* validated parking. ⊠ *900 Front St., Lahaina* ☎ *808/667–9216.*

Fodor'sChoice ★ **Whalers Village.** Chic Whalers Village has a whaling museum and more than 50 restaurants and shops. Upscale haunts include Louis Vuitton and Coach, and beautyphiles can get their fix at Sephora. Peruse some elegant koa home accessories and other local gifts at Martin and MacArthur. The complex also offers some interesting diversions: Hawaiian artisans display their crafts daily; hula dancers perform on an outdoor stage some nights from 7 to 8 pm; sunset jazz is featured every first Sunday of the month; and Polynesian rhythms resound on Saturday. ⊠ *2435 Kaanapali Pkwy., Kaanapali* ☎ *808/661–4567* ⊕ *www.whalersvillage.com.*

> **BEST MADE-ON-MAUI GIFTS**
>
> ■ *Koa* jewelry boxes from **Maui Hands.**
>
> ■ Sushi platters and bamboo chopsticks from the **Maui Crafts Guild.**
>
> ■ Black-pearl pendant from **Maui Divers.**
>
> ■ Handmade Hawaiian quilt from **Hana Coast Gallery.**
>
> ■ Jellyfish paperweight from **Hot Island Glass.**
>
> ■ Ukulele from **Mele Ukulele.**
>
> ■ Plumeria lei, made by you!

BOOKSTORES

Fodor'sChoice ★ **Maui Friends of the Library Used Book Store.** Behind the Wharf Cinema Center, this shop lets you spend a few minutes (or hours) browsing shelves filled with mystery, sci-fi, military history, and "oddball" volumes. There is also a modest shelf reserved for Hawaiian books. Finished with your vacation reading? You can donate it to benefit the island's public libraries. ⊠ *658 Front St., Lahaina* ☎ *808/667–2696* ⊕ *www.mfol.org.*

CLOTHING

Hilo Hattie Fashion Center. Hawaii's largest manufacturer of aloha shirts also carries brightly colored blouses, skirts, and children's clothing, along with gift items such as soaps and lotions. ⊠ *Lahaina Center, 900 Front St., Lahaina* ☎ *808/667–7911* ⊕ *www.hilohattie.com.*

Honolua Surf Company. If you're not in the mood for an aloha shirt, check out this surf shop—popular with young men and women for surf trunks, casual clothing, and accessories. ⊠ *845 Front St., Lahaina* ☎ *808/661–8848* ⊕ *www.honoluasurf.com.*

FOOD

Lahaina Square Shopping Center Foodland. This Foodland serves West Maui and is open daily from 6 am to midnight. ⊠ *878 Front St., Lahaina* ☎ *808/661–0975.*

Safeway. The chain has three stores on the island open 24 hours daily. ⊠ *Lahaina Cannery Mall, 1221 Honoapiilani Hwy., Lahaina* ☎ *808/667–4392.*

★ **Take Home Maui.** The folks at this colorful grocery and deli in West Maui will supply, pack, and deliver produce to the airport or your hotel. ✉ *121 Dickenson St., Lahaina* ☎ *808/661–8067* ⊕ *www.takehomemaui.com.*

GALLERIES

Lahaina Galleries. Works of both national and international artists are displayed at this well-regarded gallery. Besides the space in Lahaina, there's a second location in the Shops at Wailea. Prices start at over $2,000. ✉ *828 Front St., Lahaina* ☎ *808/661–6284* ⊕ *www. lahainagalleries.com.* ✉ *The Shops at Wailea, 3750 Wailea Alanui Dr., Wailea* ☎ *808/874–8583*

Lahaina Printsellers Ltd. Hawaii's largest selection of original antique maps and prints pertaining to Hawaii and the Pacific is available here. You can also buy museum-quality reproductions. ✉ *Whalers Village, 2435 Kaanapali Pkwy., Kaanapali* ☎ *808/667–7617* ⊕ *www.printsellers.com.*

★ **Martin Lawrence Galleries.** In business since 1975, Martin Lawrence displays the works of such world-renowned artists as Picasso, Erté, and Chagall in a bright and friendly gallery. Modern and pop-art enthusiasts will also find pieces by Miró, Haring, Warhol, and Japanese icon Takashi Murakami. ✉ *Lahaina Market Place, 790 Front St., at Lahainaluna Rd., Lahaina* ☎ *808/661–1788* ⊕ *www.martinlawrence.com.*

Village Gallery. This gallery houses the landscape paintings of popular local artists Betty Hay Freeland, George Allan, Joseph Fletcher, Pamela Andelin, Fred KenKnight, and Macario Pascual. There's a second location in Kapalua at the Ritz-Carlton. ✉ *120 Dickenson St., Lahaina* ☎ *808/661–4402* ⊕ *www.villagegalleriesmaui.com.* ✉ *Ritz-Carlton, 1 Ritz-Carlton Dr., Kapalua* ☎ *808/669–1800*

HOME FURNISHINGS

Hale Zen. If you're shopping for gifts in West Maui, don't miss this store packed with beautiful island-inspired pieces for the home. Most of the teak furniture is imported from Bali, but local purveyors supply the inventory of clothing, accessories, beauty products, kitchenware, and food. ✉ *180 Dickenson St., Suite 111, Lahaina* ☎ *808/661–4802.*

JEWELRY

Jessica's Gems. Specializing in black pearls, Jessica's also has a good selection of Hawaiian heirloom jewelry, including custom designs by Maui designers David Welty and Dave Haake. ✉ *Whalers Village, 2435 Kaanapali Pkwy., Kaanapali* ☎ *808/661–4223* ✉ *858 Front St., Lahaina* ☎ *808/661–9200.*

Lahaina Scrimshaw. Here you can buy brooches, rings, pendants, cuff links, tie tacks, and collector's items adorned with intricately carved sailors' art. The store sells a few antiques, but most pieces are modern creations. ✉ *845A Front St., Lahaina* ☎ *808/661–8820* ✉ *Whalers Village, 2435 Kaanapali Pkwy., Kaanapali* ☎ *808/661–4034.*

Maui Divers. This company has been crafting pearls, coral, and traditional gemstones into jewelry for more than 50 years. ✉ *640 Front St., Lahaina* ☎ *808/661–0988* ⊕ *www.mauidivers.com.*

CENTRAL MAUI

SHOPPING CENTERS

Maui Marketplace. On the busy stretch of Dairy Road, this behemoth mall near Kahului Airport couldn't be more conveniently located. The 20-acre complex houses several outlet stores and big retailers, such as Pier One Imports, Sports Authority, and Old Navy. Sample local and ethnic cuisines at the Kau Kau Corner food court. ⊠ *270 Dairy Rd., Kahului* ☎ *808/873–0400.*

Queen Kaahumanu Center. Maui's largest mall has 75 stores, a movie theater, and a food court. The mall's interesting rooftop, composed of a series of manta ray–like umbrella shades, is easily spotted. Stop at Camellia Seeds for what locals call "crack seed," a snack made from dried fruits, nuts, and lots of sugar. Other stops include mall standards such as Macy's, Pacific Sunwear, and American Eagle Outfitters. ⊠ *275 W. Kaahumanu Ave., Kahului* ☎ *808/877–3369* ⊕ *www.queenkaahumanucenter.com.*

ARTS AND CRAFTS

★ **Mele Ukulele.** For those looking for a professional quality, authentically Maui ukulele, skip the souvenir shops. Mele's handcrafted beauties are made of koa or mahogany and strung and finished by the store's owner, Michael Rock. ⊠ *1750 Kaahumanu Ave., Wailuku* ☎ *808/244–3938* ⊕ *www.meleukulele.com.*

CLOTHING

Bohemia. Find upscale designer resale *and* new pieces by local designers, all at affordable prices at this consignment store. ⊠ *105 N. Market St., Wailuku* ☎ *808/244–9995.*

Hi-Tech. Stop here immediately after deplaning to stock up on surf trunks, windsurfing gear, bikinis, and sundresses. ⊠ *425 Koloa St., Kahului* ☎ *808/877–2111* ⊕ *www.surfmaui.com.*

FLEA MARKETS

Maui Swap Meet. Crafts, souvenirs, fruit, shells, and more make this flea market in a college parking lot the island's biggest bargain. ⊠ *Off Kahului Beach Rd., Kahului* ☎ *808/244–3100* ⊕ *www.mauiexposition. com* 🖾 *50¢* ☉ *Sat. 7 am–1 pm.*

FOOD

Maui Coffee Roasters. The best stop for Kona and Hawaiian coffees on Maui is this café and roasting house near Kahului Airport. Salespeople give good advice and will ship items, and you even get a free cup of joe in a signature to-go cup when you buy a pound of coffee. ⊠ *444 Hana Hwy., Kahului* ☎ *808/877–2877* ⊕ *www.mauicoffeeroasters.com.*

Safeway. If you're coming from the airport, this grocery store (one of three on the island) may be a useful stop. It's open 24 hours daily. ⊠ *170 E. Kamehameha Ave., Kahului* ☎ *808/877–3377.*

THE SOUTH SHORE

SHOPPING CENTERS

Azeka Place Shopping Center. Azeka II, on the *mauka* (toward the mountains) side of South Kihei Road, has the Coffee Store (a great place for iced mochas) and the Nail Shop (for shaping, waxing, and tweezing). Azeka I, the older half on the *makai* (toward the ocean) side of the street, has a decent Vietnamese restaurant and Kihei's post office. ⊠ *1280 S. Kihei Rd., Kihei* ☎ *808/879–5000.*

Fodor's Choice ★ **Kihei Kalama Village Marketplace.** Head to this fun place to investigate. Shaded outdoor stalls sell everything from printed and hand-painted T-shirts and sundresses to jewelry, pottery, wood carvings, fruit, and gaudily painted coconut husks—some, but not all, made by local craftspeople. ⊠ *1941 S. Kihei Rd., Kihei* ☎ *808/879–6610.*

★ **The Shops at Wailea.** Stylish, upscale, and close to most of the resorts, this mall brings high fashion to Wailea. Luxury boutiques such as Gucci, Cos Bar, and Tiffany & Co. are represented, as are less-expensive chains like Gap, Guess, and Tommy Bahama's. Several good restaurants face the ocean, and regular Wednesday-night events include live entertainment, art exhibits, and fashion shows. ⊠ *3750 Wailea Alanui Dr., Wailea* ☎ *808/891–6770* ⊕ *www.shopsatwailea.com.*

Wailea Gateway Center. While lunch at chef Peter Merriman's Monkeypod is enough reason to venture to Wailea Gateway Center, you might also be enticed by the artisanal confections from Sweet Paradise Chocolate, fine cheese and charcuterie from Guava, Gouda & Caviar, and a vast collection of vintage clothing from The Aloha Shirt Museum. ⊠ *34 Wailea Gateway Pl., Wailea .*

CLOTHING

★ **Cruise.** Sundresses, swimwear, sandals, bright beach towels, and a few nice pieces of resort wear fill this upscale resort boutique. ⊠ *Grand Wailea Resort, 3850 Wailea Alanui Dr., Wailea* ☎ *808/875–1234.*

Hilo Hattie Fashion Center. Hawaii's largest manufacturer of aloha shirts also carries brightly colored blouses, skirts, and children's clothing. You can also pick up many local gift items here. ⊠ *297 Piikea Ave., Kihei* ☎ *808/875–4545* ⊕ *www.hilohattie.com.*

Sisters & Company. Opened by four sisters, this little shop has a lot to offer: contemporary lines like True Religion, XCVI and Michael Stars, plus locally produced loungewear from Island Hunny. Sister No. 3, Rhonda, runs a tiny, ultrahip hair salon in back, while Caroline, Sister No. 2, offers mani-pedis and waxing. ⊠ *The Shops at Wailea, 3750 Wailea Alanui Dr., Wailea* ☎ *808/874–0003* ⊕ *www.sistersandco.com.*

Tommy Bahama's. It's hard to find a man on Maui who *isn't* wearing a TB–logo aloha shirt. For better or worse, here's where you can get yours. And just to prove you're on vacation, grab a drink or dessert on the way out at the restaurant attached to the shop. ⊠ *The Shops at Wailea, 3750 Wailea Alanui Dr., Wailea* ☎ *808/879–7828* ⊕ *www. tommybahamas.com.*

FOOD

Foodland. In Kihei town center, this is the most convenient supermarket for those staying in Wailea. It's open around the clock. ⊠ *1881 S. Kihei Rd., Kihei* ☎ *808/879–9350.*

Safeway. Open 24 hours a day, this store is a convenient place to stock up for South Maui stays. ⊠ *277 Piikea Ave., Kihei* ☎ *808/891–9120.*

UPCOUNTRY, THE NORTH SHORE, AND HANA

CLOTHING

Alice in Hulaland. While the store is famous for its vintage tees, it also carries a lovely mix of gift items and casual wear for the whole family. Best sellers include burnout band tees, Goorin Bros. hats, Havaianas slippers, and Cosabella lingerie. ⊠ *19 Baldwin Ave., Paia* ☎ *808/579–9922* ⊕ *www.aliceinhulaland.com.*

Designing Wahine Emporium. At this Upcountry haven for Hawaiian merchandise and Balinese imports, you can find endless gift options like authentic aloha shirts, jams and jellies, bath and beauty products, and home decor crafted from wood. ⊠ *3640 Baldwin Ave., Makawao* ☎ *808/573–0990.*

Pink By Nature. Owner Desiree Martinez dresses the modern bohemian as she keeps the rustic store stocked with pieces from Indah, Mother, LA Made and Fighting Eel. ⊠ *3663 Baldwin Ave., Makawao* ☎ *808/572–9576.*

Fodor's Choice ★ **Tamara Catz.** This Maui designer has a worldwide following, and her superstylish sarongs and beachwear have appeared in many fashion magazines. If you're looking for sequined tunics, delicately embroidered sundresses, or beaded wedge sandals, this is the place. Catz also has a bridal line that is elegant and beach-appropriate. Her pieces can cost a pretty penny; if you are visiting in December, you might just catch the annual sample sale. ⊠ *83 Hana Hwy., Paia* ☎ *808/579–9184* ⊕ *www. tamaracatz.com.*

FOOD

Fodor's Choice ★ **Mana Foods.** At this bustling health-food store you can stock up on local fish and grass-fed beef for your barbecue. You'll find the best selection of organic produce on the island, as well as a great bakery and deli. ⊠ *49 Baldwin Ave., Paia* ☎ *808/579–8078* ⊕ *www.manafoodsmaui.com.*

★ **Ono Gelato.** Fresh gelato made with organic fruit is the drawing card here. You'll also find jams, jellies, and dressings from Jeff Gomes; coffees from Maui Oma Roasters; and treats from the Maui Culinary Academy. There's a second location on Front Street in Lahaina. ⊠ *115 Hana Hwy., Paia* ☎ *808/579–9201* ⊕ *www.onogelatocompany.com.*

Continued on page 274

ALL ABOUT LEI

Lei brighten every occasion in Hawaii, from birthdays to bar mitzvahs to baptisms. Creative artisans weave nature's bounty—flowers, ferns, vines, and seeds—into gorgeous creations that convey an array of heartfelt messages: "Welcome," "Congratulations," "Good luck," "Farewell," "Thank you," "I love you." When it's difficult to find the right words, a lei expresses exactly the right sentiment.

WHERE TO BUY THE BEST LEI

These florists carry a nice variety of lei: **A Special Touch** (Emerald Plaza, 142 Kupuohi St., Ste. F-1, Lahaina, 808/661–3455); **Kahului Florist** (Maui Mall, 70 E. Kaahumanu Ave., Kahului, 808/877–3951 or 800/711–8881); **Napili Florist** (5059 Napilihau St., Lahaina, 808/669–4861); and **Kihei-Wailea Flowers by Cora** (1280 S. Kihei Rd., Ste. 126, Kihei, 808/879–7249 or 800/339–0419). **Costco, Kmart, Wal-Mart**, and **Safeway** sell basic lei, such as orchid and plumeria.

LEI ETIQUETTE

■ To wear a closed lei, drape it over your shoulders, half in front and half in back. Open lei are worn around the neck, with the ends draped over the front in equal lengths.

■ Pikake, ginger, and other sweet, delicate blossoms are "feminine" lei. Men opt for cigar, crown flower, and ti leaf, which are sturdier and don't emit as much fragrance.

■ Lei are always presented with a kiss, a custom that supposedly dates back to World War II when a hula dancer fancied an officer at a U.S.O. show. Taking a dare from members of her troupe, she took off her lei, placed it around his neck, and kissed him on the cheek.

■ You shouldn't wear a lei before you give it to someone else. Hawaiians believe the lei absorbs your *mana* (spirit); if you give your lei away, you'll be giving away part of your essence.

ORCHID

Growing wild on every continent except Antarctica, orchids—which range in color from yellow to green to purple—comprise the largest family of plants in the world. There are more than 20,000 species of orchids, but only three are native to Hawaii—and they are very rare. The pretty lavender vanda you see hanging by the dozens at local lei stands has probably been imported from Thailand.

MAILE

Maile, an endemic twining vine with a heady aroma, is sacred to Laka, goddess of the hula. In ancient times, dancers wore maile and decorated hula altars with it to honor Laka. Today, "open" maile lei usually are given to men. Instead of ribbon, interwoven lengths of maile are used at dedications of new businesses. The maile is untied, never snipped, for doing so would symbolically "cut" the company's success.

ILIMA

Designated by Hawaii's Territorial Legislature in 1923 as the official flower of the island of Oahu, the golden ilima is so delicate it lasts for just a day. Five to seven hundred blossoms are needed to make one garland. Queen Emma, wife of King Kamehameha IV, preferred ilima over all other lei, which may have led to the incorrect belief that they were reserved only for royalty.

PLUMERIA

This ubiquitous flower is named after Charles Plumier, the noted French botanist who discovered it in Central America in the late 1600s. Plumeria ranks among the most popular lei in Hawaii because it's fragrant, hardy, plentiful, inexpensive, and requires very little care. Although yellow is the most common color, you'll also find plumeria lei in shades of pink, red, orange, and "rainbow" blends.

PIKAKE

Favored for its fragile beauty and sweet scent, pikake was introduced from India. In lieu of pearls, many brides in Hawaii adorn themselves with long, multiple strands of white pikake. Princess Kaiulani enjoyed showing guests her beloved pikake and peacocks at Ainahau, her Waikiki home. Interestingly, pikake is the Hawaiian word for both the bird and the blossom.

KUKUI

The kukui (candlenut) is Hawaii's state tree. Early Hawaiians strung kukui nuts (which are quite oily) together and burned them for light; mixed burned nuts with oil to make an indelible dye; and mashed roasted nuts to consume as a laxative. Kukui nut lei may not have been made until after Western contact, when the Hawaiians saw black beads from Europe and wanted to imitate them.

GALLERIES

★ **Hana Coast Gallery.** One of the best-curated galleries on the island, this 3,000-square-foot facility has fine art, handcrafted furniture, and jewelry on consignment from local artists. ✉ *Travaasa Hana, Hana Hwy., Hana* ☎ *808/248–8636, 800/637–0188* ⊕ *www.hanacoast.com.*

Fodor's Choice **Maui Crafts Guild.** Set in an old plantation building alongside the high-
★ way, the Maui Craft Guild is crammed with treasures that make it one of the island's more interesting galleries. Resident artists craft everything in the store, from lead-glazed pottery to basketry to original sculpture. The prices are surprisingly low. ✉ *69 Hana Hwy., Paia* ☎ *808/579–9697* ⊕ *www.mauicraftsguild.com.*

★ **Maui Hands.** This gallery shows work by hundreds of local artists, including exquisite woodwork, lovely ceramics, authentic Niihau shell lei, and famous wave photography by Clark Little. There are locations in Lahaina and Makawao and at the Hyatt Regency in Kaanapali. ✉ *84 Hana Hwy., Paia* ☎ *808/579–9245* ⊕ *www.mauihands.com.*

Viewpoints Gallery. Maui's only fine-arts co-op offers eclectic paintings, sculptures, photography, ceramics, and glass, along with locally made jewelry and quilts. In a courtyard across from Market Fresh Bistro, its monthly exhibits feature artists from various disciplines. ✉ *3620 Baldwin Ave., Makawao* ☎ *808/572–5979* ⊕ *www.viewpointsgallerymaui.com.*

JEWELRY

Maui Master Jewelers. The shop's exterior is as rustic as all the old buildings of Makawao, so be prepared for the elegance of the handcrafted jewelry displayed within. The store has added a diamond collection to its designs. ✉ *3655 Baldwin Ave., Makawao* ☎ *808/573–5400* ⊕ *www.mauimasterjewelers.com.*

SWIMWEAR

Hana Hwy. Surf. You can grab trunks and bikinis—and a board, if needed—at this surf shack on the North Shore. ✉ *149 Hana Hwy., Paia* ☎ *808/579–8999* ⊕ *www.hanahwysurf.com.*

Fodor's Choice **Maui Girl.** This is *the* place on Maui for swimwear, cover-ups, beach hats,
★ and sandals. Maui Girl designs its own suits, which have been spotted in *Sports Illustrated* fashion shoots, and imports teenier versions from Brazil as well. Tops and bottoms can be purchased separately, greatly increasing your chances of finding the perfect fit. ✉ *12 Baldwin Ave., Paia* ☎ *808/579–9266* ⊕ *www.maui-girl.com.*

SPAS

Updated by
Eliza Escaño-
Vasquez

Traditional Swedish massage and European facials anchor most spa menus, though you'll also find Shiatsu, Ayurveda, aromatherapy, and other body treatments drawn from cultures across the globe. *Lomilomi,* traditional Hawaiian massage involving powerful strokes down the length of the body, is a regional specialty passed down through generations. Many treatments incorporate local plants and flowers. *Awapuhi,* or Hawaiian ginger, and *noni,* a pungent-smelling fruit, are regularly used for their therapeutic benefits. *Limu*, or sea-weed, and even coffee is employed in rousing salt scrubs and soaks. And this is just the beginning.

WEST MAUI

Fodor'sChoice
★
Heavenly Spa by Westin at the Westin Maui. Pamper yourself with the exquisite 80-minute Island Indulgence treatment that combines a body scrub and a warm coconut milk bath in a hydrotherapy tub. Other options include cabana massage (for couples, too) and sunburn relief with a lavender-aloe blend. Facials use high-end lines like Priori and Eminence, while body treatments feature eco-friendly Pure Fiji products. The facility is serene and flawless. While you wait for your treatment, sip on pineapple juice in the posh, ocean-view waiting room. The open-air yoga studio and the gym offer energizing workouts, and the hair salon has braiding services. ⊠ *Westin Maui, 2365 Kaanapali Pkwy., Kaanapali* ☎ *808/661–2588* ⊕ *www.westinmaui.com* ☞ *$140 50-min massage, $265 day spa packages. Hair salon, sauna, steam room. Gym with: Cardiovascular machines, free weights, weight-training equipment. Services: aromatherapy, body wraps, facials, hydrotherapy, massage, Vichy shower. Classes and programs: Aquaerobics, Pilates, Spinning, yoga.*

Kapalua Spa. The spa's humble entrance opens onto an airy, modern beach house with a panoramic view of Kapalua Bay. The menu includes some ancient Hawaiian healing practices. The *lomi* wrap, designed by Big Island resident and healer Darrell Lapulapu, begins with a special cava tea for instant relaxation, is followed by a body wrap of cacao, ginger, sandalwood, and oats, and finishes with *lomilomi* (traditional Hawaiian massage involving strokes down the length of the body). A juice bar serves health potions that combine pure fruits and juiced veggies with natural additives like yogurt. ⊠ *100 Bay Dr., Kapalua* ☎ *808/665–8282* ⊕ *www.kapalua.com* ☞ *$160 50-min massage, $445 half-day spa package. Hair salon, sauna, steam room. Gym with: Cardiovascular machines, free weights, weight-training equipment. Services: Aromatherapy, body wraps, facials, massage. Classes and programs: Cycling, nutritional counseling, Pilates, yoga.*

Fodor'sChoice
★
Waihua Spa, Ritz-Carlton, Kapalua. At this gorgeous 17,500-square-foot spa, you enter a blissful maze where floor-to-ceiling riverbed stones lead to serene treatment rooms, couples' *hales* (cabanas), and a rain forest–like grotto with a Jacuzzi, dry cedar sauna, and eucalyptus steam rooms. Hang out in the co-ed waiting area, where sliding-glass doors open to a whirlpool overlooking a taro patch garden. Exfoliate any rough spots with a pineapple-papaya or coffee scrub; then wash off in a private outdoor shower garden before indulging in a *lomilomi* massage (traditional Hawaiian massage involving powerful strokes down the length of the body). High-end beauty treatments include advanced oxygen technology to tighten and nourish mature skin. The on-site shop has a great selection of local beauty products and jewelry. ⊠ *Ritz-Carlton, Kapalua, 1 Ritz-Carlton Dr., Kapalua* ☎ *808/669–6200, 800/262–8440* ⊕ *www.ritzcarlton.com* ☞ *$155*

50-min massage, $395 half-day spa packages. Hair salon, hot tubs (outdoor and indoor), sauna, steam room. Gym with: Cardiovascular machines, free weights, weight-training equipment. Services: Aromatherapy, body wraps, facials, massage. Classes and programs: Aquaerobics, cycling, nutritional counseling, Pilates, yoga.

SOUTH SHORE

Fodor's Choice
★
Spa Grande, Grand Wailea Resort. Built to satisfy an indulgent Japanese billionaire, this 50,000-square-foot spa makes others seem like well-appointed closets. Slathered in honey and wrapped up in the steam room (if you go for the honey steam wrap), you'll feel like royalty. All treatments include a loofah scrub and a trip to the *termé*, a hydrotherapy circuit including five therapeutic baths with Hawaii-grown essences. (Soak for 10 minutes in the moor mud to relieve sunburn or jellyfish stings.) The circuit includes a Japanese Furo bath, waterfall massage, cold plunge pool, jet showers, and a large Roman hot tub. To fully enjoy the baths, plan to arrive an hour before your treatment. Free with any treatment, the *termé* is also available separately for $55 for two hours. At times—especially during the holidays—this wonderland can be crowded. When it isn't, it is quite difficult to pry yourself away. ⊠ *Grand Wailea Resort, 3850 Wailea Alanui Dr., Wailea* ☎ *808/875– 1234, 800/888–6100* ⊕ *www.grandwailea.com* ☞ *$150 50-min massage, $298 day-spa packages. Hair salon, hot tub, sauna, steam room. Gym with: Cardiovascular machines, free weights, weight-training equipment. Services: Aromatherapy, body wraps, facials, hydrotherapy, massage, Vichy shower. Classes and programs: Aquaerobics, cycling, Pilates, Spinning, yoga.*

Fodor's Choice
★
The Spa at Four Seasons Resort Maui. The resort's hawk-like attention to detail is reflected here. Thoughtful gestures like fresh flowers beneath the massage table, organic ginger tea in the relaxation room, and your choice of music eases your mind and muscles before the treatment even begins. The spa is romantic yet modern, and the therapists are among the best. Thanks to an exclusive partnership, the spa offers excellent treatments created by skin guru Kate Somerville. The spa also features eco-friendly health and beauty products. The new Lomi Mohala massage uses muscle-relaxing oils blended exclusively for the treatment. For the ultimate indulgence, reserve one of the seaside open-air *hale hau* (traditional thatch-roof houses). You can have two therapists realign your body and spirit with a *lomilomi* massage (traditional Hawaiian massage involving powerful strokes down the length of the body). ⊠ *Four Seasons Resort Maui, 3900 Wailea Alanui Dr., Wailea* ☎ *808/874–8000, 800/334–6284* ⊕ *www.fourseasons.com/ maui* ☞ *$155 50-min massage, $370 3-treatment packages. Hair salon, steam room. Gym with: Cardiovascular machines, free weights, weight-training equipment. Services: Aromatherapy, body wraps, facials, massage. Classes and programs: Aquaerobics, meditation, personal training, Pilates, Spinning, tai chi, yoga.*

ROAD TO HANA

★ **The Spa at Travaasa Hana.** A bamboo gate opens into an outdoor sanctuary with a lava-rock basking pool and hot tub. At first glimpse, this spa seems to have been organically grown, not built. The decor can hardly be called decor—it's an abundant, living garden that overlooks Hana Bay. Ferns still wet from Hana's frequent downpours nourish the spirit as you rest with a cup of Hawaiian herbal tea, or take an invigorating dip in the cold plunge pool, or have a therapist stretch your limbs as you soak in the warm waters of the aquatic therapy pool. Luxurious skincare teatments feature organic products from Amala and essential oils from locally produced Maui Excellent. ⊠ *Travaasa Hana, 5031 Hana Hwy., Hana* ☎ *808/270–5290* ⊕ *www.travaasa.com/hana* ☞ *$130 60-min massage. Outdoor hot tub, steam room. Gym with: Cardiovascular machines, free weights, weight-training equipment. Services: Aromatherapy, body wraps, facials, hydrotherapy, massage. Classes and programs: Meditation, Pilates, yoga.*

ENTERTAINMENT AND NIGHTLIFE

Updated by
Eliza Escaño-
Vasquez

Looking for wild island nightlife? We can't promise you'll always find it here. This quiet island has little of Waikiki's after-hours decadence, and the club scene (if you want to call it that) can be quirky, depending on the season and the day of the week. But sometimes Maui will surprise you with a big-name concert, outdoor festival, or world-class DJ. Lahaina and Kihei are your best bets for action. Outside those towns, you might be able to hit an "on" night in Paia (North Shore) or Makawao (Upcountry), mostly on weekend nights. Your best bet? Pick up the free *MauiTime Weekly,* or Thursday's edition of the *Maui News,* where you'll find a listing of all your after-dark options, islandwide.

ENTERTAINMENT

Before 10 pm, there's a lot to offer by way of luau shows, dinner cruises, and tiki-lighted cocktail hours. Aside from that, you should at least be able to find some down-home DJ spinning or the strum of acoustic guitars at your nearest watering hole or restaurant.

ARTS CENTER

★ **Maui Arts & Cultural Center.** At the MACC (as it's called) you can enjoy a concert under the glass-capped Yokouchi Pavilion, rock music at the A&B Amphitheater, or theatrical and dance performances in the multitiered, 1,200-seat Castle Theater. A major draw is the free Schaeffer International Gallery, which houses superb rotating art exhibits. The building, surrounded by a lava-rock wall, incorporates works by Maui artists. ⊠ *1 Cameron Way, off Kahului Beach Rd., Kahului* ☎ *808/242–7469 box office* ⊕ *www.mauiarts.org* ☉ *Weekdays 9–5.*

DINNER CRUISES AND SHOWS

There's no better place to see the sun set on the Pacific than from one of Maui's many boat tours. You can find a tour to fit your mood, anything from a quiet, sit-down dinner to a festive, beer-swigging booze cruise. Note, however, that many cocktail cruises have recently put a cap on the number of free drinks offered with open bars, instead including a limited number of drinks per ticket.

Dinner cruises typically feature music and are generally packed—which is great if you're feeling social, but you might have to fight for a good seat. You can usually get a much better meal at one of the local restaurants. Most nondinner cruises offer *pupu* and an open bar. Winds are consistent in summer, but variable in winter—sometimes making for a rocky ride. If you're worried about seasickness, you might consider a catamaran, which is much more stable than a monohull. Take Dramamine before the trip, and if you feel sick, sit in the shade (but not inside the cabin), place a cold rag or ice on the back of your neck, and *breathe* as you look at the horizon. In the worst-case scenario, aim downwind—and shoot for distance. Tours leave from Maalaea or Lahaina harbors. Be sure to arrive at least 15 minutes early.

★   *Hula Girl* **Dinner Cruise.** This custom catamaran is one of the best-
☺   equipped boats on the island, complete with a VIP lounge for 12 people by the captain's fly bridge. Trips are on the pricier side, mainly because the initial cost doesn't include the cooked-to-order meals. But if you're willing to splurge a little for live music, an onboard chef, and upscale service, it's absolutely worth it. From mid-December to early April the cruise focuses on whale-watching. Check-in is in front of Leilani's restaurant at Whalers Village. ⊠ *2435 Kaanapali Pkwy., Kaanapali* ☎ *808/665–0344, 808/667–5980* ⊕ *www.sailingmaui.com* ✉ *$74* ☺ *Tues., Thurs., and Sat. 4:30–7.*

Pride of Maui **Charters.** A 65-foot catamaran built specifically for Maui's waters, the *Pride of Maui* has a spacious cabin, dance floor, and large upper deck for unobstructed viewing. Evening cruises include top-shelf cocktails and an impressive spread of baby back ribs, grilled chicken, roasted veggies, warm artichoke dip, garlic fettuccine, and seasonal desserts. ⊠ *Maalaea Harbor, 101 Maalaea Boat Harbor Rd., Maalaea* ☎ *877/867–7433* ⊕ *www.prideofmaui.com* ✉ *$69.65* ☺ *Tues., Thurs., and Sat. 5–7.*

Teralani Sailing Charters. These catamarans are modern, spotless, and laid out nicely for dining and lounging. They head back shortly after sunset, which means there's plenty of light to savor dinner and the view. During whale-watching season, the best seats are the corner booths by the stern of the boat. Catered by local fave Pizza Paradiso, the meal outdoes most dinner-cruise spreads, with ratatouille, chipotle-citrus rotisserie chicken, and grilled ono fish with pesto and sun-dried tomatoes. The trip departs from Kaaanapali's Dig Me Beach in front of Leilani's at Whalers Village. ⊠ *2435 Kaanapali Pkwy., Kaanapali* ☎ *808/661–1230* ⊕ *www.teralani.net* ✉ *$89.66* ☺ *Daily, hrs vary.*

The popular Old Lahaina Luau surveys Hawaii's history through music, hula, chanting, and more.

LUAU

Locals still hold luau to mark milestones or as informal, family-style gatherings. For tourists, they are a major attraction and, for that reason, have become big business. Keep in mind—some are watered-down tourist traps just trying to make a buck, others offer a night you'll never forget. As the saying goes, you get what you pay for. ■ TIP→ Many of the best luau book weeks, sometimes months, in advance, so reserve early. Plan your luau night early on in your trip to help you get into the Hawaiian spirit.

Feast at Lele. This feast redefines the luau by crossing it with island-style fine dining in an intimate beach setting. Each course of this succulent sit-down meal expresses the spirit of specific island cultures—Hawaiian, Samoan, Aotearoan, Tahitian. Don't pass up the delicious desserts. Lahaina's gorgeous sunset serves as the backdrop to the accompanying show, which forgoes gimmicks and pageantry for an authentic cultural presentation of Polynesian chants and dances. "Lele," by the way, is a more traditional name for Lahaina. ⊠ *505 Front St., Lahaina* ☎ *808/667–5353* ⊕ *www.feastatlele.com* ☒ *$112* ⌔ *Reservations essential* ☉ *Oct.–Jan., daily 5:30 pm; Feb.–Apr. and Sept., daily 6 pm; May–Aug., daily 6:30 pm.*

Grand Luau at Honuaula. At the Grand Wailea Resort and Spa, this show captivates with a contemporary interpretation of Hawaiian mythology and folklore. Indulge in pre-luau fun with Hawaiian games, lei making, and photo ops with the cast, then witness the unearthing of the *kalua* pig from the underground oven. Traditional dances share a vision of the first Polynesian voyage to the island, and there are also dancers on stilts, an iridescent aerialist suspended by silk, and many elaborate costumes. As a finale, champion fire-knife dancer Ifi Soo brings the house down with a fiery display. ⊠ *Grand Wailea Resort and Spa, 3850 Wailea Alanui Dr., Wailea* ☎ *808/875–7710* ⊕ *www. honuaula-luau.com* ✉ *$96* ☉ *Mon., Thurs., Fri. and Sat. 5 pm–8 pm.*

★ **Hyatt Regency Maui Drums of the Pacific Luau.** By Kaanapali Beach, this luau excels in every category—breathtaking location, well-made food, smooth-flowing buffet lines, and a nicely paced program that touches upon Hawaiian, Samoan, Tahitian, Fijian, Tongan, and Maori cultures. The festive show includes a solo fire-knife dancer. You'll feast on delicious Hawaiian delicacies like *huli-huli* chicken (barbecued with flavors like brown sugarcane, ginger, and soy), *lomilomi* (rubbed with onions and herbs) salmon, and Pacific ahi *poke* (pickled raw tuna, tossed with herbs and seasonings). There are also plenty of desserts. An open bar features beer, wine, and the usual tropical concoctions. ⊠ *Hyatt Regency Maui, 200 Nohea Kai Dr., Kaanapali* ☎ *808/667–4727* ⊕ *www.maui.hyatt.com* ✉ *$96* ☉ *Tues., Wed., Fri., and Sat. 5–8.*

Fodor's Choice ★ ☺ **Old Lahaina Luau.** Considered the best luau on Maui, the Old Lahaina Luau is certainly the most traditional. Immerse yourself in making *kapa* (bark cloth), weaving *lauhala* (coconut palm fronds), and pounding *poi* at the various interactive stations. Sitting either at a table or on a *lauhala* mat, you can dine on all-you-can-eat Hawaiian cuisine, including pork *laulau* (wrapped with taro sprouts in *ti* leaves), ahi *poke* (pickled raw tuna tossed with herbs and seasonings), *lomilomi* salmon (rubbed with onions and herbs), and *haupia* (coconut pudding). At sunset, the historical journey touches on the arrival of the Polynesians, the influence of missionaries and, later, the advent of tourism. The talented performers will charm you with their music, chanting, and variety of hula styles, including *kahiko*, the ancient way of communicating with the gods. You won't see fire dancers here, as they aren't considered traditional. ■TIP→ **This luau sells out regularly, so make reservations before your trip to Maui.** ⊠ *1251 Front St., near Lahaina Cannery Mall, Lahaina* ☎ *808/667–1998* ⊕ *www. oldlahainaluau.com* ✉ *$92* ⚲ *Reservations essential* ☉ *Oct.–Mar., daily 5:15 pm; Apr.–Sept., daly 5:45 pm.*

Wailea Beach Marriott Te Au Moana. Te Au Moana means "ocean tide," which is all you need to know about the simply gorgeous backdrop for this south Maui luau. The evening begins with lei making, local crafts, and an *imu* (underground oven) ceremony. The tasty buffet serves local staples, including a plethora of desserts like carrot cake, macadamia-nut brownies, and key lime squares. The performance seamlessly intertwines ancient Hawaiian stories and contemporary songs with traditional hula and Polynesian dances, concluding with a jaw-dropping solo fire-knife dance. ⊠ *Wailea Beach Marriott, 3700 Wailea Alanui Dr., Wailea* ☎ *808/879–1922* ⊕ *www.marriotthawaii. com* ⊠ *$98* ⚲ *Reservations essential* ⊘ *Mon. and Thurs.–Sat. 4:30–8.*

FILM

In the heat of the afternoon, a theater may feel like paradise. There are megaplexes showing first-run movies in Kukui Mall (Kihei), Lahaina Center, and Maui Mall and Kaahumanu Shopping Center (Kahului).

★ **Maui Film Festival.** In summer, this weeklong international festival attracts big-name celebrities to Maui for cinema and soirees under the stars. Throughout the year, the Maui Arts & Cultural Center presents art-house films on selected evenings at 5 and 7:30 pm, often accompanied by live music and poetry performances. ☎ *808/579–9244* ⊕ *www. mauifilmfestival.com.*

THEATER

For live theater, check local papers for events and showtimes.

Maui Academy of Performing Arts. Founded in 1974, this nonprofit performing-arts group offers fine productions, as well as dance and drama classes for children and teens. Recent shows have included *Peter Pan,* the *Complete Works of William Shakespeare,* and the *Wizard of Oz.* ⊠ *81 N. Church St., Wailuku* ☎ *808/244–8760* ⊕ *www.mauiacademy. org* ⊠ *$10–$35.*

★ **Ulalena at Maui Theatre.** One of Maui's hottest tickets, *Ulalena* is a Cirque ☺ du Soleil–inspired musical extravaganza that has been well received by audiences and Hawaiian-culture experts alike. The ensemble (20 singer-dancers and five musicians) mixes native rhythms and stories with acrobatic performance in the 75-minute show. High-tech stage wizardry gives an inspiring introduction to island culture. Beer and wine are for sale at the concession stand. ■TIP➔ Check out dinner-theater packages in conjunction with local restaurants. ⊠ *Maui Theatre, 878 Front St., Lahaina* ☎ *808/661–9913, 877/688–4800* ⊕ *www.mauitheatre. com* ⊠ *$59.50–$129.50 for dinner package* ⚲ *Reservations essential* ⊘ *Tues., Wed., Fri., and Sat. 6:30.*

Warren & Annabelle's. Here is one show not to miss—it's serious comedy with amazing sleight of hand. Magician Warren Gibson entices guests into his swank nightclub with red carpets and a gleaming mahogany bar, and plies them with appetizers (coconut shrimp, crab cakes), desserts (chocolate pots de crème, assorted pies and cheesecakes, crème brûlée), and "smoking cocktails." Then he performs table-side magic while his ghostly assistant, Annabelle, tickles the ivories. This is a nightclub, so no one under 21 is allowed. ⊠ *Lahaina Center, 900 Front St., Lahaina* ☎ *808/667–6244* ⊕ *www.hawaiimagic.com* ⊠ *$56 or $94.50, including food and drinks* ⚲ *Reservations essential* ⊘ *Mon.– Sat. 5 and 7:30.*

NIGHTLIFE

Your best bet when it comes to bars on Maui? If you walk by and it sounds like it's happening, go in. If you want to scope out your options in advance, be sure to check the free *Maui Time Weekly*, found at most stores and restaurants, to find out who's playing where. The *Maui News* also publishes an entertainment schedule in its Thursday edition of the "Maui Scene." With an open mind (and a little luck), you can usually find a good scene for fun.

> ### WHAT'S A LAVA FLOW?
>
> Can't decide between a piña colada or strawberry daiquiri? Go with a lava flow—a mix of light rum, coconut and pineapple juice, and a banana, with a swirl of strawberry puree. Add a wedge of fresh pineapple and a paper umbrella, and mmm . . . good. Try one at Lulu's in Kihei.

WEST MAUI

Alaloa Lounge. When atmosphere weighs heavy on the priority list, this spot at the Ritz-Carlton might just be the ticket. Nightly performances range from jazz to island rhythms. The menu includes such dishes as a fantastic seared filet mignon on a pretzel roll. Step onto the lanai for that plumeria-tinged Hawaiian air and gaze at the deep blue of the Pacific. ⊠ *Ritz-Carlton, Kapalua, 1 Ritz-Carlton Dr., Kapalua* ☎ *808/669–6200* ⊕ *www.ritzcarlton.com.*

Cheeseburger in Paradise. A chain joint on Front Street, this place is known for—what else?—big beefy cheeseburgers, not to mention a great spinach-nut burger. It's a casual place to start your evening, as they usually have live music until 10 pm and big, fruity cocktails for happy hour. There's no dance floor, but the second-floor balcony gives you a bird's-eye view of Lahaina's Front Street action. ⊠ *811 Front St., Lahaina* ☎ *808/661–4855* ⊕ *www.cheeseburgerland.com.*

Cool Cat Café. You could easily miss this casual 1950s-style diner while strolling through Lahaina. Tucked in the second floor of the Wharf Cinema Center, its semi-outdoor area plays host to rockin' local music nightly. The entertainment lineup covers jazz, contemporary Hawaiian, and traditional island rhythms. It doesn't hurt that the kitchen dishes out specialty burgers, fish that's fresh from the harbor, and delicious homemade sauces from the owner's family recipes. ⊠ *658 Front St., Lahaina* ☎ *808/667–0908* ⊕ *www.coolcatcafe.com.*

Spanky's Riptide. While 505 Plaza's Timba gets the dressy clubgoers, newly opened Spanky's draws the more casual sports bar crowd. There's no cover, the televisions stream sports nonstop, and you can check out the self-serve hotdog condiment stand. ⊠ *505 Front St., Lahaina* ☎ *808/667–2337.*

★ **Timba.** Located at Lahaina's 505 Front Street, this place has raised Maui nightlife standards more than a few notches. The space combines a charming oceanfront setting with the island's most progressive musicians. Sleek and cozy white leather couches are perfect for sipping and conversing, and the elevated dance floor will have you on your feet the

Performers in colorful costumes help make luau appealing to all ages.

night away. The upscale club attracts the bigger names in the electronic music scene, giving locals a reason to get dolled up. Co-owner Quinn Ross hosts a Friday weekly with rotating sax players, keyboardists, and vocalists to spice up the set. ⊠ *505 Front St., Lahaina* ☎ *808/661–9873* ⊕ *www.timbamaui.com.*

THE SOUTH SHORE

★ **Ambrosia.** A South Maui favorite, Ambrosia is a lively hangout for house music and old school jams, as well as the occasional absinthe drink. The art of mixology is taken more seriously here than at other venues. ⊠ *1913 S. Kihei Rd., Kihei* ☎ *808/891–1011* ⊕ *www.ambrosiamaui. com* ☾ *5 pm–2 am.*

★ **Lulu's.** A local favorite, the second-story Lulu's is an open-air sports bar with a pool table, small stage, and dance floor. The most popular night is Salsa Thursday, with dancing and lessons until 11. Friday features a live band from 7 to 10. Hawaiian music and hula kick off Saturday from 7:30 to 10. DJs close the evenings with old-school hip-hop, dub, and dance music. ⊠ *1945 S. Kihei Rd., Kihei* ☎ *808/879–9944* ⊕ *www. lulusmaui.com.*

★ **Mulligan's on the Blue.** Frothy pints of Guinness and late-night fish-and-chips—who could ask for more? Sunday nights feature foot-stomping Irish jams that will have you dancing a jig, and singing something about "a whiskey for me-Johnny." Local favorite Willie K performs every Wednesday. Other nights bring in various local bands. ⊠ *Blue Golf Course, 100 Kaukahi St., Wailea* ☎ *808/874–1131* ⊕ *www. mulligansontheblue.com.*

South Shore Tiki Lounge. Good eats are paired with cool tunes in this breezy, tropical tavern. Local acts and DJs are featured most evenings; if you're craving some old-school hip-hop, Thursday is your night. Happy hour specials run from 11 am to 6 pm. ⊠ *1913 S. Kihei Rd., Kihei* ☎ *808/874–6444* ⊕ *www.southshoretikilounge.com.*

UPCOUNTRY AND THE NORTH SHORE

Casanova Italian Restaurant & Deli. Casanova brings in some big acts, included Kool and the Gang, Los Lobos, and Taj Majal. Most Friday and Saturday nights it attracts a hip, local scene with live bands and eclectic DJs spinning house, funk, and world music. Don't miss the costumed theme nights. Wednesday is for Wild Wahines (code for ladies get in free), which can be on the smarmy side. There's a $5 to $25 cover. ⊠ *1188 Makawao Ave., Makawao* ☎ *808/572–0220* ⊕ *www. casanovamaui.com.*

Charley's. The closest thing to country Maui has to offer, Charley's is a down-home dive bar in the heart of Paia. It also hosts reggae, house, Latin soul, and jazz nights. Live bands are featured on Friday and Saturday. ⊠ *142 Hana Hwy., Paia* ☎ *808/579–9453* ⊕ *www. charleysmaui.com.*

Stopwatch Bar & Grill. This friendly dive bar books favorite local bands on Friday and charges only $3. ⊠ *1127 Makawao Ave., Makawao* ☎ *808/572–1380.*

WHERE TO EAT

Updated
by Bonnie
Friedman

From ethnic holes-in-the-wall to stunningly appointed fine dining rooms, and from seafood trucks to oceanfront fish houses with sweeping panoramic views. Much of it is excellent, but some of it is overpriced and touristy. If you're coming from a "food destination" city, you may have to adjust your expectations.

At fine and casual fine dining restaurants, choose menu items made with products that are abundant on the island, including local fish, onions, avocados, cabbage, broccoli, asparagus, hydroponic tomatoes, myriad herbs, salad greens, *kalo* (taro), bananas, papaya, guava, *lilikoi* (passionfruit), coconut, mangoes, strawberries, and Maui Gold pineapple. And items grown on neighboring islands like mushrooms, purple sweet potatoes, and watermelon.

Local cuisine is an amalgam of foods brought by the ethnic groups that have come here since the late 1700s blended, too, with the foods Native Hawaiians have enjoyed for centuries: *lomilomi* salmon, *laulau*, poi, Portuguese bean soup, kalbi ribs, chicken katsu, chow fun, hamburger steak, macaroni salad, the original "fusion" cuisine, and "everyman's" food. Always inexpensive—and always satisfying. For a food adventure, take a drive into Central Maui. Have lunch or dinner at one of the "local" spots recommended here. Or get even more adventurous. Take a drive around Wailuku or Kahului and find your own hidden gem. There are plenty out there.

Prices in the reviews are the average cost of a main course at dinner or, if dinner is not served, at lunch.

WEST MAUI

OLOWALU

$ AMERICAN 🍴 **Leoda's Kitchen and Pie Shop.** Slow down as you drive through the little roadside village of Olowalu, about 15 minutes before Lahaina town if you're coming from the airport, because you don't want to miss this adorable farmhouse-chic restaurant and pie shop where everything is prepared with care. Old photos of the area, distressed wood, and muted colors set the mood. Have a sandwich or a burger with Kula onions. All the breads are home baked and excellent, and most ingredients are sourced locally. Don't get too full: you must try the pie. The banana cream is out of this world, or dig into the yuzu-lemon tart. [$] *Average main: $13* ✉ *820 Olowalu Village Rd., Olowalu* ☎ *808/662–3600* 🌐 *www.leodas.com.*

3

LAHAINA

$ HAWAIIAN 🍴 **Aloha Mixed Plate.** From the wonderful folks who bring you Maui's best luau—the Old Lahaina Luau—comes this extremely casual, oceanfront eatery, which is open for breakfast, lunch, and dinner. If you've yet to indulge in a local-style "plate lunch," this is a good place to try it. A consistent award winner in local magazine and newspaper polls, each plate combines foods representative of Hawaii's ethnic mix. Take a plate of your Chinese chow mein noodles, marinated and grilled Korean kalbi ribs, Japanese teriyaki beef, and, of course, the requisite macaroni salad and two scoops of rice to a table so close to the ocean you just might get wet. Want to go whole hog? Try the Alii Plate of traditional Hawaiian foods: *laulau* (taro-leaf-wrapped bundles of meats and fish), *lomilomi* salmon (a cold salad of raw salmon, tomatoes, onions), poi, rice, and *haupia* (luscious coconut pudding). Oh, and don't forget the mai tai! [$] *Average main: $10* ✉ *1285 Front St., Lahaina* ☎ *808/661–3322* 🌐 *www.AlohaMixedPlate.com.*

$ MEXICAN 🍴 **Cilantro.** The flavors of Old Mexico are given new life here, where no fewer than nine chilis are used to create the salsas. The owner, a former high-end food and beverage pro, spent three years visiting authentic eateries in 40 Mexican cities before opening this place. Tucked into an older and unfancy mall, the restaurant requires you to order at the counter and fill your own disposable beverage cup at the soda fountain. But as soon as you bite into a chipotle-citrus rotisserie chicken plate or, really, anything on the menu, you'll forget all about the plastic cutlery—and the fact that the only view is of a parking lot. The brilliantly colored, clever decor—a collection of worn-from-duty tortilla presses, now hand-painted—coupled with consistently excellent food makes up for any deficiencies. [$] *Average main: $12* ✉ *Old Lahaina Center, 170 Papalaua Ave., Lahaina* ☎ *808/667–5444* 🌐 *www.cilantrogrill.com.*

$$$$ MODERN AMERICAN 🍴 **David Paul's Island Grill.** For years, he was one of Maui's most celebrated and determined chefs, winning every possible award and rave review for his original David Paul's Lahaina Grill. After an almost decade-long hiatus on Hawaii Island, David Paul opened a beautiful restaurant on Maui in 2009, where he cooks his own distinctive style of New American cuisine (think butter lettuce and bleu cheese salad, bistro chicken, Princess and the Pea diver scallops), accessing local

BEST BETS FOR MAUI DINING

Fodor's Choice★	By Price	$$$
Ba-Le Sandwiches & Plate Lunch, $, p. 297	**$**	Mala Ocean Tavern, p. 287
Café des Amis, $, p. 300	A.K.'s Café, p. 296	Market Fresh Bistro, p. 299
Mala Ocean Tavern, $$$, p. 287	Ba-Le Sandwiches & Plate Lunch, p. 297	Pineapple Grill, p. 293
Paia Fishmarket, $, p. 300	Café des Amis, p. 300	Tommy Bahama, p. 295
Roy's Kaanapali Bar & Grill, $$$$, p. 290	Cilantro, p. 285	**$$$$**
Sam Sato's, $, p. 298	Da Kitchen, p. 296	Banyan Tree, p. 292
Sansei Seafood Restaurant & Sushi Bar, $$, p. 293	Kihei Caffe, p. 294	Roy's Kaanapali Bar & Grill, p. 290
	Paia Fishmarket, p. 300	Spago, p. 295
Star Noodle, $, p. 290	Sam Sato's, p. 298	Tropica Restaurant & Bar, p. 291
Tokyo Tei, $, p. 298	Star Noodle, p. 290	
Tommy Bahama, $$$, p. 295	Tokyo Tei, p. 298	
Tropica Restaurant & Bar, $$$$, p. 291	**$$**	
	Asian Star, p. 297	
	Sansei Seafood Restaurant & Sushi Bar, p. 293	
	Tiki Terrace, p. 291	

products and adding island flavors. There's an unobstructed ocean view from the front patio, and the comfy seating out back is perfect for a cocktail and late-night bites. Service can be spotty, but it's still worth a visit. $ *Average main: $36* ⊠ *Lahaina Center, 900 Front St., Lahaina* ☎ *808/662–3000* ⊕ *www.davidpaulsislandgrill.com* ☉ *No lunch.*

$$$$ ✕**Gerard's.** For nearly three decades, classically trained French chef
FRENCH Gerard Reversade has remained true to his roots and kept his charming restaurant classically French. A native of Gascony, Reversade came up through the ranks, starting as an apprentice in acclaimed Paris restaurants when he was just 14. His exacting standards—in the dining room as well as in the kitchen—have been the hallmarks of his eponymous restaurant year in and year out. He cooks *his* way, utilizing island ingredients in such classics as mushrooms in puff pastry, escargots *forestière*, Molokai shrimp consommé, terrine of foie gras, confit of duck, and lobster pot au feu. The wine list is first-class. Floral fabrics and white tablecloths echo the look of a French country inn. $ *Average main: $45* ⊠ *Plantation Inn, 174 Lahainaluna Rd., Lahaina* ☎ *808/661–8939* ⊕ *www.gerardsmaui.com* ☉ *No lunch.*

$$$$ ✕**Honu.** Right next door to their popular Mala Ocean Tavern, celebrity
ECLECTIC chef Mark Ellman and Judy Ellman opened this oceanfront fish house and pizza restaurant in 2011. Much of the seafood comes from the East Coast and Pacific Northwest: clams, crabs, mussels—and yes, Maui

finally has lobster rolls. The pizzas are cooked in a wood-fired brick oven (is there any other way?). The wine list is fabulous. Judy designed the sleek, bright interior with white walls, abundant use of wood, and large windows: Honu makes the best of an unparalleled ocean view. All in all, it's a hot new entry on the Maui dining scene. $ *Average main: $36* ⊠ *1295 Front St., Lahaina* ☎ *808/667–9390* ⊕ *www.honumaui.com.*

$$$$ ✕ **Lahaina Grill.** At the top of many best-restaurants lists, this upscale
AMERICAN bistro is about as fashionably chic as it gets on Maui. The food and service are consistently excellent and the place is abuzz with beautiful people every night of the week. The Cake Walk (little samples of Kona lobster crab cake, sweet Louisiana rock-shrimp cake, and seared ahi cake), toy-box tomato salad, and Kona-coffee-roasted rack of lamb are a few of the classics customers demand. Newer items include Maine lobsters flown in seasonally and seared California lion-paw scallops. The full menu—including dessert—is available at the bar. The interior is as pretty as its patrons. $ *Average main: $45* ⊠ *127 Lahainaluna Rd., Lahaina* ☎ *808/667–5117* ⊕ *www.lahainagrill.com* ☾ *No lunch.*

$$$$ ✕ **Longhi's.** A Lahaina landmark created by "a man who loves to eat,"
ITALIAN Longhi's has been serving pasta and other Italian fare to throngs of visitors since 1976. That "man" is owner Bob Longhi, and although his children pretty much run the place now, his influence is still strong. Many of the classic dishes on the menu are his—prawns Amaretto, steak Longhi, and the signature lobster Longhi for two. The wine list is award winning and gigantic. Before the rest of Lahaina (or Wailea) wakes up, have yourself a cup of orange juice, a fluffy frittata, and some good, strong coffee to start the day. The in-house bakery shines with outstanding breakfast pastries, as well. There are two spacious, open-air dining levels; and there's a second Maui restaurant at the Shops at Wailea. $ *Average main: $37* ⊠ *888 Front St., Lahaina* ☎ *808/667– 2288* ⊕ *www.longhis.com.*

$$$ ✕ **Mala Ocean Tavern.** Chef-owner Mark Ellman started Maui's culinary
MODERN revolution of the late '80s with his restaurant Avalon, but Mala is a more
HAWAIIAN than satisfactory successor. The place is adorable; the best tables are
Fodor's Choice on the lanai, which actually juts out over the water. The menu reflects
★ Mark's and his wife Judy's world travels with dishes influenced by the Middle East, the Mediterranean, Italy, Bali, and Thailand. Every single item on the menu is delicious, and there's a focus on ingredients that promote local sustainability. The cocktails and wine list are great, to boot. Another location of Mala is at the Wailea Beach Marriott Resort, but the Lahaina original is highly recommended. $ *Average main: $30* ⊠ *1307 Front St., Lahaina* ☎ *808/667–9394* ⊕ *www.malaoceantavern.com.*

$$$$ ✕ **PacificO.** Sophisticated outdoor dining on the beach (no, really *on*
ASIAN the beach) and creative island cuisine using local, fresh-caught fish and greens and veggies grown in the restaurant's own Upcountry Oo Farm (and, quite possibly, picked that very morning)—this is the Maui dining experience you've been dreaming about. Start with the award-winning appetizer of prawn and basil wontons, move on to any of the fantastic fresh fish dishes, and for dessert, finish with the banana pineapple *lumpia* served hot with homemade banana ice cream. $ *Average main: $36* ⊠ *505 Front St., Lahaina* ☎ *808/667–4341* ⊕ *www.pacificomaui.com.*

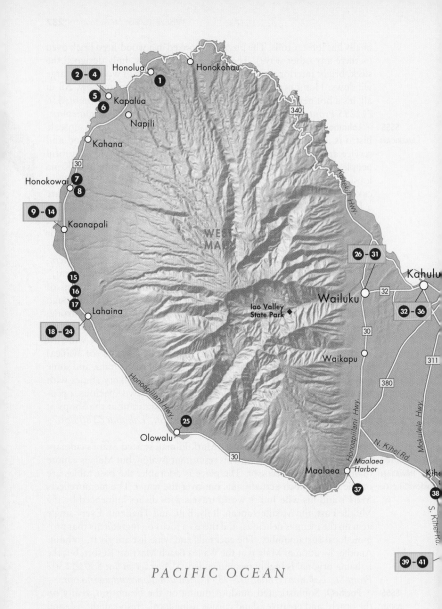

Honolua

Honokohau

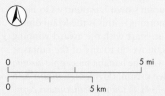 2-4

1

5

Kapalua

6

Napili

Kahana

30

Honokowai 7

8

9 - 14

Kaanapali

WEST
MAUI

26 - 31

Kahulu

15

16

17

Lahaina

18 - 24

25

Olowalu

Wailuku

32

32 - 36

30

311

Waikapu

380

Iao Valley
State Park

340

Kaileki Hwy.

Honoapiilani Hwy.

N. Kihei Rd.

Mokulele Hwy.

Honoapiilani Hwy.

Maalaea
Harbor

Maalaea

37

Kihe

38

S. Kihei Rd.

39 - 41

PACIFIC OCEAN

0   5 mi

0   5 km

Where to Eat on Maui

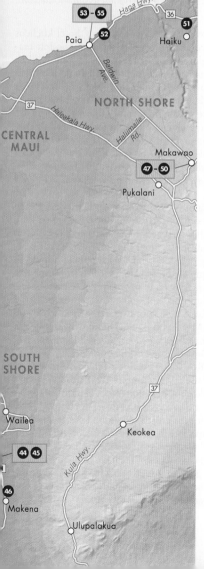

3

$　✕ **Star Noodle.** In a very short time this wonderful spot has become
ASIAN　one of Maui's best restaurants. It's way up above the highway in a
Fodor's Choice　light industrial park, but don't be discouraged by the location. Take
★　the drive and you'll find a hip place and a welcoming staff that knows
the meaning of "aloha." There's a communal table in the center of the
room, smaller tables around the perimeter and comfortable stools for
those who like to eat at a bar. Menu musts include the Ahi Avo, pan-
roasted brussels sprouts with bacon and kim chee purée, and really
any of the noodle dishes, especially the Lahaina fried soup (fat chow
fun, pork, bean sprouts). The cocktail list is fabulous and the lychee
martinis served here may be the best on Maui. $ *Average main: $10*
⊠ *286 Kupuohi St., Lahaina* ☎ *808/667–4500* ⊕ *www.starnoodle.com.*

KAANAPALI

$　✕ **CJ's Deli & Diner.** Chef Christian Jorgensen left fancy hotel kitchens
AMERICAN　behind to open a casual place serving simple, delicious food at reasonable prices. The mango-glazed ribs, burgers, and classic Reuben
sandwich are good choices, and the pineapple fried rice is *ono* (delicious); just order and pick up at the counter, and take your food to a
table. If you're traveling to Hana or the Haleakala Crater, buy a box
lunch and you're set. If you're staying in a condo, the "Chefs to Go"
service is a great alternative to picking up (run of the mill and usually
lousy) fast food. Everything is prepped and comes with easy cooking
instructions. And if you decide, even on the spur of the moment, that
Maui is a nice place for a wedding, CJ's can cater it. $ *Average main:
$10* ⊠ *Fairway Shops, 2580 Kekaa Dr., Kaanapali* ☎ *808/667–0968*
⊕ *www.cjsmaui.com.*

$$$　✕ **Hula Grill.** A bustling and family-oriented spot on Kaanapali Beach
MODERN　at Whalers Village shopping center, this restaurant designed to look
HAWAIIAN　like a sprawling '30s beach house represents a partnership between
☺　TS Restaurants group and Hawaii Regional Cuisine pioneer chef Peter
Merriman. They serve up large dinner portions of everything from fresh
local fish and Maui Cattle Company beef to Hula Grill "traditions" like
rosemary- and wood-roasted rack of lamb to sweet potato ravioli. Just
in the mood for an umbrella-adorned cocktail and some pupu? Go to
the Barefoot Bar where you can wiggle your toes in the sand while you
sip. The beach is called "Dig Me"—you'll understand why after just a
few moments. $ *Average main: $27* ⊠ *Whalers Village, 2435 Kaanapali
Pkwy., Kaanapali* ☎ *808/667–6636* ⊕ *www.hulagrill.com.*

$$$$　✕ **Roy's Kaanapali Bar & Grill.** Roy Yamaguchi is a James Beard award-
MODERN　winning chef and the granddaddy of East-meets-West cuisine. He has
HAWAIIAN　restaurants all over the world, but his eponymous Maui restaurant
Fodor's Choice　was one of the first, and it's still one of the best. It's loud and brassy
★　with a young vibe, but come for the great food, even if the atmosphere
isn't quite your thing. Signatures like fire-grilled, Szechuan-spiced baby
back pork ribs, Roy's original blackened ahi tuna, hibachi-style grilled
salmon, and the to-die-for hot chocolate soufflé have been on the menu
from the beginning, and with good reason. Roy's wine list is exception-
ally user-friendly. The service here is welcoming and professional. $ *Av-
erage main: $36* ⊠ *2990 Kaanapali Pkwy., Kaanapali* ☎ *808/669–6999*
⊕ *www.roysrestaurant.com.*

Pineapple and shrimp add local flavors to tasty grilled skewers.

$$$$ MEDITERRANEAN

🍴 **Son'z Maui at Swan Court.** If you're celebrating a special occasion and want to splurge, this just might be the place for you. You'll descend a grand staircase into an amber-lighted dining room with soaring ceilings and a massive artificial lagoon complete with swans, waterfalls, and tropical gardens. Must-haves on chef Geno Sarmiento's contemporary, Mediterranean-influenced menu include the seared scallops "BLT"; goat-cheese ravioli with Kula corn, edamame, and Hamakua mushrooms; and grilled beef tenderloin marinated in coffee and served with Parmesan-garlic fries. The restaurant claims the largest wine cellar in Hawaii with 3,000 bottles. [$] *Average main: $40* ✉ *Hyatt Regency Maui, 200 Nohea Kai Dr., Kaanapali* ☎ *808/667–4506* 🌐 *www.tristarrestaurants.com* 🕓 *No lunch.*

$$ MODERN HAWAIIAN

🍴 **Tiki Terrace.** Executive chef Tom Muromoto is a local boy who loves to cook modern, upscale Hawaiian food. He augments the various fresh fish dishes on his menu with items influenced by Hawaii's ethnic mix. This casual, open-air restaurant is the only place on Maui—maybe in Hawaii—where you can have a Native Hawaiian combination plate that is as healthful as it is authentic. Sunday brunch is renowned here, and if you're around for a holiday, chow down at the amazing holiday brunch buffets. [$] *Average main: $26* ✉ *Kaanapali Beach Hotel, 2525 Kaanapali Pkwy., Kaanapali* ☎ *808/667–0124* 🌐 *www.kbhmaui.com* 🕓 *No lunch.*

$$$$ MODERN HAWAIIAN

Fodor's Choice ★

🍴 **Tropica Restaurant & Bar.** As far as hotel restaurants go, this beautifully appointed, oceanfront restaurant serving modern Hawaiian fare is as cool, calm, comfortable, and delicious as it gets. Start with an exceptionally creative cocktail—the martinis are superb—or a glass of wine from a long, excellent list. You then must indulge in the dreamy golden potato gnocchi with Meyer lemon cream, or the Pacific bouillabaisse with Kona lobster. Fish choices are plentiful. Tropica also offers lots of specially priced cocktail and dining options that will save you some bucks. And for the dining experience of a lifetime, reserve far in advance to get one of six tables on the beach. Yes, *on* the beach. $ *Average main: $36* ✉ *The Westin Maui Resort & Spa, 2365 Kaanapali Pkwy., Kaanapali* ☎ *808/667–2525* ⊕ *www.westinmaui.com* ⊙ *Closed Mon. and Tues. No lunch.*

KAPALUA AND VICINITY

$$$$ ✕ **The Banyan Tree.** The setting is sublime, the atmosphere serene, and the
ASIAN service elegant at this signature restaurant of the Ritz-Carlton Kapalua. Drink in views of the Pailolo Channel and Molokai while enjoying perfectly prepared island cuisine full of worldly influences. The *dukka* (Middle Eastern spice mixture) delivered with your bread is just a hint of the delights to come. Chef JoJo Vasquez's recent seasonal offerings have included raw hamachi in Vietnamese marinade, grilled Colorado lamb with eggplant puree, and Maui-made Surfing Goat Dairy goat cheese tart. $ *Average main: $45* ✉ *Ritz-Carlton, Kapalua, 1 Ritz-Carlton Dr., Kapalua* ☎ *808/669–6200* ⊕ *www.ritzcarlton.com/ kapalua* ⊙ *Closed Sun. and Mon. No lunch.*

$ ✕ **The Gazebo Restaurant.** Breakfast is the reason to seek out this res-
DINER taurant located poolside at the Napili Shores Resort. The atmosphere is a little funky but the oceanfront setting and views are spectacular— including the turtle, spinner dolphin, and, in winter, humpback-whale sightings. The food is standard diner fare and portions are big. Many folks think the Gazebo serves the best pancakes on West Maui. Have them with pineapple, bananas, macadamia nuts, or chocolate chips, or make up your own combination. You will almost certainly have to wait for a table, sometimes for quite a while, but at least it's a pleasant place to do so. $ *Average main: $11* ✉ *Napili Shores Resort, 5315 Lower Honoapiilani Hwy., Napili* ☎ *808/669–5621* ⊙ *No dinner.*

$ ✕ **Honokowai Okazuya.** Sandwiched between a dive shop and a salon
ECLECTIC in a nondescript mini strip mall, this small place only has a few stools and a couple of tables outside, but it's fast and the food is consistently good—all it takes to keep the place filled with locals. The mahimahi with lemon capers, and beef black bean chow fun are the top-selling favorites. There's plenty more including vegetarian and lighter fare such as Grandma's spicy tofu, egg fu young, and even a veggie burger. The fresh chow fun noodles sell out quickly. $ *Average main: $14* ✉ *3600-D Lower Honoapiilani Hwy., Honokowai* ☎ *808/665–0512* ▭ *No credit cards* ⊙ *Closed Sun. and between 2:30 and 4:30.*

$$$ ✕ **Kai Sushi.** For a quiet, light dinner, or to meet friends for a cock-
JAPANESE tail and some ultrafresh sushi, head to this handsome restaurant on the lobby level of the Ritz-Carlton Kapalua. You have your choice of sushi, sashimi, and a list of rolls. The especially good Kai special roll combines spicy tuna, yellowtail, and green onion. In keeping with the hotel's commitment to the culture, the restaurant's design was inspired by the story of Native Hawaiians' arrival by sea; the hand-carved ceiling beams resemble outrigger canoes. $ *Average main: $30* ✉ *Ritz-Carl-*

ton, Kapalua, 1 Ritz-Carlton Dr., Kapalua ☎ *808/669–6200* 🌐 *www.ritzcarlton.com/kapalua* ⏲ *Closed Tues. and Wed. No lunch.*

$$$ MODERN HAWAIIAN 🍴 **Pineapple Grill.** High on the hill overlooking the Kapalua resort, this restaurant exudes casual elegance. Young, Lahaina-born chef Ryan Luckey makes good use of the island's bounty, with dishes featuring Maui pineapple, Roselani ice cream, Maui Cattle Company beef, greens and vegetables from Waipoli and Nalo farms, and local, sustainable fish. If you've had enough of the gorgeous ocean, mountain, or resort views, you can watch the chef and his crew in the shiny exhibition kitchen, as they assemble their specialties like pistachio-wasabi crusted rare ahi tuna, Maui farmer's chopped salad, and the Maui pineapple-glazed 14-ounce pork chop. [$] *Average main: $30* ✉ *200 Kapalua Dr., Kapalua* ☎ *808/669–9600* 🌐 *www.pineapplekapalua.com.*

3

$ ITALIAN 🍴 **Pizza Paradiso.** When it opened in 1995, this was an over-the-counter pizza place. It has evolved over the years into a local favorite serving pasta, Mediterranean comfort food and still, of course, pizza. The pies are so popular because of the top ingredients—100% pure Italian olive oil, Maui produce whenever possible, and Maui Cattle Company beef. The menu also features gyros, falafel, grilled fish, rotisserie chicken, and tiramisu. [$] *Average main: $10* ✉ *Honokowai Marketplace, 3350 Lower Honoapiilani Rd., Honokowai* ☎ *808/667–2929* 🌐 *www.pizzaparadiso.com.*

$$$ MODERN HAWAIIAN 🍴 **Plantation House Restaurant.** It's a bit of a drive to the restaurant, but chef–partner Alex Stanislaw's skills—especially with fresh fish—make it worth the trip. Here you'll find a beautiful and comfortable restaurant with expansive views of the ocean below and the majestic mountains above. Chef Alex sources the best of the island's bounty; much of the produce he uses is grown within a few miles of the kitchen. The fish preparations commonly reflect his Mediterranean heritage; think pistachio-crusted Hawaiian catch served on herbed couscous with extra virgin olive oil. Breakfast is glorious here, too. [$] *Average main: $35* ✉ *Plantation Course Clubhouse, 2000 Plantation Club Dr., Kapalua* ☎ *808/669–6299* 🌐 *www.theplantationhouse.com.*

$$ ASIAN Fodor's Choice ★ 🍴 **Sansei Seafood Restaurant & Sushi Bar.** If you are a fish or shellfish lover then this is the place for you. One of the most wildly popular restaurants in Hawaii with locations on three islands, Sansei takes sushi, sashimi, and contemporary Japanese food to a new level. Favorite dishes include the mango-and-crab-salad handroll, panko-crusted-ahi sashimi roll, Asian shrimp cake, Japanese calamari salad, and Dungeness crab ramen with Asian-truffle broth. There are great deals on sushi and small plates for early birds and night owls. This busy restaurant has several separate dining areas, a sushi bar, and a bar area, but the focus is squarely on excellent food and not the atmosphere. [$] *Average main: $26* ✉ *600 Office Rd., Kapalua* ☎ *808/669–6286* 🌐 *www.sanseihawaii.com* ⏲ *No lunch.*

THE SOUTH SHORE

KIHEI AND MAALAEA

$ ✕ **Kihei Caffe.** This small, unassuming place across the street from Kal-
AMERICAN ama Beach Park has a breakfast menu that runs the gamut from healthy
yogurt-filled papaya to the local classic, *loco moco*—two eggs, ground
beef patty, rice, and brown gravy—and everything in between. And
the best thing about it is that the breakfast menu is served all day long.
Prices are extremely reasonable and it's a good spot for people-watching. This is a popular place with locals so, depending on the time and
day, you may have to wait for a table. $ *Average main: $8* ⊠ *1945 S.
Kihei Rd., Kihei* ☎ *808/879–2230* ⊕ *www.kiheicaffe.com* ⊗ *No dinner.*

$$ ✕ **Monsoon India.** Here you can enjoy a lovely ocean view while feasting
INDIAN on authentic Indian cuisine. Appetizers like *papadum* chips and *samosas*
are served with homemade chutneys. There are 10 breads—naan and
more—that come hot from the tandoori oven, along with six mix-and-
match curries, lots of vegetarian selections, kebabs, and biryanis. Live
music on Tuesday and Saturday evenings is a big draw, as is the Sunday
brunch buffet. $ *Average main: $20* ⊠ *Menehune Shores, 760 S. Kihei
Rd., Kihei* ☎ *808/875–6666* ⊕ *www.monsoonindiamaui.com.*

$$$$ ✕ **Sarento's on the Beach.** This upscale Italian restaurant's setting right on
ITALIAN spectacular Keawakapu Beach, with views of Molokini and Kahoolawe,
is irresistible. And, to be honest, the spectacular setting is the best thing
about Sarento's. The menu has a decidedly Italian bent, with offer-
ings like linguine with clam sauce, seafood *fra diavolo* (in a tomato
sauce spiced with chilies), and portobello napoleon with local eggplant,
mozzarella, tomatoes, and arugula pesto. The food is good, if a bit
old-fashioned, and the portions may be a bit too big for some. $ *Aver-
age main: $38* ⊠ *2980 S. Kihei Rd., Kihei* ☎ *808/875–7555* ⊕ *www.
sarentosonthebeachcom* ⊗ *No lunch.*

$ ✕ **Seascape Maalaea.** A good choice for a seafood lunch, the Maui Ocean
SEAFOOD Center's signature restaurant (aquarium admission is not required to
☺ dine here) offers harbor views from its open-air perch. The restaurant
promotes heart-healthy cuisine, using sustainable seafood and trans-fat-
free items. Lunch-size salads, sandwiches, burgers, fish tacos, teriyaki
tofu, fish-and-chips, chicken, ribs, and a full kids' menu are on offer.
There's something for everyone here, and the view isn't bad either.
$ *Average main: $15* ⊠ *Maui Ocean Center, 192 Maalaea Rd., Maalaea*
☎ *808/270–7000* ⊕ *www.mauioceancenter.com* ⊗ *No dinner.*

$ ✕ **South Shore Tiki Lounge.** Come on, how can you come to Hawaii and
AMERICAN *not* go to a tiki bar? And this one—tucked into Kihei KalamaVillage—
is consistently voted "Best Bar" by the readers of *Maui Time Weekly.*
During the day, sit on the shaded lanai to enjoy a burger, sandwich, or,
better yet, one of their delicious specialty pizzas, crafted from scratch
with sauces made from fresh Roma tomatoes and Maui herbs. Seven
nights a week, the tiny bar area lights up with a lively crowd, as DJs
spin dance tunes under the glowing red eyes of the lounge's namesake
tiki. $ *Average main: $10* ⊠ *1913 S. Kihei Rd., Kihei* ☎ *808/874–6444*
⊕ *www.southshoretikilounge.com.*

$ ✕ **Thailand Cuisine.** Fragrant tea and coconut-ginger chicken soup begin
THAI a satisfying meal at this excellent Thai restaurant, set unassumingly in

the middle of a shopping mall. The care and expense that goes into the decor—glittering Buddhist shrines, elaborate hardwood facades, fancy napkin folds, and matching blue china—also applies to the cuisine. Take an exotic journey with the fantastic pad thai, special house noodles, curries, and crispy fried chicken. Can't decide? Try the family dinners for two or four. The fried bananas with ice cream are wonderful. There's a second location in Kahului's Maui Mall, a perfect choice before or after a movie at the megaplex. $ *Average main: $15* ⌧ *Kukui Mall, 1819 S. Kihei Rd., Kihei* ☎ *808/875–0839* ⊕ *www.thailandcuisinemaui.com* ⊘ *No lunch Sun.*

WAILEA AND SOUTH SHORE (MAKENA)

$$$$
ITALIAN
✕**Ferraro's Bar e Ristorante.** Overlooking the ocean from a bluff above Wailea Beach, this outdoor Italian restaurant at the Four Seasons Resort Maui at Wailea is beautiful both day and night. For lunch, indulge in a lobster sandwich or a quinoa salad topped with teriyaki-glaze tofu. At dinner try the arugula and endive salad and house-made pasta or the osso buco veal Milanese. If chef Michael Cantin is offering one of his tasting menus, you should order it. Not surprisingly, the wine list includes excellent Italian choices. Live classical music often adds to the atmosphere, and occasionally you can spot celebrities at the bar. $ *Average main: $40* ⌧ *Four Seasons Resort Maui at Wailea, 3900 Wailea Alanui Dr., Wailea* ☎ *808/874–8000* ⊕ *www.fourseasons.com/maui.*

$$$$
MODERN
AMERICAN
✕**Gannon's.** You'll love the amazing ocean and mountain views at this outpost of acclaimed chef Beverly Gannon, as well as the splashy Red Bar. Here you'll find Beverly's style of food, which consists of local products prepared with international flavors. For a starter, try the warm goat cheese Maui onion tart with roasted pears, and follow that with fennel-chilli-crusted ahi with lemon beurre blanc. Breakfast is especially nice here. The outdoor lanai seating is cool in the morning and overlooks the parade of boats heading out to Molokini. $ *Average main: $38* ⌧ *100 Golf Club Dr., Wailea* ☎ *808/875–8080* ⊕ *www. gannonsrestaurant.com.*

$$$$
ASIAN
✕**Spago.** It's a marriage made in Hawaii heaven. The California cuisine of celebrity-chef Wolfgang Puck is combined with Maui flavors and served lobby level and oceanfront at the luxurious Four Seasons Resort. Try the spicy ahi tuna *poke* in sesame-miso cones to start, and then see what the chefs-in-residence can do with some of Maui's fantastic local fishes. Finish with a little wild lilikoi (passion fruit) crème brûlée with white chocolate–macadamia nut biscotti. Oh, it'll cost you, but the service is spot-on and the smooth, Asian-inspired decor allows the food to claim the spotlight. $ *Average main: $42* ⌧ *Four Seasons Resort Maui at Wailea, 3900 Wailea Alanui Dr., Wailea* ☎ *808/879– 2999* ⊘ *No lunch.*

$$$
ASIAN
Fodor'sChoice
★
✕**Tommy Bahama.** It's more "island-style" than Hawaii, and yes, it's a chain, but the food is consistently great, the service is filled with aloha, and the atmosphere is just so island-refined. Try the Loki-Loki tuna poke (fresh ahi napoleon with guacamole, capers, soy sauce, and sesame oil), the Island Cowboy (a grilled eight-ounce tenderloin filet with red wine demi-glace, roasted garlic, and Maytag bleu cheese, served with grilled lemon garlic asparagus and roasted fingerling potatoes), or any

of the local fish preparations, equally well accompanied. The Copper Island crab bisque is worthy of a cross-island drive, as are the desserts. $ *Average main: $35* ⊠ *The Shops at Wailea, 3750 Wailea Alanui Dr., Wailea* ☎ *808/875–9983* ⊕ *www.tommybahama.com.*

CENTRAL MAUI

KAHULUI

$ ╳ **Da Kitchen.** There's an "express" location in Kihei, but do try the
ECLECTIC   happy, always-crowded Kahului location of Da Kitchen for the
☺   mahimahi tempura, the loco moco, Hawaiian plate, and chicken katsu. Everything on the menu is great and the portions are gigantic. The upbeat atmosphere is reflected in the service as well as the food. $ *Average main: $14* ⊠ *425 Koloa St., Kahului* ☎ *808/871–7782* ⊕ *www. da-kitchen.com* ⊘ *Closed Sun.*

$$ ╳ **Dragon Dragon.** Whether you're a party of 10 or 2, this is the place to
CHINESE   stop for a quality meal of Chinese food staples. Dim sum is available only during lunch, but for a real treat, try some of the house specialties like the honey walnut prawns, spicy crab Singapore-style, and the sizzling platter of fish with basil leaves. Top it all off with Maui's own Roselani lychee sherbet. $ *Average main: $20* ⊠ *Maui Mall, 70 E. Kaahumanu Ave., Kahului* ☎ *808/893–1628.*

$$ ╳ **Marco's Grill & Deli.** One of the go-to places for airport comers and
ITALIAN   goers, this popular Italian restaurant also draws a steady crowd of local residents. Meatballs, sausages, and sauces are all made fresh in-house; the owner was a butcher in his former life. There's a long list of sandwiches that are available all day, and the salads are definitely big enough to share. Note that food substitutions or special requests are not appreciated here. $ *Average main: $22* ⊠ *444 Hana Hwy., Kahului* ☎ *808/877–4446.*

$ ╳ **Ramen Ya.** Part of a Japanese chain, this outpost in a mall is the first
JAPANESE   and only location in Maui. All the ramen dishes are slurp-worthy, and the *gyoza* (dumplings) are reason enough to dine here. If you're not that hungry or just have a small appetite, you can order kid-size portions. The service is quick and friendly, and the prices are right. $ *Average main: $9* ⊠ *Queen Kaahumanu Center, 275 W. Kaahumanu Ave, Kahului* ☎ *808/873–9688.*

$ ╳ **Zippy's.** Hawaii's favorite casual, eat-in, or takeout restaurant, Zippy's
ECLECTIC   was founded more than 40 years ago. Today Oahu has more than two-
☺   dozen locations from which to choose, but Maui waited a long time to get one. It's a 24-hour-a-day, diner-type place with a big menu. Spaghetti with chili, oxtail soup, Korean chicken, chicken katsu, noodles, burgers, and burritos are just a few of the tasty menu options. Napoleon's Bakery counter up front serves its only-in-Hawaii-style turnovers, pies, cakes, and pastries. $ *Average main: $10* ⊠ *15 Hookele St., Kahului* ☎ *808/856–7599* ⊕ *www.zippys.com.*

WAILUKU

$ ╳ **A.K.'s Café.** Nearly hidden between auto-body shops and karaoke
ECLECTIC   bars is this wonderful, bright café serving good island fare. Chef-owner Elaine Nakashima not only knows how to make everything

Dig into pupu—Hawaiian appetizers—such as seaweed salad and ahi (yellowfin tuna).

taste delicious, she knows how to make local flavors more healthful, too. Her Thai chicken, local fish preparations, roast turkey plate, and even her sweet potatoes (either steamed or fried) are excellent. Elaine's crab cakes are so good—some say the best on Maui—that retail markets around the island stock them in their freezers and their prepared-food sections. The place takes on a lovely warm glow at dinnertime, and impromptu contemporary Hawaiian music is not uncommon. $ *Average main: $13* ⊠ *1237 Lower Main St., Wailuku* ☎ *808/244–8774* ⊕ *www.akscafe.com* ⊘ *Closed weekends.*

$$ ✕ **Asian Star.** This restaurant in Wailuku's Millyard (a light industrial
VIETNAMESE area) is the best choice for Vietnamese food on Maui. Owner Jason Chau grows his own Hawaiian chili peppers, mint, basil, chives, lemongrass, and green onions around the perimeter of the parking lot, and these seasonings add robust and concentrated flavors to his dishes. Try the lemongrass chicken or tofu, the garlic beef or green papaya salad, the crispy sesame or orange beef, the clay pots with crunchy, charred rice bits on the bottom, and the *bun,* bowls brimming with cold vermicelli noodles and topped with chicken. $ *Average main: $22* ⊠ *The Millyard, 1764 Wili Pa Loop, Wailuku* ☎ *808/244–1833.*

$ ✕ **Ba-Le Sandwiches & Plate Lunch.** It began as a French-Vietnamese bakery
VIETNAMESE on Oahu and has branched into popular small restaurants sprinkled
Fodor's Choice throughout the Islands. Some are kiosks in malls; others are stand-
★ alones with some picnic tables out front, as is the case at this location, which is one of four on Maui. Vietnamese *pho* (the famous soups laden with seafood or rare beef, fresh basil, bean sprouts, and lime) share menu space with local-style *saimin;* plates of barbecue or spicy chicken, beef, or pork with jasmine rice; and sandwiches. There are a slew of

tapioca flavors for dessert. ⓢ *Average main: $8* ✉ *1824 Oihana St., Wailuku* ☎ *808/249–8833* ⊕ *www.ba-le.com.*

$$ ✕ **Saeng's Thai Cuisine.** The satays, Panang curry, and crispy mahimahi
THAI   are all reason to make your way to Saeng's. Other reliable menu choices
include the angel wings (chicken wings stuffed with carrots and bean-
thread noodles), fresh summer rolls, and any of the chicken entrées.
The dining room is a bit dark but there's a courtyard with a pond and
foliage, and open-air tables. Take note: service can be slow. But it's
Maui, so who's in a hurry? ⓢ *Average main: $22* ✉ *2119 Vineyard St.,
Wailuku* ☎ *808/244–1567* ⊘ *No lunch on weekends.*

$ ✕ **Sam Sato's.** Every island has its noodle shrine and this is Maui's. Dry
HAWAIIAN mein, saimin, chow fun—they all come in different-size portions and
Fodor'sChoice with add-ins to satisfy every noodle craving. While you wait for your
★   bowl, chow down on a teriyaki beef stick or two. Save room for the
popular turnovers—pineapple, coconut, apple, or peach. At busy times,
which are most of the opening hours, you will likely have to wait for a
table or a stool at the counter. Be sure to write your name on the little
yellow pad or you'll miss your "next." ⓢ *Average main: $8* ✉ *The Mill-
yard, 1750 Wili Pa Loop, Wailuku* ☎ *808/244–7124* ▭ *No credit cards*
⊘ *No dinner. Closed Sun.*

$ ✕ **Tokyo Tei.** Getting there is half—well, maybe a quarter—of the fun.
JAPANESE   Tucked into the back corner of a covered parking garage, Tokyo Tei is
Fodor'sChoice worth seeking out for wonderful Japanese food. At lunch, you'll rub
★   elbows with bankers and construction workers; at dinner, three gen-
erations might be celebrating *Tutu's* (grandma's) birthday at the next
table. This is a bona fide local institution where, for more than six
decades, people have come for the food and the comfort of familiarity.
The freshest sashimi, feather-light yet crisp shrimp, and vegetable tem-
pura piled high are all the items that locals love. ⓢ *Average main: $12*
✉ *1063 Lower Main St., Wailuku* ☎ *808/242–9630* ⊕ *www.tokyotei.
com* ⊘ *No lunch Sun.*

UPCOUNTRY

$$$ ✕ **Casanova Italian Restaurant & Deli.** An authentic Italian dinner house
ITALIAN   and nightclub, this place is smack in the middle of Maui's *paniolo*
(cowboy) town of Makawao. The brick wood-burning oven, imported
from Italy, has been turning out perfect pies and steaming hot focaccia for more than 20 years. You can pair a pie with a salad (they're all
big enough to share) and a couple of glasses of wine without breaking the bank. The daytime deli is good for cappuccino, croissants,
and people-watching. The place turns positively raucous—in a good
way—on Wednesday, Friday, and Saturday nights. ⓢ *Average main:
$28* ✉ *1188 Makawao Ave., Makawao* ☎ *808/572–0220* ⊕ *www.
casanovamaui.com.*

$ ✕ **Grandma's Maui Coffee.** If you're taking a drive through gorgeous
AMERICAN   Upcountry Maui, this is a great place to stop for a truly homegrown
cup of coffee and snack. All of the coffee is grown right on the slopes
of Haleakala and roasted on the premises in a 100-year-old roaster
proudly on display. The baked goods and food are enjoyable and the
variety of menu items for breakfast and lunch is vast. Eggs, omelets,

crepes, and fantastic home fries are served for breakfast; salads, sandwiches, lasagna, and more can be ordered at lunch. Enjoy your coffee and goodies on the lovely deck; sometimes a Hawaiian musician is there playing a tune. [$] *Average main: $19* ✉ *9232 Kula Hwy., Kula* ☎ *808/878–2140* 🌐 *www.grandmascoffee.com* 🕒 *No dinner.*

$$$$ MODERN HAWAIIAN 🍴 **Haliimaile General Store.** Chef-restaurateur Beverly Gannon's first restaurant remains a culinary destination after more than two decades. The big, rambling former plantation store has two dining rooms: sit in the front to be seen and heard; head on back for some quiet and privacy. Classic dishes like crab boboli, Asian duck tostada, grilled lamb chops, and many more are complemented with daily and nightly specials. To get here, take the exit on the left halfway up Haleakala Highway. [$] *Average main: $38* ✉ *900 Haliimaile Rd., Haliimaile* ☎ *808/572–2666* 🌐 *www.bevgannonrestaurants.com.*

$$$ MODERN HAWAIIAN 🍴 **Market Fresh Bistro.** This hard-to-find restaurant tucked into a courtyard serves some seriously excellent food by Chef Justin Pardo, formerly of Union Square Café in New York City. He uses locally grown and produced ingredients, and in a nod to healthful eating, prefers reductions and infused oils rather than butter. Representative dishes include the cold curried watermelon gazpacho (in season) with either seared scallops or a lump crab cake, and the slow-cooked Maui Cattle Company short ribs, which are downright dreamy. [$] *Average main: $30* ✉ *3620 Baldwin Ave., Makawao* ☎ *808/572–4877* 🌐 *www.marketfreshbistromaui.com.*

THE NORTH SHORE

HAIKU

$$ AMERICAN 🍴 **Colleen's at the Cannery.** From the nondescript exterior and the location in an old pineapple cannery-cum–strip mall, you'd never anticipate what's inside. Colleen's is one of the most overlooked restaurants on Maui. It's popular with locals for breakfast and lunch, but try it at dinner when the candles come out and it's time for martinis and fresh fish. The food is excellent, in particular the huge salads made with Upcountry's best produce, the fish specials, the burgers, and the simple roast chicken. When eating here, you'll feel like you're at a hip, urban eatery. [$] *Average main: $20* ✉ *Haiku Cannery Marketplace, 810 Haiku Rd., Haiku* ☎ *808/575–9211.*

KUAU

$$$$ SEAFOOD 🍴 **Mama's Fish House.** For almost four decades, Mama's has been *the* Maui destination for special occasions. A path of gecko-shaped stones leads through the coconut grove past the giant clamshell and under the banyan arch to an ever-changing fantasyland of Hawaiiana kitsch. True, the setting couldn't be more spectacular, and yes, the menu even names the angler that reeled in your fresh catch, but the dishes are decidedly dated in terms of preparation and presentation—and the prices are off the charts. But if you're looking for an overall experience, make a reservation and celebrate your special occasion here. [$] *Average main: $48* ✉ *799 Poho Pl., Kuau* ☎ *808/579–8488* 🌐 *www.mamasfishhouse.com* ✍ *Reservations essential.*

PAIA

> **WORD OF MOUTH**
>
> "For some local flavor, try Paia Fish Market in Paia (best for lunch) or Hula Grill in Kaanapali (good lunch or dinner). More on the gourmet side, but still with local flavor, is Haliimaile General Store between Kahului and Kula. Try the Gazebo at Napili Shores for breakfast or lunch."
>
> —voyager61

$ ECLECTIC Fodor's Choice ★ 🍴 **Café des Amis.** The menu is a little neurotic—in a good way—featuring Mediterranean and Indian dishes, but the food is fresh and tasty. This budget-friendly café offers flavors and preparations not easily obtainable at other island eateries, with a nice selection of sweet and savory crepes, Indian wraps, and salads. All in all, you get delicious, good-value food, as well as excellent peope-watching from the umbrella-shaded tables outside. [$] *Average main: $14* ✉ *42 Baldwin Ave., Paia* ☎ *808/579–6323* 💳 *No credit cards.*

$$ PIZZA 👶 🍴 **Flatbread Company.** Vermont-based Flatbread Company marched right in to Paia in 2007 and instantly became a popular restaurant and a valued addition to the community. As part of the company's mission, they started "giving back" to local nonprofits immediately. Happily, along with the altruism, the food is fantastic. There's a big, primitive-looking, earthen, wood-fired oven from which emerge utterly delicious flatbread pizzas. They use organic, local, sustainable products, including 100% organically grown wheat for the made-fresh-daily products. The place is a good spot to take the kids. There's a no reservations policy but they do have "call ahead seating"—you can put your name on the wait list before you arrive. [$] *Average main: $22* ✉ *375 Hana Hwy., Paia* ☎ *808/579–8989* 🌐 *www.flatbreadcompany.com* ✍ *Reservations not accepted.*

$ SEAFOOD Fodor's Choice ★ 🍴 **Paia Fishmarket Restaurant.** If you're okay with communal picnic tables, or taking your meal to a nearby beach, this place in funky Paia town serves, arguably, the best fresh fish for the best prices on this side of the island. Four preparations are offered and, on any given day, there are at least four fresh fishes from which to choose. For the non-fish fans, there are burgers, chicken, and pasta. The side dishes—Cajun rice, home fries, and the amazing hand-cut crunchy cole slaw—are all as delectable as the main event. You can have a beer or a glass of wine, too, as long as you stay inside, of course. [$] *Average main: $15* ✉ *100 Hana Hwy., Paia* ☎ *808/579–8030* 🌐 *www.paiafishmarket.com.*

WHERE TO STAY

Updated
by Bonnie
Friedman

Maui's accommodations run the gamut from rural B&Bs to super-opulent megaresorts. In between the extremes, there's something for every vacation style and budget. The large resorts, hotels, and condominiums for which Maui is noted are on the sunny leeward southern and western shores. They bustle with activity and are near plenty of restaurants, shopping, golf, and water sports. Those seeking a different experience can try the inns, bed-and-breakfasts, and rentals in the small towns and quieter areas along the North Shore and Upcountry on the verdant slopes of Haleakala.

If the latest and greatest is your style, be prepared to spend a small fortune. Properties like the Ritz-Carlton Kapalua, the Four Seasons Resort Maui at Wailea, and newer condo complexes such as the Wailea Beach Villas may set you back at least $600 a night, though the weaker economy has brought more discounts.

Although there aren't many of them, small bed-and-breakfasts are charming. They tend to be in residential or rural neighborhoods around the island, sometimes beyond the resort areas of West Maui and the South Shore. The B&Bs offer both a personalized experience and a window onto authentic local life. The prices tend to be the lowest available on Maui, sometimes less than $200 per night.

Apartment and condo rentals are perfect for modest budgets, for two or more couples traveling together, and for families. Not only are the nightly rates lower than hotel rooms, but "eating in" (all have kitchens of some description) is substantially less expensive than dining out. There are literally hundreds of these units, ranging in size from studios to luxurious four-bedrooms with multiple baths, all over the island. The vast majority are along the sunny coasts—from Makena to Kihei on the South Shore and Lahaina up to Kapalua on West Maui. Prices depend on the size of the unit and its proximity to the beach, as well as the amenities and services offered. For about $250 a night, you can get a lovely one-bedroom apartment without many frills or flourishes, close to but probably not on the beach. Many rentals have minimum stays (usually three to five nights).

Most of Maui's resorts—several are megaresorts—have opulent gardens, fantasy swimming pools, championship golf courses, and full-service fitness centers and spas. Expect to spend at least $350 a night at the resort hotels; they are all in the Wailea and Makena resort area on the South Shore and Kaanapali and Kapalua on West Maui. At all lodgings, ask about discounts and deals (free nights with longer stays, for example), which have proliferated. Note that prices quoted do not include 13.42% tax.

Prices in the reviews are the lowest cost of a standard double room in high season or, for rentals, the lowest per-night cost of a one-bedroom unit in high season.

For expanded hotel reviews, visit Fodors.com.

WHERE TO STAY IN MAUI

	LOCAL VIBE	PROS	CONS
West Maui	Popular and busy, the West Side includes the picturesque, touristy town of Lahaina and the upscale resort areas of Kaanapali and Kapalua.	A wide variety of shopping, water sports, and historic sites provide plenty to do. To relax, there are great beaches and brilliant sunsets.	Traffic is usually congested; parking is hard to find; beaches can be crowded.
South Shore	The protected South Shore of Maui offers diverse experiences, and accommodations, from comfortable condos to luxurious resorts—and golf, golf, golf.	Many beautiful beaches; sunny weather; great snorkeling.	Numerous strip malls; crowded with condos; there can be lots of traffic.
Upcountry	Country and chic come together in farms, ranches, and trendy towns on the cool, green slopes of Haleakala.	Cooler weather at higher elevations; panoramic views of nearby Islands; distinctive shops, boutiques, galleries, and restaurants.	Fewer restaurants; no nightlife; can be very dark at night and difficult to drive for those unfamiliar with roads and conditions.
North Shore	The North Shore is a mecca for surfing, windsurfing, and kite sailing. When the surf's not up, the focus is on shopping: Paia is full of galleries, shops, and hip eateries.	Wind and waves are terrific for water sports; colorful small towns to explore without the intrusion of big resorts.	Weather may not be as sunny as other parts of the island; no nightlife; most stores in Paia close early.
Road to Hana and East Maui	Remote and rural, laid-back and tropical Hana and East Maui are special places to unwind.	Natural experience; rugged coastline and lush tropical scenery; lots of waterfalls.	Accessed by a long and winding road; no nightlife; few places to eat or shop.

LAHAINA

$$$
B&B/INN
Fodor's Choice
★

⬚ **Hooilo House.** If you want to treat yourself to a luxurious but intimate getaway and don't require resort facilities, spend a few nights at this Bali-inspired B&B; in the foothills of the West Maui Mountains, just south of Lahaina town, the stunning property exemplifies quiet perfection. **Pros:** friendly on-site hosts Amy and Dan Martin are an asset; beautiful furnishings. **Cons:** not good for families with younger children; three-night minimum; beaches are a short drive away. **TripAdvisor:** "tropical paradise," "beautiful location and privacy," "heaven on Earth." $ *Rooms from: $269* ⊠ *138 Awaiku St., Lahaina* ☎ *808/667–6669* ⊕ *www.hooilohouse.com* ⇨ *6 rooms* ⦶ *Breakfast.*

$
B&B/INN

⬚ **Lahaina Inn.** An antique jewel in the heart of town, this two-story wooden building is classic Lahaina and will transport romantics back to the turn of the 20th century; the small rooms shine with authentic period furnishings, including antique bureaus and headboards. **Pros:** a half block off Front Street, the location is within easy walking distance of shops, restaurants, and attractions; lovely antiques. **Cons:** rooms

Westin Maui Resort & Spa

Outrigger Maui Eldorado

Hooilo House

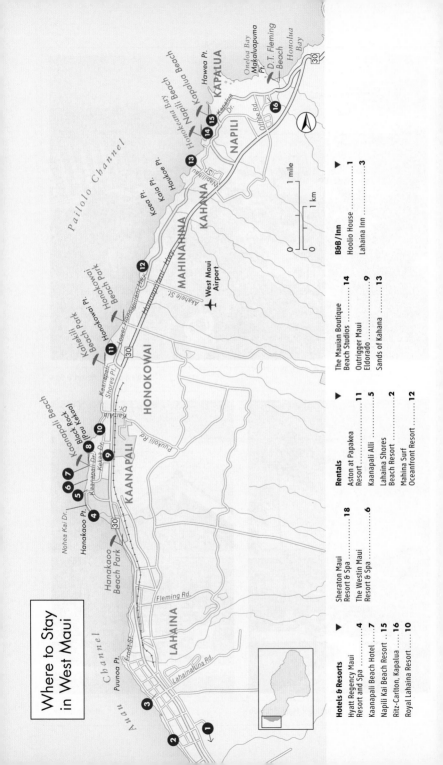

Where to Stay in West Maui

Hotels & Resorts ▶

Hyatt Regency Maui
Resort and Spa **4**
Kaanapali Beach Hotel **7**
Napili Kai Beach Resort ..**15**
Ritz-Carlton, Kapalua **16**
Royal Lahaina Resort **10**
Sheraton Maui
Resort & Spa **18**
The Westin Maui
Resort & Spa **6**

Rentals ▶

Aston at Papakea
Resort **11**
Kaanapali Alii **5**
Lahaina Shores
Beach Resort **2**
Mahina Surf **12**
Oceanfront Resort **12**

The Mauian Boutique
Beach Studios **14**
Outrigger Maui
Eldorado **9**
Sands of Kahana **13**

B&B/Inn ▶

Hoolio House **1**
Lahaina Inn **3**

BEST BETS FOR MAUI LODGING

Fodor's Choice★

Four Seasons Resort Maui at Wailea, $$$$, p. 313

Grand Wailea Resort Hotel & Spa, $$$$, p. 313

Hale Hookipa Inn, $, p. 315

Hana Kai-Maui Resort Condominiums, $$$, p. 320

Hooilo House, $$$, p. 302

Kaanapali Beach Hotel, $$$, p. 306

Luana Kai, $, p. 312

Outrigger Maui Eldorado, $$$, p. 306

The Old Wailuku Inn at Ulupono, $, p. 315

The Ritz-Carlton, Kapalua, $$$$, p. 308

The Westin Maui Resort & Spa, $$$$, p. 307

By Price

$

Banyan Tree House, p. 315

Hale Hookipa Inn, p. 315

Luana Kai, p. 312

Puu Koa Maui Rentals, p. 320

The Old Wailuku Inn at Ulupono, p. 315

$$

Hale Hui Kai, p. 308

Paia Inn Hotel, p. 319

Royal Lahaina Resort, p. 306

$$$

Hooilo House, p. 302

Kaanapali Beach Hotel, p. 306

Outrigger Maui Eldorado, p. 306

$$$$

Four Seasons Resort Maui at Wailea, p. 313

Grand Wailea Resort Hotel & Spa, p. 313

Makena Surf, p. 313

Polo Beach Club, p. 313

Ritz-Carlton, Kapalua, p. 308

The Westin Maui Resort & Spa, $$$$, p. 307

are really small, bathrooms particularly so; some street noise; the two-story property has no elevator. **TripAdvisor:** "in the heart of old town Lahaina," "small but charming," "so cute and clean." [$] *Rooms from: $125* ✉ *127 Lahainaluna Rd., Lahaina* ☎ *808/661–0577, 806/222–5642* 🌐 *www.lahainainn.com* 🛏 *9 rooms, 3 suites* 🍴 *No meals.*

$$$$ RENTAL **Lahaina Shores Beach Resort.** You really can't get any closer to the beach than this: a local landmark, this lofty (by Lahaina standards), seven-story rental property offers panoramic ocean and mountain views for a reasonable price considering the location. **Pros:** right on the beach; historical sites, attractions, and activities are a short walk away. **Cons:** older property; no up-to-date resort-type amenities. **TripAdvisor:** "great location," "comfy beds," "gorgeous." [$] *Rooms from: $355* ✉ *475 Front St., Lahaina* ☎ *808/661–4835, 866/934–9176* 🌐 *www.lahainashores.com* 🛏 *199 rooms* 🍴 *No meals.*

KAANAPALI AND VICINITY

$$$$ RESORT **Hyatt Regency Maui Resort and Spa.** Fantasy landscaping with splashing waterfalls, swim-through grottoes, a lagoonlike swimming pool, and a 130-foot waterslide "wow" guests of all ages at this bustling Kaanapali resort; stroll through the lobby past museum-quality art, brilliant parrots, and South African penguins (as we said, this is not reality). **Pros:** nightly luau show on-site; home of Astronomy Tour of the Stars; contemporary restaurant and bar. **Cons:** it can be difficult to find a space in

self-parking; service can be uneven.
TripAdvisor: "gorgeous hotel and
location," "good facilities," "fabulous and relaxing." $ *Rooms
from: $450* ⊠ *200 Nohea Kai
Dr., Kaanapali* ☎ *808/661–1234,
800/233–1234* ⊕ *www.maui.hyatt.
com* ⤳ *806 rooms* �‖ *No meals.*

<aside>
KEEP IN MIND

Most resorts now charge parking
and facility fees. What once was
complimentary is now tacked on
as a "resort fee." Thankfully, condos haven't followed suit just yet—
sometimes local calls are still free.
</aside>

$$$$
RENTAL
Kaanapali Alii. Four 11-story
buildings are laid out so well that
the feeling of seclusion can make you forget you're in a condo complex;
instead of tiny units, you'll be staying in an ample (1,500–1,900 square
feet) one- or two-bedroom apartment. **Pros:** large, comfortable units on
the beach; good location in the heart of the action in Kaanapali Resort.
Cons: elevators are notoriously slow; crowded parking; no on-site restaurant. **TripAdvisor:** "lovely beach," "a true Hawaiian experience,"
"great place for a family trip." $ *Rooms from: $450* ⊠ *50 Nohea Kai
Dr., Kaanapali* ☎ *808/667–1400, 800/642–6284* ⊕ *www.kaanapalialii.
com* ⤳ *264 units* �‖ *No meals.*

$$$
HOTEL
Fodor's Choice
★
Kaanapali Beach Hotel. Older but still attractive, this charming hotel
is full of aloha—locals say that it's one of the few resorts on the island
where you can get a true Hawaiian experience. **Pros:** exceptional
Hawaiian culture program; friendly staff; Tiki Terrace restaurant serves
delicious dinners and one of the most bountiful Sunday brunches on the
island. **Cons:** a bit run-down; fewer amenities than other places along
this beach. **TripAdvisor:** "heavenly place," "the most Hawaiian hotel
in Hawaii," "good beach." $ *Rooms from: $306* ⊠ *2525 Kaanapali
Pkwy., Kaanapali* ☎ *808/661–0011, 800/262–8450* ⊕ *www.kbhmaui.
com* ⤳ *432 rooms* �‖ *No meals.*

$$$
RENTAL
Fodor's Choice
★
Outriggger Maui Eldorado. The Kaanapali Golf Course's fairways wrap
around this fine, good-value condo complex that offers several perks,
most notably access to a fully outfitted beach cabana on a semiprivate
beach. **Pros:** privileges at Kaanapali and Kapalua resort golf courses;
maid service. **Cons:** not right on beach; some distance from attractions
of the Kaanapali Resort; two story buildings have no elevator. **TripAdvisor:** "beautiful property," "quiet oasis in paradise," "comfortable."
$ *Rooms from: $299* ⊠ *2661 Kekaa Dr., Kaanapali* ☎ *808/661–0021*
⊕ *www.mauieldorado.com* ⤳ *204 units* �‖ *No meals.*

$$
RESORT
Royal Lahaina Resort. Built in 1962 as the first hotel in the Kaanapali
Resort, this grand property toward the northern end of Kaanapali has
hosted millionaires and Hollywood stars; major room upgrades in the
12-story Lahaina Kai Tower include dark teak furnishings set against
light-color walls, plush beds with Egyptian cotton linens, sound sys-
tems with an iPod and MP3 docking station, and 32-inch flat-screen
TVs. **Pros:** on-site luau nightly; variety of accommodation types and
rates; tennis ranch with 11 courts and a pro shop. **Cons:** older prop-
erty still in need of updating. **TripAdvisor:** "beautiful hotel," "beach
front cottage is awesome," "really comfortable." $ *Rooms from:
$199* ⊠ *2780 Kekaa Dr., Kaanapali* ☎ *808/661–3611, 800/447–6925*
⊕ *www.hawaiihotels.com* ⤳ *350 rooms* �‖ *No meals.*

3

$$$$ RESORT 🏨 **Sheraton Maui Resort & Spa.** Set among dense gardens on Kaanapali's best stretch of beach, the Sheraton offers a quieter, more low-key atmosphere than its neighboring resorts; it sits next to and on top of the 80-foot-high Puu Kekaa (please don't call it "Black Rock"), from which divers leap in a nightly torch-lighting and cliff-diving ritual. **Pros:** luxury resort with terrific beach location; great snorkeling right off the beach. **Cons:** extensive property can mean a long walk from your room to the lobby, restaurants, and beach; staff not overly helpful. **TripAdvisor:** "beautiful resort," "fantastic beach," "excellence in paradise." [$] *Rooms from: $539* ✉ *2605 Kaanapali Pkwy., Kaanapali* ☎ *808/661–0031, 866/500-8313* 🌐 *www.sheraton-maui.com* 🛏 *464 rooms, 44 suites* 🍴 *No meals.*

$$$$ RESORT Fodor's Choice ★ 🖐 🏨 **The Westin Maui Resort & Spa.** The cascading waterfall in the lobby of this hotel gives way to an "aquatic playground" with five heated swimming pools, abundant waterfalls (15 at last count), lagoons complete with pink flamingos and swans, and a premier beach; the water features combined with a spa and fitness center and privileges at two 18-hole golf courses make this an active resort—great for families. **Pros:** complimentary shuttle to Westin Kaanapali Ocean Resort Villas and to Lahaina, where parking can be difficult; activity programs for all ages; one pool just for adults. **Cons:** you could end up with fantasy overload; can seem a bit stuffy at times. **TripAdvisor:** "amazing stay," "excellent hotel for families," "a little piece of heaven." [$] *Rooms from: $560* ✉ *2365 Kaanapali Pkwy., Kaanapali* ☎ *808/667–2525, 866/716–8112* 🌐 *www.westinmaui.com* 🛏 *731 rooms, 28 suites* 🍴 *No meals.*

KAPALUA AND VICINITY

$$$ RENTAL 🖐 🏨 **Aston at Papakea Resort.** Although this casual, oceanfront condominium complex with studios and one- and two-bedroom units has no beach, several are close by; Papakea has built-in privacy because its units are spread out among 11 low-rise buildings on about 13 acres of land. **Pros:** units have large rooms; lovely garden landscaping. **Cons:** no beach in front of property; pool can get crowded; no on-site shops or restaurants. **TripAdvisor:** "very friendly people," "the perfect stay," "beautiful resort." [$] *Rooms from: $325* ✉ *3543 Lower Honoapiilani Hwy., Honokowai* ☎ *808/669–4848, 866/774–2924* 🌐 *www.astonhotels.com* 🛏 *364 units* 🍴 *No meals.*

$ RENTAL 🏨 **Mahina Surf Oceanfront Resort.** One of the many condo complexes lining the ocean-side stretch of Honoapiilani Highway offers affordable accommodations; you won't be charged fees for parking or local phone use, and discount car rentals are available. **Pros:** oceanfront barbecues; no "hidden" fees. **Cons:** units need updating; oceanfront but with rocky shoreline rather than a beach. **TripAdvisor:** "fabulous ocean view," "nice condo," "comfortable and relaxing." [$] *Rooms from: $170* ✉ *4057 Lower Honoapiilani Hwy., Mahinahina* ☎ *808/669–6068, 800/367–6068* 🌐 *www.mahina-surf.com* 🛏 *56 units* 🍴 *No meals.*

$$ RENTAL 🏨 **The Mauian Boutique Beach Studios.** If you're looking for a quiet place to stay, this small, delightful property way out in Napili may be for you; the renovated and redecorated rooms have neither TVs nor phones—such noisy devices are relegated to the Ohana (Family) Room, where a Continental breakfast is served daily. **Pros:** reasonable rates; friendly

staff. **Cons:** older building; few amenities. **TripAdvisor:** "very Hawaiian feel," "superb beachfront location," "special ambience." [$] *Rooms from: $190* ✉ *5441 Lower Honoapiilani Hwy., Napili* ☎ *808/669–6205, 800/367–5034* 🌐 *www.mauian.com* 🛏 *44 rooms* 🍴 *Breakfast.*

$$$ RESORT 👶 **Napili Kai Beach Resort.** On 10 beautiful beachfront acres—the beach here is one of the best on West Maui for swimming and snorkeling—the Napili Kai draws a loyal following to its Hawaiian-style rooms that open onto private lanai. **Pros:** kids' hula performance and a Hawaiian slack-key guitar concert every week; fantastic swimming and sunning beach; Old Hawaiian feel. **Cons:** older property; some might call it "unhip." **TripAdvisor:** "low profile," "old school Maui," "relaxing and authentic." [$] *Rooms from: $270* ✉ *5900 Lower Honoapiilani Hwy., Napili* ☎ *808/669–6271, 800/367–5030* 🌐 *www.napilikai.com* 🛏 *163 units* 🍴 *No meals.*

$$$$ RESORT Fodor's Choice ★ **The Ritz-Carlton, Kapalua.** One of Maui's most notable resorts, this elegant hillside property features luxurious service, upscale accommodations, a spa, restaurants, and pool, along with an education center and an enhanced Hawaiian sense of place. **Pros:** luxury and service you'd expect from a Ritz; many cultural and recreational programs. **Cons:** expensive; can be windy on the grounds and at the pool; the hotel is not on the beach and is far from major attractions such as Haleakala. **TripAdvisor:** "beautiful property," "luxury," "great pool area." [$] *Rooms from: $759* ✉ *1 Ritz-Carlton Dr., Kapalua* ☎ *808/669–6200, 800/262–8440* 🌐 *www.ritzcarlton.com* 🛏 *463 rooms* 🍴 *No meals.*

$$$$ RENTAL **Sands of Kahana.** Meandering gardens, spacious rooms, and an on-site restaurant distinguish this large condominium complex that's primarily a time-share property; a few units are available as vacation rentals and are managed by Sullivan Properties. **Pros:** spacious units at reasonable prices; restaurant on the premises. **Cons:** you may be approached about buying a unit; street-facing units may get a bit noisy. **TripAdvisor:** "nice location," "roomy and comfortable," "panoramic sunset views." [$] *Rooms from: $445* ✉ *4299 Lower Honoapiilani Hwy., Kahana* ☎ *808/669–0400 property phone, 808/669–0423, 800/332–1137 Sullivan properties for vacation rentals* 🌐 *www.mauiresorts.com* 🛏 *196 units* 🍴 *No meals.*

THE SOUTH SHORE

KIHEI

$$ RENTAL **Hale Hui Kai.** Bargain hunters who stumble across this small three-story condo complex of mostly two-bedroom units will think they've died and gone to heaven; the beachfront units are older, but most of them have been renovated. **Pros:** far enough from the noise and tumult of "central" Kihei; close enough to all the conveniences; guest discounts at neighboring restaurants. **Cons:** nondescript 1970s architecture; a private home next door blocks the ocean view from some units. **TripAdvisor:** "a different point of view," "charming," "perfect Maui beach vacation." [$] *Rooms from: $245* ✉ *2994 S. Kihei Rd., Kihei* ☎ *808/879–1219, 800/809–6284* 🌐 *www.halehuikaimaui.com* 🛏 *40 units* 🍴 *No meals.*

Ritz-Carlton Kapalua

Grand Wailea Resort & Spa

Luana Kai

CONDO COMFORTS

Condo renters in search of food and takeout meals should try these great places around Maui.

WEST MAUI

Foodland Farms. This large supermarket combines the best of gourmet selections with all the familiar staples you need to stock your vacation kitchen. ✉ *Lahaina Gateway Shopping Center, 345 Keawe St., Lahaina* ☎ *808/662–7088.*

The Maui Fish Market. It's worth stopping by this little fish market for oysters or a cup of fresh fish chowder. You can also get live lobsters and marinated fish fillets for your barbecue. ✉ *3600 Lower Honoapiilani Hwy., Honokowai* ☎ *808/665–9895* 🌐 *www.fishmarketmaui.com.*

SOUTH SHORE

Eskimo Candy. Stop here for excellent fresh fish to cook yourself or for ready-to-eat fish-and-chips. ✉ *2665 Wai Wai Pl., Kihei* ☎ *808/879–5686* 🌐 *www.eskimocandy.com.*

Guava, Gouda & Caviar. This shop, formerly named Who Cut the Cheese, continues to offer a wide selection of cheeses, wines, and gourmet items in its new location. ✉ *10 Wailea Gateway Pl., Suite B-106, Wailea* ☎ *808/874–3930* 🌐 *www.guavagoudaandcaviar.com.*

Safeway. Find everything you could possibly need at this huge supermarket. ✉ *277 Piikea Ave., Kihei* ☎ *808/891–9120.*

Safeway. This supermarket has a deli, prepared-foods section, and bakery that are all fantastic. There's a good wine selection, tons of produce, and a flower shop where you can treat yourself to a fresh lei. ✉ *170 E. Kaahumanu Ave., Kahului* ☎ *808/877–3377.*

UPCOUNTRY

Pukalani Terrace Center. Come here if you're looking for pizza, a bank, post office, hardware store, laundromat, or Starbucks✉ *55 Pukalani St., Pukalani.*

Foodland. This member of a local supermarket chain is at Pukalani Terrace Center; it has fresh sushi and a good seafood section in addition to the usual fare. ✉ *55 Pukalani St., Pukalani* ☎ *808/572–0674.*

NORTH SHORE

Haiku Cannery. This marketplace is home to the Haiku Grocery and a few restaurants, a laundromat, and a yoga studio. The post office is across the street✉ *810 Haiku Rd., Haiku.*

Haiku Grocery. You can find the basics, such as veggies, meats, wine, snacks, and ice cream, at this local store in the Haiku Cannery. ✉ *810 Haiku Rd., Haiku* ☎ *808/575–9291.*

$$$$ RENTAL 🏊 🏨 **Kamaole Sands.** At this south Kihei property, a good choice for active families, there are tennis courts for a friendly game, and the ideal family beach (Kamaole III) is just across the street. **Pros:** in the seemingly endless strip of Kihei condos, this stands out for its pleasant grounds and well-cared-for units. **Cons:** the complex of buildings may seem a bit too "citylike"; all buildings look the same, so remember a landmark to help you find your unit. **TripAdvisor:** "beautiful grounds," "nice clean condo," "great location." [$] *Rooms from: $345* ✉ *2695 S. Kihei*

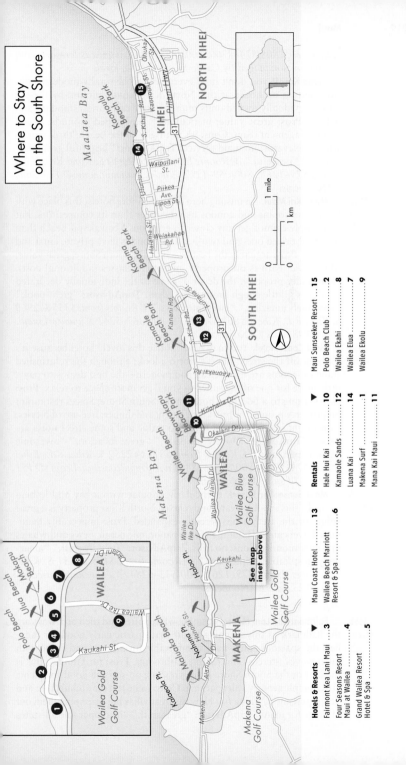

Where to Stay on the South Shore

3

Hotels & Resorts ▼

Fairmont Kea Lani Maui ... 3
Four Seasons Resort
Maui at Wailea ... 4
Grand Wailea Resort
Hotel & Spa ... 5
Maui Coast Hotel ... 13
Wailea Beach Marriott
Resort & Spa ... 6

Rentals ▼

Hale Hui Kai ... 10
Kamaole Sands ... 12
Luana Kai ... 14
Makena Surf ... 1
Mana Kai Maui ... 11

Maui Sunseeker Resort ... 15
Polo Beach Club ... 2
Wailea Ekahi ... 8
Wailea Elua ... 7
Wailea Ekolu ... 9

Rd., Kihei ☎ *808/874–8700, 800/367–5004* 🌐 *www.castleresorts.com* 🛏 *205 units managed by Castle Resorts* 🍴 *No meals.*

$ RENTAL Fodor's Choice ★ 🏨 **Luana Kai.** If you don't need everything to be totally modern, consider setting up house at this North Kihei condominium-by-the-sea with individually owned units offered in two categories: standard and deluxe. **Pros:** great value; meticulously landscaped grounds; excellent management team. **Cons:** it's not right on the beach; three stories with no elevator; no maid service. **TripAdvisor:** "beautiful grounds," "quiet," "peaceful." [$] *Rooms from: $139* ✉ *940 S. Kihei Rd., Kihei* ☎ *808/879–1268, 800/669–1127* 🌐 *www.luanakai.com* 🛏 *113 units* 🍴 *No meals.*

$$$$ RENTAL 👶 🏨 **Mana Kai Maui.** An unsung hero of South Shore hotels, this place with both hotel rooms and condos may be older than its competitors, but you simply cannot get any closer to gorgeous Keawakapu Beach than this; well-priced one- and two-bedroom condos have private lanai and kitchens. **Pros:** arguably the best beach on the South Shore; great value; Maui Yoga Path is on property and offers classes (additional cost). **Cons:** older property; the decor of some of the individually decorated condos is a little rough around the edges. **TripAdvisor:** "great pool," "absolutely amazing," "awesome views." [$] *Rooms from: $355* ✉ *2960 S. Kihei Rd., Kihei* ☎ *808/879–2778, 800/367–5242* 🌐 *www.crhmaui.com* 🛏 *98 units* 🍴 *No meals.*

$$$ HOTEL 🏨 **Maui Coast Hotel.** You may never notice this lovely hotel because it's set back off the street, but it's worth a look; although the refurbished standard rooms are fine—clean and modern—the best deal is to pay a little more for one of the suites so you'll get more space to relax. **Pros:** closest thing to a boutique hotel on the South Shore; Spices restaurant on property is open for breakfast, lunch, and dinner; free use of bicycles. **Cons:** right in the center of Kihei, so traffic and some street noise are issues. **TripAdvisor:** "lovely property," "great location," "awesome Maui experience." [$] *Rooms from: $315* ✉ *2259 S. Kihei Rd., Kihei* ☎ *808/874–6284, 800/895–6284* 🌐 *www.mauicoasthotel.com* 🛏 *151 rooms, 114 suites* 🍴 *No meals.*

$ RENTAL 🏨 **Maui Sunseeker Resort.** Particularly popular with a gay and lesbian clientele, this small, private, and relaxed North Kihei property is a great value for the area; it has recently expanded. **Pros:** impeccably maintained; webcam on building videos panoramic ocean views and whales in winter months. **Cons:** no frills. **TripAdvisor:** "friendly staff," "amazingly hospitable," "pleasant." [$] *Rooms from: $175* ✉ *551 S. Kihei Rd., Kihei* ☎ *808/879–1261, 800/532–6284* 🌐 *www.mauisunseeker.com* 🛏 *23 units* 🍴 *No meals.*

WAILEA

$$$$ RESORT 👶 🏨 **Fairmont Kea Lani Maui.** Gleaming white spires and tiled archways are the hallmark of this stunning resort that's particularly good for families; the spacious suites have comfortable furnishings and come with microwaves, stereos, and marble bathrooms. **Pros:** for families, this is the best of the South Shore luxury resorts; on-site deli good for picnic fare; complimentary valet parking. **Cons:** some feel the architecture and design scream anything *but* Hawaii; great villas but price puts them out of range for many. **TripAdvisor:** "great staff," "incomparable all-suites

hotel," "beautiful." $\boxed{\$}$ *Rooms from: $499* ✉ *4100 Wailea Alanui Dr., Wailea* ☎ *808/875–4100, 866/540–4456* ⊕ *www.fairmont.com/kealani* ↘ *413 suites, 37 villas* |◯| *No meals.*

$$$$ 🏨 **Four Seasons Resort Maui at Wailea.** *Impeccably stylish, subdued,* and
RESORT   *relaxing* describe most Four Seasons properties, and this one fronting
Fodor's Choice   award-winning Wailea beach is no exception; thoughtful luxuries—
★   like Evian spritzers poolside and twice-daily housekeeping—earned this
Maui favorite its reputation. **Pros:** no resort fee—children's program,
poolside cabanas, tennis, and other activities are complimentary; the
most low-key elegance on Maui; known for exceptional service. **Cons:**
expensive; a bit pretentious for some. **TripAdvisor:** "first-class resort,"
"perfection," "nothing this resort could improve upon." $\boxed{\$}$ *Rooms
from: $485* ✉ *3900 Wailea Alanui Dr., Wailea* ☎ *808/874–8000,
800/332–3442* ⊕ *www.fourseasons.com/maui* ↘ *305 rooms, 75 suites*
|◯| *No meals.*

$$$$ 🏨 **Grand Wailea Resort Hotel & Spa.** "Grand" is no exaggeration for this
RESORT   opulent, sunny, 40-acre resort with elaborate water features such as a
Fodor's Choice   "canyon riverpool" with slides, caves, a Tarzan swing, and a water ele-
★   vator. **Pros:** you can meet every vacation need without ever leaving the
property; many shops. **Cons:** at these prices, service should be extraordinary, and it isn't; room prices don't include a resort fee, parking fee,
and more; sometimes too much is too much. **TripAdvisor:** "beyond
amazing," "wonderful luxury," "idyllic." $\boxed{\$}$ *Rooms from: $785* ✉ *3850
Wailea Alanui Dr., Wailea* ☎ *808/875–1234, 800/888–6100* ⊕ *www.
grandwailea.com* ↘ *728 rooms, 52 suites* |◯| *No meals.*

$$$$ 🏨 **Makena Surf.** For travelers who've done all there is to do on Maui and
RENTAL   just want simple but luxurious relaxation at a rental, this is the spot;
the security-gate entrance gives way to tropical landscaping dotted with
palm trees. **Pros:** away from it all, yet still close enough to "civilization";
laundry facilities in every unit. **Cons:** too secluded and "locked-up" for
some; Hawaiian legend has it that spirits may have been disturbed here.
TripAdvisor: "fantastic beach location," "great view," "comfortable
condo." $\boxed{\$}$ *Rooms from: $429* ✉ *34 Wailea Gateway Pl., Suite A102,
Wailea* ☎ *808/801–6249, 800/367–5246* ⊕ *www.drhmaui.com* ↘ *107
units* |◯| *No meals.*

$$$$ 🏨 **Polo Beach Club.** Lording over a hidden section of Polo Beach, this
RENTAL   wonderful older eight-story rental property somehow manages to stay
under the radar. **Pros:** you can pick fresh herbs for dinner out of the garden; beach fronting the building is a beautiful, private crescent of sand.
Cons: some may feel isolated. **TripAdvisor:** "wonderful view and lovely
condo," "a magic spot," "perfect family vacation." $\boxed{\$}$ *Rooms from:
$650* ✉ *3750 Wailea Alanui Dr., Wailea* ☎ *808/891–6249, 800/367–
5246* ⊕ *www.drhmaui.com* ↘ *71 units* |◯| *No meals.*

$$$$ 🏨 **Wailea Beach Marriott Resort & Spa.** The Marriott was built before cur-
RESORT   rent construction laws, so rooms sit much closer to the crashing surf
than at most resorts; Wailea Beach is a few steps away, as are the Shops
at Wailea. **Pros:** spa is one of the best in Hawaii; near good shopping;
luau four nights a week. **Cons:** it's not quite beachfront and has a rocky
shore, so you must walk left or right to sit on the sand; there can be
a lot of foot traffic on the beach walk along the coast. **TripAdvisor:**

Four Seasons Resort Maui at Wailea

Old Wailuku Inn at Ulupono

"beautiful location," "incredible ocean view," "well maintained." [$] *Rooms from: $550* ✉ *3700 Wailea Alanui Dr., Wailea* ☎ *808/879–1922* 🌐 *www.waileamarriott.com* 🛏 *497 rooms, 47 suites* 🍴 *No meals.*

$$$$ RENTAL **Wailea Ekahi, Elua, and Ekolu.** The Wailea Resort started out with three upscale condominium complexes named, appropriately, Ekahi, Elua, and Ekolu (One, Two, and Three); today the individually owned units, managed by Destination Resorts Hawaii, represent some of the best values in this high-class neighborhood, with a wide range of prices. **Pros:** probably the best value in this high-rent district; close to good shopping and dining. **Cons:** the oldest complexes in the neighborhood; it can be tricky to find your way around the buildings. **TripAdvisor:** "very relaxing," "beautiful grounds," "lovely view." [$] *Rooms from: $500* ✉ *34 Gateway Plaza, Suite A102, Wailea* ☎ *808/891–6249, 800/367–5246* 🌐 *www.drhmaui.com* 🛏 *594 units* 🍴 *No meals.*

CENTRAL MAUI

$ B&B/INN Fodor's Choice ★ **The Old Wailuku Inn at Ulupono.** Built in 1924 and listed on the State of Hawaii Register of Historic Places, this home may be the ultimate Hawaiian B&B; each room is decorated with the theme of a Hawaiian flower, and the flower motif appears in the heirloom Hawaiian quilt on each bed. **Pros:** the charm of Old Hawaii; knowledgeable innkeepers; walking distance to Maui's best ethnic restaurants. **Cons:** closest beach is a 20-minute drive away; you may hear some traffic at certain times. **TripAdvisor:** "sheer perfection," "lovely," "a warm welcome to Maui." [$] *Rooms from: $165* ✉ *2199 Kahookele St., Wailuku* ☎ *808/244–5897, 800/305–4899* 🌐 *www.mauiinn.com* 🛏 *10 rooms* 🍴 *Breakfast.*

UPCOUNTRY

$ B&B/INN 👶 **The Banyan Tree House.** If a taste of rural Hawaii life in plantation days is what you crave, you can find it at this pastoral spot—the 2-acre property is lush with tropical foliage, has an expansive lawn, and is fringed with huge monkeypod and banyan trees. **Pros:** two cottages and the pool are outfitted for travelers with disabilities; you can walk to Makawao town for dining and shopping. **Cons:** the furniture in the cottages is pretty basic; few amenities. **TripAdvisor:** "peaceful retreat," "beautiful setting," "renewing." [$] *Rooms from: $165* ✉ *3265 Baldwin Ave., Makawao* ☎ *808/572–9021* 🌐 *www.bed-breakfast-maui.com* 🛏 *7 rooms* 🍴 *Breakfast.*

$ B&B/INN Fodor's Choice ★ **Hale Hookipa Inn.** A handsome 1924 Craftsman-style house in the heart of Makawao town, this inn on both the Hawaii and the National Historic Registers provides a great base for excursions to Haleakala or to Hana. **Pros:** genteel rural setting; price includes buffet breakfast with organic fruit from the garden. **Cons:** a 20-minute drive to the nearest beach; this is not the sun, sand, and surf surroundings of travel posters. **TripAdvisor:** "very accommodating," "loving and lovely place," "homey and comfortable." [$] *Rooms from: $128* ✉ *32 Pakani Pl., Makawao* ☎ *808/572–6698, 877/572-6698* 🌐 *www.maui-bed-and-breakfast.com* 🛏 *3 rooms, 1 suite* 🍴 *Breakfast.*

VACATION RENTAL COMPANIES

There are many real-estate companies that specialize in short-term vacation rentals. They may represent an entire resort property, most of the units at one property, or even individually owned units. The companies listed here have a long history of excellent service to Maui visitors.

AA Oceanfront Rentals and Sales. As the name suggests, the specialty is "oceanfront." With rental units in more than 25 condominium complexes on the South Shore from the northernmost reaches of Kihei all the way to Wailea, there's something for everyone at prices that range from $130 to $435 a night. ⊠ *1279 S. Kihei Rd., #107, Kihei* ☎ *808/879-7288, 800/488-6004* ⊕ *www.aaoceanfront.com.*

Bello Maui Vacations. The Bellos are Maui real-estate experts and have a full range of vacation rentals in 20 South Shore condominium complexes. They also have gorgeous houses for rent. Condos start at right around $100 per night (most are $200 or less); a beautiful oceanfront villa rents for $1,950 per night. ⊠ *95 E. Lipoa, No. 201, Kihei* ☎ *808/879-3328, 800/541-3060* ⊕ *www.bellomauivacations.com.*

Chase 'n Rainbows. Family-owned and -operated, this is the largest property management company on West Maui, with the largest selection of rentals from studios to three bedrooms. Rentals are everywhere from Lahaina town up to Kapalua. Prices range from about $100 to $1500 per night. The company has been in business since 1980, and is good at what it does. ⊠ *118 Kupuohi St., Lahaina* ☎ *808/667-7088, 800/367-6092* ⊕ *www.chasenrainbows.com.*

Destination Resorts Hawaii. If it's the South Shore luxury of Wailea and Makena you seek, look no further. This company has dozens of condominiums and villas ranging in size from studios to four bedrooms, and in price from $260 a night for a studio at Wailea Ekahi, an older property, to more than $3,000 for the new Wailea Beach Villas. The company offers excellent personalized service and is known for particularly fine housekeeping services. ⊠ *34 Wailea Gateway Pl., Suite A102, Wailea* ☎ *808/891-6249, 800/367-5246* ⊕ *www.drhmaui.com.*

Maalaea Bay Realty and Rentals. A little strip of condominiums within the isthmus that links Central and West Maui, Maalaea is often overlooked, but it shouldn't be. This company has 140 one- and two-bedroom units from $100 to $300 per night. The wind is usually strong here, but there's a nice beach, a harbor, and some good shopping and decent restaurants. ⊠ *280 Hauoli St., Maalaea* ☎ *808/244-5627, 800/367-6084* ⊕ *www.maalaeabay.com.*

Maui Condo & Home Vacations. This Maui-based agency, part of Interval Acquisition Corporation, manages more than 3,000 individually owned condos. Most of the units are near the beach or golf courses, and are located throughout South Maui. Studios to three-bedroom units range in price from $100 to $450 per night. ⊠ *1819 S. Kihei Rd., Suite D103, Kihei* ☎ *808/879-5445, 800/822-4409* ⊕ *www.mauicondo.com.*

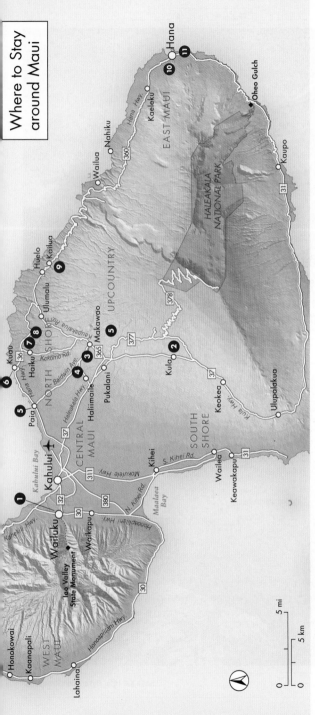

Where to Stay around Maui

3

Banyan Tree House **4**
Haiku Plantation Inn **7**
Hale Hookipa Inn **3**
Hana Kai-Maui Resort
Condominiums **10**
The Inn at Mama's
Fish House **6**

Maui Ocean Breezes **9**
Old Wailuku Inn
at VIupono **1**
Paia Inn Hotel **5**
Puu Koa Maui Rentals **8**
Travaasa Hana **11**
Upcountry B&B **2**

Hale Hookipa Inn

Hana Kai-Maui Resort Condominiums

$ B&B/INN 🏨 **Upcountry Bed & Breakfast.** Spacious rooms and unobstructed views are two reasons to experience Upcountry Maui at this B&B, into which owner Michael Sullivan has put a lot of heart and soul; he designed his house to take advantage of natural cooling and heating techniques, based on the principles of noted Hawaii architect C. W. Dickey. **Pros:** at 3,000 feet above sea level, it's closer to Haleakala than most accommodations; two rooms are ADA accessible; local store and restaurant nearby; rates include taxes. **Cons:** can be cool in Kula; far from beach; not everyone may enjoy the mellow and friendly resident dog. **TripAdvisor:** "beautiful house," "super friendly," "great location for sunrise." [$] *Rooms from: $150* ✉ *4925 Lower Kula Rd., Kula* ☎ *808/878–8083* 🌐 *www.upcountrybandb.com* 🛏 *4 rooms* 🍴 *Breakfast.*

3

THE NORTH SHORE

HAIKU

$ B&B/INN 🏨 **Haiku Plantation Inn.** Water lilies and a shade tree bedecked in orchids greet you at this forested bend in the road; a remnant of Haiku's plantation history, this gracious estate was built in 1870 for the company doctor. **Pros:** quiet setting; close to restaurants, gas station, and post office; opportunities to experience authentic Hawaiian culture. **Cons:** no resort amenities; 10-minute drive from closest beach. **TripAdvisor:** "authentic in so many ways," "absolute gem," "awesome bed-and-breakfast." [$] *Rooms from: $119* ✉ *555 Haiku Rd., Haiku* ☎ *808/575–7500* 🌐 *www.haikuleana.net* 🛏 *4 rooms* 🍴 *Breakfast.*

KUAU

$$ B&B/INN 🏨 **The Inn at Mama's Fish House.** Nestled in gardens adjacent to one of Maui's most popular dining spots, Mama's Fish House, these well-maintained one- and two-bedroom cottages have a retro-Hawaiian style with rattan furnishings and local artwork. **Pros:** daily maid service; free parking; next to Hookipa Beach. **Cons:** three-night minimum stay; Mama's Fish House is popular, so there can be many people around in the evenings (it's more mellow during the day). **TripAdvisor:** "quiet relaxation," "a special place," "hidden gem." [$] *Rooms from: $250* ✉ *799 Poho Pl., Kuau* ☎ *808/579–9764, 800/860–4852* 🌐 *www.mamasfishhouse.com* 🛏 *12 units* 🍴 *No meals.*

$ RENTAL 🏨 **Maui Ocean Breezes.** The warm ocean breeze rolls through these pretty eco-friendly rentals, making this a perfect spot to relax and enjoy the gorgeous scenery. **Pros:** one of few licensed rentals in area; expansive lawn with ocean views. **Cons:** 15 minutes from closest beach; the owner prefers stays of seven nights or longer, though will negotiate depending on availability. **TripAdvisor:** "relaxing and out of the way," "almost indescribable," "peaceful getaway." [$] *Rooms from: $155* ✉ *240 N. Holokai Rd., Haiku* ☎ *808/283–8526* 🌐 *www.mauivacationhideaway.com* 🛏 *3 units* 🍴 *No meals.*

$$ B&B/INN 🏨 **Paia Inn Hotel.** Reopened as an inn in 2008, the original part of the property was built in 1927 as a boarding house when Pa'ia was a bustling plantation town; two more buildings between the street and the beach have been added and offer oceanfront and ocean-view accommodations. **Pros:** friendly and knowledgeable staff; no minimum stay

required; guests receive a complimentary membership at Upcountry Fitness in Haiku. **Cons:** no elevator; guest rooms are extraordinarily small and have no closets. **TripAdvisor:** "gorgeous property," "perfect reflection of Paia town," "quaint little hotel." [$] *Rooms from: $189* ✉ *93 Hana Hwy., Paia* ☎ *808/579–6000, 800/721–4000* 🌐 *www.paiainn.com* 🛏 *15 rooms* 🍴 *No meals.*

$ RENTAL 🏨 **Puu Koa Maui Rentals.** Off a peaceful cul-de-sac in a residential area, these two well-maintained and immaculately clean homes offer studio and one-bedroom accommodations. **Pros:** very clean; reasonable rates; good spot for a group. **Cons:** 10-minute drive to the beach; set in quiet residential area. [$] *Rooms from: $90* ✉ *66 Puu Koa Pl., Haiku* ☎ *808/573–2884* 🌐 *www.puukoa.com* 🛏 *7 rooms* 🍴 *No meals.*

SHOPPING IN HANA

Hasegawa General Store. Do stop at Hana's charming, filled-to-the-rafters, one-stop shopping option. Buy fishing tackle, hot dogs, ice cream, and eggs here. You can rent videos and buy the newspaper, which isn't always delivered on time. Check out the bulletin board for local events. ✉ *5165 Hana Hwy., Haiku* ☎ *808/248–8231.*

ROAD TO HANA

$$$ RENTAL Fodor's Choice ★ 🏨 **Hana Kai-Maui Resort Condominiums.** Perfectly situated on Hana Bay, this resort complex has a long history (it opened in 1970) and an excellent reputation for visitor hospitality. **Pros:** it's a stone's throw to Hana Bay, where you can take a swim or have a Roselani mac-nut ice-cream cone at Tutu's; one-night rentals are accepted; daily housekeeping. **Cons:** early to bed and early to rise—no nightlife or excitement here; no elevator. **TripAdvisor:** "a quiet escape," "beautiful place," "outstanding view." [$] *Rooms from: $275* ✉ *1533 Uakea Rd., Hana* ☎ *808/248–8426, 800/346–2772* 🌐 *www.hanakaimaui.com* 🛏 *18 units* 🍴 *No meals.*

$$$$ RESORT 🏨 **Travaasa Hana.** Formerly the Hotel Hana-Maui, this property has a new name but remains secluded and quietly luxurious, with unobstructed views of the Pacific; it now has two types of accommodation plans, one an all-inclusive option unique on Maui. **Pros:** if you want to get away from it all, there's no better or more beautiful place; spa is incredibly relaxing. **Cons:** everything moves slowly; if you can't live without your BlackBerry, this is not the place for you; it's oceanfront but does not have a sandy beach (red- and black-sand beaches are nearby). **TripAdvisor:** "a unique Hawaiian experience," "pure paradise," "beautiful property." [$] *Rooms from: $375* ✉ *5031 Hana Hwy., Hana* ☎ *808/248–8211, 855/868–7282* 🌐 *www.travaasa.com/hana* 🛏 *47 cottages, 23 garden suites* 🍴 *Multiple meal plans.*

The Big Island

WORD OF MOUTH

"[Hawaii Volcanoes National Park] itself was magnificent and eerie even though the lack of fresh flowing lava was the major disappointment of our vacation. We spent one day driving first on Kilauea Crater Drive, then on the Chain of Craters road to the sea. On both drives, there are several half mile to mile long walks."

—cmstraf

WELCOME TO THE BIG ISLAND

TOP REASONS TO GO

★ **Hawaii Volcanoes National Park:** Catch the lava fireworks at night and explore newly made land, lava tubes, steam vents, and giant craters.

★ **Waipio Valley:** Experience a real-life secret garden, the remote spot known as the Valley of the Kings.

★ **Kealakekua Bay:** Kayak past spinner dolphins to the Captain Cook Monument, then go snorkeling along the fabulous coral reef.

★ **The Heavens:** Stargaze through gigantic telescopes on snow-topped Mauna Kea.

★ **Hidden Beaches:** Discover one of the Kohala Coast's lesser-known gems.

1 Kailua-Kona. A seaside town packed with tons of restaurants, shops, and a busy waterfront bustling with tourists along the main street, Alii Drive.

2 The Kona Coast. An area that stretches a bit north of Kailua-Kona and much farther south includes the gorgeous Kealakekua Bay. This is the place to come for world-famous Kona Coffee, to take farm tours, and taste samples.

3 The Kohala Coast. The sparking coast is where all those long, white-sand beaches are found, and the expensive resorts to go with them.

4 Waimea. Ranches sprawl across the cool, upland meadows of Waimea, known as paniolo (cowboy) country.

5 Mauna Kea. Climb (or drive) this 13,796-foot mountain for what's considered the world's best stargazing, with 13 telescopes perched on top.

6 The Hamakua Coast. Waterfalls, dramatic cliffs, ocean views, ancient hidden valleys, and rainforests and the stunning Waipio Valley are just a few of the treats that await you here.

7 Hilo. Known as the City of Rainbows for all its rain,

Hilo is often skipped by tourists in favor of the sunny Kohala Coast. But for what many consider the "real" Hawaii, as well as incredible rainforests, waterfalls, and the best farmers' market on the island, Hilo can't be beat.

8 Puna. This section of the island was most recently covered by lava, and so it has brand-new jet-black beaches with volcanic hot springs.

9 Hawaii Volcanoes National Park and Vicinity. The land around the park is continually expanding, as the active Kilauea Volcano sends lava spilling into the ocean. The nearby town of Volcano provides a great base for exploring the park.

10 Kau and Ka Lae (South Point). Round the southernmost part of the island for two of Big Island's most famous beaches: Papakolea (Green Sand) Beach, and Punaluu (Black Sand) Beach.

GETTING ORIENTED

You could fit all the other Hawaiian Islands into the Big Island and still have some room left over—hence the name. Locals refer to the island by side: Kona to the west and Hilo to the east. Most of the resorts, condos, and restaurants are crammed into 30 miles of the sunny Kona side, while rainy, tropical Hilo is much more residential.

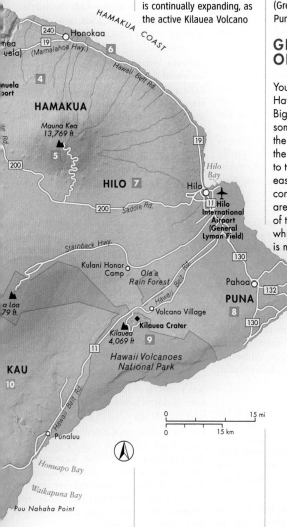

GREAT ITINERARIES

Yes, the Big Island is big, and yes, there's a lot to see. If you're short on time, consider flying into one airport and out the other. That will give you the opportunity to see both sides of the island without ever having to go backwards. Decide what sort of note you'd rather end on to determine your route—if you'd prefer to spend your last few days sleeping on the beach, go from east to west; if hiking through rain forests and showering in waterfalls sounds like a better way to wrap up the trip, move from west to east. If you're short on time, head straight for Hawaii Volcanoes National Park and briefly visit Hilo before traveling the Hamakua Coast route and making your new base in Kailua-Kona.

Hike Volcanoes

Devote a full day (at least) to exploring Hawaii Volcanoes National Park. Head out on the Kilauea Iki trail—a 4-mile loop at the summit—by late morning. Leave the park to grab lunch at nearby restaurants in Volcano Village just a few minutes away, or plan ahead and pack your own picnic lunch before you start your morning hike. Later you can take a stroll through the expansive Thurston Lava Tube and then hit the Jagger Museum, which offers great views of Halemaumau Crater's glow at night.

Black and Green Sand

Check out some of the unusual beaches you'll find only on the Big Island. Start with a hike into Green Sands Beach near South Point and plan to spend some time sitting on the beach, dipping into the bay's turquoise waters, and marveling at the surreal beauty of this spot.

When you've had your fill, hop back in the car and head south about half an hour to Punaluu, the island's best-known black-sand beach and favorite nesting place of the endangered Hawaiian green sea turtle. Although the surf is often too rough to go swimming with the turtles, there are typically at least two or three napping on the beach at any given time of the day.

Majestic Waterfalls and Valley of the Kings

Take a day to enjoy the splendors of the Hamakua Coast—any gorge you see on the road is an indication of a waterfall waiting to be explored. For a sure bet, head to beautiful Waipio Valley. Book a horseback, hiking, or four-wheel-drive tour, or walk on in yourself (just keep in mind that it's an arduous hike back up—a 25% grade for a little over a mile).

Once in the valley, take your first right to get to the black-sand beach. Take a moment to sit here—the ancient Hawaiians believed this was where souls crossed over to the afterlife. Whether you believe it or not, there's something unmistakably special about this place.

Sun and Stars

Spend the day lounging on a Kohala Coast beach (Hapuna, Kaunaoa—also known as Mauna Kea—or Kua Bay), but throw jackets and boots in the car because you'll be catching the sunset from Mauna Kea's summit. Bundle up and stick around after darkness falls for some of the world's best stargazing.

For the safest, most comfortable experience, book a summit tour or stop in at the Onizuka Center for International Astronomy, a visitor center located at about 9,000 feet, or join the free summit tour at 1 pm on Saturday or Sunday, and return to the center to use the telescopes for evening stargazing.

4

Nicknamed "The Big Island," Hawaii the island is a microcosm of Hawaii the state. From long white-sand beaches and crystal clear bays to rain forests, waterfalls, luau, exotic flowers, and birds, all things quintessentially Hawaiian are well represented here. An assortment of happy surprises also distinguishes the Big Island from the rest of Hawaii—an active volcano (Kilauea) oozing red lava and creating new earth every day, the clearest place in the world to view stars in the night sky (Mauna Kea), and some seriously good coffee from the famous Kona district and also from neighboring Kau.

GEOLOGY

Home to 11 climate zones, this is the land of fire (thanks to active Kilauea volcano) and ice (compliments of not-so-active Mauna Kea, topped with snow and expensive telescopes). At just under a million years old, Hawaii is the youngest of the Hawaiian Islands. The east rift zone on Kilauea has been spewing lava intermittently since January 3, 1983; an eruption began at Kilauea's summit caldera in March 2008 for the first time since 1982. Mauna Loa's explosions caused some changes back in 1984, and it could blow again any minute—or not for years. The third of the island's five volcanoes still considered active is Hualalai. It last erupted in 1801, and geologists say it will probably erupt again within 100 years. Mauna Kea is currently considered dormant, but may very well erupt again. Kohala, which last erupted some 120,000 years ago, is likely dead, but on volatile Hawaii Island, you can never be sure.

FLORA AND FAUNA

Sugar was the main agricultural and economic staple of all the Islands, but especially the Big Island. The drive along the Hamakua Coast, from Hilo or Waimea, illustrates recent agricultural developments on the

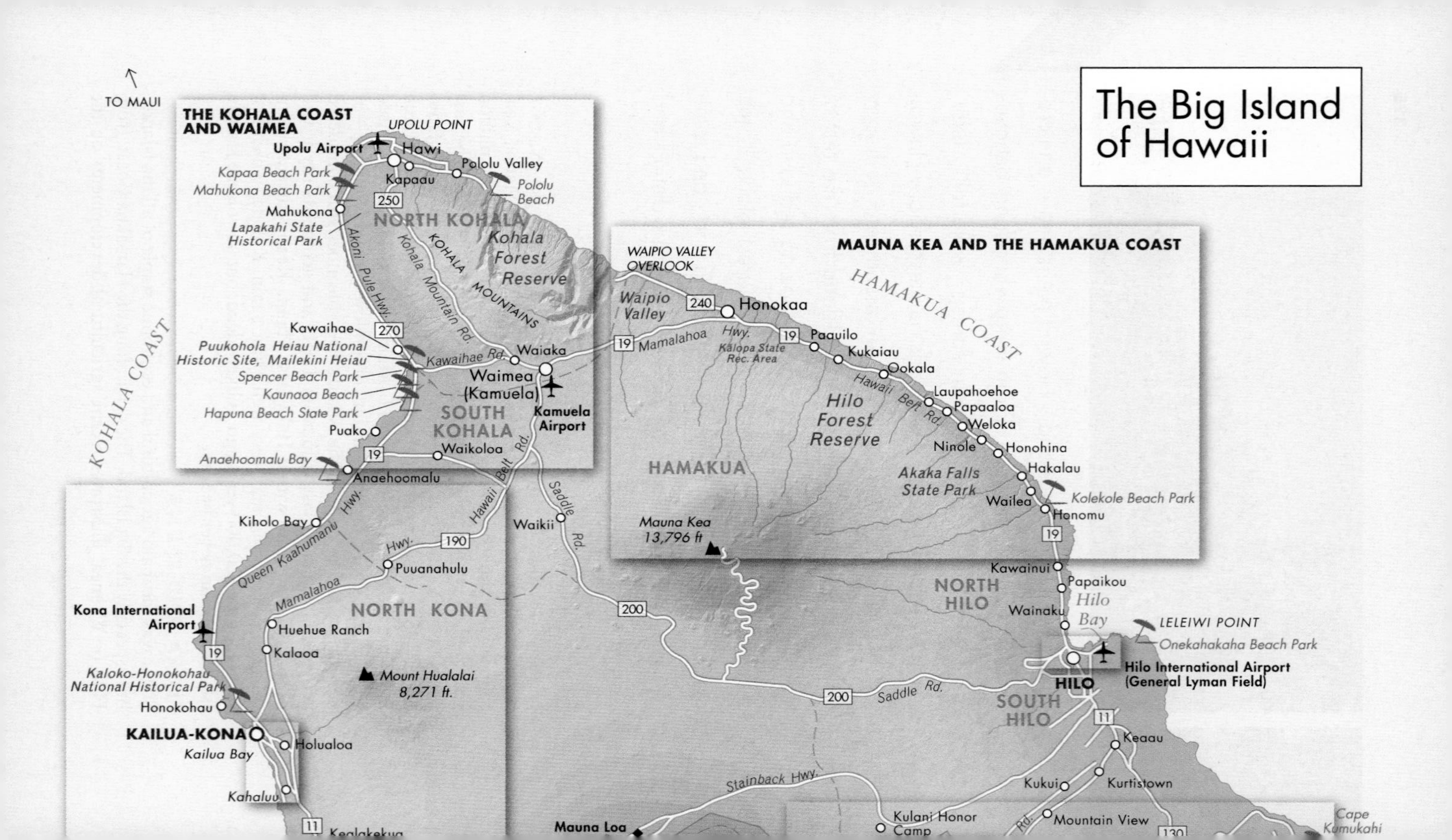

The Big Island of Hawaii

TO MAUI

THE KOHALA COAST AND WAIMEA

Kapaa Beach Park
Mahukona Beach Park
Lapakahi State Historical Park

Kawaihae
Puukohola Heiau National Historic Site, Mailekini Heiau
Spencer Beach Park
Kaunaoa Beach
Hapuna Beach State Park

UPOLU POINT
Upolu Airport
Hawi
Pololu Valley
Pololu Beach
Kapaa Beach Park
Kapaau
Mahukona
250
NORTH KOHALA
Kohala Forest Reserve
KOHALA MOUNTAINS
Akoni Pule Hwy.
270
Kawaihae
Kohala Mountain Rd.
Waiaka
Waimea (Kamuela)
Kamuela Airport
SOUTH KOHALA
Waikoloa
Kawaihae Rd.
Puako
Anaehoomalu Bay
19
Waikoloa
Anaehoomalu

KOHALA COAST

Kiholo Bay
Kaloa
Huehue Ranch
Queen Kaahumanu Hwy.
190
Puuanahulu
NORTH KONA
Mamalahoa Hwy.
▲ Mount Hualalai 8,271 ft.
Kona International Airport
Kaloko-Honokohau National Historical Park
Honokohau
KAILUA-KONA
Kailua Bay
Kahaluu
Holualoa
11
Keauhou
Kealakekua

MAUNA KEA AND THE HAMAKUA COAST

HAMAKUA COAST

WAIPIO VALLEY OVERLOOK
240
Honokaa
19
Hwy.
Kalopa State Rec. Area
Mamalahoa Hwy.
Waipio Valley
Paauilo
Kukaiau
Ookala
Hawaii Belt Rd.
Laupahoehoe
Papaaloa
Weloka
Ninole
Honohina
Hakalau
Honomu
Kolekole Beach Park
Wailea
Wailea
Kawainui
Papaikou
Hilo Bay
Wainaku
LELEIWI POINT
Onekahakaha Beach Park
Hilo International Airport (General Lyman Field)
HILO
Hilo Forest Reserve
Akaka Falls State Park
NORTH HILO
HAMAKUA
▲ Mauna Kea 13,796 ft
200
Saddle Rd.
Saddle Rd.
Waikii
Hawaii Belt Rd.
Saddle Rd.
200
SOUTH HILO
Kulani Honor Camp
Stainback Hwy.
11
Keaau
Kurtistown
Kukui
Mountain View
130
▲ Mauna Loa
Cape Kumukahi

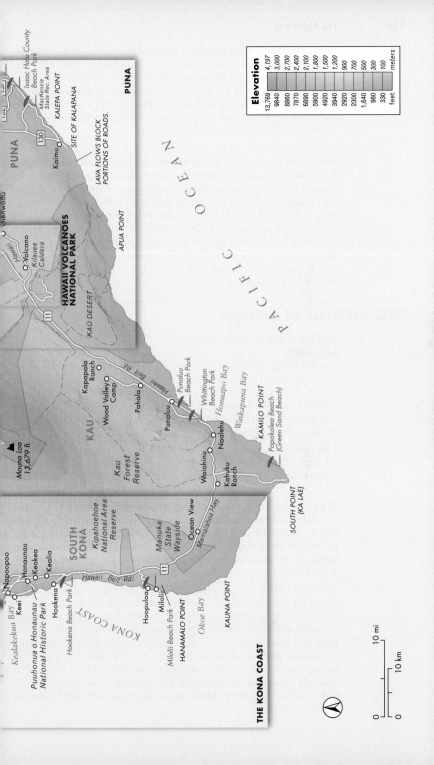

THE KONA COAST

PUNA

Isaac Hale County Beach Park
MacKenzie State Rec. Area
KALEPA POINT

130

Kaimu
SITE OF KALAPANA

LAVA FLOWS BLOCK
PORTIONS OF ROADS.

APUA POINT

Glenwood

Hawaii
Volcano
Kilauea Caldera

HAWAII VOLCANOES
NATIONAL PARK

KAU DESERT

11

Kappapala Ranch
Wood Valley Camp
Pahala

Hawaii Belt Rd.

Punaluu
Punaluu Beach Park
Whittington Beach Park
Honuapo Bay
Naalehu
Waikapuna Bay
KAMILO POINT

Waiohinu
Kahuku Ranch
Papakolea Beach
(Green Sand Beach)

KAU

Kau Forest Reserve

Mauna Loa
13,679 ft.

SOUTH KONA

Kipahoehoe National Area Reserve

Manuka State Wayside

Ocean View

Mamalahoa Hwy.

SOUTH POINT
(KA LAE)

Napoopoo
Keei
Honaunau
Keokea
Keolia

Kealakekua Bay

Puuhonua o Honaunau
National Historic Park

Hookena Beach Park
Hookena

Hawaii Belt Rd.

Hoopuloa
Milolii
Milolii Beach Park
HANAMALO POINT

Okoe Bay

KAUNA POINT

KONA COAST

PACIFIC OCEAN

Elevation

feet	meters
13,769	4,197
9840	3,000
8860	2,700
7870	2,400
6890	2,100
5900	1,800
4920	1,500
3940	1,200
2920	900
2300	700
1640	500
980	300
330	100
feet	meters

0   10 mi

0   10 km

island. Sugarcane stalks have been replaced by orchards of macadamia-nut trees, eucalyptus, and specialty crops from lettuce to strawberries. Macadamia nuts on the Big Island supply 90% of the state's yield, and coffee continues to be big business, dominating the mountains above Kealakekua Bay. Orchids keep farmers from Honoka to Pahoa afloat, and small organic farms produce meat, fruits, vegetables, and even goat cheese for high-end resort restaurants.

HISTORY

Though no longer home to the capital, the state's history is nonethe-less rooted in that of its namesake island, Hawaii. Kamehameha, the greatest king in Hawaiian history and the man credited with uniting the Islands, was born here, raised in Waipio Valley, and died peace-fully in Kailua-Kona. The other man who most affected the history of Hawaii, Captain James Cook, spent the bulk of his time in the Hawaiian Islands here, docked in Kealakekua Bay (he landed first on Kauai, but had little contact with the natives there). Thus it was here that Western influence was first felt, and from here that it spread to the rest of the Islands.

BIG ISLAND PLANNER

GETTING HERE AND AROUND

AIR TRAVEL

The Big Island's two main airports are almost directly across the island from each other. Kona International Airport on the west side is about a 10-minute drive from Kailua-Kona and 30 to 45 minutes from the Kohala Coast. On the east side, Hilo International Airport, 2 miles from downtown Hilo, is about 40 minutes from Volcanoes National Park. A 2½-hour drive connects Hilo and Kailua-Kona.

CAR TRAVEL

It's a good idea to rent a car with four-wheel drive, such as a Jeep, while visiting the Big Island. Some of the island's best sights (and most beauti-ful beaches) are at the end of rough or unpaved roads.

Most rental agencies require you sign an agreement that you won't drive to certain locations, such as over the Saddle Road or up to Mauna Kea and its observatories. Though a good portion of the road is smoothly paved (and being upgraded), the Saddle Road is remote, winding, and bumpy in certain areas, unlighted and bereft of gas stations. Harper's, a local rental company, is the sole exception.

As a result of multiple microclimates and varying elevations, the Big Island experiences its share of extreme weather. During the same circle-the-island trip you may experience combinations of the following: intensely heavy tropical downpours; cold, windy conditions; searing heat; and even snow flurries. Be cautious on the mostly single-lane roads through rural areas, as these can be slick, winding, poorly lit, and prone to sudden flash floods. Pull over to the side of the road to wait out intense bursts of rain that may obscure vision and contribute to hazardous conditions. These are usually brief and might even end with a rainbow.

See Travel Smart Hawaii for more information on renting a car and driving.

ISLAND DRIVING TIMES Due to the Big Island's size, it can take a long time to get from one region to another. And the island's increasing traffic is making driving times even longer, particularly between Kona and the Kohala Coast on weekday afternoons.

The state is widening portions of Highway 11 and Highway 19, which circle the island, and has opened a long-awaited bypass road between Keauhou and Kealakekua, both of which have alleviated congestion considerably. In general, you can expect the following average driving times.

ISLAND DRIVING TIMES	
Kailua-Kona to Kealakekua Bay	14 miles/30 min
Kailua-Kona to Kohala Coast	32 miles/50 min
Kailua-Kona to Waimea	40 miles/1 hr, 15 min
Kailua-Kona to Hamakua Coast	53 miles/1 hr, 40 min
Kailua-Kona to Hilo	75 miles/2 hrs
Kohala Coast to Waimea	16 miles/33 min
Kohala Coast to Hamakua Coast	29 miles/55 min
Hilo to Volcano	30 miles/45 min

RESTAURANTS

Hawaii is a melting pot of cultures, and nowhere is this more apparent than in its cuisine. From luau and "plate lunches" to sushi and steak, there's no shortage of interesting flavors and presentations. The same "grow local, buy local" trend that is spreading through the rest of the country is also taking hold on the Big Island. This is a welcome shift from years past, in which all foods were imported, and it's a happy trend for visitors, who get to taste juicy, flavorful Waimea tomatoes, handmade Hamakua goat cheese, locally raised beef, or even island-grown wine. Whether you're looking for a quick snack or a multicourse meal, we cover the best eating experiences the island has to offer.

Prices in the reviews are the average cost of a main course at dinner or, if dinner is not served, at lunch.

HOTELS

Consider spending part of your vacation at a resort and some of it at small inns or bed-and-breakfasts. The big resorts sit squarely on some of the best beaches on the Big Island, and they have a lot to offer—spas, golf, and great restaurants for starters. The B&Bs provide a more intimate experience in settings as diverse as an Upcountry ranch, a rain-forest tree house, or a Victorian mansion perched on a dramatic sea cliff. Several romantic B&Bs nestle in the rain forest surrounding Hawaii Volcanoes National Park—very convenient (and romantic) after a nighttime lava hike.

Prices in the reviews are the lowest cost of a standard double room in high season. Prices for rentals are the lowest per-night cost for a one-bedroom unit in high season.

WILL I SEE FLOWING LAVA?

Without question, the best time to see lava is at night. However, you may not know until the day of your visit whether the lava flow will be in an accessible location. Your best bet is to call the visitor center at Hawaii Volcanoes National Park before you head out. No matter what's happening at the active lava flows, there's plenty to see and do inside the national park, where the Halemaumau Crater is located.

At times when lava is flowing inside the park, the hike out to the closest viewing might take a couple of hours. If it is expected to take longer than that, park rangers will usually advise against making the trek. Pay attention to all warning signs, and take safety advice from park rangers seriously. ■TIP→ **Bring a flashlight, water, and sturdy shoes, and be prepared for some rough going over the lava fields at night.**

When lava is flowing outside the park boundaries, hiking is strictly regulated because trails pass through private land.

For more information about visiting Hawaii Volcanoes National Park, see Hawaii National Park.

For expanded hotel reviews, visit www.Fodors.com

VISITOR INFORMATION

Before you go, contact the Big Island Visitors Bureau to request a free official vacation planner. The Hawaii Island Chamber of Commerce also has links to dozens of museums, attractions, bed-and-breakfasts, and parks on its website. The Kona-Kohala Chamber of Commerce also has resources for the west side of the island.

Contacts Big Island Visitors Bureau ☎ *808/961–5797, 800/648–2441* ⊕ *www.bigisland.org.* **Hawaii Island Chamber of Commerce** ☎ *808/935–7178* ⊕ *www.hicc.biz.*

EXPLORING

KAILUA-KONA

Updated by Cynthia Sweeney

Kailua-Kona is about 7 miles south of the Kona airport.

A fun and bustling seaside town, Kailua-Kona has the souvenir shops and open-air restaurants you'd expect in a major tourist hub, with the added bonus of a surprising number of historic sites. There are a few great restaurants here that are far more affordable than those at the resorts on the Kohala Coast and in Waimea.

Except for the rare deluge, the sun shines year-round. Mornings offer cooler weather, smaller crowds, and more birds singing in the banyan trees; you'll see tourists and locals out running on Alii Drive, the town's main drag, by about 5 am every day. Afternoons sometimes bring clouds and drizzly rain, but evenings are great for cool drinks, brilliant sunsets, gentle trade winds, and lazy hours spent gazing out over the ocean. Though there are better beaches north of the town on the Kohala Coast,

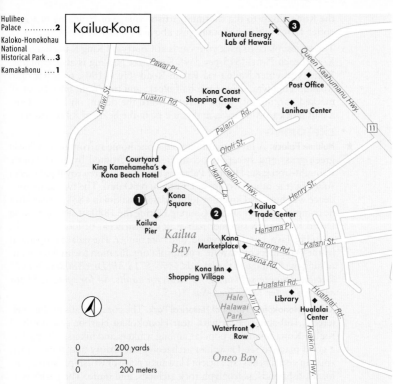

Kailua-Kona

Natural Energy
Lab of Hawaii

Queen Kaahumanu Hwy.

Pawai Pl.

Kuakini Rd.

Kona Coast
Shopping Center

Post Office

Lanihau Center

Palani Rd.

Otoli St.

11

Courtyard
King Kamehameha's
Kona Beach Hotel

Kaiwi St.

Likana La.

Kuakini Hwy.

Henry St.

Kona
Square

Kailua
Trade Center

Kailua
Pier

*Kailua
Bay*

Kona
Marketplace

Hanama Pl.

Sarona Rd.

Kalani St.

Kakina Rd.

Kona Inn
Shopping Village

Hualalai Rd.

Hale
Halawai
Park

Alii Dr.

Library

Hualalai Center

Hualalai Rd.

Waterfront
Row

Kuakini Hwy.

Ōneo Bay

0   200 yards

0   200 meters

Kailua-Kona is home to a few gems, including a fantastic snorkeling beach (Kahaluu) and a tranquil bay perfect for kids (Kamakahonu Beach, in front of the King Kamehameha Hotel).

Scattered among the shops, restaurants, and condo complexes of Alii Drive are the replica of the homestead where King Kamehameha I spent his last days (he died here in 1819), the last royal palace in the United States (Hulihee Palace), and a battleground dotted with the graves of ancient Hawaiians who fought for their land and lost. It was also here in Kailua-Kona that Kamehameha's successor, King Liholiho, broke and officially abolished the ancient *kapu* (roughly translated as "forbidden," it was the name for the strict code of conduct islanders were compelled to follow) system by publicly sitting and eating with women. The following year, on April 4, 1820, the first Christian missionaries came ashore here, changing the islands forever.

GETTING HERE AND AROUND

Half a day is plenty of time to explore Kailua-Kona, as most of the town's sights are located in or near the downtown area. Still, if you add in a beach trip (Kahaluu Beach has some of the best and easiest snorkeling on the island), it's easy to while away the bulk of a day here. Another option for making a day of it is to tack on a short trip down the Kona Coast to the charming artists' village of Holualoa or to the coffee farms in the mountains just above Kealakekua Bay.

The easiest place to park your car is at Courtyard King Kamehameha's Kona Beach Hotel ($15 per day). Some free parking is also available: When you enter Kailua via Palani Road (Hwy. 190), turn left onto Kuakini Highway, drive for a half block, and turn right into the small marked parking lot. Walk *makai* (toward the ocean) on Likana Lane a half block to Alii Drive, and you'll be in the heart of Kailua-Kona.

EXPLORING

★ **Hulihee Palace.** A lovely rambling old stone home surrounded by jewel green grass and sweeping ocean views and fronted by an elaborate wrought-iron gate, Hulihee Palace is one of only three royal palaces in America (the other two are in Honolulu on Oahu). The two-story residence was built by Governor John Adams Kuakini in 1838, a year after he completed Mokuaikaua Church. During the 1880s it served as King David Kalakaua's summer palace. It's constructed of local materials, including lava, coral, koa wood, and *ohia* timber. The palace is operated by the Daughters of Hawaii, a nonprofit organization focused on maintaining the heritage of the Islands. ⊠ *75-5718 Alii Dr.* ☎ *808/329–1877* ⊕ *www.daughtersofhawaii.org* ⊠ *$6 for adults, $4 for seniors, $1 for children under 18* ☉ *Tues.–Sat. 10–3.*

Kaloko–Honokohau National Historical Park. The coastal trails at this sheltered 1,160-acre coastal park near Honokohau Harbor, just north of Kailua-Kona town, are popular among walkers and hikers. The park is a good place to see Hawaiian archaeological history and ruins intact; you can visit a *heiau* (an ancient Hawaiian place of worship), house platforms, fishponds, petroglyph rock etchings, and more. The park's wetlands provide refuge to a number of waterbirds, including the endemic Hawaiian stilt and coot. There are two beaches here that are good for swimming, walking, and sea turtle spotting—**Aiopio**, a few yards north of the harbor, is a small beach with calm, protected swimming areas (good for kids) near the archaeological site of Hale o Mono, while **Honokohau Beach**, a ¾-mile stretch with ruins of ancient fishponds, is also north of the harbor. There are three entrances to the park; the middle entrance provides access to park headquarters, where the rangers are very helpful. ⊠ *Honokohau Harbor, 74-425 Kealakehe Pkwy., off Hwy. 19* ☎ *808/329–6881* ⊕ *www.nps.gov* ☉ *Park road gate 8–4.*

Kamakahonu. King Kamehameha I spent his last years, from 1812 to 1819, near what is now King Kamehameha's Kona Beach Hotel. Part of what was once a 4-acre homestead, complete with several houses and religious sites, has been swallowed by Kailua Pier, but a replica of the temple, **Ahuena Heiau**, keeps history alive. ⊠ *75-5660 Palani Rd.* ☎ *808/329–2911.*

THE KONA COAST

South of Kailua-Kona, Highway 11 hugs splendid coastlines, leaving busy streets behind. A detour along the winding narrow roads in the mountains above takes you straight to the heart of coffee country, where lush plantations and jaw-dropping views offer a taste of what Hawaii was like before

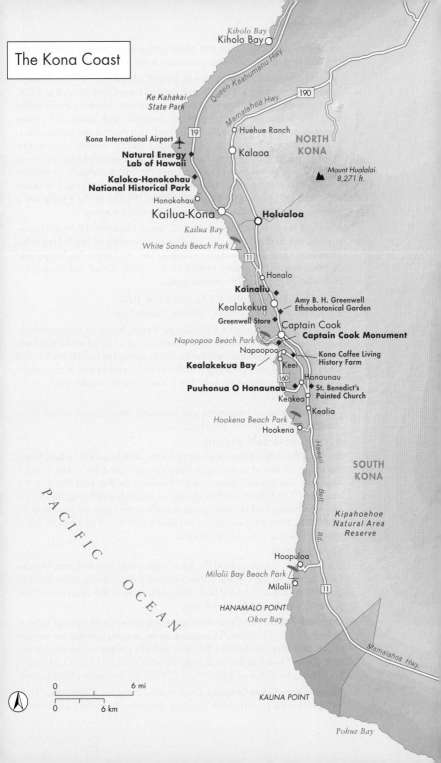

The Kona Coast

Kiholo Bay
Kiholo Bay

Queen Kaahumanu Hwy.

Mamalahoa Hwy.

190

Ke Kahakai State Park

19

Huehue Ranch

NORTH KONA

Kona International Airport

Kalaoa

▲ *Mount Hualalai 8,271 ft.*

Natural Energy Lab of Hawaii

Kaloko-Honokohau National Historical Park

Honokohau

Holualoa

Kailua-Kona

Kailua Bay

11

White Sands Beach Park

Honalo

Kainaliu

Amy B. H. Greenwell Ethnobotanical Garden

Kealakekua

Greenwell Store

Captain Cook

Captain Cook Monument

Napoopoo Beach Park

Napoopoo

Kona Coffee Living History Farm

Kealakekua Bay

Keei

160

Honaunau

Puuhonua O Honaunau

St. Benedict's Painted Church

Keokea

Kealia

Hookena Beach Park

Hookena

Hawaii Belt Rd.

SOUTH KONA

Kipahoehoe Natural Area Reserve

PACIFIC

OCEAN

Hoopuloa

Milolii Bay Beach Park

Milolii

11

HANAMALO POINT

Okoe Bay

Mamalahoa Hwy.

0   6 mi

0   6 km

KAUNA POINT

Pohue Bay

the resorts took over. Tour one of the coffee farms to find out what the big deal is about Kona coffee, and enjoy a free sample while you're at it.

A half-hour drive on the highway from Kailua-Kona will lead you to beautiful Kealakekua Bay, where Captain James Cook arrived in 1778, changing the Islands forever. Hawaiian spinner dolphins frolic in the bay, now a marine preserve nestled alongside high green cliffs more reminiscent of popular images of Ireland than posters of Hawaii. Snorkeling is superb here, as it is a protected marine reserve, so you may want to bring your gear and spend an hour or so exploring the coral reefs. This is also a nice kayaking spot; the bay is normally extremely calm. ■TIP→ **One of our favorite ways to spend a morning is to throw some snorkel gear in a kayak, paddle across the bay, go for a swim and a snorkel, and paddle back, dodging dolphins along the way.**

North of Kona International Airport, along Highway 19, brightly colored bougainvillea stand out in relief against miles of black-lava fields stretching from the mountain to the sea. The dry, barren landscape may not be what you'd expect to find on a tropical island, but it's a good reminder of the island's volcanic past.

SOUTH KONA AND KEALAKEKUA BAY
Kealakekua Bay is 14 miles south of Kailua-Kona.

The winding road above Kealakekua Bay is home to a quaint little painted church, as well as several reasonably priced bed-and-breakfasts with great views. The communities surrounding the bay (Kainaliu and Captain Cook) are brimming with local and transplanted artists, making them great places to stop for a meal, some unique gifts, or an afternoon stroll.

After a morning of swimming and kayaking, head to one of the great cafés in nearby Kainaliu to refuel.

GETTING HERE AND AROUND
Between the coffee plantations, artsy towns, and Kealakekua Bay, South Kona has plenty of activities to keep you occupied for a day. Bring a swimsuit and snorkel gear, and hit Kealakekua Bay first thing in the morning. You'll have a better chance of a dolphin sighting, and you'll beat the large snorkel cruise groups. Follow the signs off Highway 11 to the bay, then park at Napoopoo Beach (not much of a beach, but it provides easy access into the water).

COFFEE FARMS
Several coffee farms around the Kona coffee-belt area welcome visitors to watch all or part of the coffee process, from harvest to packaging. Some tours are self-guided and most are free, with the exception of the Kona Coffee Living History Farm.

Greenwell Farms. This 20-minute tour of a working Hawaiian farm is great for the entire family. Depending on the season, you will see various stages of coffee production, but you will always get to sample Greenwell Farms' Kona coffee at the end of your tour. ✉ *81-6581 Mamalahoa Hwy., Kealakekua* ☎ *808/323–2295* ⊕ *www.greenwellfarms.com.*

Holualoa-Kona Coffee Company. There is a lot going on at this coffee farm and processing facility, from growing the beans to milling and drying.

Kona Coast

CLOSE UP

Kona Coffee

From the cafés, stores, and restaurants selling Kona coffee, to the farm tours, to the annual Kona Coffee Cultural Festival, coffee is a major part of life on this side of the Big Island. More than 600 farms, most from just three to seven acres in size, grow the delicious—and luxurious, at generally more than $25 per pound—beans. Only coffee from the North and South Kona Districts can be called Kona.

Hawaii is the only U.S. producer of commercially grown coffee, and it has been growing in Kona since 1828, when Reverend Samuel Ruggles, an American missionary, brought a cutting over from the Oahu farm of Chief Boki, Oahu's governor. That coffee plant was a strain of Ethiopian coffee called coffee Arabica, and it is the same coffee still produced today, although a Guatemalan strain of Arabica introduced in the late 1800s is produced in far higher quantities.

In the early 1900s, the large Hawaiian coffee plantations subdivided their lots and began leasing parcels to local tenant farmers, a practice that continues today. Many tenant farmers were Japanese families. In the 1930s, local schools switched summer vacation to "coffee vacation" from August to November so that the kids could help with the coffee harvest, a practice that held until 1969.

Coffee is harvested as "cherries"— the beans are encased in a hard red shell. Kona beans are handpicked several times each season to guarantee the best product. The cherries are shelled and the beans roasted to a dark brown. Today most farms— owned and operated by Japanese-American families, West Coast mainland transplants, Native Hawaiians, and descendants of Portuguese and Chinese immigrants—control production from harvest to cup.

The processing plant next door to the farm lets you see how the beans are roasted and packaged as well. Holuakoa also processes beans for many other coffee farms in the area. The partially self-guided tours are weekdays only. ⊠ 77-6261 Old Mamalahoa Hwy., Hwy. 180, Holualoa ☎ 808/322–9937, 800/334–0348 ⊕ www.konalea.com ☞ Free.

Hula Daddy. Learn the history of the farm and view different aspects of the coffee-making process here. You will get to pick and pulp your own coffee bean. Hours are 10 am to 4 pm. ⊠ 74-4944 Mamalahoa Hwy., Holualoa ☎ 808/327–9744, 888/553–2339 ⊕ www.huladaddy. com ☞ Free.

Kona Coffee Living History Farm. Known as the D. Uchida Farm, this site is on the National Register of Historic Places. Completely restored by the Kona Historical Society, it includes a 1913 farmhouse surrounded by coffee trees, a Japanese bathhouse, *kuriba* (coffee-processing mill), and *hoshidana* (traditional drying platform). ⊠ 82-6199 Mamalahoa Hwy., Kealakekua ☎ 808/323–2006 ⊕ www.konahistorical.org ☞ $20 ⊙ Farm tours Mon.–Thurs. 10–2.

Kealakekua Bay is one of the most beautiful spots on the Big Island.

Mountain Thunder. The largest organic coffee farm in Hawaii, this property in the rain forest above Kona teaches you about coffee from "bean to cup." The tour includes a tasting and access to the processing plant, where you can see everything from dry milling, sizing, coloring, sorting, and roasting. Hourly tours run daily from 10–4. ⊠ *79-7469 Hawaii Belt Rd., Kainaliu* ☎ *888/414–5662* ⊕ *www.mountainthunder.com.*

Royal Kona Coffee Museum & Coffee Mill. Take this easy self-guided tour by following the descriptive plaques located around the coffee mill, then stop off at the small museum to see coffee-making relics and watch an informational film. Tours are weekdays only. ⊠ *83-5427 Mamalahoa Hwy., next to tree house, Honaunau* ☎ *808/328–2511* ⊕ *www. hawaiicoffeeco.com.*

COFFEE
FESTIVAL
Kona Coffee Cultural Festival. The fun annual Kona Coffee Cultural Festival runs for 10 days in November and includes parades and concerts, special tours, an art stroll and coffee tasting in Holualoa, and the Gevalia Kona Cupping Competition (a judged tasting). ⊕ *www. konacoffeefest.com.*

EXPLORING

★ **Captain Cook Monument.** No one knows for sure what happened on February 14, 1779, when English explorer Captain James Cook was killed on this spot. He had chosen Kealakekua Bay as a landing place in November 1778. Cook, arriving during the celebration of Makahiki, the harvest season, was welcomed at first. Some Hawaiians saw him as an incarnation of the god Lono. Cook's party sailed away in February 1779, but a freak storm forced his damaged ship back to Kealakekua Bay. Believing that no god could be thwarted by a mere rainstorm, the

Hawaiians were not so welcoming this time, and various confrontations arose between them and Cook's sailors. The theft of a longboat brought Cook and an armed party ashore to reclaim it. One thing led to another: shots were fired, daggers and spears were thrown, and Captain Cook fell, mortally wounded.

A 27-foot-high obelisk marks the spot where Captain Cook died on the shore of Kealakekua Bay. The October 2006 earthquake caused the hillside above the monument to be come unstable, and as a result, there is no land access to the monument. You can see it from a vantage point across the bay at Kealakekua Bay State Park, or there are several licensed kayak tour operators that run trips to the monument. You can also get a one-day permit to land a noncommercial kayak by the monument. ✉ *Captain Cook.*

Holualoa. Hugging the hillside along the Kona Coast, the tiny village of Holualoa is just up winding Hualalai Road from Kailua-Kona. It's comprised almost entirely of galleries in which all types of artists, from woodworkers to jewelry makers and more traditional painters, work in their studios in back and sell the finished product up front. Formerly the exclusive domain of coffee plantations, it still has quite a few coffee farms offering free tours and cups of joe. ✉ *Kailua-Kona.*

Kainaliu. Like many of the Big Island's old plantation towns, Kainaliu is experiencing a bit of a renaissance. In addition to a ribbon of funky old stores, a handful of new galleries and shops have sprung up in the last few years. Browse around Oshima's, established in 1926, and Kimura's, established in 1927, to find authentic Japanese goods beyond tourist trinkets, then pop into one of the local cafés for a tasty vegetarian snack. Cross the street to peek into the 1932 Aloha Theatre, where community-theater actors might be practicing a Broadway revue. ✉ *Hwy. 11, mile markers 112–114, Kainaliu.*

Fodor's Choice ★ **Kealakekua Bay.** This is one of the most beautiful spots on the island. Dramatic cliffs surround crystal clear, turquoise water chock-full of stunning coral and tropical fish. The term *beach* is used a bit liberally for **Napoopoo Beach,** on the south side of the bay. There's no real beach to speak of, but there are easy ways to enter the water. This is a nice place to swim as it's well protected from weather or currents, so the water is almost always calm and clear. Excellent snorkel cruises can be booked through Fair Wind Cruises, the only company allowed to moor in Kealakekua Bay. ✉ *Bottom of Napoopoo Rd.*

★ **Puuhonua O Honaunau** (*City of Refuge*). This 180-acre National Historic Park was once a safe haven for women in times of war as well as for *kapu* (taboo) breakers, criminals, and prisoners of war—anyone who could get inside the 1,000-foot-long wall, which was 10 feet high and 17 feet thick, could avoid punishment. **Hale-o-Keawe Heiau,** built in 1650 as the burial place of King Kamehameha I's ancestor Keawe, has been restored. If this place doesn't give you "chicken skin" (goose bumps), nothing will. ✉ *Rte. 160, about 20 miles south of Kailua-Kona* ☎ *808/328–2288* ⊕ *www.nps.gov/puho* ⌨ *$5 per vehicle* ☉ *Park daily 7 am–8 pm; visitor center daily 8 am–5:30 pm.*

NORTH KONA

Most of the lava flows in North Kona are from the last eruptions of Mt. Hualalai, in 1800 and 1801. You will no doubt notice the miles of white-coral graffiti in the vast lava fields. This has been going on for decades, and locals still get a kick out of it, as do tourists. The first thing everyone asks is "where do the white rocks come from?" and the answer is this: they're bits of coral and they come from the ocean. If you want to write a message in the lava, you've got to use the coral that's already out there. This means that no one's message lasts for long, but that's all part of the fun. Some local couples even have a tradition of writing their names in the same spot on the lava fields every year on their anniversary.

GETTING HERE AND AROUND

Head north from Kona International Airport and follow Highway 19 along the coast. Take caution driving at night between the airport and where resorts begin on the Kohala Coast; it's extremely dark and there are few road signs and traffic lights.

EXPLORING

Natural Energy Lab of Hawaii. Driving south from the Kona International Airport towards Kailua-Kona, you'll spot a large mysterious group of buildings with an equally large and mysterious photovoltaic (solar) panel installation just inside its gate. Although it looks like some sort of top-secret military station, this is the site of the Natural Energy Lab of Hawaii, NELHA for short, where scientists, researchers, and entrepreneurs are developing and marketing everything from new uses for solar power to energy-efficient air-conditioning systems and environmentally friendly aquaculture techniques. Visitors are welcome at the lab, and there are 1½-hour tours for those interested in learning more about the experiments being conducted. ⊠ 73-4460 Queen Kaahumanu Hwy., #101, Kailua-Kona ☎ 808/329–8073 ⊕ www.friendsofnelha.org ☑ $8 donation for tours ⊙ Tours Mon.–Thurs. at 10 am.

THE KOHALA COAST

The Kohala Coast is about 32 miles north of Kailua-Kona.

If you had only a weekend to spend on the Big Island, this is probably where you'd want to go. The Kohala Coast is a mix of the island's best beaches and swankiest hotels just minutes from ancient valleys and temples, waterfalls, and funky artist enclaves.

The resorts on the Kohala Coast lay claim to some of the island's finest restaurants and its only destination spas. But the real attraction here is the island's best beaches. On a clear day, you can see Maui and during the winter months, glistening humpback whales cleave the waters just offshore.

Rounding the northern tip of the island, the arid coast shifts rather suddenly to green villages and hillsides, leading to lush Pololu Valley in North Kohala, and the hot sunshine along the coast gives way to cooler temperatures.

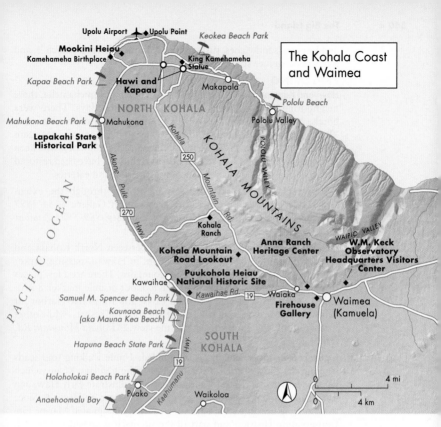

The Kohala Coast and Waimea

As you drive north, you'll find the quaint sugar-plantations-turned-artsy-enclaves of Hawi and Kapaau, where new galleries are interspersed with charming reminders of Old Hawaii—wooden boardwalks, quaint local stores, delicious neighborhood restaurants, friendly locals, and a delightfully slow pace. There's great shopping for everything from designer beachwear to authentic Hawaiian crafts.

GETTING HERE AND AROUND

Two days is sufficient time for experiencing each unique side of Kohala—one day for the resort perks: the beach, the spa, the golf, the restaurants; one day for hiking and admiring the waterfalls and valleys of North Kohala, coupled with a wander around Hawi and Kapaau.

Diving and snorkeling are great along this coast, so bring or rent equipment. If you're staying at one of the resorts, they will usually have any equipment you could possibly want. If you're feeling adventurous, get your hands on a four-wheel-drive vehicle and head to one of the unmarked beaches along the Kohala Coast—you may end up with a beach to yourself.

The best way to explore the valleys of North Kohala is with a hiking tour. Look for one that includes lunch and a dip in one of the area's waterfall pools. There are a number of casual lunch options in Hawi and Kapaau (sandwiches, sushi, seafood, local-style "plate lunch"), and a few good dinner spots.

EXPLORING

Hawi and Kapaau. Home to the birthplace of King Kamehameha, these neighboring towns thrived during the plantation days. There were hotels, saloons, and theaters—even a railroad. They took a hit when "Big Sugar" left the island, but both towns are blossoming once again today, thanks to strong local communities and an influx of artists keen on honoring the towns' past. Old historic buildings have been restored and now boast a wide variety of shops, galleries, and eateries.

Ackerman Gift Gallery. In Kapaau, browse through the extensive Hawaiian collection of the Ackerman Gift Gallery. ⊠ *54-3897 Akoni Pule Hwy., Hwy. 270, North Kohala* ☎ *808/889–5971* ⊕ *www. ackermangalleries.com.*

★ **Kohala Mountain Road Lookout.** The road between North Kohala and Waimea is one of the most scenic drives in Hawaii, passing Parker Ranch, open pastures, and tree-lined mountains. There are a few places to pull over and take in the view; the lookout at mile marker 8 provides a splendid vista of the Kohala Coast and Kawaihae Harbor far below. On clear days, you can see well beyond the resorts, while other times an eerie, thick mist drifts over the view. ⊠ *Kohala Mountain Rd. (Hwy. 250), Kamuela.*

★ **Lapakahi State Historical Park.** A self-guided, 1-mile walking tour leads through the ruins of the once-prosperous fishing village Koaie, which dates as far back as the 15th century. Displays illustrate early Hawaiian fishing and farming techniques, salt gathering, games, and legends. Since the shoreline near the state park is an officially designated Marine Life Conservation District, and part of the site itself is considered sacred, swimming is discouraged. ⊠ *Hwy. 270, mile marker 14 between Kawaihae and Mahukona, North Kohala* ☎ *808/974–6200, 808/327–4958* ⊕ *www.hawaiistateparks.org* ⊠ *Free* ☉ *Daily 8–4.*

★ **Mookini Heiau.** This National Historic Landmark, an isolated *heiau* (an ancient place of worship), is so impressive in size it may give you what locals call "chicken skin" (goose bumps)—especially after you learn its history. The heiau's foundations date to about AD 480, but the high priest Paao from Tahiti expanded it several centuries later to offer sacrifices to please his gods. You can still see the lava slab where hundreds of people were sacrificed, which gives this place a truly haunted feel. The road is unpaved, and even with four-wheel-drive you could easily get stuck in the mud. Then it is a half-mile hike to the site. ⊠ *North Kohala* ✛ *Turn off Hwy. 270 at sign for Upolu Airport, near Hawi, and hike or drive in a four-wheel-drive vehicle 1½ miles southwest* ☎ *808/974–6200.*

★ **Puukohola Heiau National Historic Site.** In 1790 a prophet told King Kamehameha to build a *heiau* on top of Puukohola (Hill of the Whale) and dedicate it to the war god Kukailimoku by sacrificing his principal rival, Keoua Kuahuula. By doing so the king would achieve his goal of conquering the Hawaiian Islands. The prophecy came true in 1810. A short walk over arid landscape leads from the impressive, recently

Take a tour of one of the many Kona coffee farms on the Big Island.

renovated visitor center to temples **Puukohola Heiau** and **Mailekini Heiau.** An even older temple, dedicated to the shark gods, lies submerged just offshore. Bring along your cellular phone to listen to a free audio tour while you visit the site. ✉ *62-3601 Kawaihae Rd., Kawaihae* ☎ *808/882–7218* ⊕ *www.nps.gov/puhe/index.htm* 🎫 *Free* ⊙ *Daily 7:45–5.*

WAIMEA

Waimea is 40 miles northeast of Kailua-Kona and 10 miles east of the Kohala Coast.

Thirty minutes over the mountain from Kohala, Waimea offers a completely different experience from the rest of the island. Rolling green hills, large open pastures, cool evening breezes and morning mists, abundant cattle, horses, and regular rodeos are just a few of the surprises you'll stumble upon here in *paniolo* (Hawaiian for "cowboy") country.

In addition to the horses and cattle, Waimea is also where some of the island's top Hawaii regional-cuisine chefs practice their art using local ingredients, which makes it an ideal place to find yourself at dinnertime. In keeping with the recent Big Island restaurant trend toward locally farmed ingredients, a handful of Waimea farms and ranches supply most of the restaurants on the island, and many sell to the public as well. With its galleries, restaurants, beautiful countryside, and paniolo culture, Waimea is well worth a stop if you're heading to Hilo or Mauna Kea. ■TIP→ And the short highway, or mountain road, that connects Waimea to North Kohala (Hwy. 250) affords some of our favorite Big Island views.

GETTING HERE AND AROUND

You can see most of what Waimea has to offer in one day, but if you're heading up to Mauna Kea for stargazing (which you should), it could easily be stretched to two. If you stay in Waimea overnight (there are a few bed-and-breakfast options), spend the afternoon browsing through town or touring some of the area's ranches and historic sites, then indulge in a gourmet dinner—all before heading up Saddle Road for world-renowned stargazing atop Mauna Kea.

> ## WAIMEA OR KAMUELA?
>
> Both, actually. Everyone knows it as Waimea, but the sign on the post office says Kamuela, which is Hawaiian for "Samuel," referring to Samuel Parker, the son of the founder of Parker Ranch. That designation is used to avoid confusion with communities named Waimea on the islands of Kauai and Oahu. But the official name of the town is Waimea.

A word to the wise—there are no services or gas stations on Saddle Road, the only way to reach the summit of Mauna Kea. Fill up on gas and bring water, snacks, and warm clothes with you (there are plenty of gas stations, cafés, and shops in Waimea).

EXPLORING

★ **Anna Ranch Heritage Center.** Named after the "First Lady" of Hawaii ranching, Anna Lindsey Perry-Fiske, this ranch offers a rare opportunity to see a fully restored cattle ranch house on the Big Island. Wander the picturesque grounds and gardens on a self-guided walk, watch a master saddle maker and an ironsmith in action, and take a tour of the historic house, where Anna's elaborate *pau* (riding) costumes are on display. The knowledgeable staff will share anecdotes about Anna's amazing life. The ranch is on the National Register of Historic Places. On Wednesday afternoon a farmers' market is held here. ⊠ *65-1480 Kawaihae Rd.* ☎ *808/885–4426* ⊕ *www.annaranch.org* ⊠ *Guided tours $10* ☉ *Tues.–Sat. 10–4.*

Firehouse Gallery. Walk across the Parker Ranch Shopping Center parking lot to a historic 79-year-old fire station, now a gallery, to glimpse what the artists in Hamakua and Kohala are up to. The Waimea Arts Council sponsors free *kaha kiis* (one-person shows). ⊠ *67-1201 Mamalahoa Hwy.* ☎ *808/887–1052* ⊕ *www.waimeaartscouncil.org.* ☉ *Wed.–Sat. 11–3.*

W. M. Keck Observatory Headquarters Vistors Center. If you are keen on astronomy but don't have time to go all the way to the summit, visit Keck Observatory headquarters right in Waimea, with its educational exibits and informed staff. You can see models and images of the twin 10-meter Keck telescopes on Mauna Kea and learn about the latest discoveries. ⊠ *65-1120 Kawaihae Rd., across from the hospital* ☎ *808/885–7887* ☉ *Tues.–Fri. 10–2.*

MAUNA KEA

Mauna Kea's summit is 18 miles southeast of Waimea and 34 miles northwest of Hilo.

Mauna Kea ("white mountain") is the antithesis of the typical island experience. Freezing temperatures and arctic conditions are common at the summit, and snow can fall year-round.

Mauna Kea's summit—at 13,796 feet—is reputedly the best place in the world for viewing the night sky. For this reason, the summit is home to the largest and most productive astronomical observatory in the world. Research teams from 11 different countries operate 13 telescopes on Mauna Kea, several of which are record holders: the world's largest optical–infrared telescopes (the dual Keck telescopes), the world's largest dedicated infrared telescope (UKIRT), and the largest submillimeter telescope (the JCMT). A still-larger 30-meter telescope has just been cleared for construction, and is slated to open its record-breaking eye to the heavens in 2018.

GETTING HERE AND AROUND

The summit of Mauna Kea is only 34 miles from Hilo and 18 from Waimea, but the drive takes about an hour and a half from Hilo and an hour from Waimea thanks to the steep road. Between the ride there, sunset on the summit, and stargazing, we recommend allotting at least four hours for your Mauna Kea visit.

To reach the summit, you must drive on Saddle Road, which used to be a narrow, rough, winding highway, but has recently been rerouted and repaved, and is now a beautiful shortcut across the middle of the island (except for that stretch near Waimea). The road to the visitor center at Mauna Kea is fine, but the road from there to the summit is a bit more precarious because it's unpaved and very steep: although most cars can make it up slowly, four-wheel-drive vehicles are recommended. If you're worried about your rental making the drive, you can still head for the summit with one of a handful of tour operators who will take care of everything. If you plan to drive yourself, fill up on gas and bring water and snacks and warm clothes with you, as there is nowhere along the way to stock up.

The second thing, which is extremely important to remember, is the altitude. ■TIP➤ **Take the change in altitude seriously—stop at the visitor center for at least half an hour, and don't overexert yourself, especially at the top.** Scuba divers must wait at least 24 hours before attempting a trip to the summit to avoid getting the bends. The observatory recommends that children under 16, pregnant women, and those with heart, respiratory, or weight problems not go higher than the visitor center.

The last potential obstacle: it's cold, as in freezing. Military personnel stationed in Hawaii do their cold-weather training atop Mauna Kea. Most summit tours provide parkas, but it's difficult to find cold-weather clothing in Hawaii, so, if you plan to visit Mauna Kea, pack your favorite warm things from home.

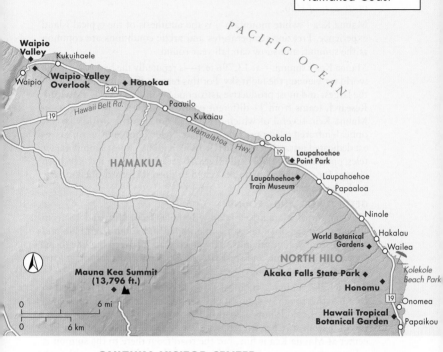

PACIFIC OCEAN

Waipio Valley
Kukuihaele

Waipio
Waipio Valley Overlook ◆ **Honokaa**
[240]

Paauilo

Hawaii Belt Rd. Kukaiau

[19]

(Mamalahoa Hwy.)
Ookala

[19]
Laupahoehoe Point Park

Laupahoehoe Train Museum ◆ Laupahoehoe
Papaaloa

Ninole

HAMAKUA

Hakalau
World Botanical Gardens ◆ Wailea

NORTH HILO

Kolekole Beach Park

Mauna Kea Summit (13,796 ft.)
◆ ▲

Akaka Falls State Park ◆
Honomu ◆

[19] Onomea

Hawaii Tropical Botanical Garden
Papaikou

0 — 6 mi

0 — 6 km

ONIZUKA VISITOR CENTER

★ **Onizuka Center for International Astronomy Visitor Information Station.** At a 9,300-foot elevation, this is an excellent amateur observation site, with a handful of telescopes and a knowledgeable staff. It hosts nightly stargazing sessions from 6 to 10. This is also where you should stop for a while to acclimate to the altitude if you're heading for the summit. This is a pleasure to do as you drink hot chocolate and peruse the exhibits on ancient Hawaiian celestial navigation, the ancient history of the mountain as not only a quarry for the best basalt in the Hawaiian Islands, but also as one of its most revered spiritual retreats. Other exhibits cover modern astronomy and the unique natural history of the summit.

The gift shop is full of great books, posters, and other mementos. On weekends the Onizuka Center offers free escorted summit tours, heading up the mountain in a caravan. Participants must arrive at 1 pm, in your own all-wheel or four-wheel-drive vehicle. After watching a one-hour video, the caravan begins.

To get here from Hilo, which is about 34 miles away, take Highway 200 (Saddle Road), and turn right at mile marker 28 onto John A. Burns Way, which is the only access road to the summit. ☎ *808/961–2180* ⊕ *www.ifa.hawaii.edu/info/vis* ☾ *Daily 9 am–9:30 pm.*

THE SUMMIT

Head to the summit before sunset so you're already there to witness the stunning sunset and emerging star show. Only the astronomers are allowed to use the telescopes and equipment up here, but the scenery is free for everybody. So, watch the sun sink into the horizon and then head down to the visitor center to warm up and stargaze some more. Or do your stargazing first and then head up here to get a different perspective—if you were blown away by the number of stars crowding the sky over the visitor center, this vantage point will really make you speechless. Just take it easy if you're driving back down in the dark— slow and cautious is the name of the game on this steep road.

If you haven't rented a four-wheel-drive vehicle, don't want to deal with driving to the summit, or don't want to wait in line to use the handful of telescopes at the visitor center, consider booking a tour. Operators provide transportation to and from the summit, and expert guides; some also provide parkas, gloves, telescopes, dinner, hot beverages, and snacks. Excursion fees range from $90 to $189.

GOING WITH A GUIDE

Arnott's Lodge & Hiking Adventures. Arnott's Mauna Kea summit tour focuses more on the experience of the mountain than astronomy. Each guest gets to use a pair of binoculars while the guide provides an informative lesson on major celestial objects and Polynesian navigational stars. The excursion departs from Hilo and costs $175 per person, including parkas and hot beverages. The outfitter also offers lava and waterfall tours. ⊠ *Hilo* ☎ *808/969–7097* ⊕ *www. arnottslodge.com.*

Hawaii Forest & Trail. This outfitter leaves from Kona and also picks up guests at the Hilton Waikoloa Resort and at the Paniolo Greens Condominiums in Waikoloa Village. You'll stop for dinner along the way at a historic ranch. Hawaii Forest & Trail supplies parkas, gloves, and brings a telescope along. Cookies and hot chocolate make cold stargazing more pleasant. The price is $189 per person. ⊠ *74-5035 Queen Kaahumanu Hwy., 3 mi. south of Kona airport, Kailua-Kona* ☎ *808/331–8505, 800/464–1993* ⊕ *www.hawaii-forest.com.*

Mauna Kea Summit Adventures. As the first company to specialize in tours to the mountain and the only company to offer only Mauna Kea tours, Mauna Kea Summit Adventures has a bit more cred than the rest of the pack. Expect cushy new van coaches for the tours, parkas and gloves provided, and dinner at the visitor center before heading up to view the sunset on the summit. A powerful telescope is also supplied. Find directions for pickup spots on the website; these include downtown Kona, the Hilton Waikoloa Resort, and the junction of Highway 190 and Saddle Road. The price is $200 per person, including tax. ⊠ *Hilo* ☎ *808/322–2366* ⊕ *www.maunakea.com.*

THE HAMAKUA COAST

The Hamakua Coast is about 25 miles east of Waimea.

The spectacular waterfalls, mysterious jungles, emerald fields, and stunning ocean vistas along Highway 19 northwest of Hilo are collectively referred to as the Hilo–Hamakua Heritage Coast. Brown signs featuring a sugarcane tassel reflect the area's history: thousands of acres of sugarcane are now idle, with no industry to support since "King Sugar" left the island in the early 1990s.

The 45-mile drive winds through little plantation towns, Papaikou, Laupahoehoe, and Paauilo among them. It's a great place to wander off the main road and see "real" Hawaii—untouched valleys, overgrown banyan trees, tiny coastal villages. ■TIP→ The "Heritage Drive," a 4-mile loop just off the main highway, is well worth the detour. Signs mark various sites of historical interest, as well as scenic views along the 40-mile stretch of coastline. Keep an eye out for them and try to stop at the sights mentioned—you won't be disappointed.

Once back on Highway 19, you'll pass the road to Honokaa, which leads to the end of the road bordering Waipio Valley, ancient home to Hawaiian royalty. The isolated valley floor has maintained the ways of Old Hawaii, with taro patches, wild horses, and a handful of houses. The view from the lookout is breathtaking.

GETTING HERE AND AROUND

Any turn off along this coast could lead to an incredible view, so take your time and go exploring up and down the side roads. You'll find small communities still hanging on quite nicely, well after the demise of the big sugar plantations that first engendered them. You'll find homey cafés, gift shops, and galleries—and a way of life from a time gone by. If you're driving from Kailua-Kona, rather than driving around the northern tip of the island, cut across on the Mamalahoa Highway (190) to Waimea, and then catch Highway 19 to the coast. It takes a little longer but is well worth it.

If you've stopped to explore the quiet little villages with wooden boardwalks and dogs dozing in backyards, or if you've spent several hours in Waipio Valley, night will undoubtedly be falling by the time you've had your fill of the Hamakua Coast. Don't worry: the return to Hilo via Highway 19 only takes about an hour, or you can go in the other direction on the same road to stop for dinner in Waimea before heading back to the Kohala Coast resorts (another 25 to 45 minutes). Although you shouldn't have any trouble exploring the Hamakua Coast in a day, a handful of romantic bed-and-breakfasts are available along the coast if you want to spend more time.

TOURS

A guided tour is the best way to see Waipio Valley. You can walk down and up the steep narrow road yourself, but you won't see as much. Costs range from about $50 to $150, depending on the company and the transport mode.

Hawaiian Walkways. If you are serious about hiking, this is the company for you. Knowledgeable guides lead various personalized tours, from

Waipio waterfall hikes to volcano discovery walks to a unique Saddle Road excursion. Tours range from 3½ to 7½ hours and from $119 for the Waipio hike to $185 for the Saddle Road excursion. Hikes include a light lunch and hiking gear. It's best to call for reservations. ⊠ *Honokaa* ☎ *808/775–0372, 800/457–7759* ⊕ *www.hawaiianwalkways.com.*

Naalapa Stables. Friendly horses and friendly guides take guests on tours of the valley floor. The 2½-hour tours run Monday through Saturday (the valley rests on Sunday) with check-in times of 9 am and 12:30 pm. Cost is $88.50 per person. ⊠ *Waipio Valley, Honokaa* ☎ *808/775–0419* ⊕ *www.naalapastables.com.*

Waipio on Horseback. This is a great outfit offering guided horseback-riding trips on the valley floor for $85. It also offers ATV ranch tours for those 16 years and older, with awesome views of the valley and surrounding areas, for $100. ⊠ *WOH Ranch, Hwy. 240, mile marker 7.5, northwest of Honokaa* ☎ *808/775–7291, 877/775–7291* ⊕ *www. waipioonhorseback.com.*

Waipio Valley Shuttle. These informative 1½–2-hour four-wheel-drive tours explore the valley Monday through Saturday. The cost is $52. ⊠ *48-5416 Government Main Rd., Honokaa* ☎ *808/775–7121.*

EXPLORING

★ **Akaka Falls State Park.** A meandering 10-minute loop trail takes you to the best spots to see the two cascades, **Akaka** and **Kahuna.** The 400-foot Kahuna Falls is on the lower end of the trail. The majestic upper Akaka Falls drops more than 442 feet, tumbling far below into a pool drained by Kolekole Stream amid a profusion of fragrant white, yellow, and red torch ginger. ⊠ *4 miles inland, off Hwy. 19, near Honomu* ☎ *808/974–6200* ⬛ *$5 per vehicle (non-residents); $1 for walk-ins* ⊙ *Daily 7–7.*

★ **Hawaii Tropical Botanical Garden.** Eight miles north of Hilo, stunning coastline views appear around each curve of the 4-mile scenic jungle drive that accesses the privately owned nature preserve beside Onomea Bay. Paved pathways in the 17-acre botanical garden lead past ponds, waterfalls, and more than 2,000 species of plants and flowers, including palms, bromeliads, ginger, heliconia, orchids, and ornamentals. ⊠ *27-717 Old Mamalahoa Hwy., Papaikou* ☎ *808/964–5233* ⊕ *www. hawaiigarden.com* ⬛ *$15* ⊙ *Daily 9–4.*

Honokaa. In 1881 Australian William Purvis planted the first macadamia-nut trees in Hawaii near what is now a very friendly, funky little town with a great antique shop, a few interesting galleries, and good cafés. But Honokaa's true heyday came when sugar was king in the early part of the 20th century. During World War II, this was the place for soldiers stationed around Waimea to cut loose. Today, it's still worth a look at its historic buildings, and a chat with its friendly residents. ⊠ *Hwy. 240, Honokaa.*

Honomu. Its sugar-plantation past is reflected in the wooden boardwalks and tin-roof buildings of this small community. It's fun to poke through old dusty shops such as Glass from the Past, where you'll find an assortment of old bottles. The Woodshop Gallery/Café showcases local artists. ⊠ *1 mile inland from Hwy. 19 en route to Akaka Falls State Park.*

DID YOU KNOW?

The dramatic Akaka Falls is only one of the hundreds of waterfalls on the Hamakua Coast. Many falls tumble into pristine swimming holes, so bring your swimsuit when you explore this area.

Fodor's Choice **Waipio Valley.** Bounded by 2,000-foot cliffs, the "Valley of the Kings"
★ was once a favorite retreat of Hawaiian royalty. Waterfalls drop 1,200
feet from the Kohala Mountains to the valley floor, and the sheer cliff
faces make access difficult. Though completely off the grid today,
Waipio was once a center of Hawaiian life; somewhere between 4,000
and 20,000 people made it their home between the 13th and 17th centuries. To preserve this pristine part of the island, commercial-transporta-
tion permits are limited—only five outfitters offer organized valley trips
and they're not allowed to take visitors to the beach: environmental
laws protect the swath of black sand. And on Sunday the valley rests.
A road leads down from the **Waipio Valley Overlook**, but only four-
wheel-drive vehicles should attempt the *very* steep road. There are no
roads on the valley floor, and the going is often muddy. The walk down
into the valley is less than a mile from the lookout point—just keep
in mind the climb back up is strenuous. ⊠ *Follow Hwy. 240 8 miles
northwest of Honokaa.*

4

HILO

*Hilo is 55 miles southeast of Waimea, 95 miles northeast of Kailua-
Kona, and just north of the Hilo Airport.*

When compared to Kailua-Kona, Hilo is often described as "the real
Hawaii." With significantly fewer tourists than residents, more historic
buildings, and a much stronger identity as a long-established community, life does seem more authentic on this side of the island. This quaint,
traditional town stretches from the banks of the Wailuku River to Hilo
Bay, where a few hotels line stately Banyan Drive. The characteristic
old buildings that make up Hilo's downtown have been spruced up as
part of a revitalization effort.

One of the main reasons visitors have tended to steer clear of the east
side of the island is its weather. With an average rainfall of 130 inches
per year, it's easy to see why Hilo's yards are so green, and its buildings so weatherworn. Outside town, the Hilo District has rain forests
and waterfalls, very unlike the hot and dry white-sand beaches of the
Kohala Coast. But when the sun does shine—usually part of nearly
every day—the town sparkles, and, during winter, the snow glistens on
Mauna Kea, 25 miles in the distance. Best of all is when the mists fall
and the sun shines at the same time, leaving behind the colorful arches
that earn Hilo its nickname: the City of Rainbows.

GETTING HERE AND AROUND

Hilo is a great base for exploring the eastern and southern parts of
the island—just be sure to bring an umbrella for sporadic showers. If
you're just passing through town or making a day trip, make the first
right turn into the town off Highway 19 (it comes up fast) and grab a
parking spot in the lot on your left or on any of the surrounding streets.
Downtown Hilo is best experienced on foot.

There are plenty of gas stations and restaurants in the area. Hilo is a
good spot to load up on food and supplies—just south of downtown
there are several large budget chains. If you're here on Wednesday or
Saturday, be sure to stop by the expansive Hilo Farmers' Market. The

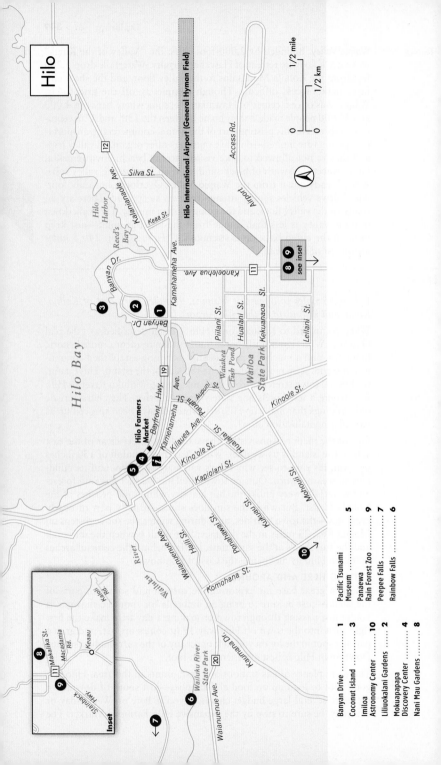

Hilo

Hilo Bay

Hilo Harbor

Reed's Bay

Hilo Farmers Market

Hilo International Airport (General Hyman Field)

Wailoa State Park

Waiakea Fish Pond

Wailuku River State Park

Inset

Keaau

- Banyan Dr.
- Silva St.
- Kalanianaole Ave.
- Keaa St.
- Kamehameha Ave.
- Kanoelehua Ave.
- Silva St.
- Piilani St.
- Hualani St.
- Kekuanaoa St.
- Leilani St.
- Bayfront Hwy.
- Aupuni St.
- Pauahi St.
- Kilauea Ave.
- Kino'ole St.
- Kapiolani St.
- Kukau St.
- Mohouli St.
- Kinoole St.
- Hualalai St.
- Hall St.
- Ponahawai St.
- Komohana St.
- Waianuenue Ave.
- Waianuenue Ave.
- Kaumana Dr.
- Makalika St.
- Macadamia Rd.
- Keaau Rd.
- Steinback Hwy.

see inset

1/2 mile
1/2 km

N

Banyan Drive 1	Pacific Tsunami Museum 5
Coconut Island 3	Panaewa Rain Forest Zoo 9
Imiloa Astronomy Center ... 10	Peepee Falls 7
Liliuokalani Gardens 2	Rainbow Falls 6
Mokuapapapa Discovery Center 4	
Nani Mau Gardens 8	

Merrie Monarch Hula Festival takes place in Hilo every year during the second week of April, and dancers and admirers flock to the city from all over the world. If you're planning a stay in Hilo during this time, be sure to book your room well in advance.

TOP ATTRACTIONS

Imiloa Astronomy Center. Part Hawaiian cultural center, part astronomy museum, the Imiloa Astronomy Center provides an educational and cultural complement to the research being conducted atop Mauna Kea. Although visitors are welcome at Mauna Kea, its primary function is as a research center—not observatory, museum, or education center. Those roles have been taken on by Imiloa in a big way. With its interactive exhibits, full-dome planetarium shows, and regularly scheduled talks and events, the center is a must-see for anyone interested in the stars, the planets, or Hawaiian culture and history. The center, five minutes from downtown Hilo, also provides an important link between the scientific research being conducted at Mauna Kea and its history as a sacred mountain for the Hawaiian people. Admission includes one planetarium show. The lunch buffet at the adjoining Sky Garden Cafe is popular. ⊠ *600 Imiloa Pl., at the UH Hilo Science & Technology Park, off Nowelo and Komohana* ☎ *808/969–9700* ⊕ *www.imiloahawaii.org* ⊠ *$17.50* ☉ *Tues.–Sun. 9–5.*

★ **Liliuokalani Gardens.** Designed to honor Hawaii's first Japanese immigrants, Liliuokalani's 30 acres of fish-filled ponds, stone lanterns, half-moon bridges, elegant pagodas, and ceremonial teahouse make it a favorite Sunday destination. The surrounding area used to be a busy residential neighborhood until a tsunami in 1960 swept the buildings away, taking the lives of 60 people in the process. ⊠ *Banyan Dr. at Lihiwai St.* ☎ *808/961–8311.*

Peepee Falls (*Boiling Pots*). Four separate streams fall into a series of circular pools, forming the Peepee Falls. The resulting turbulent action—best seen after a good rain—has earned this stretch of the Wailuku River the name Boiling Pots. ■TIP→ **There's no swimming allowed at Peepee Falls or anywhere in the Wailuku river, due to dangerous currents and undertows.** ⊠ *3 miles northwest of Hilo, Waianuenue Ave., keep to right when road splits and look for a green sign for Boiling Pots.*

★ **Rainbow Falls.** After a hard rain, these falls thunder into the Wailuku River gorge, often creating magical rainbows in the mist. ⊠ *Take Waianuenue Ave. west of town 1 mile; when the road forks, stay right and look for the Hawaiian warrior sign.*

WORTH NOTING

Banyan Drive. The more than 50 leafy banyan trees with aerial roots dangling from their limbs were planted some 60 to 70 years ago by visiting celebrities. You'll find such names as Amelia Earhart and Franklin Delano Roosevelt on plaques affixed to the trees. ⊠ *Begin at Hawaii Naniloa Resort, 93 Banyan Dr.*

Coconut Island. This small island, just offshore from Liliuokalani Gardens, is accessible via a footbridge. It was considered a place of healing in ancient times. Today children play in the tide pools, while fisherfolk try their luck. ⊠ *Liliuokalani Gardens, Banyan Dr.*

Mokupapapa Discovery Center. Visitors to this small but informative center will learn about the Papahanaumokuakea Marine National Monument, which encompasses about 140,000 square miles in the waters northwest of the main Hawaiian Islands, and is a UNESCO World Heritage site. Wall maps depict the northwestern Hawaiian Islands' extensive coral reefs and the more than 7,000 marine species that live there, one in four of which are found only in the Hawaiian archipelago. This center is run by devoted volunteers who are knowledgeable and give daily tours of the exhibits. Interactive programs and short films describe marine life and reef conditions. It's worth a stop just to get an up-close look at the center's huge stuffed albatross, with wings outstretched. ⊠ *S. Hata Bldg. fronting Hilo Bay, 308 Kamehameha Ave., Suite 109* ☎ *808/933–8195* ⛶ *Free* ◔ *Tues.–Sat. 9–4.*

Nani Mau Gardens. The name means "forever beautiful" in Hawaiian, and that's a good description of this 20-acre botanical garden filled with several varieties of fruit trees and hundreds of varieties of ginger, orchids, anthuriums, and other exotic plants. Guided tours by tram are available for groups. There is also a restaurant with a lunch buffet. ⊠ *421 Makalika St., off Hwy. 11* ☎ *808/959–3500* ⊕ *www.nanimaugardens.com* ⛶ *$10* ◔ *Daily 9:30–4.*

☾ **Pacific Tsunami Museum.** A memorial to all those who lost their lives in tsunamis that have struck the Big Island, Hawaii, and the world, this small but informative museum offers a poignant history of the devastating waves. In a 1931 C. W. Dickey–designed building—the former home of the First Hawaiian Bank—you'll find an interactive computer center, a science room, a theater, a replica of Old Hilo Town, a children's corner, and a knowledgeable, friendly staff. In the background, a striking quilt tells a silent story. ⊠ *130 Kamehameha Ave.* ☎ *808/935–0926* ⊕ *www.tsunami.org* ⛶ *$8* ◔ *Mon.–Sat. 9–4:15.*

☾ **Panaewa Rain Forest Zoo.** Advertised as "the only natural tropical rain forest zoo in the United States," this is the home of white Bengal tiger, Namaste. There is a variety of native Hawaiian species, such as the state bird, the *nene* (Hawaiian goose), as well as a small petting zoo every Saturday 1:30–2:30. Come in the afternoon and watch Namaste's feeding at 3:30 daily. ⊠ *Left on Mamaki off Hwy. 11, just past the "Kulani 19, Stainback Hwy." sign* ☎ *808/959–7224* ⊕ *www.hilozoo.com* ⛶ *Free* ◔ *Daily 9–4.*

PUNA

Puna is about 6 miles south of Hilo.

The Puna District is wild in every sense of the word. The jagged black coastline is changing all the time; the trees are growing out of control, forming canopies over the few paved roads; the land is dirt cheap and there are no building codes; and the people—well, there's something about living in an area that could be destroyed by lava at any moment (as Kalapana was in 1990) that makes the laws of modern society seem silly. So it is that Puna has its well-deserved reputation as the "outlaw" region of the Big Island.

That said, it's a unique place that's well worth a detour, especially if you're in this part of the island anyway. There are volcanically heated springs, tide pools bursting with interesting sea life, and some mighty fine people-watching opportunities in Pahoa, a funky little town that the outlaws call home.

When night falls here, the air fills with the high-pitched symphony of hundreds of coqui frogs. Though they look cute on the signs and sound harmless, the coqui frogs

are pests both to local crops and to locals tired of their loud, shrill, all-night song.

GETTING HERE AND AROUND

The sprawling Puna District includes part of the volcano area and stretches northeast down to the coast. If you're staying in Hilo for the night, driving around wild lower Puna is a great way to spend a morning.

The roads connecting Pahoa to Kapoho and the Kalapana coast form a loop that's about 25 miles long; driving times are from two to three hours, depending on the number of stops you make and the length of time at each stop. There are restaurants, stores, and gas stations in Pahoa, but services elsewhere in the region are spotty. There are long stretches of the road that may be completely isolated at any given point; this can be a little scary at night but beautiful and tranquil during the day.

Compared to big-city living, it's pretty tame, but there is a bit of a "locals-only" vibe in parts of Puna, and a drug problem in Pahoa, so don't go wandering around at night.

EXPLORING

Cape Kumukahi Lighthouse. This lighthouse was miraculously unharmed during the 1960 volcano eruption here that destroyed the town of Kapoho. The lava flowed directly up to the lighthouse's base, but instead of pushing it over, actually flowed around it—an impressive sight now that the lava flows have hardened. Locals say that Pele, the volcano goddess, protected the Hawaiian fisherfolk by sparing the lighthouse. The building itself is a simple metal-frame structure with a light on top, similar to a tall electric-line transmission tower. To reach the lighthouse, keep going straight for 1½ miles when Highway 132 meets Highway 137 and turns into an unpaved road. ⊠ *Past intersection of Hwys. 132 and 137, Kapoho.*

Pahoa. Sort of like a town from the Wild West, this little town even has some wooden boardwalks and rickety buildings—not to mention a reputation as a wild and woolly place where pot growers make up a significant part of the community. Now things are more civilized in town, but there are still plenty of hippies and other colorful characters pursuing alternative lifestyles. The secondhand stores, tie-dye

clothing boutiques, and art galleries in quaint old buildings are fun to wander through during the day. Pahoa's main street boasts a handful of island eateries, the best of which is **Luquin's Mexican Restaurant.** ⊠ *Turn southeast onto Hwy. 130 at Keaau, drive 11 miles to a right turn marked Pahoa, Pahoa.*

HAWAII VOLCANOES NATIONAL PARK AND VICINITY

Hawaii Volcanoes National Park is about 22 miles southwest from the start of the Puna district, and about 27 miles southwest of Hilo.

Few visitors realize that in addition to "the volcano" (Kilauea)—that mountain oozing new layers of lava onto its flanks—there's also Volcano, the village. Conveniently located next to Hawaii Volcanoes National Park, Volcano village is a charming little hamlet in the woods that offers a dozen or so excellent inns and bed-and-breakfasts, a decent (although strangely expensive) Thai restaurant, some killer (although strangely expensive) pizza, and a handful of things to see and do that don't include the village's namesake.

GETTING HERE AND AROUND

There are a handful of dining options, a couple of stores, and gas stations available in Volcano, so most of your needs should be covered. If you can't find what you're looking for, Hilo is about a 35-minute drive away, and the Keeau grocery store and fast-food joints are 25 minutes away.

Bring a fleece or a sweater if you plan to stay the night in Volcano; temperatures drop at night and mornings are usually cool and misty. One of the main reasons people choose to stay the night in Volcano is to see the dramatic glow at the summit vent and to drive to the coast to see the lava flow into the sea. ■TIP→ **Make sure you have enough gas to get down to the flow and back up.** The entrance to Volcanoes National Park is about one minute from Volcano village, but the drive down is a good 30 minutes. Remember that you'll be coming back around midnight, long after the rangers have gone home.

Speed limits in this area are low for a reason. Paved roads can become unpaved within a few feet; heed the speed limits so that you don't go flying onto a bumpy dirt road at 70 mph. There are also occasionally farm kids riding around on ATVs (and some of them might be going way faster than you're allowed to). It's best to be able to dodge them without ending up crashing into a lava rock.

EXPLORING

For information on the park, see Hawaii Volcanoes National Park.

Kilauea Caverns of Fire. Strap on a miner's hat and gloves and get ready to explore the underbelly of the world's largest active volcano. Tours through these fascinating caves and lava tubes underneath the volcano must be arranged in advance, but are well worth a little extra planning. Located off Highway 11 between Hilo and Volcanoes National Park, the caverns are comprised of four main tubes, each 500–700 years old and full of stalactites, stalagmites, and a variety of different-colored flowstone. The largest lava tube in the world is here—40 miles

Continued on page 362

HAWAII VOLCANOES NATIONAL PARK

Exploring the surface of the world's most active volcano—from the moonscape craters at the summit to the red-hot lava flows on the coast to the kipuka, pockets of vegetation miraculously left untouched—is the ultimate ecotour and one of Hawaii's must-dos.

The park sprawls over 520 square miles and encompasses Kilauea and Mauna Loa, two of the five volcanoes that formed the Big Island nearly half a million years ago. Kilauea, youngest and most rambunctious of the Hawaiian volcanoes, erupted at its summit from the 19th century through 1982. Since then, the top of the volcano had been more or less quiet, frequently shrouded in mist; an eruption in the Halemaumau Crater in 2008 ended this period of relative inactivity.

Kilauea's eastern side sprang to life on January 3, 1983, shooting molten lava four stories high. This eruption has been ongoing, and lava flows are generally steady and slow, appearing and disappearing from view. Over 500 acres have been added to Hawaii's eastern coast since the activity began, and scientists say this eruptive phase is not likely to end anytime soon.

If you're lucky, you'll be able to catch creation at its most elemental—when molten lava meets the ocean, cools, and solidifies into brand-new stretches of coastline. Even if lava-viewing conditions aren't ideal, you can hike 150 miles of trails and camp amid wide expanses of *aa* (rough) and *pahoehoe* (smooth) lava. There's nothing quite like it.

📮 P.O. Box 52, Hawaii Volcanoes National Park, HI 96718

☎ 808/985–6000

🌐 www.nps.gov/havo

💲 $10 per vehicle; $5 for pedestrians and bicyclists. Ask about passes. Admission is good for seven consecutive days.

🕐 The park is open daily, 24 hours. Kilauea Visitor Center: 7:45 am–5 pm. Thomas A. Jaggar Museum: 8:30–5. Volcano Art Center Gallery: 9–5.

(top) Kilauea Iki Trail
(left) Fuming rim of Puu Oo, source of the current eruption

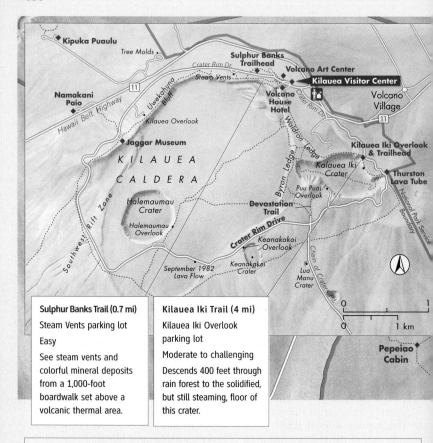

Sulphur Banks Trail (0.7 mi)

Steam Vents parking lot

Easy

See steam vents and colorful mineral deposits from a 1,000-foot boardwalk set above a volcanic thermal area.

Kilauea Iki Trail (4 mi)

Kilauea Iki Overlook parking lot

Moderate to challenging

Descends 400 feet through rain forest to the solidified, but still steaming, floor of this crater.

SEEING THE SUMMIT

The best way to explore the summit of Kilauea is to cruise along Crater Rim Drive to Kilauea Overlook. From Kilauea Overlook you can see all of Kilauea Caldera and Halemaumau Crater, an awesome depression in Kilauea Caldera measuring 3,000 feet across and nearly 300 feet deep. It's a huge and breathtaking view with pluming steam vents. At this writing, lava flows in the Southwest Rift Zone have closed parts of the 11-mile loop road indefinitely, including Halemaumau Overlook.

Near Kilauea Overlook is the Thomas A. Jaggar Museum, which offers simi-lar views, plus geologic displays, video presentations of volcanic eruptions, and exhibits of seismographs once used by volcanologists at the adjacent Hawaiian Volcano Observatory (not open to the public).

Other Highlights along Crater Rim Drive include sulfur and steam vents, a walk-through lava tube, and deep fissures, fractures, and gullies along Kilauea's flanks. Kilauea Iki Crater, on the way down to Chain of Crater's Road, is smaller, but just as fascinating when seen from Puu Pai Overlook.

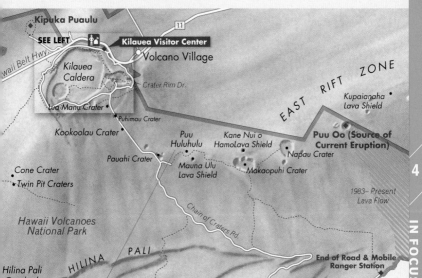

Kipuka Puaulu

SEE LEFT

Kilauea Visitor Center

Volcano Village

11

Hawaii Belt Hwy.

Kilauea Caldera

Crater Rim Dr.

Lua Manu Crater

Puhimau Crater

Kookoolau Crater

EAST RIFT ZONE

Kupaianaha Lava Shield

Puu Huluhulu

Kane Nui o HamoLava Shield

Puu Oo (Source of Current Eruption)

Pauahi Crater

Napau Crater

Cone Crater

Mauna Ulu Lava Shield

Makaopuhi Crater

Twin Pit Craters

1983– Present Lava Flow

Hawaii Volcanoes National Park

Chain of Craters Rd.

HILINA PALI

Hilina Pali Overlook

End of Road & Mobile Ranger Station

Puu Loa

Holei Sea Arch

Kaena Point

Pacific Ocean

4

IN FOCUS HAWAII VOLCANOES NATIONAL PARK

Puu Huluhulu Trail (2.5 mi)

Mauna Ulu parking lot

Moderate

Great view of the ocean, Mauna Kea, Mauna Loa, Kilauea, and Puu Oo cinder cone from atop this cinder cone formed 400 years ago.

Puu Loa Petroglyphs Trail (1.5 mi)

Puu Loa Petroglyphs parking lot

Easy to moderate

Spotlighted here: ancient petroglyphs the Hawaiians created on smooth lava flows to ensure the health and safety of their children.

SEEING LAVA

Before you head out to find flowing lava, pinpoint the safe viewing spots at the Visitor Center. One of the best places usually is at the end of 18-mile Chain of Craters Road. Magnificent plumes of steam rise where the rivers of liquid fire meet the sea.

There are three guarantees about lava flows in HVNP. First: They constantly change. Second: Because of that, you can't predict when and where you'll be able to see them. Third: New land formed when lava meets the sea is highly unstable and can collapse at any time. Never go into areas that have been closed.

■ TIP➔ The view of brilliant red-orange lava flowing from Kilauea's east rift zone is most dramatic at night.

People watching lava flow at HVNP

PLANNING YOUR TRIP TO HVNP

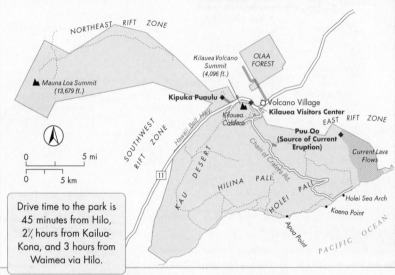

NORTHEAST RIFT ZONE

Kilauea Volcano Summit (4,096 ft.)

OLAA FOREST

◆ Mauna Loa Summit (13,679 ft.)

Kipuka Puaulu ◆

Volcano Village

Kilauea Visitors Center

Kilauea Caldera

EAST RIFT ZONE

SOUTHWEST RIFT ZONE

Hawaii Belt Hwy.

Puu Oo (Source of Current Eruption) ◆

Current Lava Flows

0 — 5 mi

0 — 5 km

11

KAU DESERT

HILINA PALI

Chain of Craters Rd.

HOLEI PALI

Holei Sea Arch

Kaena Point

Apua Point

PACIFIC OCEAN

Drive time to the park is 45 minutes from Hilo, 2¼ hours from Kailua-Kona, and 3 hours from Waimea via Hilo.

Lava entering the ocean

WHERE TO START

Begin your visit at the Visitor Center, where you'll find maps, books, and DVDs; information on trails, ranger-led walks, and special events; and current weather, road, and lava-viewing conditions. Free volcano-related film showings, lectures, and other presentations are regularly scheduled.

WEATHER

Weather conditions fluctuate daily, sometimes hourly. It can be rainy and chilly even during the summer; the temperature usually is 14° cooler at the 4,000-foot-high summit of Kilauea than at sea level.

Expect hot, dry, and windy coastal conditions at the end of Chain of Craters Road. Bring rain gear, and wear layered clothing, sturdy shoes, sunglasses, a hat, and sunscreen.

Photographer on lava table filming lava flow into ocean

FOOD

It's a good idea to bring your own favorite snacks and beverages; stock up on provisions in Volcano Village, 1½ miles away.

PARK PROGRAMS

Rangers lead daily walks at 10:30 and 1:30 into different areas; check with the Visitor Center for details as times and destinations depend on weather conditions.

Over 60 companies hold permits to lead hikes at HVNP. Good choices are Hawaii Forest & Trail (www.hawaii-forest.com), Hawaiian Walkways (www.hawaiianwalkways.com), and Native Guide Hawaii (www.nativeguide hawaii.com).

CAUTION

"Vog" (volcanic smog) can cause headaches; breathing difficulties; lethargy; irritations of the skin, eyes, nose, and throat; and other health problems. Pregnant women, young children, and people with asthma and heart conditions are most susceptible, and should avoid areas such as Halemaumau Crater where fumes are thick.

Wear long pants and boots or closed-toe shoes with good tread for hikes on lava. Stay on marked trails and step carefully. Lava is composed of 50% silica (glass) and can cause serious injury if you fall.

Carry at least 2 quarts of water on hikes. Temperatures near lava flows can rise above 100°F, and dehydration, heat exhaustion, and sunstroke are common consequences of extended exposure to intense sunlight and high temperatures.

Remember that these are active volcanoes, and eruptions can cause parts of the park to close at any time. Check the park's website or call ahead for last-minute updates before your visit.

Volcanologists inspecting a vent in the East Rift Zone

"I learned that the best viewing area was at the end of the Pahoa Kalapana Road past the Keauohana Forest Reserve." —NickiGgert, Fodors.com photo contest participant

long, it has 80-foot ceilings and is 80 feet wide. Tours can range from safe and easy (safe enough for children five years old and up) to long and adventurous. ⊠ *16-1953 7th Rd., Hawaiian Acres, off Hwy. 11, between Kurtistown and Mountain View* ☎ *808/217–2363* ⊕ *www. kilaueacavernsoffire.com* ✉ *$29 for walking tour, $79 for adventure tour* ☺ *By appointment only.*

Volcano Farmers' Market. Local produce, flowers, and food products are on offer every Sunday morning at one of the better farmers' markets on the island. It's best to get there early, before 8 am, as vendors tend to sell out of the best stuff quickly. There's also a great bookstore (paperbacks 25¢, hardbacks 50¢, and magazines 10¢), and a thrift store with clothes and knickknacks. ■ TIP→ There are also more prepared-food vendors at the Volcano market than Hilo, with such temptations as fresh baked breads and pastries, vegetarian lunch items, and homemade Thai food. ⊠ *Cooper Center, 19-4030 Wright Rd., Volcano* ☎ *808/936–9705* ⊕ *www.thecoopercenter.org* ☺ *Sun. 6–10 am.*

KAU AND KA LAE

Ka Lae (South Point) is 50 miles south of Kailua-Kona.

The most desolate region of the island, Kau, is home to spectacular sights. Mark Twain wrote some of his finest prose here, where macadamia-nut farms, remote green-sand beaches, and tiny communities offer rugged, largely undiscovered beauty. The 50-mile drive from Kailua-Kona to the turnoff for windswept Ka Lae (South Point), where the first Polynesians came ashore as early as AD 750, winds away from the ocean through a surreal moonscape of lava plains and patches of scrub forest. Coming from Volcano, as you near South Point, the barren lavascape gives way to lush vistas from the ocean to the hills.

At the end of the 12-mile two-lane road to Ka Lae, you can park and hike about an hour to Papakolea Beach (Green Sand Beach). Back on the highway, the coast passes verdant cattle pastures and sheer cliffs and the village of Naalehu on the way to the black-sand beach of Punaluu, a common nesting place of the Hawaiian green sea turtle.

GETTING HERE AND AROUND

Kau and Ka Lae are destinations usually combined with a quick trip to the volcano from Kona. This is probably cramming too much into one day, however. The volcano fills up at least a day (two is better), and the sights of this southern end of the island are worth more than a cursory glance.

Our recommendation? Make Green Sand Beach or Punaluu your destination for a beach day at some point during your stay, and stop to see some of the other sights on the way there or back. Bring sturdy shoes, water, and a sun hat if Green Sand Beach is your choice (reaching the beach requires a hike). And be careful in the surf here. Don't go in unless you're used to ocean waves. There are no lifeguards at this remote beach. It's decidedly calmer at Punaluu. Don't forget your snorkeling gear.

The drive from Kailua-Kona to Ka Lae is a long one (roughly 2½ hours); from Volcano it's approximately 45 minutes. It's a good idea to fill up on gas and pack a lunch before you leave, as there are few amenities along the way. Or you can eat or get picnic fixings in Naalehu. Weather tends to be warm, dry, and windy.

EXPLORING

★ **Ka Lae (South Point).** Windswept Ka Lae is the southernmost point of land in the United States. It's thought that the first Polynesians came ashore here. Check out the old canoe-mooring holes that are carved through the rocks, possibly by settlers from Tahiti as early as AD 750. Some artifacts, thought to have been left by early voyagers who never settled here, date to AD 300. Driving down to the point, you pass rows of giant electricity-producing windmills powered by the nearly constant winds sweeping across this coastal plain. Continue down the road (parts at the end are unpaved, but driveable), bear left when the road forks and park in the lot at the end; walk past the boat hoists toward the little lighthouse. South Point is just past the lighthouse at the southernmost cliff. ■ TIP→ Don't leave anything of value in your car, and know that you don't have to pay for parking. It's a free, public park, so anyone trying to charge you is likely running some sort of scam. ⊠ *Turn right past mile marker 70 on Mamalahoa Hwy., then drive 12 miles down South Point Rd., Kau.*

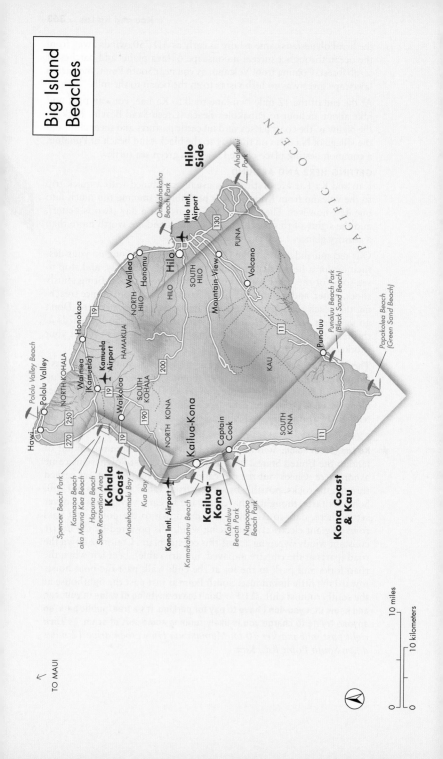

Big Island
Beaches

TO MAUI

PACIFIC OCEAN

Hilo Side

Ahalanui Park

Onekahakaha Beach Park

Hilo Intl. Airport

Hilo

130

NORTH HILO

SOUTH HILO

PUNA

Honomu

Wailea

HILO

Volcano

Papaikou

Mountain View

11

Honokaa

HAMAKUA

19

Waimea [Kamuela]

Kamuela Airport

200

KAU

Punaluu Beach Park
(Black Sand Beach)

Papakolea Beach
(Green Sand Beach)

SOUTH KOHALA

Waikoloa

Punaluu

NORTH KOHALA

Pololu Valley Beach

Pololu Valley

Hawi

250

270

19

NORTH KONA

190

SOUTH KONA

11

Spencer Beach Park

Kaunaoa Beach
aka Mauna Kea Beach

Hapuna Beach
State Recreation Area

Anaehoomalu Bay

Kua Bay

Kohala
Coast

Kona Intl. Airport

Kamakahonu Beach

Kailua-
Kona

Kailua-Kona

Captain Cook

Kahaluu
Beach Park

Napoopoo
Beach Park

Kona Coast
& Kau

10 miles

10 kilometers

0

0

BEACHES

Updated
by Cynthia
Sweeney

Don't believe anyone who tells you that the Big Island lacks beaches. It's just one of the myths about Hawaii's largest island that has no basis in fact. It's not so much that the Big Island has fewer beaches than the other islands, just that there's more island, so getting to the beaches can be slightly less convenient.

That said, there are plenty of those perfect white-sand stretches you think of when you hear "Hawaii," and the added bonus of black-and green-sand beaches, thanks to the age of the island and its active volcanoes. New beaches appear and disappear regularly, created and destroyed by volcanic activity. In 1989 a black-sand beach, Kamoamoa, formed when molten lava shattered as it hit cold ocean waters; it was closed by new lava flows in 1992. It's part of the ongoing process of the volcano's creation-and-change dynamic.

The bulk of the island's beaches are on the northwest part of the island, along the Kohala Coast. Black-sand beaches and green-sand beaches are in the southern region, along the coast nearest the volcano. On the eastern side of the island, beaches tend to be of the rocky-coast–surging-surf variety, but there are still a few worth visiting, and this is where the Hawaiian shoreline is at its most picturesque.

KAILUA-KONA

There are a few good sandy beaches in the area near Kailua-Kona town. However, the coastline is generally rugged black lava rock, so don't expect long stretches of wide golden sand. The beaches near Kailua-Kona get lots of use by local residents, and visitors will enjoy them, too. Excellent opportunities for snorkeling, scuba diving, swimming, kayaking, and other water sports are easy to find.

Kahaluu Beach Park. This salt-and-pepper beach is a combination of white and black sand mixed with lava and coral pebbles. It's one of the Big Island's most popular swimming and snorkeling sites, thanks to the fringing reef that helps keep the waters calm. But outside the reef there are very strong rip currents, so caution is advised. Some snorkelers hand-feed the unusually tame reef fish here, but we advise against it: the fish can become dependent and lose their natural survival instincts. ■TIP➔ Experienced surfers find good waves beyond the reef, and scuba divers like the shore dives—shallow ones inside the breakwater, deeper ones outside. This beach is very busy, and, consequently, littered. Snorkel equipment and boards are available for rent across the street. Hawaiian craft vendors set up on the beach but are unobtrusive. Kahaluu was a favorite of King Kalakaua, whose summer cottage is on the grounds of the neighboring Outrigger Keauhou Beach Resort. **Amenities:** food and drink; lifeguards; parking (no fee); shower; toilets; water sports. **Best for:** snorkeling; swimming. ⊠ 78-6720 Alii Dr., 5½ miles south of Kailua-Kona, across from the Beach Villas, ½ mile north of the Keahou Resort ☎ 808/961–8311.

Kamakahonu Beach. This is where King Kamehameha spent his final days—his Ahuena Heiau sits next to the sand. Fronting Courtyard's

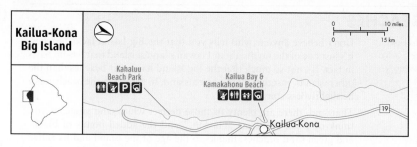

King Kamehameha's Kona Beach Hotel and next to Kailua Pier, this little crescent of white sand is the only beach in downtown Kailua-Kona. Protected by the harbor, the water here is almost always calm and the beach is clean, making this a perfect spot for kids. For adults it's a great place for a swim, some stand-up paddleboarding, or just a lazy beach day, although it can get crowded in the afternoon. Though surrounded by an active pier, the water is surprisingly clear. Snorkeling can be good north of the beach, and snorkeling and kayaking equipment can be rented nearby. ■TIP→ **A little family of sea turtles likes to hang out next to the seawall, so keep an eye out.** Park at the hotel for $15 a day. **Amenities:** food and drink; showers; toilets; water sports. **Best for:** snorkeling; swimming. ✉ *75-5660 Palani Rd., at Alii Dr.*

BEACHES KEY
👬 *Restroom*
🚿 *Showers*
🏄 *Surfing*
🤿 *Snorkel/Scuba*
👫 *Good for kids*
🅿 *Parking*

THE KONA COAST

The rugged beauty of this coastline harbors a couple of scenic beaches that take you off the beaten track. Napoopoo and Hookena offer great swimming, snorkeling, diving, and kayaking.

Kua Bay. This lovely beach is on the northernmost portion of the stretch of coastline that comprises Kekaha Kai State Park. At one time you had to hike over a few miles of unmarked, rocky trail to get here, which kept many people out. Today, there's a separate entrance and a parking lot, making this bay much more accessible, and, as a result, more crowded. This is one of the most beautiful bays you'll ever see—the water is crystal clear, deep aquamarine, and peaceful in summer. The beach is a stretch of fine white sand and little shade. Rocky shores on either side keep the beach from getting too windy in the afternoon. ⚠ **The surf can get very rough in winter. Amenities:** parking (no fee); showers; toilets. **Best for:** surfing; swimming. ✉ *Hwy. 19, north of mile marker 88, directly across from the Veterans Cemetery, Kailua-Kona.*

Napoopoo Beach Park. The shoreline is rocky with only a sliver of beach, but don't let that deter you—this is a popular park and a historically significant one. Captain James Cook first landed in Hawaii here in 1778 to refurbish his ships. When he returned a year later, he was killed in a skirmish with Hawaiians, now marked by a monument on the north end of Kealakekua Bay. The area is surrounded by high green cliffs, and when the water is calm the swimming, snorkeling, and diving is superb.

Kua Bay is protected from wind by the rocky shores that surround it.

You"ll see a variety of marine life here, including colorful reef fish, corals, and, most likely, dolphins. This is also a great place to kayak. The trails behind the shore, leading to Hikiau Heiau, are rocky but walkable. ⚠ **Be aware of the off-limits area (in case of rockfalls) marked by orange buoys. Amenities:** parking (no fee); toilets. **Best for:** snorkeling; swimming. ⊠ *Kealakekua Bay, Napoopoo Rd., off Hwy. 11, just south of mile marker 111, Kealakekua* ☎ *808/961–8311.*

THE KOHALA COAST

Most of the Big Island's white sandy beaches are found on the Kohala Coast, which is also called the "Gold Coast," and is, understandably, home to the majority of the island's first-class resorts. Hawaii's beaches are public property and the resorts are required to provide public access to the beach, so don't be frightened off by a guard shack and a fancy sign. There is some limited public parking as well. The resort beaches aside, there are some real hidden gems on the Kohala Coast accessible only by boat, four-wheel drive, or a 15- to 20-minute hike. It's well worth the effort to get to at least one of these. ■ TIP→ **The west side of the island tends to be calmer, but the surf still gets rough in winter.**

★ **Anaehoomalu Beach** (*A-Bay*). Also known as "A-Bay," this expansive
Ⓒ stretch of white sand mixed with black lava grains fronts the Waikoloa Beach Marriott and is a perfect spot for swimming, windsurfing, snorkeling, and diving. Although damaged by the 2011 tsunami (about 50% of the beach is gone), it's still a vital and popular beach. The bay is well protected, so even when surf is rough on the rest of the island, it's fairly calm here. Snorkel gear, kayaks, and body boards

The calm Kailua Bay is an excellent spot for rowing, snorkeling, and swimming.

are available for rent at the north end, and the vendors are friendly and helpful. Snorkel cruises and glass-bottom boat tours also depart from this bay. Behind the beach are two ancient Hawaiian fishponds, **Kuualii** and **Kahapapa**, that served the Hawaiian royalty in the old days. A walking trail follows the coastline to the Hilton Waikoloa Village next door, passing by tide pools, ponds, and a turtle sanctuary where you will often see sea turtles sunbathing on the sand. Footwear is recommended for the trail. **Amenities:** food and drink; parking (no fee); showers; toilets; water sports. **Best for:** snorkeling; swimming; walking. ⊠ *69-275 Waikoloa Beach Dr., follow Waikoloa Beach Dr. to Kings' Shops, then turn left; parking lot and beach just south of Waikoloa Beach Marriott, Kohala Coast.*

Fodor's Choice **Hapuna Beach State Recreation Area.** One of Hawaii's finest white-sand
★ beaches, Hapuna is a half-mile-long stretch of perfect white sand. The
🅒 turquoise water is calm in summer with just enough rolling waves to make bodysurfing and body boarding fun. Watch for the undertow; in winter the water can be rough. There is some excellent snorkeling

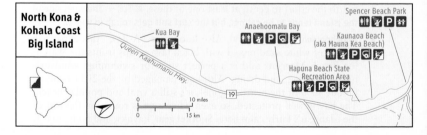

around the jagged rocks that border the beach on either side, but watch for strong currents when the surf is high. Come here for awesome sunsets—it's one of the best places on the island to see the "green flash" as the sun dips below the horizon. The north end of the beach fronts the Hapuna Beach Prince Hotel. You can rent water-sports equipment here, or stop by the food concession and have lunch at the shaded picnic tables. There is ample parking, although the lot can fill up by midday, and the beach can be crowded on holidays. **Amenities:** food and drink; lifeguards; parking (no fee); showers; toilets; water sports. **Best for:** sunset; swimming; surfing; walking. ⊠ *Hwy. 19, near mile marker 69, just south of the Hapuna Beach Prince Hotel, Kohala Coast* ☎ *808/974–6200.*

Fodor'sChoice
★
☺
Kaunaoa Beach (*Mauna Kea Beach*). Hands-down one of the most beautiful beaches on the island, Kaunaoa is a long crescent of pure white sand. The beach, which fronts the Mauna Kea Beach Hotel, slopes very gradually, and along the rocks it's a great place for snorkeling. This is a great spot to watch the sun set. When conditions permit, waves are good for body- and board surfing also. Currents can be strong and powerful in winter so be careful. ■TIP➜ Public parking is limited to 40 spaces, so arrive before 10 am or after 3 pm. If the lot is full, head to nearby Hapuna Beach, where there's a huge parking lot. Try this spot again another day—it's worth it! **Amenities:** lifeguards; parking (no fee); showers; toilets; water sports. **Best for:** sunset; swimming; walking. ⊠ *62-100 Mauna Kea Beach Dr., entry through gate to Mauna Kea Beach Hotel, Kohala Coast.*

Pololu Valley Beach. On the North Kohala peninsula, this is one of the Big Island's most scenic black-sand beaches. After about 8 miles of lush, winding road past Hawi town, Highway 270 ends at the overlook of Pololu Valley. Snap a few photos of the stunning view, then take the 15-minute hike down (twice as long back up) to the beach. The trail is steep and rocky; it can also be muddy and slippery, so watch your step. The beach itself is a wide expanse of fine black sand surrounded by sheer green cliffs and backed by high dunes and pine trees. A gurgling stream leads from the beach to the back of the valley. ⚠ This is not a particularly safe swimming beach even though locals do swim, body board, and surf here. Dangerous rip currents and usually rough surf pose a real hazard. And because this is a remote, isolated area far from emergency help, extreme caution is advised. **Amenities:** none. **Best for:** hiking. ⊠ *Hwy. 270, end of the road, Kapaau.*

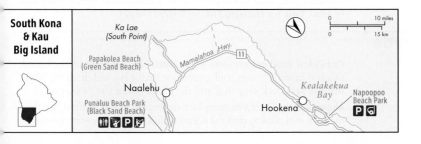

Hilo Side Big Island — Onekahakaha Beach Park — Ahalanui Park — Hilo — Pahoa — 11 — 130 — 132 — 137 — 0 10 miles / 0 15 km

⟲ **Spencer Beach Park.** This white-sand beach is popular with local families because of its reef-protected waters. ■TIP→ **It's probably the safest beach in west Hawaii for young children.** It's also safe for swimming year-round, which makes it an excellent spot for a lazy day at the beach. There is a little shade, plus a volleyball court and pavilion, and the soft sand is perfect for sand castles. It does tend to get crowded with families and campers on weekends, and the beach can be spotted with litter. Although you won't see a lot of fish if you're snorkeling here, in winter you can usually catch sight of a breaching whale or two. The beach park lies just below Puukohola Heiau National Historic Park, site of the historic temple built by King Kamehameha the Great in 1795. **Amenities:** lifeguards (weekends and holidays only); parking (no fee); showers; toilets. **Best for:** sunset; swimming. ⊠ *Hwy. 270, towards Kawaihae Harbor, just after the road forks from Hwy. 19, Kawaihae* ☎ *808/961–8311.*

HILO

Hilo isn't exactly known for its beautiful white beaches, but there are a few in the area that provide good swimming and snorkeling opportunities, and most are surrounded by lush rain forest.

⟲ **Onekahakaha Beach Park.** Shallow, rock-wall-enclosed tide pools and an adjacent grassy picnic area make this park a favorite among Hilo families with small children. The protected pools are great places to look for Hawaiian marine life like sea urchins and anemones. There isn't much white sand, but access to the water is easy. The water is usually rough beyond the line of large boulders protecting the inner tide pools, so be careful if the surf is high. This beach gets crowded on weekends. **Amenities:** lifeguards (weekends and holidays only); parking (no fee); showers; toilets. **Best for:** swimming. ⊠ *Onekahakaha Rd. and Kalanianaole Ave., take Kanoelehua St. to Kalanianaole Ave. 3 miles east of Hilo, look for the sign, Hilo* ☎ *808/961–8311.*

PUNA

Puna's few beaches have some unique attributes—swaths of black sand, volcano-heated springs, and a coastline that is beyond dramatic (sheer walls of lava rock dropping into the bluest ocean you've ever seen).

⟲ **Ahalanui Park.** There's nothing like swimming in this natural, geothermally heated pool next to the ocean with palm trees swaying overhead.

Popular with locals, this 3-acre beach park has a ½-acre pond of fresh spring water mixed with seawater that's heated by volcanic steam. There's no sand, but there is smooth rocky access to the ocean as well as the pool. ■TIP→ **The pool has had ongoing bacterial contamination problems that are typical of some ocean tidal pools in Hawaii.** Those with skin-lesion problems, or chronic conditions like psoriasis, may want to avoid the water here. Others should have no problem. Check with the lifeguard on duty, and heed all posted signs. The parking lot fills up quickly. **Amenities:** lifeguards; parking (no fee); showers; toilets. **Best for:** swimming. ⊠ *Hwy. 137, 2½ miles south of Hwy. 132 junction, Puna* ☎ *808/961–8311* ⊗ *Closed Wed.*

KAU

4

You shouldn't expect to find sparkling white-sand beaches on the rugged and rocky coasts of Kau, and you won't. What you will find is something a bit rarer and well worth the visit: black- and green-sand beaches. And there's the chance to see the endangered Hawaiian green sea turtles close up.

★ **Papakolea Beach** (*Green Sand Beach*). Tired of the same old gold-, white-, or black-sand beach? Then how about a green-sand beach? You'll need good hiking shoes or sneakers to get to this olive-green crescent, one of the most unusual beaches on the island. It lies at the base of Puu O Mahana, at Mahana Bay, where a cinder cone formed during an early eruption of Mauna Loa. The greenish tint is caused by an accumulation of olivine crystals that form in volcanic eruptions. The dry, barren landscape is totally surreal. The surf is often rough, and swimming is hazardous due to strong currents, so caution is advised. Take the road off Highway 11 down to Ka Lae (South Point); at the end of the 12-mile "paved" road, take the road to the left and park at the end. ■TIP→ **Anyone trying to charge you for parking is running a scam.** To reach the beach, follow the 2¼-mile coastal trail, which ends in a steep and dangerous descent down the cliff side on an unimproved trail. The hike takes about two hours each way and it can get windy, so make sure to bring lots of drinking water. (Four-wheel-drive vehicles are no longer permitted on the trail). **Amenities:** none. **Best for:** solitude. ⊠ *Hwy. 11, 2½ miles northeast of South Point, Naalehu.*

★ **Punaluu Beach Park** (*Black Sand Beach*). This park is known for the endangered Hawaiian green sea turtles that nest here. Easily accessible, the beach is a long crescent of black sand backed by low dunes with some rocky outcroppings at the shoreline. You can see turtles feeding on the seaweed along the surf break or napping on the sand. If you swim with the turtles (they're used to people and will swim right next to you), resist the urge to touch or disturb them—they're protected by federal and state law and fines for touching them can be hefty. Don't venture too far from the shore; avoid going out past the boat ramp as very strong rip currents are active. ■TIP→ **It's quite rocky in the water, even close to shore—you might want to bring a pair of reef shoes if you plan to swim.** Popular with locals and tour buses alike, this beach can be very busy, especially on weekends (the north parking lot is usually quieter). Shady palm trees provide an escape from the sun, and at the northern end of the beach, near the boat ramp, lie the ruins of Kaneeleele Heiau, an Old Hawaiian temple. This area used to be a sugar port until the tidal wave of 1946 destroyed the buildings. Inland is a memorial to Henry Opukahaia. In

1809, when he was 17, Opukahaia swam out to a fur-trading ship in the harbor and asked to sign up as a cabin boy. When he reached New England, he entered the Foreign Mission School in Connecticut, but he died of typhoid fever in 1818. His dream of bringing Christianity to the Islands inspired the American Board of Missionaries to send the first Protestant missionaries to Hawaii in 1820. **Amenities:** parking (no fee); showers; toilets. **Best for:** snorkeling; walking. ⊠ *Hwy. 11, 27 miles south of Hawaii Volcanoes National Park between mile markers 55 and 56, Naalehu* ☎ *808/961–8311.*

WATER SPORTS AND TOURS

Updated by Cynthia Sweeney

From any point on the Big Island, the ocean is never far away. With the variety of water sports that can be enjoyed—from body boarding and snorkeling to kayaking and surfing—there is something for everyone. For most activities, you can rent gear and go it alone or sign up for a group excursion with an experienced guide who can offer security as well as special insights into Hawaiian marine life and culture. Want to try surfing? You can take lessons as well.

The Kona and Kohala coasts of west Hawaii have the largest number of ocean sports outfitters and tour operators. They operate from the small-boat harbors and piers in Kailua-Kona, Keauhou, and at the Kohala Coast resorts. There are also several outfitters in the east Hawaii and Hilo areas.

BODY BOARDING AND BODYSURFING

According to the movies, in the Old West there was always friction between cattle ranchers and sheep ranchers. Sometimes a similar situation exists between surfers and body boarders. That's why they generally keep to their own separate surfing areas. Often the body boarders, who lie on their stomachs on shorter boards, stay closer to shore and leave the outside breaks to the board surfers. Or the board surfers may stick to one side of the beach and the body boarders to the other. The truth is, body boarding (often called "boogie boarding," in homage to the first commercial manufacturer of this slick, little, flexible-foam board) is a blast. The only surfers who don't also sometimes carve waves on a body board are hard-core purists, and almost none of that type lives on this island.

■TIP→ Novice body boarders should catch shore-break waves only. Ask lifeguards or locals for the best spots. You'll need a pair of short fins to get out to the bigger waves offshore (not recommended for newbies). As for bodysurfing, just catch a wave and make like Superman going faster than a speeding bullet.

BEST SPOTS

Hapuna Beach State Recreation Area. When conditions are right, Hapuna Beach State Recreation Area, north of Kailua-Kona, is fabulous. The water is very calm in summer, with just enough rolling waves for body-surfing or body boarding. But this beach isn't known as the "broken-neck capital" for nothing. Ask the lifeguards about conditions before heading into the water, and remember that if almost no one is in the water, there's a good reason for it. ⊠ *Hwy. 19, near mile marker 69, just south of the Mauna Kea Hotel, Kailua-Kona.*

Honolii Cove. North of Hilo, Honolii Cove is the best body boarding–surfing spot on the east side of the island. ⊠ *Off Hwy. 19, near mile marker 4, Hilo.*

White Sands, Magic Sands, or Disappearing Sands Beach Park. This is a great place for beginning and intermediate snorkelers, and in winter it's a good place to spot whales. Much of the sand at White Sands, Magic Sands, or Disappearing Sands Beach Park washes out to sea and forms a sandbar just offshore. This causes the waves to break in a way that's ideal for intermediate or advanced body boarding. There can be nasty rip currents at high tide. ■TIP➔ If you're not using fins, wear reef shoes because of the rocks. ⊠ *Alii Dr., 4½ miles south of Kailua-Kona.*

EQUIPMENT

Equipment-rental shacks are located at many beaches and boat harbors, along the highway, and at most resorts. Body board rental rates are around $12–$15 per day and around $60 per week. Ask the vendor if he'll throw in a pair of fins—some will for no extra charge.

Orchid Land Surf Shop. This shop has a wide variety of water sports and surf equipment for sale or rent. They stock professional custom surf-boards, body boards, and surf apparel, and do repairs. You can rent a body board here for $12 a day, or a surfboard for $20 a day. ⊠ *262 Kamehameha Ave., Hilo* ☎ *808/935–1533* ⊕ *www.orchidlandsurf.com.*

Pacific Vibrations. This family-owned surf shop has it all, from casual clothing to surf gear. This place stocks tons of equipment and is enthu-siastic about GoPro digital cameras. You can rent a Morey or LMNOP body board for $5 a day, but you have to buy or bring your own fins. If you keep your board for more than five days, the rental rate drops to $3 a day. The shop rents surfboards, too. ⊠ *75-5702 Likana La., at Alii Dr., Kailua-Kona* ☎ *808/329–4140.*

DEEP-SEA FISHING

Along the Kona Coast you can find some of the world's most exciting "blue-water" fishing. Although July, August, and September are peak months, with the best fishing and a number of tournaments, charter fishing goes on year-round. You don't have to compete to experience the thrill of landing a Pacific blue marlin or other big-game fish. Some

60 charter boats, averaging 26 to 58 feet, are available for hire, most of them out of **Honokohau Harbor,** north of Kailua-Kona.

For an exclusive charter, prices generally range from $500 to $750 for a half-day trip (about four hours) and $800 to $1,300 for a full day at sea (about eight hours). For share charters, rates range from about $100 to $140 per person for a half day and $200 for a full day. If fuel prices increase, expect charter costs to rise. Most boats are licensed to take up to six passengers, in addition to the crew. Tackle, bait, and ice are furnished, but you'll usually have to bring your own lunch. You won't be able to keep your catch, although if you ask, many captains will send you home with a few fillets.

Honokohau Harbor's Fuel Dock. Big fish are weighed in at Honokohau Harbor's Fuel Dock. Show up around 11:30 am and watch the weigh-in of the day's catch from the morning charters, or around 3:30 pm for the afternoon charters. Weigh-ins are not a sure thing, but are fun when the big ones come in. If you're lucky, you'll get to see a "grander," a fish weighing in at 1,000-plus pounds. A surprising number of these are caught just outside Kona Harbor. ■ TIP➜ On Kona's Waterfront Row, look for the "Grander's Wall" of anglers with their prizes. ⌂ *Honokohau Harbor, Kealakekua Pkwy., Kailua-Kona.*

BOATS AND CHARTERS

Captain Teddy Hoogs Big Game Fishing. Full-, half-, and quarter-day charters are available on the 46-foot *Bwana.* Built in 2008, the boat has all the latest electronics, top-of-the-line equipment, and air-conditioned cabins. Overnight fishing is also a possibility. Captain Teddy comes from a fishing family; father Peter, formerly of Pamela Big Game Fishing, is semiretired but still operates the Kona Charter Skippers Association. Rates start at $750. ⌂ *Honokohau Harbor, just south of Kona airport, 74-381 Kealakehe Pkwy., Kailua-Kona* ☎ *808/936–5168* ⊕ *www.teddyhoogs.com.*

Charter Locker. This company can provide information on various charter-boat fishing trips and make all the arrangements—it can even book you on the luxurious *Blue Hawaii,* which has air-conditioned staterooms for overnight trips. ⌂ *Honokohau Harbor, just south of the Kona airport, 74-381 Kealakehe Pkwy., Kailua-Kona* ☎ *808/326–2553* ⊕ *www.charterlocker.com.*

Honokohau Harbor Charter Desk. With about 60 boats on the books, this place can take care of almost anyone. You can make arrangements through your hotel activity desk, but we suggest you go down to the desk at the harbor and look things over for yourself. ⌂ *74-381 Kealakehe Pkwy., Kailua-Kona* ☎ *808/329–5735, 888/566–2487* ⊕ *www.charterdesk.com.*

Humdinger Sportfishing. This game fisher guide has more than three decades of fishing experience in Kona waters. The experienced crew are marlin specialists. The 37-foot *Humdinger* has the latest in electronics and top-line rods and reels. Half-day exclusive charters begin at $600, full-day exclusives at $950. ⌂ *Honokohau Harbor, Slip B-4, Kailua-Kona* ☎ *808/936–3034, 800/926–2374* ⊕ *www.humdinger-online.com.*

Illusions Sportfishing. Captain Steve Sahines is one of Kona's top fishing tourney producers with several years of experience. The 39-foot *Illusions* is fully equipped with galley, restrooms, an air-conditioned cabin for guest comfort, plus the latest in fishing equipment. Half-day exclusive charters begin at $500, full-day exclusives at $800. ⌂ *Honokohau Harbor, just south of Kona airport, 74-381 Kealakehe Pkwy., Kailua-Kona* ☎ *808/960–7371* ⊕ *www.illusionssportfishing.com.*

KAYAKING

The leeward west coast areas of the Big Island are protected for the most part from the northeast trade winds, making for ideal near-shore kayaking conditions. There are miles and miles of uncrowded Kona and Kohala coastline to explore, presenting close-up views of stark, raw, lava-rock shores and cliffs, lava-tube sea caves, pristine secluded coves, and deserted beaches.

BEST SPOTS

Hilo Bay. Hilo Bay is a favorite kayak spot, and the best place to put in is at **Reeds Bay Beach Park.** Most afternoons you can share the bay with local paddling clubs. Stay inside the breakwater unless the ocean is calm (or you're feeling unusually adventurous). Conditions range from extremely calm to quite choppy. ⌂ *Banyan Way and Banyan Dr., 1 mile from downtown Hilo.*

Kailua Bay and Kamakahonu Beach. The small, sandy beach that fronts the King Kamehameha Kona Beach Hotel is a perfect place to launch your kayak. Because the bay is protected by the harbor, the water here is especially calm and teeming with ocean life. It's easy to get to and great for all skill levels. ⌂ *Alii Dr., next to Kailua Pier, Kailua-Kona.*

★ **Kealakekua Bay.** The excellent snorkeling and the likelihood of seeing dolphins makes Kealakekua Bay one of the most popular kayak spots on the Big Island. The bay is usually calm, and the kayaking is not difficult—except during high surf. If you're there in the morning, you may very well see spinner dolphins. Depending on your strength and enthusiasm, you'll cross the bay in 30 to 60 minutes. You can snorkel from your kayak to the ancient canoe landing about 50 yards to the left of the **Captain Cook Monument,** but you need a special permit to land your canoe. Hawaii State Parks (⊕ *www.hawaiistateparks.org/announcements*) has information about obtaining a permit. The coral around the monument makes for fabulous snorkeling. ⌂ *Bottom of Napoopoo Rd., Kailua-Kona.*

EQUIPMENT, LESSONS, AND TOURS

There are several rental outfitters on Highway 11 between mile markers 110 and 113.

Aloha Kayak Co. This Honalo outfitter offers guided tours out of Keauhou Bay—a four-hour morning tour ($89 per person) and a 2½-hour afternoon version ($69 per person). Both include snacks and beverages. There's also an hour-long evening tour ($99 per person). Daily kayak rental rates are $35 for a single, $60 for a double, and $85 for a triple. ✉ *79-7248 Mamalahoa Hwy., Honalo* ☎ *808/322–2868, 877/322–1444* ⊕ *www.alohakayak.com.*

Kohala Ditch Adventures. Formerly Flumin' Da Ditch, this 2½-hour guided kayak cruise through an old irrigation ditch reveals a dramatic part of Kohala history. The tour begins with an off-road excursion high in the Kohala Mountains, followed by a short hike to the ditch, where you'll paddle along with the guides through 2½ miles of rain forest, tunnels, and water flumes. The valleys beyond provide water for the Kohala Ditch, which once brought water to the area's sugar plantations. The tour costs $129 per person. ✉ *Akoni-Pule Hwy., 1 mile past King Kamehameha Statue, Kapaau* ☎ *808/889–6000, 888/288–7288* ⊕ *www.kohaladitchadventures.com* ☉ *Tours Mon.– Sat. at 8:30 and 1.*

Kona Boys. On the highway above Kealakekua Bay, this full-service outfitter handles kayaks, body boards, surfboards, stand-up paddleboards, and snorkeling gear. Single-seat kayaks are $47 daily, while doubles are $67. If you want to learn surfing and stand-up paddling, the prices are $75 per person for group instruction or $150 for private lessons. The Kona Boys also lead two different half-day guided kayaking and snorkeling trips ($159 per person, including lunch, snacks, and beverages). One skirts the Kona coastline, and the other explores Kamakahonu Cove and Pawai Bay. There's also a sunset kayak and snorkel tour for $125 per person. Overnight camping trips are available. The Kona Boys also run a beach shack next to Kailua Pier, behind the King Kamehameha Kona Beach Hotel. ■TIP➡ This location offers the same rental equipment as well as Hawaiian outrigger canoe rides and charters, a uniquely Hawaiian experience. ✉ *79-7539 Mamalahoa Hwy., Kealakekua* ☎ *808/328–1234* ⊕ *www.konaboys.com* ✉ *75–5660 Palani Rd., Kailua-Kona.*

Ocean Safari's Kayak Adventures. On the guided 3½-hour morning seacave tour that begins in Keauhou Bay, you can visit lava-tube sea caves along the coast then swim ashore for a snack. The kayaks will already be on the beach, so you won't have to hassle with transporting them. The cost is $64 per person. A two-hour dolphin-spotting tour leaves at 7 am on Tuesday. It's $35 per person. Kayak daily rental rates are $25 for singles and $40 for doubles. ✉ *End of Kamehameha III Rd., Kailua-Kona* ☎ *808/326–4699* ⊕ *www.oceansafariskayaks.com.*

Pineapple Park. Pineapple Park is actually a hostel with locations in Hilo, Kona, and Mountain View, but it's also one of the only outfitters for kayak rentals in Hilo. Kayaks are $38 for a single and $58 for a double, and the rental price includes oars, life jackets, bags to keep all your gear dry, and harnesses to strap your kayak to your car. ■TIP➡ There's a 10% discount if you book ahead. ✉ *860 Piilani St., Hilo* ☎ *808/323–2224, 877/800–3800* ⊕ *pineapple-park.com.*

SAILING

For old salts and novice sailors alike, there's nothing like a cruise on the Kona or Kohala coasts of the Big Island. Calm waters, serene shores, and the superb scenery of Mauna Kea, Mauna Loa, and Hualalai, the

Big Island's primary volcanic peaks, make for a great sailing adventure. You can drop a line over the side and try your luck at catching dinner, or grab some snorkel gear and explore when the boat drops anchor in one of the quiet coves and bays. A cruise may well be the most relaxing and adventurous part of a Big Island visit.

BOATS AND CHARTERS

Maile Charters. Private sailing charters for two to six passengers are available on the *Maile*, a 50-foot GulfStar sloop. You choose the itinerary, whether it's watching for dolphins and whales, snorkeling around coral reefs, or enjoying appetizers as the sun sinks below the horizon. Prices start at $997 for a sunset sail. You can also book daylong jaunts or overnight trips. Snorkeling equipment is provided, and food can be catered. ⊠ *Kawaihae Harbor, Hwy. 270, Kawaihae* ☎ *808/960–9744* ⊕ *www.adventuresailing.com.*

4

SCUBA DIVING

The Big Island's underwater world is the setting for a dramatic diving experience. With generally calm waters, vibrant coral reefs and rock formations, and plunging underwater drop-offs, the Kona and Kohala coasts provide some great scuba diving. There are also some good dive locations in east Hawaii, not far from the Hilo area. Divers will find much to occupy their time, including marine reserves teeming with unique Hawaiian reef fish, Hawaiian green sea turtles, an occasional and rare Hawaiian monk seal, and even some playful Hawaiian spinner dolphins. On special night dives to see manta rays, divers descend with bright underwater lights that attract plankton, which in turn attract these otherworldly creatures. The best spots to dive are listed in order from north to south; all are on the west coast.

BEST SPOTS

Garden Eel Cove. A great spot to see manta rays is Garden Eel Cove. At this site you're likely to spot hundreds of tiny garden eels darting out from their sandy homes, as well as manta rays somersaulting overhead as they feast on a plankton supper. There's a steep drop-off and lots of marine life. ⊠ *Near Kona International Airport, Rte. 19, Kailua-Kona.*

Manta Village. One of Kona's best night-dive spots is Manta Village. Booking with a night-dive operator is required for the short boat ride to the area. If you're a diving or snorkeling fanatic, it's well worth it for the experience of seeing the manta rays. ⊠ *Off Sheraton Keauhou Bay Resort & Spa, 78-128 Ehukai St., Kailua-Kona.*

Pawai Bay Marine Reserve. The water is usually very clear at Pawai Bay Marine Reserve. This bay near Kailua-Kona has numerous underwater sea caves, arches, and rock formations, plus lots of marine life. It can be busy with snorkel boats, but is an easy dive spot. ⊠ *Kuakini Hwy., north of Old Kona Airport Beach Park, Kailua-Kona.*

Puako. Just south of Hapuna Beach State Recreation Area is Puako, which offers easy entry to some fine reef diving. Deep chasms, sea caves, and rock arches abound with varied marine life. ⊠ *Puako Rd., off Hwy. 19, Kohala Coast.*

The Kona Coast's relatively calm waters and colorful coral reefs are excellent for scuba diving.

EQUIPMENT, LESSONS, AND TOURS

There are quite a few good dive shops on the Kona Coast. Most are happy to take on all customers, but a few focus on specific types of trips. Trip prices vary, depending on whether you're already certified and whether you're diving from a boat or from shore. Instruction with PADI, SDI, or TDI certification in three to five days costs $600 to $850. Most instructors rent out dive equipment and snorkel gear, as well as underwater cameras. A few organize otherworldly manta ray dives at night or whale-watching cruises in season.

Jack's Diving Locker. The best place for novice and intermediate divers, Jack's Diving Locker has trained and certified tens of thousands of divers since opening in 1981. A massive operation, it has classrooms and a dive pool for beginning instruction. The company has four boats that can accommodate 10 to 24 divers. Heading to more than 80 established dive sites along the Kona coast, Jack's has plenty to offer, whether you want to see turtles, manta rays, garden eels, or schools of barracuda. It does a good job looking out for customers and protecting the coral reef. Daytime rates are $55 for snorkelers, $125 for divers. Night dives to see manta rays are $95 for snorkelers, $145 for divers. Snorkel charters, for a minimum of four passengers, cost $125 per person. ■ TIP➜ Kona's best deal for scuba newbies is the introductory dive from Kailua Pier. It costs $80, including pool instruction. ✉ 75-5813 Alii Dr., Kailua-Kona ☎ 808/329–7585 ⊕ www.jacksdivinglocker.com.

★ **Ocean Eco Tours and Harbor Dive Center.** This eco-friendly outfit is eager to share a wealth of knowledge to beginners and advanced divers. It's close to a number of good reefs and other prime underwater locations.

Divers and snorkelers head out on one of two 30-foot crafts. Excursions start at $129 for a four-hour daytime dive or for a nighttime dive to spot manta rays. The PADI open-water certification classes can be completed in three to four days for $650. Seasonal whale-watch tours are $95. ⊠ *Honokohau Harbor, 74-425 Kealakehe Pkwy., Kailua-Kona* ☎ *808/324–7873* ⊕ *www.oceanecotours.com.*

★ **Torpedo Tours.** Mike and Nikki Milligan specialize in small groups, which means you'll spend more time diving and less time hanging out on the boat waiting to dive. Morning excursions featuring two-tank dives run $110 ($79 for snorkeling). Boat snorkelers and divers can try out the namesake torpedo scooters for $30. The scooters allow you to cover more ground with less kicking. ⊠ *Honokohau Harbor, 74-425 Kealakehe Pkwy., Kailua-Kona* ☎ *808/938–0405* ⊕ *www.torpedotours.com.*

4

SNORKELING

A favorite pastime on the Big Island, snorkeling is perhaps one of the easiest and most enjoyable water activities for visitors. By floating on the surface, looking through your mask, and breathing through your snorkel, you can see lava rock formations, sea arches, sea caves, and coral reefs teeming with colorful tropical fish. While the Kona and Kohala coasts have more beaches, bays, and quiet coves to snorkel, the east side around Hilo and at Kapoho has also great places to get in the water.

If you don't bring your own equipment, you can easily rent all the gear needed from a beach activities vendor, who will happily provide directions to the best sites for snorkeling in the area. For access to deeper water and assistance from an experienced crew, you can opt for a snorkel cruise. Excursions generally range from two to five hours; be sure you know what equipment and food is included.

BEST SPOTS

Kahaluu Beach Park. Since ancient times, the waters around Kahaluu Beach Park have been a traditional net-fishing area (the water is shallower here than at Kealakekua). The swimming is good, and the snorkeling is even better. You'll see angelfish, parrot fish, needlefish, puffer fish, and a lot more. ■TIP→ **Stay inside the breakwater and don't stray too far, as dangerous and unpredictable currents swirl outside the bay.** ⊠ *Alii Dr., Kailua-Kona.*

Kapoho Tide Pools. Kapoho Tide Pools has the best snorkeling on the Hilo side. Fingers of lava from the 1960 flow that destroyed the town of Kapoho jut into the sea to form a network of tide pools. Conditions near the shore are excellent for beginners and challenging enough farther out for experienced snorkelers. ⊠ *End of Kapoho-Kai Rd., off Hwy. 137, Hilo.*

Fodor'sChoice
★

Kealakekua Bay. Kealakekua Bay is, hands-down, the best snorkel spot on the island, with fabulous coral reefs around the Captain Cook monument and generally calm waters. And with any luck, you'll probably get to swim with dolphins. Overland access is difficult, so opt for one of several guided snorkel cruises or kayak across the bay to get to the monument. ■TIP→ Be on the lookout for kayakers who might not notice you swimming beneath them, and stay on the ocean side of the buoys near the cliffs. ⊠ *Bottom of Napoopoo Rd., Kailua-Kona.*

Puuhonua O Honaunau (*City of Refuge*). There is no swimming inside the actual park, but just north is a boat launch where the snorkeling is almost as good as at Kealakekua Bay, and it's much easier to reach. It's also a popular scuba diving spot. ⊠ *Hwy. 160, 20 miles south of Kailua-Kona* ⊕ *www.nps.gov/puho.*

EQUIPMENT, LESSONS, AND TOURS

★ **Body Glove Cruises.** This operator is a good choice for families, par-
ↄ ticularly if at least one member is a certified diver and the rest want to snorkel. Kids love the waterslide and the high-dive platform, and parents appreciate the reasonable prices. The 51-foot catamaran sets off from Kailua-Kona pier daily for morning and afternoon dive and snorkel cruises that include breakfast and lunch buffets. Snorkelers pay $78 per person. A three-hour dinner cruise to Kealakekua Bay is a great way to relax, watch the sunset, and learn about Kona's history. Including a buffet and live music, it's $98 per person. Seasonal whale-watch cruises are $78. ⊠ *75-5629 Kuakini Hwy., Kailua-Kona* ☎ *808/326–7122, 800/551–8911* ⊕ *www.bodyglovehawaii.com.*

Captain Zodiac Raft Expedition. A four-hour trip on an inflatable raft takes you along the Kona Coast to explore gaping lava-tube caves, search for dolphins and turtles, and snorkel around Kealakekua Bay. The captain often throws in some Hawaiian folklore and Kona history, too. The morning trip departs at 8:15 am, the afternoon trip at 1 pm. The fee for the trips starts at $94 per person. A seasonal three-hour whale-watching cruise is $65. ⊠ *Honokohau Harbor, Hwy. 19, Kailua-Kona* ☎ *808/329–3199* ⊕ *www.captainzodiac.com.*

★ **Fair Wind Cruises.** In business since 1971, Fair Wind offers morning
ↄ and afternoon snorkel trips. The company's custom-built 60-foot cata-
maran has two 15-foot waterslides, freshwater showers, and a stair-case descending directly into the water for easy access. Snorkel gear is included (ask about prescription masks). These trips are great for families with small kids—there's lots of pint-size flotation equipment. Morning cruises are $129 per person; afternoon cruises are less, at $109 per person (but you're less likely to see dolphins).

The company also operates the adults-only *Hula Kai* snorkel cruise, a 55-foot luxury hydrofoil catamaran with theater-style seats for pan-oramic views. A five-hour morning snorkel cruise that includes a gour-met breakfast buffet and barbecue lunch is $165 for snorkelers, $196 for divers. ⊠ *Keauhou Bay, 78-7130 Kaleiopapa St., Kailua-Kona* ☎ *808/322–2788, 800/677–9461* ⊕ *www.fair-wind.com.*

Continued on page 386

SNORKELING IN HAWAII

The waters surrounding the Hawaiian Islands are filled with life—from giant manta rays cruising off the Big Island's Kona Coast to humpback whales giving birth in Maui's Maalaea Bay. Dip your head beneath the surface to experience a spectacularly colorful world: pairs of milletseed butterflyfish dart back and forth, redlipped parrotfish snack on coral algae, and spotted eagle rays flap past like silent spaceships. Sea turtles bask at the surface while tiny wrasses give them the equivalent of a shave and a haircut. The water quality is typically outstanding; many sites afford 30-foot-plus visibility. On snorkel cruises, you can often stare from the boat rail right down to the bottom.

Certainly few destinations are as accommodating to every level of snorkeler as Hawaii. Beginners can tromp in from sandy beaches while more advanced divers descend to shipwrecks, reefs, craters, and sea arches just offshore. Because of Hawaii's extreme isolation, the island chain has fewer fish species than Fiji or the Caribbean—but many of the fish that are here exist nowhere else. The Hawaiian waters are home to the highest percentage of endemic fish in the world.

The key to enjoying the underwater world is slowing down. Look carefully. Listen. You might hear the strange crackling sound of shrimp tunneling through coral, or you may hear whales singing to one another during winter. A shy octopus may drift along the ocean's floor beneath you. If you're hooked, pick up a waterproof fishkey from Long's Drugs. You can brag later that you've looked the Hawaiian turkeyfish in the eye.

Picasso Triggerfish

Milletseed Butterflyfish*

Yellow Tang

Moorish Idol

Hawaiian Whitespotted Toby*

Saddleback Wrasse*

Redlip Parrotfish

Hawaiian Turkeyfish*

Zebra Moray Eel

Stocky Hawkfish

Green Sea Turtle (Honu)

Spotted Eagle Ray

*endemic to Hawaii

POLYNESIA'S FIRST CELESTIAL NAVIGATORS: HONU

Honu is the Hawaiian name for two native sea turtles, the hawksbill and the green sea turtle. Little is known about these dinosaur-age marine reptiles, though snorkelers regularly see them foraging for *limu* (seaweed) and the occasional jellyfish in Hawaiian waters. Most female honu nest in the uninhabited Northwestern Hawaiian Islands, but a few sociable ladies nest on Maui and Big Island beaches. Scientists suspect that they navigate the seas via magnetism—sensing the earth's poles. Amazingly, they will journey up to 800 miles to nest—it's believed that they return to their own birth sites. After about 60 days of incubation, nestlings emerge from the sand at night and find their way back to the sea by the light of the stars.

SNORKELING

Many of Hawaii's reefs are accessible from shore.

The basics: Sure, you can take a deep breath, hold your nose, squint your eyes, and stick your face in the water in an attempt to view submerged habitats . . . but why not protect your eyes, retain your ability to breathe, and keep your hands free to paddle about when exploring underwater? That's what snorkeling is all about.

Equipment needed: A mask, snorkel (the tube attached to the mask), and fins. In deeper waters (any depth over your head), life jackets are advised.

Steps to success: If you've never snorkeled before, it's natural to feel a bit awkward at first, so don't sweat it. Breathing through a mask and tube, and wearing a pair of fins take getting used to. Like any activity, you build confidence and comfort through practice.

If you're new to snorkeling, begin by submerging your face in shallow water or a swimming pool and breathing calmly through the snorkel while gazing through the mask.

Next you need to learn how to clear water out of your mask and snorkel, an essential skill since splashes can send water into tube openings and masks can leak. Some snorkels have built-in drainage valves, but if a tube clogs, you can force water up and out by exhaling through your mouth. Clearing a mask is similar: lift your head from water while pulling forward on mask to drain. Some masks have built-in purge valves, but those without can be cleared underwater by pressing the top to the forehead and blowing out your nose (charming, isn't it?), allowing air to bubble into the mask, pushing water out the bottom. If it sounds hard, it really isn't. Just try it a few times and you'll soon feel like a pro.

Now your goal is to get friendly with fins—you want them to be snug but not too tight—and learn how to propel yourself with them. Fins won't help you float, but they will give you a leg up, so to speak, on smoothly moving through the water or treading water (even when upright) with less effort.

Flutter stroking is the most efficient underwater kick, and the farther your foot bends forward the more leg power you'll be able to transfer to the water and the farther you'll travel with each stroke. Flutter kicking movements involve alternately separating the legs and then drawing them back together. When your legs separate, the leg surface encounters drag from the water, slowing you down. When your legs are drawn back together, they produce a force pushing you forward. If your kick creates more forward force than it causes drag, you'll move ahead.

Submerge your fins to avoid fatigue rather than having them flailing above the water when you kick, and keep your arms at your side to reduce drag. You are in the water—stretched out, face down, and snorkeling happily away—but that doesn't mean you can't hold your breath and go deeper in the water for a closer look at some fish or whatever catches your attention. Just remember that when you do this, your snorkel will be submerged, too, so you won't be breathing (you'll be holding your breath). You can dive head-first, but going feet-first is easier and less scary for most folks, taking less momentum. Before full immersion, take several long, deep breaths to clear carbon dioxide from your lungs.

If your legs tire, flip onto your back and tread water with inverted fin motions while resting. If your mask fogs, wash condensation from lens and clear water from mask.

TIPS FOR SAFE SNORKELING

- Snorkel with a buddy and stay together.

- Plan your entry and exit points prior to getting in the water.

- Swim into the current on entering and then ride the current back to your exit point.

- Carry your flippers into the water and then put them on, as it's difficult to walk in them.

- Make sure your mask fits properly and is not too loose.

- Pop your head above the water periodically to ensure you aren't drifting too far out, or too close to rocks.

- Think of the water as someone else's home—don't take anything that doesn't belong to you, or leave any trash behind.

- Don't touch any sea creatures; they may sting.

- Wear a T-shirt over your swimsuit to help protect you from being fried by the sun.

- When in doubt, don't go without a snorkeling professional; try a guided tour.

Green sea turtle (Honu)

STAND-UP PADDLING

Stand-up paddling (or SUP for short), a sport with roots in the Hawaiian Islands, has grown popular worldwide over the past few years. It's available for all skill levels and ages, and even novice stand-up paddleboarders can get up, stay up, and have a great time paddling around a protected bay or exploring the gorgeous coastline. All you need is a large body of water, a board, and a paddle. The workout will test your core strength as well as your balance, but truly offers a unique vantage point from which to enjoy the beauty of the island and the ocean.

BEST SPOTS

Anaehoomalu Beach (*A-Bay*). This is a well-protected bay, so even when surf is rough on the rest of the island, it's fairly calm here. Boards are available for rent at the north end and the safe area for stand-up paddling is marked off by buoys. ⊠ *Off Waikoloa Beach Dr., south of Waikoloa Beach Marriott.*

Kailua Bay and Kamakahonu Beach. The small, sandy beach that fronts the King Kamehameha Kona Beach Hotel is protected by the harbor; the water here is especially calm and teeming with ocean life. If you're more daring, you can easily paddle out of the bay and along the coast for some great scenic views. ⊠ *Alii Dr., next to Kailua Pier, Kailua-Kona.*

Kealakekua Bay. The most protected deepwater bay in the islands, conditions at Kealakekua Bay are typically calm. You might see spinner dolphins (in the morning) or even the occasional whale in season. There aren't any shacks for rentals right at the bay, so you'll have to load up your board and transport it there yourself. ⊠ *Bottom of Napoopoo Rd., Kailua-Kona.*

EQUIPMENT AND LESSONS

Kona Boys. If you rent from the main location above Kealakekua Bay, your rental comes with the necessary gear to transport your board to the water on your car; or visit the beach-shack location and carry your board straight from the shack to the water. Board rentals at this outfitter are $25 per hour or $65 per day. Kona Boys also offers group lessons for $75 per person, private lessons for $125 per person. ⊠ *79-7539 Mamalahoa Hwy., Kealakekua* ☎ *808/328–1234, 808/329–2345* ⊕ *www.konaboys.com* ✉ *75–5660 Palani Rd., Kailua-Kona.*

Ocean Sports. At the Waikoloa Beach Marriott, this outfitter rents equipment, offers lessons, and has the perfect location for easy access to A-Bay. Stand-up paddleboard rentals are $30 per hour. Ocean Sports also has rental shacks at the Hilton Waikoloa Village, the Mauna Kea Beach Hotel, and the Waikoloa Queen's Marketplace. ⊠ *Waikoloa Beach Marriott, 69-275 Waikoloa Beach Dr., Waikoloa* ☎ *808/886–6666* ⊕ *www.hawaiioceansports.com.*

SUBMARINE TOURS

FodorsChoice
★
☾
Atlantis Adventures. Want to stay dry while exploring the undersea world? Climb aboard the 48-foot *Atlantis VII* submarine anchored off Kailua Pier, across from King Kamehameha's Kona Beach Hotel in Kailua-Kona. A large glass dome in the bow and 13 viewing ports on the

"Anaehoomalu Beach Surf Shack—classic Hawaii." —travel192, Fodors.com photo contest participant

sides allow clear views of the aquatic world more than 100 feet down. This is a great trip for kids and nonswimmers. Each one-hour voyage costs $109 for adults. The company also operates on Oahu and Maui. ⊠ *Kailua Pier, Alii Dr., Kailua-Kona* ☎ *808/326–7939, 800/548–6262* ⊕ *www.atlantisadventures.com.*

SURFING

The Big Island does not have the variety of great surfing spots found on Oahu or Maui, but it does have decent waves and a thriving surf culture. Local kids and avid surfers frequent a number of places up and down the Kona and Kohala coasts of west Hawaii. Expect high surf in winter and much calmer activity during summer. The surf scene is much more active on the Kona side.

BEST SPOTS

Honolii Cove. North of Hilo, Honolii Cove is the best surfing spot on the eastern side of the island. ⊠ *Off Hwy. 19, near mile marker 4, Hilo.*

Kahaluu Beach Park. Slightly north of Kahaluu Beach Park, intermediate surfers brave the rocks to get out to a popular break just past the beach's calm lagoons and snorkelers. ⊠ *Alii Dr., next to Sheraton Keauhou Beach Hotel, Kailua-Kona.*

Pine Trees. Among the best places to catch the waves is Pine Trees. Keep in mind that this is a very popular local surf spot on an island where there aren't all that many surf spots, so be very respectful. ⊠ *Off Hwy. 11, about 2 miles south of Kona Airport, Kailua-Kona.*

EQUIPMENT AND LESSONS

Hawaii Lifeguard Surf Instructors. This certified school with experienced instructors helps novices become wave riders and offers tours that take more experienced riders to Kona's top surf spots. There's a one-hour introductory lesson ($75 for groups, $98 for individuals), but the two-hour lesson ($98 for groups, $175 for individuals) is recommended to get you ready to surf. ⊠ *75-5909 Alii Dr., Kailua-Kona* ☎ *808/324–0442, 808/936–7873* ⊕ *www.surflessonshawaii.com.*

Ocean Eco Tours Surf School. Kona's oldest surf school emphasizes the basics and specializes in beginners. All lessons are taught by certified instructors, and the school guarantees that you will surf. Lessons start at $95 per person. If you're hooked, sign up for a three-day package for $270. ⊠ *Honokohau Harbor, 74-425 Kealakehe Pkwy., Kailua-Kona* ☎ *808/324–7873* ⊕ *www.oceanecotours.com.*

Orchid Land Surf Shop. The shop has a wide variety of water sports and surf equipment for sale or rent. It stocks custom surfboards, body boards, and surf apparel. The staff also handles repairs. ⊠ *262 Kamehameha Ave., Hilo* ☎ *808/935–1533* ⊕ *www.orchidlandsurf.com.*

WHALE-WATCHING

Each winter, some two-thirds of the North Pacific humpback whale population (about 4,000–5,000 animals) migrate over 3,500 miles from the icy Alaska waters to the warm Hawaiian ocean to give birth to and nurse their calves. Recent reports indicate that the whale population is on the upswing—a few years ago one even ventured into the mouth of Hilo Harbor, which marine biologists say is quite rare. Humpbacks are spotted here from early December through the end of April, but other species, like sperm, pilot, and beaked whales, can be seen year-round. Most ocean tour companies offer whale outings during the season, but two owner-operators *(listed below)* do it full-time. They are much more familiar with whale behavior and you're more likely to have a quality whale-watching experience. ■ **TIP→** If you take the morning cruise, you're likely to see dolphins as well. *See Snorkeling for additional outfitters that offer whale-watching cruises.*

Blue Sea Cruises. The 46-foot *Makai* and the 70-foot *Spirit of Kona* cruise along the Kona Coast catching sight of dolphins, whales, and manta rays. Both boats have snack bars and restrooms, and the double-decker *Spirit of Kona* also has a glass bottom. Seasonal humpback whale watches are $79, dolphin cruises are $84, and night manta ray cruises are $69. Cruises last about three hours. ⊠ *Kailua-Kona Pier, 75-5660 Palani Rd., Kailua-Kona 808/331–8875* ⊕ *www.blueseacruisesinc.com.*

Captain Dan McSweeney's Year-Round Whale Watching Adventures. This is probably the most experienced small operation on the island. Captain Dan McSweeney offers three-hour trips on his double-decker, 40-foot cruise boat. In addition to humpbacks in the winter, he'll show you dolphins and some of the six other whale species that live off the Kona Coast throughout the year. Three-hour tours cost $89.50. McSweeney guarantees you'll see a whale or he'll take you out again free. ⊠ *Honokohau Harbor, 74-381 Kealakehe Pkwy., Kailua-Kona* ☎ *808/322–0028, 888/942–5376* ⊕ *www.ilovewhales.com.*

GOLF, HIKING, AND OUTDOOR ACTIVITIES

Updated
by Kristina
Anderson

With the Big Island's predictably mild year-round climate, it's no wonder you'll find an emphasis on outdoor activities. After all, this is the home of the annual Ironman World Championship triathlon. Whether you're an avid hiker or a beginning bicyclist, a casual golfer or a tennis buff, you'll find plenty of land-based activities to lure you away from the sun and surf.

You can explore by bike, helicopter, ATV, or on horseback, or you can put on your hiking boots and use your own horsepower. No matter how you get around, you'll be treated to breathtaking backdrops along the Big Island's 266-mile coastline and within its 4,028 square miles (and still growing!). Aerial tours take in the latest eruption activity and lava flows, as well as the island's gorgeous tropical valleys, gulches, and coastal areas. Trips into the backcountry wilderness explore the rain forest, private ranch lands, coffee farms, and old sugar-plantation villages that offer a glimpse of Hawaii's earlier days.

AERIAL TOURS

There's nothing quite like the aerial view of a waterfall crashing down a couple of thousand feet into cascading pools, or watching lava flow to the ocean, where clouds of steam billow into the air. You can get this bird's-eye view from a helicopter or a small plane. Most operators are reputable and fly with strict adherence to FAA safety rules. How to get the best experience for your money? Before you choose a company, be a savvy traveler and ask the right questions. What kind of aircraft do they fly? What is their safety record?

Blue Hawaiian Helicopters. The Eco-Star helicopters here live up to their reputation, with a smooth, comfortable ride and a great view from every seat. Pilots are knowledgeable about the island and offer accurate information about the sights, but are not excessively chatty. Flights into the Waimanu Valley, passing 2,500-foot cliffs and dramatic waterfalls, will take your breath away. Prices are between $396 and $495 per person (depending on the type of helicopter) for the two-hour Big Island Spectacular, which also includes the Kilauea Volcano area. ⊠ *Waikoloa Heliport, Hwy. 19, Waikoloa* ☎ *808/961–5600* ⊕ *www.bluehawaiian.com.*

Fodor's Choice
★

Paradise Helicopters. This company offers a few great options no one else does. On landing tours, departing from Kona Airport, you can either touch down for a hike along the Hamakua Coast or for lunch in Hilo. In the six-passenger Bell 407, you can open small side windows for a little more air or to take photos without reflections on the glass. These aircraft can easily maneuver in the valleys, ensuring great views. In the four-passenger MD 500 helicopters, you can experience a very cool "doors off" adventure. Departing from the Hilo Airport, these flights allow you to feel the heat from the volcanoes. Flights start at $200 for

Take an off-road ATV adventure to see remote areas of Big Island's wilderness.

a 50-minute flight to $495 for a three-hour landing tour. Pilots, many of whom come from Coast Guard backgrounds, are knowledgeable and personable. Free shuttles are available to and from the aiports. ☎ *808/969–7392, 866/876–7422 ⊕ www.paradisecopters.com.*

ATV TOURS

A different way to experience the Big Island's rugged coastline and wild ranch lands is through an off-road adventure—a real backcountry experience. At higher elevations, the weather can be nippy and rainy, but views can be awesome. Protective gear is provided. Generally, you have to be 16 or older to ride your own ATV, though some outfitters allow children seven and older to be passengers.

ATV Outfitters Hawaii. These trips take in the scenic beauty of the rugged North Kohala Coast, traveling along coastal cliffs and into the forest in search of waterfalls. ATV Outfitters also offers double-seater ATVs for parents traveling with children or adults who don't feel comfortable operating their own vehicle. ⊠ *Old Sakamoto Store, Hwy. 270, Kapaau* ☎ *808/889–6000, 888/288–7288 ⊕ www.atvoutfittershawaii.com.*

Waipio Ride the Rim. This is one of the best ways to experience the extraordinary beauty at the top of the lush Waipio Valley. Fun and knowledgeable guides lead you to a gorgeous swimming pond, a lava-tube grotto, and a place to stand under a refreshing waterfall. You'll travel up to a series of lookouts where you can gaze all the way down to the black-sand beach. Bring a bathing suit and be prepared to get wet and muddy. The semichallenging terrain offers the ideal ATV experience. Prices start at $159 per person. ✉ *Waipio Valley Artworks Bldg., 48-5416 Kukuihaele Rd., Kukuihaele* ☎ *808/775–1450, 877/775–1450* ⊕ *www. RideTheRim.com.*

BIKING

The Big Island's biking trails and road routes range from easy to moderate coastal rides to rugged backcountry wilderness treks that will challenge the most serious cyclists. You can soak up the island's storied scenic vistas and varied geography—from tropical rain forest to rolling ranch country, from high country mountain meadows to dry lava deserts. It's dry, windy, and hot on Kona's and Kohala's coastal trails and cool, wet, and muddy in the Upcountry Waimea and Volcano areas, as well as in lower Puna. There are long distances between towns and few services available in the Kau, Puna, South Kona and Kohala Coast areas, so plan accordingly for weather, water, food, and lodging before setting out.

BEST SPOTS

Fodor'sChoice **Kulani Trails.** Kulani Trails has been called the best ride in the state—if
★ you really want to get gnarly. To reach the trailhead from the intersection of Highway 11 and Highway 19, take Highway 19 south about 4 miles, then turn right onto Stainback Highway and continue on 2½ miles, then turn right at the Waiakea Arboretum. Park near the gate. This technically demanding ride, which passes majestic eucalyptus trees, is for advanced cyclists.

Old Puna Trail. The Old Puna Trail is a 10½-mile ride through the subtropical jungle in Puna, one of the island's most isolated areas. You'll start out on a cinder road, which becomes a four-wheel-drive trail. If it's rained recently, you'll have to deal with some puddles—the first few of which you'll gingerly avoid until you give in and go barreling through the rest of them for the sheer fun of it. This is a great ride for all abilities and takes about 90 minutes. To get to the traihead from Highway 130, take Kaloli Road to Beach Road .

EQUIPMENT AND TOURS

If you want to strike out on your own, there are several rental shops in Kailua-Kona and a couple in Waimea and Hilo. Many resorts rent bicycles that can be used around the properties. Most outfitters can provide a bicycle rack for your car. All offer reduced rates for rentals longer than one day.

Cycle Station. This shop has a variety of bikes for rent, from hybrids to racing models. Rental runs from $20 to $75 per day, and can be delivered to your hotel. ✉ *73-4976 Kamanu St., Kailua-Kona* ☎ *808/327– 0087* ⊕ *www.cyclestationhawaii.com.*

Volcano Bike Tours. Volcano Bike Tours takes you on a three- or five-hour bike ride through the rain forests and past the craters of Hawaii Volcanoes National Park. After a mostly downhill ride through the park, the five-hour tour ends at the Volcano Winery for a tasting at one of the country's most unique wineries. The three-hour tour costs $99, and the five-hour tour costs $129. There's also a spectacular seven-hour

The rainy Hilo side of the Big Island means lush hills and valleys and many waterfalls.

sunset tour that takes you to the active lava flow. ⊠ *2352 Kalanianaole St., Hilo* ☎ *808/934–9199, 888/934–9199* ⊕ *www.bikevolcano.com.*

CAVING

The Kanohina Lava Tube system is about 1,000 years old and was used by the ancient Hawaiians for water collection and for shelter. More than 30 miles of these braided lava tubes have been mapped so far in the Kau District of the Big Island, near South Point. About 45 miles south of Kailua-Kona, these lava tubes are a great experience for cavers of all age levels and abilities.

Fodor'sChoice **Kula Kai Caverns.** Embark on a fantastic adventure with expert cav-
★ ers (not "spelunkers") at Kula Kai Caverns, located near South Point. Braided lava tubes attract scientists from around the world, who come to study and map them (more than 30 miles have been mapped so far). Tours start at $15 and range from strolls along walkways in the lighted sections to down-and-dirty adventures lasting two to four hours. Tours are tailored to your group's interest and abilities, and all gear is provided. Knowledgeable guides provide great information about the caves. Advance reservations are required. ⊠ *Kula Kai Estates, Lauhala at Kona Kai* ☎ *808/929–9725* ⊕ *kulakaicaverns.com.*

GOLF

For golfers, the Big Island is a big deal—starting with the Mauna Kea Golf Course, which opened in 1964 and remains one of the state's top courses. Black lava and deep blue sea are the predominant themes on the island. In the roughly 40 miles from the Kona Country Club out to the Mauna Kea Resort, nine courses are carved into sunny seaside lava plains, with four more in the hills above. Indeed, most of the Big Island's best courses are concentrated along the Kona Coast, statistically the sunniest spot in Hawaii. Vertically speaking, although the majority of courses are seaside or at least near sea level, three are located above 2,000 feet, another one at 4,200 feet. This is significant because in Hawaii temperatures drop 3°F for every 1,000 feet of elevation gained.

Greens Fees: Greens fees listed here are the highest course rates per round on weekdays for U.S. residents. Courses with varying weekend rates are noted in the individual listings. (Some courses charge non–U.S. residents higher prices.) Discounts are often available for resort guests and for those who book tee times on the Web, as well as for those willing to play in the afternoon instead of the morning. Twilight fees are also usually offered; call individual courses for information.

★ **Big Island Country Club.** Set 2,000 feet above sea level on the slopes of Mauna Kea, the Big Island Country Club is rather out of the way but well worth the drive. In 1997, Pete and Perry Dye created a gem that plays through upland woodlands—more than 2,500 trees line the fairways. On the par-5 15th, a giant tree in the middle of the fairway must be avoided with the second shot. Five lakes and a meandering natural mountain stream mean water comes into play on nine holes. The most dramatic is on the par-3 17th, where Dye creates a knockoff of his infamous 17th at the TPC at Sawgrass. ⊠ *71-1420 Mamalahoa Hwy., Kailua-Kona* ☎ *808/325–5044* ⊕ *www.bigislandcountryclub.com* ⅄ *18 holes. 7075 yds. Par 72. Greens fee: $70* ☞ *Facilities: Driving range, putting green, rental clubs, golf carts, pro shop, lessons.*

Hapuna Golf Course. Hapuna's challenging play and environmental sensitivity make it one of the island's most unique courses. Designed by Arnold Palmer and Ed Seay, the course is nestled into the natural contours of the land from the shoreline to about 700 feet above sea level. There are spectacular views of mountains and sea (Maui is often visible in the distance). Holes wind through kiawe scrub, beds of jagged lava, and tall fountain grasses. Hole 12 is favored for its beautiful views and challenging play. ⊠ *62-100 Kaunaoa Dr., Kamuela* ☎ *808/880–3000* ⊕ *www.princeresortshawaii.com/hapuna-golf* ⅄ *18 holes 6875 yds. Par 72. Greens fee: $125* ☞ *Facilities: Driving range, putting green, chipping green, golf carts, rental clubs, rental shoes, locker rooms, pro shop, lessons, restaurant.*

★ **Hualalai Resort.** Named for the volcanic peak that is the target off the first tee, the Nicklaus Course at Hualalai is semiprivate, open only to guests of the adjacent Four Seasons Resort Hualalai. From the forward and resort tees, this is perhaps Jack Nicklaus's most friendly course in Hawaii, but the back tees play a full mile longer. The par-3 17th plays across convoluted lava to a seaside green, and the view from the tee is so lovely, you may be tempted to just relax on the koa bench and enjoy the scenery. ⊠ *100 Kaupulehu Dr., Kohala Coast* ☎ *808/325–8480* ⊕ *www. fourseasons.com/hualalai* ⅄ *18 holes. 7117 yds. Par 72. Greens fee:*

$250 for all-day access ☞ *Facilities: Driving range, putting green, pull carts, golf carts, rental clubs, lessons, pro shop, restaurant, bar.*

★ **Kona Country Club.** This venerable country club offers two very different tests with the aptly named Ocean and Alii Mountain courses. The Ocean Course (William F. Bell, 1967) is a bit like playing through a coconut plantation, with a few remarkable lava features—such as the "blowhole" in front of the par-4 13th, where seawater propelled through a lava tube erupts like a geyser. The Alii Mountain Course (front nine, William F. Bell, 1983: back nine, Robin Nelson and Rodney Wright, 1992) plays a couple of strokes tougher than the Ocean and is the most delightful split personality you may ever encounter. Both nines share breathtaking views of Keauhou Bay, and elevation change is a factor in most shots. The most dramatic view on the front nine is from the tee of the par-3 fifth hole, one of the best golf vistas on the island. The back nine is links style, with less elevation change—except for the par-3 14th, which drops 100 feet from tee to green, over a lake. The routing, the sight lines and framing of greens, and the risk-reward factors on each hole make this one of the single best nines in Hawaii. ⊠ *78-7000 Alii Dr., Kailua-Kona* ☎ *808/322–2595* ⊕ *www.konagolf.com* ⚊ *Ocean Course: 18 holes. 6613 yds. Par 72. Greens fee: $165. Mountain Course: 18 holes. 6509 yds. Par 72. Greens fee: $150* ☞ *Facilities: Driving range, putting green, golf carts, rental clubs, lessons, restaurant, bar.*

★ **Mauna Kea Golf Course.** Originally opened in 1964, this golf course is one of the most revered in the state. It recently underwent a tee-to-green renovation by Rees Jones, son of the original architect, Robert Trent Jones Sr. New hybrid grasses were planted, the number of bunkers increased, and the overall yardage was expanded. The par-3 third hole is one of the most famous holes in the world (and one of the most photographed); you play from a cliff-side tee across a bay to a cliff-side green. Getting across the ocean is just half the battle because the third green is surrounded by seven bunkers, each one large and undulated. The course is definitely a shot-maker's paradise and follows Jones' "easy bogey/tough par" philosophy. Greens fees drop after 11 am. ⊠ *62-100 Mauna Kea Beach Dr., Kohala Coast* ☎ *808/882–5400* ⊕ *www.maunakeagolf.com* ⚊ *18 holes 7250 yds. Par 72. Greens fee: $250* ☞ *Facilities: Driving range, putting green, chipping green, golf carts, rental clubs, locker rooms, pro shop, lessons, shoe shine service, restaurant.*

Fodor'sChoice ★ **Mauna Lani Resort.** Black lava flows, lush green turf, white sand, and the Pacific's multihues of blue define the 36 holes at Mauna Lani. The South Course includes the par-3 15th across a turquoise bay, one of the most photographed holes in Hawaii. But it shares "signature hole" honors with the seventh. A long par 3, it plays downhill over convoluted patches of black lava, with the Pacific immediately to the left and

Most of the Big Island's top golf courses are located on the sunny Kona Coast.

a dune to the right. The North Course plays a couple of shots tougher. Its most distinctive hole is the 17th, a par 3 with the green set in a lava pit 50 feet deep. The shot from an elevated tee must carry a pillar of lava that rises from the pit and partially blocks your view of the green. ⌗ *68-1310 Mauna Lani Dr., Kohala Coast* ☎ *808/885–6655* ⊕ *www. maunalani.com* ⅄ *North Course: 18 holes. 6057 yds. Par 72. Greens fee: $215. South Course: 18 holes. 6025 yds. Par 72. Greens fee: $215* ☞ *Facilities: Driving range, putting green, golf carts, rental clubs, pro shop, lessons, restaurant, bar.*

Volcano Golf & Country Club. Just outside Volcanoes National Park—and barely a stone's throw from Halemaumau Crater—Volcano is by far Hawaii's highest course. At 4,200-feet elevation, shots tend to fly a bit farther than at sea level, even in the often cool, misty air. Because of the elevation and climate, Volcano is one of the few Hawaii courses with bent-grass putting greens. The course is mostly flat and holes play through stands of Norfolk pines, flowering *lehua* trees, and multitrunk *hau* trees. The uphill par-4 15th doglegs through a tangle of *hau*. ⌗ *Pii Mauna Dr., off Hwy. 11, Volcanoes National Park* ☎ *808/967–7331* ⊕ *www.volcanogolfshop.com* ⅄ *18 holes. 6106 yds. Par 72. Greens fee: $55* ☞ *Facilities: Driving range, putting green, golf carts, rental clubs, restaurant, bar.*

Fodor's Choice **Waikoloa Beach Resort.** Robert Trent Jones Jr. built the Beach Course at
★ Waikoloa (1981) on an old flow of crinkly *aa* lava, which he used to create holes that are as artful as they are challenging. The par-5 12th hole is one of Hawaii's most picturesque and plays through a chute of black lava to a seaside green. At the King's Course at Waikoloa (1990), Tom

Weiskopf and Jay Morrish built a very links-esque track. It turns out lava's natural humps and declivities remarkably replicate the contours of seaside Scotland. But there are a few island twists—such as seven lakes. This is "option golf," as Weiskopf and Morrish provide different risk-reward tactics on each hole. Beach and King's have separate clubhouses. ⊠ *600 Waikoloa Beach Dr., Waikoloa* 🕾 *808/886–7888* ⊕ *www.waikoloagolf.com* 🏌. *Beach Course: 18 holes. 6566 yds. Par 70. Greens fees: $135 for guests, $165 for nonguests. King's Course: 18 holes. 7074 yds. Par 72. Greens fees: $135 for guests, $165 for nonguests.* ⌲ *Facilities: Driving range, putting green, golf carts, rental clubs, lessons, restaurant, bar.*

Waikoloa Village Golf Course. Robert Trent Jones Jr., the same designer who created some of the most expensive courses on the Kohala Coast, designed this little gem, which is 20 minutes from the coast, in 1973. At a 450-foot elevation, it offers ideal playing conditions year-round. Holes run across rolling hills with sweeping mountain and ocean views. ⊠ *68-1792 Melia St., Waikoloa* 🕾 *808/883–9621* ⊕ *www.waikoloa.org* 🏌. *18 holes. 6230 yds. Par 72. Greens fee: $83.50* ⌲ *Facilities: Driving range, putting green, golf carts, rental clubs, lessons, restaurant, bar.*

HIKING

Meteorologists classify the world's weather into 13 climates. Eleven are here on the Big Island, and you can experience them all by foot on the many trails that lace the island. The ancient Hawaiians cut trails across the lava plains, through the rain forests, and up along the mountain heights. Many of these paths are still in use today. Part of the King's Trail at Anaehoomalu winds through a field of lava rocks covered with prehistoric carvings called petroglyphs. Many other trails, historic and modern, crisscross the huge Hawaii Volcanoes National Park and other parts of the island. Plus, the serenity of remote beaches, such as Papakolea Beach (Green Sand Beach), is accessible only to hikers.

Department of Land and Natural Resources, State Parks Division. For information on all the Big Island's state parks, contact the Department of Land and Natural Resources, State Parks Division. ⊠ *75 Aupuni St., Hilo* 🕾 *808/587–0300* ⊕ *www.hawaiistateparks.org.*

BEST SPOTS

Fodor'sChoice
★

Hawaii Volcanoes National Park. Hawaii Volcanoes National Park is perhaps the Big Island's premier area for hikers. The 150 miles of trails provide close-up views of fern and rainforest environments, cinder cones, steam vents, lava fields, rugged coastline and current lava flow activity. Day hikes range from easy to moderately difficult, and from one or two hours to a full day. For a bigger challenge, consider an overnight or multiday backcountry hike with a stay in a park cabin (available by a remote coast, in a lush forest, or atop frigid Mauna Loa). To do so, you must first obtain a free permit at the Kilauea Visitor Center. There are also daily guided hikes led by knowledgeable and friendly park rangers. ⊠ *Hwy. 11, 30 miles south of Hilo* 🕾 *808/985–6000* ⊕ *www. nps.gov/havo/index.htm.*

Keep an eye out for flora and fauna unique to the Big Island while hiking through the island's varied microclimates.

Kekaha Kai (Kona Coast) State Park. A pair of 1½-mile-long, unpaved roads lead to the Mahaiula Beach and Kua Bay, on opposite sides of the park. Connecting the two is the 4½-mile Ala Kahakai historic coastal trail. At Mahaiula, you'll find picnic tables and luas. Midway between the two white sand beaches you can hike to the summit of Puu Kuili, a 342-foot-high cinder cone with an excellent view of the coastline. It's dry and hot with no drinking water, so be sure to pack sunblock and water. ⊠ *Trailhead: Hwy. 19, about 2 miles north of Keahole–Kona International Airport.*

GUIDED HIKES

To get to some of the best trails and places, it's worth going with a skilled guide. Costs range from $95 to $185, and some hikes include picnic meals or refreshments, and gear such as binoculars, ponchos, and walking sticks. The outfitters mentioned here also offer custom-ized adventure tours.

Hawaii Forest & Trail. This locally owned and operated company has a reputation for great nature tours and eco-adventures of all kinds. The company has access to thousands of acres of restricted or private lands and employs certified guides who are experts in their fields. Try the Hakalau Forest National Wildlife Refuge Birdwatching Adventure, Kilauea Volcano Adventure, Kohala Waterfall Adventure, or the fun Kona Coffee & Craters Adventure. One of the most popular tours takes you to the top of Hawaii's tallest volcano for a sunset you'll never forget—as well as dinner and stargazing. ⊠ *74-5035B Queen Kaahahumanu Hwy., Kailua-Kona* ☎ *808/331–8505, 800/464–1993* ⊕ *www.hawaii-forest.com.*

Hawaiian Walkways. With the aid of knowledgeable guides, this company conducts several tours in unique spots—a Kona Cloud Forest botanical walk, a hike on Saddle Road between Mauna Kea and Mauna Loa, waterfall hikes and jaunts through Hawaii Volcanoes National Park—as well as custom-designed trips. ⊠ *45-3625 Mamane St., Honokaa* ☎ *808/775–0372, 800/457–7759* ⊕ *www.hawaiianwalkways.com.*

Kapoho Kine Adventures. This outfitter offers several interesting tours of Hawaii Volcanoes National Park and surrounding areas, including a 14-hour tour that allows you to explore the region by day and see the lava at night. There is also a shorter day tour and a separate evening tour complete with a Hawaiian-style barbecue dinner. Prices range from $89 to $179 per person. ⊠ *25 Waianuinui Ave., Hilo* ☎ *808/964–1000, 866/965–9552* ⊕ *kapohokine.com.*

HORSEBACK RIDING

With its *paniolo* (cowboy) heritage and the ranches it spawned, the Big Island is a great place for equestrians. Riders can gallop through green pastures, or saunter through Waipio Valley for a taste of Old Hawaii. *See Tours in the Hamakua Coast Exploring section for Waipio Valley rides.*

Cowboys of Hawaii. Take a horseback ride at historic Parker Ranch, one of the largest privately held cattle ranches in the country and the spot where *paniolo* (Hawaiian cowboys) rode for the first time. Along the way, you might see some of the more than 5,000 head of Hereford cattle as they are driven down from the slopes of Mauna Kea. Morning and afternoon rides start at $79 per person. ⊠ *Parker Ranch, 67-133 Pukalani Rd., Waimea* ☎ *808/885–5006* ⊕ *www.cowboysofhawaii.com.*

King's Trail Rides. Take a four-hour excursion down an Old Hawaiian trail to a small, uncrowded stretch of sand near Kealakekua Bay for snorkeling and lunch. A mask and snorkel is provided. The price is $135 per person. ⊠ *Hwy. 11, mile marker 111, Kealakekua* ☎ *808/323–2388* ⊕ *www.konacowboy.com.*

Continued on page 402

BIRTH OF THE ISLANDS

How did the volcanoes of the Hawaiian Islands evolve here, in the middle of the Pacific Ocean? The ancient Hawaiians believed that the volcano goddess Pele's hot temper was the key to the mystery; modern scientists contend that it's all about plate tectonics and one very hot spot.

Plate Tectonics & the Hawaiian Question: The theory of plate tectonics says that the Earth's surface is comprised of plates that float around slowly over the planet's molten interior. The vast majority of earthquakes and volcanic eruptions occur near plate boundaries—the San Francisco earthquakes in 1906 and 1989, for example, were the result of activity along the nearby San Andreas Fault, where the Pacific and North American plates meet. Hawaii, more than 1,988 miles from the nearest plate boundary, is a giant exception. For years scientists struggled to explain the island chain's existence—if not a fault line, what caused the earthquakes and volcanic eruptions that formed these islands?

What's a hotspot? In 1963, J. Tuzo Wilson, a Canadian geophysicist, argued that the Hawaiian volcanoes must have been created by small concentrated areas of extreme heat beneath the plates. Wilson hypothesized that there is a hotspot beneath the present-day position of the Big Island. Its heat produced a persistent source of magma by partly melting the Pacific Plate above it. The magma, lighter than the surrounding solid rock, rose through the mantle and crust to erupt onto the sea floor, forming an active seamount. Each flow caused the seamount to grow until it finally emerged above sea level as an island volcano. Plausible so far, but why then, is there not one giant Hawaiian island?

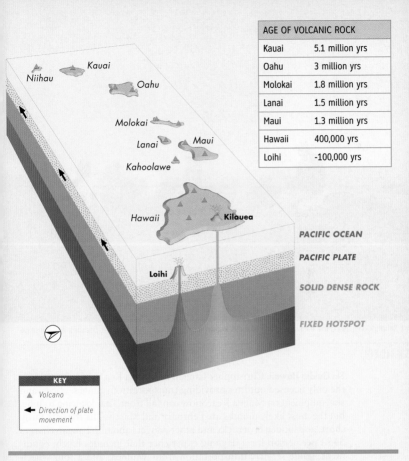

AGE OF VOLCANIC ROCK	
Kauai	5.1 million yrs
Oahu	3 million yrs
Molokai	1.8 million yrs
Lanai	1.5 million yrs
Maui	1.3 million yrs
Hawaii	400,000 yrs
Loihi	-100,000 yrs

PACIFIC OCEAN

PACIFIC PLATE

SOLID DENSE ROCK

FIXED HOTSPOT

KEY
▲ Volcano
◄ Direction of plate movement

Volcanoes on the Move: Wilson further suggested that the movement of the Pacific Plate itself eventually carries the island volcano beyond the hotspot. Cut off from its magma source, the island volcano becomes dormant. As the plate slowly moved, one island volcano would become extinct just as another would develop over the hotspot. After several million years, there is a long volcanic trail of islands and seamounts across the ocean floor. The oldest islands are those farthest from the hotspot. The exposed rocks of Kauai, for example, are about 5.1 million years old, but those on the Big Island are less than .5 million years old, with new volcanic rock still being formed.

An Island on the Way: Off the coast of the Big Island, the volcano known as Loihi is still submerged but erupting. Scientists long believed it to be a retired seamount volcano, but in the 1970s they discovered both old and new lava on its flanks, and in 1996 it erupted with a vengeance. It is believed that several thousand years from now, Loihi will be the newest addition to the Hawaiian Islands.

The Kohala Coast along the east side of Big Island is known for its shimmering blue water, beaches, and sunshine.

SKIING

Ski Guides Hawaii. Christopher Langan of Mauna Kea Ski Corporation is the only licensed outfitter providing transportation, guide services, and ski equipment on Mauna Kea. Snow can fall from Thanksgiving to June, but the most likely months are February and March. The runs are fairly short, and hidden lava rocks and other dangers abound. Langan charges $450 per person for a daylong experience that includes lunch, equipment, guide service, transportation from Waimea, and a four-wheel-drive shuttle back up the mountain after each ski run. Ski or snowboard rentals are $50 per day. *808/885–4188 ⊕ www.skihawaii.com.*

ZIPLINE TOURS

One of the few ways you can really see the untouched beauty of the Big Island is by flying over its lush forests, dense tree canopies, and glorious rushing waterfalls on a zipline course. You strap into a harness, get clipped to a cable and then zip, zip, zip your way through paradise. Most guide companies start you out easy on a slower, shorter line and by the end you graduate to faster, longer zips. It's an exhilarating adventure for all ages and has even been known to help some put aside their fear of heights (at least for a few minutes) to participate in the thrill ride. Check company credentials and specifics before you book to make sure your safety is their number one concern.

Big Island Eco Adventures II. This company knows ziplines—it built the first one on the Big Island. The three-hour tour takes you on eight ziplines and a 200-foot suspension bridge. You'll experience exhilarating crisscrossing thrills over the mountains and gulches of historic North Kohala, including the enormous Waianae Gulch. Along the way you get awesome views of the ocean, and, on clear days, all the way to Maui. If you are short on time, you can do the "quickie" Wiki Wiki Zip. ✉ *55-514 Hawi Rd., Hawi* ☎ *808/889–5111* ⊕ *thebigislandzipline.com.*

Kohala Zipline. This company features nine zips, five suspension bridges, and a thrilling, above-the-canopy adventure in the forest. Designed for all ability levels, the Kohala Zipline offers plenty of safety equipment, including a dual line allowing for easy braking. You'll be hundreds of feet above the ground and feel like a pro by the time you reach the last line. Two certified guides accompany groups of no more than eight. The price includes transportation from your hotel in a six-wheel-drive, military-style vehicle. This course is especially fun for older kids. ✉ *54-3676 Akoni Pule Hwy., Kapaau* ☎ *808/331–3620, 800/464–1993* ⊕ *www.kohalazipline.com.*

SHOPPING

Updated by Karen Anderson

Residents like to complain that there isn't a lot of great shopping on the Big Island, but unless you're searching for winter coats or high-tech toys, you can find plenty to deplete your pocketbook.

Dozens of shops in Kailua-Kona offer a range of souvenirs from far-flung corners of the globe and plenty of local coffee and foodstuffs to take home to everyone you left behind. Housewares and artworks made from local materials (lava rock, coconut, koa, and milo wood) fill the shelves of small boutiques and galleries throughout the island. Upscale shops in the resorts along the Kohala Coast carry high-end clothing and accessories, as do a few boutiques scattered around the island. Galleries and gift shops, many showcasing the work of local artists, fill historic buildings in Waimea, Kainaliu, Holualoa, and Hawi. Hotel shops generally offer the most attractive and original resort wear but, as with everything else at resorts, the prices run higher than elsewhere on the island.

In general, stores on the Big Island open at 9 or 10 am and close by 6 pm. Hilo's Prince Kuhio Plaza stays open until 8 pm on weekdays and 9 pm on Friday and Saturday. In Historic Kona Village, most shopping plazas geared to tourists remain open until 9 pm. Grocery stores such as KTA Superstore are open until 11 pm.

KAILUA-KONA

SHOPPING CENTERS

Coconut Grove Marketplace. This meandering labyrinth of buildings includes cafés, restaurants, boutiques, a frozen-yogurt shop, and several art galleries. At night, locals gather to watch the outdoor sand volleyball games held in the courtyard or to grab a couple of beers at one of several sports bars. Jack's Diving Locker offers gear and scuba lessons. ✉ *75-5795 Alii Dr.*

Kaloko Light Industrial Park. This large retail complex includes Costco—the best place to stock up on food if you're staying in a condo for a week or more. For lunch, stop at Ceviche Dave's and enjoy some fresh fish. ⊠ *Off Hwy. 19 and Hina Lani St., near Keahole-Kona International Airport.*

Kona Commons. This new center features big-box retailers like Sports Authority (for snorkel and swim gear), as well as an array of fast-food standbys like Dairy Queen, Subway, Taco Del Mar, and Panda Express. The best-kept secret is Ultimate Burger, featuring locally produced beef and delicious homemade fries. Take the kids to Genki Sushi, where fresh sushi is delivered to patrons via a conveyer belt. Relocated from its previous site in Kailua Village, Kona Wine Market offers the best selection of premium wines, liquors, and spirits in Kona, along with some gourmet and gift items. ⊠ *75-5450 Makala Blvd.*

Kona Marketplace. On the *mauka* (mountain) side of Alii Drive, this tourist destination in the heart of Kailua Village includes galleries, clothing shops, souvenirs, and a dive-y karaoke bar, Sam's Hideaway. The best-kept secret here is You Make the Roll sushi shop, offering shaded outdoor seating and affordable sushi to go. ⊠ *75-5744 Alii Dr.*

Makalapua Center. This shopping center attracts islanders for the great bargains at Kmart, plus island-influenced clothing, jewelry, and housewares at the upscale Macy's. There's also one of the island's largest movie theaters here. ⊠ *Kamakaeha Ave. at Hwy. 19.*

ARTS AND CRAFTS

★ **Antiques and Orchids.** Housed in a historic building, this shop lives up to its name by offering a comprehensive collection of antiques and Hawaiiana interspersed with orchids of assorted colors and varieties. If you're on your way to Volcano, stop to enjoy a cup of Kona coffee served in antique china cups at the store's quaint coffee shop. ⊠ *81-6224 Mamalahoa Hwy., Captain Cook* ☎ *808/323–9851.*

Fodor'sChoice ★ **Eclectic Craftsman.** This longtime favorite occupies a beautiful space at the Kona Inn Shopping Village. Brimming with handmade Hawaiian collectibles, the boutique focuses on local art and crafts. The 60 Big Island artists represented here include woodworker Craig Nichols and renowned painter Avi Kiraty. Affordable gifts range from bookmarks to salad servers to wine-bottle toppers. You won't find these items anywhere else, and they're all made in Hawaii. ⊠ *Kona Inn Shopping Village, 75-5744 Alii Dr.* ☎ *808/334–0562.*

Fodor'sChoice ★ **Hula Lamps of Hawaii.** Located in Kailua-Kona, this one-of-a-kind shop features the bronze creations of Charles Moore. Inspired by the vintage hula-girl lamps of the 1930s, Moore creates art pieces sought by visitors and residents alike. Mix and match with an array of hand-painted lamp shades. ⊠ *74-5599 Luhia St., Unit F-5* ☎ *808/326–9583.*

CLOTHING

★ **Hilo Hattie.** The well-known clothier matches his-and-her aloha wear and carries a huge selection of casual clothes, local art, books, music, jewelry, and souvenirs. ■TIP→ **Call for free transportation from nearby hotels.** ⊠ *75-5597 Palani Rd.* ☎ *808/329–7200* ⊕ *www.hilohattie.com.*

Honolua Surf Company. Surfer chic, compliments of Roxy, Volcom, and the like is on offer here for both men and women. This is a great place to look for a bikini or board shorts, or to pick up a cool, casual T-shirt or beautifully embroidered sweat jacket. A second location at the Waikoloa Beach Resort focuses on *wahine* (women's) apparel. ⊠ *Kona Inn Shopping Village, 75-5744 Alii Dr.* ☎ *808/329–1001* ⊕ *www. honoluasurf.com.*

Paradise Found. This reputable shop carries contemporary silk and rayon clothing for women. Located in the Upcountry town of Kainaliu, there's also a branch at Keauhou Shopping Center. ⊠ *79-740 Mamalahoa Hwy., Kainaliu* ☎ *808/322–2111*

FOOD AND WINE

Kailua Candy Company. This chocolate company has been satisfying sweet tooths for more than three decades with decadent desserts and sinful bites of chocolate heaven. Many truffles and candies incorporate local ingredients (passion-fruit truffles and chocolate-covered mango—yum). There are also a variety of cheesecakes and mousse cakes that will melt in your mouth. Of course, tasting is part of the fun. Through a glass wall you can watch the chocolate artists at work Monday to Saturday from 9 to 5. ⊠ *Kamanu St. and Kauholo St.* ☎ *808/329–2522* ⊕ *www. kailuacandy.com.*

Kona Coffee & Tea Company. Its location across from the Honokohau Harbor makes this family-owned coffee company's retail outlet a good bet for some easy gourmet gift shopping—or just a coffee or tea stop. Try different roasts or a selection of flavored coffees from the coffee bar, and shop for other Hawaiian-made treats, from honey and jams to chocolate-covered coffee beans. The shop is behind the Tesoro gas station. ⊠ *74-5035 Queen Kaahumanu Hwy., 4 miles south of the airport, Kailua-Kona* ☎ *808/329–6577* ⊕ *www.konacoffeeandtea.com.*

Kona Wine Market. Kona's only wine market carries both local and imported varietals, gourmet foods, and local products (coffee or macadamia nuts, for example). As a bonus, the shop will deliver wine or any other product to your hotel. ⊠ *Kona Commons, 74-5450 Makala Blvd.* ☎ *808/329–9400* ⊕ *www.konawinemarket.com.*

GALLERIES

Pacific Fine Art. One of the oldest and largest galleries in Kona, Pacific Fine Art represents 42 artists from across the globe. The gallery features everything from original oil and acrylic paintings to limited editions, sculptures, glass, and raku ceramic pieces. ⊠ *Kona Inn Shopping Village, 75-5744 Alii Dr.* ☎ *808/329–5009.*

MARKETS

Alii Gardens Marketplace. This cluster of about 50 vendor stalls has beautiful tropical flowers, produce, coffee, jewelry, clothing, and even ukuleles. It's open Wednesday to Sunday 9 to 5. ⊠ *75-6129 Alii Dr., 1½ miles south of Kona Inn Shopping Village.*

Keauhou Farmers' Market. This cheerful market is the place to go on Saturday morning, and for good reason: live music, plus local produce (much of it organic), goat cheese, honey, meat, flowers, coffee, and macadamia nuts. Be sure to try Earthly Delight's fresh-baked pastries. Sample Lotus Cafe's savory breakfast offerings and fresh-squeezed sugarcane juice. ⊠ *Keauhou Shopping Center, 78-6831 Alii Dr.* ⊕ *www. keauhoufarmersmarket.com.*

Kona Inn Farmers' Market. An awesome flower vendor creates custom arrangements while you wait at this touristy farmers' market. A glass artist offers nice works of fine art. Here you can find the best prices on fresh produce anywhere in Kona. The market is held in the parking lot at the corner of Hualalai Road and Alii Drive, Wednesday to Sunday from 7 to 3. ⊠ *75-7544 Alii Dr.*

Kona International Market. Vendors come from other islands to sell fresh flowers, local produce, handmade crafts, and random collectibles at this open-air tourist destination. It's open daily 9 to 5. There's also a shaded food court. Be sure to check out Mike's Just Barbecuing for fantastic pulled pork and brisket, slow-cooked over kiawe wood for a savory flavor. ⊠ *Luhia St.* ⊕ *www.konainternationalmarket.com.*

THE KOHALA COAST

SHOPPING CENTERS

Kawaihae Harbor Center. This oceanfront shopping plaza houses the exquisite Harbor Gallery, which represents more than 150 Big Island artists. Take a look inside before or after your meal at the acclaimed Cafe Pesto, Kohala Burger and Taco, or Kawaihae Kitchen Sushi and Take-Out. Also here are Mountain Gold Jewelers, the Kawaihae Deli, and Kohala Divers. ⊠ *Hwy. 270, Kawaihae.*

Kings' Shops at Waikoloa Beach Resort. Here you can find fine stores such as Under the Koa Tree, with its upscale gift items crafted by artisans, along with such high-end chains as Coach, Tiffany, L'Occitane, and Louis Vuitton. Gourmet offerings include Merriman's Market Cafe, Roy's Waikoloa Bar & Grill, and the Eddie Aikau Restaurant and Surf Museum. Oahu-based Martin and MacArthur joined the tenant roster in late 2011, featuring koa furniture and fine accessories. ⊠ *Waikoloa Beach Resort, 250 Waikoloa Beach Dr., Waikoloa* ☎ *808/886–8811* ⊕ *www.waikoloabeachresort.com.*

The Shops at Mauna Lani. This best part about this complex is its roster of restaurants, including Tommy Bahama's Tropical Café, Ruth's Chris Steakhouse, and Monstera. The boutiques are a bit overpriced, but you can find tropical apparel at Jams World, high-end housewares at Oasis, and original art at Lahaina Galleries and the Third Dimension Gallery. Kids love the movie theater, with the first "4-D" screens in Hawaii. ⊠ *68-1330 Mauna Lani Dr., Kohala Coast* ☎ *808/885–9501* ⊕ *www. shopsatmaunalani.com.*

Waikoloa Queens' Marketplace. The largest shopping complex on the Kohala Coast, Queens' Marketplace houses several clothing shops, a jewelry store, a gallery, several gift shops, a food court, and a few restaurants, including Sansei Seafood Restaurant & Sushi Bar and Romano's Macaroni Grill. Island Gourmet Markets is a 20,000-square-foot grocery store. The marketplace sits adjacent to a performing arts amphitheater. ⊠ *Waikoloa Beach Resort, 201 Waikoloa Beach Dr., Waikoloa* ☎ *808/886–8822* ⊕ *www.waikoloabeachresort.com.*

ARTS AND CRAFTS

Elements Jewelry & Fine Crafts. John Flynn showcases his exquisite jewelry pieces from his shop in Hawi. Look for the delicate silver lei and gold waterfalls. The shop also carries carefully chosen gifts, including unusual ceramics, paintings, prints, and glass items. ⊠ *55-3413 Akoni Pule Hwy., Hawi* ☎ *808/889–0760* ⊕ *www.elementsjewelryandcrafts.com.*

Hawaiian Quilt Collection. The Hawaiian quilt is a work of art that is prized and passed down through generations. At this store you find everything from hand-quilted purses and bags to wall hangings and blankets. You can even get a take-home kit and make your very own Hawaiian quilt, if you have the time. ⊠ *Waikoloa Queens' Marketplace, 201 Waikoloa Beach Dr., Waikoloa* ☎ *808/886–0494* ⊕ *www. hawaiianquilts.com.*

Island Pearls. This boutique carries a wide selection of fine pearl jewelry, including Tahitian black pearls, South Sea white and golden pearls, and chocolate Tahitian pearls. Also look for freshwater pearls in the shell. Prices are high but you're paying for quality and beauty. ⊠ *Waikoloa Queens' Marketplace, 201 Waikoloa Beach Dr., Waikoloa* ☎ *808/886– 4817* ⊕ *www.waikoloabeachresort.com.*

CLOTHING

As Hawi Turns. This North Kohala shop, housed in the historic 1932 Toyama Building, adds a sophisticated touch to resort wear with items made of hand-painted silk in tropical designs by local artists. There are vintage and secondhand treasures, jewelry, and handmade ukuleles by David Gomes. ⊠ *55-3412 Akoni Pule Hwy., Hawi* ☎ *808/889–5023.*

Blue Ginger. The Waikoloa branch of this 25-year fashion veteran offers really sweet matching aloha outfits for the entire family. ⊠ *Waikoloa Queens' Marketplace, 201 Waikoloa Beach Dr., Waikoloa* ☎ *808/886– 0022* ⊕ *www.blueginger.com.*

Cinnamon Girl. Popular for its original print dresses, skirts, and tops for women and girls, this store's feminine, flirty outfits are all designed in Hawaii and offer a contemporary twist on traditional aloha wear. In addition to clothing, the boutique carries jewelry, hats, slippers, stuffed animals, and other trinkets and toys. ⊠ *Kings' Shops at Waikoloa Beach Resort, 250 Waikoloa Beach Dr., Waikoloa* ☎ *808/886–0241* ⊕ *www. cinnamongirl.com.*

Persimmon. This darling little boutique that's stocked with trendy women's clothing from lines such as Three Dots, Trinity, Sky, Michael Stars, Hard Tail, and Zen Knits also carries fantastic purses imported from Indonesia, as well as locally made jewelry. Other gift items include funky stationery and cards, and island-themed bath and body products. ⊠ *Waikoloa Queens' Marketplace, 201 Waikoloa Beach Dr., Waikoloa* ☎ *808/886–0303* ⊕ *www.persimmonboutique.com* ⊠ *Waikoloa Queens' Marketplace, 201 Waikoloa Beach Dr., Waikoloa* ☎ *808/886– 0303* ⊕ *www.persimmonboutique.com.*

Reyn's. Reyn Spooner's clothing has been well known throughout Hawaii since 1959. The store offers aloha shirts for both men and boys, men's shorts, and some dresses for women and girls. The aloha shirts, by the way, are high quality—and high price. ⊠ *Waikoloa Queens' Marketplace, 201 Waikoloa Beach Dr., Waikoloa* ☎ *808/886–1162* ⊕ *www.reyns.com.*

GALLERIES

Ackerman Fine Art Gallery. This gallery is truly a family affair. Painter Gary Ackerman's daughter, Alyssa, and her husband, Ronnie, run the gallery that showcases several family members' art. Don't miss the fine and varied collection of gifts for sale in their side-by-side gallery, cafe, and gift shop near the King Kamehameha statue. ⊠ *54-3897 Akoni Pule Hwy., Kapaau* ☎ *808/889–5971* ⊕ *www.ackermangalleries.com.*

Gallery at Bamboo. Inside Bamboo, one of the island's favorite eateries, this gallery seduces visitors with elegant koa-wood furniture pieces. It also has a wealth of gift items such as boxes, jewelry, and even aloha shirts. ⊠ *Hwy. 270, Hawi* ☎ *808/889–1441* ⊕ *www. bamboorestaurant.info.*

Rankin Gallery. Watercolorist and oil painter Patrick Louis Rankin showcases his own work in his shop in a restored plantation store next to the bright-green Chinese community-and-social hall, on the way to Pololu Valley. The building sits right on the road at the curve, in the Palawa *ahupuaa* (land division) near Kapaau. ⊠ *53-4380 Akoni Pule Hwy., Kapaau* ☎ *808/889–6849* ⊕ *www.patricklouisrankin.net.*

WAIMEA

SHOPPING CENTERS

Parker Ranch Center. With a snazzy ranch-style motif, this shopping hub includes a supermarket, some great local eateries, a coffee shop, natural foods store, and some clothing boutiques. The Parker Ranch Store and Parker Ranch Visitor Center and Museum are also here, and the Kahilu Center next door hosts plays and musical entertainment most nights. Check out Village Burgers and the Liliokoi Cafe for delicious and affordable meals. ⊠ *67-1185 Mamalahoa Hwy.* ⊕ *www. parkerranchcenterads.com.*

Parker Square. Browse the boutiques here, where you may find books and beads at Sweet Wind, locally crafted gold jewelry at Kamuela Goldsmiths, or salads, sandwiches, and Kona coffee at Waimea Coffee Company. Although Gallery of Great Things is the center's star attraction, Waimea General Store is packed with cool Hawaiian collectibles, books, cookware, and designer toiletries. ⊠ *65-1279 Kawaihae Rd.*

ARTS AND CRAFTS

Fodor's Choice
★
Gallery of Great Things. At this Parker Square shop, you might lose yourself exploring the treasure trove of fine art and collectibles in every price range. For almost three decades, the gallery has represented hundreds of local artists and has provided a low-key, unhurried atmosphere for customers. The "things" include: hand-stitched quilts, ceramic sculptures, vintage kimonos, original paintings, koa-wood furniture, etched

glassware, Niihau shell lei, and feather art by Beth McCormick. ⊠ *65-1279 Kawaihae Rd.* ☏ *808/885–7706.*

Harbor Gallery. Though it carries some of the usual ocean-scene schlock, the Harbor Gallery has one of the better and more unique selections of art on the island. Expect to find fine art, furniture, and decorative pieces made with koa and other native woods. ⊠ *Kawaihae Harbor Center, Hwy. 270, Kawaihae* ☏ *808/882–1510* ⊕ *www.harborgallery.biz.*

FOOD AND WINE

Kamuela Liquor Store. From the outside it doesn't look like much, but this shop sells the best selection of spirits, wines, and gourmet foods on the island. Wine-and-cheese tastings take place Friday afternoons—the store offers an extensive selection of artisanal cheeses from around the world, including France, Italy, Spain, England, Switzerland, and Wales. Favorites like pâté and duck mousse round out the inventory, and everything is priced within reason. ⊠ *64-1010 Mamalahoa Hwy.* ☏ *808/885–4674.*

THE HAMAKUA COAST

ARTS AND CRAFTS

Glass from the Past. The best place to shop for a quirky gift or just to poke around, Glass from the Past is a truly unique store chock-full of antiques, vintage clothing, a colorful assortment of old bottles, and ephemera. ⊠ *28-1672 Old Mamalahoa Hwy., Honomu* ☏ *808/963–6449.*

GALLERIES

Waipio Valley Artworks. In this remote gallery you can find finely crafted wooden bowls, koa furniture, paintings, and jewelry—all made by local artists. There's also a great little café where you can pick up a sandwich or ice cream before descending into Waipio Valley. ⊠ *Off Hwy. 240, Kukuihaele* ☏ *808/775–0958* ⊕ *www.waipiovalleyartworks.com.*

Woodshop Gallery. Run by local artists Peter and Jeanette McLaren, this Honomu gallery showcases their woodwork and photography collections along with beautiful ceramics, woodwork, photography, glass, and paintings from other Big Island artists. The McLarens also serve up plate lunches, shave ice, homemade ice cream, and espresso to hungry tourists in the adjoining café. Their shop next door, called Same-Same, But Different, features made-in-Hawaii clothing and small gifts. The historic building still has a soda fountain dating from 1935. ⊠ *28-1692 Old Government Rd., Honomu* ☏ *808/963–6363* ⊕ *www.woodshopgallery.com.*

HILO

SHOPPING CENTERS

Hilo Shopping Center. This shopping plaza encloses 40 shops, including Lanky's Pastries and Island Naturals Market and Deli. Restaurants include Happy Valley Seafood, Sunlight Cafe, and Restaurant Niwa. You'll also find everyhing from a day spa to a pharmacy to a trendy boutique. There's plenty of free parking. ⊠ *345 Kekuanaoa St., at Kilauea Ave.*

Prince Kuhio Plaza. Hilo's most comprehensive mall, Prince Kuhio Plaza is an indoor shopping center where you'll find entertainment and dining options including KFC, Kuhio Grille, Hot Dog on a Stick, Cinnabon, and the Big Island's only IHOP. Grab a bite at Maui Tacos before heading to the multiplex, stadium-seating movie theater, or drop the kids off at the arcade (located near the food court) while you browse the stores. ⊠ *111 E. Puainako St., at Hwy. 11* ☎ *808/959–3555* ⊕ *www.princekuhioplaza.com.*

ARTS AND CRAFTS

Most Irresistible Shop. This place lives up to its name by stocking unique gifts from around the Pacific, be it pure Hawaiian ohia lehua honey, Kau coffee, or tinkling wind chimes. ⊠ *256 Kamehameha Ave.* ☎ *808/935–9644.*

BOOKS AND MAGAZINES

♻ **Basically Books.** More than a bookstore, this bay-front shop stocks one of Hawaii's largest selections of maps, including topographical and relief maps. You'll find books about Hawaii, including great choices for children. It also has the largest selection of Hawaiian music in Hilo. ⊠ *160 Kamehameha Ave.* ☎ *808/961–0144, 800/903–6277* ⊕ *www.basicallybooks.com.*

CLOTHING AND SHOES

★ **Hilo Hattie.** The east-coast outlet of the well-known clothier is slightly smaller than its Kailua-Kona cousin, but offers plenty of the same his-and-her aloha wear, casual clothes, slippers, jewelry, and souvenirs. ⊠ *Prince Kuhio Plaza, 111 E. Puainako St.* ☎ *808/961–3077* ⊕ *www.hilohattie.com.*

★ **Sig Zane Designs.** This acclaimed boutique sells distinctive island wearables with bold colors and motifs designed by the legendary Sig Zane, well-known for his artwork honoring native flora and fauna. All apparel is handcrafted in Hawaii and is found nowhere else. ⊠ *122 Kamehameha Ave.* ☎ *808/935–7077* ⊕ *www.sigzane.com.*

FOOD

★ **Big Island Candies.** A local legend in the cookie- and chocolate-making business, Big Island Candies is a must-see if you have a sweet tooth. Enjoy a free cookie sample and a cup of Kona coffee as you watch sweets being made through a plate-glass window. Big Island Candies has a long list of interesting and tasty products, but it is best known for its chocolate-dipped shortbread cookies. ⊠ *585 Hinano St.* ☎ *808/935–8890* ⊕ *www.bigislandcandies.com.*

Two Ladies Kitchen. This hole-in-the-wall confections shop has made a name for itself thanks to its pillowy *mochi* (Japanese rice pounded into a sticky paste and molded into shapes). The proprietors are best known for their huge ripe strawberries wrapped in a white mochi covering. These won't last as long as a box of chocolates—most mochi items are only good for two or three days. To guarantee you get your fill, call and place your order ahead of time. ⊠ *274 Kilauea Ave.* ☎ *808/961–4766* ☽ *Closed Sun.–Tues.*

HOME DECOR

Dragon Mama. Step into this popular downtown Hilo spot to find authentic Japanese fabrics, futons, and antiques, along with a limited but elegant selection of clothing, sleepwear, and slippers for women. Handmade comforters, pillows, and futon pads are made of natural fibers. ⊠ *266 Kamehameha Ave.* ☎ *808/934–9081* ⊕ *www. dragonmama.com.*

MARKETS

Fodor'sChoice
★

Hilo Farmers' Market. The 200 vendors here sell a profusion of tropical flowers, locally grown produce, aromatic honey, tangy goat cheese, and fresh baked goods at extraordinary prices. This colorful, open-air market—the most popular on the island—opens for business Wednesday and Saturday from 6 am to 4 pm. A smaller market on the other days features 20 to 30 vendors. ⊠ *Kamehameha Ave. and Mamo St.* ☎ *808/933–1000* ⊕ *www.hilofarmersmarket.com.*

SPAS

Updated
by Karen
Anderson

The Big Island's spa directors have produced menus full of "only in Hawaii" treatments well worth a holiday splurge. Local specialties include *lomilomi* massages, hot-lava-stone massages, and scrubs and wraps that incorporate plenty of coconut, ginger, orchids, and macadamia nuts. Also expect to find Swedish and deep-tissue massages and, at some spas, Thai massage. And in romantic Hawaii, couples can be pampered side by side in a variety of offerings. ■TIP→ **Lomilomi massage is a quintessential Hawaiian deep-tissue massage, and most practitioners are happy to adjust the pressure to your needs.** Most of the full-service spas on the Big Island are located at the resorts. With the exception of the Four Seasons Spa at Hualalai, these spas are open to anyone. In fact, many of the hotels outsource management of their spas, and there is no difference in price for guests and nonguests, although guests have the bonus of receiving in-room services.

KAILUA-KONA

Hoola Spa at the Sheraton Keauhou Bay. The Sheraton Keauhou Bay occupies one of the prettier corners of the island. That said, it's too bad that the Hoola Spa doesn't fully take advantage of its location, although there are plenty of windows with pretty views of the bay, and several outdoor treatment balconies. The spa menu includes a variety of locally influenced treatments, and the warm lava-rock massage is a little slice of heaven. The packages are an excellent deal, combining several services for far less than you would pay à la carte. For couples, the spa offers an ocean-side massage on a balcony overlooking the water, followed by a dip in a whirlpool bath. ⊠ *Sheraton Keauhou Bay, 78-128 Ehukai St.,*

Kailua-Kona ☎ *808/930–4848* ⊕ *www.sheratonkeauhou.com* ☞ *$120 50-min lomilomi massage; $225–$380 packages. Hair salon, hot tub, sauna, steam room. Services: Aromatherapy, body scrubs and wraps, facials, massage, waxing.*

THE KONA COAST

Fodor'sChoice ★ **Mamalahoa Hot Tubs and Massage.** Tucked into a residential neighborhood above Kealekekua, this little gem is a welcome alternative to the large resort spas. Soaking tubs are made of the finest quality wood, and they are enclosed in their own thatched gazebo with portholes in the roof for your stargazing pleasure. Tastefully laid out and run, there's no "hot tub party" vibe here, just a pleasant soak followed by, if you like, an hour-long massage. Mamalahoa offers *lomilomi,* Swedish, deep-tissue, and a Hawaiian hot-stone massage performed with lava rocks collected from around the island. Indulge in some romance with a twilight soak from 7:30 to 9 pm at $40 per couple. In addition to its secret-hideaway ambience, Mamalahoa's prices are lower than any other spa on the island. Call ahead for appointments. ⊠ *81-1016 St. John's Rd., Kealakekua* ☎ *808/323–2288* ⊕ *www.mamalahoa-hottubs. com* ⊗ *Wed.–Sat. noon–9 pm* ☞ *$30 60-min soak; $95 30-min soak plus 60-min lomilomi, Swedish, or deep-tissue massage, $150 30-min soak plus 90-min hot-stone massage.*

THE KOHALA COAST

★ **Kohala Spa at the Hilton Waikoloa Village.** The orchids that you'll find all over the Big Island suffuse the signature treatments at the Kohala Spa. By the end of the relaxing Orchid Isle Wrap, you're completely immersed in the scent. The island's volcanic character is also expressed in several treatments, as well as in the design of the lava-rock soaking tubs. Locker rooms are outfitted with a wealth of beauty and bath products; the spa's retail facility offers a signature line of Coco-Mango lotions, body washes, and shampoos. Open-air cabanas provide a delightful spot for a massage overlooking the ocean. The fitness center is equipped with the latest generation of machines, and group classes are plentiful, with everything from water aerobics to yoga. ⊠ *Hilton Waikoloa Village, 69-425 Waikoloa Beach Dr., Hilo* ☎ *808/886–2828, 800/445–8667* ⊕ *www.kohalaspa.com* ☞ *$145 50-min lomilomi massage, $489–$599 half-day packages. Hair salon, hot tubs, sauna, steam room. Gym with: Cardiovascular machines, free weights, weight-training equipment. Services: Aromatherapy, body scrubs and wraps, facials, massage. Classes and programs: aquaerobics, personal training, Pilates, Spinning, yoga.*

★ **Mandara Spa at the Waikoloa Beach Marriott Resort.** Overlooking the hotel's main pool with a distant view of the ocean, Mandara offers a very complete, if not unique, spa menu, with more facial options than you'll find at the island's other spas. Mandara, which operates spas all over the world, uses Elemis and La Therapie products in spa and salon treatments. The spa menu contains the usual suspects—*lomilomi,* scrubs, and wraps—but it incorporates local ingredients (lime and ginger in the scrubs, warm coconut milk in the wraps), and the facility, which fuses contemporary and traditional Asian motifs, is beautiful. ⊠ *Waikoloa Beach Marriott Resort, 69-275 Waikoloa Beach Dr., Waikoloa* ☎ *808/886–8191 ⊕ www.mandaraspa.com ⌣ $145 50-min lomilomi massage; $450–$500 half-day packages. Steam room. Gym with: Cardiovascular machines, free weights, weight-training equipment.*

Mauna Kea Spa by Mandara. Mandara Spas blends European, Balinese, and indigenous treatments to create the ultimate spa experience. Things are no different at this spa at the Mauna Kea Beach Hotel. Though the facility is on the smaller side, the excellent treatments are up to the company's exacting standards. Try the Elemis Tri-Enzyme Resurfacing Facial or, even better, the Mandara Four Hand Massage, where two therapists work out the kinks simultaneously. Hawaiian traditional *lomilomi* is also available. The hotel operates a separate hair salon that offers manicures and pedicures in addition to standard salon services. ⊠ *Mauna Kea Beach Hotel, 69-100 Mauna Kea Beach Dr., Kohala Coast* ☎ *808/882–5630 ⊕ www.mandaraspa.com ⌣ $181 50-min lomilomi. Services: Body treatments, facials, massage, waxing. Gym with: Cardiovascular machines, weight-training equipment. Classes and programs: Yoga.*

Fodor'sChoice
★

Mauna Lani Spa. If you're looking for a one-of-a-kind experience, this is your destination. Most treatments take place in outdoor *hales* (houses) surrounded by lava rock. Wonderful therapists offer a mix of the traditional standbys (*lomilomi* massage, moisturizing facials) and innovative treatments influenced by ancient traditions and incorporating local products. One exfoliating body treatment is self-administered in one of the outdoor saunas. Watsu therapy, which mimics the feeling of being in the womb, takes place in a 1,000-square-foot grotto between two lava tubes. You feel totally weightless, thanks to some artfully applied weights and the buoyancy of the warm salt water. It's a great treatment for people with disabilities that keep them from enjoying a traditional massage. The aesthetic treatments on the menu incorporate high-end products from Epicuran and Emminence, so a facial will have a real and lasting therapeutic effect on your skin. The spa also offers a full regimen of fitness and yoga classes. ⊠ *Mauna Lani Resort, 68-1365 Pauoa Rd., Kohala Coast* ☎ *808/881–7922 ⊕ www.maunalani.com ⌣ $159 50-min lomilomi massage; $345–$799 packages. Hair salon, hot tub, sauna, steam room. Gym with: Cardiovascular machines, free weights, weight-training equipment. Services: Aquatic therapy, baths, body wraps, facials, massage, nail treatment, scrubs, waxing and tinting. Classes and programs: body sculpting, kickboxing, personal training, Pilates, Spinning, weight training, yoga.*

Paul Brown Salon & Spa at the Hapuna Beach Prince Hotel. It's not unusual for locals to drive an hour each way to get their hair styled here. The salon is still the center of the operation, but today it's joined by a full-service spa—nicely designed to let in lots of light—that has an extensive menu of massages, facials, and body treatments. The most popular massage is the *lomilomi* (traditional Hawaiian massage), but don't overlook the spa's unique body treatments. Consider the seaweed wrap, the detoxifying volcanic clay treatment, or the salt-and-aloe exfoliation. This is the best place for waxing. You can use the gym at the Hapuna Golf Course's clubhouse, accessible via a free shuttle. ✉ *62-100 Kaunaoa Dr., Kohala Coast* ☎ *808/880–3335* ⊕ *www.paulbrownhawaii.com* ✆ *$115 50-min lomilomi massage, $338–$410 half-day package; $575 full-day package. Hair salon, sauna, steam room. Services: Acupuncture, body wraps, facials, massage.*

Fodor's Choice **Spa Without Walls at the Fairmont Orchid Hawaii.** This ranks among the ★ best massage facilities on the island, partially due to the superlative setting—private massage areas are situated amid the waterfalls, salt-water pools, and meandering gardens, as well as right on the beach. In fact, the Fairmont Orchid is one of the few resorts to offer beach-side massage. Splurge on the 110-minute Alii Experience featuring hot-coconut-oil treatments, *lomilomi,* and hot-stone massage. There are other great treatments, including caviar facials, fragrant herbal wraps, and coffee-and-vanilla scrubs. And where else can you relax to the sounds of cascading waterfalls while watching tropical yellow tang swim beneath you through windows in the floor? ✉ *Fairmont Orchid Hawaii, 1 N. Kaniku Dr., Kohala Coast* ☎ *808/887–7540, 808/885–2000* ⊕ *www.fairmont.com/orchid* ✆ *$159–$179 50-min lomilomi massage. Sauna, steam room. Services: Baths, body wraps, facials, massage, scrubs. Classes and programs: Aquaerobics, guided walks, meditation, personal training, yoga.*

ENTERTAINMENT AND NIGHTLIFE

Updated by Karen Anderson

If you're the sort of person who doesn't come alive until after dark, you might be a little lonely on the Big Island. Blame it on the plantation heritage. People did their cane raising in the morning, thus no late-night fun. Still, there are a few lively bars on the island, a handful of great local playhouses, half a dozen or so movie houses (including those that play foreign and independent films), and plenty of musical entertainment to keep you occupied. Also, many resorts have bars and late-night activities and events as well, and keep pools and gyms open late so there's something to do after dinner. And let's not forget the luau. These fantastic dance and musical performances are combined with some of the best local food on the island and are plenty of fun for the whole family.

ENTERTAINMENT

DINNER CRUISES AND SHOWS

★ **Evening on the Reef Glass Bottom Dinner Cruise.** Blue Sea Cruises offers a classier alternative to the booze cruise, with a buffet dinner, tropical cocktails, live entertainment, hula show, and open dancing. The focus is on the sunset and the scenery, with the chance to see spinner dolphins and manta rays, as well as whales from November to May. You can also enjoy what's below the surface through the boat's glass bottom. ✉ *Kailua Pier, Alii Dr., next to King Kamehameha's Kona Beach Hotel, Kailua-Kona* ☎ *808/331–8875* ⊕ *www.blueseacruisesinc.com* ✆ *$98* ⊙ *Mon., Wed., Fri., and Sat., departure times vary.*

LUAU AND POLYNESIAN REVUES

KAILUA-KONA

Courtyard King Kamehameha's Kona Beach Hotel. Witness a dramatic fire-knife performance at the Island Breeze Luau, an oceanfront event that features live music and a bounty of food that includes kalua pig cooked in an authentic underground *imu*. ⊠ *75-5660 Palani Rd.* ☎ *808/326–4969, 808/329–8111* ⊕ *www.islandbreezeluau.com* ▭ *$67.85* ⊗ *Tues., Thurs., and Sun. 5–8.*

Royal Kona Resort. This resort lights its torches for a spectacular show and an oceanfront buffet four times a week. It's also one of a handful of luau on the island that feature food cooked in a traditional underground *imu* (oven). A fire-knife dancer caps off the show. Prices are cheaper if you book ahead. ⊠ *75-5852 Alii Dr.* ☎ *808/329–3111* ⊕ *www. royalkona.com* ▭ *$78* ⊗ *Mon., Tues. Wed., and Fri. at 5.*

Sheraton Keauhou Bay Resort & Spa. On the graceful grounds of the Sheraton Keauhou Bay, this luau takes you on a journey of song and dance, highlighted by a dramatic fire-knife finale. Before the show, you can participate in workshops on topics ranging from coconut-frond weaving to poi ball techniques. The excellent buffet features a feast of local favorites like kalua pig, poi, and ahi poke. Generous refills on the mai tais don't hurt, either. ⊠ *75-5852 Alii Dr.* ☎ *808/930–4900* ⊕ *www. sheratonkeauhou.com* ▭ *$83* ⊗ *Mon. at 5.*

KOHALA COAST

Fairmont Orchid. The Fairmont's "Gathering of the Kings Polynesian Feast" offers the most bang for your buck. The show is slickly produced and well choreographed, incorporating both traditional and modern dance and an array of beautiful costumes. The meal offers the most variety of any island luau, with four buffet tables representing New Zealand, Hawaii, Tahiti, and Samoa. ⊠ *1 N. Kaniku Dr., Kohala Coast* ☎ *808/885–2000* ⊕ *www.fairmont.com/orchid* ▭ *$103* ⊗ *Sat. at 6.*

Fodor's Choice
★
Hapuna Beach Prince Hotel's Let's Go Crabbing. While the Mauna Kea Beach Hotel's clambake gets all the acclaim, Let's Go Crabbing at the Hapuna Beach Prince Hotel is tastier, and at a fraction of the price. Held every Friday night on the hotel's terrace, the all-you-can-eat buffet features everything from prime rib and roasted breast of turkey to Washington mussels, steamed Manila clams, excellent shrimp salads, and corn-and-crab bisque. Expect an array of crab offerings, including wok-fried Dungeness crab and chilled snow-crab claws. Homemade ice cream is the star attraction of the dessert bar, which features hot fudge and other toppings. ⊠ *Hapuna Beach Prince Hotel, 62-100 Kaunaoa Dr., Kohala Coast* ☎ *808/880–1111* ⊕ *www.princeresortshawaii.com.*

Hilton Waikoloa Village. This venue seats 400 people outdoors at the Kamehameha Court, where it presents the "Legends of the Pacific" review. A buffet dinner provides samplings of Hawaiian food as well as fish, beef, and chicken dishes that appeal to all tastes. ⊠ *425 Waikoloa Beach Dr., Waikoloa* ☎ *808/886–1234* ⊕ *www.hiltonwaikoloavillage. com* ▭ *$99, includes two cocktails* ⊗ *Tues., Fri., and Sun. at 6.*

Mauna Kea Beach Hotel Clambake. The Mauna Kea Beach Hotel's weekly clambake features an extensive menu that includes oysters on the half shell, Manila clams, Dungeness crab legs, and Keahole lobster sashimi. There's even prime rib for meat lovers. Live Hawaiian music is often accompanied by a graceful hula dancer. ⌧ *62-100 Mauna Kea Beach Dr., Kohala Coast* ☎ *808/882–5810, 808/882–7222* ⊕ *www.maunakeabeachhotel.com* ⌧ *$86* ☉ *Sat. at 6.*

Waikoloa Beach Marriott. At this celebration, the entertainment includes a Samoan fire-knife presentation as well as songs and dances from various Pacific cultures. Traditional dishes are served alongside more familiar fare, and there's also an open bar. ⌧ *69-275 Waikoloa Beach Dr., Waikoloa* ☎ *808/886–6789* ⊕ *www.marriott.com* ⌧ *$88* ☉ *Wed. and Sat. 5–8:30.*

FESTIVALS

There is a festival dedicated to just about everything on the Big Island. Some of them are small community affairs, but a handful of film, food, and music festivals provide quality entertainment for visitors and locals alike. *The following is a list of our favorites:*

Black and White Night. This lovely annual outdoor party takes place in downtown Hilo. The stores stay open late, the sidewalks are dotted with live jazz bands, and everyone dresses in black and white, some in shorts and tees and others in gowns and tuxes, to enter the "best dressed" contest. ⌧ *329 Kamehameha Ave., Hilo* ☎ *808/935–8850* ⊕ *www.downtownhilo.com* ☉ *First Friday in Nov.*

Chinese New Year. Every February, Hilo throws a big free party complete with live music, food, and fireworks to commemorate this holiday. There's a smaller celebration along Alii Drive in Kona. ⌧ *329 Kamehameha Ave., Hilo* ☎ *808/935–8850* ⊕ *www.downtownhilo.com* ☉ *Feb.*

Kona Brewers Festival. At this great annual celebration, roughly 30 breweries and 25 restaurants offer samples of their craft beer and ale. There's also live music, fashion shows, and a home-brewer contest. The event is usually held on the grounds of Courtyard King Kamehameha's Kona Beach Hotel. ☎ *808/331–3033* ⊕ *www.konabrewersfestival.com* ☉ *Early Mar.*

Kona Coffee Cultural Festival. Held over 10 days, the oldest food festival in Hawaii includes a coffee-recipe contest, coffee-picking competition, and a colorful parade. A highlight is the Holualoa Village Coffee and Art Stroll, during which you can enjoy original art and sample different cups of java. ☎ *808/323–2006* ⊕ *www.konacoffeefest.com* ☉ *Early Nov.*

★ **Merrie Monarch Festival.** The mother of all Big Island festivals, the Merrie Monarch celebrates all things hula and completely overtakes Hilo for one fantastic weekend a year. The largest event of its kind in the

Catch a Big Island sunset while hiking on mountaintops covered with lava fields.

world honors the legacy of King David Kalakaua, the man responsible for reviving fading Hawaiian traditions like the hula. The festival is staged at the spacious Edith Kanakaole Tennis Stadium during the first week following Easter Sunday. Hula *halau* (schools) compete in *kahiko* (ancient) and *auana* (modern) dance styles. ■TIP➜ You need to reserve accommodations and tickets up to a year in advance. ✉ *Edith Kanakaole Tennis Stadium, 350 Kalanikoa St., Hilo* ☎ *808/935–9168* ⊕ *www. merriemonarchfestival.org* ⊗ *Apr.*

Taste of the Hawaiian Range. Since 1995, this culinary event has given locals and visitors a taste of what the region's best chefs and ranches have to offer, from grass-fed beef, lamb, and mutton to succulent veal. ☎ *808/981–5199* ⊕ *www.tasteofthehawaiianrange.com* ⊗ *Sept. or Oct.*

THEATER

Aloha Angel Performing Arts Center. Local talent stages musicals and Broadway plays at this charming old plantation center near Kailua-Kona. ✉ *Aloha Angel Theatre Café, 79-7384 Mamalahoa Hwy., Kainaliu* ☎ *808/322–2122.*

Kahilu Theater. For legitimate theater, the little town of Waimea is your best bet. The Kahilu Theater regularly hosts internationally acclaimed performers, interspersed with a variety of top-notch national and regional acts. In a recent season, Terence Blanchard, Ben Vereen, and the Martha Graham Company shared the calendar with modern dance performances and traditional Hawaiian dance shows. ✉ *Parker Ranch Center, 67-1185 Mamalahoa Hwy., Waimea* ☎ *808/885–6868* ⊕ *www. kahilutheatre.org.*

★ **Volcano Art Center.** Hawaiian music and dance, as well as theater performances, are hosted by this local art center. Locals drive here from all over the island for the concerts. ✉ *19-4744 Old Volcano Rd., Volcano* ☎ *808/967–8222* ⊕ *www.volcanoartcenter.org.*

NIGHTLIFE

KAILUA-KONA

BARS

Kona Brewing Co. This place has been a local favorite practically since it opened. Good food, great locally brewed beer (go for the sampler and try them all), and an outdoor patio with live music on Sunday nights make sure it stays that way. ✉ *75-5629 Kuakini Hwy.* ☎ *808/334–2739* ⊕ *www.konabrewingco.com.*

Oceans Sports Bar & Grill. A popular gathering place, this sports bar in the back of the Coconut Grove Marketplace has a pool table and an outdoor patio, along with dozens of TVs screening the big game (whatever it happens to be that day). It really gets hopping on the weekends and for karaoke on Tuesday and Thursday. ✉ *Coconut Grove Marketplace, 75-5811 Alii Dr.* ☎ *808/327–9494.*

Okolemaluna Tiki Lounge. This addition to the Kailua-Kona cocktail scene is a cool, retro tiki bar where you can sip an exotic cocktail made with fresh, local, seasonal ingredients while munching on tasty tropical pupus. Happy hour, on weekdays from 3 pm to 6 pm, features $5 mai tais and $4 local draft beers. It's open Sunday to Thursday from 3 to 11 and Friday and Saturday 3 pm to midnight. ✉ *Alii Sunset Plaza, 75-5799 Alii Dr., by Lava Java* ☎ *808/883–8454* ⊕ *www. okolemalunalounge.com.*

CLUBS

Huggo's on the Rocks. Jazz, country, and rock bands perform at this popular place, so call ahead to find out who's on the bill. Outside you might see people dancing in the sand to Hawaiian songs. The crowd is slightly older and better behaved than at Lulu's across the street. ✉ *75-5828 Kahakai Rd., at Alii Dr.* ☎ *808/329–1493* ⊕ *www.huggos.com.*

Lulu's. On weekends, a young crowd gyrates to hot dance music—hip-hop, R&B, and rock—spun by a professional DJ. The party lasts well into the evening. ✉ *Coconut Grove Marketplace, 75-5819 Alii Dr.* ☎ *808/331–2633.*

THE KOHALA COAST

BARS

Luana Terrace. This wood-paneled lounge in the Fairmont Orchid has a large terrace and an impressive view. The bartenders are skilled, and service is impeccable. The crowd is subdued, so it's a nice place for an early evening cocktail or an after-dinner port. ✉ *Fairmont Orchid, 1 N. Kaniku Dr., Kohala Coast* ☎ *808/885–2000* ⊕ *www.fairmont.com/orchid.*

Malolo Lounge. A favorite after-work spot for employees from the surrounding hotels, this lounge in the Hilton Waikoloa Village offers decent music (usually jazz), friendly bartenders, and a pool table. ✉ *Hilton*

BEST SUNSET MAI TAIS

Huggo's on the Rocks (Kailua-Kona). Table dining in the sand, plus live music Friday and Saturday.

Kona Inn (Kailua-Kona). Wide, unobstructed view of the Kailua-Kona coastline.

Manta Ray Bar & Grill at the Sheraton Keauhou (Kailua-Kona). Fantastic sunset views from plush lounge

chairs, followed by spotlighted glimpses of nearby manta rays.

Waioli Lounge in the Hilo Hawaiian Hotel (Hilo). A nice view of Coconut Island, live music Friday and Saturday nights.

Waikoloa Village, 425 Waikoloa Beach Dr., Waikoloa ☎ *808/886–1234* ⊕ *www.hiltonwaikoloavillage.com.*

HILO

BARS

Cronie's Bar & Grill. A sports bar and hamburger joint by day, Cronie's is a local favorite when the lights go down, when the bar gets packed. ⊠ *11 Waianuenue Ave.* ☎ *808/935–5158.*

Mask-querade Bar. Hidden away in a little strip mall, this is one of the Big Island's most venerable gay bars. Drag shows, hot DJs, and Sunday barbecues are included in the roster of weekly events. ⊠ *Kopiko Plaza, 75-5660 Kopiko St., behind Longs Drugs, Kailua-Kona* ☎ *808/329–8558* ⊕ *http://themask-queradebar.com.*

WHERE TO EAT

Updated by Karen Anderson

Between star chefs and myriad local farms, the Big Island restaurant scene has really heated up in the last 10 years. Food writers from national magazines are praising the chefs of the Big Island for their ability to turn the local bounty into inventive blends of the island's cultural heritage. The Big Island has become a destination for vacationing foodies who are drawn by the innovative offerings and reputations of some world-renowned chefs.

Hotels along the Kohala Coast have long invested in celebrated chefs who know how to make a meal memorable, from inventive entrées to spot-on wine pairings. But great food on the Big Island doesn't begin and end with the resorts. A handful of cutting-edge chefs have retired from the fast-paced hotel world and opened up their own small bistros closer to the farms in Upcountry Waimea, or other places off the beaten track. And, as some historic towns transform into vibrant arts communities, unique and wonderful restaurants have cropped up in Hawi, Kainaliu, and Holualoa, and on the east side of the island in Hilo.

Though the larger, gourmet restaurants (especially those at the resorts) tend to be very pricey, there are still *ono grindz* (Hawaiian slang for

BEST BETS FOR BIG ISLAND DINING

Fodor'sChoice ★	$$	KPC (Kamuela Provision Company), p. 432
Bamboo Restaurant, $$, p. 430	Bamboo Restaurant, p. 430	Manta & Pavilion Wine Bar, p. 432
Beach Tree, $$$, p. 430	Jackie Rey's Ohana Grill, p. 426	Pahuia, p. 430
Brown's Beach House, $$$$, p. 431	Keei Café, p. 429	Monettes, p. 433
CanoeHouse, $$$$, p. 431	Kenichi Pacific, p. 426	**By Cuisine**
Keei Café, $$, p. 429	Kiawe Kitchen, p. 439	
Kona Brewing Co. Pub & Brewery, $, p. 427	Merriman's Market Café, p. 432	PLATE LUNCH
Pahuia, $$$$, p. 430	Sam Choy's Kai Lanai, p. 428	Blane's Drive-In, $, p. 437
		Big Island Grill, $, p. 422
By Price	$$$	Café 100, $, p. 437
	Beach Tree, p. 430	
$	Kilauea Lodge, p. 439	SUSHI
Island Lava Java, p. 426	$$$$	Kenichi Pacific, $$ p. 426
Kona Brewing Co. Pub & Brewery, p. 427	Brown's Beach House, p. 431	Monstera, $$, p. 433
Lilikoi Café, p. 435	CanoeHouse, p. 431	Norio's Sushi Bar, $$$ p. 433
Pau, p. 436		Sansei Seafood Restaurant & Sushi Bar, $$$, p. 434

tasty local food) to be found at budget prices throughout the island, from greasy plate lunch specials to reasonably priced organic fare at a number of cafés and health food markets. Less populated areas like Kau, the Hamakua Coast, and Puna offer limited choices for dinner, but there are usually at least one or two spots that have a decent plate lunch or surprisingly good food.

Prices in the reviews are the average cost of a main course at dinner or, if dinner is not served, at lunch.

KAILUA-KONA

$ ✕ **Ba-Le.** Hidden away in a strip mall on Palani Road near KTA, Ba-Le
HAWAIIAN serves a decent plate lunch. It also offers Vietnamese-influenced food such as pho, though there are more authentic options elsewhere. Ba-Le's sandwiches are served on croissants or French baguettes, stuffed with pickled daikon and carrots, cucumber, cilantro, homemade mayo, and your choice of a variety of Asian-style meats. $ *Average main: $8* ⊠ *Kona Coast Shopping Center, 74-5588 Palani Rd.* ☎ *808/327–1212* ⊕ *www.ba-le.com.*

$ ✕ **Big Island Grill.** This typical, local Hawaiian restaurant looks like an
HAWAIIAN old coffee shop or a Denny's—it's dark and nondescript inside, with

booths along the walls and basic tables with bingo-hall chairs in the middle of the room. Local families love it for the huge portions of pork chops, *loco moco* (two eggs, ground beef patty, rice, and brown gravy), and an assortment of fish specialties at very reasonable prices. "Biggie's" also serves a decent breakfast—the prices and portions make this a good place to take large groups or families, if you want to feel like a real *kamaaina* (local), that is. [$] *Average main: $16* ✉ *75-5702 Kuakini Hwy.* ☎ *808/326–1153* ⏲ *Closed Sun.*

$ SEAFOOD 🍴 **Bite Me Fish Market Bar & Grill.** This cool sit-down bar and grill overlooks the boat ramp of the Bite Me Fish Market in Honokohau Harbor. Sit at the outdoor picnic tables and watch the day's catch get hoisted from the boats; chances are it will end up on your plate that day. Sandwiches are named after famous fishing lures in Kona (try the Kaya Bait Fish Reuben). Fish tacos can be ordered à la carte for a couple of bucks. [$] *Average main: $12* ✉ *Gentrys Kona Marina at Honokohau Harbor, 74-425 Kealakehe Pkwy., No. 17* ☎ *808/327–3474* 🌐 *www.bitemefishmarket.com.*

$ AMERICAN 👪 🍴 **Bubba Gump Shrimp Company.** Okay, it's a chain, and a chain that centers on an old Tom Hanks movie, no less. However, it has one of the nicest oceanfront patios in Kailua-Kona, and the food's not bad, providing you know what to order. Anything with popcorn shrimp in it is a good bet, and the pear and berry salad (a combination of chicken, strawberries, pears, and glazed pecans) is the perfect size for lunch. [$] *Average main: $10* ✉ *75-5776 Alii Dr.* ☎ *808/331–8442* 🌐 *www.bubbagump.com.*

$ AMERICAN 🍴 **Harbor House.** This open-air restaurant on the docks at Kona's busy harbor is a fun place to grab a beer and a bite after a long day fishing, surfing, or diving. The venue is nothing fancy but Harbor House is a local favorite for fresh-fish sandwiches and a variety of fried fish-and-chip combos. The icy schooners of Kona Brewing Company ale don't hurt, either. [$] *Average main: $10* ✉ *74-425 Kealakehe Pkwy., Suite 4, Honokohau Harbor* ☎ *808/326–4166* 🌐 *harborhouserestaurantkona.com.*

$$$ HAWAIIAN 🍴 **Honu's on the Beach.** Featuring al fresco dining near the sand, Honu's on the Beach is one of the only true beachfront restaurants in Kailua Village. Part of Courtyard King Kamehameha's Kona Beach Hotel, the newly transformed open-air venue offers prime views of Kailua Pier and Kamakahonu Bay. Steak and seafood dominate the menu, highlighted by the rib-eye, fresh catch, and the delicious seafood chowder made with fish, clams, scallops, and shrimp. For lighter fare, there's an excellent selection of entrée salads, including the grilled chicken and papaya salad. A prime rib seafood buffet is available Friday and Saturday nights. [$] *Average main: $28* ✉ *Courtyard King Kamehameha's Kona Beach Hotel, 75-5660 Palani Road* ☎ *808/331–6388* 🌐 *www.konabeachhotel.com/dining.htm.*

$$$$ HAWAIIAN 🍴 **Huggo's.** This is one of the only restaurants in town with prices and atmosphere comparable to the splurge restaurants at the Kohala Coast resorts. The dinner offerings sometimes fall short, considering the high prices, but lunch is usually a good bet. Windows open out over the rocks at the ocean's edge, and at night you can almost touch the marine

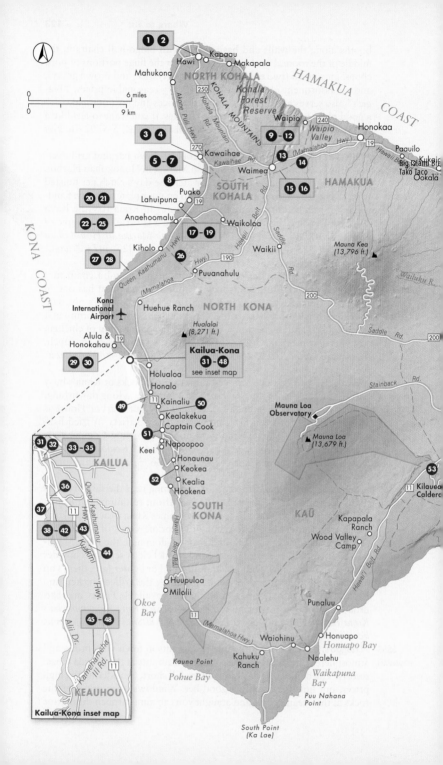

Papa'aloa
aloka
Ninole
Hakalau
Wailea
Honomu
NORTH HILO
19

Papaikou
Wainaku
Hilo Bay
Leleiwi Point
Hilo International Airport (General Lyman Field)
Hilo
61 – 68
ee inset map
59 60
SOUTH HILO
11
Keaau
Kukui
Kurtistown
130
Mountain View
Cape Kumakahi
Glenwood
Pahoa
132
PUNA
58
Volcano
– 56
Kaimu
Kalapana
Hawaii Volcanoes National Park

PACIFIC OCEAN

Where to Eat on the Big Island

Hilo inset map
Hilo Bay
Wainuenue Ave.
61 62
65
Bayfront Hwy.
67
64
Kamehameha Ave.
19
66
63
68
Ponahawai St.
Kilauea Ave.
Kinoole St.
Kapiolani St.
Manono St.
Kanoelehua Ave.
9

4

life swimming below. Relax with cocktails for two and feast on fresh local seafood; the nightly chef's special is always changing. If you're on a budget, try Huggo's happy hour: pupus are half price from 5:30 to 6 pm and drink specials run from 4 to 6 pm daily. **Huggo's on the Rocks,** next door, is a popular outdoor bar in the sand, and the burgers are pretty darn good, too. It's also Kailua-Kona's hot spot for drinks and live music on Friday nights. $ *Average main: $36* ⊠ *75-5828 Kahakai Rd., off Alii Dr.* ☎ *808/329–1493* ⊕ *www.huggos.com.*

$ × **Island Lava Java.** This place is always busy, especially on weekends.
AMERICAN   Order your food at the counter then sit outside at one of the wooden, umbrella-shaded tables where you can sip 100% Kona coffee and take in the ocean view. The variety-filled menu includes island-style pancakes for breakfast, fresh-fish tacos for lunch, and braised lamb shanks for dinner, plus towering, fresh bistro salads. There are also pizzas, sandwiches, and plenty of choices for both vegetarians and meat eaters. The giant cinnamon rolls are hugely popular. Portions are large and most of the menu is fresh, local, and organic. $ *Average main: $14* ⊠ *75-5799 Alii Dr.* ☎ *808/327–2161* ⊕ *www.islandlavajava.com.*

$$ × **Jackie Rey's Ohana Grill.** This brightly decorated, open-air restaurant
MODERN   is a favorite lunch destination and popular for dinner as well, thanks
HAWAIIAN   to the chef's chicken and angel hair pasta, nicely prepared local seafood dishes, and a few juicy meat standouts, including six bone rack of lamb. Be sure to pair your meal with a selection from Jackie Rey's well-rounded wine list. At lunchtime, the fresh-fish sandwiches with wasabi mayo are excellent, and the fries are crisped to perfection. On the lighter side, inventive salads keep it healthy but flavorful. $ *Average main: $23* ⊠ *Pottery Terrace, 75-5995 Kuakini Hwy.* ☎ *808/327–0209* ⊕ *www.jackiereys.com* ☾ *No lunch weekends.*

$ × **Kanaka Kava.** This is a popular local hangout and not just because
HAWAIIAN   the kava makes you mellow. Their *pupu* (appetizers) rock! Fresh poke, smoky, tender bowls of pulled kalua pork, and healthy organic greens are available in fairly large portions for less than you'll pay elsewhere. The restaurant also offers fresh-fish plates, vegetarian options, and even traditional Hawaiian *lau lau* (pork and butterfish wrapped in taro leaves and steamed). Seating is at a premium, but don't be afraid to share a table and make friends. $ *Average main: $12* ⊠ *75-5803 Alii Dr., Space B-6, in Coconut Grove Marketplace* ☎ *808/327–1660* ⊕ *www. kanakakava.com.*

$$ × **Kenichi Pacific.** With its black-lacquer tables and lipstick-red ban-
JAPANESE   quettes, Kenichi provides one of the few upscale choices in town. Its location at Keauhou Shopping Center might feel like a secret, but visitors should seek it out. This is where residents go when they feel like splurging on top-notch sushi. It's a little on the pricey side, but you'll leave feeling satisfied. The signature rolls are inventive and tasty, especially the always-popular Dynamite Shrimp. If you're looking to save a buck or two, go early for happy hour (4:30 to 6:30 pm daily) when all sushi rolls are half price, or hang out in the cocktail bar where menu items average $6. $ *Average main: $25* ⊠ *Keauhou Shopping Center, 78-6831 Alii Dr., D-125* ☎ *808/322–6400* ⊕ *www.kenichirestaurants. com* ☾ *Closed Mon.*

WORD OF MOUTH

"There are a number of restaurants along Alii Drive, south of King Kamehameha Hotel. Most are active, noisy, and crowded. They have dining on the second floor, looking out over Alii Drive to sunsets and the Kona harbor."

—BillJ

$ AMERICAN Fodor's Choice ★ 🍴 **Kona Brewing Co. Pub & Brewery.** This megapopular destination with a huge outdoor patio features an excellent and varied menu, including pulled-pork quesadillas, gourmet pizzas, and a killer spinach salad with Gorgonzola cheese, macadamia nuts, and strawberries. Your best bet for lunch or dinner is the veggie slice and salad for under $8—the garden salad is generous and the pizza is the best in town. Go for the beer-tasting menu—your choice of four of the eight available microbrews in miniature glasses that add up to about two regular-size mugs for the price of one. The Hefeweizen is excellent. If you're staying in town, purchase beer to go in a half-gallon jug ("growler") filled on-site from the brewery's own taps. The Growler Shack also sells beer by the keg. [$] *Average main: $12* ✉ *75-5629 Kuakini Hwy., off Kaiwi St. at end of Pawai Pl.* ☎ *808/329–2739* 🌐 *www.konabrewingco.com.*

$$$ FRENCH 🍴 **La Bourgogne.** A genial husband-and-wife team owns this quiet, country-style bistro with dark-wood walls and private, romantic booths (no windows; it's located in a nondescript office building). The traditional French cuisine might not impress visitors from France, but the average guest can enjoy classics such as escargots, beef with a cabernet sauvignon sauce, rack of lamb with roasted garlic and rosemary, and the less traditional venison with a pomegranate glaze. Call well in advance for reservations. [$] *Average main: $30* ✉ *77-6400 Nalani St.* ☎ *808/329–6711* 👔 *Reservations essential* 🕒 *Closed Sun. and Mon. No lunch.*

$ MEXICAN 🍴 **Los Habaneros.** A surprising find in the corner of Keauhou Shopping Center adjacent to the movie theater, Habaneros serves up fast Mexican food for low prices. Favorites are usually combos, which can be anything from enchilada plates to homemade sopes and chiles rellenos. The burritos are a solid pick, stuffed with meat, beans, cheese, and all the fixings. Wash it down with imported beer from Mexico. [$] *Average main: $7* ✉ *78-631 Alii Dr., Keauhou Shopping Center* ☎ *808/324–4688* 🕒 *Closed Sun.*

$ FRENCH 🍴 **Peaberry & Galette.** This little creperie is a welcome addition to the neighborhood. The menu includes Illy espresso, teas, excellent sweet and savory crepes, and rich desserts like lemon cheesecake and chocolate mousse that are made fresh daily. The small venue has a relaxed, urban-café vibe, and is a nice place to hang for a bit if you're waiting for a movie at the theater next door, or just feel like taking a break from paradise to sip a decent espresso and flip through the latest *W*. [$] *Average main: $12* ✉ *Keauhou Shopping Center, 78-6831 Ali'i Dr.* ☎ *808/322–6020.*

$ AMERICAN 🍴 **Quinn's Almost by the Sea.** With the bar in the front and the dining patio in the back, Quinn's may seem like a bit of a dive at first glance, but this venerable restaurant serves up the best darn cheeseburger and fries in town. Appropriate for families, the restaurant stays busy for lunch and dinner, while the bar attracts a cast of colorful regulars.

4

The menu has many tasty options, like fish-and-chips, meat loaf, or beef tenderloin tips. Quinn's stays open until 11 pm, later than almost any other restaurant in Kailua-Kona. If time gets away from you on a drive to the north beaches, Quinn's awaits your return with a cheap beer and a basket of fried calamari. Drinks are strong; there are no watered-down cocktails served here. Park across the street at the Courtyard King Kamehameha's Kona Beach Hotel and get free one-hour parking with validation. $ *Average main: $15* ⊠ *75-5655 Palani Rd.* ☎ *808/329–3822* ⊕ *quinnsalmostbythesea.com.*

$$
HAWAIIAN
✕ **Sam Choy's Kai Lanai.** Perched on the bluff above Keauhou Shopping Center, the newly opened Sam Choy's Kai Lanai is already a Kona classic. Celebrity-chef Sam Choy has transformed an old Wendy's into a beautiful open-air restaurant complete with an awesome bar, The Short Bait, designed to look like a charter-fishing boat. Granite-topped tables offer sweeping ocean views from every seat in the house. Open for breakfast, lunch, and dinner, the venue presents reasonably priced entrées, highlighted by the macadamia-nut-crusted chicken, Oriental lamb chops, or Sam's trio of fish served with shiitake-mushroom cream sauce. The ahi salad (served in a deep-fried flour tortilla bowl) is a great deal for $14. *Keiki* (children's) menus accommodate families. Parking is at a premium, so you might have to park in the shopping center below. The restaurant can be noisy. ■ TIP➔ Arrive at 5 pm to nab the best patio seating. $ *Average main: $22* ⊠ *Keauhou Shopping Center, 78-6831 Alii Dr., Suite 1000* ☎ *808/333–3434* ⊕ *www.samchoy.com.*

$
MEXICAN
✕ **Tacos El Unico.** This place offers an array of authentic soft-taco choices (beef and chicken, among others), burritos, quesadillas, and excellent homemade tamales. Order at the counter, take a seat outside at one of a dozen yellow tables with blue umbrellas, and enjoy all the good flavors served up in those red plastic baskets. $ *Average main: $9* ⊠ *Kona Marketplace, 75-5729 Alii Dr.* ☎ *808/326–4033.*

$
THAI
✕ **Thai Rin Restaurant.** The owner at this dependable joint adjacent to Lava Java is likely to take your order, cook it, and bring it to your table himself, but that doesn't mean the service is slow—just the opposite. Everything is cooked to order, and the menu is brimming with choices, including five curries, a green-papaya salad, and a popular platter that combines spring rolls, satay, beef salad, and *tom yum* (lemongrass soup). For a real treat, try the deep-fried fish. Piña colada fans will appreciate the excellent cocktails served here, and you can't beat the beautiful ocean view. Indoor and outdoor seating is available. $ *Average main: $11* ⊠ *75-5799 Alii Dr.* ☎ *808/329–2929* ⊕ *www.aliisunsetplaza.com.*

$
JAPANESE
✕ **Wasabi's.** A tiny place hidden in the back of the Coconut Plaza on Alii Drive, Wasabi's features indoor and outdoor seating. Prices may seem steep, but the fish is of the highest quality, highlighted by a large selection of rolls and authentic Japanese offerings, along with a few unique inventions. And for those who will never be hip to the raw-fish thing, teriyaki, udon, and sukiyaki options abound. $ *Average main: $14* ⊠ *75-5803 Alii Dr., Coconut Grove Marketplace* ☎ *808/326–2352* ⊕ *www.wasabishawaii.com.*

THE KONA COAST

SOUTH KONA

$
AMERICAN

☓ The Coffee Shack. Visitors enjoy stopping here for lunch after a morning of snorkeling at Kealakekua Bay, and for good reason: the views of the Honaunau coast from this roadside restaurant in South Kona are stunning. Breads are all homemade, and you get to choose your favorite when ordering a generously sized sandwich brimming with Black Forest ham and the like. If you're in the mood for a Hawaiian smoothie, iced honey-mocha latte, or homemade luau bread, it's worth the detour, even though the parking lot can be tricky to maneuver. $ *Average main: $11* ✉ *83-5799 Mamalahoa Hwy., Captain Cook* ☎ *808/328–9555* ⊕ *www.coffeeshack.com* ☽ *No dinner.*

$$
ECLECTIC
Fodor'sChoice
★

☓ Keei Café at Hokukano. This beautiful restaurant, perched above the highway just 15 minutes south of Kailua-Kona, serves delicious dinners with Brazilian, Asian, and European flavors highlighting fresh ingredients from local farmers. Favorites are the Brazilian seafood chowder or peanut-miso salad, followed by pasta primavera smothered with a basil-pesto sauce. There's an extensive wine list. Bob Miyashiro, the owner, is a Kona native, and his wife, Gina, is Brazilian. The husband-and-wife cooking team is also from Brazil and has been with the restaurant since its humble beginnings at its previous location in Honaunau. Toast your friendly hosts with a refreshing mojito before dinner. $ *Average main: $20* ✉ *79-7511 Mamalahoa Hwy., ½ mile south of Kainaliu, Kealakekua* ☎ *808/322–9992* ⊕ *www.keeicafe.net* ⌔ *Reservations essential* ▭ *No credit cards* ☽ *Closed Sun. and Mon.*

$
AMERICAN

☓ Manago Hotel. About 20 minutes Upcountry of Kailua-Kona, the historic Manago Hotel is a time-warp experience. A vintage neon sign identifies the hotel, while Formica tables and old photos add to the authentically retro flavor. The T-shirts (which are great souvenirs for friends at home) brag that the hotel's restaurant has the best pork chops in town, and it's not false advertising. The fresh fish is excellent as well, especially the ono and butterfish. Unless you request otherwise, the fish is sautéed with a tasty house butter–soy sauce concoction. Meals come with rice for the table and an assortment of side dishes that changes from time to time, but usually includes a macaroni, potato, and tuna salad, and a braised tofu and sautéed veggie dish. $ *Average main: $10* ✉ *82-6155 Mamalahoa Hwy., Captain Cook* ☎ *808/323–2642* ⊕ *www.managohotel.com* ☽ *Closed Mon.*

$
JAPANESE

☓ Teshima's. Locals show up at this small, historic restaurant 15 minutes south of Kailua-Kona whenever they're in the mood for fresh sashimi, puffy shrimp tempura, or *hekka* (beef and vegetables cooked in an iron pot) at a reasonable price. Teshima's doesn't look like much, inside or out, but it's been a *kamaaina* (local) favorite since 1929 for a reason. You might want to try *teishoku* (tray) No. 3, featuring sashimi, tempura, sukiyaki beef, rice, miso soup, sunomono, and more. Or order the popular bento box lunch. The service is laid-back and friendly, and the restaurant has been family owned and operated by five generations of Teshimas. $ *Average main: $15* ✉ *79-7251 Mamalahoa Hwy., Honalo* ☎ *808/322–9140* ▭ *No credit cards.*

4

NORTH KONA

$$$ MODERN ITALIAN Fodor's Choice ★ ☺ 🍴 **Beach Tree at the Four Seasons Resort Hualalai.** This beautifully designed venue provides a relaxed and elegant setting for alfresco dining near the sand, with its boardwalk-style deck, outdoor seating under the trellis, and enormous vaulted ceiling. Chef Nick Mastrascusa is a transplant from the Four Seasons Hotel New York, bringing Italian and Spanish influences to his inventive menu. Outstanding entrées include the seafood paella for two and the grilled rib eye with shoestring fries. The tropical Peletini martini is a favorite, and at dinner, the premium wine list includes the Beach Tree's own signature reds and whites. There's also a great children's menu and activities to keep them busy, like a fun, rotating pasta fork, and an ice-cream-cone spinner. Live Hawaiian music is featured nightly. [$] *Average main: $35* ✉ *72-100 Kaupulehu Dr. 808/325–8000* 🌐 *www.fourseasons.com/hualalai.*

> **WORD OF MOUTH**
>
> "In Hawi, we really like Bamboo. The people there are very friendly and love to chat with you. We go there every year when we are in Kona, and they always remember us and greet us like old friends. And we really like the food. Try something with their coconut sauce. Divine!"
>
> —charnees

$$$$ MODERN HAWAIIAN Fodor's Choice ★ 🍴 **Pahuia at the Four Seasons Resort Hualalai.** *Pahuia* means aquarium, so it's fitting that a 9- by 4-foot aquarium in the entrance casts a dreamy light through this exquisite restaurant. Presentation is paramount, and the cuisine is first rate. Asian-influenced dishes stand out for their layers of flavor. Chef Jacob Anaya creates something spectacular with each plate. Opt for a tasting menu of up to seven small items or go for a full entrée–you'll be happy with whatever you choose. The chef changes the menu four times a year and focuses on showcasing local ingredients. You're likely to find unique preparations of your favorite dishes, such as baby abalone, white shrimp, Keahole lobster, Big Island moi, Hawaiian snapper, lamb, and prime beef. Breakfasts are superb; the lemon ricotta pancakes are so good they should be illegal. Reserve a table on the patio and you may be able to spot whales while dining. It's pricey, but worth the splurge, at least once. [$] *Average main: $44* ✉ *Four Seasons Resort Hualalai, 100 Kaupulehu Dr., North Kona* ☎ *808/325–8000* 🌐 *www.fourseasons.com/hualalai* ⏲ *No lunch.*

THE KOHALA COAST

$$ ASIAN Fodor's Choice ★ 🍴 **Bamboo Restaurant.** It's out of the way, but the food at this spot in the heart of Hawi is good and the service and ambience have a Hawaiian–country flair. Creative entrées feature fresh island fish prepared several ways. The Thai-style fish, for example, combines lemongrass, Kaffir lime leaves, and coconut milk; it's best washed down with a passion-fruit margarita or passion-fruit iced tea. Bamboo accents, bold local artwork, and an old unfinished wooden floor make the restaurant cozy. Local musicians entertain on Friday or Saturday evenings. [$] *Average main: $25* ✉ *55-3415 Akoni Pule Hwy, Hwy. 270, Hawi* ☎ *808/889–5555* 🌐 *www.bamboorestaurant.info* ⏲ *Closed Mon. No dinner Sun.*

$$$$
MODERN
HAWAIIAN
Fodor'sChoice
★

✕ **Brown's Beach House at the Fairmont Orchid Hawaii.** Nestled alongside the resort's sandy bay, Brown's Beach House offers beautiful sunset dining and innovative cuisine by chef "TK" Keosavang. Attention to detail is evident in the sophisticated cuisine, like the delicious Manilla clams infused with subtle hints of tomato, onion, fennel, saffron, and white wine. Try the yummy tom yum soup with poached ono in coconut-lemongrass broth, or the tender braised short ribs with veggie risotto. The menu includes choices that accommodate diet-specific preferences such as macrobiotic, raw, vegan, gluten-free, and diabetic—amazingly, these offerings are as flavorful and inventive as everything on the main menu. $ *Average main: $40* ⊠ *Fairmont Orchid Hawaii, 1 N. Kaniku Dr., Kohala Coast* ☎ *808/885–2000* ⊕ *www.fairmont.com/orchid* ⊗ *No lunch.*

$$$$
ECLECTIC
Fodor'sChoice
★

✕ **CanoeHouse at the Mauna Lani Bay Hotel & Bungalows.** This landmark restaurant on the ocean showcases the inventive cuisine of executive chef Sandy Tuason, who previously served at the prestigious L'Atelier de Joël Robuchon restaurant in Manhattan. The progressive menu draws its influences from around the world while incorporating the flavors of the Islands. Dishes are artfully presented and feature delicious offerings like the Duo of Lamb, comprised of roasted loin and spiced lamb sausage; or the Keahole lobster salad with avocado-mango relish and crispy greens from Waimea. Don't miss the exquisite desserts, especially the homemade sorbets or the Waialua Chocolate Dome. The wine list is great, and the open-air beachfront setting makes the hefty price tag worth it on clear evenings. $ *Average main: $45* ⊠ *Mauna Lani Bay Hotel & Bungalows, 68-1400 Mauna Lani Dr., Kohala Coast* ☎ *808/885–6622* ⊕ *www.maunalani.com.*

$$$
MODERN
HAWAIIAN

✕ **Coast Grille at Hapuna Beach Prince Hotel.** This open-air venue has high ceilings and a lanai that overlooks the pool and beach. American bistro-style dishes showcase the bounty of Big Island ingredients, including fresh Kona shrimp and lobster (raised at the Natural Energy Lab), seasonal fresh oysters, and specially prepared seafood. Every Friday is "Let's Go Crabbing" night, a splendid buffet with everything from steamed Manilla clams and soft-shell crab tempura to crab-and-corn bisque and a full salad bar. $ *Average main: $30* ⊠ *Hapuna Beach Prince Hotel, 62-100 Kaunaoa Dr., Kohala Coast* ☎ *808/880–3192* ⊕ *www.princeresortshawaii.com* ⊗ *No lunch.*

$$$
HAWAIIAN

✕ **Eddie Aikau Restaurant and Surf Museum.** The lastest addition to the upscale Kings' Shops in Waikoloa, this two-level venue commemorates the late, big-wave-surfing legend of "Eddie Would Go" fame. The restaurant is owned and operated by Eddie's family in partnership with a group of Hawaiian-born restaurateurs. Although the menu approaches resort prices, the restaurant is fun and casual, with cocktail bars upstairs and downstairs, plus lakeside seating. Don't miss the 16-oz. grilled Aikau rib eye or the Kalua spring rolls laden with special sauce. Chef Scott Lutey's take on contemporary Hawaiian cuisine includes an inventive Luau Plate with taro hash. Memorabilia including Eddie's red surf trunks are on display. $ *Average main: $35* ⊠ *Kings' Shops Waikoloa, 69-250 Waikoloa Beach Dr., Suite C1, Kohala Coast* ☎ *808/886–8433* ⊕ *www.eddieaikaurestaurant.com.*

4

$$ ✕ **Kawaihae Seafood Bar.** Upstairs in a structure that dates from the
SEAFOOD   1850s, this seafood bar has been a hot spot since it opened in 2003,
serving up a dynamite and well-priced bar menu with tasty *pupu* (appe-
tizers), and an always expanding dinner menu that includes at least
four fresh-fish specials daily. There's fare for landlubbers, too, includ-
ing boneless braised short ribs, rib-eye steak, specialty pizza and lots
of salad options. Don't miss their escargot, oysters Rockefeller, and
ginger steamed clams. At lunch, the menu ranges from sandwiches and
burgers to sashimi and poke. Breakfast is served only on weekends,
and happy hour runs daily from 3 to 5:30 pm, and again from 10
pm until close (2 am). If you've got the late-night munchies, this is
a great spot—they serve food until 11:30 pm. $ *Average main: $19*
⊠ *61-3642 Kawaihae Harbor, Hwy. 270, Kawaihae* ☎ *808/880–9393*
⊕ *www.seafoodbargrill.com.*

$$$$ ✕ **KPC (Kamuela Provision Company) at the Hilton Waikoloa Village.** The
MODERN   breezy lanai with a sweeping view of the Kohala Coast is the perfect
HAWAIIAN   accompaniment to the elegant yet down-to-earth Hawaii regional cui-
sine. The lanai offers the best seats in the house—get there by 5:30 if
you want to score a seat for the sunset, because KPC offers a better
view than any other restaurant on the Big Island. The specialty cocktails
are some of the best on the island, as well; ask for the mango martini.
Entrées are on the pricy side, but the ginger-steamed monchong (a deep-
water Hawaiian fish) is a winner. If you're in the mood for appetizers,
the Kona lobster and Hokkaido pumpkin bisque tastes as good as it
sounds. The restaurant's number one seller is the Kona Coffee Mud
Slide; don't miss it. The Baked Mauna Kea (KPC's take on a Baked
Alaska) is equally decadent. $ *Average main: $40* ⊠ *Hilton Waiko-
loa Village, 69-425 Waikoloa Beach Dr., Waikoloa* ☎ *808/886–1234*
⊕ *www.hiltonwaikoloavillage.com* ☉ *No lunch.*

$$$$ ✕ **Manta & Pavilion Wine Bar at the Mauna Kea Beach Hotel.** Perched on
MODERN   the edge of a bluff overlooking the sparkling waters of Kaunaoa
HAWAIIAN   Beach, this is an amazing spot for a romantic meal at sunset, espe-
cially at one of the outside tables. The restaurant's Enomatic wine
system allows guests to sample 48 different wines by the glass. Main
dishes include macadamia nut–crusted lamb, Big Island butterfish,
Kau coffee beef filet, butter-poached Keahole lobster, and a perfectly
prepared seared ahi with Molokai sweet-potato puree and foie-gras
spring roll. The crispy pork-belly appetizer with Kona baby abalone
is not to be missed; try the squash soup topped with ohelo berry.
This is also the spot for Sunday brunch, with an impressive spread
that includes an omelet station, prime rib, smoked salmon, tempura,
lobster bisque, and a build-your-own-sundae bar. $ *Average main:
$40* ⊠ *62-100 Mauna Kea Beach Dr., Kohala Coast* ☎ *808/882–5810*
⊕ *www.maunakeabeachhotel.com* ☉ *No lunch.*

$$ ✕ **Merriman's Market Café.** From Peter Merriman, one of Hawaii's star
MEDITERRANEAN   chefs, comes a more affordable alternative to his upscale Waimea and
Maui restaurants. The Mediterranean-influenced menu includes a variety of pasta dishes, tasty appetizers, and salads teeming with fresh ingredients from nearby Waimea farms. Its outdoor patio beckons locals and
visitors alike. It's open daily for lunch, followed by happy hour from

3 pm to 5:30 pm, then dinner until 8:45 pm. $ *Average main: $25* ⊠ *Kings' Shops at Waikoloa Beach Resort, 250 Waikoloa Beach Dr., Waikoloa* ☎ *808/886–1700* ⊕ *merrimanshawaii.com/market_cafe.htm.*

$$$$ ✕ **Monettes.** Chef Michael Minshull has arrived, and with him comes
MODERN a refined and lightened menu to which he's adding new favorites. This
AMERICAN superpricey restaurant at the Mauna Kea Beach Hotel unveils a beautiful koa-and-mahogany bar, plus a huge, glass-fronted wine cellar that houses an award-winning selection of more than 4,500 premium wines. Signature dishes range from Kobe beef to Colorado rack of lamb. Try the rich and buttery lobster bisque. Be sure to sample one of the delicious martinis served in a cone-shaped glass embedded in a bowl of crushed ice. $ *Average main: $45* ⊠ *Mauna Kea Beach Hotel, 62-100 Mauna Kea Beach Dr., Kohala Coast* ☎ *808/443–2850* ⊕ *www. monetteshawaii.com.*

$$ ✕ **Monstera.** It may not be beachfront with a view of the sunset, but this
JAPANESE addition to the Shops at Mauna Lani is worth a visit for its casual Japanese pub food with a touch of local inspiration. Chef Norio Yamamoto's tasty lunch and dinner menu includes his signature tuna *tataki* (seared raw fish slices), crispy whole moi, *hamachi kama* (broiled Japanese yellowtail cheek), and seafood papaya (shrimp and scallops with veggies baked in a papaya). There are excellent sizzling plate items like short ribs and rib-eye steak, hot and cold noodle dishes, and, of course, the outstanding sushi. Most people make a meal out of sharing several small plate items so you can sample a bit of everything. Save room for the tempura banana drizzled with chocolate and caramel for dessert. It's best to make a reservation; you can also get some of the menu to go. $ *Average main: $25* ⊠ *The Shops at Mauna Lani, 68-1330 Mauna Lani Dr., Waikoloa* ☎ *808/887–2711* ⊕ *www.monterasushi.com.*

$$$ ✕ **Norio's Japanese Restaurant and Sushi Bar.** Located inside the Fairmont
JAPANESE Orchid at the garden level, this restaurant appeals to both steak and seafood lovers. Chef Darren Ogasawara has completely revamped the former Norio's menu, highlighting everything from Australian A6 wagyu rib eye (seasoned with five different kinds of Hawaiian sea salt) to the delicious hamachi-and-avocado sashimi served with ponzu-garlic sauce. Everything on the menu is made from scratch, including the sauces, plus the fish is as fresh as it gets. $ *Average main: $35* ⊠ *Fairmont Orchid Hawaii, 1 N. Kaniku Dr., Kohala Coast* ☎ *808/885–2000* ⊕ *www. fairmont.com/orchid* ⊘ *Closed Tues. and Wed. No lunch.*

$$ ✕ **Number 3 at the Mauna Kea Beach Hotel.** Though it sits right on the
AMERICAN edge of the hotel's golf course, this is not just a restaurant for golfers. A short walk from the main entrance to the hotel, the newly renovated, spacious dining room has seating both inside and out, and service is quick and correct. Number 3 serves up a great lunch menu with dishes such as ahi sashimi and beer-battered fresh-fish tacos. $ *Average main: $18* ⊠ *62-100 Mauna Kea Beach Dr., Kohala Coast* ☎ *808/882–5810* ⊕ *www.maunakeabeachhotel.com* ⊘ *No dinner.*

$$$ ✕ **Roy's Waikoloa Bar & Grill.** If you're looking for consistently decent
MODERN food and you're staying nearby, Roy's fits the bill. The venue overlooks
HAWAIIAN the lake at the Kings' Shops, which, granted, is not an oceanfront setting by any means. If you're simply in the mood for a light meal, you

can easily fill up on the enormous selection of great appetizers, and the extensive wine-by-the-glass list offers good pairing options. The three-course meal is a good bet, or try the butterfish for a melt-in-your mouth encounter. $ *Average main: $30* ⊠ *Kings' Shops at Waikoloa Village, 250 Waikoloa Beach Dr., Kohala Coast* ☎ 808/886–4321 ⊕ *www. roysrestaurant.com* ⊗ *No lunch.*

$$$
JAPANESE
✕ **Sansei Seafood Restaurant & Sushi Bar.** This restaurant serves heavenly interpretations of sushi and contemporary Asian cuisine. More than a few dishes have won awards, including the shrimp dynamite in a creamy garlic masago aioli and unagi glaze, and the Dungeness crab ramen with Asian truffle broth. There are tried-and-true favorites that are mainstays, however, the menu is consistently updated to include new and exciting options such as the Hawaiian *moi* sashimi rolls and the Japanese yellowtail nori aioli poke. You can certainly make a meal out of the appetizers and sushi rolls, or try some of Sansei's great entrées from both land and sea. Go for an early dinner on Sunday and Monday when sushi and other food items are half off from 5 to 6 pm (limited seating; first come, first served). Or opt for a late-night meal on Friday and Saturday when sushi and appetizers are half off from 10 pm until 1:30 am (you just have to put up with the karaoke singers; 21 and older). $ *Average main: $35* ⊠ *201 Waikoloa Beach Dr., 801 Queens' MarketPlace, Waikoloa* ☎ 808/886–6286 ⊕ *www. dkrestaurants.com* ⊗ *No lunch.*

$$
JAPANESE
✕ **Sushi Rock.** In the funky Without Boundaries shop in Hawi, Sushi Rock isn't big on atmosphere—its narrow dining room is brightly painted and casually decorated with various Hawaiian and Japanese knickknacks—but hungry locals and visiting couples flock here for some of the island's best sushi. The restaurant prides itself on using fresh local ingredients like grass-fed beef tenderloin, goat cheese, macadamia nuts, and mango in their island-inspired sushi rolls. They also serve up a variety of cooked seafood, chicken, noodle dishes, and salads for lunch and dinner. Everything is plated beautifully and served either at the sushi bar, at one of the handful of indoor tables in the restaurant's narrow dining room, or on the covered front patio. There's also a full bar. $ *Average main: $23* ⊠ *55-3435 Akoni Pule Hwy., Hawi* ☎ 808/889–5900 ⊕ *sushirockrestaurant.net* ⊗ *Closed Wed.*

$$$
MODERN
HAWAIIAN
✕ **Tommy Bahama Tropical Café.** This breezy, open-air restaurant, located upstairs at the Shops at Mauna Lani, offers an excellent roster of appetizers: don't miss the seared-scallop sliders or the coconut-crusted crab cakes. The chef here has freedom to cook up his own daily specials, and the macadamia-crusted *opakapaka* (Pacific red snapper) is a standout. Other entrées include maple-brined pork chops and crab-stuffed shrimp. Homemade breads and creamy butters set the stage for a nice meal, which most definitely should include one of Tommy's outstanding martinis, the tastiest and strongest anywhere on the island. Desserts are decadent and meant for sharing. $ *Average main: $34* ⊠ *Shops at Mauna Lani, 68-1330 Mauna Lani Dr., No. 102, Kohala Coast* ☎ 808/881–8686 ⊕ *www.tommybahama.com.*

WAIMEA

$$$ HAWAIIAN 🍴 **Allen's Table.** Formerly executive chef at the acclaimed Merriman's restaurant in Waimea, Chef Allen Hess recently opened his own namesake restaurant at the former Huli Sue's down the highway. Foodies will appreciate his "slow food" take on regional cuisine inspired by Hawaii's plantation era. Don't miss the braised short ribs, the fried pork chop, the goat tacos, and the Kona lobster bouillabaisse. Chef Allen makes everything in-house, including sausages, patés, and dry-aged meats sourced from Big Island beef producers. As for seafood, his broiled local kampachi is the highlight of the fresh-catch offerings. [$] *Average main: $30* ✉ *64-957 Mamalahoa Hwy.* ☎ *808/885–6268* 🌐 *www.allenstable.com* 🕒 *Closed Sun.*

$ MEXICAN 🍴 **Big Island Brewhaus/Tako Taco.** Tako Taco has always been a favorite Waimea eatery, and owner Tom Kerns is a veteran brewer. He's now churning out some decent ales, lagers, and specialty beers from his on-site brewery. With a focus on fresh ingredients, Tako Taco whips up excellent tacos, burritos, Mexican salads, enchiladas, rellenos, and quesadillas fresh to order. You'll want refills on the habanero salsa, perhaps accompanied by a top-shelf margarita, either classic or *lilikoi* (passion fruit). And nothing beats a cold local brew to wash down that spicy enchilada. [$] *Average main: $11* ✉ *64-1066A Mamalahoa Hwy.* ☎ *808/887–1717* 🌐 *www.bigislandbrewhaus.com.*

$$ MODERN HAWAIIAN 🍴 **Daniel's.** This fine-dining restaurant features the creations of respected local chef Daniel Thiebaut in a quaint yellow building that once housed the historic Chock In Store, which catered to the ranching community beginning in 1900. Collectibles abound, such as antique porcelain pieces. Under new ownership, but still retaining the services of chef Daniel, the revamped establishment has unveiled an all-organic, locally sourced, sustainable menu that includes everything from handmade pastas to eggplant napoleon with hamakua mushrooms to Cajun-style ahi nicoise, pan-seared scallops, and a variety of sautéed seafood options. The place to be in Waimea on a Sunday afternoon, Daniel's offers a popular Sunday brunch from 10 to 2, featuring live local music and slack-key players. [$] *Average main: $25* ✉ *65-1259 Kawaihae Rd.* ☎ *808/881–8282* 🌐 *www.danielthiebaut.com* 🕒 *Closed Mon. No dinner Sun.*

$ MODERN HAWAIIAN 🍴 **Huli Sue's BBQ and Grill.** Huli Sue's serves large portions of updated Hawaiian classics in a casual little restaurant along the highway in Waimea. The barbecue menu, which includes your choice of meat (classics like ribs, pork roast, brisket) with one of four sauces, is melt-in-your-mouth delicious. The menu includes many other options, including a baked potato stuffed with your choice of meat, cilantro sour cream, and Fontina cheese, a variety of curry dishes, and a handful of fantastic appetizers. [$] *Average main: $12* ✉ *64-957 Mamalahoa Hwy. (Hwy. 11).* ☎ *808/885–6268* 🌐 *www.hulisues.com.*

$ EUROPEAN 🍴 **Lilikoi Café.** This gem of a café is tucked away in the back of the Parker Ranch Shopping Center. Locals love that it's hard to find because they want to keep Lilikoi Café's delicious breakfast crepes, freshly made soups, and croissants Waimea's best-kept secret. Owner and chef John Lorda puts out an impressive display of salad choices daily, including chicken curry, beet, fava bean, chicken pesto, and Mediterranean pasta. The Israeli couscous with tomato, red onion, cranberry, and basil is a hit, as is the half avocado stuffed with tuna salad. There's also a nice selection of sandwiches and hot entrées. The food is fresh, many of the ingredients are organic, and everything is homemade. $ *Average main: $9 ⊠ 67-1185 Mamalahoa Hwy. (Hwy. 11)* ☎ *808/887–1400* ⊙ *Closed Sun. No dinner.*

$$$$
MODERN
HAWAIIAN

✕ **Merriman's.** By far one of the best restaurants in Waimea, this is the signature restaurant of Peter Merriman, one of the pioneers of Hawaiian regional cuisine. Merriman's is the home of the original wok-charred ahi, usually served with buttery Wainaku corn. If you prefer meat, try the Kahua Ranch lamb, raised locally to the restaurant's specifications, or the prime bone-in New York steak, grilled to order. The extensive wine list is impressive and includes many selections poured by the glass. Be forewarned: Merriman's is pricey, so prepare to splurge. $ *Average main: $45 ⊠ Opelo Plaza, 65-1227 Opelo Rd.* ☎ *808/885–6822* ⊕ *www.merrimanshawaii.com* ⊲ *Reservations essential.*

$
ITALIAN

✕ **Pau.** The name here is the Hawaiian word for "done," which we're guessing alludes to how eagerly you will gobble up their sensational pizzas. You order at the counter and find your own seat in the small but neat inside dining area. The big draw is the wide selection of appetizers, salads, sandwiches, pastas, and pizzas loaded with lots of local, fresh ingredients. Try the "Superfood" salad with quinoa, brown rice, edamame, grapes, and spiced nuts or the tangy vintner's salad with local organic greens, spiced pecans, apples, Gorgonzola, and Pau's champagne vinaigrette. All sauces and salad dressings are made in-house. When it comes to the pizzas, anything goes: order one of Pau's 16-inch signature pies or create your own. Lunch is a deal if you order the Slice of Italy: a quarter pizza cut into three slices plus a side salad for just $9. The restaurant is a little tricky to find, but it's right next to Merriman's in Waimea. $ *Average main: $12 ⊠ 65-1227 Opelo Rd.* ☎ *808/885–6325* ⊕ *www.paupizza.com* ⊙ *Closed Sun.*

$
AMERICAN

✕ **Village Burger.** Village Burger brings a whole new meaning to gourmet hamburgers. This little eatery in Parker Ranch Center serves up locally raised, grass-fed, hormone-free beef that is ground fresh, hand-shaped daily at their restaurant, and grilled to perfection right before your eyes. Top your burger (be it ahi, veal, Kahua Ranch wagyu beef, Hamakua mushroom, or Waipio Taro) with everything from local avocados, baby greens, and chipotle goat cheese to tomato marmalade. Even the ice cream for their milkshakes is made right in Waimea, and the delicious brioche buns that house these juicy burgers are baked fresh in nearby Hawi. At this place, you really can taste the difference. $ *Average main: $10 ⊠ Parker Ranch Center, 67-1185 Mamalahoa Highway* ☎ *808/885–7319* ⊕ *villageburgerwaimea.com.*

HILO

$
ITALIAN

✕ **Big Island Pizza.** Gourmet pizza is the star here, topped with things like shrimp and smoked salmon. They also serve sandwiches, wraps, pastas, and salads. There are only a handful of tables for eating in, but they do a brisk take-out business and also deliver to the eastern side of the island. There's another brand-new location above Costco in Kailua-Kona, where they specialize in European-style pizzas with artisan crusts. [$] *Average main: $15* ✉ *760 Kilauea Ave.* ☎ *808/934–8000* 🌐 *www.bigislandpizza.com.*

$ HAWAIIAN 🍴 **Blane's Drive-In.** With a vast menu second only to Ken's House of Pancakes, Blane's serves up everything from standard hamburgers to chicken *katsu.* There's a mean plate lunch with tons of fresh fish for only $8. At one point it was a real drive-in, with car service. Now, customers park, order at the window, and then eat at one of the few picnic tables provided or take their food to go. [$] *Average main: $8* ✉ *217 Wainuenue Ave.* ☎ *808/969–9494.*

$ HAWAIIAN 🍴 **Café 100.** Established in 1948, this family-owned restaurant is famous for its tasty *loco moco,* prepared in more than a three-dozen ways, and its dirt-cheap breakfast and lunch specials. (You can stuff yourself for $3 if you order right.) The word "restaurant," or even "café," is used liberally here—you order at a window and eat on one of the outdoor benches provided—but you come here for the food and prices, not the ambience. [$] *Average main: $6* ✉ *969 Kilauea Ave.* ☎ *808/935–8683* 🕓 *Closed Sun.*

$$ ITALIAN 🍴 **Café Pesto.** One of the better restaurants in Hilo, Café Pesto offers exotic pizzas (with fresh Hamakua mushrooms, artichokes, and rosemary Gorgonzola sauce, for example), Asian-inspired pastas and risottos, fresh seafood, delicious salads, and appetizers that you could make a meal of. Products from local farmers feature heavily on the menu here—everything from the Kulana free-range beef to the Kawamata Farms tomatoes to the Kapoho Farms lehua-blossom honey made on the island. Live local musicians provide entertainment at dinner Thursday through Sunday. [$] *Average main: $20* ✉ *308 Kamehameha Ave.* ☎ *808/969–6640* 🌐 *www.cafepesto.com.*

$ THAI 🍴 **Full Moon Cafe.** This cozy restaurant in a newly renovated downtown Hilo building offers a small American menu of burgers, fish, and steak, but where the eatery truly stands out is in its fresh and tasty traditional Thai fare. The owners grow their own spices, herbs, and papayas organically on their Puna farm. The chefs here also sauté with olive oil to keep things heart-healthy. Try the hot and sour Tom Yum soup that is loaded with fresh veggies, pineapple curry, and the Thai basil eggplant. Wash it all down with a Thai iced tea or coffee as a musician strums relaxing Hawaiian music (weekends from 6 to 8:30). Also look for outdoor seating on the lanai and a new coffee shop next door that serves breakfast. [$] *Average main: $13* ✉ *51 Kalakaua St.* ☎ *808/961–0599* 🌐 *www.fullmooncafe.net.*

$ AMERICAN 🍴 **Hilo Bay Café.** What this eatery lacks in setting—it's in a strip mall that contains Office Max and Wal-Mart—it makes up for with modern decor and fantastic food. It's a popular restaurant among locals for "special" occasions like birthdays and anniversaries due to the high quality of food, but truth be told, the prices are reasonable enough you can come just to celebrate a Tuesday. Highly recommended are the roasted eggplant-Parmesan custard and the peppered local beef carpaccio with horseradish cream. The vegan offerings, like potpie, are good enough to seduce meat eaters. Daily specials always include a vegetarian, meat, and fish choice, and the menu changes twice a year to keep things fresh. The chef tries to use organic and local products wherever possible. $ *Average main: $15* ⊠ *315 Makaala St.* ☎ *808/935–4939* ⊕ *www.hilobaycafe.com* ☉ *No dinner Sun.*

$ ✕ **Ken's House of Pancakes.** For years, this 24-hour diner on Banyan Drive
AMERICAN   between the airport and the hotels has been a gathering place for Hilo residents and visitors. Breakfast is the main attraction: Ken's serves more than 11 different types of pancakes, plus all kinds of fruit waffles (banana, peach), and popular omelets, like "Da Bradda," teeming with a variety of meats. The menu features 180 other tasty local specialties (*loco moco*, tripe stew, oxtail soup) and American-diner-inspired items from which to choose. Sunday is all-you-can-eat spaghetti night, Tuesday is all-you-can-eat tacos, and Wednesday is prime rib night. $ *Average main: $10* ⊠ *1730 Kamehameha Ave.* ☎ *808/935–8711* ⊕ *kenshouseofpancakes-hilohi.com.*

$ ✕ **Kuhio Grille.** There's no atmosphere to speak of, and water is served in
HAWAIIAN   unbreakable plastic, but if you're searching for local fare—that eclectic and undefinable fusion of ethnic cuisines—Kuhio Grille is a must. Sam Araki serves a 1-pound *laulau* (a steamed bundle of taro leaves and pork) that is worth the trip. Other *grindz* include *loco moco*, oxtail soup, plate lunch specialties, pork chops, steaks, saimin, stir-fry, and daily specials. This local diner opens at 6 am, and is at the edge of Hilo's largest mall above the parking lot near Longs. $ *Average main: $9* ⊠ *Prince Kuhio Shopping Plaza, 111 E. Puainako St., at Hwy. 11* ☎ *808/959–2336* ⊕ *www.kuhiogrill.com.*

$ ✕ **Ocean Sushi.** What this restaurant lacks in ambience it certainly makes
JAPANESE   up for in quality and price. We're talking about light and crispy tempura; tender, moist teriyaki chicken; and about 25 specialty sushi rolls that, on average, will cost you a mere $5 per roll. If you're a sushi lover, be sure to try the "hospital roll" with shrimp tempura, cream cheese, cucumber, and spicy ahi, or the "volcano roll," a California roll topped with flying fish eggs, dried fish shavings, green onions, and spicy mayo. Don't let the low price tag fool you—the service is friendly and the food here is fresh, filling, and delicious. Open Monday through Saturday, 10 am to 2 pm, and 5 pm to 9 pm. $ *Average main: $9* ⊠ *250 Keawe St.* ☎ *808/961–6625* ☉ *Closed Sun.*

$$ ✕ **The Seaside Restaurant & Aqua Farm.** The Nakagawa family has been
SEAFOOD   running this eatery since the early 1920s. The latest son to manage the
☉   restaurant has transformed both the menu and the decor, and that, paired with the setting (the restaurant sits on a 30-acre natural brackish water fishpond) makes this one of the most romantic and interesting places to eat in Hilo. You can't get fish fresher than this. Islanders travel great distances for the fried *aholehole* (young Hawaiian flagtail) that's raised on the aqua-farm. Other great dishes from the sea include furikake salmon, miso butterfish, and macadamia nut–crusted mahimahi. The Pacific Rim menu includes plenty of selections for landlubbers, too. Arrive before sunset and request a table by the window for a view of the egrets roosting around the fishponds. $ *Average main: $23* ⊠ *1790 Kalanianaole Ave.* ☎ *808/935–8825* ⊕ *www.seasiderestaurant. com* ☉ *Closed Mon. No lunch.*

PUNA

$ ✕ **Luquin's Mexican Restaurant.** Long an island favorite for tasty, albeit
MEXICAN   greasy, Mexican grub, Luquin's is still going strong in the funky town
of Pahoa. Tacos are great here (go for crispy), especially when stuffed
with grilled, seasoned local fish on occasion. Chips are warm and salty,
the salsa's got some kick, and the beans are thick with lard and topped
with melted cheese. Not something you'd eat before a long swim, but
perfect after a long day of exploring. $ *Average main: $9* ✉ *15-2942
Pahoa Village Rd., Pahoa* ☎ *808/965–9990* ⊕ *luquinsmexicanrestau-
ranthawaii.com.*

HAWAII VOLCANOES NATIONAL PARK AND VICINITY   4

VOLCANO

$$ ✕ **Kiawe Kitchen.** Everyone around here says the same thing: "Kiawe has
ITALIAN   awesome pizza, but it's a little expensive." And it's true—the wood-fired
pizza at this warm and pretty Italian eatery, with red walls and wood
floors, has a perfect thin crust and an authentic Italian taste, but you
have to be prepared to spend around $20 on a typical pie. Food options
are limited in this area, though. Go for it. $ *Average main: $20* ✉ *19-
4005 Old Volcano Rd.* ☎ *808/967–7711.*

$$$ ✕ **Kilauea Lodge.** Chef Albert Jeyte combines contemporary trends with
EUROPEAN   traditional cooking styles from the mainland, France, and his native
Hamburg, Germany. The menu changes daily, and features such entrées
as venison, duck à l'orange with an apricot-mustard glaze, and authentic *hasenpfeffer* (braised rabbit). The coconut-crusted Brie appetizer is
huge, melty, and absolutely delicious, as are Jeyte's made-from-scratch
soups and breads. Built in 1937 as a YMCA camp, the restaurant
still has the original "Friendship Fireplace" embedded with coins and
plaques from around the world. The roaring fire, koa-wood tables, and
warm lighting make the dining room feel like a cozy lodge. $ *Average
main: $30* ✉ *19-3948 Old Volcano Hwy., Volcano Village* ☎ *808/967–
7366* ⊕ *www.kilauealodge.com.*

$ ✕ **Lava Rock Café.** This is an affordable place to grab a sandwich or a
DINER   coffee and check your email (Wi-Fi is free with purchase of meal) before
🕐   heading to HVNP. The homey, sit-down diner caters to families, serving
up heaping plates of pancakes and French toast for breakfast. For lunch,
burgers highlight the menu—everything from bacon-cheese to turkey
to Paniolo burgers made with Hawaii grass-fed beef. There are also
generous-sized sandwiches, *loco moco,* and soups, plus beef or chicken
teriyaki. Try the haupia cake for dessert. Bottled beer is served here too.
If you're looking for a place to take the kids, Lava Rock Café is the only
real option in Volcano Village. $ *Average main: $10* ✉ *19-3972 Old
Volcano Hwy., behind Kilauea General Store* ☎ *808/967–8526* ⊘ *No
dinner Sun. and Mon.*

$ ✕ **Thai Thai Restaurant.** The food is authentic, and the prices are reason-
THAI   able at this little Volcano Village find. A steaming hot plate of curry is
the perfect antidote to a chilly day on the volcano. The chicken satay
is excellent—the peanut dipping sauce the perfect match of sweet and
spicy. Be careful when you order, as "medium" is more than spicy

enough even for hard-core chili addicts. The service is warm and friendly and the dining room is pleasant, with white tablecloths, Thai art, and a couple of silk wall hangings. [$] *Average main: $15* ✉ *19-4084 Old Volcano Rd.* ☎ *808/967–7969* 🕒 *No lunch Wed.*

$ AMERICAN 🍴 **Volcano Golf & Country Club.** This restaurant doesn't feel much like a country club—it's simple and not at all fancy, with oak tables filled with local old-timers talking story and chowing down on greasy local favorites. Locals love this spot for its large portions and classic breakfasts: ordering the breakfast burger (with fried egg, cheese, and your choice of meat) and a cup of Kona coffee is the way to go. If it's lunchtime, you can't beat the burgers. [$] *Average main: $9* ✉ *Pii Mauna Dr., off Hwy. 11* ☎ *808/967–8228* 🕒 *No dinner Fri. and Sun.*

WHERE TO STAY

Updated by Karen Anderson

Even among locals, there is an ongoing debate about which side of the Big Island is "better," so don't worry if you're having a tough time deciding where to stay. Our recommendation? Do both. Each side of the island offers a different range of accommodations, restaurants, and activities.

Consider staying at one of the upscale resorts along the Kohala Coast or in a condo in Kailua-Kona for half of your trip. Then, shift gears and check into a romantic bed-and-breakfast on the Hamakua Coast, South Kona, Hilo, or near the volcano. If you've got children in tow, opt for a vacation home or a stay at one of the island's many family-friendly hotels. On the west side, explore the island's most pristine beaches or try some of the fine-dining restaurants; on the east side, hike through rain forests, witness majestic waterfalls, or go for a plate lunch.

Some locals like to say that the east is "more Hawaiian," but we argue that King Kamehameha himself made Kailua-Kona his final home during his sunset years. Another reason to try a bit of both: your budget. You can justify splurging on a stay at a Kohala Coast resort for a few nights because you'll spend the rest of your time paying one-third that rate at a cozy cottage in Volcano or a condo on Alii Drive. And although food at the resorts is very expensive, you don't have to eat every meal there. Condos and vacation homes can be ideal for a family trip or for a group of friends looking to save money and live like *kamaainas* (local residents) for a week or two. Many of the homes also have private pools and hot tubs, lanai, ocean views, and more—you can go as budget or as high-end as you like.

If you choose a bed-and-breakfast, inn, or an out-of-the-way hotel, explain your expectations fully and ask plenty of questions before booking. Be clear about your travel and location needs. Some places require stays of two or three days. No matter where you stay, you'll want to rent a car. Some rental car companies do have restrictions about taking their vehicles to certain Big Island scenic spots, so make sure to ask about rules before you book.

Prices in the reviews are the lowest price of a standard double room in high season. Prices for rentals are the lowest per-night cost for a one-bedroom unit in high season.For expanded hotel reviews, visit Fodors.com.

BEST BETS FOR BIG ISLAND LODGING

Fodor's Choice ★

Fairmont Orchid Hawaii, $$$, p. 448

Four Seasons Resort Hualalai, $$$$, p. 446

Holualoa Inn, $$, p. 444

Mauna Kea Beach Hotel, $$$$, p. 448

Mauna Lani Bay Hotel and Bungalows, $$$$, p. 450

Puakea Ranch, $$$, p. 450

Waianuhea, $$, p. 453

By Price

$

Courtyard King Kamehameha's Kona Beach Hotel, p. 441

Hale Ohia Cottages, p. 457

Kilauea Lodge, p. 457

Kona Tiki Hotel, p. 445

Manago Hotel, p. 446

Royal Kona Resort, p. 446

Waimea Gardens Cottage, p. 451

$$

Hilton Waikoloa Village, p. 448

Holualoa Inn, p. 444

Waianuhea, p. 453

$$$

Fairmont Orchid Hawaii, p. 448

Puakea Ranch, p. 450

Waikoloa Beach Marriott, p. 451

$$$$

Four Seasons Resort Hualalai, p. 446

Mauna Kea Beach Hotel, p. 448

Mauna Lani Bay Hotel and Bungalows, p. 450

By Experience

BEST BEACH

Hapuna Beach Prince Hotel, $$, p. 448

Mauna Kea Beach Hotel, $$$$, p. 448

Waikoloa Beach Marriott, $$$, p. 451

KAILUA-KONA

$$
RENTAL
Aston Kona by the Sea. Complete modern kitchens, tile lanai, and washer-dryer units can be found in every suite of this comfortable oceanfront condo complex. **Pros:** oceanfront; swimming pool and Jacuzzi. **Cons:** no beach. **TripAdvisor:** "what a great view," "secret getaway," "peaceful." $ *Rooms from: $210* ✉ *75-6106 Alii Dr.* ☎ *808/327–2300, 877/997–6667* ⊕ *www.astonhotels.com* ⤤ *73 units* ⦿ *No meals.*

$
RENTAL
Casa de Emdeko. A large and pretty complex on the *makai* (oceanfront) side of Alii Drive, Casa de Emdeko offers a few more amenities than most condo complexes, including a florist, hair salon, and an on-site convenience store that makes sandwiches. **Pros:** oceanfront fresh- and saltwater pools; hidden from the street; very private. **Cons:** quality and prices depend on owner; not kid-friendly. **TripAdvisor:** "relaxing," "great seaside location," "awesome condo." $ *Rooms from: $110* ✉ *75-6082 Alii Dr.* ☎ *808/329–2160* ⊕ *www.casadeemdeko.org* ⤤ *106 units* ⦿ *No meals.*

$
HOTEL
Courtyard King Kamehameha's Kona Beach Hotel. A splendid renovation has given new life to this previously aging landmark hotel in Kailua-Kona; new highlights include modern room decor that evokes a quintessential Hawaiian charm, plus a jazzed-up lobby that displays historical artifacts. **Pros:** central location; tastefully appointed rooms; historic ambience; aloha-friendly staff. **Cons:** most rooms have partial

WHERE TO STAY ON THE BIG ISLAND

	Local Vibe	Pros	Cons
Kailua-Kona	Kailua-Kona is a bustling little village. Alii Drive is brimming with hotels and condo complexes.	Plenty to do, day and night; main drag of shops, historic landmarks, and seaside attractions within easy walking distance of most hotels; many grocery stores in the area.	More traffic than anywhere else on the island; limited number of beaches; traffic noise on Alii Drive.
South Kona and Kau	A great place to stay if you want to be near some of the best water attractions on the island; there are plenty of bed-and-breakfasts and vacation rentals at or near Kealakekua Bay.	Kealakekua Bay is one of the most popular destinations on the island for kayaking and snorkeling; several good dining options nearby; coffee-farm tours in Captain Cook and Kainaliu towns.	Vog from Kilauea often settles here; fewer sand beaches in the area; farther south, the Kau district is quite remote.
The Kohala Coast	The Kohala Coast is home to most of the Big Island's major resorts. Blue, sunny skies prevail here, along with the island's best beaches.	Beautiful beaches; high-end shopping and dining; lots of activities for adults and children.	Pricey; long driving distances to Volcano, Hilo, and Kailua-Kona.
Waimea	Though it seems a world away, Waimea is only about a 15- to 20-minute drive from the Kohala Coast.	Beautiful scenery, paniolo (cowboy) culture; home to some exceptional local restaurants.	Can be cool and rainy year-round; nearest beaches are a 20-minute drive away.
The Hamakua Coast	The Hamakua Coast is a nice spot for those seeking peace, tranquility, and an alternative to the tropical-beach-vacation experience.	Close to Waipio Valley; foodie and farm tours in the area; good spot for honeymooners.	Beaches are an hour's drive away; convenience shopping is nonexistent.
Hilo	Hilo is the wetter, more lush eastern side of the Big Island. It is also less touristy than the west side.	Proximity to waterfalls, rain-forest hikes, museums, and botanical gardens; good bed-and-breakfast options.	The best white-sand beaches are on the other side of the island; noise from coqui frogs can be distracting at night.
Puna	Puna doesn't attract nearly as many visitors as other regions on the island, so you'll find good deals on rentals and B&Bs here.	A few black-sand beaches; off the beaten path with lots of outdoor wilderness to explore; lava flows into the sea here.	Few dining and entertainment options; no resorts or resort amenities; noisy coqui frogs at night.
Hawaii Volcanoes National Park and Vicinity	If you are going to visit Hawaii Volcanoes National Park, stay the night at any number of enchanting bed-and-breakfast inns in the fern-shrouded Volcano Village.	Good location for watching lava at night bubbling inside Halemaumau Crater; great for hiking, nature tours, and bike riding; close to Hilo and Puna.	Not many dining options; not much nightlife; can be cold and wet.

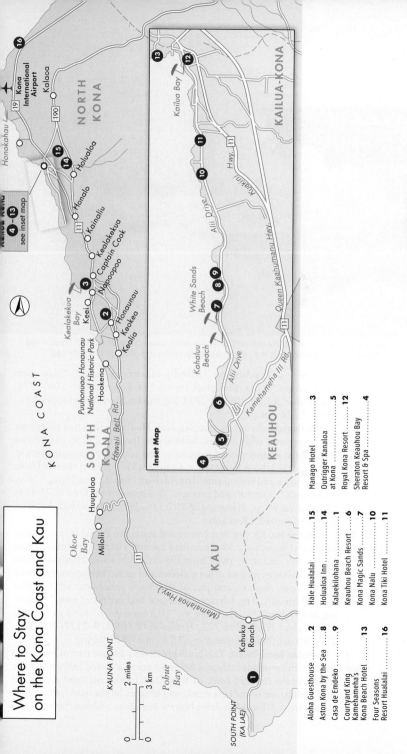

Where to Stay on the Kona Coast and Kau

KONA COAST

KAU

SOUTH POINT (KA LAE)

KAUNA POINT

Pohue Bay

Okoe Bay

Miloli'i

Huʻpuloa

Kahuku Ranch

(Mamalahoa Hwy.)

NORTH KONA

SOUTH KONA

Kona International Airport

Kalaoa

Holualoa

Honalo

Kainaliu

Kealakekua

Captain Cook

Napoʻopoʻo

Honaunau

Keokea

Kealia

Hoʻokena

Keʻei

Kealakekua Bay

Puʻuhonua o Honaunau National Historic Park

Hawaii Belt Rd.

Honokohau

Kona Kona
see inset map

Inset Map

KAILUA-KONA

Kailua Bay

White Sands Beach

Kahaluʻu Beach

Alii Drive

Kuakini

Queen Kaʻahumanu Hwy.

Kamehameha III Rd.

KEAUHOU

Hwy. 11

Aloha Guesthouse **2**	Manago Hotel **3**
Aston Kona by the Sea **8**	Outrigger Kanaloa at Kona **5**
Casa de Emdeko **9**	
Courtyard King Kamehameha's Kona Beach Hotel **13**	Royal Kona Resort **12**
	Sheraton Keauhou Bay Resort & Spa **4**
Four Seasons Resort Hualalai **16**	
Hale Hualalai **15**	
Holualoa Inn **14**	
Kalaekilohana **1**	
Keauhou Beach Resort **6**	
Kona Magic Sands **7**	
Kona Nalu **10**	
Kona Tiki Hotel **11**	

4

"We saw lava flowing into the sea. The sun went down, the steam turned shades of red and orange. It was one of the most memorable moments in my life." —disneydan, Fodors.com photo contest participant

ocean views. **TripAdvisor:** "friendly full-service hotel," "nice room and location," "beautiful place to stay." [$] *Rooms from: $160* ✉ *75-5660 Palani Rd.* ☎ *808/329–2911* 🌐 *www.konabeachhotel.com* 🛏 *457 rooms* 🍴 *No meals.*

$ B&B/INN **Hale Hualalai.** Perfect for couples, Hale Hualalai offers two exceptionally large suites with exposed beams, whirlpool bathtubs, and private lanai. **Pros:** gourmet breakfasts; new and tastefully decorated house; whirlpool tubs; large living space. **Cons:** not kid-friendly; removed from local beaches and restaurants. **TripAdvisor:** "terrific breakfasts," "very nice owner," "comfort and privacy." [$] *Rooms from: $160* ✉ *74-4968 Mamalahoa Hwy., Holualoa* ☎ *808/326–2909* 🌐 *www.hale-hualalai.com* 🛏 *2 suites* 🍴 *Breakfast.*

$$ B&B/INN Fodor's Choice ★ **Holualoa Inn.** Six spacious rooms and suites are available in this beautiful cedar home on a 30-acre coffee-country estate, a few miles above Kailua Bay and steps away from the artists' town of Holualoa. **Pros:** within walking distance of art galleries and cafés; well-appointed, with wood floors, fine art, and lots of windows; panoramic views. **Cons:** not kid-friendly. **TripAdvisor:** "best bed and breakfast ever," "amazing hospitality," "lovely property." [$] *Rooms from: $260* ✉ *76-5932 Mamalahoa Hwy., Box 222, Holualoa* ☎ *808/324–1121, 800/392–1812* 🌐 *www.holualoainn.com* 🛏 *6 rooms* 🍴 *Breakfast.*

$ RESORT **Keauhou Beach Resort.** This hotel preserves a unique part of Hawaiian history (the grounds include a *heiau* (temple), a sacred fishpond, and a replica of the summer home of King David Kalakaua) and is adjacent to Kahaluu, one of the best snorkeling beaches on the island. **Pros:** large rooms; free full breakfast daily; historic Hawaiian ambience; great tennis center. **Cons:** limited dining options. **TripAdvisor:** "great Hawaiian heritage," "fabulous grounds," "paradise found." [$] *Rooms from: $175* ✉ *78-6740 Alii Dr.* ☎ *808/322–3441, 866/326–6803* 🌐 *www.keauhoubeachresort.com* 🛏 *306 rooms, 3 suites* 🍴 *Breakfast.*

$ RENTAL 🏨 **Kona Magic Sands.** Cradled between a lovely grass park on one side and White Sands Beach on the other, this condo complex is great for swimmers, surfers, and sunbathers. **Pros:** next door to popular beach; affordable; oceanfront view from all units. **Cons:** studios only; some units are dated. **TripAdvisor:** "great location," "lots of amenities," "like sleeping on the beach." [$] *Rooms from: $115* ✉ *77-6452 Alii Dr.* ☎ *808/329–9393, 800/622–5348* 🌐 *www.konahawaii.com/ms.htm* 🛏 *37 units* 🍴 *No meals.*

KAILUA-KONA CONDO COMFORTS

The **Safeway** at Crossroads Shopping Center (✉ *75-1000 Henry St., Kailua-Kona* ☎ *808/329–2207*) offers an excellent inventory of groceries and produce, although prices can be steep.

You can rent DVDs at **Blockbuster** in the Kona Coast Shopping Center (✉ *74-5588 Palani Rd., Kailua-Kona* ☎ *808/326–7694*).

For pizza, **Kona Brewing Co. Pub & Brewery** (✉ *75-5629 Kuakini Hwy., just past Palani intersection on right, Kailua-Kona* ☎ *808/329–2739*) is the best bet, if you can pick it up. Otherwise, for delivery, try **Domino's** (☎ *808/329–9500*).

$$ RENTAL 🏨 **Kona Nalu.** One of the smaller complexes on the ocean side of Alii Drive, Kona Nalu features large, beautifully furnished units with super-size lanai, and ocean views from all units. **Pros:** extra-large units; ocean views. **Cons:** not within walking distance to stores or restaurants; sandy cove doesn't provide easy ocean entry. **TripAdvisor:** "perfect sunsets," "nice décor and amenities," "great condo." [$] *Rooms from: $250* ✉ *76-6212 Alii Dr.* ☎ *808/329–6438* 🌐 *www.sunquest-hawaii.com* 🛏 *15 units* 🍴 *No meals.*

$ HOTEL 🏨 **Kona Tiki Hotel.** The best thing about this three-story walk-up budget hotel, about a mile south of downtown Kailua Village, is that all the units have lanai right next to the ocean. **Pros:** very low price; oceanfront lanai and pool; friendly staff; free parking. **Cons:** older hotel in need of update; no TV; doesn't accept credit cards, but will take Paypal. **TripAdvisor:** "nice small hotel," "great price and view," "feet from gorgeous crashing waves." [$] *Rooms from: $80* ✉ *75-5968 Alii Dr.* ☎ *808/329–1425* 🌐 *www.konatikihotel.com* 🛏 *15 rooms* 💳 *No credit cards* 🍴 *Breakfast.*

$$$ RENTAL 🏨 **Outrigger Kanaloa at Kona.** The 16-acre grounds provide a peaceful and verdant background for this low-rise condominium complex bordering the Keauhou-Kona Country Club. **Pros:** across the street from acclaimed golf course and within walking distance of Keauhou Bay; three pools with hot tubs. **Cons:** no restaurant on property. **TripAdvisor:** "excellent view," "spacious condos," "excellent facilities." [$] *Rooms from: $305* ✉ *78-261 Manukai St.* ☎ *808/322–9625, 808/322–2272, 800/688–7444* 🌐 *www.outrigger.com* 🛏 *166 units* 🍴 *No meals.*

4

$ RESORT **Royal Kona Resort.** This is a great option if you're on a budget—the location is central; the bar, lounge, pool, and restaurant are right on the water; and the rooms feature contemporary Hawaiian decor with Polynesian accents. **Pros:** convenient location; waterfront pool; low prices. **Cons:** can be crowded; parking is tight. **TripAdvisor:** "wonderful Old Hawaiian feel," "beautiful views," "comfortable." [$] *Rooms from: $160* ✉ *75-5852 Alii Dr.* ☎ *808/329–3111, 800/222–5642* 🌐 *www.royalkona.com* 🛏 *436 rooms, 8 suites* 🍴 *No meals.*

$ RESORT 👶 **Sheraton Keauhou Bay Resort & Spa.** What it might lack in architectural ambience (it's a big concrete structure), the Sheraton makes up for with its beautifully manicured grounds, a historic sense of place, and stunning location on Keauhou Bay. **Pros:** cool pool; manta rays on view nightly; resort style at lower price. **Cons:** no beach; daily resort fee for Wi-Fi and parking; only one restaurant. **TripAdvisor:** "beautiful location," "big fun," "unexpected pleasure." [$] *Rooms from: $169* ✉ *78-128 Ehukai St.* ☎ *808/930–4900* 🌐 *www.sheratonkeauhou.com* 🛏 *510 rooms, 11 suites* 🍴 *No meals.*

THE KONA COAST

SOUTH KONA

$ B&B/INN **Aloha Guesthouse.** In the hills above Honaunau, Aloha Guesthouse offers quiet elegance, complete privacy, and ocean views from every room. **Pros:** eco-conscious; full breakfast; views of the South Kona coastline. **Cons:** remote location up a bumpy 1-mile dirt road. **TripAdvisor:** "quiet," "a paradise," "quirky but very nice." [$] *Rooms from: $110* ✉ *Old Tobacco Rd., off Hwy. 11 near mile marker 104, Honaunau* ☎ *808/328–8955* 🌐 *www.alohaguesthouse.com* 🛏 *5 rooms* 🍴 *Breakfast.*

$ HOTEL **Manago Hotel.** This historic hotel is a good option if you want to escape the touristy thing but still be close to the water and attractions like Kealakekua Bay and Puuhonua O Honaunau National Historical Park. **Pros:** local color; rock-bottom prices; terrific on-site restaurant. **Cons:** not the best sound insulation between rooms. **TripAdvisor:** "simple and convenient," "experience authentic Old Hawaii," "yummy and good service." [$] *Rooms from: $40* ✉ *81-6155 Mamalahoa Hwy., Box 145, Captain Cook* ☎ *808/323–2642* 🌐 *www.managohotel.com* 🛏 *64 rooms, 42 with bath* 🍴 *No meals.*

NORTH KONA

$$$$ RESORT Fodor's Choice ★ 👶 **Four Seasons Resort Hualalai.** Beautiful views everywhere, polished wood floors, custom furnishings and linens in warm earth and cool white tones, and Hawaiian fine artwork make Four Seasons Resort Hualalai a peaceful retreat. **Pros:** beautiful location; excellent restaurants. **Cons:** not the best beach among the resorts. **TripAdvisor:** "relaxed and beautiful," "another trip to paradise," "finest luxury resort." [$] *Rooms from: $625* ✉ *72-100 Kaupulehu Dr., Box 1269, Kailua-Kona* ☎ *808/325–8000, 800/819–5053, 888/340–5662* 🌐 *www.fourseasons.com/hualalai* 🛏 *243 rooms, 51 suites* 🍴 *No meals.*

Four Seasons Resort Hualalai

Holualoa Inn

THE KOHALA COAST

$$$
RESORT
Fodor'sChoice
★

Fairmont Orchid Hawaii. You can't go wrong booking a stay at The Fairmont Orchid, a first-rate resort that overflows with tropical gardens, cascading waterfalls, beautiful wings with "open sesame" doors, a meandering pool, and nicely appointed rooms with all the amenities. **Pros:** oceanfront location; great restaurants; excellent pool; aloha hospitality. **Cons:** top resort features come at a high price. **TripAdvisor:** "wonderful staff," "comfortable," "beautiful grounds." $ *Rooms from: $329* ⊠ *1 N. Kaniku Dr., Kohala Coast* ☎ *808/885–2000, 800/845–9905* ⊕ *www.fairmont.com/orchid* ⤳ *486 rooms, 54 suites* ⦿| *No meals.*

$$
HOTEL
☾

Hapuna Beach Prince Hotel. More reasonably priced than its neighbor resorts, Hapuna Beach Prince Hotel occupies the northern corner of the largest sand beach on the Big Island. **Pros:** extra-large rooms; all ocean-facing rooms; direct access to one of the island's best beaches. **Cons:** fitness center located off-site at the golf course; daily fees for Wi-Fi and parking. **TripAdvisor:** "a break from reality," "beautiful beach," "glitz from a bygone era." $ *Rooms from: $250* ⊠ *62-100 Kaunaoa Dr., Kohala Coast* ☎ *808/880–1111, 800/882–6060* ⊕ *www.princeresortshawaii.com* ⤳ *350 rooms, 61 suites* ⦿| *No meals.*

$$$
B&B/INN

Hawaii Island Retreat at Ahu Pohaku Hoomaluhia. Here, sustainability meets luxury without sacrificing comfort. **Pros:** stunning location; new and beautiful construction with no expense spared; eco-friendly. **Cons:** not within walking distance of restaurants; off the beaten path. **TripAdvisor:** "peaceful Hawaiian getaway," "a true oasis," "pampered luxury with a conscience." $ *Rooms from: $275* ⊠ *250 Maluhia Rd., Kapaau* ⊹ *Follow signs off Hwy. 270 in Kapaau, North Kohala* ☎ *808/889–6336* ⊕ *www.hawaiiislandretreat.com* ⤳ *9 rooms* ⦿| *Breakfast.*

$$
RESORT
☾

Hilton Waikoloa Village. Dolphins swim in the lagoon; a pint-size daredevil zooms down the 175-foot waterslide; a bride poses on the grand staircase; a fire-bearing runner lights the torches along the seaside path at sunset—these are some of the scenes that may greet you at this 62-acre megaresort. **Pros:** family-friendly; lots of restaurant and activity options. **Cons:** gigantic, crowded; restaurants are pricey. **TripAdvisor:** "excellent quality service," "endless amenities," "huge resort with beautiful landscaping." $ *Rooms from: $249* ⊠ *69-425 Waikoloa Beach Dr., Waikoloa* ☎ *808/886–1234, 800/445–8667* ⊕ *www.hiltonwaikoloavillage.com* ⤳ *1,240 rooms, 57 suites* ⦿| *No meals.*

$$$
RENTAL

Kolea at Waikoloa Beach Resort. Kolea appeals to the high-end visitor typically associated with the Mauna Lani Resort. **Pros:** high design; close to beach and activities; some resort amenities. **Cons:** pricey; no on-property restaurants. **TripAdvisor:** "well appointed," "perfect location," "gorgeous condos with over-the-top amenities." $ *Rooms from: $300* ⊠ *Waikoloa Beach Resort, 69-1000 Kolea Kai Circle, Waikoloa* ☎ *808/987-4519* ⊕ *www.waikoloavacationrentals.com/kolea-rentals* ⤳ *28 villas, 1 home* ⦿| *No meals.*

$$$$
HOTEL
Fodor'sChoice
★

Mauna Kea Beach Hotel. The grande dame of Kohala Coast, the Mauna Kea Beach Hotel was designed by Laurance S. Rockefeller in the early 1960s and opened in 1965. **Pros:** beautiful beach; extra-large contemporary rooms; excellent restaurants. **Cons:** small swimming

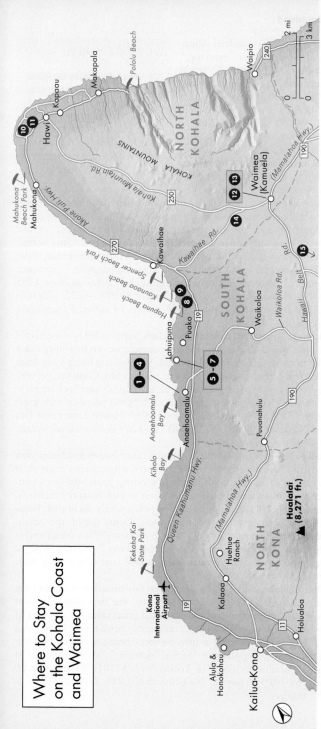

Where to Stay on the Kohala Coast and Waimea

Aaah The Views B&B **15**
Aloha Vacation
Cottages **14**
Fairmont Orchid
Hawaii **5**
Hapuna Beach
Prince Hotel **8**

Hawaii Island Retreat
at Ahu Pohaku
Hoomaluhia **11**
Hilton Waikoloa Village **1**
Kolea at Waikoloa
Beach Resort **3**
Mauna Kea Beach Hotel **9**

Mauna Lani Bay
Hotel & Bungalows **6**
Mauna Lani Point &
Islands of Mauna Lani **7**
Puakea Ranch **10**
Vista Waikoloa **4**

Waikoloa Beach Marriott ... **2**
Waimea Country Lodge .. **13**
Waimea Gardens
Cottage **12**

pool; overpriced sundries shop. **TripAdvisor:** "super relaxing," "best beach anywhere," "great architecture." [$] *Rooms from: $525* ✉ *62-100 Mauna Kea Beach Dr., Kohala Coast* ☎ *808/882–7222, 800/882–6060* 🌐 *www.maunakeabeachhotel.com* 🛏 *258 rooms, 10 suites* 🍴 *No meals.*

WORD OF MOUTH

"We had 10 days on the Big Island, and split it with 4 on the Hilo side and 6 on the Kona side. I was very glad we did both. It's really very long to do day trips, and there are lots of things to see and do on the west side. I would split the time."
—china_cat

$$$$ HOTEL Fodor'sChoice ★ 🏨 **Mauna Lani Bay Hotel & Bungalows.** A Kohala Coast classic, popular with honeymooners and anniversary couples for decades, the elegant Mauna Lani Bay Hotel & Bungalows is still one of the most beautiful resorts on the island, highlighted by a breathtaking, open-air lobby with cathedral-like ceilings, Zen-like koi ponds, and illuminated sheets of cascading water. **Pros:** beautiful design; award-winning spa; no hidden fees; complimentary valet parking. **Cons:** no luau. **TripAdvisor:** "relaxing property," "romance and magic," "neat hotel with historic grounds." [$] *Rooms from: $395* ✉ *68-1400 Mauna Lani Dr., Kohala Coast* ☎ *808/885–6622, 800/367–2323* 🌐 *www.maunalani.com* 🛏 *324 rooms, 14 suites, 5 bungalows* 🍴 *No meals.*

$$$$ RENTAL 🏨 **Mauna Lani Point and Islands of Mauna Lani.** Surrounded by the emerald greens of a world-class ocean-side golf course, spacious two-story suites at Islands of Mauna Lani offer a private, independent home away from home. **Pros:** privacy; soaking tubs; extra-large units. **Cons:** can get very pricey; no access to nearby resort amenities. **TripAdvisor:** "perfect paradise retreat," "relaxing and reenergizing," "great property with great location." [$] *Rooms from: $395* ✉ *68-1050 Mauna Lani Point Dr., Kohala Coast* ☎ *808/885–5022, 800/642–6284* 🌐 *www.classicresorts.com* 🛏 *61 units* 🍴 *No meals.*

$$$ RENTAL Fodor'sChoice ★ 🏨 **Puakea Ranch.** Four beautifully restored ranch houses and bungalows occupy this historic country estate in Hawi, where guests enjoy their own private swimming pools, horseback riding, round-the-clock concierge availability, and plenty of fresh fruit to pick from the orchards. **Pros:** horseback lessons and trail riding; charmingly decorated; beautiful bathrooms; private swimming pools. **Cons:** not on the beach. **TripAdvisor:** "fantastic views," "a true getaway," "luxurious exclusivity." [$] *Rooms from: $289* ✉ *56-2864 Akoni Pule Hwy., Kohala Coast* ☎ *808/315–0805* 🌐 *www.puakearanch.com* 🛏 *4 private bungalows* 🍴 *No meals.*

$$ RENTAL 🏨 **Vista Waikoloa.** Older and more reasonably priced than most of the condo complexes along the Kohala Coast, the two-bedroom, two-bath Vista condos offer ocean views and a great value for this part of the island. **Pros:** centrally located; reasonably priced; very large units; 75-foot lap pool. **Cons:** hit or miss on decor because each unit is individually owned. **TripAdvisor:** "perfect location," "all the comforts of home," "paradise revisited." [$] *Rooms from: $180* ✉ *Waikoloa Beach Resort, 69-1010 Keana Pl., Waikoloa* ☎ *808/886–3594* 🛏 *122 units* 🍴 *No meals.*

$$$ RESORT **Waikoloa Beach Marriott.** The most affordable resort on the Kohala Coast, the Waikoloa Beach Marriott covers 15 acres and encompasses ancient fishponds, historic trails, and petroglyph fields. **Pros:** more low-key than the Hilton Waikoloa; well-designed interiors. **Cons:** only one restaurant. **TripAdvisor:** "good service," "wonderful place to relax," "good contemporary hotel." [$] *Rooms from: $330* ✉ *69-275 Waikoloa Beach Dr., Waikoloa* ☎ *808/886–6789, 800/228–9290* 🌐 *www.marriott.com* 🛏 *523 rooms, 22 suites* 🍴 *No meals.*

WAIMEA

$ B&B/INN **Aaah The Views Bed and Breakfast.** The name aptly sums up the experience at this tranquil, stream-side inn built specifically to be a bed-and-breakfast—and it's the only lodging in Waimea that includes breakfast. **Pros:** away from it all; friendly hosts; beautiful countryside views; free beach gear. **Cons:** no pool. **TripAdvisor:** "very pleasant," "magical spot," "lovely hosts." [$] *Rooms from: $125* ✉ *66-1773 Alaneo St., off Akulani, just past mile marker 60 on Hwy. 19* ☎ *808/885–3455* 🌐 *www.aaahtheviews.com* 🛏 *3 suites* 🍴 *Breakfast.*

$ RENTAL **Aloha Vacation Cottages.** Set on several acres in upper South Kohala, these two rental cottages are clean, comfortable, and well stocked with beach toys, towels and mats, snorkel gear, body boards, kayaks, fishing gear, laptop computers, books, cable TV, videos, you name it. **Pros:** each cottage equipped with gas grill; free Wi-Fi; 10-minute drive from great beaches. **Cons:** somewhat remote location; can't walk to restaurants or stores; no pool. **TripAdvisor:** "everything you'd ever need," "like being at home," "our hosts were so thoughtful." [$] *Rooms from: $125 877/875–1722, 808/885–6535* 🌐 *www.alohacottages.net* 🛏 *2 units* 🍴 *No meals.*

$ HOTEL **Waimea Country Lodge.** In the heart of cowboy country, this modest ranch house–style lodge offers views of the green, rolling slopes of Mauna Kea. **Pros:** affordable; large rooms equipped with kitchenettes. **Cons:** rooms could use some updating; no pool. **TripAdvisor:** "better than expected," "haunted," "great potential but very dated." [$] *Rooms from: $129* ✉ *65-1210 Lindsey Rd.* ☎ *808/885–4100, 800/367–5004* 🌐 *www.castleresorts.com* 🛏 *21 rooms* 🍴 *No meals.*

$ RENTAL **Waimea Gardens Cottage.** Surprisingly luxe, yet cozy and quaint, three charming country cottages at this historic Hawaiian homestead are surrounded by flowering private gardens and a backyard stream. **Pros:** no detail left out; beautiful

KOHALA COAST CONDO COMFORTS

If you require anything not provided by the management, both the **Kings' Shops** (✉ *250 Waikoloa Beach Dr., Waikoloa* ☎ *808/886–8811*) and the **Queens' Marketplace** (✉ *201 Waikoloa Beach Dr., Waikoloa* ☎ *808/886–8822*) in the Waikoloa Beach Resort are good places to go. There are a small grocery store, a liquor store, and several nice restaurants at the Kings' Shops. The newer Queens' Marketplace also has a food court, as well as a gourmet market where you can get pizza baked to order. It's not exactly cheap, but you're paying for the convenience of not having to drive into town.

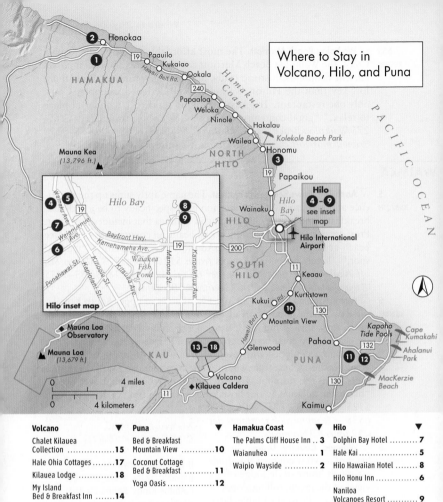

Where to Stay in Volcano, Hilo, and Puna

Volcano ▼

Chalet Kilauea
Collection 15

Hale Ohia Cottages 17

Kilauea Lodge 18

My Island
Bed & Breakfast Inn 14

Volcano Places 16

Volcano Teapot
Cottage 13

Puna ▼

Bed & Breakfast
Mountain View 10

Coconut Cottage
Bed & Breakfast 11

Yoga Oasis 12

Hamakua Coast ▼

The Palms Cliff House Inn .. **3**

Waianuhea **1**

Waipio Wayside **2**

Hilo ▼

Dolphin Bay Hotel **7**

Hale Kai **5**

Hilo Hawaiian Hotel **8**

Hilo Honu Inn **6**

Naniloa
Volcanoes Resort **9**

Shipman House Bed &
Breakfast Inn **4**

self-contained cottages; gardens; complete privacy. **Cons:** requires payment in full six weeks prior to arrival. **TripAdvisor:** "delightful hosts," "perfect studio," "beautiful grounds and room." [$] *Rooms from: $150 808/885–8550 🌐 www.waimeagardens.com 🛏 2 cottages, 1 studio 💳 No credit cards 🍴 Breakfast.*

THE HAMAKUA COAST

$$ B&B/INN 🏨 **The Palms Cliff House Inn.** This handsome Victorian-style mansion, 15 minutes north of downtown Hilo, is perched on the sea cliffs 100 feet above the crashing surf of the tropical coast. **Pros:** stunning views; terrific breakfast; comfortable rooms with every amenity; all rooms have private entrances from the exterior. **Cons:** no pool; no lunch or dinner on site; remote location means you have to drive to Hilo town for dinner. **TripAdvisor:** "relaxing and comfortable," "great service and great views," "perfect Hawaii accommodations." [$] *Rooms from: $199 ✉ 28-3514 Mamalahoa Hwy., Honomu ☎ 866/963–6076, 808/963–6076 🌐 www.palmscliffhouse.com 🛏 4 rooms, 4 suites 🍴 Breakfast.*

$$ B&B/INN Fodor's Choice ★ 🏨 **Waianuhea.** Defining Hawaiian Upcountry elegance, this gorgeous country inn, which is fully self-contained and runs off solar power, sits in a forested area on the Hamakua Coast in Ahualoa. **Pros:** eco-friendly hotel; hot and healthy breakfast; beautiful views. **Cons:** very remote location; unreliable phone access. **TripAdvisor:** "a gorgeous getaway," "beautiful and tasty breakfasts," "off the grid." [$] *Rooms from: $210 ✉ 45-3503 Kahana Dr., Honokaa ☎ 888/775–2577, 808/775–1118 🌐 www.waianuhea.com 🛏 4 rooms, 1 suite 🍴 Breakfast.*

$ B&B/INN 🏨 **Waipio Wayside.** Nestled amid the avocado, mango, coffee, and kukui trees of a historic plantation estate (circa 1932), this serene inn provides a retreat close to the Waipio Valley. **Pros:** close to Waipio; authentic Hawaiian feel; hammocks with views. **Cons:** remote location; no lunch or dinner on property. **TripAdvisor:** "nicely furnished," "peaceful and comfortable," "classy and romantic." [$] *Rooms from: $110 ✉ 46-4226 Honokaa-Waipio Road off Hwy. 240, Honokaa ☎ 808/775–0275, 800/833–8849 🌐 www.waipiowayside.com 🛏 5 rooms 🍴 Breakfast.*

HILO

$ HOTEL 👶 🏨 **Dolphin Bay Hotel.** Units in this circa-1950s motor lodge are modest, but charming, clean, and inexpensive. **Pros:** great value; full kitchens in all units; extremely helpful and pleasant staff; weekly rates are a good deal. **Cons:** no pool; no phones in the rooms. **TripAdvisor:** "in the heart of Hilo," "quaint hotel with Hawaiian charm," "delightful gardens." [$] *Rooms from: $109 ✉ 333 Iliahi St. ☎ 808/935–1466 🌐 www.dolphinbayhotel.com 🛏 18 rooms, 12 studios, 4 1-bedroom units, 1 2-bedroom unit 🍴 No meals.*

$ B&B/INN 🏨 **Hale Kai.** On a bluff above Hilo Bay, this 5,400-square-foot modern home is 2 miles from downtown Hilo, and features four rooms—each with patios, deluxe bedding, and grand ocean views within earshot of the surf. **Pros:** delicious hot breakfast; panoramic views; hot tub. **Cons:** no kids under 13. **TripAdvisor:** "great food," "B&B

The Fairmont Orchid Hawaii

Mauna Kea Beach Hotel

in paradise," "beautiful view." $ *Rooms from: $165* ⊠ *111 Honolii Place* ☎ *808/935–6330* ⊕ *www.halekaihawaii.com* ↝ *3 rooms, 1 suite* |◎| *Breakfast.*

$$
HOTEL

▦ **Hilo Hawaiian Hotel.** Though it does show its age and some of the rooms are in dire need of a refresh, this older hotel has large bay-front rooms offering spectacular views of Mauna Kea and Coconut Island on Hilo Bay. **Pros:** Hilo Bay views; private lanai in most rooms; large rooms. **Cons:** worse for wear; prices high for quality of rooms. **TripAdvisor:** "simple but very comfortable," "wonderful staff," "great views." $ *Rooms from: $200* ⊠ *71 Banyan Dr.* ☎ *808/935–9361, 800/367–5004 from mainland, 800/272–5275 interisland* ⊕ *www.castleresorts.com* ↝ *264 rooms, 21 suites* |◎| *No meals.*

$
B&B/INN

▦ **Hilo Honu Inn.** A charming old Craftsman home lovingly restored by a friendly and hospitable couple from North Carolina, the Hilo Honu offers quite a bit of variety. **Pros:** beautifully restored home; spectacular Hilo Bay views; delicious breakfast; free Wi-Fi. **Cons:** no toddlers in the upstairs suite. **TripAdvisor:** "lovely hosts," "first class and fabulous," "unforgettable Southern hospitality." $ *Rooms from: $140* ⊠ *465 Haili St.* ☎ *808/935–4325* ⊕ *www.hilohonu.com* ↝ *3 rooms* |◎| *Breakfast.*

$
RESORT

▦ **Naniloa Volcanoes Resort.** The Naniloa's recently renovated guest rooms in the Mauna Kea tower are a vast improvement over the old ones at this landmark hotel, which is a great home base for exploring the Big Island's unspoiled east side. **Pros:** some renovated rooms; great views of Hilo Bay and Mauna Kea and Mauna Loa volcanoes from some rooms. **Cons:** ongoing renovations; limited dining options. **TripAdvisor:** "great view out to the ocean," "a proud tourist standard," "pretty room." $ *Rooms from: $105* ⊠ *93 Banyan Dr.* ☎ *808/969–3333* ⊕ *www.volcanohousehotel.com/naniloa_volcanoes_resort.htm* ↝ *313 rooms, 7 suites* |◎| *No meals.*

$$
B&B/INN

▦ **Shipman House Bed & Breakfast Inn.** This bed-and-breakfast is on 5½ verdant acres on Reed's Island; the house is furnished with antique koa and period pieces, some dating from the days when Queen Liliuokalani came to tea. **Pros:** 10-minute walk to downtown Hilo; historic home; friendly and knowledgeable local hosts. **Cons:** not a great spot for kids. **TripAdvisor:** "charming," "romantic and historical," "such a beautiful home." $ *Rooms from: $219* ⊠ *131 Kaiulani St.* ☎ *808/934–8002, 800/627–8447* ⊕ *www.hilo-hawaii.com* ↝ *3 rooms, 2 cottage rooms* |◎| *Breakfast.*

PUNA

$
B&B/INN

▦ **Bed & Breakfast Mountain View.** This modern home on a secluded 4-acre estate has extensive floral gardens and a fishpond and is surrounded by rolling forest and farmland. **Pros:** reasonable prices; local artist hosts; beautiful landscaping. **Cons:** rooms could use some updating; location is remote. **TripAdvisor:** "pleasant accommodations," "quiet location," "wonderful hosts." $ *Rooms from: $90* ⊠ *18-3717 South Kulani Rd., Kurtistown* ☎ *808/968–6868, 888/698–9896* ⊕ *www.bbmtview.com* ↝ *4 rooms, 2 with shared bath* |◎| *Breakfast.*

Mauna Lani Bay Hotel & Bungalows

Puakea Ranch

Waianuhea

$ B&B/INN **Coconut Cottage Bed & Breakfast.** Coconut Cottage has quickly become a favorite among visitors for its beautiful grounds, the hosts' attention to detail, and its proximity to different island adventures. **Pros:** great breakfast; convenient to the lava-flow area, black-sand beach, and Kapoho tide pools for snorkeling. **Cons:** some may have a hard time sleeping with the coqui frogs chirping. **TripAdvisor:** "paradise at its best," "charming and breathtaking," "excellent hospitality." [$] *Rooms from: $110* ✉ *13-1139 Leilani Ave., Pahoa* ☎ *808/965–0973, 866/204–7444* 🌐 *www.coconutcottagehawaii.com* 🛏 *3 rooms, 1 bungalow* 🍴 *Breakfast.*

$ B&B/INN **Yoga Oasis.** With its exposed redwood beams, Balinese doorways, and imported art, Yoga Oasis draws those who seek relaxation and rejuvenation, and perhaps a free morning yoga lesson or two. **Pros:** daily yoga; focus on relaxation; very low prices. **Cons:** remote location; shared bathrooms in the main building. **TripAdvisor:** "the perfect yoga retreat," "all the healing in one place," "unique adventure." [$] *Rooms from: $75* ✉ *13-677 Pohoiki Rd., Pahoa808/936-7710, 800/274–4446* 🌐 *www.yogaoasis.org* 🛏 *4 rooms with shared bath, 4 deluxe cabins, 1 Bali house* 🍴 *No meals.*

HAWAII VOLCANOES NATIONAL PARK AND VICINITY

$ B&B/INN **Chalet Kilauea Collection.** The Collection comprises three inns and lodges and five vacation houses in and around Volcano Village. **Pros:** free Wi-Fi at all facilities; free afternoon tea at main office; large variety of lodging types to choose from; hot tub; fireplace. **Cons:** office closes at 5 pm—late arrivals allowed but you need to formally check in the following morning. **TripAdvisor:** "peaceful and romantic," "comfortable room," "very charming and clean." [$] *Rooms from: $63* ✉ *Wright Rd., 19-4178 Wright Rd.* ☎ *808/967–7786, 800/937–7786* 🌐 *www.volcanohawaii.com* 🛏 *14 rooms, 3 suites, 5 houses* 🍴 *No meals.*

$ RENTAL **Hale Ohia Cottages.** A stately and comfortable Queen Anne–style mansion, Hale Ohia was built in the 1930s as a summer home for a wealthy Scotsman (the property is listed on the State Historic Register). **Pros:** unique architecture; central, quiet location; privacy. **Cons:** no TVs. **TripAdvisor:** "comfortable and charming," "beautiful cottage," "a gem in the woods." [$] *Rooms from: $109* ✉ *11-3968 Hale Ohia Rd., off Hwy. 11* ☎ *808/967–7986, 800/455–3803* 🌐 *www.haleohia.com* 🛏 *4 rooms, 3 cottages, 1 suite* 🍴 *Breakfast.*

$ HOTEL **Kilauea Lodge.** A mile from the entrance of Hawaii Volcanoes National Park, this lodge was initially built as a YMCA camp in the 1930s. **Pros:** great restaurant; close to volcano; fireplaces. **Cons:** a little pricey for the area; no TV or phone in room. **TripAdvisor:** "convenient location for touring the volcano," "beautiful lush area," "great food." [$] *Rooms from: $170* ✉ *19-3948 Old Volcano Rd., 1 mile northeast of Volcano Store* ☎ *808/967–7366* 🌐 *www.kilauealodge.com* 🛏 *12 rooms, 4 cottages (off property)* 🍴 *Breakfast.*

$ B&B/INN **My Island Bed & Breakfast Inn.** This three-story, family-operated inn is in a historic home built in 1886 by the Lyman missionary family and set on a 7-acre botanical estate. **Pros:** historic home; full breakfast. **Cons:** some shared bathrooms; not every room has a TV. **TripAdvisor:** "beautiful gardens," "great folks," "can't beat the breakfast." $ *Rooms from: $80* ✉ *19-3896 Old Volcano Hwy., Volcano Village* ☎ *808/967–7216* ⊕ *www.myislandinnhawaii.com* ⤴ *6 rooms, 1 guesthouse* |○| *Breakfast.*

$ | RENTAL ░ **Volcano Places.** A collection of lovely vacation rental cottages, these accommodations range from a simple cottage in the rain forest to the stunning cedar-paneling Nohea, with its own hot tub. **Pros:** unique architecture; accommodates families; competitively priced; total privacy. **Cons:** no nightlife nearby. **TripAdvisor:** "beautiful property in the rainforest," "unique cottage," "magical." $ *Rooms from: $125* ✉ *19-3951 Laukapu Rd.* ☎ *808/967–7990, 877/967–7990* ⊕ *www. volcanoplaces.com* ⤴ *2 2-bedroom cottages, 1 1-bedroom unit, 1 studio* |○| *No meals.*

$$ | RENTAL ░ **Volcano Teapot Cottage.** A near-perfect spot for couples seeking a romantic getaway in Volcano Village, this cute two-bedroom red-and-white cottage is completely private and lovingly decorated. **Pros:** claw-foot tub; hot tub; fireplace; laundry facilities. **Cons:** single or double occupancy only. **TripAdvisor:** "an immaculately kept dollhouse," "comfortable and romantic," "absolutely gorgeous in the rainforest." $ *Rooms from: $195* ✉ *19-4041 Kilauea Rd., Volcano Village* *808/967–7112* ⊕ *www.volcanoteapot.com* ⤴ *1 cottage* |○| *Breakfast.*

KAU

$$ | B&B/INN ░ **Kalaekilohana.** You wouldn't really expect to find a top-notch bed-and-breakfast in Kau, but just up the road from South Point, this grand yellow residence offers large, comfortable private suites with beautiful, locally harvested hardwood floors, private lanai with ocean and mountain views, and big, comfy beds decked out with high-thread-count sheets and fluffy down comforters. **Pros:** luxurious beds; beautiful decor reminiscent of Old Hawaii; delicious breakfast. **Cons:** not for children under 10; no pool. **TripAdvisor:** "relaxing and beautiful," "wonderful taste of Hawaii," "heavenly retreat." $ *Rooms from: $219* ✉ *94-2152 South Point Rd., Naalehu* ☎ *808/939–8052* ⊕ *www.kau-hawaii.com* ⤴ *4 rooms* |○| *Breakfast.*

Kauai

WORD OF MOUTH

"Napali, Napali, and Napali—by air, by boat, and by hikes. All are worth it. Also remember Kokee is actually more of seeing Napali. Waimea is okay but Kokee is exceptional."

—lifeisbeautiful

WELCOME TO KAUAI

TOP REASONS TO GO

★ **Napali Coast:** On foot, by boat, or by air—explore what is unarguably one of the most beautiful stretches of coastline in all Hawaii.

★ **Kalalau Trail:** Hawaii's ultimate adventure hike will test your endurance but reward you with lush tropical vegetation, white-sand beaches, and unforgettable views.

★ **Kayaking:** Kauai is a mecca for kayakers, with four rivers plus the spectacular coastline to explore.

★ **Waimea Canyon:** Dramatic, colorful rock formations and frequent rainbows make this natural wonder one of Kauai's most stunning features.

★ **Birds:** Birds thrive on Kauai, especially at the Kilauea Point National Wildlife Refuge.

1 **North Shore.** Dreamy beaches, green mountains, breathtaking scenery, and abundant rain, waterfalls, and rainbows characterize the North Shore, which includes the communities of Kilauea, Princeville, and Hanalei.

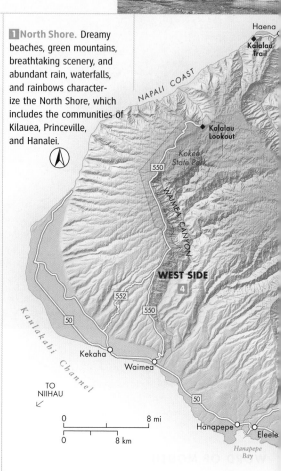

2 **East Side.** This is Kauai's commercial and residential hub, dominated by the island's largest town, Kapaa. The airport, harbor, and government offices are found in the county seat of Lihue.

3 **South Shore.** Peaceful landscapes, sunny weather, and beaches that rank among the best in the world make the South Shore the resort capital of Kauai. The Poipu resort area is here, along with the main towns of Koloa, Lawai, and Kalaheo.

GETTING ORIENTED

Despite its small size—550 square miles—Kauai has four distinct regions, each with its own unique characteristics. The windward coast, which catches the prevailing trade winds, consists of the North Shore and East Side, while the drier leeward coast encompasses the South Shore and West Side. One main road nearly encircles the island, except for a 15-mile stretch of sheer cliffs called Napali Coast. The center of the island—Mt. Waialeale, completely inaccessible by car and rarely viewable except from above due to nearly year-round cloud cover—is reported to be the wettest spot on Earth, getting about 450 inches of rain per year.

4 West Side. Dry, sunny, and sleepy, the West Side includes the historic towns of Hanapepe, Waimea, and Kekaha. This area is ideal for outdoor adventurers because it's the entryway to the Waimea Canyon and Kokee State Park, and the departure point for most Napali Coast boat trips.

GREAT ITINERARIES

As small as Kauai may be, you still can't do it all in one day: hiking Kalalau Trail, kayaking Wailua River, showering in a waterfall, watching whales at Kilauea Lighthouse, waking to the sunrise above Kealia, touring underwater lava tubes at Tunnels, and shopping for gifts at Koloa Town shops. Rather than trying to check everything off your list in one fell swoop, we recommend choosing your absolute favorite and devoting a full day to the experience.

Adventure Galore

For big-time adventure, kayak Napali Coast or spend a day learning to fly a microlight. For those whose idea of adventure is a good walk, take the flat, coastal trail along the East Side—you can pick it up just about anywhere starting at the southern end of Lydgate Park, heading north. It'll take you all the way to Anahola, if you desire. After it's all over, recuperate with a massage by the ocean—or in the comfort of your own room, so you can crash immediately afterward.

Shop Till You Drop

You could actually see a good many of the island's sights by browsing in our favorite island shops. Of course, you can't see the entire island, but this itinerary will take you through Kapaa and north to Hanalei. Don't miss Marta's Boat—high-end clothing for mom and child—across from Foodland in Waipouli. A mile north, Kela's Glass has great art pieces. From there, a leisurely drive north will reveal the rural side of Kauai. If you enjoy tea, sake, or sushi, stop at Kilauea's Kong Lung, where you can stock up on complete place settings for each. Then, head down the road to Hanalei. If you're inspired by surf, stop in Hanalei Surf Company. Our favorite for one-of-a-kind keepsakes—actually antiques and authentic memorabilia—is Yellow Fish Trading Company, and we never head into Hanalei without stopping at On the Road to Hanalei.

Relax Kauai-Style

If you're headed to Kauai for some peace and quiet, you'll want to start your day with yoga at Yoga Hanalei (⊕ www.yogahanalei.com) or Kapaa's Bikram Yoga Kauai (⊕ www.birkamyogakapaa.com). If you're staying on the South Shore, try yoga on the beach (actually a grassy spot just off the beach) with long-time yoga instructor Joy Zepeda (⊕ www.aloha-yoga.com). If it happens to be the second or last Sunday of the month, you might then head to the Lawai International Center (⊕ www.lawaicenter.org) for an afternoon stroll among 88 Buddhist shrines. On the North Shore, Limahuli Gardens is the perfect place to wander among native plants. Then watch the sun slip into the sea on any west-facing beach and call it a day with a glass of wine.

Have a Little Romance

We can't think of a better way to ensure a romantic vacation for two than to pop a bottle of champagne and walk the Mahaulepu shoreline at sunrise, hand in hand with a loved one. Make this a Sunday and follow your walk with brunch at the Grand Hyatt. Then spend the afternoon luxuriating with facials, body scrubs, and massage in the Hyatt ANARA Spa's Garden Treatment Village, in a private, thatched hut just for couples. That'll put you in the mood for a wedding ceremony or renewal of vows on the beach followed by a sunset dinner overlooking the ocean at the Beach House restaurant. Can it get any more romantic than this?

Even a nickname like "The Garden Island" fails to do justice to Kauai's beauty. Verdant trees grow canopies over the few roads, and brooding mountains are framed by long, sandy beaches, coral reefs, and sheer sea cliffs. Pristine trade winds moderate warm daily temperatures while offering comfort for deep, refreshing sleep through gentle nights.

5

For adventure seekers, Kauai offers everything from difficult hikes to helicopter tours. The island has top-notch spas and golf courses, and its beaches are known to be some of the most beautiful in the world. Even after you've spent days lazing around drinking mai tais or kayaking your way down a river, there's still plenty to do, as well as see: Plantation villages, a historic lighthouse, wildlife refuges, a fern grotto, a colorful canyon, and deep rivers are all easily explored.

GEOLOGY

Kauai is the oldest and northernmost of the main Hawaiian Islands. Five million years of wind and rain have worked their magic, sculpting fluted sea cliffs and whittling away at the cinder cones and caldera that prove its volcanic origin. Foremost among these is Waialeale, one of the wettest spots on Earth. Its approximate 450-inch annual rainfall feeds the mighty Wailua River, the only navigable waterway in Hawaii. The vast Alakai Swamp soaks up rain like a sponge, releasing it slowly into the watershed that gives Kauai its emerald sheen.

FLORA AND FAUNA

Kauai offers some of the best birding in the state, due in part to the absence of the mongoose. Many nene (the endangered Hawaiian state bird) reared in captivity have been successfully released here, along with an endangered forest bird called the puaiohi. The island is also home to a large colony of migratory nesting seabirds and has two refuges protecting endangered Hawaiian waterbirds. Kauai's most noticeable fowl, however, is the wild chicken. A cross between jungle fowl (*moa*) brought by the Polynesians and domestic chickens and fighting cocks that escaped during the last two hurricanes, they are everywhere, and the roosters crow when they feel like it, not just at dawn.

HISTORY

Kauai's residents have had a reputation for independence since ancient times. Called "the separate kingdom," Kauai alone resisted King Kamehameha's charge to unite the Hawaiian Islands. In fact, it was only by kidnapping Kauai's king, Kaumualii, and forcing him to marry Kamehameha's widow that the Garden Isle was joined to the rest of Hawaii. That spirit lives on today as Kauai residents try to resist the lure of tourism dollars captivating the rest of the Islands. Local building rules maintain that no structure may be taller than a coconut tree, and Kauai's capital city, Lihue, is still more small town than city.

KAUAI PLANNER

GETTING HERE AND AROUND

AIR TRAVEL

All commercial and cargo flights use the Lihue Airport, 2 miles east of the town of Lihue.

GROUND TRANSPOR- TATION A rental car is the best way to get to your hotel, though taxis and some hotel shuttles are available. From the airport it will take you about 15 to 25 minutes to drive to Wailua or Kapaa, 30 to 40 minutes to reach Poipu, and 45 minutes to an hour to get to Princeville or Hanalei.

CAR TRAVEL

Unless you plan to stay strictly at a resort or do all of your sightseeing as part of guided tours, you'll need a rental car. There is bus service on the island, but the buses tend to be slow and run limited hours.

You most likely won't need a four-wheel-drive vehicle anywhere on the island, so save yourself the money. And although convertibles look like fun, the frequent, intermittent rain showers and intense tropical sun make hardtops a better (and cheaper) choice.

If possible, avoid the "rush" hours when the local workers go to and from their jobs. Kauai has some of the highest gas prices in the Islands.

ISLAND DRIVING TIMES Driving around Kauai will take longer than you'd expect, and Kauai roads are subject to some heavy traffic, especially going through Kapaa and Lihue.

DRIVING TIMES	
Haena to Hanalei	5 mi/15 mins
Hanalei to Princeville	4 mi/10 mins
Princeville to Kilauea	5 mi/12 mins
Kilauea to Anahola	8 mi/15 mins
Anahola to Kapaa	5 mi/10 mins
Kapaa to Lihue	10 mi/20 mins
Lihue to Poipu	13 mi/25 mins
Poipu to Kalaheo	8 mi/20 mins
Kalaheo to Hanapepe	4 mi/10 mins
Hanapepe to Waimea	7 mi/10 mins

RESTAURANTS

Kauai's cultural diversity is apparent in its restaurants, which offer authentic Vietnamese, Chinese, Korean, Japanese, Thai, Mexican, Italian, and Hawaiian specialties. Less specialized restaurants cater to the tourist crowd, serving standard American fare—burgers, pizza, sandwiches, surf-and-turf combos, and so on. Kapaa offers the best selection of restaurants, with options for a variety of tastes and budgets; most fast-food joints are in Lihue.

Parents will be relieved to encounter a tolerant attitude toward children, even if they're noisy. Men can leave their jackets and ties at home; attire tends toward informal, but if you want to dress up, you can. Reservations are accepted in most places and required at some of the top restaurants.

Prices in the reviews are the average cost of a main course at dinner or, if dinner is not served, at lunch.

HOTELS

If you want to golf, play tennis, or hang at a spa, stay at a resort. You'll also be more likely to find activities for children at resorts, including camps that allow parents a little time off. The island's hotels tend to be smaller and older, with fewer on-site amenities. Some of the swankiest places to stay on the island are the St. Regis Princeville Resort on the North Shore, where rooms run more than $900 per night in high season, and the Grand Hyatt Kauai on the South Shore for a bit less; of course, those with views of the ocean book faster than those without.

Condos and vacation rentals on Kauai tend to run the gamut from fabulous luxury estates to scruffy little dives. It's buyer-beware in this totally unregulated sector of the visitor industry, though the County of Kauai is in the process of developing new regulations for these types of properties, particularly those in agricultural and rural areas. If you're planning to stay at one of these, be sure to contact the operator prior to traveling to ensure it's still open.

Properties managed by individual owners can be found on online vacation-rental directories such as CyberRentals and Vacation Rentals By Owner, as well as on the Kauai Visitors Bureau's website. There are also several Kauai-based management companies with vacation rentals.

The island's bed-and-breakfasts allow you to meet local residents and more directly experience the aloha spirit. Many have oceanfront settings and breakfasts with everything from tropical fruits and juices, Kauai coffee, and macadamia-nut waffles to breads made with local bananas and mangoes. Some have pools, hot tubs, services such as *lomilomi* massage, and breakfasts delivered to your lanai. Some properties have stand-alone units on-site.

Prices in the reviews are the lowest cost of a standard double room in high season. Prices for rentals are the lowest per-night cost for a one-bedroom unit in high season. For expanded hotel reviews visit www.Fodors.com.

VISITOR INFORMATION

The Kauai Visitors Bureau has an office at 4334 Rice Street, Lihue's main thoroughfare, near the Kauai Museum.

Information Kauai Visitors Bureau ⊠ *4334 Rice St., Suite 101, Lihue*
☎ *808/245–3971, 800/262–1400* ⊕ *www.kauaidiscovery.com.* **Poipu Beach
Resort Association***808/742–7444, 888/744–0888* ⊕ *www.poipu-beach.org.*

EXPLORING

Updated by
Charles E.
Roessler

The main road tracing Kauai's perimeter takes you past much more scenery than would seem possible on one small island. Chiseled mountains, thundering waterfalls, misty hillsides, dreamy beaches, lush vegetation, and small towns make up the physical landscape. Perhaps the most stunning piece of scenery is a place no road will take you—the breathtakingly beautiful Napali Coast, which runs along the northwest side of the island.

■TIP→ While exploring the island, try to take advantage of the many roadside scenic overlooks and pull over to take in the constantly changing view. Don't try to pack too much into one day. Kauai is small, but travel is slow. The island's sights are divided into four geographic areas, in clockwise order: the North Shore, the East Side, the South Shore, and the West Side.

THE NORTH SHORE

The North Shore of Kauai includes the environs of Kilauea, Princeville, Hanalei, and Haena. Traveling north on Route 56 from the airport, the coastal highway crosses the Wailua River and the busy towns of Wailua and Kapaa before emerging into a decidedly rural and scenic landscape, with expansive views of the island's rugged interior mountains. As the two-lane highway turns west and narrows, it winds through spectacular scenery and passes the posh resort community of Princeville before dropping down into Hanalei Valley. Here it narrows further and becomes a federally recognized scenic roadway, replete with one-lane bridges (the local etiquette is for six or seven cars to cross at a time, before yielding to those on the other side), hairpin turns, and heart-stopping coastal vistas. The road ends at Kee, where the ethereal rain forests and fluted sea cliffs of Napali Coast Wilderness State Park begin.

In winter Kauai's North Shore receives more rainfall than other areas of the island. Don't let this deter you from visiting. The clouds drift over the mountains of Namolokama creating a mysterious mood and then, in a blink, disappear, rewarding you with mountains laced with a dozen waterfalls or more. The views of the mountain—as well as the sunsets over the ocean—from the St. Regis Bar, adjacent to the lobby of the St. Regis Princeville Resort, are fantastic.

HANALEI, HAENA, AND WEST

Haena is 40 miles northwest of Lihue; Hanalei is 5 miles southeast of Haena.

Crossing the historic one-lane bridge into Hanalei reveals old-world Hawaii, including working taro farms, poi making, and evenings of throwing horseshoes at Black Pot Beach Park—found unmarked (as many places are on Kauai) at the east end of Hanalei Bay Beach Park.

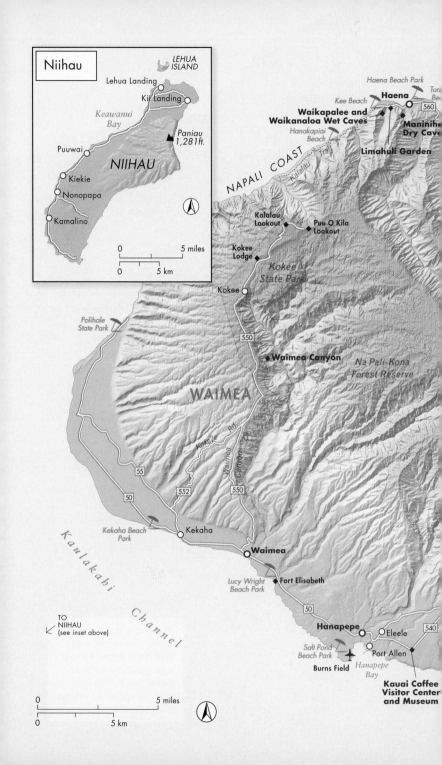

Niihau

LEHUA ISLAND

Lehua Landing

Kii Landing

Keawanui Bay

Puuwai

Kiekie

Nonopapa

Kamalino

▲ Paniau 1,281 ft.

NIIHAU

0   5 miles

0   5 km

Haena Beach Park

Kee Beach

Haena

Turn Be

Waikapalee and Waikanaloa Wet Caves

Manini Dry Cave

Hanakapiai Beach

Limahuli Garden

560

NAPALI COAST

Kalalau Trail

Kalalau Lookout

Puu O Kila Lookout

Kokee Lodge

Kokee State Park

Kokee

Polihale State Park

550

Waimea Canyon

WAIMEA

Na Pali-Kona Forest Reserve

Kokee Rd.

Waimea Canyon Dr.

55

552

550

Kekaha Beach Park

Kekaha

50

Waimea

Lucy Wright Beach Park

Fort Elisabeth

Kaulakahi Channel

TO NIIHAU (see inset above)

50

Hanapepe

Eleele

540

Salt Pond Beach Park

Burns Field

Hanapepe Bay

Port Allen

Kauai Coffee Visitor Center and Museum

0   5 miles

0   5 km

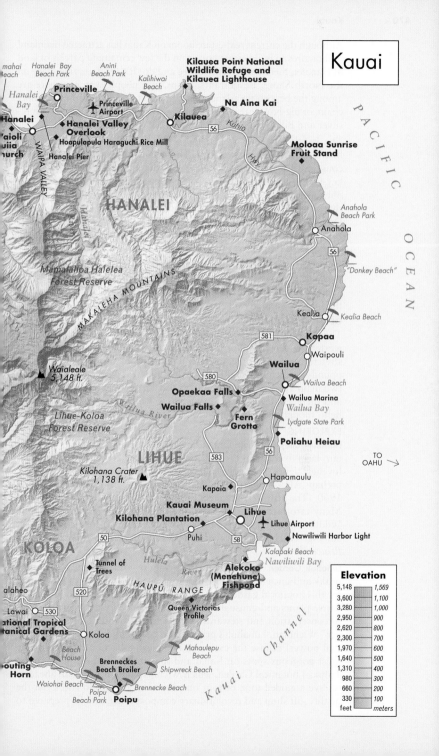

Kauai

PACIFIC OCEAN

...mahai ...each
Hanalei Bay Beach Park
Anini Beach Park
Kalihiwai Beach
Kilauea Point National Wildlife Refuge and Kilauea Lighthouse
Princeville
Princeville Airport
Na Aina Kai
Hanalei Bay
Hanalei
'aioli 'uia 'urch
Hanalei Valley Overlook
Kilauea
Hoopulapula Haraguchi Rice Mill
Hanalei Pier
56 Kuhio
Moloaa Sunrise Fruit Stand

WAIPA VALLEY

HANALEI

Hanalei

Kuhio Hwy

Anahola Beach Park
Anahola
56
"Donkey Beach"

Mamalahoa Halelea Forest Reserve

MAKALEHA MOUNTAINS

Kealia Kealia Beach

581 Kapaa
Waipouli
Wailua
580
Wailua Beach

Waialeale 5,148 ft.

Lihue-Koloa Forest Reserve

Opaekaa Falls
Wailua Falls
Fern Grotto
Wailua Marina
Wailua Bay
Lydgate State Park
Poliahu Heiau

Wailua River

LIHUE

Kilohana Crater 1,138 ft.

583

56

TO OAHU →

Hanamaulu

Kapaia

Kauai Museum
Kilohana Plantation
Lihue
Lihue Airport
Nawiliwili Harbor Light
Kapaia
Puhi
58
Kalapaki Beach
Nawiliwili Bay

KOLOA

50

Huleia

Tunnel of Trees

HAUPU RANGE

Huleia River

Alekoko (Menehune) Fishpond

alaheo

520

Queen Victoria's Profile

Lawai
530

Kauai Channel

...ational Tropical ...anical Gardens
Koloa

Mahaulepu Beach

Beach House

Brenneckes Beach Broiler
Shipwreck Beach

...outing Horn

Waiohai Beach
Poipu Beach Park
Brennecke Beach
Poipu

Elevation	
5,148	1,569
3,600	1,100
3,280	1,000
2,950	900
2,620	800
2,300	700
1,970	600
1,640	500
1,310	400
980	300
660	200
330	100
feet	meters

Although the current real-estate boom on Kauai has attracted mainland millionaires to build estate homes on the few remaining parcels of land in Hanalei, there's still plenty to see and do. It's *the* gathering place on the North Shore. Restaurants, shops, and people-watching here are among the best on the island, and you won't find a single brand name, chain, or big-box store around—unless you count surf brands like Quiksilver and Billabong.

The beach and river at Hanalei offer swimming, snorkeling, body boarding, surfing, and kayaking. Those hanging around at sunset often congregate at the Hanalei Pavilion, where a husband-and-wife-slack-key-guitar-playing combo makes impromptu appearances. There's an old rumor, since quashed by the local newspaper, the *Garden Island*, that says Hanalei was the inspiration for the song "Puff the Magic Dragon," performed by the 1960s singing sensation Peter, Paul & Mary. Even with the newspaper's clarification, some tours still point out the shape of the dragon carved into the mountains encircling the town.

Once you pass through Hanalei town, the road shrinks even more as you skirt the coast and pass through Haena. Blind corners, quick turns, and one-lane bridges force slow driving along this scenic stretch across the Lumahai and Wainiha valleys.

GETTING HERE AND AROUND

There is only one road leading beyond Princeville to Kee Beach at the western end of the North Shore: Route 560. Hanalei's commercial stretch fronts this route, and you'll find parking at the shopping compounds on each side of the road. After Hanalei, parking is restricted to two main areas, Haena Beach Park and a new lot at Haena State Park, and there are few pullover areas along Route 560. Traffic is usually light, though the route can become congested right after sunset.

EXPLORING

Hanalei Valley Overlook. Dramatic mountains and a patchwork of neat taro farms bisected by the wide Hanalei River make this one of Hawaii's loveliest sights. The fertile Hanalei Valley has been planted in taro since perhaps AD 700, save for a century-long foray into rice that ended in 1960. (The historic Haraguchi Rice Mill is all that remains of the era.) Many taro farmers lease land within the 900-acre Hanalei National Wildlife Refuge, helping to provide wetland habitat for four species of endangered Hawaiian waterbirds. ⌧ *Rte. 56, across from Foodland, Princeville.*

Limahuli Garden. Narrow Limahuli Valley, with its fluted mountain peaks and ancient stone taro terraces, creates an unparalleled setting for this botanical garden and nature preserve. Dedicated to protecting native plants and unusual varieties of taro, it represents the principles of conservation and stewardship held by its founder, Charles "Chipper" Wichman. Limahuli's priomordial beauty and strong *mana* (spiritual power) eclipse the extensive botanical collection. It's one of the most gorgeous spots on Kauai and the crown jewel of the National Tropical Botanical Garden, which Wichman now heads. Call ahead to reserve a guided tour, or tour on your own. Be sure to check out the quality gift shop and revolutionary compost toilet, and be prepared to walk a somewhat steep hillside. ✉ *Rte. 560, Haena* ☎ *808/826–1053* ⊕ *www.ntbg.org* 🎫 *Self-guided tour $15, guided tour $30 (reservations required)* 🕙 *Tues.–Sat. 9:30–4.*

Maniniholo Dry Cave. Kauai's North Shore caves echo an enchanting, almost haunting, alternative to sunny skies and deep blue seas. Steeped in legend, Maniniholo Dry Cave darkens and becomes more claustro-phobic as you glide across its sandy floor, hearing the drips down the walls and wondering at its past. Legend has it that Maniniholo was the head fisherman of the Menehune—Kauai's quasi-mythical first inhabit-ants. After gathering too much food to carry, his men stored the excess in the dry cave overnight. When he returned in the morning, the food had vanished and he blamed the imps living in the cracks of the cave. He and his men dug into the cliff to find and destroy the imps, leaving behind the cave. Across the highway from Maniniholo Dry Cave is Haena State Park. ✉ *Rte. 560, Haena.*

Waikapalae and Waikanaloa Wet Caves. These wet caves are smaller (and wetter) than Maniniholo but are still visually worth a short jaunt. Said to have been dug by Pele, goddess of fire, these watering holes used to be clear, clean, and great for swimming. Now stagnant, they're never-theless a photogenic example of the many haunting natural landmarks of Kauai's North Shore. Waikanaloa is visible right beside the highway, near the end of the road. Waikapalae is back a few hundred yards and is accessed by a five-minute uphill walk. ✉ *Western end of Rte. 560.*

Waioli Huiia Church. Designated a National Historic Landmark, this little church—affiliated with the United Church of Christ—doesn't go unno-ticed right alongside Route 560 in downtown Hanalei, and its doors are often wide open (from 9 to 5, give or take) inviting inquisitive visitors in for a look around. Like the Waioli Mission House next door, it's an exquisite representation of New England architecture crossed with Hawaiian thatched buildings. During Hurricane Iniki's visit in 1992, which brought sustained winds of 160 mph and wind gusts up to 220 mph, this little church was lifted off its foundation but, thankfully, lov-ingly restored. Services are held at 10 am on Sunday with many hymns sung in Hawaiian. ✉ *5-5393A Kuhio Hwy., Hanalei* ☎ *808/826–6253.*

PRINCEVILLE, KILAUEA, AND AROUND

Princeville is 4 miles northeast of Hanalei; Kilauea is 5 miles east of Princeville.

Built on a bluff offering gorgeous sea and mountain vistas, including Hanalei Bay, Princeville is the creation of a 1970s resort development. The area is anchored by a few large hotels, world-class golf courses, and lots of condos and time-shares.

Five miles down Route 56, a former plantation town, Kilauea, maintains its rural flavor in the midst of unrelenting gentrification encroaching all around it. Especially noteworthy are its historic lava-rock buildings, including **Christ Memorial Episcopal Church** on Kolo Road and, on Keneke and Kilauea Road (commonly known as Lighthouse Road), the Kong Lung Company, which is now an expensive shop.

GETTING HERE AND AROUND

There is only one main road through the Princeville resort area, so maneuvering a car here can be a nightmare. If you're trying to find a smaller lodging unit, be sure to get specific driving directions. Ample parking is available at the Princeville Shopping Center at the entrance to the resort. Kilauea is about 5 miles east on Route 56. There's a public parking lot in the town center as well as parking at the end of Kilauea Road for access to the lighthouse.

EXPLORING

Fodor's Choice ★ **Kilauea Point National Wildlife Refuge and Kilauea Lighthouse.** A beacon for sea traffic since it was built in 1913, this National Historic Landmark has the largest clamshell lens of any lighthouse in the world. It's within a national wildlife refuge, where thousands of seabirds soar on the trade winds and nest on the steep ocean cliffs. Seeing endangered nene geese, white- and red-tailed tropic birds, and more (all identifiable by educational signboards) as well as native plants, dolphins, humpback whales, huge winter surf, and gorgeous views of the North Shore are well worth the modest entry fee. The gift shop has a great selection of books about the island's natural history and an array of unique merchandise, with all proceeds benefiting education and preservation efforts. ⊠ *Kilauea Lighthouse Rd., Kilauea* ☎ *808/828–0168* ⊕ *www. fws.gov/kilaueapoint* ⊡ *$5* ⊘ *Daily 10–4.*

Moloaa Sunrise Fruit Stand. Don't let the name fool you; they don't open at sunrise (more like 7:30 am, so come here after you watch the sun rise elsewhere). And it's not just a fruit stand. Breakfast is light and includes bagels, granola, smoothies, coffee, espresso, cappuccino, latte, and, of course, tropical-style fresh juices (pineapple, carrot, watermelon, guava, even sugarcane, in season). This is also a great spot to get out and stretch, take in the mountain view, and pick up sandwiches to go. Select local produce is available, although the variety is not as good as at the island's farmers' markets. What makes this fruit stand different is the fresh, natural ingredients like multigrain breads and *nori* (seaweed) wraps. ⊠ *Rte. 56, just past mile marker 16* ⊘ *Mon.–Sat. 7:30–5, Sun. 10–5.*

Na Aina Kai. One small sign along the highway is all that promotes this once-private garden gone big time. Joyce Doty's love for plants and art now spans 240 acres and includes 13 different gardens, a hardwood plantation, a canyon, lagoons, a Japanese teahouse, a Poinciana maze, a waterfall, and a sandy beach. Throughout are more than 100 bronze sculptures, reputedly one of the nation's largest collections. One popular project is a children's garden with a 16-foot-tall Jack and the Beanstalk bronze sculpture, gecko maze, tree house, kid-size train and, of course, a tropical jungle. Located in a residential neighborhood and hoping to maintain good neighborly relations, the garden, which is now a nonprofit organization, limits tours (guided only). Tour lengths vary widely, from 1½ to 5 hours. Reservations are strongly recommended.

Stop by the farmers' market in Kapaa to pick up locally grown mangoes and other fruits.

THE EAST SIDE

The East Side encompasses Lihue, Wailua, and Kapaa. It's also known as the Coconut Coast, as there was once a coconut plantation where today's aptly named Coconut Marketplace is located. A small grove still exists on both sides of the highway. *Mauka* (toward the mountains), a fenced herd of goats keeps the grass tended; on the *makai* (toward the ocean) side, you can walk through the grove, although it's best not to walk directly under the trees—falling coconuts can be dangerous. Lihue is the county seat, and the whole East Side is the island's center of commerce, so early-morning and late-afternoon drive times (or rush hour) can get congested. (Because there's only one main road, if there's a serious traffic accident the entire roadway may be closed, with no way around. Not to worry; it's a rarity.)

KAPAA AND WAILUA

Kapaa is 16 miles southeast of Kilauea; Wailua is 3 miles southwest of Kapaa.

Old Town Kapaa was once a plantation town, which is no surprise—most of the larger towns on Kauai once were. Old Town Kapaa is made up of a collection of wooden-front shops, some built by plantation workers and still run by their progeny today. Kapaa houses the two biggest grocery stores on the island, side by side: Foodland and Safeway. It also offers plenty of dining options for breakfast, lunch, and dinner, and gift shopping. To the south, Wailua comprises a few restaurants and shops, a few midrange resorts along the coastline, and a housing community *mauka*.

GETTING HERE AND AROUND

Turn to the right out of the airport at Lihue for the road to Wailua. A bridge—under which the very culturally significant Wailua River gently flows—marks the beginning of town. It quickly blends into Kapaa; there's no real demarcation. Careful, though—the zone between Lihue and Wailua has been the site of many car accidents. Pay attention and drive carefully, always knowing where you are going and when to turn off.

EXPLORING

Fern Grotto. The Fern Grotto has a long history on Kauai. For some reason, visitors seem to like it. It's really nothing more than a yawning lava tube swathed in lush fishtail ferns 3 miles up the Wailua River. Though it was significantly damaged after Hurricane Iniki and again after heavy rains in 2006, the greenery has completely recovered. Smith's Motor Boat Services is the only way to legally see the grotto. You can access the entrance with a kayak, but if boats are there, you may not be allowed to land. ⊠ *Rte. 56, just south of Wailua River, Kapaa* ☎ *808/821–6893* 💰 *$20* ⊙ *Daily departures 9:30–3:30.*

★ **Opaekaa Falls.** The mighty Wailua River produces many dramatic waterfalls, and Opaekaa (pronounced oh-pie-kah-ah) is one of the best. It plunges hundreds of feet to the pool below and can be easily viewed from a scenic overlook with ample parking. *Opaekaa* means "rolling shrimp," which refers to tasty native crustaceans that were once so abundant they could be seen tumbling in the falls. ■**TIP**→ **Just before reaching the parking area for the waterfalls, turn left into a scenic pullout for great views of the Wailua River valley and its march to the sea.** ⊠ *Kuamoo Rd. From Rte. 56, turn mauka onto Kuamoo Rd. and drive 1½ mi, Wailua.*

Poliahu Heiau. Storyboards near this ancient *heiau* (sacred site) recount the significance of the many sacred structures found along the Wailua River. It's unknown exactly how the ancient Hawaiians used Poliahu Heiau—one of the largest pre-Christian temples on the island—but legend says it was built by the Menehune because of the unusual stonework found in its walled enclosures. From this site, drive downhill toward the ocean to *pohaku hanau*, a two-piece birthing stone said to confer special blessings on all children born there, and *pohaku piko*, whose crevices were a repository for umbilical cords left by parents seeking a clue to their child's destiny, which reportedly was foretold by how the cord fared in the rock. Some Hawaiians feel these sacred stones shouldn't be viewed as tourist attractions, so always treat them with respect. Never stand or sit on the rocks or leave any offerings. ⊠ *Rte. 580, Kuamoo Rd., Wailua.*

Wailua Falls. You may recognize this impressive cascade from the opening sequences of the *Fantasy Island* television series. Kauai has plenty of noteworthy waterfalls, but this one is especially gorgeous, easy to find, and easy to photograph. ⊠ *End of Rte. 583, 4 miles from Rte. 56, Kapaa.*

Continued on page 478

HAWAII'S PLANTS 101

Hawaii is a bounty of rainbow-colored flowers and plants. The evening air is scented with their fragrance. Just look at the front yard of almost any home, travel any road, or visit any local park and you'll see a spectacular array of colored blossoms and leaves. What most visitors don't know is that many of the plants they are seeing are not native to Hawaii; rather, they were introduced during the last two centuries as ornamental plants, or for timber, shade, or fruit.

Hawaii boasts nearly every climate on the planet, excluding the two most extreme: arctic tundra and arid desert. The Islands have wine-growing regions, cactus-speckled ranchlands, icy mountaintops, and the rainiest forests on earth.

Plants introduced from around the world thrive here. The lush lowland valleys along the windward coasts are predominantly populated by non-native trees including yellow- and red-fruited **guava**, silvery-leafed **kukui**, and orange-flowered **tulip trees**.

The colorful **plumeria flower**, very fragrant and commonly used in lei making, and the giant multicolored **hibiscus flower** are both used by many women as hair adornments, and are two of the most common plants found around homes and hotels. The umbrella-like **monkeypod tree** from Central America provides shade in many of Hawaii's parks including Kapiolani Park in Honolulu. Hawaii's largest tree, found in Lahaina, Maui, is a giant **banyan tree**. Its canopy and massive support roots cover about two-thirds of an acre. The native **ohia tree**, with its brilliant red brush-like flowers, and the **hapuu**, a giant tree fern, are common in Hawaii's forests and are also used ornamentally in gardens.

Bougainvillea

Guava

Monkeypod

Banyan

Ohia Lehua*

Tulip Tree

Plumeria

Pandanus

Hibiscus

Anthurium

Kukui

Hapuu

*endemic to Hawaii

DID YOU KNOW?

More than 2,200 plant species are found in the Hawaiian Islands, but only about 1,000 are native. Of these, 320 are so rare, they are endangered. Hawaii's endemic plants evolved from ancestral seeds arriving in the Islands over thousands of years as baggage with birds, floating on ocean currents, or drifting on winds from continents thousands of miles away. Once here, these plants evolved in isolation, creating many new species known nowhere else in the world.

LIHUE

7 miles southwest of Wailua.

The commercial and political center of Kauai County, which includes the islands of Kauai and Niihau, Lihue is home to the island's major airport, harbor, and hospital. This is where you can find the state and county offices that issue camping and hiking permits and the same fast-food eateries and big-box stores that blight the mainland. The county is seeking help in reviving the downtown; for now, once your business is done, there's little reason to linger in lackluster Lihue.

GETTING HERE AND AROUND

Route 56 leads into Lihue from the north and Route 50 comes here from the south and west. The road from the airport (where Kauai's car rental agencies are) leads to the middle of Lihue. Many of the area's stores and restaurants are on and around Rice Street, which also leads to Kalapaki Bay and Nawiliwili Harbor.

EXPLORING

Alekoko (Menehune) Fishpond. No one knows just who built this intricate aquaculture structure in the Huleia River. Legend attributes it to the Menehune, a mythical—or real, depending on whom you ask—ancient race of people known for their small stature, industrious nature, and superb stoneworking skills. Volcanic rock was cut and fit together into massive walls 4 feet thick and 5 feet high, forming an enclosure for raising mullet and other freshwater fish that has endured for centuries. ⊠ *Hulemalu Rd., Niumalu.*

Kauai Museum. Maintaining a stately presence on Rice Street, the historic museum building is easy to find. It features a permanent display, "The Story of Kauai," which provides a competent overview of the Garden Island and Niihau, tracing the island's geology, mythology, and cultural history. Local artists are represented in changing exhibits in the second-floor Mezzanine Gallery. The recently expanded gift shop alone is worth a visit, with a fine collection of authentic Niihau shell lei, feather hatband lei, hand-turned wooden bowls, reference books, and other quality arts, crafts, and gifts, many of them locally made. ⊠ *4428 Rice St.* ☎ *808/245–6931* 🖅 *$10* ⊙ *Mon.–Sat. 9–5, closed Sun.*

ᘓ **Kilohana Plantation.** This estate dates back to 1896, when plantation manager Albert Spencer Wilcox first developed it as a working cattle ranch. His nephew, Gaylord Parke Wilcox, took over in 1936, building Kauai's first mansion. Today the 16,000-square-foot, Tudor-style home houses specialty shops, art galleries, and 22 North, a pretty restaurant with courtyard seating. Nearly half the original furnishings remain, and the gardens and orchards were replanted according to the original plans. You can tour the grounds for free; children enjoy visiting the farm animals. A train runs 2½ miles through 104 acres of lands representing the agricultural story of Kauai—then and now. ⊠ *3-2087 Kaumualii Hwy.* ☎ *808/245–5608* ⊙ *Mon.–Sat. 9:30–9:30, Sun. 9:30–3:30.*

KAUAI SIGHTSEEING TOURS

Aloha Kauai Tours. You get *way* off the beaten track on these four-wheel-drive van excursions. Choose from several options, including the half-day Backroads Tour covering mostly haul-cane roads behind the locked gates of Grove Farm Plantation, and the half-day Rainforest Tour, which follows the Wailua River to its source, Mt. Waialeale. The expert guides are some of the best on the island. Rates are $80. ⊠ *Check in at Kilohana Plantation on Rte. 50 in Puhi* ☎ *808/245–6400, 800/452–1113* ⊕ *www.alohakauaitours.com.*

Roberts Hawaii Tours. The Round-the-Island Tour, sometimes called the Wailua River–Waimea Canyon Tour, gives a good overview of half the island, including Fort Elisabeth and Opaekaa Falls. Guests are transported in air-conditioned, 25-passenger minibuses. The $79.50 trip includes a boat ride up the Wailua River to the Fern Grotto and a visit to the lookouts above Waimea Canyon. ☎ *808/245–9101, 800/831–5541* ⊕ *www.robertshawaii.com.*

Waimea Historic Walking Tour. Led by a *kupuna*, a respected Hawaiian elder, this 2½- to 3-hour tour begins promptly at 9:30 am, every Monday at the West Kauai Visitor Center. While sharing her personal remembrances, Aletha Kaohi leads an easy walk that explains Waimea's distinction as a recipient of the 2006 National Trust for Historic Preservation Award. The tour is free, but a reservation is required. ⊠ *Waimea* ☎ *808/338–1332.*

THE SOUTH SHORE

As you follow the main road south from Lihue, the landscape becomes lush and densely vegetated before giving way to drier conditions that characterize Poipu, the South Side's major resort area. Poipu owes much of its popularity to a steady supply of sunshine and a string of sandy beaches, although the beaches are smaller and more covelike than those on the West Side. With its extensive selection of accommodations, services, and activities, the South Shore attracts more visitors than any other area of Kauai. It's also attracting developers with big plans for the onetime sugarcane fields that are nestled in this region and enveloped by mountains. There are few roads in and out, and local residents are concerned about increased traffic as well as noise and dust pollution as a result of chronic construction. If you're planning to stay on the South Side, be sure to ask if your hotel, condo, or vacation rental will be impacted by the ongoing development during your visit.

Both Poipu and nearby Koloa (site of Kauai's first sugar mill) can be reached via Route 520 (Maluhia Road) from the Lihue area. Route 520 is known locally as Tree Tunnel Road, due to the stand of eucalyptus trees lining the road that were planted at the turn of the 20th century by Walter Duncan McBryde, a Scotsman who began cattle ranching on Kauai's South Shore. The canopy of trees was ripped to literal shreds twice—in 1982 during Hurricane Iwa and again in 1992 during Hurricane Iniki. And, true to Kauai, both times the trees grew back into an impressive tunnel. It's a distinctive way to announce, "You are now on

"Jungle fowl were all over some of the scenic stops in Kauai. They had beautiful colors, and it was cool just to see them walking around." —jedivader

vacation," for there's a definite feel of leisure in the air here. There's still plenty to do—snorkel, bike, walk, horseback ride, take an ATV tour, surf, scuba dive, shop, and dine—everything you'd want on a tropical vacation. From the west, Route 530 (Koloa Road) slips into downtown Koloa, a string of fun shops and restaurants, at an intersection with the only gas station on the South Shore.

POIPU

13 miles southwest of Lihue.

Thanks to its generally sunny weather and a string of golden-sand beaches dotted with oceanfront lodgings, Poipu is a top choice for many visitors. Beaches are user-friendly, with protected waters for *keiki* (children) and novice snorkelers, lifeguards, clean restrooms, covered pavilions, and a sweet coastal promenade ideal for leisurely strolls. Some experts have even ranked Poipu Beach Park number one in the nation. It depends on your preferences, of course, though it certainly does warrant high accolades.

GETTING HERE AND AROUND

Poipu is the one area on Kauai where you could get by without a car, though that could mean an expensive taxi ride from the airport and limited access to other parts of the island. To reach Poipu by car, follow Poipu Road south from Koloa. After the traffic circle, the road curves to follow the coast, leading to some of the popular South Shore beaches.

EXPLORING

National Tropical Botanical Gardens (*NTBG*). Tucked away in Lawai Valley, these gardens include lands and a cottage once used by Hawaii's Queen Emma for a summer retreat. Visitors can take a self-guided tour of the rambling 252-acre **McBryde Gardens** to see and learn about plants collected throughout the tropics. It is known as a garden of "research and conservation." The 100-acre **Allerton Gardens,** which can be visited only on a guided tour, artfully display statues and water features that were originally developed as part of a private estate. Reservations are required for tours of Allerton Gardens, but not for the self-guided tours of McBryde Gardens. The visitor center has a high-quality gift shop with botany-theme merchandise.

Besides harboring and propagating rare and endangered plants from Hawaii and elsewhere, NTBG functions as a scientific research and education center. The organization also operates gardens in Limahuli, on Kauai's North Shore, and in Hana, on Maui's east shore. ⊠ *Lawai Rd., across from Spouting Horn parking lot, Poipu* ☎ *808/742–2623* ⊕ *www. ntbg.org* 🖃 *McBryde self-guided tour $15, Allerton guided tour $45* ⊗ *McBryde Gardens daily at 12:45 ($25). Allerton Gardens tours (by reservation) daily at 9, 10, 1, and 2. Sunset Tour Tues., Thurs., Sat. ($70).*

Spouting Horn. If the conditions are right, you can see a natural blowhole in the reef behaving like Old Faithful, shooting saltwater high into the air and making a cool, echoing sound. It's most dramatic during big summer swells, which jam large quantities of water through an ancient lava tube with great force. ∎TIP➜ Stay on the paved walkways as rocks can be slippery and wave action unpredictable. Vendors hawk inexpensive souvenirs and collectibles in the parking lot. You may find good deals on shell jewelry, but ask for a certificate of authenticity to ensure it's a genuine Niihau shell lei before paying the higher price that these intricate creations command. ⊠ *End of Lawai Rd., Poipu.*

QUICK BITES

Brennecke's Beach Broiler. Stop in at Brennecke's Beach Broiler, a long-time fixture on the beach in Poipu. After a day of sun, this is a perfect spot to chill out with a mango margarita or mai tai, paired with a yummy pupu platter. ⊠ *2100 Hoone Rd., Poipu* ☎ *808/742–7588.*

THE WEST SIDE

Exploring the West Side is akin to visiting an entirely different world. The landscape is dramatic and colorful: a patchwork of green, blue, black, and orange. The weather is hot and dry, the beaches are long, the sand is dark. Niihau, a private island and the last remaining place in Hawaii where Hawaiian is spoken exclusively, can be glimpsed offshore. This is rural Kauai, where sugar is making its last stand and taro is still cultivated in the fertile river valleys. The lifestyle is slow, easy, and traditional, with many folks fishing and hunting to supplement their diets. Here and there modern industry has intruded into this pastoral scene: huge generators turn oil into electricity at Port Allen; scientists cultivate experimental crops of genetically engineered plants in Kekaha; the navy launches rockets at Mana to test the "Star Wars" missile defense system; and NASA mans a tracking station in the wilds of Kokee. It's a region of contrasts that simply shouldn't be missed.

Heading west from Lihue or Poipu, you pass through a string of tiny towns, plantation camps, and historic sites, each with a story to tell of centuries past. There's Hanapepe, whose coastal salt ponds have been harvested since ancient times; Kaumakani, where the sugar industry still clings to life; Fort Elisabeth, from which an enterprising Russian tried to take over the island in the early 1800s; and Waimea, where Captain Cook made his first landing in the Islands, forever changing the face of Hawaii.

From Waimea town you can head up into the mountains, skirting the rim of magnificent Waimea Canyon and climbing higher still until you reach the cool, often-misty forests of Kokee State Park. From the vantage point at the top of this gemlike island, 3,200 to 4,200 feet above sea level, you can gaze into the deep, verdant valleys of the North Shore and Napali Coast. This is where the "real" Kauai can still be found: the native plants, insects, and birds that are found nowhere else on Earth.

HANAPEPE
15 miles west of Poipu.

In the 1980s Hanapepe was fast becoming a ghost town, its farm-based economy mirroring the decline of agriculture. Today it's a burgeoning art colony with galleries, crafts studios, and a lively art-theme street fair on Friday nights. The main street has a new vibrancy enhanced by the restoration of several historic buildings. The emergence of Kauai Coffee as a major West Side crop and expanded activities at Port Allen, now the main departure point for tour boats, also gave the town's economy a boost.

GETTING HERE AND AROUND
Hanapepe, locally known as Kauai's "biggest little town," is just past the Eleele Shopping Center on the main highway (Route 50). A sign leads you to the town center, where street parking is easy and there's an enjoyable walking tour.

EXPLORING
Kauai Coffee Visitor Center and Museum. Two restored camp houses, dating from the days when sugar was the main agricultural crop on the Islands, have been converted into a museum, visitor center, and gift shop. About 3,400 acres of McBryde sugar land have become Hawaii's largest coffee plantation. You can walk among the trees, view old grinders and roasters, watch a video to learn how coffee is processed, sample various estate roasts, and check out the gift store. The center offers a 15-minute or so self-guided tour with well-marked signs through a small coffee grove. From Eleele, take Highway 50 in the direction of Waimea Canyon and veer right onto Highway 540, west of Kalaheo. It's located 2½ miles from the Highway 50 turnoff. ⊠ *870 Halawili Rd., Kalaheo* ☎ *808/335–0813* ⊕ *www.kauaicoffee.com* ☜ *Free* ☾ *Daily 9–5.*

SUNSHINE MARKETS

If you want to rub elbows with the locals and purchase fresh produce and flowers at very reasonable prices, head for Sunshine Markets, also known as Kauai's farmers' markets. These busy markets are held weekly, usually in the afternoon, at locations all around the island. They're good fun, and they support neighborhood farmers. Arrive a little early, bring dollar bills to speed up transactions and your own shopping bags to carry your produce, and be prepared for some pushy shoppers. Farmers are usually happy to educate visitors about unfamiliar fruits and veggies, especially when the crowd thins. ☎ 808/241–6303 ⊕ www.kauai.gov.

North Shore Sunshine Markets ⊠ Waipa, mauka of Rte. 560 north of Hanalei after mile marker 3, Hanalei ⊘ Tues. 2 pm ⊠ Kilauea Neighborhood Center, on Keneke St., Kilauea ⊘ Thurs. 4:30 pm ⊠ Hanalei Community Center ⊘ Sat. 9:30 am noon.

East Side Sunshine Markets ⊠ Vidinha Stadium, Lihue, ½ mile south of airport on Rte. 51 ⊘ Fri. 3 pm ⊠ Kapaa, turn mauka on Rte. 581/ Olohena Rd. for 1 block ⊘ Wed. 3 pm.

South Shore Sunshine Markets ⊠ Ballpark, Koloa, north of intersection of Koloa Road and Rte. 520 ⊘ Mon. noon.

West Side Sunshine Markets ⊠ Kalaheo Community Center, on Papalina Rd. just off Kaumualii Hwy., Kalaheo ⊘ Tues. 3 pm ⊠ Hanapepe Park, Hanapepe ⊘ Thurs. 3 pm ⊠ Kekaha Neighborhood Center, Elepaio Rd., Kekaha ⊘ Sat. 9 am.

QUICK BITES

Lappert's Ice Cream. It's not ice cream on Kauai if it's not Lappert's Ice Cream. Guava, mac nut, pineapple, mango, coconut, banana—Lappert's is the ice-cream capital of Kauai. Warning: Even at the factory store in Hanapepe, the prices are no bargain. But, hey, you gotta try it. ⊠ On Hwy. 50 mauka, Hanapepe ☎ 808/335–6121 ⊕ www.lappertshawaii.com.

WAIMEA, WAIMEA CANYON, AND AROUND

Waimea is 7 miles northwest of Hanapepe; Waimea Canyon is approximately 10 miles northeast of Waimea.

Waimea is a serene, pretty town that has the look of the Old West and the feel of Old Hawaii, with a lifestyle that's decidedly laid-back. It's an ideal place for a refreshment break while sightseeing on the West Side. The town has played a major role in Hawaiian history since 1778, when Captain James Cook became the first European to set foot on the Hawaiian Islands. Waimea was also the place where Kauai's King Kaumualii acquiesced to King Kamehameha's unification drive in 1810, averting a bloody war. The town hosted the first Christian missionaries, who hauled in massive timbers and limestone blocks to build the sturdy Waimea Christian Hawaiian and Foreign Church in 1846. It's one of many lovely historic buildings preserved by residents who take great pride in their heritage and history.

North of Waimea town, via Route 550, you'll find the vast and gorgeous Waimea Canyon, also known as the Grand Canyon of the Pacific. The

The sunny South Shore beaches have some good surf breaks. Head to Poipu Beach for board rentals or lessons.

spectacular vistas from the lookouts along the road culminate with an overview of Kalalau Valley. There are various hiking trails leading to the inner heart of Kauai. A camera is a necessity in this region.

GETTING HERE AND AROUND

Route 50 continues northwest to Waimea and Kekaha from Hanapepe. You can reach Waimea Canyon and Kokee State Park from either town—the way is clearly marked. Some pull-off areas on Route 550 are fine for a quick view of the canyon, but the designated lookouts have bathrooms and parking.

EXPLORING

Fodor's Choice ★ **Waimea Canyon.** Carved over countless centuries by the Waimea River and the forces of wind and rain, Waimea Canyon is a dramatic gorge nicknamed the "Grand Canyon of the Pacific"—but not by Mark Twain, as many people mistakenly think.

Hiking and hunting trails wind through the canyon, which is 3,600 feet deep, 2 miles wide, and 10 miles long. The cliff sides have been sharply eroded, exposing swatches of colorful soil. The deep red, brown, and green hues are constantly changing in the sun, and frequent rainbows and waterfalls enhance the natural beauty.

This is one of Kauai's prettiest spots, and it's worth stopping at both the **Puu ka Pele** and **Puu hinahina** lookouts. Clean public restrooms and parking are at both lookouts. ⊠ *Waimea*.

QUICK BITES

Kokee Lodge. There's only one place to buy food and hot drinks in Kokee State Park, and that's the dining room of rustic Kokee Lodge. It's known for its corn bread, of all things. Peruse the gift shop for T-shirts, postcards,

Waimea Canyon: You don't have to hike to see sweeping Waimea Canyon vistas. Many overlooks, like the one pictured above, are reachable by car, right off the main road.

or campy Kokee memorabilia. ⊠ *Kokee State Park, 3600 Kokee Rd., mile marker 15, Kokee* ☎ *808/335–6061* ⊗ *No dinner.*

BEACHES

Updated by Charles E. Roessler

With more sandy beaches per mile of coastline than any other Hawaiian Island, Kauai could be nicknamed the Sandy Island just as easily as it's called the Garden Island. Totaling more than 50 miles, Kauai's beaches make up 44% of the island's shoreline—almost twice that of Oahu, second on this list. It is, of course, because of Kauai's age as the eldest sibling of the inhabited Hawaiian Islands, allowing more time for water and wind erosion to break down rock and coral into sand.

But not all Kauai's beaches are the same. Each beach is unique unto itself, for that day, that hour. Conditions, scenery, and intrigue can change throughout the day and certainly throughout the year, transforming, say, a tranquil lakelike ocean setting in summer into monstrous waves drawing internationally ranked surfers from around the world in winter.

There are sandy beaches, rocky beaches, wide beaches, narrow beaches, skinny beaches, and alcoves. Generally speaking, surf kicks up on the North Shore in winter and the South Shore in summer, although summer's southern swells aren't nearly as frequent or big as the northern winter swells that attract those surfers. Kauai's longest and widest beaches are found on the North Shore and West Side and are popular with beachgoers, although during winter's rains, everyone heads to

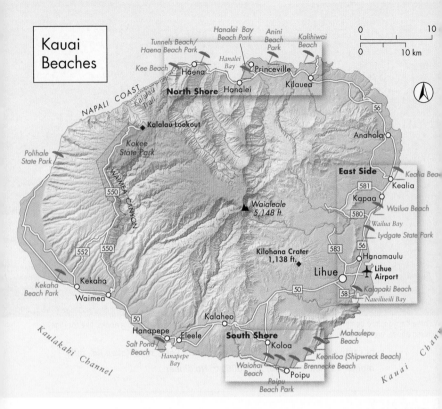

the dryer South and West Sides. The East Side beaches tend to be narrower and have onshore winds less popular with sunbathers, yet fishers abound. Smaller coves are characteristic of the South Shore and attract all kinds of water lovers year-round, including monk seals.

In Hawaii, all beaches are public, but their accessibility varies greatly. Some require an easy ½-mile stroll, some require a four-wheel-drive vehicle, others require boulder hopping, and one takes an entire day of serious hiking. And then there are those "drive-in" beaches onto which you can literally pull up and park your car. Kauai is not Disneyland, so don't expect much signage to help you along the way. One of the top-ranked beaches in the whole world—Hanalei—doesn't have a single sign in town directing you to the beach. Furthermore, the majority of Kauai's beaches on Kauai's vast coastline are remote, offering no facilities. ■TIP→ **If you want the convenience of restrooms, picnic tables, and the like, stick to county beach parks.**

THE NORTH SHORE

If you've ever dreamed of Hawaii—and who hasn't—you've dreamed of Kauai's North Shore. *Lush, tropical,* and *abundant* are just a few words to describe this rugged and dramatic area. And the views to the sea aren't the only attraction—the inland views of velvety-green valley

folds and carved mountain peaks will take your breath away. Rain is the reason for all the greenery on the North Shore, and winter is the rainy season. Not to worry, though; it rarely rains *everywhere* on the island at one time. ■ TIP➔ **The rule of thumb is to head south or west when it rains in the north.**

The waves on the North Shore can be big—and we mean huge—in winter, drawing crowds to witness nature's spectacle. By contrast, in summer the waters can be completely serene.

BEACHES KEY	
🚻	*Restroom*
🚿	*Showers*
🏄	*Surfing*
🤿	*Snorkel/Scuba*
👫	*Good for kids*
🅿	*Parking*

Anini Beach Park. A great family park, Anini is unique in that it features one of the longest and widest fringing reefs in all Hawaii, creating a shallow lagoon that is good for snorkeling and following the occasional turtle. It is quite safe in all but the highest of winter surf. The reef follows the shoreline for some 2 miles and extends 1,600 feet offshore at its widest point. During times of low tide—usually occurring around the full moon of the summer months—much of the reef is exposed. Anini is inarguably the windsurfing mecca of Kauai, even for beginners, and it also attracts participants in the growing sport of kiteboarding. **Amenities:** parking; showers; toilets; food and drink. **Best For:** walking; swimming; windsurfing; sunrise. ⊠ *Anini Rd., off Rte. 56, Princeville.*

Fodor'sChoice ★

Haena Beach Park (*Tunnels Beach*). This is a drive-up beach park popular with campers year-round. The wide bay here—named Makua and commonly known as "Tunnels"—is bordered by two large reef systems creating favorable waves for surfing during peak winter conditions. In July and August, waters at this same beach are as calm as a lake, usually, and snorkelers enjoy the variety of fish life found in a hook-shape reef made up of underwater lava tubes, on the east end of the bay. ■ TIP➔ **During the summer months only, this is a premier snorkeling site on Kauai.** It's not unusual to find a food vendor parked here selling sandwiches and drinks out of a converted bread van. **Amenities:** lifeguards; parking; showers; toilets; food and drink. **Best For:** walking; snorkeling; surfing. ⊠ *Near end of Rte. 560, across from lava-tube sea caves, Haena.*

Fodor'sChoice ★

Hanalei Bay Beach Park. This 2-mile crescent beach surrounds a spacious bay that is quintessential Hawaii. After gazing out to sea and realizing you have truly arrived in paradise, look landward. The site of the mountains, ribboned with waterfalls, will take your breath away. All this beauty accounts for why coastal expert "Dr. Beach" named Hanalei number one in the United States in 2009. In winter Hanalei Bay boasts some of the biggest onshore surf breaks in the state,

Be sure to set aside time to catch a sunset over Napali Coast from Kee Beach on Kauai's North Shore.

attracting world-class surfers. The beach itself is wide enough to have safe real estate for your beach towel even in winter. In summer the bay is transformed—calm waters lap the beach, sailboats moor in the bay, and outrigger-canoe paddlers ply the sea. Pack the cooler, haul out the beach umbrellas, and don't forget the beach toys, because Hanalei Bay is worth scheduling for an entire day, maybe two. **Amenities:** lifeguards; parking; showers; toilets. **Best For:** surfing; swimming; walking; windsurfing. ⊠ *Weli Weli Rd.* ✛ *In Hanalei, turn makai at Aku Rd. and drive 1 block to Weli Weli Rd. Parking areas are on makai side of Weli Weli Rd.*

Kalihiwai Beach. A winding road leads down a cliff face to this picture-perfect beach. A jewel of the North Shore, Kalihiwai Beach is on par with Hanalei, just without the waterfall-ribbon backdrop. It's another one of those drive-up beaches, so it's very accessible. Most people park on the sand under the grove of ironwood trees. Families set up camp for the day at the west end of the beach, near the stream, where young kids like to splash and older kids like to body board. On the eastern edge of the beach, from which the road descends, there's a locals' favorite surf spot during winter's high surf. The onshore break can be dangerous during this time. During the calmer months of summer, Kalihiwai Beach is a good choice for beginning board riders and swimmers. The toilets here are the portable kind. No showers. **Amenities:** parking; toilets. **Best For:** surfing; swimming; walking. ⊠ *Kalihiwai Rd., on Kilauea side of Kalihiwai Bridge, Kilauea.*

Kee Beach. Highway 560 on the North Shore literally dead-ends at this beach, which is also the trailhead for the famous Kalalau Trail and the

CLOSE UP

Best Beaches

He says "to-mah-toe," and she says "to-may-toe." When it comes to beaches on Kauai, the meaning behind that axiom holds true: People are different. What rocks one person's world wreaks havoc for another's. Here are some additional tips on how to choose a beach that's right for you.

BEST FOR FAMILIES
Lydgate State Park, East Side. The kid-designed playground, the protected swimming pools, and Kamalani Bridge guarantee you will not hear these words from your child: "Mom, I'm bored."

Poipu Beach Park, Poipu, South Shore. The *keiki* (children's) pool and lifeguards make this a safe spot for kids. The near-perpetual sun isn't so bad, either.

BEST STAND-UP PADDLING
Anini Beach Park, North Shore. The reef and long stretch of beach give beginners to stand-up paddling a calm place to give this new sport a try. You won't get pummeled by waves here.

Wailua Beach, East Side. On the East Side, the Wailua River bisects the beach and heads inland 2 miles, providing stand-up paddlers with a long and scenic stretch of water before they have to figure out how to turn around.

BEST SURFING
Hanalei Bay Beach Park, North Shore. In winter, Hanalei Bay offers a range of breaks, from beginner to advanced. Hanalei is where surfing legends such as Laird Hamilton and the Irons Brothers—international surf champions—began their shredding careers as they grew up surfing these waters.

Waiohai Beach, South Shore. Surf instructors flock to this spot with their students for its gentle, near-shore break. Then, as students advance, they can paddle out a little farther to an intermediate break—if they dare.

BEST SUNSETS
Kee Beach, North Shore. Even in winter, when the sun sets in the south and out of view, you won't be disappointed here, because the "magic hour," as photographers call the time around sunset, paints Napali Coast with a warm gold light.

Polihale State Park, West Side. This due-west-facing beach may be tricky to get to, but it does offer the most unobstructed sunset views on the island. The fact that it's so remote means you won't have strangers in your photos, but you will want to depart right after sunset or risk getting lost in the dark.

BEST FOR SEEING AND BEING SEEN
Haena Beach Park, North Shore. Behind those gated driveways and heavily foliaged yards that line this beach live—at least, part-time—some of the world's most celebrated music and movie moguls. Need we say more?

Hanalei Bay Beach Park, North Shore. We know we tout this beach often, but it deserves the praise. It's a mecca for everyone—regular joes, surfers, fishers, young, old, locals, visitors, and, especially, the famous. You may also recognize Hanalei Bay from the movie *The Descendants*.

5

site of an ancient *heiau* dedicated to hula. The beach is protected by a reef—except during high surf—creating a small sandy-bottom lagoon and making it a popular snorkeling destination. If there's a current, it's usually found on the western edge of the beach as the incoming tide ebbs back out to sea. Makana (a prominent peak also known as Bali Hai after the blockbuster musical *South Pacific*) is so artfully arranged, you'll definitely want to capture the memory, so don't forget your camera. The popularity of this beach often makes parking quite difficult. Start extra early or, better yet, arrive at the end of the day, in time to witness otherworldly sunsets sidelighting Napali Coast. **Amenities:** lifeguards; parking; showers, toilets. **Best For:** swimming; snorkeling; sunset; walking. ⊠ *End of Rte. 560, 7 miles west of Hanalei.*

THE EAST SIDE

The East Side of the island is considered the "windward" side, a term you'll often hear in weather forecasts. It simply means the side of the island receiving onshore winds. The wind helps break down rock into sand, so there are plenty of beaches here. Unfortunately, only a few of those beaches are protected, so many are not ideal for beginning ocean-goers, though they are perfect for long sunrise ambles. On super-windy days, kiteboarders sail along the east shore, sometimes jumping waves and performing acrobatic maneuvers in the air.

★ **Kalapaki Beach.** Five minutes south of the airport in Lihue, you'll find this wide, sandy-bottom beach fronting the Kauai Marriott. One of the big attractions is that this beach is almost always safe from rip currents and undertows because it's around the backside of a peninsula, in its own cove. There are tons of activities here, including all the usual water sports—beginning and intermediate surfing, body boarding, bodysurfing, and swimming—plus, there are two outrigger canoe clubs paddling in the bay and the Nawiliwili Yacht Club's boats sailing around the harbor. Kalapaki is the only place on Kauai where sailboats—in this case Hobie Cats—are available for rent (at Kauai Beach Boys, which fronts the beach next to Duke's Canoe Club restaurant). Visitors can also rent snorkel gear, surfboards, body boards, and kayaks from Kauai Beach Boys. A volleyball court on the beach is often used by a loosely organized group of local players; visitors are always welcome.
■ **TIP→** Families prefer the stream end of the beach, whereas those seeking more solitude will prefer the cliff side of the beach. Duke's Canoe Club restaurant is one of only a couple of restaurants on the island actually on a beach; the restaurant's lower level is casual, even welcoming beach attire and sandy feet, perfect for lunch or an afternoon cocktail. **Amenities:** parking; showers; toilets; water sports; food and drink. **Best For:** swimming; surfing; partiers; walking. ⊠ *Off Wapaa Rd., Lihue.*

Kealia Beach. A half-mile long and adjacent to the highway heading north out of Kapaa, Kealia Beach attracts body boarders and surfers year-round (possibly because the local high school is just up the hill). Kealia is not generally a great beach for swimming or snorkeling. The waters are usually rough and the waves crumbly because of an onshore break (no protecting reef) and northeasterly trade winds.

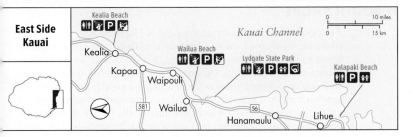

A scenic lookout on the southern end, accessed off the highway, is a superb location for saluting the morning sunrise or spotting whales during winter. A level, paved trail follows the coastline north and is one of the most scenic coastal trails on the island for walking, running, and biking. **Amenities:** Lifeguard; parking; showers; toilets. **Best For:** surfing; swimming; walking; sunrise. ⊠ *Rte. 56, at mile marker 10, Kealia.*

★ **Lydgate State Park.** This is by far the best family beach park on Kauai.
The waters off the beach are protected by a hand-built breakwater creating two boulder-enclosed saltwater pools for safe swimming and snorkeling year-round. A recent dredging finds the pools in a recovery stage as sand had to be removed leaving mud off shore. But the numerous schools of fish are slowly returning. The smaller of the two pools is perfect for *keiki* (children). Behind the beach is Kamalani Playground, designed by the children of Kauai and built by the community. Children of all ages—that includes you—enjoy the swings, lava-tube slides, tree house, and more. Picnic tables abound in the park, and a large covered pavilion is available by permit for celebrations. The Kamalani Kai Bridge is a second playground—also built by the community — south of the original. (The two are united by a bike and pedestrian path that is part of the Nawiliwili-to-Anahola multi-use path project currently under construction.) ■ TIP→ **This park system is perennially popular; the quietest times to visit are early mornings and weekdays. If you want to witness a "baby luau," Lydgate State Park attracts them year-round, especially in summers.** **Amenities:** Lifeguards; parking; showers; toilets. **Best For:** partiers; walking; swimming; sunrise. ⊠ *Nalu Rd., just south of Wailua River, Wailua.*

Wailua Beach. Some say the first Polynesians to migrate to Hawaii landed at Wailua Beach. At the river's mouth, petroglyphs carved on boulders are sometimes visible during low surf and tide conditions. Surfers, body boarders, and bodysurfers alike enjoy this beach year-round thanks to its dependable waves (usually on the north end); however, because of Hawaii's northeast trade winds, these waves are not the "cleanest" for surf aficionados. Many families spend the weekend days under the Wailua Bridge at the river mouth, even hauling out their portable grills and tables to go with their beach chairs. The great news about Wailua Beach is that it's almost impossible to miss; however, parking can be a challenge. The best parking for the north end of the beach is on Papaloa Road behind the Shell station. For the southern end of the beach, park at Wailua River State Park. **Amenities:** Parking; showers; toilets. **Best For:** swimming; surfing; walking; windsurfing. ⊠ *Kuamoo Rd., Wailua.*

THE SOUTH SHORE

The South Shore's primary access road is Highway 520, a tree-lined, two-lane, windy road. As you drive along it, there's a sense of tunneling down a rabbit hole into another world, à la Alice. And the South Shore is certainly a wonderland. On average, it rains only 30 inches per year, so if you're looking for fun in the sun, this is a good place to start. The beaches with their powdery-fine sand are consistently good year-round, except during high surf, which, if it hits at all, will be in summer. If you want solitude, this isn't it; if you want excitement—well, as much excitement as quiet Kauai offers—this is the place for you.

Brennecke Beach. There's little beach here on the eastern end of Poipu Beach Park, but Brennecke Beach is synonymous on the island with board surfing and bodysurfing, thanks to its shallow sandbar and reliable shore break. Because the beach is small and often congested, surfboards are prohibited near shore. The water on the rocky eastern edge of the beach is a good place to see the endangered green sea turtles noshing on plants growing on the rocks. **Amenities:** parking; food and drink. **Best For:** surfing; sunset. ⊠ *Hoone Rd., off Poipu Rd., Poipu.*

Keoniloa Beach (*Shipwreck Beach*). Few—except the public relations specialists at the Grand Hyatt Kauai Resort and Spa, which backs the beach—refer to this beach by anything other than its common name: Shipwreck Beach. Its Hawaiian name means "long beach." Both make sense. It is a long stretch of crescent-shape beach punctuated by cliffs on both ends, and, yes, a ship once wrecked here. With its onshore break, the waters off Shipwreck are best for body boarding and bodysurfing; however, the beach itself is plenty big for sunbathing, sand-castle building, Frisbee, and other beach-related fun. Fishers pole fish from shore and off the cliff and sometimes pick *opihi* (limpets) off the rocks lining the foot of the cliffs. The eastern edge of the beach is the start of an interpretive dune walk (complimentary) held by the hotel staff; check with the concierge for dates and times. **Amenities:** Parking, showers, toilets; food and drink. **Best for:** surfing; walking; sunrise ⊠ *Ainako Rd. Continue on Poipu Rd. past Hyatt, turn makai on Ainako Rd., Poipu.*

Fodor's Choice
★
Mahaulepu Beach. This 2-mile stretch of coast with its sand dunes, limestone hills, sinkholes, and caves is unlike any other on Kauai. Remains of a large, ancient settlement, evidence of great battles, and the discovery of a now-underwater petroglyph field indicate that Hawaiians lived in this area as early as 700 AD. Mahaulepu's coastline is unprotected and rocky, which makes venturing into the ocean hazardous. There are three beach areas with bits of sandy-bottom swimming; however, we think the best way to experience Mahaulepu is simply to roam, especially at sunrise. ■ TIP→ Access to this beach is via private property. The owner allows access during daylight hours, but be sure to depart before sunset or risk getting locked in for the night. **Amenities:** parking. **Best For:** walking; solitude; sunrise. ⊠ *Poipu Rd., past the Hyatt Hotel, Poipu.*

★
☾
Poipu Beach Park. The most popular beach on the South Shore, and perhaps on all of Kauai, is Poipu Beach Park. The snorkeling's good, the body boarding's good, the surfing's good, the swimming's good, and the fact that the sun is almost always shining is good, too. The beach

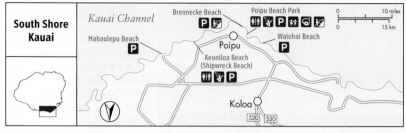

can be crowded at times, especially on weekends and holidays, but that just makes people-watching that much more fun. You'll see *keiki* (children) experiencing the ocean for the first time, snorkelers trying to walk with their flippers on, ukulele players, birthday party revelers, young and old, visitors and locals. Even the endangered Hawaiian monk seal often makes an appearance. **Amenities:** lifeguards; parking; showers; toilets; food and drink. **Best For:** swimming, snorkeling, partiers, walking. ⊠ *Hoone Rd., off Poipu Rd., Poipu.*

Waiohai Beach. The first hotel built in Poipu in 1962 overlooked this beach, adjacent to Poipu Beach Park. Actually, there's little to distinguish where one starts and the other begins other than a crescent reef at the eastern end of Waiohai Beach. That crescent, however, is important. It creates a small, protected bay—good for snorkeling and beginning surfers. If you're a beginner, this is the spot. However, when a summer swell kicks up, the near-shore conditions become dangerous; offshore, there's a splendid surf break for experienced surfers. The beach itself is narrow and, like its neighbor, gets very crowded in summer. **Amenities:** parking. **Best For:** surfing; sunrise; sunset. ⊠ *Hoone Rd., off Poipu Rd., Poipu.*

THE WEST SIDE

The West Side of the island receives hardly enough rainfall year-round to water a cactus, and because it's also the leeward side, there are few tropical breezes. That translates to sunny and hot with long, languorous, and practically deserted beaches. You'd think the leeward waters—untouched by wind—would be calm, but there's no reef system, so the waters are not as inviting as one would like. ■TIP→ **The best place to gear up for the beaches on the West Side is on the South Shore or East Side.** Although there's some catering to visitors here, it's not much.

Kekaha Beach Park. This is one of the premier spots on Kauai for sunset walks and the start of the state's longest beach. We don't recommend much water activity here without first talking to a lifeguard: The beach is exposed to open ocean and has an onshore break that can be hazardous any time of year. However, there are some excellent surf breaks—for experienced surfers only. Or, if you would like to run on a beach, this is the one—the hard-packed sand goes on for miles, all the way to Napali Coast, but you won't get past the Pacific Missile Range Facility and its post-9/11 restrictions. Another bonus for this beach is its relatively dry weather year-round. If it's raining where you are, try Kekaha Beach

Seal-Spotting on the South Shore

When strolling on one of Kauai's lovely beaches, don't be surprised if you find yourself in the rare company of Hawaiian monk seals. These are among the most endangered of all marine mammals, with perhaps fewer than 1,200 remaining. They primarily inhabit the northwestern Hawaiian Islands, although more are showing their sweet faces on the main Hawaiian Islands, especially on Kauai. They're fond of hauling out on the beach for a long snooze in the sun, particularly after a night of gorging on fish. They need this time to rest and digest, safe from predators.

During the past several summers, female seals have birthed young on the beaches around Kauai, where they stay to nurse their pups for upward of six weeks. It seems the seals enjoy particular beaches for the same reasons we do: the shallow, protected waters.

If you're lucky enough to see a monk seal, keep your distance and let it be. Although they may haul out near people, they still want and need their space. Stay several hundred feet away, and forget photos unless you've got a zoom lens. It's illegal to do anything that causes a monk seal to change its behavior, with penalties that include big fines and even jail time. In the water, seals may appear to want to play. It's their curious nature. Don't try to play with them. They are wild animals—mammals, in fact, with teeth.

If you have concerns about the health or safety of a seal, or just want more information, contact the **Hawaiian Monk Seal Conservation Hui** (☎ *808/651–7668* ⊕ *www.kauaiseals.com*).

Park. Toilets here are the portable kind. **Amenities:** lifeguards; showers; toilets; parking. **Best For:** sunset; walking; surfing. ⊠ *Rte. 50, near mile marker 27, Kekaha.*

Fodor'sChoice ★ **Polihale State Park.** The longest stretch of beach in Hawaii starts in Kekaha and ends about 15 miles away at the start of Napali Coast. At the Napali end of the beach is the 5-mile-long, 140-acre Polihale State Park. In addition to being long, this beach is 300 feet wide in places and backed by sand dunes 50 to 100 feet tall. Polihale is a remote beach accessed via a rough, 5-mile haul-cane road (four-wheel drive preferred but not required) at the end of Route 50 in Kekaha. ■ TIP→ Be sure to start the day with a full tank of gas and a cooler filled with food and drink. Many locals wheel their four-wheel-drive vehicles up and over the sand dunes right onto the beach, but don't try this in a rental car. You're sure to get stuck and found in violation of your rental car agreement.

On weekends and holidays Polihale is a popular locals' camping location, but even on "busy" days this beach is never crowded. On days of high surf, only experts surf the waves. In general, the water here is extremely rough and not recommended for recreation; however, there's one small fringing reef, called Queen's Pond, where swimming is sometimes safe. Neighboring Polihale Beach is the Pacific Missile Range Facility (PMRF), operated by the U.S. Navy. Since September 11, 2001, access to the beaches fronting PMRF has been restricted. **Amenities:**

5

Lydgate State Park is a great place for families. Kids love watching fish in the nearby koi ponds and blowing off steam on the two playgrounds designed by local *keiki* (children).

parking; showers; toilets. **Best For:** walking; solitude; sunset. ⊠ *Dirt road at end of Rte. 50, Kekaha.*

Salt Pond Beach Park. A great family spot, Salt Pond Beach Park features a naturally made, shallow swimming pond behind a curling finger of rock where keiki splash and snorkel. This pool is generally safe except during a large south swell, which usually occurs in summer, if at all. The center and western edge of the beach is popular with body boarders and bodysurfers. On a cultural note, the flat stretch of land to the east of the beach is the last spot in Hawaii where ponds are used to harvest salt in the dry heat of summer. The beach park is popular with locals and can get crowded on weekends and holidays. **Amenities:** lifeguard; parking; showers, toilets. **Best For:** swimming; sunset; walking. ⊠ *Lolokai Rd., off Rte. 50, Hanapepe.*

WATER SPORTS AND TOURS

Updated by David Simon

So, you've decided to vacation on an island. That means you're going to run into a little water at some time. Ancient Hawaiians were notorious water sports fanatics—they invented surfing, after all—and that proclivity hasn't strayed far from today's mind-set. Even if you're not into water sports or sports in general, there's a slim chance that you'll leave this island without getting out on the ocean, as Kauai's top attraction—Napali Coast—is something not to be missed.

BOAT TOURS

Deciding to see Napali Coast by boat is an easy decision. Choosing the outfitter to go with is not. There are numerous boat-tour operators to choose from, and, quite frankly, they all do a good job. Before you even start thinking about whom to go out with, answer these three questions: What kind of boat do I prefer? Where am I staying? Do I want to go in the morning or afternoon? Once you settle on these three, you can easily zero in on the tour outfitter.

First, the boat. The most important thing is to match your personality and that of your group with the personality of the boat. If you like thrills and adventure, the rubber, inflatable rafts—often called Zodiacs, which Jacques Cousteau made famous and which the U.S. Coast Guard uses—will entice you. They're fast, sure to leave you drenched, and quite bouncy. If you prefer a smoother, more leisurely ride, then the large catamarans are the way to go. The next boat choice is size. Both the rafts and catamarans come in small and large. Again—think smaller, more adventurous; larger, more leisurely. ■ TIP➜ Do not choose a smaller boat because you think there will be fewer people. There might be fewer people, but you'll be jammed together sitting atop strangers. If you prefer privacy over socializing, go with a larger boat, so you'll have more room to spread out. The smaller boats will also take you along the coast at a higher rate of speed, making photo opportunities a bit more challenging. One advantage to smaller boats, however, is that—depending on ocean conditions—some may slip into a sea cave or two. If that sounds interesting to you, call the outfitter and ask their policy on entering sea caves. Some won't, no matter the conditions, because they consider the caves sacred or because they don't want to cause any environmental damage.

There are three points boats leave from around the island (Hanalei, Port Allen, and Waimea), and all head to the same spot: Napali Coast. Here's the inside skinny on which is the best: If you're staying on the North Shore, choose to depart out of the North Shore. If you're staying anywhere else, depart out of the West Side. It's that easy. Sure, the North Shore is closer to Napali Coast; however, you'll pay more for less overall time. The West Side boat operators may spend more time getting to Napali Coast; however, they'll spend about the same amount of time along Napali, plus you'll pay less. Finally, you'll also have to decide whether you want to go on a morning tour, which includes a deli lunch and a stop for snorkeling, or an afternoon tour, which does not stop to snorkel but does include a sunset over the ocean. The morning tours with snorkeling are more popular with families and those who love dolphins, which enjoy the "waves" created by the front of the catamarans and might just escort you down the coast. The winter months will also be a good chance to spot some whales breaching. You don't have to be an expert snorkeler or even have any prior experience, but if it is your first time, note that although there will be some snorkeling instruction, there might not be much. Hawaiian spinner dolphins are so plentiful in the mornings that some tour companies guarantee you'll see them, though you won't get in the water and swim with them. The afternoon tours are more popular with nonsnorkelers—obviously— and photographers interested in capturing the setting sunlight on the coast. ■TIP→ No matter which tour you select, book it online whenever possible. Most companies offer Web specials, usually around $10 to $20 off per person.

CATAMARAN TOURS

Fodor's Choice
★

Blue Dolphin Charters. This company operates 63-foot and 65-foot sailing (rarely raised and always motoring) catamarans designed with three decks of spacious seating with great visibility. ■TIP→ The lower deck is best for shade seekers. Upgrades from snorkeling to scuba diving—no need for certification—are available and run $35, but the diving is really best for beginners or people who need a refresher course. On Tuesday and Friday a tour of Napali Coast includes a detour across the channel to Niihau for snorkeling and diving. Blue Dolphin likes to say they have the best mai tais "off the island," and truth is, they probably do. Morning snorkel tours of Napali include a deli lunch, and afternoon sunset sightseeing tours include a meal of kalua pork, teriyaki chicken, Caesar salad, and chocolate-chip cookies. Prices range from $105 to $196, depending on the tour. Two-hour whale-watching/sunset tours, offered during winter, run $63. Book online for cheaper deals on every tour offered. ⊠ *In Port Allen Marina Center Turn makai onto Rte. 541 off Rte. 50, at Eleele* ☎ *808/335–5553, 877/511–1311* ⊕ *www. kauaiboats.com.*

Capt. Andy's Sailing Adventures. Departing from Port Allen and running two 55-foot sailing catamarans, Capt. Andy's runs the same five-hour snorkeling and four-hour sunset tours along Napali Coast as everyone else, though we're not crazy about its seating, which exists mostly in the cabin. It also operates a six-hour snorkel BBQ sail aboard a new addition—its "Southern Star" yacht—originally built for private charters. The new boat now operates as host for two of Capt. Andy's daily sailing trips for an upgraded feel. For a shorter adventure, they have a two-hour sunset sail, embarking out of Kukuiula Harbor in Poipu along the South Shore—with live Hawaiian music—on select days (*check website for particulars*). ■TIP→ If the winds and swells are up on the North Shore, this is usually a good choice—especially if you're prone to seasickness. This is the only tour boat operator that allows infants on board—but only on the two-hour trip. Note, if you have reservations for the shorter tour, you'll check in at their Kukuiula Harbor office. Prices range from $69 to $159. ⊕ *www.napali.com.*

Captain Sundown. If you're staying on the North Shore, Captain Sundown is a worthy choice, especially for the nonadventurous. Get this: Captain Bob has been cruising Napali Coast since 1971—six days a week, sometimes twice a day. (And right alongside Captain Bob is his son Captain Larry.) To say he knows the area is a bit of an understatement. Here's the other good thing about this tour: they take only 15 to 17 passengers. Now, you'll definitely pay more, but it's worth it. The breathtaking views of the waterfall-laced mountains behind Hanalei and Haena start immediately, and then it's around Kee Beach and the magic of Napali Coast unfolds before you. All the while, the captains are trolling for fish, and if they catch any, guests get to reel 'em in.

Get out on the water and see Napali Coast in style on a luxe cruising yacht.

Afternoon sunset sails (seasonal) run three hours and check in around 3 pm—these are BYOB. Prices range from $144 to $199. Meet in the Tahiti Nui parking lot. During the winter months, Captain Bob moves his operation to Nawiliwili Harbor, where he runs four- to five-hour whale-watching tours. ⊠ *5-5134 Kuhio Hwy., Hanalei* ☎ *808/826–5585* ⊕ *www.captainsundown.com.*

Catamaran Kahanu. This Hawaiian-owned-and-operated company has been in business since 1985 and runs a 40-foot power catamaran with 18-passenger seating. The five-hour tour includes snorkeling at Nualolo Kai, plus a deli lunch and soft drinks. The four-hour afternoon tour includes a hot dinner and sunset. The boat is smaller than most and may feel a tad crowded, but the tour feels more personal, with a laid-back, *ohana* style. Saltwater runs through the veins of Captain Lani. Guests can witness the ancient cultural practice of coconut weaving or other Hawaiian craft demonstrations on board. There's no alcohol allowed. Prices range from $105 to $135. ⊠ *4353 Waialo Rd., near Port Allen Marina Center, Eleele* ☎ *808/645–6176, 888/213–7711* ⊕ *www.catamarankahanu.com.*

HoloHolo Charters. Choose between the 50-foot catamaran called *Leila* for a morning snorkel sail to Napali Coast, or the 65-foot *Holo Holo* catamaran trip to the "forbidden island" of Niihau. Both boats have large cabins and little outside seating. Originators of the Niihau tour, HoloHolo Charters built their 65-foot powered catamaran with a wide beam to reduce side-to-side motion, and twin 425 HP turbo diesel engines specifically for the 17-mile channel crossing to Niihau. ■ TIP→ It's the only outfitter running daily Niihau tours. The *Holo Holo* also embarks on a daily sunset and sightseeing tour of the Napali Coast. *Leila* can hold 37 passengers, while her big brother can take a maximum of 49. Prices range from $99 to $179. Check in at Port Allen Marina Center. ⊠ *4353 Waialo Rd., Eleele* ☎ *808/335–0815, 800/848–6130* ⊕ *www.holoholocharters.com.*

★ **Kauai Sea Tours.** This company operates a 60-foot sailing catamaran designed almost identically to that of Blue Dolphin Charters—with all the same benefits—including great views and spacious seating. Snorkeling tours anchor near Makole (based on the captain's discretion). If snorkeling isn't your thing, try the four-hour sunset tour, with beer, wine, mai tais, pupu, and a hot buffet dinner. Prices range from $115 to $149. Check in at Port Allen Marina Center. ⊠ *4353 Waialo Rd., Eleele* ☎ *808/826–7254, 800/733–7997* ⊕ *www.kauaiseatours.com.*

RAFT TOURS

Capt. Andy's Rafting Expeditions. This company used to be known as Captain Zodiac; however, the outfit has changed hands over the years. It first started running Napali in 1974, and currently, Capt. Andy's (as in the sailing catamaran Capt. Andy's) is operating the business. Departing out of Kikiaola Harbor in Kekaha, this tour is much like the other raft tours, offering both snorkeling and beach-landing excursions. The rafts are on the smaller side—24 feet with a maximum of 14 passengers—and all seating is on the rubber hulls, so hang on. They operate three different rafts, so there's a good chance of availability. Price is $185 in summer; $159 in winter, including snorkeling at Nualolo Kai (ocean conditions permitting), sightseeing along Napali Coast, a hiking tour through an ancient Hawaiian fishing village, and a hot buffet lunch on the beach. You're closer to the water on the Zodiacs, so you'll have great views of humpbacks, spinner dolphins, sea turtles, and other wildlife. ⊠ *Kikiaola Small Boat Harbor, Hwy. 50, Waimea* ☎ *808/335–6833, 800/535–0830* ⊕ *www.napali.com.*

Fodor'sChoice **Napali Explorer.** Owned by a couple of women, these tours operate out
★ of Waimea, a tad closer to Napali Coast than most of the other West Side catamaran tours. Departing out of the West Side, the company runs two different sizes of inflatable rubber raft: a 48-foot, 36-passenger craft with an onboard toilet, freshwater shower, shade canopy, and seating in the stern (which is surprisingly smooth and comfortable) and bow (which is where the fun is); and a 26-foot, 14-passenger craft for the all-out fun and thrills of a white-knuckle ride in the bow. The smaller vessel stops at Nualolo Kai and ties up onshore for a tour of the ancient fishing village. Though they used to operate out of Hanalei Bay during the summer, the company is now strictly a West Side operation. Rates are $105 to $149, including snorkeling. Charters are available. ⊠ *9643 Kaumalii Hwy., Waimea* ☎ *808/338–9999, 877/335–9909* ⊕ *www.napaliexplorer.com.*

★ **Z-Tourz.** What we like about Z-Tourz is that it is the only boat company to make snorkeling its priority. As such, it focuses on the South Shore's abundant offshore reefs, stopping at two locations. If you want to see Napali, this boat is not for you; if you want to snorkel with the myriad of Hawaii's tropical reef fish and turtles (pretty much guaranteed), this is your boat. Z-Tourz runs daily three-hour tours on a 26-foot rigid-hull inflatable (think Zodiac) with a maximum of 16 passengers. These snorkel tours are guided, so someone actually identifies what you're seeing. Rate is $94, which includes lunch and snorkel gear. Check in at the business center then ride to Kukuiula Harbor in Poipu. ✉ *3417 Poipu Rd., Poipu* ☎ *808/742–7422, 888/998–6879* ⊕ *www.ztourz.com.*

RIVER BOAT TOURS TO FERN GROTTO

Smith's Motor Boat Services. This 2-mile, upriver trip culminates at a yawning lava tube that is covered with enormous fishtail ferns. During the boat ride, guitar and ukulele players regale you with Hawaiian melodies and tell the history of the river. It's a kitschy bit of Hawaiiana, worth the little money ($20) and short time required. Flat-bottom, 150-passenger riverboats (that rarely fill up) depart from Wailua Marina at the mouth of the Wailua River. ■**TIP→** It's extremely rare, but occasionally after heavy rains the tour doesn't disembark at the grotto; if you're traveling in winter, ask beforehand. Round-trip excursions take 1½ hours, including time to walk around the grotto and environs. Tours run at 9:30, 11, 2, and 3:30 daily. Reservations are not required. Contact Smith's Motor Boat Services for more information. ✉ *5971 Kuhio Hwy, Kapaa* ☎ *808/821–6892* ⊕ *www.smithskauai.com.*

BODY BOARDING AND BODYSURFING

The most natural form of wave riding is bodysurfing, a popular sport on Kauai because there are many shore breaks around the island. Wave riders of this style stand waist-deep in the water, facing shore, and swim madly as a wave picks them up and breaks. It's great fun and requires no special skills and absolutely no equipment other than a swimsuit. The next step up is body boarding, also called Boogie boarding. In this case, wave riders lie with their upper body on a foam board about half the length of a traditional surfboard and kick as the wave propels them toward shore. Again, this is easy to pick up, and there are many places around Kauai to practice. The locals wear short-finned flippers to help them catch waves, although they are not necessary for and even hamper beginners. It's worth spending a few minutes watching these experts as they spin, twirl, and flip—that's right—while they slip down the face of the wave. Of course, all beach safety precautions apply, and just because you see wave riders of any kind in the water doesn't mean the water is safe for everyone. Any snorkeling-gear outfitter also rents body boards.

BEST SPOTS

Some of our favorite bodysurfing and body-boarding beaches are **Brennecke, Wailua, Kealia, Kalihiwai,** and **Hanalei.** *For directions, see Beaches.*

DEEP-SEA FISHING

Simply step aboard and cast your line for mahimahi, ahi, ono, and marlin. That's about how quickly the fishing—mostly trolling with lures—begins on Kauai. The water gets deep quickly here, so there's less cruising time to fishing grounds. Of course, your captain may elect to cruise to a hot location where he's had good luck lately.

5

There are oodles of charter fishermen around; most depart from Nawiliwili Harbor in Lihue, and most use lures instead of live bait. Inquire about each boat's "fish policy," that is, what happens to the fish if any are caught. Some boats keep all; others will give you enough for a meal or two, even doing the cleaning themselves. On shared charters, ask about the maximum passenger count and about the fishing rotation; you'll want to make sure everyone gets a fair shot at reeling in the big one. Another option is to book a private charter. Shared and private charters run four, six, and eight hours in length.

BOATS AND CHARTERS

Captain Don's Sport Fishing & Ocean Adventure. Captain Don is very flexible and treats everyone like family—he'll stop to snorkel or whale-watch if that's what the group (four to six) wants. Saltwater fly-fishermen (bring your own gear) are welcome. He'll even fish for bait and let you keep part of whatever you catch. The *June Louise* is a 34-foot twin diesel. Rates start at $140 for shared, $595 for private charters. ⊠ *Nawiliwili Small Boat Harbor, off Nawiliwili Rd., Nawiliwili* ☎ *808/639–3012* ⊕ *www.captaindonsfishing.com.*

Explore Kauai Sportfishing. If you're staying on the West Side, you'll be glad to know that Napali Explorer (of the longtime rafting tour business) is now running fishing trips out of Port Allen under the name Explore Kauai Sportfishing. It offers shared and exclusive charters of four, six, and eight hours in a 41-foot Concord called *Happy Times.* The shared tours max out at six fishermen, and a portion of the catch is shared with all. The boat is also used for specialty charters—that is, film crews, surveys, burials, and even Niihau fishing. Rates range from $130 to $179 per person. ⊠ *Port Allen Small Boat Harbor, Waialo Rd., Eleele* ☎ *808/338–9999, 877/335–9909* ⊕ *www.napali-explorer.com.*

Hana Paa. The advantage with Hana Paa is that it takes fewer people (minimum two, maximum four for a nonprivate excursion), but you pay for it. Rates start at $310 for shared, $600 for private charters, which can accommodate up to six people. The company's fish policy is flexible, and the boat is roomy. The *Maka Hou II* is a 38-foot Bertram. ⊠ *Nawiliwili Small Boat Harbor, off Nawiliwili Rd., Nawiliwili* ☎ *808/823–6031, 866/776–3474.*

KAYAKING

Kauai is the only Hawaiian island with navigable rivers. As the oldest inhabited island in the chain, Kauai has had more time for wind and water erosion to deepen and widen cracks into streams and streams into rivers. Because this is a small island, the rivers aren't long, and there are no rapids; that makes them perfectly safe for kayakers of all levels, even beginners.

For more advanced paddlers, there aren't many places in the world more beautiful for sea kayaking than Napali Coast. If this is your draw to Kauai, plan your vacation for the summer months, when the seas are at their calmest. ■ TIP→ Tour and kayak-rental reservations are recommended at least two weeks in advance during peak summer and holiday seasons. In general, tours and rentals are available year-round,

Monday through Saturday. Pack a swimsuit, sunscreen, a hat, bug repellent, water shoes (sport sandals, aqua socks, old tennis shoes), and motion sickness medication if you're planning on sea kayaking.

RIVER KAYAKING

Tour outfitters operate on the Huleia, Wailua, and Hanalei rivers with guided tours that combine hiking to waterfalls, as in the case of the first two, and snorkeling, as

WORD OF MOUTH

"My husband and I kayaked the Wailua River and did the one-mile hike to the Uluwehi Falls (aka Secret Falls), and I highly recommend it. This is the only kayaking we have ever done. We were in okay shape, and did not have much trouble." —jcb

in the case of the third. Another option is renting kayaks and heading out on your own. Each has its advantages and disadvantages, but it boils down as follows:

If you want to swim at the base of a remote 100-foot waterfall, sign up for a five-hour kayak (4-mile round-trip) and hiking (2-mile round-trip) tour of the **Wailua River.** It includes a dramatic waterfall that is best accessed with the aid of a guide, so you don't get lost. ■ TIP→ Remember—it's dangerous to swim under waterfalls no matter how good a water massage may sound. Rocks and logs are known to plunge down, especially after heavy rains.

If you want to kayak on your own, choose the **Hanalei River.** It's most scenic from the kayak itself—there are no trails to hike to hidden waterfalls. And better yet, a rental company is right on the river—no hauling kayaks on top of your car.

If you're not sure of your kayaking abilities, head to the **Huleia River;** 3½-hour tours include easy paddling upriver, a nature walk through a rain forest with a cascading waterfall, a rope swing for playing Tarzan and Jane, and a ride back downriver—into the wind—on a motorized, double-hull canoe.

As for the kayaks themselves, most companies use the two-person sit-on-top style that is quite buoyant—no Eskimo rolls required. The only possible danger comes in the form of communication. The kayaks seat two people, which means you'll share the work (good) with a guide, or your spouse, child, parent, or friend (the potential danger part). On the river, the two-person kayaks are known as "divorce boats." Counseling is not included in the tour price.

SEA KAYAKING

In its second year and second issue, *National Geographic Adventure* ranked kayaking Napali Coast second on its list of America's Best 100 Adventures, right behind rafting the Colorado River through the Grand Canyon. That pretty much says it all. It's the adventure of a lifetime in one day, involving eight hours of paddling. Although it's good to have some kayaking experience, feel comfortable on the water, and be reasonably fit, it doesn't require the preparation, stamina, or fortitude of, say, climbing Mt. Everest. Tours run May through September, ocean conditions permitting. In the winter months sea-kayaking tours operate on the South Shore—beautiful, but not Napali.

In summer you can reach Kalalau Beach by sea kayaking along Napali Coast. "[We had a] great day at the river by Kalalau." —clitopower

EQUIPMENT AND TOURS

Kayak Kauai. Based in Hanalei, this company offers guided tours on the Hanalei and Wailua rivers, and along Napali Coast. It has a great shop right on the Hanalei River for kayak rentals and camping gear. The guided Hanalei River Kayak and Snorkel Tour starts at the shop and heads downriver, so there's not much to see of the scenic river valley. (For that, rent a kayak on your own.) Instead, this three-hour tour paddles down to the river mouth, where the river meets the sea. Then, it's a short paddle around a point to snorkel at either Princeville Hotel Beach or, ocean conditions permitting, a bit farther at Hideaways Beach. This is a great choice if you want to try your paddle at a bit of ocean kayaking.

A second location on Kuhio Highway in Kapaa is the base for Wailua River guided tours and kayak rentals. It's not right on the river, however, so shuttling is involved. For rentals, the company provides the hauling gear necessary for your rental car. Guided tours range from $60 to $214. Kayak rentals range from $28 to $75, depending on the river, depending on kayak size (single or double). ⊠ *5-5070 Kuhio Hwy., 1 mile past Hanalei Bridge, Hanalei* ☎ *808/826–9844, 800/437–3507* ⊕ *www.kayakkauai.com* ⊠ *Kapaa: south end of Coconut Marketplace, 4-484 Kuhio Hwy, Kapaa.*

Kayak Wailua. We can't quite figure out how this family-run business offers pretty much the same Wailua River kayaking tour as everyone else—except for lunch and beverages, which are BYO—for half the price, but it does. They say it's because they don't discount and don't offer commission to activities and concierge desks. Their 4½-hour kayak, hike, and waterfall swim costs $39.95, and their three-hour kayak-to-a-swimming-hole costs $34.95. We say fork over the extra $5 for the longer tour and hike to the beautiful 150-foot Secret Falls. Six tours a day are offered, beginning at 8 am and running on each hour until 1 pm. With the number of boats going out, large groups can be accommodated. ✉ *4565 Haleilio Rd., behind the old Coco Palms hotel, Kapaa* ☎ *808/822–3388* 🌐 *www.kayakwailua.com.*

Fodor's Choice ★ **Napali Kayak.** A couple of longtime guides ventured out on their own a few years back to create this company, which focuses solely on sea kayaking—Napali Coast in summer, as the name implies, and the South Shore in winter (during peak times only). These guys are highly experienced and still highly enthusiastic about their livelihood. So much so, that REI Adventures hires them to run their multiday, multisport tours. Now, that's a feather in their cap, we'd say. Prices start at $200. You can also rent kayaks; price range from $25 to $75. If you want to try camping on your own at Kalalau (you'll need permits), Napali Kayak will provide kayaks outfitted with dry bags, extra paddles, and seat backs, while also offering transportation drop-off and pickup. ✉ *5-5075 Kuhio Hwy., next to Postcards Café, Hanalei* ☎ *808/826–6900, 866/977–6900* 🌐 *www.napalikayak.com.*

Outfitters Kauai. This well-established tour outfitter operates year-round river-kayak tours on the Huleia and Wailua rivers, as well as sea-kayaking tours along Napali Coast in summer and the South Shore in winter. Outfitters Kauai's specialty, however, is the Kipu Safari. This all-day adventure starts with kayaking up the Huleia River and includes a rope swing over a swimming hole, a wagon ride through a working cattle ranch, a picnic lunch by a private waterfall, hiking, and two "zips" across the rain-forest canopy (strap on a harness, clip into a cable, and zip over a quarter of a mile). They then offer a one-of-a-kind Waterzip Zipline at their mountain stream–fed blue pool. The day ends with a ride on a motorized double-hull canoe. It's a great tour for the family, because no one ever gets bored. The Kipu Safari costs $182; other guided tours range from $102 to $229. ✉ *2827-A Poipu Rd., Poipu* ☎ *808/742–9667, 888/742–9887* 🌐 *www.outfitterskauai.com.*

Wailua Kayak & Canoe. This is the only purveyor of kayak rentals on the Wailua River, which means no hauling your kayak on top of your car (a definite plus). Rates are $45 for a single, $75 for a double, for either a morning or afternoon. Guided tours are also available with rates ranging from $55 to $90. This outfitter promotes itself as "Native Hawaiian owned and operated." ✉ *169 Wailua Rd., Kapaa* ☎ *808/821–1188* 🌐 *www.wailuariverkayaking.com.*

KITEBOARDING

Several years ago, the latest wave-riding craze to hit the Islands was kiteboarding, and the sport is still going strong. As the name implies, there's a kite and a board involved. The board you strap on your feet; the kite is attached to a harness around your waist. Steering is accomplished with a rod that's attached to the harness and the kite. Depending on conditions and the desires of the kiteboarder, the kite is played out some 30 to 100 feet in the air. The result is a cross between waterski-ing—without the boat—and windsurfing. Speeds are fast and aerobatic maneuvers are involved. Unfortunately, neither lessons nor rental gear are available for the sport on Kauai (Maui is a better bet), so if you aren't a seasoned kiteboarder already, you'll have to be content with watching the pros—who can put on a pretty spectacular show. The most popular year-round spots for kiteboarding are **Kapaa Beach Park, Anini Beach Park,** and **Mahaulepu Beach.** ■TIP➜ Many visitors come to Kauai dreaming of parasailing. If that's you, make a stop at Maui or the Big Island. There's no parasailing on Kauai.

SCUBA DIVING

The majority of scuba diving on Kauai occurs on the South Shore. Boat and shore dives are available, although boat sites surpass the shore sites for a couple of reasons. First, they're deeper and exhibit the complete symbiotic relationship of a reef system, and second, the visibility is bet-ter a little farther offshore.

The dive operators on Kauai offer a full range of services, including certification dives, referral dives, boat dives, shore dives, night dives, and drift dives. ■TIP➜ As for certification, we recommend completing your confined-water training and classroom testing before arriving on the island. That way, you'll spend less time training and more time diving.

BEST SPOTS
The best and safest scuba-diving sites are accessed by boat on the South Shore of the island, right off the shores of Poipu. The captain selects the actual site based on ocean conditions of the day. Beginners may prefer shore dives, which are best at **Koloa Landing** on the South Shore year-round and **Makua (Tunnels) Beach** on the North Shore in the calm summer months. Keep in mind, though, that you'll have to haul your gear a ways down the beach.

For the advanced diver, the island of Niihau—across an open ocean channel in deep and crystal clear waters—beckons and rewards, usually with some big fish. Seasport Divers and Fathom Five venture the 17 miles across the channel in summer when the crossing is smoothest. Div-ers can expect deep dives, walls, and strong currents at Niihau, where conditions can change rapidly. To make the long journey worthwhile, three dives and Nitrox are included.

EQUIPMENT, LESSONS, AND TOURS
Kauai Down Under Scuba. Though this company is now offering boat diving, it definitely specializes in shore diving, typically at Koloa Land-ing (year-round) and Tunnels (summers). They're not only geared toward beginning divers—for whom they provide a very thorough and gentle certification program as well as the Discover Scuba pro-gram—but also offer night dives and scooter (think James Bond) dives. Their main emphasis is a detailed review of marine biology, such as pointing out rare dragon eel and harlequin shrimp tucked away in pockets of coral. One reason is that their instructor-to-student ratio never exceeds 1:4—that's true of all their dive groups. Rates range

If you get up close with a Hawaiian monk seal, consider yourself lucky—they're endangered. But look, don't touch—it's illegal.

from $79 for a one-tank certified dive to $450 for certification—all dive gear included. ☎ 877/441–3483, 808/742–9534 ⊕ *www.kauaidownunderscuba.com.*

Fodor'sChoice
★ **Ocean Quest Watersports/Fathom Five.** A few years ago, Fathom Five, the South Shore boat-diving specialist, teamed up with Ocean Quest Watersports, a separate company specializing in shore dives at Tunnels on the North Shore. Today, they offer it all: boat dives, shore dives, night dives, certification dives. They're pretty much doing what everyone else is with a couple of twists. First, they offer a three-tank premium charter for those really serious about diving. Second, they operate a Nitrox continuous-flow mixing system, so you can decide the mix rate. Third, they tag on a twilight dive to the standard, one-tank night dive, making the outing worth the effort. Fourth, their shore diving isn't an afterthought. Finally, we think their dive masters are pretty darn good, too. They even dive Niihau in the summer aboard their 35-foot *Force*. Prices start at $75 for a one-tank shore dive and top out at $495 for full certification. The standard two-tank boat dive runs $125 plus $40 for gear rental, if needed. ■ TIP→ **In summer, book well in advance.** ✉ *3450 Poipu Rd., Koloa* ☎ *808/742–6991, 800/972–3078* ⊕ *www.fathomfive.com.*

Seasport Divers. Rated highly by readers of *Scuba Diving* magazine, Seasport Divers' 48-foot *Anela Kai* tops the chart for dive-boat luxury. But owner Marvin Otsuji didn't stop with that. A second boat—a 32-foot catamaran—is outfitted for diving, but we like it as an all-around charter. The company does a brisk business, which means it won't cancel at the last minute because of a lack of reservations, like some other companies, although they may book up to 18 people per boat. ■TIP→ **There are slightly more challenging trips in the morning; mellower dive sites are in the afternoon.** The company also runs a good-size dive shop for purchases and rentals, as well as a classroom for certification. Niihau trips are available in summer. All trips leave from Kukuiula Harbor in Poipu. Rates start at $125 for a two-tank boat dive; rental gear is $25 extra. ⊠ *2827 Poipu Rd., look for yellow submarine in parking lot, Poipu* ☎ *808/742–9303, 800/685–5889* ⊕ *www.seasportdivers.com.*

SNORKELING

Generally speaking, the calmest water and best snorkeling can be found on Kauai's North Shore in summer and South Shore in winter. The East Side, known as the windward side, has year-round, prevalent northeast trade winds that make snorkeling unpredictable, although there are some good pockets. The best snorkeling on the West Side is accessible only by boat.

A word on feeding fish: Don't. As Captain Ted with HoloHolo Charters says, fish have survived and populated reefs for much longer than we have been donning goggles and staring at them. They will continue to do so without our intervention. Besides, fish food messes up the reef and—one thing always leads to another—can eliminate a once-pristine reef environment. As for gear, if you're snorkeling with one of the Napali boat-tour outfitters, they'll provide it. However, depending on the company, it might not be the latest or greatest. If you have your own, bring it. On the other hand, if you're going out with SeaFun or Z-Tourz *(see Boat Tours)*, the gear is top-notch. If you need to rent, hit one of the "snorkel-and-surf" shops such as Snorkel Bob's in Koloa and Kapaa, Nukumoi in Poipu, or Seasport in Poipu and Kapaa, or shop Wal-Mart or Kmart if you want to drag it home. Typically, though, rental gear will be better quality than that found at Wal-Mart or Kmart. ■TIP→ **If you wear glasses, you can rent prescription masks at the rental shops—just don't expect them to match your prescription exactly.**

BEST SPOTS

Just because we say these are good places to snorkel doesn't mean that the exact moment you arrive, the fish will flock—they are wild, after all.

Beach House (*Lawai Beach*). Don't pack the beach umbrella, beach mats, or cooler for snorkeling at Beach House. Just bring your snorkeling gear. The beach—named after its neighbor the Beach House restaurant—is on the road to Spouting Horn. It's a small slip of sand during low tide and a rocky shoreline during high tide. However, it's right by the road's edge, and its rocky coastline and somewhat rocky bottom make it great for snorkeling. Enter and exit in the sand channel (not over the rocky reef) that lines up with the Lawai Beach Resort's center atrium. Stay within the rocky points anchoring each end of the beach. The current runs east to west. ⊠ *5017 Lawai Rd., near Lawai Beach Resort, Koloa.*

Kee Beach. Although it can get quite crowded, Kee Beach is quite often a good snorkeling destination. Just be sure to come during the off-hours, say early in the morning or later in the afternoon. ■TIP➔ Snorkeling here in winter can be hazardous. Summer is the best and safest time, although you should never swim beyond the reef. During peak times, a parking lot is available back down the road away from the beach. ⊠ *End of Rte. 560, Haena.*

⟳ **Lydgate Beach Park.** Lydgate Beach Park is the absolute safest place to snorkel on Kauai. With its lava-rock wall creating a protected swimming pool, this is the perfect spot for beginners, young and old. The fish are so tame here it's almost like swimming in a saltwater aquarium. There is also a playground for children, plenty of parking and full-service restrooms with showers. ⊠ *4470 Nalu Rd., off Rte. 56, Kapaa.*

Fodor's Choice **Niihau.** With little river runoff and hardly any boat traffic, the waters off
★ the island of Niihau are some of the clearest in all Hawaii, and that's good for snorkeling. Like Nualolo Kai, the only way to snorkel here is to sign on with one of the two tour boats venturing across a sometimes rough open ocean channel: Blue Dolphin Charters and HoloHolo (*see Boat Tours*).

★ **Nualolo Kai.** Nualolo Kai was once an ancient Hawaiian fishpond and is now home to the best snorkeling along Napali Coast (and perhaps on all of Kauai). The only way to access it is by boat, and only a few Napali snorkeling-tour operators are permitted to do so. We recommend Napali Explorer and Kauai Sea Tours (see Boat Tours).

Poipu Beach Park. You'll generally find good year-round snorkeling at Poipu Beach Park, except during summer's south swells (which are not nearly as frequent as winter's north swells). The best snorkeling fronts the Marriott Waiohai Beach Club. Stay inside the crescent created by the sandbar and rocky point. The current runs east to west. ⊠ *Hoone Rd., off Poipu Rd., Koloa.*

★ **Tunnels (Makua).** The search for Tunnels (Makua) is as tricky as the snorkeling. Park at Haena Beach Park and walk east—away from Napali Coast—until you see a sand channel entrance in the water, almost at the point. Once you get here, the reward is fantastic. The name of this beach comes from the many underwater lava tubes, which always attract marine life. The shore is mostly beach rock interrupted by three sand channels. You'll want to enter and exit at one of these channels (or risk stepping on a sea urchin or scraping your stomach on the reef). Follow the sand channel to a drop-off; the snorkeling along here is always full of nice surprises. Expect a current running east to west. Snorkeling here in winter can be hazardous; summer is the best and safest time for snorkeling. ⊠ *Haena Beach Park, end of Rte. 560, Kilauea.*

TOURS

⟳ **SeaFun Kauai.** This guided snorkeling tour, for beginners and intermediates alike, is led by a marine expert, so there's instruction plus the guide actually gets into the water with you and identifies marine life. You're guaranteed to spot tons of critters you'd never see on your own. This is a land-based operation and the only one of its kind on Kauai. (Don't think those snorkeling cruises are guided snorkeling tours—they rarely are. A member of the boat's crew serves as lifeguard, not a marine life *guide.*) A half-day tour includes all your snorkeling gear—and a wet suit to keep you warm—and stops at one or two snorkeling locations, chosen based on ocean conditions. They will come pick up customers at some of the resorts, so inquire within. The cost is $80. Check in at Kilohana Plantation in Puhi, next to Kauai Community College. ⊠ *3-2087 Kaumualii Hwy.* ☎ *808/245–6400, 800/452–1113* ⊕ *www. alohakauaitours.com.*

STAND-UP PADDLING

Unlike kiteboarding, this is a new sport that even a novice can pick up—*and* have fun doing. Technically, it's not really a new sport but a reinvigorated one from the 1950s. Beginners start with a heftier surfboard and a longer-than-normal canoe paddle. And, just as the name implies, stand-up paddlers stand on their surfboards and paddle out from the beach—no timing a wave and doing a push-up to stand. The perfect place to learn is a river (think **Hanalei** or **Wailua**) or a calm lagoon (try **Anini** or **Kalapaki**). But this sport isn't just for beginners. Tried-and-true surfers turn to it when the waves are not quite right for their preferred sport, because it gives them another reason to be on the water. Stand-up paddlers catch waves earlier and ride them longer than long-board surfers. In the past couple of years, professional stand-up paddling competitions have popped up, and surf shops and instructors have adapted to its quick rise in popularity.

EQUIPMENT

Not all surf instructors teach stand-up paddling, but more and more are, like Blue Seas Surf School and Titus Kinimaka Hawaiian School of Surfing (⇨ *see Surfing*).

Hawaiian Surfing Adventures. This Hanalei location has a wide variety of stand-up boards and paddles for rent, with a few options depending on your schedule. A 2.5-hour rental is $30, 4.5 hours goes for $40 and $50 gets you a full day's use. Check in at the storefront and then head down to the beach where your gear will be waiting. Lessons are also available on the scenic Hanalei River or in Hanalei Bay, and include one hour of instruction and two hours to practice with the board (lessons range from $55 to $75, depending on group size). The company also offers surfboard rentals and surfing lessons. ⊠ *5134 Kuhio Hwy., Hanalei* ☎ *808/482–0749* ⊕ *www.hawaiiansurfingadventures.com.*

Kauai Beach Boys. This outfitter is located right on the beach at Kalapaki, so there's no hauling your gear on your car. The rates are reasonable ($25 an hour, $60 for the day) and the convenience is essential. ⊠ *Kalapaki Beach, off Rice St., Lihue* ☎ *808/246–6333.*

SURFING

Good ol' stand-up surfing is alive and well on Kauai, especially in winter's high-surf season on the North Shore. If you're new to the sport, we highly recommend taking a lesson. Not only will this ensure you're up and riding waves in no time, but instructors will provide the right board for your experience and size, help you time a wave, and give you a push to get your momentum going. ■ TIP→ **You don't need to be in top**

Winter brings big surf to Kauai's North Shore. You can see some of the sport's biggest celebrities catching waves at Haena and Hanalei Bay.

physical shape to take a lesson. Because your instructor helps push you into the wave, you won't wear yourself out paddling. If you're experienced and want to hit the waves on your own, most surf shops rent boards for all levels, from beginners to advanced.

BEST SPOTS

Perennial-favorite beginning surf spots include **Poipu Beach** (the area fronting the Marriott Waiohai Beach Club); **Hanalei Bay** (the area next to the Hanalei Pier); and the stream end of **Kalapaki Beach.** More advanced surfers move down the beach in Hanalei to an area fronting a grove of pine trees known as **Pine Trees.** When the trade winds die, the north ends of **Wailua** and **Kealia** beaches are teeming with surfers. Breaks off **Poipu** and **Beach House/Lawai Beach** attract intermediates year-round. During high surf, the break on the cliff side of **Kalihiwai** is for experts only. Advanced riders will head to **Polihale** to face the heavy West Side waves when conditions are right.

LESSONS

Blue Seas Surf School. Surfer and instructor Charlie Smith specializes in beginners (especially children) and will go anywhere on the island to find just the right surf. His soft-top longboards are very stable, making it easier to stand up. He specializes in one-on-one or family lessons, so personal interaction is a priority. He has also added stand-up paddling to his operation. Rates start at $65 for a 1½-hour lesson. (Transportation provided, if needed.) ⊠ *Marriott's Waiohai Beach Club, 2249 Poipu Rd., Koloa* ☎ *808/634–6979* ⊕ *www.blueseassurfingschool.com.*

Margo Oberg Surfing School. Seven-time world surfing champion and hall of famer Margo Oberg runs a surf school that meets on the beach in front of the Sheraton Kauai in Poipu. Lessons are $68 for two hours, though Margo's staff teaches more than she does these days. ⊠ *2440 Hoonani Rd., Koloa* ☎ *808/332–6100* ⊕ *www.surfonkauai.com.*

Titus Kinimaka Hawaiian School of Surfing. Famed as a pioneer of big-wave surfing, this Hawaiian believes in giving back to his sport. Beginning, intermediate, and advanced lessons are available. If you want to learn to surf from a living legend, this is the man. ■ TIP→ He employs other instructors, so if you want Titus, be sure to ask for him. (And good luck, because if the waves are going off, he'll be surfing, not teaching.) Rates are $55 for a 90-minute group lesson; $65 for a 90-minute group stand-up paddle lesson. Customers are also able to use the board for a while after the lesson is complete. ⊠ *Quicksilver, 5-5088 Kuhio Hwy., Hanalei* ☎ *808/652–1116.*

EQUIPMENT

Hanalei Surf Company. You can rent boards here and shop for rash guards, wet suits, and some hip surf-inspired apparel. ⊠ *Hanalei Center, 5-5161 Kuhio Hwy., Hanalei* ☎ *808/826–9000.*

Progressive Expressions. This full-service shop has a choice of rental boards and a whole lotta shopping. ⊠ *5428 Koloa Rd., Koloa* ☎ *808/ 742–6041.*

Tamba Surf Company. This is your best bet for surf rentals on the East Side and the biggest name in local surf apparel. ⊠ *4-1543 Kuhio Hwy., across from Scotty's Beachside BBQ, Kapaa* ☎ *808/823–6942* ⊕ *www. tambasurfcompany.com.*

WHALE-WATCHING

Every winter North Pacific humpback whales swim some 3,000 miles over 30 days, give or take a few, from Alaska to Hawaii. Whales arrive as early as November and sometimes stay through April, though they seem to be most populous in February and March. They come to Hawaii to breed, calve, and nurse their young.

Of course, nothing beats seeing a whale up close. During the season, any boat on the water is looking for whales; they're hard to avoid, whether the tour is labeled "whale-watching" or not. Consider the whales a lucky-strike extra to any boating event that may interest you. If whales are definitely your thing, though, you can narrow down your tour boat decision by asking a few whale-related questions like whether there's a hydrophone on board, how long the captain has been running tours in Hawaii, and if anyone on the crew is a marine biologist or trained naturalist.

Several boat operators will add two-hour, afternoon whale-watching tours during the season that run on the South Shore (not Napali). Operators include **Blue Dolphin, Catamaran Kahanu, HoloHolo,** and **Napali Explorer** (⇨ *see Boat Tours*). Trying one of these excursions is a good option for those who have no interest in snorkeling or sightseeing along Napali Coast, although keep in mind, the longer you're on the water, the more likely you'll be to see the humpbacks.

Humpback whales arrive at Kauai in December and stick around until early April. Head out on a boat tour for a chance to see these majestic creatures breach.

One of the more unique ways to, *possibly,* see some whales is atop a kayak. For such an encounter, try **Outfitters Kauai**'s South Shore kayak trip (⇨ *see Kayaking Tours).* There are a few lookout spots around the island with good land-based viewing: Kilauea Lighthouse on the North Shore, the Kapaa Scenic Overlook just north of Kapaa town on the East Side, and the cliffs to the east of Keoniloa (Shipwreck) Beach on the South Shore.

GOLF, HIKING, AND OUTDOOR ACTIVITIES

Updated by
David Simon

For those of you who love ocean sports but need a little break from all that sun, sand, and salt, there are plenty of options on Kauai to keep you busy on the ground. You can hike the island's many trails, or consider taking your vacation into flight with a treetop zipline. You can have a backcountry adventure in a four-wheel drive, or relax in an inner tube floating down the cane-field irrigation canals.

AERIAL TOURS

If you only drive around Kauai in your rental car, you will not see *all* of Kauai. There is truly only one way to see it all, and that's by air. Helicopter tours are the favorite way to get a bird's-eye view of Kauai—they fly at lower altitudes, hover above waterfalls, and wiggle their way into areas that a fixed-wing aircraft cannot.

★ **Blue Hawaiian Helicopters.** This multi-island operator flies the latest in helicopter technology, the Eco-Star, costing $1.8 million. It has 23%

more interior space for its six passengers, has unparalleled viewing, and offers a few extra safety features. As the name implies, the helicopter is also a bit more environmentally friendly, with a 50% noise-reduction rate. Flights run a tad shorter than others (50 to 55 minutes instead of the 55 to 65 minutes that other companies tout), but the flight feels very complete. The rate is $240 and includes taxes and fuel surcharge. A DVD of your actual tour is available for an additional $25. ⊠ *Harbor Mall, 3501 Rice St., Nawiliwili* ☎ *808/245–5800, 800/745–2583.*

Inter-Island Helicopters. This company flies four-seater Hughes 500 helicopters *with the doors off.* It can get chilly at higher elevations, so bring a sweater and wear long pants. Tours depart from Hanapepe's Port Allen Airport, so if you're staying on the West Side, this is a good bet. Prices range from $260 to $310 per person. ⊠ *Port Allen Airport, 3441 Kuiloko Rd., Hanapepe* ☎ *808/335–5009, 800/656–5009* ⊕ *www.interislandhelicopters.com.*

Fodor'sChoice
★

Jack Harter Helicopters. Jack Harter was the first company to offer helicopter tours on Kauai. The company flies the six-passenger ASTAR helicopter with floor-to-ceiling windows, and the four-person Hughes 500, which is flown with no doors. The doorless ride can get windy, but it's the best bet for taking reflection-free photos. Pilots provide information on the Garden Island's history and geography through two-way intercoms. The company flies out of Lihue and has a second office at the Kauai Marriott. Tours are 60 to 65 minutes and 90 to 95 minutes and cost $259 to $384, including taxes and fuel surcharge. ⊠ *4231 Ahukini Rd.* ☎ *808/245–3774, 888/245–2001* ⊕ *www.helicopters-kauai.com.*

Safari Helicopters. This company flies the "Super" ASTAR helicopter, which offers floor-to-ceiling windows on its doors, four roof windows, and Bose X-Generation headphones. Two-way microphones allow passengers to converse with the pilot. A major perk Safari can offer is its 90-minute "eco-tour," which adds a landing in Olokele Canyon. Passengers will then be met by Keith Robinson of *the* Robinson family, who will provide a brief tour of the Kauai Wildlife Refuge, with endangered, endemic plants. The once daily tour goes out Monday through Friday at 3:30 p.m. Flight prices range from $224 to $304, including taxes and fuel surcharge; a DVD is $40 extra. ⊠ *3225 Akahi St., Lihue* ☎ *808/246–0136, 800/326–3356* ⊕ *www.safarihelicopters.com.*

Sunshine Helicopter Tours. If the name of this company sounds familiar, it may be because its pilots fly on all the main Hawaiian Islands. On Kauai, Sunshine Helicopters departs out of two different locations:

Lihue and Princeville. They fly the six-passenger FX STAR and super roomy six-passenger WhisperSTAR birds. Prices for the 45–55 minute Lihue flights range from $244 to $294, including tax and fuel surcharges. The 40–50 minute Princeville flights will run from $289 to $364. ■TIP→ Discounts can be substantial by booking online and taking advantage of the "early-bird" seating during off hours. ✉ *3416 Rice St., Lihue* ☎ *808/240–2577, 888/245–4354* ⊕ *www.sunshinehelicopters. com* ✉ *Princeville Airport, Princeville.*

ATV TOURS

Although all the beaches on the island are public, much of the interior land—once sugar and pineapple plantations—is privately owned. This is really a shame, because the valleys and mountains that make up the vast interior of the island easily rival the beaches in sheer beauty. The good news is some tour operators have agreements with landowners that make exploration possible, albeit a bit bumpy, and unless you have back troubles, that's half the fun. ■TIP→ If it looks like rain, book an ATV tour ASAP. That's the thing about these tours: the muddier, the better.

★ **Kauai ATV Tours.** This is *the* thing to do when it rains on Kauai. Consider it an extreme mud bath. Kauai ATV in Koloa is the originator of the island's all-terrain-vehicle tours. Its $125 three-hour Koloa tour takes you through a private sugar plantation and historic cane-haul tunnel. The $155 four-hour waterfall tour visits secluded waterfalls and includes a picnic lunch. This popular option includes a hike through a bamboo forest and a swim in a freshwater pool at the base of the falls—to rinse off all that mud. You must be 16 or older to operate your own ATV, but Kauai ATV also offers its four-passenger "Ohana Bug" and two-passenger "Mud Bugs" to accommodate families with kids ages five and older. There are price breaks ($105 for the three-hour tour, $135 for the four-hour) for passengers. ✉ *3477A Weliweli Rd., Koloa* ☎ *808/742–2734, 877/707–7088* ⊕ *www.kauaiatv.com.*

Kipu Ranch Adventures. This 3,000-acre property extends from the Huleia River to the top of Mt. Haupu. *Jurassic Park, Indiana Jones,* and *Mighty Joe Young* were filmed here, and you'll see the locations for all of them on the $125 three-hour Ranch Tour. The $150 four-hour Waterfall Tour includes a visit to two waterfalls and a picnic lunch. Kipu Ranch was once a sugar plantation, but today it is a working cattle ranch, so you'll be in the company of bovines as well as pheasants, wild boars, and peacocks. ✉ *235 Kipu Rd., off Hwy. 50, Lihue* ☎ *808/246–9288* ⊕ *www.kiputours.com.*

BIKING

Kauai is a labyrinth of cane-haul roads, which are fun for exploring on two wheels. The challenge is finding roads where biking is allowed and then not getting lost in the maze. Maybe that explains why Kauai is not a hub for the sport . . . yet. Still, there are some epic rides for those who are interested—both the adrenaline-rush and the mellower beach-cruiser kind. If you want to grind out some mileage, the main highway that skirts the coastal areas is generally safe, though there are only a few designated bike lanes. It's hilly, but you'll find that keeping your eyes on the road and not the scenery is the biggest challenge. "Cruisers" should head to Kapaa. A new section of Ke Ala Hele Makalae, a pedestrian trail that runs along the East Side of Kauai, was completed in the summer of 2009, totaling 6½ miles of completed path. You can rent bikes (with helmets) from the activities desks of certain hotels, but these are not the best quality. You're better off renting from Kauai Cycle in Kapaa, Outfitters Kauai in Poipu, or Pedal 'n' Paddle in Hanalei.

★ **Ke Ala Hele Makalae** (*Nawiliwili to Anahola Bike/Pedestrian Path*). For the cruiser, this path follows the coastline on Kauai's East Side. Eventually, it will run some 20 miles and offer scenic views, picnic pavilions, and restroom facilities along the way—all in compliance with the Americans with Disabilities Act. For now, there are 2.5 miles of path in Lydgate Beach Park to secluded Kuna Bay (aka Donkey Beach). The easiest way to access the completed sections of the path is from Kealia Beach. Park here and head north into rural lands with spectacular coastline vistas or head south into Kapaa for a more interactive experience. ⊠ *Trailhead: 1 mile north of Kapaa; park at north end of Kealia Beach.*

Wailua Forest Management Road. For the novice mountain biker, this is an easy ride, and it's also easy to find. From Route 56 in Wailua, turn mauka on Kuamoo Road and continue 6 miles to the picnic area, known as Keahua Arboretum; park here. The potholed four-wheel-drive road includes some stream crossings—⚠ stay away during heavy rains, because the streams flood—and continues for 2 miles to a T-stop, where you should turn right. Stay on the road for about 3 miles until you reach a gate; this is the spot where the gates in the movie *Jurassic Park* were filmed, though it looks nothing like the movie. Go around the gate and down the road for another mile to a confluence of streams at the base of Mt. Waialeale. Be sure to bring your camera. ⊠ *Kuamoo Rd., Kapaa.*

Waimea Canyon Road. For those wanting a very challenging road workout, climb this road, also known as Route 550. After a 3,000-foot climb, the road tops out at mile 12 adjacent to Waimea Canyon, which will pop in and out of view on your right as you ascend. From here it continues several miles (mostly level) past the Kokee Museum and ends at the Kalalau Lookout. It's paved the entire way, uphill 100%, and curvy. ⚠ There's not much of a shoulder on either road—sometimes none—so be extra cautious. The road gets busier as the day wears on, so you may want to consider a sunrise ride. A slightly more moderate uphill climb is Kokee Road, Route 552, from Kekaha, which intersects with Route 550. By the way, bikes aren't allowed on the hiking trails in and around Waimea Canyon and Kokee State Park, but there are miles of wonderful 4WD roads perfect for mountain biking. Check at Kokee Lodge for a map and conditions. ⊠ *Off Rte. 50, near grocery store, Waimea.*

One of the most visited sites on Kauai is Waimea Canyon. Make sure to stop at Puu ka Pele and Puu hinahina lookouts.

EQUIPMENT AND TOURS

★ **Kauai Cycle.** This reliable, full-service bike shop rents, sells, and repairs bikes. Cruisers, mountain bikes (front- and full-suspension), and road bikes are available for $20 to $45 per day and $110 to $250 per week with directions to trails. The Ke Ala Hele Makalae is right out their back door. ⊠ *934 Kuhio Hwy., across from Taco Bell, Kapaa* ☎ *808/821–2115* ⊕ *www.kauaicycle.com.*

Outfitters Kauai. Hybrid "comfort" and mountain bikes (both full-suspension and hardtails), as well as road bikes, are available at this shop in Poipu. You can ride right out the door to tour Poipu, or get information on how to do a self-guided tour of Kokee State Park and Waimea Canyon. The company also leads sunrise and evening coasting tours (under the name **Bicycle Downhill**) from Waimea Canyon past the island's West Side beaches. Rentals cost $25 to $45 per day. Tours cost $102 plus tax. Stand-up paddle tours are also available. ⊠ *2827-A Poipu Rd., near turnoff to Spouting Horn, Poipu* ☎ *808/742–9667, 888/742–9887* ⊕ *www.outfitterskauai.com.*

★ **Pedal 'n' Paddle.** This company rents old-fashioned, single-speed beach cruisers and hybrid road bikes for $15 to $20 per day; $60 to $80 per week, with a discount for more than one week's use. In the heart of Hanalei, this is a great way to cruise the town; the more ambitious cyclist can head to the end of the road. Be careful, though, because there are no bike lanes on the twisting and turning road to Kee. ⊠ *Ching Young Village, 5-5190 Kuhio Hwy., Hanalei* ☎ *808/826–9069* ⊕ *www.pedalnpaddle.com.*

GOLF

For golfers, the Garden Isle might as well be known as the Robert Trent Jones Jr. Isle. Four of the island's nine courses, including Poipu Bay—onetime home of the PGA Grand Slam of Golf—are the work of Jones, who maintains a home at Princeville. Combine these four courses with those from Jack Nicklaus, Robin Nelson, and local legend Toyo Shirai, and you'll see that golf sets Kauai apart from the other Islands as much as the Pacific Ocean does. ■ TIP→ Afternoon tee times can save you big bucks.

Kauai Lagoons Golf Club. With the development of the Kauai Lagoons Resort, the golf club is getting a face-lift, albeit a slow one due to the economy. Yes, Jack is back. When Nicklaus is done with this course, 27 championship-style holes (the links-style course is gone) will await golfers. For now, 18 holes are playable including a half mile of ocean-hugging holes redesigned to take advantage of the obvious visual splendor of Kalapaki Bay. Number 18 is the island green named "The Bear" for its challenging play into the trade winds. ⊠ *3351 Hoolaulea Way* ☎ *808/241–6000, 800/634–6400* ⊕ *www.kauailagoonsgolf.com* ⅃ *18 holes. 6977 yds. Par 72. Greens fees: $155–195* ☞ *Facilities: Driving range, putting green, golf carts, rental clubs, lessons.*

Kiahuna Plantation Golf Course. A meandering creek, lava outcrops, and thickets of trees give Kiahuna its character. Robert Trent Jones Jr. was given a smallish piece of land just inland at Poipu, and defends par with smaller targets, awkward stances, and optical illusions. In 2003 a group of homeowners bought the club and brought Jones back to renovate the course (it was originally built in 1983), adding tees and revamping bunkers. The pro here boasts his course has the best putting greens on the island. This is the only course on Kauai with a complete set of Junior's tee boxes. ⊠ *2545 Kiahuna Plantation Dr., Koloa* ☎ *808/742–9595* ⊕ *www.kiahunagolf.com* ⅃ *18 holes. 6214 yds. Par 70. Greens fee: $103* ☞ *Facilities: Driving range, putting green, rental clubs, lessons, pro shop, restaurant, bar.*

Kukuiolono Golf Course. Local legend Toyo Shirai designed this fun, funky 9-holer where holes play across rolling, forested hills that afford views of the distant Pacific. Though Shirai has an eye for a good golf hole, Kukuiolono is out of the way and a bit rough, and so probably not for everyone. But at $9 for the day, it's a deal—bring cash, though, as they don't accept credit cards. No tee times. ⊠ *854 Puu Rd., Kalaheo* ☎ *808/332–9151* ⅃ *9 holes. 3173 yds. Par 36. Greens fee: $9* ☞ *Facilities: Driving range, putting green, golf carts, pull carts, rental clubs.*

Poipu Bay Golf Course. Poipu Bay has been called the Pebble Beach of Hawaii, and the comparison is apt. Like Pebble Beach, Poipu is a links course built on headlands, not true links land. And as at Monterey Bay, there's wildlife galore—except that the animals are not quite as intrusive to play. It's not unusual for golfers to see monk seals sunning on the beach below, sea turtles bobbing outside the shore break, and humpback whales leaping offshore. From 1994 to 2006, the course (designed by Robert Trent Jones Jr.) hosted the annual PGA Grand

Slam of Golf. That means Tiger was a frequent visitor—and winner—here. Call ahead to take advantage of varying prices for tee times. ✉ *2250 Ainako St., Koloa* ☎ *808/742–8711* ⊕ *www.poipubaygolf. com* ⚑ *18 holes. 6612 yds. Par 72. Greens fee: $240* ✆ *Facilities: Driving range, putting green, rental clubs, golf carts, golf academy/ lessons, restaurant, bar.*

Fodor'sChoice
★
Princeville Resort. Robert Trent Jones Jr. built two memorable courses overlooking Hanalei Bay, the 27-hole Princeville Makai Course (1971) and the 18-hole Prince Course (1990). The combination earned Princeville Resort the 20th spot in *Golf Digest's* list of the "Best 75 Golf Resorts in North America." The Makai Course underwent extensive renovations in 2009, including new turf throughout, reshaped greens and bunkers, refurbished cart paths and comfort stations, and the creation of an extensive practice facility. They also offer free rounds for junior golfers (15 and under) when accompanied by one paying adult. Rated Hawaii's second toughest course (behind Oahu's Koolau), this is jungle golf, with holes running through dense forest and over tangled ravines, out onto headlands for breathtaking ocean views, then back into the jungle.

Makai Golf Course ✉ *4080 Lei O Papa Rd., Princeville* ☎ *808/826– 3580* ⊕ *www.makaigolf.com* ⚑ *27 holes. 6886 yds. Par 72. Greens fee: $220* ✆ *Facilities: Driving range, putting green, rental clubs, golf carts, pro shop, golf academy/lessons, snack bar.*

Prince Golf Course ✉ *5-3900 Kuhio Hwy., Princeville* ☎ *808/826– 5001* ⊕ *www.princeville.com* ⚑ *18 holes. 6960 yds. Par 72. Greens fee: $170* ✆ *Facilities: Driving range, putting green, rental clubs, golf carts, pro shop, golf academy/lessons, restaurant, bar.*

Wailua Municipal Golf Course. Voted by *Golf Digest* as one of Hawaii's 15 best golf courses, this seaside course was first built as a 9-hole golf course in the 1930s. The second 9 holes were added in 1961. Course designer Toyo Shirai created a course that is fun but not punishing. Not only is this an affordable game with minimal water hazards, but it is challenging enough to have been chosen to host three USGA Amateur Public Links Championships. The trade winds blow steadily on the East Side of the island and make the game all the more challenging. An ocean view and affordability make this one of the most popular courses on the island. Tee times are accepted up to seven days in advance. ✉ *3-5350 Kuhio Hwy., Lihue* ☎ *808/241–6666* ⚑ *18 holes. 6585 yds. Par 72. Greens fees: $48 weekdays, $60 weekends. Half price after 2 pm. Cart rental: $18. Cash or traveler's checks only* ✆ *Facilities: Driving range, rental clubs, golf carts, pro shop, lessons, snack bar.*

HIKING

The best way to experience the *aina*—the land—on Kauai is to step off the beach and hike into the remote interior. You'll find waterfalls so tall you'll strain your neck looking, pools of crystal clear water for swimming, tropical forests teeming with plant life, and ocean vistas that will make you wish you could stay forever.

■ TIP→ For your safety wear sturdy shoes—preferably water-resistant ones. All hiking trails on Kauai are free, so far. There's a development plan in the works that will turn the Waimea Canyon and Kokee state parks into admission-charging destinations. Whatever it may be, it will be worth it.

★ **Hanalei-OkolehaoTrail.** *Okolehao* basically translates to "moonshine" in Hawaiian. This trail follows the Hihimanu Ridge, which was established in the days of Prohibition, when this backyard liquor was distilled from the roots of ti plants. The 2-mile hike climbs 1,200 feet and offers a 360-degree view of Hanalei Bay and Waioli Valley. Thanks to Kauai Sierra Club volunteers, this trail survived Hurricane Iniki. It took eight years of hauling chain saws and weed whackers up the ridge to clear the trail. Your ascent begins at the China Ditch off the Hanalei River. Follow the trail through a lightly forested grove, at the Y take the first right, and then take the next left up a steep embankment. From here the trail is well marked. Most of the climb is lined with hala, ti, wild orchid, and eucalyptus. You'll get your first of many ocean views at mile marker 1. ⊠ *Follow Ohiki Rd. (north of the Hanalei Bridge) 7 miles to the U.S. Fish and Wildlife Service parking area. Directly across the street is a small bridge that marks the trailhead, Hanalei.*

Fodor'sChoice
★ **Kalalau Trail.** Of all the hikes on the island, Kalalau Trail is by far the most famous and in many regards the most strenuous. A moderate hiker can handle the 2-mile trek to Hanakapiai Beach, and for the seasoned outdoorsman, the additional 2 miles up to the falls is manageable. But be prepared to rock-hop along a creek and ford waters that can get waist high during the rain. Round-trip to Hanakapiai Falls is 8 miles. This steep and often muddy trail is best approached with a walking stick. If there has been any steady rain, waiting for drier days would provide a more enjoyable trek. The narrow trail will deliver one startling ocean view after another along a path that is alternately shady and sunny. Wear hiking shoes or sandals, and bring drinking water since the creeks on the trail are not potable. Plenty of food is always encouraged on a strenuous hike such as this one. If your plan is to venture the full 11 miles into Kalalau, you need to acquire a camping permit. ⊠ *Drive north past Hanalei to end of road. Trailhead is directly across from Kee Beach.*

Mahaulepu Heritage Trail. This trail offers the novice hiker an accessible way to appreciate the rugged southern coast of Kauai. A cross-country course wends its way along the water, high above the ocean, through a lava field and past a sacred *heiau* (stone structure). Walk all the way to Mahaulepu, 2 miles north for a two-hour round-trip. ⊠ *Drive north on Poipu Rd., turn right at Poipu Bay Golf Course sign. The street name is Ainako, but the sign is hard to see. Drive down to beach and park in lot* ⊕ *www.hikemahaulepu.org.*

Sleeping Giant Trail. An easy and easily accessible trail practically in the heart of Kapaa, the Sleeping Giant Trail—or simply Sleeping Giant—gains 1,000 feet over 2 miles. We prefer an early-morning—say, sunrise—hike, with sparkling blue-water vistas, up the east-side trailhead. At the top you can see a grassy grove with a picnic table. Experienced hikers may want to go a step farther, all the way to the giant's nose and chin. From here there are 360-degree views of the island. It is a local favorite with many east-siders meeting here to exercise. ⊠ *Haleilio Rd., off Rte. 56, Wailua.*

Waimea Canyon and Kokee State Parks. This park contains a 50-mile network of hiking trails of varying difficulty that take you through acres of native forests, across the highest-elevation swamp in the world, to the river at the base of the canyon, and onto pinnacles of land sticking their necks out over Napali Coast. All hikers should register at Kokee Natural History Museum, where you can find trail maps, current trail information, and specific directions.

All mileage mentioned below is one-way.

The **Kukui Trail** descends 2½ miles and 2,200 feet into Waimea Canyon to the edge of the Waimea River—it's a steep climb. The **Awaawapuhi Trail,** with 1,600 feet of elevation gains and losses over 3¼ miles, feels more gentle than the Kukui Trail, but it offers its own huffing-and-puffing sections in its descent along a spiny ridge to a perch overlooking the ocean.

The 3½-mile **Alakai Swamp Trail** is accessed via the **Pihea Trail** or a four-wheel-drive road. There's one strenuous valley section, but otherwise it's a pretty level trail—once you access it. This trail is a bird-watcher's delight and includes a painterly view of Wainiha and Hanalei valleys at the trail's end. The trail traverses the purported highest-elevation swamp in the world on a boardwalk so as not to disturb the fragile plant- and wildlife. It is typically the coolest of the hikes due to the tree canopies, elevation and cloud coverage.

The **Canyon Trail** offers much in its short trek: spectacular vistas of the canyon and the only dependable waterfall in Waimea Canyon. The easy 2-mile hike can be cut in half if you have a four-wheel-drive vehicle. If you were outfitted with a headlamp, this would be a great hike at sunset as the sun's light sets the canyon walls ablaze in color. ⊠ *Kokee Natural History Museum, 3600 Kokee Rd., Kekaha* ☎ *808/335–9975 for trail conditions.*

EQUIPMENT AND TOURS

Fodor's Choice

★ **Kauai Nature Tours.** Father and son scientists started this hiking tour business. As such, their emphasis is on education and the environment. If you're interested in flora, fauna, volcanology, geology, oceanography, and the like, this is the company for you. They offer daylong hikes along coastal areas, beaches, and in the mountains. ■ TIP→ **If you have a desire to see a specific location, just ask. They will do custom hikes to spots they don't normally hit if there is interest.** Hikes range from easy to strenuous and rates range from $125 to $150. Transportation is often provided from hotel. ☎ *808/742–8305, 888/233–8365* ⊕ *www. kauainaturetours.com.*

Continued on page 530

NAPALI COAST: EMERALD QUEEN OF KAUAI

If you're coming to Kauai, Napali ("cliffs" in Hawaiian) is a major must-see. More than 5 million years old, these sea cliffs rise thousands of feet above the Pacific, and every shade of green is represented in the vegetation that blankets their lush peaks and folds. At their base, there are caves, secluded beaches, and waterfalls to explore.

The big question is how to explore this gorgeous stretch of coastline. You can't drive to it, through it, or around it. You can't see Napali from a scenic lookout. You can't even take a mule ride to it. The only way to experience its magic is from the sky, the ocean, or the trail.

FROM THE SKY

If you've booked a helicopter tour of Napali, you might start wondering what you've gotten yourself into on the way to the airport. Will it feel like being on a small airplane? Will there be turbulence? Will it be worth all the money you just plunked down?

Your concerns will be assuaged on the helipad, once you see the faces of those who have just returned from their journey: Everyone looks totally blissed out. And now it's your turn.

Climb on board, strap on your headphones, and the next thing you know the helicopter gently lifts up, hovers for a moment, and floats away like a spider on the wind—no roaring engines, no rumbling down a runway. If you've chosen a flight with music, you'll feel as if you're inside your very own IMAX movie.

Pinch yourself if you must, because this is the real thing. Your pilot shares history, legend, and lore. If you miss something, speak up: pilots love to show off their island knowledge. You may snap a few pictures (not too many or you'll miss the eyes-on experience!), nudge a friend or spouse, and point at a whale breeching in the ocean, but mostly you stare, mouth agape. There is simply no other way to take in the immensity and greatness of Napali but from the air.

Helicopter flight over Napali Coast

GOOD TO KNOW

Helicopter companies depart from the north, east, and west side of the island. Most are based in Lihue, near the airport.

If you want more adventure—and air—choose one of the helicopter companies that flies with the doors off.

Some companies offer flights without music. Know the experience you want ahead of time. Some even sell a DVD of your flight, so you don't have to worry about taking pictures.

Wintertime rain grounds some flights; plan your trip early in your stay in case the flight gets rescheduled.

IS THIS FOR ME?

Taking a helicopter trip is the most expensive way to see Napali—as much as $280 for an hour-long tour.

Claustrophobic? Choose a boat tour or hike. It's a tight squeeze in the helicopter, especially in one of the middle seats.

Short on time? Taking a helicopter tour is a great way to see the island.

WHAT YOU MIGHT SEE

■ Nualolo Kai (an ancient Hawaiian fishing village) with its fringed reef

■ The 300-foot Hanakapiai Falls

■ A massive sea arch formed in the rock by erosion

■ The 11-mile Kalalau Trail threading its way along the coast

■ The amazing striations of aa and pahoehoe lava flows that helped push Kauai above the sea

FROM THE OCEAN

Napali from the ocean is two treats in one: spend a good part of the day on (or in) the water, and gaze up at majestic green sea cliffs rising thousands of feet above your head.

There are three ways to see it: a mellow pleasure-cruise catamaran allows you to kick back and sip a mai tai; an adventurous raft (Zodiac) tour will take you inside sea caves under waterfalls, and give you the option of snorkeling; and a daylong outing in a kayak is a real workout, but then you can say you paddled 16 miles of coastline.

Any way you travel, you'll breathe ocean air, feel spray on your face, and see pods of spinner dolphins, green sea turtles, flying fish, and, if you're lucky, a rare Hawaiian monk seal.

Napali stretches from Kee Beach in the north to Polihale beach on the West Side. If your departure point is Kee, you are already headed toward the lush Hanakapiai Valley. Within a few minutes, you'll see caves and waterfalls galore. About halfway down the coast just after the Kalalau Trail ends, you'll come to an immense arch—formed where the sea eroded the less dense basaltic rock—and a thundering 50-foot waterfall. And as the island curves near Nualolo State Park, you'll begin to notice less vegetation and more rocky outcroppings.

(left and top right) Kayaking on Napali Coast
(bottom right) Dolphin on Napali Coast

GOOD TO KNOW

If you want to snorkel, choose a morning rather than an afternoon tour—preferably during a summer visit—when seas are calmer.

If you're on a budget, choose a non-snorkeling tour.

If you want to see whales, take any tour, but be sure to plan your vacation for December through March.

If you're staying on the North Shore or East Side, embark from the North Shore. If you're staying on the South Shore, it might not be worth your time to drive to the north, so head to the West Side.

IS THIS FOR ME?

Boat tours are several hours long, so if you have only a short time on Kauai, a helicopter tour is a better alternative.

Even on a small boat, you won't get the individual attention and exclusivity of a helicopter tour.

Prone to seasickness? A large boat can be surprisingly rocky, so be prepared.

WHAT YOU MIGHT SEE

■ Hawaii's state fish—the humuhumunukunukuapuaa—otherwise known as the reef triggerfish

■ Waiahuakua Sea Cave, with a waterfall coming through its roof

■ Tons of marine life, including dolphins, green sea turtles, flying fish, and humpback whales, especially in February and March

■ Waterfalls—especially if your trip is after a heavy rain

FROM THE TRAIL

If you want to be one with Napali—feeling the soft red earth beneath your feet, picnicking on the beaches, and touching the lush vegetation—hiking the Kalalau Trail is the way to do it.

Most people hike only the first 2 miles of the 11-mile trail and turn around at Hanakapiai. This 4-mile round-trip hike takes three to four hours. It starts at sea level and doesn't waste any time gaining elevation. (Take heart—the uphill lasts only a mile and tops out at 400 feet; then it's downhill all the way.) At the half-mile point, the trail curves west and the folds of Napali Coast unfurl.

Along the way you might share the trail with feral goats and wild pigs. Some of the vegetation is native; much is introduced.

After the 1-mile mark the trail begins its drop into Hanakapiai. You'll pass a couple of streams of water trickling across the trail, and maybe some banana, ginger, the native uluhe fern, and the Hawaiian ti plant. Finally the trail swings around the eastern ridge of Hanakapiai for your first glimpse of the valley and then switchbacks down the mountain. You'll have to boulder-hop across the stream to reach the beach. If you like, you can take a 4-mile, round-trip fairly strenuous side trip from this point to the gorgeous Hanakapiai Falls.

(left) Awaawapuhi mountain biker on razor-edge ridge
(top right) Feral goats in Kalalau Valley
(bottom right) Napali Coast

GOOD TO KNOW

Wear comfortable, amphibious shoes. Unless your feet require extra support, wear a self-bailing sort of shoe (for stream crossings) that doesn't mind mud. Don't wear heavy, waterproof hiking boots.

During winter the trail is often muddy, so be extra careful; sometimes it's completely inaccessible.

Don't hike after heavy rain—flash floods are common.

If you plan to hike the entire 11-mile trail (most people do the shorter hike described at left) you'll need a permit to go past Hanakapiai.

IS THIS FOR ME?

Of all the ways to see Napali (with the exception of kayaking the coast), this is the most active. You need to be in decent shape to hit the trail.

If you're vacationing in winter, this hike might not be an option due to flooding—whereas you can take a helicopter or boat trip year-round.

WHAT YOU MIGHT SEE

■ Big dramatic surf right below your feet

■ Amazing vistas of the cool blue Pacific

■ The spectacular Hanakapiai Falls; if you have a permit don't miss Hanakoa Falls, less than 1/2 mile off the trail

■ Wildlife, including goats and pigs

■ Zany-looking ohia trees, with aerial roots and long, skinny serrated leaves known as hala. Early Hawaiians used them to make mats, baskets, and canoe sails.

HORSEBACK RIDING

Most of the horseback-riding tours on Kauai are primarily walking tours with little trotting and no cantering or galloping, so no experience is required. Zip. Zilch. Nada. If you're interested, most of the stables offer private lessons. The most popular tours are the ones including a picnic lunch by the water. Your only dilemma may be deciding what kind of water you want—waterfalls or ocean. You may want to make your decision based on where you're staying. The "waterfall picnic" tours are on the wetter North Shore, and the "beach picnic" tours take place on the South Side.

CJM Country Stables. Just past the Hyatt in Poipu, CJM Stables offers a three-hour picnic ride with noshing on the beach, as well as their more popular two-hour trail ride. The landscape here is rugged and beautiful, featuring sand dunes and limestone bluffs. They can get you as close as anyone to the secluded Mahaulepu Bay. CJM sponsors seasonal rodeo events that are free and open to the public. Prices range from $103 to $135. ✉ *Poipu Rd. 1½ miles from Grand Hyatt Kauai, Koloa* ☎ *808/742–6096* ⊕ *www.cjmstables.com.*

Esprit de Corps. If you ride, this is the company for you. Esprit de Corps has three- to eight-hour rides for experienced riders who know how to trot and canter. They also have a two-hour beginner ride that requires no experience. What's also nice is the maximum group size: six. Weddings on horseback can be arranged (in fact, Dale, the owner, is a wedding officiant, specializing in Jewish and interfaith marriages), and custom rides for less experienced and younger riders (as young as two) are available, as well as private lessons (starting at age six). Make sure to call ahead because they are by appointment only. Rates range from $130 to $390. ✉ *1491 Kualapa Pl., Kapaa* ☎ *808/822–4688* ⊕ *www.kauaihorses.com.*

Fodor'sChoice
★ **Princeville Ranch Stables.** A longtime *kamaaina* (resident) family operates Princeville Ranch. They originated the waterfall picnic tours, which run three or four hours and include a short but steep hike down to Kalihiwai Falls, a dramatic three-tier waterfall, for swimming and picnicking. Princeville also has shorter, straight riding tours and private rides, and if they're moving cattle while you're visiting, you can sign up for a cattle drive. Prices range from $135 up to $245 for some private tours. ✉ *Kuhio Hwy., between mile markers 27 and 28, Princeville* ☎ *808/826-7669* ⊕ *www.princevilleranch.com.*

MOUNTAIN TUBING

♻ **Kauai Backcountry Adventures.** Popular with all ages, this laid-back adventure can book up two weeks in advance in busy summer months. Here's how it works: you recline in an inner tube and float down fern-lined irrigation ditches that were built more than a century ago—the engineering is impressive—to divert water from Mt. Waialeale to sugar and pineapple fields around the island. They'll even give you a headlamp so you can see as you float through five covered tunnels. The scenery from the island's interior at the base of

LEPTOSPIROSIS

The sparkling waters of those babbling brooks trickling around the island can be life threatening, and we're not talking about the dangers of drowning, although they, too, exist. Leptospirosis is a bacterial disease that is transmitted from animals to humans. It can survive for long periods of time in freshwater and mud contaminated by the urine of infected animals, such as mice, rats, and goats. The bacteria enter the body through the eyes, ears, nose, mouth, and broken skin. To avoid infection, do not drink untreated water from the island's streams; do not wade in waters above the chest or submerge skin with cuts and abrasions in island streams or rivers. Symptoms are often mild and resemble the flu—fever, diarrhea, chills, nausea, headache, vomiting, and body pains—and may occur two to 20 days after exposure. If you think you have these symptoms, see a doctor right away.

Mt. Waialeale on Lihue Plantation land is superb. Ages five and up are welcome. The tour takes about three hours and includes a picnic lunch and a swim in a swimming hole. ■ TIP→ You'll definitely want to pack water-friendly shoes (or rent some from the outfitter), sunscreen, a hat, bug repellent, and a beach towel. Tours cost $102 per person and are offered morning and afternoon, daily. ⊠ 3-4131 Kuhio Hwy., across from gas station, Hanamaulu ☎ 808/245–2506, 888/270–0555 ⊕ www. kauaibackcountry.com.

SKYDIVING

Skydive Kauai. Ten thousand feet over Kauai and falling at a rate of 120 mph is probably as thrilling as it gets while airborne. First, there's the 25-minute plane ride to altitude in a Cessna 182, then the exhilaration of the first step into sky, the sensation of sailing weightless in the air over Kauai, and finally the peaceful buoyancy beneath the canopy of your parachute. A tandem free-fall rates among the most unforgettable experiences of a lifetime. Wed that to the aerial view over Kauai and you've got a winning marriage that you can relive with an HD video memory. Tandem dive: $229. ⊠ Port Allen Airport, 3666 Kuiloko Rd., Hanapepe ☎ 808/335–5859 ⊕ skydivekauai.com.

TENNIS

If you're interested in booking some court time on Kauai, there are public tennis courts in Waimea, Kekaha, Hanapepe, Koloa, Kalaheo, Puhi, Lihue, Wailua Homesteads, Wailua Houselots, and Kapaa New Park.

Many hotels and resorts have tennis courts on property; even if you're not staying there, you can still rent court time. Rates range from $10 to $15 per person per hour. On the South Shore, try the **Grand Hyatt Kauai** (☎ 808/742–1234) and **Kiahuna Swim and Tennis Club** (☎ 808/742–9533). On the North Shore try the **Hanalei Bay Resort** (☎ 808/826–6522 Ext. 8225).

For specific directions or more information, call the **County of Kauai Parks and Recreation Office** (☎ *808/241–4463*). Many hotels and resorts have tennis courts on property; even if you're not staying there, you can still rent court time. Rates range from $10 to $15 per person per hour. On the South Side, try the **Grand Hyatt Kauai** (☎ *808/742–1234*) and **Kiahuna Swim and Tennis Club** (☎ *808/742–9533*). On the North Shore, try the **Princeville Racquet Club** (☎ *808/826–1230*).

ZIPLINE TOURS

The latest adventure on Kauai is "zipping," or "ziplining." Regardless of what you call it, chances are you'll scream like a rock star while trying it. Strap on a harness, clip onto a cable running from one side of a river or valley to the other, and zip across. The step off is the scariest part. ■ TIP→ Pack knee-length shorts or pants, athletic shoes, and courage for this adventure.

Fodor's Choice ★ **Just Live.** When Nichol Baier and Julie Lester started Just Live in 2003, their market was exclusively school-age children, but soon they added visitor tours. Experiential education through adventure is how they describe it. Whatever you call it, sailing 70 feet above the ground for 3½ hours will take your vacation to another level. This is the only treetop zipline in the state where your feet never touch ground once you're in the air: Seven zips and four canopy bridges make the Tree Top Tour ($120) their most popular one. For the heroic at heart, there's the Zipline Eco Adventure ($125), which includes three ziplines, two canopy bridges, a climbing wall, a 100-foot rappelling tower, and a "Monster Swing." If you're short on time—or courage—you can opt for the Wikiwiki Zipline Tour ($79), which includes three ziplines and two canopy bridges in under two hours. They still incorporate team building in the visitor tours, although their primary focus remains community programming. Enjoy knowing that money spent here serves Kauai's children. ⊠ *Hwy. 50, Luhue* ☎ *808/482–1295.*

★ **Outfitters Kauai.** This company added new zipline offerings in the summer of 2009. They still have a half-day, multisport adventure of ziplining, suspension bridge crossings, and aerial walkways with hiking in between. Their most popular tour (Zipline Trek Nui Loa) features a 1,800-foot tandem zip—that's right, you don't have to go it alone. Plus, a unique WaterZip cools things off if you work up a sweat. The price is $152. A shorter version of this adventure—the Zipline Trek Iki Mua—is available and runs $112. Outfitters Kauai also includes ziplining as part of its Kipu Safari tour (*see Kayaking*). ⊠ *2827-A Poipu Rd., Poipu* ☎ *808/742–9667, 888/742–9887* ⊕ *www. outfitterskauai.com.*

Princeville Ranch Adventures. The North Shore's answer to ziplining is a nine-zipline course with a bit of hiking, and suspension bridge crossing thrown in for a half-day adventure. The 4½-hour Zip N' Dip tour includes lunch and swimming at a waterfall pool, while the Zip Express whizzes you through the entire course in three hours. Both excursions conclude with a 1,200-foot tandem zip across a valley. Guides are energetic and fun and can offer good dining and nightlife recommendations.

This is as close as it gets to flying; just watch out for the albatross. Prices start at $125 for the Zip Express and $145 for the Zip N' Dip. ⊠ *Rte. 56, between mile markers 27 and 28, Princeville* ☎ *808/826–7669, 888/955–7669* ⊕ *www.adventureskauai.com.*

SHOPPING

Updated by
Lois Ann Ell

There aren't a lot of shops on Kauai, but what you will find here are a handful of places very much worth checking out for the quality of their selection of items sold and services rendered. Many shops now make an effort to sell as many locally made products as possible. When buying an item, ask where it was made or even who made it.

Often you will find that a product handcrafted on the island may not be that much more expensive than a similar product made overseas. You can also look for the purple "Kauai Made" sticker many merchants display.

Along with one major shopping mall, a few shopping centers, and a growing number of big-box retailers, Kauai has some delightful mom-and-pop shops and specialty boutiques with lots of character. The Garden Isle also has a large and talented community of artisans and fine artists, with galleries all around the island showcasing their creations. You can find many island-made arts and crafts in the small shops, and it's worthwhile to stop in at crafts fairs and outdoor markets to look for bargains and mingle with island residents.

If you're looking for a special memento of your trip that is unique to Kauai County, check out the distinctive Niihau shell lei. The tiny shells are collected from beaches on Kauai and Niihau, pierced, and strung into beautiful necklaces, chokers, and earrings. It's a time-consuming and exacting craft, and these items are much in demand, so don't be taken aback by the high price tags. Those made by Niihau residents will have certificates of authenticity and are worth collecting. You often can find cheaper versions made by non-Hawaiians at crafts fairs.

Stores are typically open daily from 9 or 10 am to 5 pm, although some stay open until 9 pm, especially those near resorts. Don't be surprised if the posted hours don't match the actual hours of operation at the smaller shops, where owners may be fairly casual about keeping to a regular schedule.

THE NORTH SHORE

The North Shore has three main shopping areas, all in towns off the highway. Hanalei has two shopping centers directly across from each other, which offer more than you would expect in a remote, relaxed town. Princeville Shopping Center is a bustling little mix of businesses, necessities, and some unique shops, often pricey. Kilauea is a bit more sprawled out and offers a charming, laid-back shopping scene with a neighborhood feel.

SHOPPING CENTERS

Ching Young Village. This popular shopping center looks a bit worn, but that doesn't deter business. Hanalei's only grocery store is here along with a number of other shops useful to locals and visitors, such as a Hawaiian music outlet, jewelry stores, art galleries, a surf shop, and several restaurants. ⊠ *5-5190 Kuhio Hwy., near mile marker 2, Hanalei* ⊕ *www.chingyoungvillage.com.*

Hanalei Center. Once an old Hanalei schoolhouse, the Hanalei Center is now a bevy of boutiques and restaurants. You can dig through '40s and '50s vintage memorabilia, find Polynesian artifacts or search for that unusual gift. Buy beach gear as well as island wear and women's clothing. Find a range of fine jewelry and paper art jewelry. There is a full-service salon and a yoga studio in the two-story modern addition to the center, which also houses a well-stocked health food store. ⊠ *5-5161 Kuhio Hwy., near mile marker 2, Hanalei* ☏ *808/826–7677.*

Princeville Shopping Center. The big draws at this small center are a full-service grocery store and a hardware store, but there's also a wine market, a yoga studio, a sandal boutique, a comic-book store, and an ice-cream shop. This is also the last stop for gas and banking on the North Shore. ⊠ *5-4280 Kuhio Hwy., near mile marker 28, Princeville* ☏ *808/826–9497.*

SHOPS

Kong Lung Co. Sometimes called the Gump's of Kauai, this gift store sells elegant clothing, exotic glassware, ethnic books, gifts, and artwork—all very lovely and expensive. The shop is housed in a beautiful 1892 stone building right in the heart of Kilauea. It's the showpiece of the pretty little Kong Lung Center, where everything from handmade soaps to hammocks to excellent pizza can be found. Next door is the Kilauea Town Market & Deli, a good place to buy natural and gourmet foods, wines, and sandwiches. ⊠ *2484 Keneke St., Kilauea* ☏ *808/828–1822.*

THE EAST SIDE

KAPAA AND WAILUA

Kapaa is the most heavily populated area on Kauai, so it's not surprising that it has the most diverse shopping opportunities on the island. Unlike the North Shore's retail scene, shops here are not neatly situated in centers; they are spread out along a long stretch of road, with many local retail gems tucked away that you may not find if you're in a rush.

SHOPPING CENTERS

Kauai Village Shopping Center. The buildings of this Kapaa shopping village are in the style of a 19th-century plantation town. **ABC Discount Store** sells sundries; **Safeway** carries groceries and alcoholic beverages; **Longs Drugs** has a pharmacy, health and beauty products, and a good selection of Hawaiian merchandise; **Papaya's** has health foods and an excellent cafe. There's also a **Vitamin World** and a **UPS store**. Other shops sell jewelry, art, and home decor. Check out the **Children of the Land Cultural Center,** which holds workshops, classes, and other events. Restaurants include Chinese, vegetarian, and Vietnamese options, and there's also a **Starbucks.** ☒ *4-831 Kuhio Hwy., Kapaa* ☎ *808/822–3777.*

Kinipopo Shopping Village. Kinipopo is a tiny little center on Kuhio Highway. **Korean Barbeque** fronts the highway, as does **Goldsmith's Kauai Gallery,** which sells handcrafted Hawaiian-style gold jewelry. **Monaco's** has authentic Mexican food, and **Cakes by Kristin** is a new pastry shop specializing in cakes. There's also a clothing shop, an art gallery, and a cafe open for breakfast and lunch called **Tutu's Soup Hale.** ☒ *4-356 Kuhio Hwy., Kapaa.*

SHOPS AND GALLERIES

★ **Bambulei.** Two 1930s-style plantation homes have been transformed into a boutique featuring vintage and contemporary clothing, antiques, jewelry, and accessories. You'll also find rare Hawaiian collectibles and furniture here. ☒ *4-369 Kuhio Hwy., Wailua* ☎ *808/823–8641* ⊕ *www. bambulei.com.*

Deja Vu Surf Outlet. This mom-and-pop operation has a great assortment of surfwear and clothes for outdoor fanatics, including tank tops, visors, swimwear, and Kauai-style T-shirts. They also carry body boards and water-sports accessories. Good deals can be found at sidewalk sales. ☒ *4-1419 Kuhio Hwy., Kapaa* ☎ *808/822–4401.*

Jim Saylor Jewelers. Jim Saylor has been designing beautiful keepsakes for over 30 years on Kauai. Gems from around the world, including black pearls, diamonds and more, appear in his unusual settings. ☒ *1318 Kuhio Hwy., Kapaa* ☎ *808/822–3591.*

Kauai Products Fair. Open daily, the Kauai Products Fair outdoor market features fresh produce, tropical plants and flowers, a red dirt shirt shop, a coffee shop, aloha wear, jewelry and gifts. ☒ *Outside on north side of Kapaa, across from Otsuka's Furniture* ☎ *808/246–0988.*

Kela's Glass Gallery. The colorful vases, bowls, and other fragile items sold in this distinctive gallery are definitely worth viewing at Kela's Glass Gallery if you appreciate quality handmade glass art. It's expensive, but if something catches your eye, they'll happily pack it for safe transport home. They also ship worldwide. ☒ *4-1354 Kuhio Hwy., Kapaa* ☎ *808/822–4527* ⊕ *www.glass-art.com.*

Vicky's Fabric Shop. This small store is packed full of tropical and Hawaiian prints, silks, slinky rayons, soft cottons, and other fine fabrics. A variety of sewing patterns and notions are featured as well at Vicky's Fabric Shop, making it a must-stop for any seamstress. If you're seeking something that's truly one-of-a-kind, check out the selection of purses, aloha wear, and other quality hand-sewn items. ☒ *4-1326 Kuhio Hwy., Kapaa* ☎ *808/822–1746.*

LIHUE

Lihue is the business area on Kauai, as well as home to all the big-box stores and the only real mall. Do not mistake this town as lacking in rare finds, however. Lihue is steeped in history and diversity while simultaneously welcoming new trends and establishments.

SHOPPING CENTERS

Kilohana Plantation. This 16,000-square-foot Tudor mansion contains art galleries, a jewelry store, and the farm-to-table restaurant 22 North. Kilohana Plantation is filled with antiques from its original owner and the restored outbuildings house a craft shop and a Hawaiian-style clothing shop. Train rides on a restored railroad are available, with knowledgeable guides reciting the history of sugar on Kauai. The site is also now the home of Luau Kalamaku and Koloa Rum Company. ⊠ *3-2087 Kaumualii Hwy.* ☎ *808/245–5608* ⊕ *www.kilohanakauai.com.*

Kukui Grove Center. This is Kauai's only true mall. Besides **Sears Roebuck** and **Kmart,** anchor tenants are **Longs Drugs, Macy's,** and **Times Supermarket.** The mall's stores offer women's clothing, surf wear, art, toys, athletic shoes, jewelry, a hair salon, and locally made crafts. Restaurants range from fast food and sandwiches to Mexican and Korean. The center stage often has entertainment, and there is a farmers' market on Mondays, and "Toddler Thursdays" offers entertainment for young children. ⊠ *3-2600 Kaumualii Hwy.* ☎ *808/245–7784* ⊕ *www.kukuigrovecenter.com.*

SHOPS AND GALLERIES

Hilo Hattie, The Store of Hawaii, Fashion Factory. This is the big name in aloha wear for tourists throughout the Islands, and Hilo Hattie, The Store of Hawaii, Fashion Factory only has a store on Kauai. Located a mile from Lihue Airport, come here for cool, comfortable aloha shirts and muumuu in bright floral prints, as well as other souvenirs. Also, be sure to check out the line of Hawaii-inspired home furnishings. ⊠ *3252 Kuhio Hwy.* ☎ *808/245–3404* ⊕ *www.hilohattie.com.*

Fodor's Choice ★ **Kapaia Stitchery.** Hawaiian quilts made by hand and machine, a beautiful selection of fabrics, quilting kits, and fabric arts fill Kapaia Stitchery, a cute little red plantation-style building. There are also many locally made gifts for sale. The staff is friendly and helpful, even though a steady stream of customers keeps them busy. ⊠ *3-3551 Kuhio Hwy.* ☎ *808/245–2281.*

Kauai Fruit and Flower Company. At this shop near Lihue and five minutes away from the airport, you can buy fresh Hawaii-grown sugarloaf pineapple, sugarcane, ginger, tropical flowers, coconuts, local jams, jellies, and honey, plus papayas, bananas, and mangoes from Kauai. All the fruit at Kauai Fruit and Flower Company has been inspected and approved to ship out-of-state. ⊠ *3-4684 Kuhio Hwy., Kapaa* ☎ *808/245–1814.*

★ **Kauai Museum.** The gift shop at the museum sells some fascinating books, maps, and prints, as well as lovely feather lei hatbands, Niihau shell jewelry, handwoven *lau hala* hats, and koa wood bowls. Also featured at the Kauai Museum are tapa cloth, authentic *tikis* (hand-carved wooden figurines), as well as other good-quality local crafts at reasonable prices. ⊠ *4428 Rice St.* ☎ *808/246–2470.*

THE SOUTH SHORE

The South Shore, like the North Shore, has convenient shopping clusters, including Poipu Shopping Village and the new Kukuiula Shopping Village. There are many high-priced shops but some unique clothing and gift selections.

SHOPPING CENTERS

Poipu Shopping Village. Convenient to nearby hotels and condos on the South Shore, the two-dozen shops at Poipu Shopping Village sell resort wear, gifts, souvenirs, and art. This complex also has great food choices, from hot dog stands to excellent restuarants. There are a few upscale and appealing jewelry stores and fun clothing stores. A Tahitian dance troupe performs in the open-air courtyard Tuesday and Thursday at 5 pm. ⊠ *2360 Kiahuna Plantation Dr., Poipu Beach* ☎ *808/742–2831.*

The Shops at Kukuiula. This is the South Shore's newest shopping center, with chic, high-end shops, exclusive galleries, restaurants, and cafés. Check out the Kauai Culinary Market on Wednesday from 4 to 6, to see cooking demonstrations, listen to live Hawaiian music, visit the beer and wine garden, and browse wares from local vendors. This attractive open-air, plantation-style center is just beyond the roundabout as you enter Poipu. ⊠ *2829 Kalanikaumaka St., Poipu* ☎ *808/742–2831.*

SHOPS AND GALLERIES

Fodor's Choice ★ **Galerie 103.** This gallery sells art, but the owners want you to experience it as well. Sparse and dramatic, the main room at Galerie 103 consists of concrete floors and walls of featured pieces, from internationally acclaimed artists and local Kauai ones. Most of the artwork is contemporary or modern with a focus on environmental issues. ⊠ *2829 Kalanikaumaka Rd., Kohala* ☎ *808/742–0103* ⊕ *www.galerie103.com* ☺ *Tuesday through Saturday 12–8.*

THE WEST SIDE

The West Side is years behind the South Shore in development, offering charming, simple shops with authentic local flavor.

SHOPPING CENTERS

Eleele Shopping Center. Kauai's West Side has a scattering of stores, including those at this no-frills strip-mall, Eleele Shopping Center. It's a good place to rub elbows with local folk at **Big Save** grocery store or to grab a quick bite to eat at the casual **Grinds Cafe** or **Tois Thai Kitchen.** ⊠ *Rte. 50, Eleele.*

Waimea Canyon Plaza. As Kekaha's retail hub and the last stop for supplies before heading up to Waimea Canyon, Waimea Canyon Plaza is a tiny, tidy complex of shops surprisingly busy. Look for local foods, souvenirs, and island-made gifts for all ages. ⊠ *Kokee Rd., at Rte. 50, Kekaha.*

SHOPS AND GALLERIES

Kauai Coffee Visitor Center and Museum. Kauai produces more coffee than any other island in the state. The local product can be purchased from grocery stores or here at the Kauai Coffee Visitor Center and Museum, where a sampling of the nearly one-dozen coffees is available. Be sure to try some of the estate-roasted varieties. ⊠ *870 Halawili Rd., off Rte. 50, Kalaheo* ☎ *808/335–0813, 800/545–8605* ⊕ *www.kauaicoffee.com.*

Kauai Tropicals. You can have Kauai Tropicals ship heliconia, anthuriums, ginger, and other tropicals in 5-foot-long boxes directly from its flower farm in Kalaheo. ⊠ *3870 Waha Rd., Kalaheo* ☎ *800/303–4385.*

Paradise Sportswear. This is the retail outlet of the folks who invented Kauai's popular "red dirt" shirts, which are dyed and printed with the characteristic local soil. Ask the salesperson at Paradise Sportswear to tell you the charming story behind these shirts. Sizes from infants up to 5X are available. ⊠ *4350 Waialo Rd., Port Allen* ☎ *808/335–5670.*

SPAS

Updated by
Lois Ann Ell

Though most spas on Kauai are associated with resorts, none are restricted to guests only. And there's much by way of healing and wellness to be found on Kauai beyond the traditional spa—or even the day spa. More and more retreat facilities are offering what some would call alternative healing therapies. Others would say there's nothing alternative about them; you can decide for yourself.

Alexander Day Spa & Salon at the Kauai Marriott. This sister spa of Alexander Simson's Beverly Hills spa focuses on body care rather than exercise, so don't expect any fitness equipment or exercise classes. The Alexander Day Spa & Salon at the Kauai Marriott has the same ambience of stilted formality as the rest of the resort, but it is otherwise a sunny, pleasant facility. Massages are available in treatment rooms and on the beach, although the beach locale isn't as private as you might imagine. Wedding-day and custom spa packages can be arranged. ⊠ *Kauai Marriott Resort & Beach Club, 3610 Rice St., Suite 9A, Lihue* ☎ *808/246–4918* ⊕ *www.alexanderspa.com* ☞ *$65–$190 massage. Facilities: Hair salon, steam room. Services: Body treatments—including masks, scrubs, and wraps—facials, hair styling, makeup, manicures, massage, pedicures, waxing.*

Fodor's Choice
★

ANARA Spa. The luxurious ANARA Spa has all the equipment and services you expect from a top resort spa, along with a pleasant, professional staff. Best of all, it has indoor and outdoor areas that capitalize on the tropical locale and balmy weather, further distinguishing it from the Marriott and St. Regis spas. Its 46,500 square feet of space includes the new Garden Treatment Village, an open-air courtyard with private thatched-roof huts, each featuring a relaxation area, misters, and open-air shower in a tropical setting. Ancient Hawaiian remedies and local ingredients are featured in many of the treatments, such as a Lokahi Garden facial, and a Hawaiian Herbal Aromatherapy body wrap. The open-air lava-rock showers are wonderful, introducing many guests to the delightful island practice of showering outdoors. The spa, which includes a full-service salon, adjoins the Hyatt's legendary swimming pool. ⊠ *Hyatt Regency Kauai Resort and Spa, 1571 Poipu Rd., Poipu* ☎ *808/240–6440* ⊕ *www.anaraspa.com* ☞ *Massages start at $160. Facilities: Hair salon, outdoor hot tubs, sauna, steam room. Gym with: Cardiovascular machines, free weights, weight-training equipment. Services: Body scrubs and wraps, facials, manicures, massage, pedicures. Classes and programs: Aerobics, aquaerobics, body sculpting, fitness analysis, flexibility training, personal training, Pilates, step aerobics, weight training, yoga.*

Angeline's Muolaulani Wellness Center. It doesn't get more authentic than this. In the mid-1980s Aunty Angeline Locey opened her Anahola home to offer traditional Hawaiian healing practices. Now her son and granddaughter carry on the tradition. At Angeline's Muolaulani Wellness Center, there's a two-hour treatment ($150) that starts with a steam, followed by a sea-salt-and-clay body scrub and a two-person massage. The real treat, however, is relaxing on Aunty's open-air garden deck. Hot-stone lomi is also available. Aunty's mission is to promote a healthy body image; as such, au naturel is the accepted way here, so if you're nudity-shy, this may not be the place for you. On second thought, Aunty would say it most definitely is, as *muolaulani* translates to "a place for young buds to bloom." Detailed directions are given when you book a treatment. ⊠ *Kamalomaloo Pl., Anahola* ☎ *808/822–3235* ⊕ *www.angelineslomikauai.com* ☞ *Facilities: Steam room. Services: Body scrubs and massage.*

Fodor's Choice ★ Halelea Spa. This superb spa at The St. Regis Princeville Resort is indeed a House of Joy, as its Hawaiian name translates. Opened in 2009, the 11,000-square-foot Halelea Spa transports users to a place of utter tranquillity. The spa's 12 luxurious treatment rooms afford a subdued indoor setting only outmatched by the professional service. Take advantage of the dedicated couples' room and enjoy a taro butter pohaku hot stone massage. Follow that with a few hours sipping tea in the relaxation lounge, sweating in the sauna, and rinsing in an overhead rain shower. There is a qualified wellness consultant and spa programs are inspired by Native Hawaiian healing rituals. You can find health, beauty, and inner peace at this spa, but expect to pay for it. ⊠ *The St. Regis Princeville Resort, 5520 Ka Haku Rd., Princeville* ☎ *877/787–3447, 808/826–9644* ⊕ *www.stregisprinceville.com* ☞ *Massage $170–$245. Services: Body scrubs and wraps, facials, massage, waxing.*

Hanalei Day Spa. As you travel beyond tony Princeville, life slows down. The single-lane bridges may be one reason. Another is the Hanalei Day Spa (opened in 2004), an open-air, thatched-roof, Hawaiian-style hut nestled just off the beach on the grounds of Hanalei Colony Resort in Haena. Though this no-frills day spa offers facials, waxing, wraps, scrubs, and the like, its specialty is massage: Ayurveda, Zen Shiatsu, Swedish, and even a baby massage (and lesson for Mom, to boot). Owner Darci Frankel teaches yoga, a discipline she started as a young child. That practice led her to start the Ayurveda Center of Hawaii, which operates out of the spa and offers an ancient Indian cleansing and rejuvenation program known as Pancha Karma. Think multiday

Continued on page 546

HULA: MORE THAN A FOLK DANCE

Hula has been called "the heartbeat of the Hawaiian people" and also "the world's best-known, most misunderstood dance." Both are true. Hula isn't just dance. It is storytelling.

Chanter Edith McKinzie calls it "an extension of a piece of poetry." In its adornments, implements, and customs, hula integrates every important Hawaiian cultural practice: poetry, history, genealogy, craft, plant cultivation, martial arts, religion, protocol. So when 19th century Christian missionaries sought to eradicate a practice they considered depraved, they threatened more than just a folk dance.

With public performance outlawed and private hula practice discouraged, hula went underground for a generation, to rural villages. The fragile verbal link by which culture was transmitted from teacher to student hung by a thread. Even increasing literacy did not help because hula's practitioners were a secretive and protected circle.

As if that weren't bad enough, vaudeville, Broadway, and Hollywood got hold of the hula, giving it the glitz treatment in an unbroken line from "Oh, How She Could Wicky Wacky Woo" to "Rock-A-Hula Baby." Hula became shorthand for paradise: fragrant flowers, lazy hours. Ironically, this development assured that hundreds of Hawaiians could make a living performing and teaching hula. Many danced *auana* (modern form) in performance; but taught *kahiko* (traditional), quietly, at home or in hula schools.

Today, 30 years after the cultural revival known as the Hawaiian Renaissance, language immersion programs have assured a new generation of proficient—and even eloquent—chanters, songwriters, and translators. Visitors can see more, and more authentic, traditional hula than at any other time in the last 200 years.

Like the culture of which it is the beating heart, hula has survived.

Lei *poo*. Head lei. In kahiko, greenery only. In auana, flowers.

Face emotes appropriate expression. Dancer should not be a smiling automaton.

Shoulders remain relaxed and still, never hunched, even with arms raised. No bouncing.

Eyes always follow leading hand.

Lei. Hula is rarely performed without a shoulder lei.

Arms and hands remain loose, relaxed, below shoulder level—except as required by interpretive movements.

Traditional hula skirt is loose fabric, smocked and gathered at the waist.

Hip is canted over weight-bearing foot.

Knees are always slightly bent, accentuating hip sway.

Kupee. Ankle bracelet of flowers, shells, or—traditionally—noise-making dog teeth.

In kahiko, feet are flat. In auana, they may be more arched, but not tiptoes or bouncing.

BASIC MOTIONS

Speak or Sing

Moon or Sun

Grass Shack or House

Mountains or Heights

Love or Caress

At backyard parties, hula is performed in bare feet and street clothes, but in performance, adornments play a key role, as do rhythm-keeping implements.

In hula *kahiko* (traditional style), the usual dress is multiple layers of stiff fabric (often with a pellom lining, which most closely resembles *kapa*, the paperlike bark cloth of the Hawaiians). These wrap tightly around the bosom but flare below the waist to form a skirt. In pre-contact times, dancers wore only kapa skirts. Men traditionally wear loincloths.

Monarchy-period hula is performed in voluminous muumuu or high-necked muslin blouses and gathered skirts. Men wear white or gingham shirts and black pants.

In hula *auana* (modern), dress for women can range from grass skirts and strapless tops to contemporary tea-length dresses. Men generally wear aloha shirts, but sometimes grass skirts over pants or even everyday gear.

SURPRISING HULA FACTS

■ Grass skirts are not traditional; workers from Kiribati (the Gilbert Islands) brought this custom to Hawaii.

■ In olden-day Hawaii, *mele* (songs) for hula were composed for every occasion—name songs for babies, dirges for funerals, welcome songs for visitors, celebrations of favorite pursuits.

■ Hula *mai* is a traditional hula form in praise of a noble's genitals; the power of the *alii* (royalty) to procreate gave *mana* (spiritual power) to the entire culture.

■ Hula students in old Hawaii adhered to high standards: scrupulous cleanliness, no sex, daily cleansing rituals, certain food prohibitions, and no contact with the dead. They were fined if they broke the rules.

WHERE TO WATCH

■ Coconut Marketplace, ⊠ 4-484 Kuhio Hwy., Kapaa, ⊙ Sat. 1 PM.

■ Poipu Shopping Village, ⊠ 2360 Kiahuna Plantation Dr., Poipu Beach, ☎ 808/742–7444 ⊙ Tues. and Thurs. 5 pm.

■ Smith's Tropical Paradise, ⊠ 174 Wailua Rd., Kapaa, ☎ 808/821–6895, ⊙ Mon., Wed., and Fri. 5–9:15. Dinner included.

■ Festivals: There are many festivals on the island year-round where you can see hula performed. For more information visit www.kauaifestivals.com.

wellness retreat. ⊠ *Hanalei Colony Resort, Rte. 560, 6 milespast Hanalei, Haena* ☎ *808/826–6621* ⊕ *www.hanaleidayspa.com* ☞ *Massage $95–$210. Services: Body scrubs and wraps, facials, massage, waxing. Classes and programs: Yoga.*

★ **A Hideaway Spa.** This is the only full-service day spa on the laid-back West Side. A Hideaway Spa is in one of the restored plantation cottages that make up the guest quarters at Waimea Plantation Cottages, creating a cozy and comfortable setting you won't find elsewhere. The overall feel is relaxed, casual, and friendly, as you'd expect in this quiet country town. The staff is informal, yet thoroughly professional. Beach yoga and massages are available, as well as a full-service salon with hair, nails, and makeup services. Try the kava kava ginger wrap followed by the lomi *iliili*—hot-stone massage. ⊠ *Waimea Plantation Cottages, 9400 Kaumualii Hwy., Cottage No. 30, Waimea* ☎ *808/338–0005* ⊕ *www. ahideawayspa.com* ☞ *Massage $50–$170. Facilities: Outdoor hot tub, steam room. Services: Acupuncture, body scrubs and wraps, facials, hydrotherapy, massage. Classes and programs: Yoga.*

Tri Health Ayurveda Spa. The goal at the Tri Health Ayurveda Spa isn't a one-time massage for momentary bliss, although relaxation is a key ingredient. Rather, this spa's focus is a multiweek, multitreatment, intensive program designed to eliminate toxins stored in the body and increase the flow and energy of all systems. Treatments are designed around the ancient Ayurvedic tradition of heat to open the pores, oil to deliver nutrients to tissues and nerve endings, and massage (by two therapists working in synchronized movement) to accelerate circulation. Note: Because the massage strokes are long and can run the length of the body, there is no draping involved. Ayurvedic doctors, food, and treatments are available, as is lodging in the 10-bedroom retreat facility, on 25 acres hidden by design for privacy—hence, no glaring signs. Single sessions are available. ⊠ *Kilauea* ☎ *808/828–2104* ⊕ *www.trihealthayurvedaspa.com* ☞ *Massage $130–$275. Facilities: Steam room. Services: Herbal body scrubs, massage.*

ENTERTAINMENT AND NIGHTLIFE

Updated by
David Simon

Kauai has never been known for its nightlife. It's a rural island, where folks tend to retire early, and the streets are dark and deserted well before midnight. The island does have its nightspots, though, and the after-dark entertainment scene may not be expanding, but it is consistently present in areas frequented by tourists.

Most of the island's dinner and luau shows are held at hotels and resorts. Hotel lounges are a good source of live music, often with no cover charge, as are a few bars and restaurants around the island.

Check the local newspaper, the *Garden Island*, as well as its own *Kauai Times* entertainment guide, for listings of weekly happenings, or tune in to community radio station KKCR—found at 90.9, 91.9, or 92.7 on the FM dial, depending on where on the island you are at that moment—at 5:30 pm for the arts and entertainment calendar. Free publications such as *Kauai Gold, This Week on Kauai,* and

Essential Kauai also list entertainment events. You can pick them up at Lihue Airport near the baggage claim area, as well as at numerous retail areas on the island.

ENTERTAINMENT

Although luau remain a primary source of evening fun for families on vacation, there are a handful of other possibilities. There are no traditional dinner cruises, but some boat tours do offer an evening buffet with music along Napali Coast. A few times a year, Women in Theater (WIT), a local women's theater group, performs dinner shows at the Hukilau Lanai in Wailua. You can always count on a performance of *South Pacific* at the Kauai Beach Resort, and the Kauai Community College Performing Arts Center draws well-known artists.

Kauai Community College Performing Arts Center. This is a main venue for island entertainment, hosting a concert music series, visiting musicians, dramatic productions, and special events such as the International Film Festival. ✉ *3-1901 Kaumualii Hwy., Lihue* ☎ *808/245–8352* ⊕ *kauai. hawaii.edu/pac.*

DINNER SHOW

South Pacific Dinner Show. It seems a fitting tribute to see the play that put Kauai on the map. Rodgers and Hammerstein's original *South Pacific* has been playing at the Kauai Beach Resort to rave reviews since 2002. The full musical production, accompanied by a buffet dinner, features local talent. ✉ *Jasmine Ballroom, Kauai Beach Resort, 4331 Kauai Beach Dr., Lihue* ☎ *808/346–6500* ⊕ *www.southpacifickauai.com* 🎫 *$85* ☉ *Wed., doors open at 5:30 pm, show at 6:45.*

LUAU

Although the commercial luau experience is a far cry from the backyard luau thrown by local residents to celebrate a wedding, graduation, or baby's first birthday, they're nonetheless entertaining and a good introduction to the Hawaiian food that isn't widely sold in restaurants. Besides the feast, there's often an exciting dinner show with Polynesian-style music and dancing. It all makes for a fun evening that's suitable for couples, families, and groups, and the informal setting is conducive to meeting other people. Every luau is different, reflecting the cuisine and tenor of the host facility, so compare prices, menus, and entertainment before making your reservation. Most luau on Kauai are offered only on a limited number of nights each week, so plan ahead to get the luau you want. We tend to prefer those *not* held on resort properties, because they feel a bit more authentic.

Grand Hyatt Kauai Luau. What used to be called Drums of Paradise has a new name and a new dance troupe but still offers a traditional luau buffet and an exceptional performance. This oceanfront luau comes with a view of the majestic Keoneloa Bay. ✉ *Grand Hyatt Kauai Resort and Spa, 1571 Poipu Rd., Poipu* ☎ *808/240–6456* ⊕ *www.hyatt.com/ gallery/kauailuau* 🎫 *$94* ☉ *Thurs. and Sun., doors open at 5 pm, show begins at 6.*

★ **Luau Kalamaku.** Set on historic sugar-plantation land, this new luau bills itself as the only "theatrical" luau on Kauai. The luau feast is served buffet-style, there's an open bar, and the performers aim to both entertain and educate about Hawaiian culture. Guests sit at tables around a circular stage; tables farther from the stage are elevated, providing unobstructed views. Additional packages offer visitors the opportunity to tour the 35-acre plantation via train or special romantic perks like a lei greeting and champagne. ⊠ *3-2087 Kaumualii St., Lihue* ☎ *877/622–1780* ⊕ *www.luaukalamaku.com* ☒ *$99* ⊗ *Tues. and Fri. check-in begins at 5, dinner at 6:30, show at 7:30.*

Fodor'sChoice **Smith's Tropical Paradise Luau.** A 30-acre tropical garden provides the ★ lovely setting for this popular luau, which begins with the traditional blowing of the conch shell and *imu* (pig roast) ceremony, followed by cocktails, an island feast, and an international show in the amphitheater overlooking a torch-lighted lagoon. It's fairly authentic and a better deal than the pricier resort events. ⊠ *174 Wailua Rd., Kapaa* ☎ *808/821–6895* ☒ *$88* ⊗ *Sept.–May, Mon., Wed., and Fri. 5–9:15; June–Aug., weekdays 5–9:15.*

MUSIC

Check the local papers for outdoor reggae and Hawaiian-music shows, or one of the numbers listed below for more formal performances.

Hanalei Slack Key Concerts. Relax to the instrumental music form created by Hawaiian *paniolo* (cowboys) in the early 1800s. Shows are at Hale Halawai Ohana O Hanalei, which is *mauka* down a dirt access road across from St. William's Catholic Church (Malolo Road) and then left down another dirt road. Look for a thatched-roof *hale* (house), several little green plantation-style buildings, and the brown double-yurt community center around the gravel parking lot. There is also a weekly Saturday show in Kapaa town. ⊠ *Hanalei Family Community Center, 5-5299 Kuhio Hwy., Hanalei* ☎ *808/826–1469* ⊕ *www. hawaiianslackkeyguitar.com* ☒ *$20* ⊗ *Fri. at 4, Sun. at 3.*

Kauai Concert Association. This group offers a seasonal program at the Kauai Community College Performing Arts Center. A range of big-name artists, from Ricky Lee Jones to Taj Mahal, have been known to show up on Kauai for planned or impromptu performances. ⊠ *3-1901 Kaumualii Hwy., Lihue* ☎ *808/245–7464* ⊕ *www.kauai-concert.org.*

NIGHTLIFE

For every new venue that opens on Kauai, another one closes. Perhaps it's simply the result of the island's ubiquitous but little-known epidemic: paradise paralysis. Symptoms include a slight fragrance of coconut wafting from the pores, pink cheeks and nose, a relaxed gait, and a slight smile curving on the lips. Let's face it: Kauai lulls people into a stupor that puts them to bed before 10 pm. But if you are one of those immune to the disease, Kauai may have a place or two for you to while away your spare hours.

Nightclubs that stay open until the wee hours are rare on Kauai, and the bar scene is pretty limited. The major resorts generally host their own live entertainment and happy hours. All bars and clubs that serve alcohol must close by 2 am, except those with a cabaret license, which allows them to close at 4 am. For information on events or specials, check out the local newspaper's nightlife section, *Kauai Times* (⊕ *kauaitimes.net*).

THE NORTH SHORE

Hanalei Gourmet. The sleepy North Shore stays awake—until 10:30, that is—each evening in this small, convivial setting inside Hanalei's restored old school building. The emphasis here is on local live Hawaiian, jazz, rock, and folk music. ⊠ *Hanalei Center, 5-5161 Kuhio Hwy., Hanalei* ☎ *808/826–2524* ⊕ *www.hanaleigourmet.com.*

★ **St. Regis Bar.** This spacious lounge overlooking Hanalei Bay offers drinks daily from 3:30 to 11. Stop by between 5:30 and 10 for *pupu* (hors d'oeuvres), acoustic guitar or piano music, and an ocean view. ⊠ *Princeville Resort, 5520 Ka Haku Rd., Princeville* ☎ *808/826–9644.*

Tahiti Nui. This venerable and decidedly funky institution in sleepy Hanalei no longer offers its famous luau, ever since owner and founder Auntie Louise Marston died. But spirits are always high at this popular hangout for locals and visitors alike, which houses live nightly entertainment, including Hawaiian music earlier in the evening and rock and roll starting around 9. Patrons can show off their own pipes during Monday karaoke festivities. For a more intimate setting, don't miss the new wine bar, Tahiti Iti, located right next door. ⊠ *5-5134 Kuhio Hwy., Hanalei* ☎ *808/826–6277* ⊕ *www.thenui.com.*

THE EAST SIDE

Duke's Barefoot Bar. This is one of the liveliest bars in Nawiliwili. Contemporary Hawaiian music is usually performed at this beachside bar every day during "Aloha Hours" from 4 to 6 pm. Thursday, Friday and Saturday nights also feature more music from 8:30 to 10:30. ⊠ *Kalapaki Beach, 3610 Rice St., Lihue* ☎ *808/246–9599* ⊕ *www. dukeskauai.com.*

Hukilau Lanai. This open-air bar and restaurant is on the property of the Kauai Coast Resort but operates independently. Trade winds trickle through the modest little bar, which looks out into a coconut grove. If the mood takes you, go on a short walk to the sea, or recline in big, comfortable chairs while listening to mellow jazz or Hawaiian slack-key guitar. Live music plays every night, though the bar is closed on Mondays. Poolside happy hour runs from 3 to 5. Freshly infused tropical martinis—perhaps locally grown lychee and pineapple or a Big Island vanilla bean infusion—are house favorites. ⊠ *520 Aleka Loop, Wailua* ☎ *808/822–0600* ⊕ *www.hukilaukauai.com.*

Rob's Good Times Grill. Let loose at this popular sports bar, which features DJs spinning Friday and Saturday from 10 pm to 2 am with the occasional live band. Tuesday offers swing dancing, while Wednesday you can kick up your heels with country line dancing from 8 to 10 pm. Karaoke follows both, while Sunday and Monday are full-on karaoke all night. ⊠ *4303 Rice St., Lihue* ☎ *808/246–0311* ⊕ *www. kauaisportsbarandgrill.com.*

CLOSE UP

Kauai: Undercover Movie Star

Though Kauai has played itself in the movies, most recently starring in *The Descendants* (2011), most of its screen time has been as a stunt double for a number of tropical paradises. The island's remote valleys portrayed Venezuelan jungle in Kevin Costner's *Dragonfly* (2002) and a Costa Rican dinosaur preserve in Steven Spielberg's *Jurassic Park* (1993). Spielberg was no stranger to Kauai, having filmed Harrison Ford's escape via seaplane from Menehune Fishpond in *Raiders of the Lost Ark* (1981).

The fluted cliffs and gorges of Kauai's rugged Napali Coast play the misunderstood beast's island home in *King Kong* (1976), and a jungle dweller of another sort, in *George of the Jungle* (1997), frolicked on Kauai. Harrison Ford returned to the island for 10 weeks during the filming of *Six Days, Seven Nights* (1998), a romantic adventure set in French Polynesia. Part-time Kauai resident Ben Stiller used the island as a stand-in for the jungles of Vietnam in *Tropic Thunder* (2008) and Johnny Depp came here to film some of *Pirates of the Caribbean: On Stranger Tides* (2011). But these are all relatively contemporary movies. What's truly remarkable is that Hollywood discovered Kauai in 1933 with the making of *White Heat*, which was set on a sugar plantation and—like another more memorable movie filmed on Kauai—dealt with interracial love stories.

Then, it was off to the races, as Kauai saw no fewer than a dozen movies filmed on island in the 1950s, not all of them Oscar contenders. Rita Hayworth starred in *Miss Sadie Thompson* (1953) and no one you'd recognize starred in the tantalizing *She Gods of Shark Reef* (1956).

The movie that is still immortalized on the island in the names of restaurants, real estate offices, a hotel, and even a sushi item is *South Pacific* (1957). (You guessed it, right?) That mythical place called Bali Hai is never far away on Kauai.

In the 1960s Elvis Presley filmed *Blue Hawaii* (1961) and *Girls! Girls! Girls!* (1962) on the island. A local movie tour likes to point out the stain on a hotel carpet where Elvis's jelly doughnut fell.

Kauai has welcomed a long list of Hollywood's A-List: John Wayne in *Donovan's Reef* (1963); Jack Lemmon in *The Wackiest Ship in the Army* (1961); Richard Chamberlain in *The Thorn Birds* (1983); Gene Hackman in *Uncommon Valor* (1983); Danny DeVito and Billy Crystal in *Throw Momma from the Train* (1987); and Dustin Hoffman, Morgan Freeman, Renee Russo, and Cuba Gooding Jr. in *Outbreak* (1995).

Yet the movie scene isn't the only screen on which Kauai has starred. A long list of TV shows, TV pilots, and made-for-TV movies make the list as well, including *Gilligan's Island, Fantasy Island, Starsky & Hutch, Baywatch Hawaii*—even reality TV shows *The Bachelor* and *The Amazing Race 3*.

For the record, just because a movie did some filming here doesn't mean the entire movie was filmed on Kauai. *Honeymoon in Vegas* filmed just one scene here, while the murder mystery *A Perfect Getaway* (2009) was set on the famous Kalalau Trail and featured beautiful Kauaian backdrops but was shot mostly in Puerto Rico.

Trees Lounge. Behind the hokey Coconut Marketplace and next to the Kauai Coast Resort in Kapaa, you'll find Trees Lounge. For a while, this chic wood-filled bar and restaurant hosted good live music but didn't allow any dancing, to the chagrin of its patrons. Now with the proper liquor licenses in hand, Trees will let you move much more than just some solo toe tapping as live bands, singer-songwriters and open mikers all take the stage. Closed Sundays. ⊠ *440 Aleka Pl., Kapaa* ☎ *808/823–0600* ⊕ *www.treesloungekauai.com.*

THE SOUTH SHORE

Keoki's Paradise. A young, energetic crowd makes this a lively spot on Friday and Saturday nights. There's live music every night, usually for two hours between 6 pm and 9 pm. When the dining room clears out, there's a bit of a bar scene for singles. The bar closes at 10:30 pm. ⊠ *Poipu Shopping Village, 2360 Kiahuna Plantation Dr., Poipu* ☎ *808/742–7534* ⊕ *www.keokisparadise.com.*

Lavas at Sheraton Kauai. This is *the* place to be on the South Shore to celebrate sunset with a drink; the ocean view is unsurpassed. There is live music every night from 9 until closing at 11. The lineup isn't set in stone, so call before you arrive to see who's playing that night. ⊠ *Sheraton Kauai Resort, 2440 Hoonani Rd., Poipu* ☎ *808/742–1661* ⊕ *www. sheraton-kauai.com/dining.*

THE WEST SIDE

The Grove Cafe. Formerly the Waimea Brewing Company, this location allows you to sip on some locally brewed beers in an airy plantation-style house on the grounds of Waimea Plantation Cottages. Outdoor seating and a wraparound lanai make this eatery a worthwhile West Side experience. Expect slow service and mediocre fare. There is usually live music Wednesday through Friday, or grab a growler to go, take a stroll out back to the beach, and enjoy views of Ni'ihau while the sun sets. ⊠ *9400 Kaumualii Hwy., Waimea* ☎ *808/338–1625.*

WHERE TO EAT

Updated by Charles E. Roessler

On Kauai, if you're lucky enough to win an invitation to a potluck, baby luau, or beach party, don't think twice—just accept. The best grinds (food) are homemade, and so you'll eat until you're full, then rest, eat some more, and make a plate to take home, too.

But even if you can't score a spot at one of these parties, don't despair. Great local-style food is easy to come by at countless low-key places around the island. As an extra bonus, these eats are often inexpensive, and portions are generous. Expect plenty of meat—usually deep-fried or marinated in a teriyaki sauce and grilled *pulehu*-style (over an open fire)—and starches. Rice is standard, even for breakfast, and often served alongside potato-macaroni salad, another island specialty. Another local favorite is *poke,* made from chunks of raw tuna or octopus seasoned with sesame oil, soy sauce, onions, and pickled seaweed. It's a great *pupu* (appetizer) when paired with a cold beer.

■ TIP ➔ **One cautionary note: most restaurants stop serving dinner at 8 or 9 pm, so plan to eat early.**

BEST BETS FOR KAUAI DINING

Fodor's Choice ★	Hanamaulu Restaurant, p. 561	Pomodoro Ristorante Italiano, p. 568
Bar Acuda, $$$$, p. 552	Joe's on the Green, p. 567	Wrangler's Steakhouse, p. 568
Beach House, $$$, p. 562	Lihue Barbecue Inn, p. 561	**$$$**
Dondero's, $$$, p. 562		
Hukilau Lanai, $$, p. 557	Mema Thai Chinese Cuisine, p. 558	Beach House, p. 562
Restaurant Kintaro, $$, p. 558		Dondero's, p. 562
	Mermaid's Café, p. 558	Roy's Poipu Bar & Grill, p. 568
By Price	**$$**	Tidepools, p. 568
$	Hukilau Lanai, p. 557	**$$$$**
Dani's Restaurant, p. 560	Kauai Pasta, p. 558	Bar Acuda, p. 552
Hamura Saimin, p. 560	Plantation Gardens, p. 567	Kauai Grill, p. 553

Prices in the reviews are the average cost of a main course at dinner or, if dinner is not served, at lunch.

THE NORTH SHORE

Because of the North Shore's isolation, restaurants have enjoyed a captive audience of visitors who don't want to make the long, dark trek into Kapaa town for dinner. As a result, dining in this region has been characterized by expensive fare that isn't especially tasty, either. Fortunately, the situation is slowly improving as new restaurants open and others change hands or menus.

Still, dining on the North Shore can be pricier than other parts of the island, and not especially family-friendly. Most of the restaurants are found either in Hanalei town or the Princeville resorts. Consequently, you'll encounter delightful mountain and ocean views, but just one restaurant with oceanfront dining.

$$$$
MEDITERRANEAN
Fodor's Choice
★

✕ **Bar Acuda.** This tapas bar is a very welcome addition to the Hanalei dining scene, rocketing right near top place in the categories of tastiness, creativity, and pizzazz. Owner-chef Jim Moffat's brief menu changes regularly: You might find *banderillas* (grilled flank steak skewers with honey and chipotle chili oil), Gorgonzola endive salad, or Spanish chorizo with grilled apples. The food is consistently remarkable, but it's the subtly intense sauces that elevate the cuisine to outstanding. It's super casual, but chic, with a nice porch for outdoor dining. $ *Average main: $40 ✉ Hanalei Center, 5-5161 Kuhio Hwy., Hanalei ☎ 808/826–7081 ⊕ www.restaurantbaracuda.com ✆ Closed Mon.*

$$
AMERICAN

✕ **Hanalei Gourmet.** This spot in Hanalei's restored old schoolhouse offers dolphin-safe tuna, low-sodium meats, fresh-baked breads, and homemade desserts as well as a casual atmosphere where both families and the sports-watching crowds can feel equally comfortable. Early birds can order coffee and toast or a hearty breakfast. Lunch and dinner menus feature sandwiches, burgers, filling salads, and nightly specials of fresh local fish. They also will prepare a picnic and give it to you in an insulated backpack. A full bar and frequent live entertainment keep things hopping even after the kitchen closes. Thursday evenings fill up for fish taco night, which begins at 6. $ *Average main: $25* ⊠ *Hanalei Center, 5-5161 Kuhio Hwy., Hanalei* ☎ *808/826–2524* ⊕ *www. hanaleigourmet.com.*

$$$$
ECLECTIC

✕ **Kauai Grill.** Savor an artful meal created by world-renowned chef Jean-Gorges Vongerichten, surrounded by a dramatic Hanalei Bay scene. Located at the recently renovated St. Regis Princeville Resort, Kauai Grill has dark wood decor and an ornate red chandelier, the centerpiece of the room. The attention here is on the flavors of robust meat and local, fresh seafood. Most dishes are plainly grilled, accompanied by exotic sauces and condiments. The specials change frequently and use as many Hawaiian-grown ingredients as possible. Expect attentive service with the somewhat stiff feel of an exclusive hotel, and an expertly created meal. $ *Average main: $45* ⊠ *St. Regis Princeville, 5520 Ka Haku Rd., Princeville* ☎ *808/826–9644* ⚐ *Reservations essential* ☉ *No lunch. Closed Sun.–Mon.*

$
AMERICAN
☺

✕ **Kilauea Bakery and Pau Hana Pizza.** This bakery has garnered tons of well-deserved good press for its starter of Hawaiian sourdough made with guava as well as its specialty pizzas topped with such yummy ingredients as smoked *ono* (a Hawaiian fish), Gorgonzola-rosemary sauce, barbecued chicken, goat cheese, and roasted onions. Open from 6:30 am, the bakery serves coffee drinks, delicious fresh pastries, bagels, and breads in the morning. Late risers beware: breads and pastries sell out quickly on weekends. Pizza, soup, and salads can be ordered for lunch or dinner. If you want to hang out or do the Wi-Fi coffee shop bit in Kilauea, this is the place. A cute courtyard with covered tables is a pleasant place to linger. $ *Average main: $15* ⊠ *Kong Lung Center, 2484 Keneke St., Kilauea* ☎ *808/828–2020.*

$$$$
HAWAIIAN

✕ **Makana Terrace.** Enjoy dining while gazing at one of the most exquisite snapshots of Hanalei Bay. There's no doubt it's pricey, but you're paying for the view—sit on the terrace if you can—and for an attentive staff. There is a focus on local, Hawaiian-grown foods here, including the fish plate of a fresh Pacific catch, which is your best bet for lunch. Feast at the extensive breakfast buffet for $34 per person from 6:30 to 11:00 am, but note that it's traditional fare: nothing spectacular or exotic. For a special evening, splurge on the surf and turf (around $45) and time your dinner around sunset for an unforgettable Hawaiian vista. $ *Average main: $40* ⊠ *5520 Ka Haku Rd., Princeville* ☎ *808/826–9644.*

$$
AMERICAN

✕ **Postcards Café.** With its vintage photos of the North Shore, beamed ceilings, and light interiors, this plantation-cottage restaurant has a menu stressing seafood but also offering additive-free vegetarian and vegan options. But don't get the wrong idea—this isn't simple cooking: specials might include carrot-ginger soup, taro fritters, or fresh fish

Where to Eat
on Kauai

Haena Beach Park

Tunnels
Beach

Kee Beach

Haena

Princeville

32

560

*Hanalei
Bay*

34

*Hanakapiai
Beach*

Hanalei

35

36

WAIPA VALLEY

NAPALI COAST

Kalalau Trail

Kalalau
Lookout

Puu O Kila
Lookout

Kokee
Lodge

*Kokee
State Park*

Kokee

550

WAIMEA CANYON

*NaPali-Kona
Forest Reserve*

Waialeale
5,148 ft.

WAIMEA

Kokee Rd.

Waimea Canyon Dr.

55

552

550

KOLOA

Kekaha Beach
Park

Kekaha

Menehune
Ditch

1

Waimea

Lucy Wright
Beach Park

2 Kalaheo

Lawa

Kaulakahi Channel

50

Hanapepe

Eleele

540

Burns Field

Port Allen

Spouting
Horn

*Hanapepe
Bay*

Beach
House

0		5 miles
0		5 km

5

Mahimahi is a popular fish dish on Kauai. The Beach House adds a macadamia-nut crust for local flavor.

served with peppered pineapple-sage sauce, or blackened ahi. Desserts are made without refined sugar. Try the chocolate silk pie made with barley malt chocolate, pure vanilla, and creamy tofu with a gingery crust. This is probably your best bet for dinner in Hanalei town. $ *Average main: $21* ⊠ *5-5075A Kuhio Hwy., Hanalei* ☎ *808/826–1191* ⊕ *www.postcardscafe.com* ⊗ *No lunch.*

$$ ╳ **The Tavern at Princeville.** Roy Yamaguchi's tasteful restaurant overlook-
AMERICAN ing the beautiful Prince Golf Course offers a convivial, lively atmo-
sphere to dine in. Though it lacks ambience after the sun goes down, the food is high-quality, with specialties like parmesan-crusted ono, ahi poke spiked with a kukui-nut base, an excellent onion soup gratin, plus steak, burger, and chicken choices. Kid- and small group–friendly, the Tavern lends itself to a casual come-and-go vibe. $ *Average main: $25* ⊠ *5-3900 Kuhio Hwy, Princeville* ☎ *808/826–8700.*

THE EAST SIDE

Since the East Side is the island's largest population center, it makes sense that it should boast the widest selection of restaurants. It's also a good place to get both cheaper meals and the local-style cuisine that residents favor.

Most of the eateries are found along Kuhio Highway between Kapaa and Wailua; a few are tucked into shopping centers and resorts. In Lihue, it's easier to find lunch than dinner because many restaurants cater to the business crowd.

The Beach House on the South Shore is a prime spot to watch the sun set.

You'll find all the usual fast-food joints in both Kapaa and Lihue, as well as virtually every ethnic cuisine available on Kauai. Although fancy gourmet restaurants are less abundant in this part of the island, there's plenty of good, solid food, and a few stellar attractions. But unless you're staying on the East Side, or passing through, it's probably not worth the long drive from the North Shore or Poipu resorts to eat here.

KAPAA AND WAILUA

$ ✕ **Caffé Coco.** A restored plantation cottage set back off the highway
CAFÉ and surrounded by tropical foliage is the setting for this island café. You'll know it by its bright blue storefront. An attached black-light art gallery and an apparel shop called Bambulei make this a fun stop for any meal. Outdoor seating in the vine-covered garden is pleasant during nice weather, although on calm nights, it can get buggy. Acoustic music is offered regularly, attracting a laid-back local crowd. Potstickers filled with tofu and chutney, ahi wraps, Greek and organic salads, fresh fish and soups, and a daily list of specials are complemented by wonderful desserts. Allow plenty of time, because the tiny kitchen can't turn out meals quickly. $ *Average main: $15* ⊠ *4-369 Kuhio Hwy., Wailua* ☎ *808/822–7990* ⊘ *Closed Mon.*

$$ ✕ **Hukilau Lanai.** Relying heavily on super-fresh island fish and locally
AMERICAN grown vegetables, this restaurant offers quality food that is compe-
Fodor's Choice tently and creatively prepared. The fish—grilled, steamed, or sautéed
★ and served with succulent sauces—shines here. Other sound choices are the savory meat loaf and prime rib. Mac-nut crusted chicken and a few pasta dishes round out the menu. The ahi nachos appetizer is not to be missed, nor is the warm chocolate dessert soufflé. The spacious dining

room looks out to the ocean, and it's lovely to eat at the outdoor tables when the weather is nice. Overall, it's a solid choice on the East Side. $ *Average main: $23* ⊠ *Kauai Coast Resort, Coconut Marketplace, 520 Aleka Loop, Kapaa* ☎ *808/822–0600* ⊕ *www.hukilaukauai.com* ⊗ *No lunch. Closed Mon.*

$$ ✕ **Kauai Pasta.** If you don't mind a no-frills atmosphere for affordable
ITALIAN food, this is the place. The husband of the husband-and-wife team that runs the restaurant left his executive-chef position at Roy's to open a catering business. He leased a kitchen that happened to have a small dining area and gradually upgraded and expanded it. Rather than let it go to waste, they open for dinner every evening. Their specials are satisfying and delicious, and their 10-inch pizzettas make a fine meal for one. The locals have this place figured out; they show up in droves. The chic KP Lounge stays open late, offering a handsome hideout for tasty nighttime grinds and cocktails. There's a branch in Lihue that also serves lunch. $ *Average main: $18* ⊠ *4-939B Kuhio Hwy., Kapaa* ☎ *808/822–7447* ⊕ *www.kauaipasta.com* ⊗ *No lunch.*

$ ✕ **Kountry Kitchen.** If you're big on breakfast, try Kountry Kitchen, which
AMERICAN serves breakfast and lunch items until 1:30 pm daily. Across the street
ⓒ from the library in Kapaa, this family-friendly restaurant has a sunny interior, and a cozy, greasy-spoon atmosphere with friendly service. It is a great spot for omelets, banana pancakes, and eggs Benedict in two sizes. Lunch selections include sandwiches, burgers, and *loco mocos* (a popular local rice, beef, gravy, and eggs concoction). Take-out orders are also available. $ *Average main: $12* ⊠ *1485 Kuhio Hwy., Kapaa* ☎ *808/822–3511* ⊗ *No dinner.*

$ ✕ **Mema Thai Chinese Cuisine.** Refined and intimate, Mema Thai serves
THAI its dishes on crisp white linens accented by tabletop orchid sprays. Menu items such as broccoli with oyster sauce and cashew chicken reveal Chinese origins, but the emphasis is on Thai dishes. A host of curries—red, green, yellow, and house—made with coconut milk and kaffir-lime leaves run from mild to mouth searing. The traditional green-papaya salad adds a cool touch for the palate. $ *Average main: $14* ⊠ *Wailua Shopping Plaza, 369 Kuhio Hwy., Kapaa* ☎ *808/823–0899* ⊗ *No lunch weekends.*

$ ✕ **Mermaid's Café.** Sit and watch as your meal is prepared at this café
ECLECTIC in Kapaa. The small yet diverse menu of sophisticated dishes features homemade sauces and local ingredients. Try the ahi nori wrap with fresh seared tuna, rice, cucumber, and wasabi cream sauce with pickled ginger and soy sauce—their most popular pick. Other dishes include rice, fresh vegetables, and either tofu or chicken served with a peanut sauce or coconut curry sauce. Everything can be made either vegetarian or vegan. Fish is caught daily by local fisherman, and produce is grown on the island. $ *Average main: $9* ⊠ *1384 Kuhio Hwy., Kapaa* ☎ *808/821–2026.*

$$ ✕ **Restaurant Kintaro.** If you want to eat someplace that's a favorite with
JAPANESE locals, visit Kintaro's. But be prepared to wait on weekends, because
Fodor'sChoice the dining room and sushi bar are always busy. Try the unbeatable
★ Bali Hi Bomb, a roll of crab and smoked salmon, baked and topped with wasabi mayonnaise. For an "all-in-one-dish" meal, consider the

Some of the best eats on Kauai come from the sea. Ask what the local catch of the day is for the freshest option.

Yosenabe, a single pot filled with a healthful variety of seafood and vegetables. *Teppanyaki* dinners are meat, seafood, and vegetables flash-cooked on tabletop grills in an entertaining display. Tatami-mat seating is available behind shoji screens that provide privacy for groups. Like many longtime restaurants, it's an enduring favorite. [$] *Average main: $22* ✉ *4-370 Kuhio Hwy., Wailua* ☎ *808/822–3341* 🕒 *No lunch. Closed Sun.*

$ SEAFOOD 🍴 **Wailua Marina Restaurant.** Offering the island's only river view, this marina restaurant—an island fixture for almost 40 years—is a good spot to stop for lunch after a boat ride up the Wailua River to the Fern Grotto, and worth a visit on its own merit. With more than 40 selections, the menu is a mix of comfort food and more sophisticated dishes; portions are gigantic. The chef is fond of stuffing: You'll find stuffed baked pork chops, stuffed chicken baked in plum sauce, and ahi stuffed with crab. The steamed mullet is a classic island dish. [$] *Average main: $17* ✉ *Wailua River State Park, Wailua Rd., Wailua* ☎ *808/822–4311* 🕒 *Closed Mon.*

LIHUE

$$ ITALIAN 🍴 **Café Portofino.** The menu at this mostly authentic northern Italian restaurant is as impressive as the views of Kalapaki Bay and the Hauupu range. Owner Giuseppe Avocadi's better-sounding-than-tasting dishes have managed to garner a host of culinary awards and raves from dining critics. The fresh ahi carpaccio is a signature dish, and pasta, scampi, and veal are enhanced by sauces. Linger over coffee and ice cream-filled profiteroles or traditional tiramisu while enjoying romantic harp music. Solid service and a soothing, dignified ambience complete the dining

experience, making this a great place for a date if only the food was better and wine less overpriced. $ *Average main: $25* ✉ *Kauai Marriott Resort & Beach Club, 3610 Rice St., Kalipaki Beach.*

$ ✗ **Dani's Restaurant.** Kauai residents frequent this big, sparsely fur-
HAWAIIAN   nished eatery near the Lihue Fire Station for hearty, local-style at breakfast and lunch. Dani's is a good place to try traditional luau cuisine without commercial luau prices. You can order Hawaiian-style *laulau* (pork and taro leaves wrapped in ti leaves and steamed) or kalua pig, slow roasted in an underground oven. Other island-style dishes include Japanese-prepared *tonkatsu* (pork cutlet) and teriyaki beef, and there's always the all-American New York steak. Omelets are whipped up with fish cake, kalua pig, or seafood; everything is served with rice. $ *Average main: $8* ✉ *4201 Rice St.* ☎ *808/245–4991* ⊗ *Closed Sun. No dinner.*

$$ ✗ **Duke's Canoe Club.** Surfing legend Duke Kahanamoku is immortal-
SEAFOOD   ized at this casual bi-level restaurant set on Kalapaki Bay. Guests can admire surfboards, photos, and other memorabilia marking the Duke's long tenure as a waterman. It's an interesting collection, and an indoor garden and waterfall add to the pleasing sights. You'll find simple fare ranging from fish tacos and stir-fried cashew chicken to hamburgers, served 11 am to 11 pm. At dinner, fresh fish prepared in a variety of styles is the best choice. Duke's claims to have the biggest salad bar on the island, though given the lack of competition, that isn't saying much. A happy-hour drink and appetizer is a less expensive way to enjoy the moonrises and ocean views here—though it can get pretty crowded. The Barefoot Bar is a hot spot for after-dinner drinks, too. $ *Average main: $25* ✉ *Kauai Marriott Resort & Beach Club, 3610 Rice St., Kalapaki Beach* ☎ *808/246–9599* ⊕ *www.dukeskauai.com.*

$$$ ✗ **Gaylord's.** This restaurant recently received a welcome overhaul.
ECLECTIC   Located in what was at one time Kauai's most expensive plantation estate, Gaylord's pays tribute to the elegant dining rooms of 1930s high society. Tables with candlelight sit on a cobblestone patio surrounding a fountain and overlooking a wide lawn. The sustainability-minded menu features classic American cooking with a focus on locally produced ingredients. Try the quiche ceviche with avocado and citrus, followed with a Wailua lamb chop, stuffed eggplant or Aakukui Ranch beef tenderloin with gorgonzola-stuffed potato cake. Lunches feature the tasty (grilled eggplant and peppers with pickled vegetables, rouille, and smoked provolone) and the daily burger, the chef's "whimsical preparation" of ground local meat. The lavish Sunday brunch includes a variety of eggs Benedict offerings in addition to standard omelets with farm-fresh eggs and a pancake station. Before or after dining you can wander around the estate grounds. $ *Average main: $27* ✉ *Kilohana Plantation, 3-2087 Kaumualii Hwy* ☎ *808/245–9593* ⊕ *www.gaylordskauai.com.*

$ ✗ **Hamura Saimin.** Folks just love this funky old plantation-style diner.
HAWAIIAN   Locals and tourists stream in and out all day long, and Neighbor Islanders stop in on their way to the airport to pick up take-out orders for friends and family back home. *Saimin* is the big draw, and each day the Hiraoka family dishes up about 1,000 bowls of steaming broth

and homemade noodles, topped with a variety of garnishes. The barbecued chicken and meat sticks adopt a smoky flavor during grilling. The landmark eatery is also famous for its *lilikoi* (passion fruit) chiffon pie. ■ TIP→ **As one of the few island restaurants open late, until 8:30 pm on weeknights and midnight on Friday and Saturday, it's favored by night owls.** [$] *Average main: $7* ✉ *2956 Kress St.* ☎ *808/245–3271* 💳 *No credit cards.*

$ JAPANESE 🍴 **Hanamaulu Restaurant, Tea House, Sushi Bar, and Robatayaki.** Business is brisk at this landmark Kauai eatery. The food is a mix of Japanese, Chinese, and local-style cooking, served up in hearty portions. The ginger chicken and fried shrimp are wildly popular, as are the fresh sashimi and sushi. Other choices include tempura, chicken *katsu* (Japanese-style fried chicken), beef broccoli, and *robatayaki* (grilled seafood and meat). The main dining room is rather unattractive, but the private rooms in back look out on the Japanese garden and fishponds and feature traditional seating on tatami mats at low tables. These tearooms can be reserved and are favored for family events and celebrations. [$] *Average main: $12* ✉ *3-4291 Kuhio Hwy., Hanamaulu* ☎ *808/245–2511* 🕐 *Closed Mon.*

$$ AMERICAN 🍴 **JJ's Broiler.** This spacious, low-key restaurant serves hearty fare, with dinner specials such as lobster and Slavonic steak, a broiled sliced tenderloin dipped in buttery wine sauce. On sunny afternoons, ask for a table on the lanai overlooking Kalapaki Bay and try one of the generous salads. The upstairs section is currently only available for private events, but you can still eat at the restaurant's lower level, which is open-air and casual. JJ's is a relaxed place to enjoy lunch, dinner, or just sit at the bar for a drink, with one of the best ocean views in Lihue. [$] *Average main: $25* ✉ *Anchor Cove, 3416 Rice St., Nawiliwili* ☎ *808/246–4422* 🌐 *www.jjsbroiler.com.*

$ AMERICAN 🍴 **Kalapaki Joe's.** Hit the original Kalapaki Joe's down in Nawiliwili for happy hour and enjoy 25-cent wings and $3 fish tacos at this well-situated sports bar. Whoop it up with the crowd of locals and tourists watching everything from football to rugby on strategically placed TVs. Stay for dinner to have generous portions of sports bars fare, plus local fish dishes including an excellent seared ahi sashimi plate, and take in the postcard-perfect view of Kalapaki Bay. [$] *Average main: $13* ✉ *3501 Rice St, #208* ☎ *808/245-6266.*

$ AMERICAN 🍴 **Lihue Barbecue Inn.** Few Kauai restaurants are more beloved than this family-owned eatery, a mainstay of island dining since 1940. The menu runs from traditional American to Asian. The dishes are decent but nothing to send a postcard home about. Try the baby back ribs, or fried *loco moco*, or choose a full Japanese dinner from the other side of the menu. If you can't make up your mind, strike a compromise with the inn's tri-sampler. Opt for the fruit cup—fresh, not canned—instead of soup or salad, and save room for a hefty slice of homemade cream pie, available in all sorts of flavors. [$] *Average main: $15* ✉ *2982 Kress St.* ☎ *808/245–2921* 🕐 *Closed Sun.*

THE SOUTH SHORE

Most South Shore restaurants are more upscale and located within the Poipu resorts. If you're looking for a gourmet meal in a classy setting, the South Shore is where you'll find it. Poipu has a number of excellent restaurants in dreamy settings and decidedly fewer family-style, lower-price eateries.

$$$
AMERICAN
Fodor'sChoice
★

✕ **Beach House.** This restaurant partners a dreamy ocean view with impressive cuisine. Few Kauai experiences are more delightful than sitting at one of the outside tables and savoring a delectable meal while the sun sinks into the glassy blue Pacific. It's the epitome of tropical dining, and no other restaurant on Kauai can offer anything quite like it. Chef Robin Moe's menu changes often, but the food is consistently creative and delicious. A few trademark dishes appear regularly, such as mint-coriander lamb rack, fire-roasted ahi, and lemongrass and kaffir-lime sea scallops. Seared macadamia-nut-crusted mahimahi, a dish ubiquitous on island menus, gets a refreshing new twist when served with a *lilikoi* (passion fruit)–lemongrass beurre blanc. Save room for the signature molten chocolate desire, a decadent finale at this pleasing and deservedly popular restaurant. $ *Average main: $30* ⊠ *5022 Lawai Rd., Koloa 808/742–1424* ⊕ *www.the-beach-house.com* ⚐ *Reservations essential* ⊗ *No lunch.*

$$$
STEAKHOUSE

✕ **Brennecke's Beach Broiler.** Brennecke's is decidedly casual and fun, with a busy bar, windows overlooking the beach, and a cheery blue-and-white interior. It specializes in big portions in a wide range of offerings including rib-eye steak, prime rib, crab legs, shrimp, and the fresh catch of the day. Can't decide? Then, create your own combination meal. This place is especially good for happy hours (3 pm to 5 pm and 8 to 9:30), as the drink and pupu menus bring the prices closer to reality. The fare is fair, but the ocean view and convenient location compensate for the food's shortcomings. There's a take-out deli downstairs. $ *Average main: $27* ⊠ *2100 Hoone Rd., Poipu* ☎ *808/742–7588* ⊕ *www.brenneckes.com.*

$$
ITALIAN

✕ **Casa di Amici.** Tucked away in a quiet neighborhood above Poipu Beach, this "House of Friends" has live classical piano music on Saturday nights and an outside deck open to sweeping ocean views. Entrées from the internationally eclectic menu include a saffron-vanilla paella risotto made with black tiger prawns, fresh fish, chicken breast, and homemade Italian sausage. For dessert, take the plunge with a baked Hawaii: a chocolate-macadamia-nut brownie topped with coconut and passion-fruit sorbet and flambéed Italian meringue. $ *Average main: $25* ⊠ *2301 Nalo Rd., Poipu* ☎ *808/742–1555* ⊕ *www.casadiamici.com* ⊗ *No lunch.*

$$$
ITALIAN
Fodor'sChoice
★

✕ **Dondero's.** The inlaid marble floors, ornate tile work, and Italianate murals that compose the elegant interior at this restaurant compete with a stunning ocean view. In addition to the beautiful setting, Dondero's offers outstanding food, a remarkable wine list, and impeccable service, making this one of Kauai's best restaurants. Chef Patrick Shimada's elegant tasting menu features Italian dishes, including homemade pastas, risotto, and flatbread pizza. Try the four-cheese risotto

Continued on page 567

LUAU: A TASTE OF HAWAII

The best place to sample Hawaiian food is at a backyard luau. Aunts and uncles are cooking, the pig is from a cousin's farm, and the fish is from a brother's boat.

But even locals have to angle for invitations to those rare occasions. So your choice is most likely between a commercial luau and a Hawaiian restaurant.

Some commercial luau are less authentic; they offer little of the traditional diet and are more about umbrella drinks, spectacle, and fun.

For greater authenticity, folksy experiences, and rock-bottom prices, visit a Hawaiian restaurant (most are in anonymous storefronts in residential neighborhoods). Expect rough edges and some effort negotiating the menu.

In either case, much of what is known today as Hawaiian food would be as foreign to a 16th-century Hawaiian as risotto or chow mien. The pre-contact diet was simple and healthy—mainly raw and steamed seafood and vegetables. Early Hawaiians used earth ovens and heated stones to cook seafood, taro, sweet potatoes, and breadfruit and seasoned their food with sea salt and ground kukui nuts. Seaweed, fern shoots, sweet potato vines, coconut, banana, sugarcane, and select greens and roots rounded out the diet.

Successive waves of immigrants added their favorites to the ti leaf–lined table. So it is that foods as disparate as salt salmon and chicken long rice are now Hawaiian—even though there is no salmon in Hawaiian waters and long rice (cellophane noodles) is Chinese.

AT THE LUAU: KALUA PORK

The heart of any luau is the *imu*, the earth oven in which a whole pig is roasted. The preparation of an imu is an arduous affair for most families, who tackle it only once a year or so, for a baby's first birthday or at Thanksgiving, when many Islanders prefer to imu their turkeys. Commercial luau operations have it down to a science, however.

THE ART OF THE STONE

The key to a proper imu is the *pohaku*, the stones. Imu cook by means of long, slow, moist heat released by special stones that can withstand a hot fire without exploding. Many Hawaiian families treasure their imu stones, keeping them in a pile in the backyard and passing them on through generations.

PIT COOKING

The imu makers first dig a pit about the size of a re-frigerator, then lay down *kiawe* (mesquite) wood and stones, and build a white-hot fire that is allowed to burn itself out. The ashes are raked away, and the hot stones covered with banana and ti leaves. Well-wrapped in ti or banana leaves and a net of chicken wire, the pig is lowered onto the leaf-covered stones. *Laulau* (leaf-wrapped bundles of meats, fish, and taro leaves) may also be placed inside. Leaves—ti, banana, even ginger—cover the pig followed by wet burlap sacks (to create steam). The whole is topped with a canvas tarp and left to steam for the better part of a day.

OPENING THE IMU

This is the moment everyone waits for: The imu is unwrapped like a giant present and the imu keep-ers gingerly wrestle out the steaming pig. When it's unwrapped, the meat falls moist and smoky-flavored from the bone, looking just like Southern-style pulled pork, but without the barbecue sauce.

WHICH LUAU?

Grand Hyatt Kauai Luau. Choose this oceanfront luau if it's a romantic evening you're after.

Luau Kalamaku. This luau is on a former sugar planta-tion and has a more theatrical style than the resort type.

Paina o Hanalei. Lavish, with upscale Pacific Rim cuisine.

Smith's Tropical Paradise. Our top pick, set on a lovely 30-acre tropical garden.

MEA AI ONO.
GOOD THINGS TO EAT.

LAULAU
Steamed meats, fish, and taro leaf in ti-leaf bundles: fork-tender, a medley of flavors; the taro resembles spinach.

Laulau

LOMI LOMI SALMON
Salt salmon in a piquant salad or relish with onions, tomatoes.

POI
Poi, a paste made of pounded taro root, may be an acquired taste, but it's a must-try during your visit.

Consider: The Hawaiian Adam is descended from *kalo* (taro). Young taro plants are called "keiki"–children. Poi is the first food after mother's milk for many Islanders. Ai, the word for food, is synonymous with poi in many contexts.

Lomi Lomi Salmon

Not only that, we love it. "There is no meat that doesn't taste good with poi," the old Hawaiians said.

But you have to know how to eat it: with something rich or powerfully flavored. "It is salt that makes the poi go in," is another adage. When you're served poi, try it with a mouthful of smoky kalua pork or salty lomi lomi salmon. Its slightly sour blandness cleanses the palate. And if you don't like it, smile and say something polite. (And slide that bowl over to a local.)

Poi

E HELE MAI AI! COME AND EAT!

Hawaiian restaurants tend to be inconveniently located in well-worn storefronts with little or no parking, outfitted with battered tables and clattering Melmac dishes, but they personify aloha, invariably run by local families who welcome tourists who take the trouble to find them.

Many are cash-only operations and combination plates are a standard feature: one or two entrées, a side such as chicken long rice, choice of poi or steamed rice and—if the place is really old-style—a tiny portion of coarse Hawaiian salt and some raw onions for relish.

Most serve some foods that aren't, strictly speaking, Hawaiian, but are beloved of ka-maaina, such as salt meat with watercress (preserved meat in a tasty broth), or *akubone*

(skipjack tuna fried in a tangy vinegar sauce).

Our favorite: **Dani's Restaurant** (✉ 4201 Rice St., Lihue, ☎ 808/245–4991).

MENU GUIDE

Much of the Hawaiian language encountered during a stay in the Islands will appear on restaurant menus and lists of luau fare. Here's a quick primer.

ahi: *yellowfin tuna.*

aku: *skipjack, bonito tuna.*

amaama: *mullet; it's hard to get but tasty.*

bento: *a box lunch.*

chicken luau: *a stew made from chicken, taro leaves, and coconut milk.*

haupia: *a light, pudding-like sweet made from coconut.*

imu: *the underground oven in which pigs are roasted for luau.*

kalua: *to bake underground.*

kau kau: *food. The word comes from Chinese but is used in the Islands.*

kimchee: *Korean dish of pickled cabbage made with garlic and hot peppers.*

Kona coffee: *coffee grown in the Kona district of the Big Island.*

laulau: *literally, a bundle. Laulau are morsels of pork, chicken, butterfish, or other ingredients wrapped with young taro leaves and then bundled in ti leaves for steaming.*

lilikoi: *passion fruit, a tart, seedy yellow fruit that makes delicious desserts, juice, and jellies.*

lomi lomi: *to rub or massage; also a massage. Lomi lomi salmon is fish that has been rubbed with onions and herbs; commonly served with minced onions and tomatoes.*

luau: *a Hawaiian feast; also the leaf of the taro plant used in preparing such a feast.*

luau leaves: *cooked taro tops with a taste similar to spinach.*

mahimahi: *mild-flavored dolphinfish, not the marine mammal.*

mai tai: *potent rum drink with orange liqueurs and pineapple juice, from the Tahitian word for "good."*

malasada: *a Portuguese deep-fried doughnut without a hole, dipped in sugar.*

manapua: *steamed chinese buns filled with pork, chicken, or other fillings.*

mano: *shark.*

niu: *coconut.*

onaga: *pink or red snapper.*

ono: *a long, slender mackerel-like fish; also called wahoo.*

ono: *delicious; also hungry.*

opihi: *a tiny shellfish, or mollusk, found on rocks; also called limpets.*

papio: *a young ulua or jack fish.*

poha: *Cape gooseberry. Tasting a bit like honey, the poha berry is often used in jams and desserts.*

poi: *a paste made from pounded taro root, a staple of the Hawaiian diet.*

poke: *cubed raw tuna or other fish, tossed with seaweed and seasonings.*

pupu: *appetizers or small plates.*

saimin: *long thin noodles and vegetables in broth, often garnished with small pieces of fish cake, scrambled egg, luncheon meat, and green onion.*

sashimi: *raw fish thinly sliced and usually eaten with soy sauce.*

ti leaves: *a member of the agave family. The leaves are used to wrap food while cooking and removed before eating.*

uku: *deep-sea snapper.*

ulua: *a member of the jack family that also includes pompano and amberjack. Also called crevalle, jack fish, and jack crevalle.*

with Kauai cherry tomatoes, or the grilled Pacific swordfish filet, served with oregeno, lemon, olive oil, and baby bell pepper relish. The waitstaff deserves special praise for its thoughtful, discrete service. $ *Average main: $33* ⊠ *Grand Hyatt Kauai Resort and Spa, 1571 Poipu Rd., Koloa* ☎ *808/240–6456* ◷ *No lunch.*

$ ✕ **Joe's on the Green.** Eat an open-air breakfast or lunch with an expan-
AMERICAN sive vista of Poipu. Located on the Kiahuna Golf Course, this restaurant boasts such favorites as eggs Benedict, tofu scramble, and banana-macadamia-nut pancakes. For lunch, try the Reuben sandwich or ribs, or build your own salad. The small-plates menu and happy-hour drink specials are available from 3 to 6, including favorites such as herb and garlic chicken skewers, seared ahi tacos, and homemade chili nachos, all accompanied by live Hawaiian music. With a casual atmosphere and generous portions, Joe's is a refreshing alternative to the pricier hotel brunch venues in this area. $ *Average main: $11* ⊠ *2545 Kiahuna Plantation Dr., Poipu* ☎ *808/742–9696* ◷ *No dinner.*

$$$ ✕ **Josselin's Tapas Bar and Grill.** Chef Jean-Marie Josselin, one of the
CONTEMPORARY pioneers of Hawaiian regional cuisine, has a winner with this local favorite. After the roaming sangria cart rolls up with concoctions containing lilikoi and lychee, the feast is on. Daily selections depend on local availability, but there's a wide range of Hawaiian-influenced, Asian and Western choices to satisfy all palates. The ahi poke and sashimi dish is special but the menu also features more traditional steak and lamb options. But the fun is in savoring the variety of complex smaller plates. $ *Average main: $30* ⊠ *2829 Ala Kalani Kaumaka, St, Koloa* ☎ *808/742-7117.*

$$ ✕ **Keoki's Paradise.** Built to resemble a dockside boathouse, this active,
STEAKHOUSE boisterous place fills up quickly at night thanks to the live music. Sea-
◷ food appetizers span the tide from sashimi to Thai shrimp sticks, crab cakes, and scallops crusted in *panko* (Japanese-style bread crumbs). The day's fresh catch is available in half a dozen styles and sauces. And there's a sampling of beef, chicken, and pork-rib entrées for the committed carnivore. A lighter menu is available at the bar for lunch and dinner. $ *Average main: $25* ⊠ *Poipu Shopping Village, 2360 Kiahuna Plantation Dr., Koloa* ☎ *808/742–7534* ⊕ *www.keokisparadise.com.*

$$ ✕ **Plantation Gardens.** A historic plantation manager's home has been
ITALIAN converted to a restaurant that serves seafood and kiawe-grilled meats with a Pacific Rim and Italian influence. You'll walk through a tropical setting of torch-lighted orchid gardens and lotus-studded koi ponds to a cozy, European-style dining room with cherry wood floors and a veranda. The menu is based on fresh, local foods: fish right off the boat, herbs and produce picked from the plantation's gardens, fruit delivered by neighborhood farmers. The result is cuisine with an island flair—seafood *laulau* (seafood wrapped in ti leaves and steamed)—served alongside traditional classics such as sugar-cane-skewered pork tenderloin. Definitely save room for dessert: The lilikoi cheesecake is a dream. In short, the food is excellent and the setting charming. $ *Average main: $24* ⊠ *Kiahuna Plantation, 2253 Poipu Rd., Koloa* ☎ *808/742-2121* ⊕ *www.pgrestaurant.com* ◷ *No lunch.*

$$ ITALIAN 🍴 **Pomodoro Ristorante Italiano.** Two walls of windows brighten this intimate second-story restaurant in the heart of Kalaheo, where there's good food at reasonable prices. Begin with prosciutto and melon, then proceed directly to the multilayer meat lasagna, a favorite of the chefs—two Italian-born brothers. Other highlights include eggplant or veal parmigiana, chicken saltimbocca, and scampi in a garlic, caper, and white wine sauce. [$] *Average main: $20* ✉ *Rainbow Plaza, Kaumualii Hwy., Kalaheo* ☎ *808/332–5945* 🕓 *Closed Sun. No lunch.*

$$$ MODERN HAWAIIAN 🍴 **Roy's Poipu Bar & Grill.** Hawaii's culinary superstar, Roy Yamaguchi, is fond of sharing his signature Hawaiian fusion cuisine by cloning the successful Honolulu restaurant where he got his start. You'll find one of these copycat eateries on Kauai's South Side in a shopping-center locale that feels too small and ordinary for the exotic food. The menu changes daily, and the hardworking kitchen staff dreams up 5 to 10 (or more) specials each night—an impressive feat. Though the food reflects the imaginative pairings and high-quality ingredients of the original Roy's and the presentation is spectacular, the atmosphere is a little different. As with most restaurant branches, it just doesn't have the heart and soul of the original. [$] *Average main: $35* ✉ *Poipu Shopping Village, 2360 Kiahuna Plantation Dr., Koloa* ☎ *808/742–5000* 🌐 *www.roysrestaurant.com* 🕓 *No lunch.*

$$$ SEAFOOD 🍴 **Tidepools.** The Grand Hyatt Kauai is notable for its excellent restaurants, which differ widely in their settings and cuisine. This one is definitely the most tropical and campy, sure to appeal to folks seeking a bit of island-style romance and adventure. Private grass-thatch huts seem to float on a koi-filled pond beneath starry skies while torches flicker in the lushly landscaped grounds nearby. The equally distinctive food has an island flavor that comes from the chef's advocacy of Hawaii Regional Cuisine and extensive use of Kauai-grown products including fresh herbs from the resort's organic garden. You won't go wrong ordering one of the signature dishes, such as the Hawaiian opah with a tangerine yuzu sauce; macadamia-nut crusted mahimahi; or the Hawaiian-salt and garlic-rubbed prime rib. Start with Tidepools' pupu platter for two—with a crab cake, Kauai shrimp, and ahi sashimi—to wake up your taste buds. If you're still hungry at the end of the meal, the molten chocolate lava cake is sure to satisfy. [$] *Average main: $33* ✉ *Grand Hyatt Kauai Resort and Spa, 1571 Poipu Rd., Koloa* ☎ *808/240–6456* 🕓 *No lunch.*

THE WEST SIDE

West Side eateries tend to be more local-style and are generally found along Kaumualii Highway. Pickings start to get slimmer the farther west you travel, and dining choices often are dictated by what's open. Fortunately, West Side restaurants are generally worth patronizing, so you won't go too far wrong if your hunger demands to be satisfied while you're out enjoying the sights.

$$ STEAKHOUSE 🍴 **Wrangler's Steakhouse.** Denim-covered seating, decorative saddles, and a stagecoach in a loft helped to transform the historic Ako General Store in Waimea into a West Side steak house. You can eat under the

BEST BETS FOR KAUA'I LODGING

Fodor'sChoice★	By Price	$$
Grand Hyatt Kauai Resort and Spa, $$$$, p. 577	**$**	**Aston Aloha Beach Hotel**, p. 573
Waimea Plantation Cottages, $, p. 580	**Garden Island Inn**, p. 576	**Hanalei Bay Resort**, p. 570
Sheraton Kauai Resort, $$$$, p. 580	**Kauai Coast Resort**, p. 573	**Hanalei Colony Resort**, p. 570
St. Regis Princeville Resort, $$$$, p. 571	**Kokee Lodge**, p. 580	**Hotel Coral Reef**, p. 573
	Plantation Hale Suites, p. 576	**$$$$**
	Poipu Plantation Resort, p. 577	**Grand Hyatt Kauai Resort and Spa**, p. 577
	Poipu Shores, p. 577	**St. Regis Princeville Resort**, p. 571
	Rosewood Bed and Breakfast, p. 576	**Whalers Cove**, p. 580
	Waimea Plantation Cottages, p. 580	

stars on the deck out back or inside the old-fashioned, wood-panel dining room. The 16-ounce New York steak comes sizzling, and the rib eye is served with capers. A tasty salad is part of each meal. Those with smaller appetites might consider the vegetarian or Japanese-style tempura or the ahi served on penne pasta. Local folks love the special lunch: rice, beef teriyaki, and shrimp tempura with kimchee served in a three-tier *kaukau* tin, or lunch pail, just like the ones sugar-plantation workers once carried. A gift shop has local crafts. $ *Average main: $25* ✉ *9852 Kaumualii Hwy., Waimea* ☎ *808/338–1218* ⊕ *wranglersrestaurant.com* ☾ *Closed Sun.*

WHERE TO STAY

Updated by
Charles E.
Roessler

The Garden Isle has lodgings for every taste, from swanky resorts to rustic cabins, and from family-friendly condos to romantic bed-and-breakfasts. The savvy traveler can also find inexpensive places that are convenient, safe, and accessible to Kauai's special places and activities.

When you're choosing a place to stay, location is an important consideration. Kauai may seem small on a map, but because it's circular with no through roads, it can take more time than you think to get from place to place. If at all possible, stay close to your desired activities. This way, you'll save time to squeeze in all the things you'll want to do.

Time of year is also a factor. If you're here in winter or spring, consider staying on the South Shore, as the surf on the North Shore and East Side tends to be rough, making many ocean beaches too rough for swimming or water sports.

Where to Stay on the North Shore

Before booking accommodations, think hard about what kind of experience you want to have for your island vacation. There are several top-notch resorts to choose from, and Kauai also has a wide variety of condos, vacation rentals, and bed-and-breakfasts. The Kauai Visitors Bureau provides a comprehensive listing of accommodation choices to help you decide.

Prices shown in reviews are the lowest price of a standard double room in high season. Rental prices are the one-bedroom rate per night.

For expanded hotel reviews, visit Fodors.com.

THE NORTH SHORE

$$ **Hanalei Bay Resort.** This time-share condominium resort has a lovely
RESORT   location overlooking Hanalei Bay and Napali Coast. **Pros:** beautiful views; tennis courts on property; tropical pool. **Cons:** steep walkways; long walk to beach. **TripAdvisor:** "great pool," "a little bit of heaven," "beautiful view." *$ Rooms from: $225 ⊠ 5380 Honoiki Rd., Princeville* ☎ *808/826–6522, 866/507–1428* ⊕ *www.hanaleibayresort.com* ⤵ *134 units.*

$$ **Hanalei Colony Resort.** This 5-acre property, the only true beachfront
HOTEL   resort on Kauai's North Shore, is a laid-back, go-barefoot kind of place

WHERE TO STAY IN KAUAI

	Local Vibe	Pros	Cons
The North Shore	Properties here have the "wow" factor with ocean and mountain beauty; laid-back Hanalei and Princeville set the high-end pace.	When the weather is good (summer) this side has it all. Epic winter surf, gorgeous waterfalls, and verdant vistas create some of the best scenery in Hawaii.	Lots of rain (being green has a cost) means you may have to travel south to find the sun; expensive restaurants and shopping offer few deals.
The East Side	The most reasonably priced area to stay for the practical traveler; lacks the pizzazz of expensive resorts on North and South shores; more traditional Hawaiian hotels.	The best travel deals show up here; more direct access to the local population; plenty of decent restaurants with good variety, along with delis in food stores.	Beaches aren't the greatest (rocky, reefy) at many of the lodging spots; bad traffic at times; some crime issues in parks.
The South Shore	Resort central; plenty of choices where the consistent sunshine is perfect for those who want to do nothing but play golf or tennis and read a book by the pool.	Beautiful in its own right; many enchanted evenings with stellar sunsets; summer surf easier for beginners to handle.	Some areas are deserty with scrub brush; construction can be brutal on piece of mind.
The West Side	There are few options for lodging in this mostly untouristlike setting with contrasts such as the extreme heat of a July day in Waimea to a frozen winter night up in Kokee.	A gateway area for exploration into the wilds of Kokee or for boating trips on Napali Coast; main hub for boat and helicopter trips; outstanding sunsets.	Least convenient side for most visitors; daytime is languid and dry; river runoff can ruin ocean's clarity.

5

sandwiched between towering mountains and the sea. **Pros:** oceanfront setting; private, quiet; seventh night free. **Cons:** remote location; damp in winter. **TripAdvisor:** "picture-perfect paradise," "great privacy," "a view that can't be beat." [$] *Rooms from: $255* ✉ *5-7130 Kuhio Hwy., Haena* ☎ *808/826–6235, 800/628–3004* 🌐 *www.hcr.com* 🛏 *48 units.*

$ RENTAL 🏨 **Hanalei Inn.** If you're looking for low-priced lodgings a block from gorgeous Hanalei Bay, look no further, as this is the only choice. **Pros:** quick walk to beach. **Cons:** strict cancellation policy; very modest amenities; daytime traffic noise. **TripAdvisor:** "very comfortable and relaxing," "best place on Earth," "good location." [$] *Rooms from: $139* ✉ *5-5468 Kuhio Hwy., Hanalei* ☎ *808/826–9333* 🌐 *www.hanaleiinn.com* 🛏 *4 studios.*

$$$$ RESORT Fodor's Choice ★ 🏨 **St. Regis Princeville Resort.** Built into the cliffs above Hanalei Bay, this unbeatable Starwood resort offers expansive views of the sea and mountains, including Makana, the landmark peak immortalized as the mysterious Bali Hai island in the film *South Pacific*. **Pros:** great views; excellent restaurants; attractive lobby; professional staff. **Cons:** minimal grounds; reefy beach for swimming. **TripAdvisor:** "magical location," "most beautiful view in the world," "strong customer service." [$] *Rooms from:*

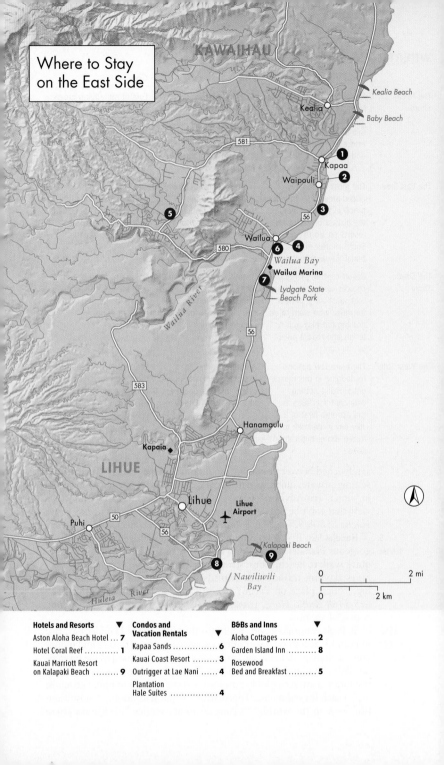

Where to Stay on the East Side

Kealia Beach

Baby Beach

KAWAIHAU

Kealia

581

Kapaa ❶

Waipouli ❷

56

❸

581

Wailua

580

❻ ❹

Wailua Bay

◆ Wailua Marina

❼

Lydgate State Beach Park

Wailua River

56

583

Hanamaulu

Kapaia ◆

LIHUE

Lihue

✈ Lihue Airport

Puhi

50

56

Kalapaki Beach

❽ ❾

Nawiliwili Bay

Huleia River

| 0 | | 2 mi |
| 0 | | 2 km |

$1,000 ✉ 5520 Ka Haku Rd., Princeville ☎ 877/787–3447, 808/826–9644 🌐 www.stregisprinceville.com 🛏 201 rooms, 51 suites.

THE EAST SIDE

KAPAA AND WAILUA

$$$$ RENTAL 🏨 **Aloha Cottages.** Owners Charlie and Susan Hoerner restored a three-bedroom plantation home on Kapaa's Baby Beach to reflect the charm of yesteryear with the conveniences of today. **Pros:** comfortable, home-like ambience; good for large groups; safe children's beach. **Cons:** can be windy at times; not great for swimming. **TripAdvisor:** "laid-back," "lush garden retreat," "clean with good view." [$] *Rooms from: $371 ✉ 1041 Moana Kai Rd., Kapaa ☎ 808/823–0933, 877/915–1015 🌐 www.alohacottages.com 🛏 2 cottages.*

$$ RESORT 🏨 **Aston Aloha Beach Hotel.** Nestled alongside Wailua Bay and the Wailua River, this low-key, low-rise resort is an easy, convenient place to stay. **Pros:** excellent cultural program; walk to beach and park; convenient locale. **Cons:** exiting hotel parking lot onto highway can be difficult; restaurant meals are average. **TripAdvisor:** "nice grounds," "cool old hotel by beach," "clean and affordable." [$] *Rooms from: $201 ✉ 3-5920 Kuhio Hwy., Kapaa ☎ 808/823–6000, 888/823–5111 🌐 www.astonhotels.com 🛏 216 rooms, 10 suites, 24 beach cottages.*

$$ HOTEL 🦢 🏨 **Hotel Coral Reef.** Coral Reef has been in business since the 1960s and is something of a beachfront landmark. **Pros:** nice pool; sauna; oceanfront setting; convenient location. **Cons:** located in a busy section of Kapaa; ocean swimming is marginal. **TripAdvisor:** "small and excellent," "paradise found," "great view." [$] *Rooms from: $245 ✉ 4-1516 Kuhio Hwy., Kapaa ☎ 808/822–4481, 800/843–4659 🌐 www.hotelcoralreefresort.com 🛏 19 rooms, 2 suites.*

$ RENTAL 🏨 **Kapaa Sands.** An old rock etched with *kanji,* Japanese characters, reminds you that the site of this condominium gem was formerly occupied by a Shinto temple. **Pros:** discounts for extended stays; walking distance to shops, restaurants, and beach; turtle and monk seal sightings common. **Cons:** no-frills lodging; traffic noise in mountain-facing units. **TripAdvisor:** "wonderful condo," "a bargain gem," "well furnished." [$] *Rooms from: $135 ✉ 380 Papaloa Rd., Kapaa ☎ 808/822–4901, 800/222–4901 🌐 www.kapaasands.com 🛏 21 units.*

$ RENTAL 🏨 **Kauai Coast Resort.** Fronting an uncrowded stretch of beach, this three-story primarily time-share resort is convenient and a bit more upscale than nearby properties. **Pros:** lovely pool; excellent restaurant; convenient. **Cons:** area is a bit touristy. **TripAdvisor:** "wonderful room," "restful stay," "exceptionally maintained." [$] *Rooms from: $135 ✉ 520 Aleka Loop, Kapaa ☎ 808/822–3441, 866/678–3289 🌐 www.shellhospitality.com 🛏 108 units.*

$ RENTAL 🏨 **Outrigger at Lae Nani.** Ruling Hawaiian chiefs once returned from ocean voyages to this spot, now host to condominiums comfortable enough for minor royalty. **Pros:** nice swimming beach; walking distance to playground; attractively furnished. **Cons:** tricky driving in area. **TripAdvisor:** "great condos," "beautiful setting," "spacious." [$] *Rooms from: $179*

The St. Regis Princeville Resort

FodorśChoice ★

Grand Hyatt Kauai Resort and Spa

Grand Hyatt Kauai Resort and Spa

Waimea Plantation Cottages

✉ *410 Papaloa Rd., Kapaa* ☎ *808/822–4938, 800/688–7444* 🌐 *www.outrigger.com* 🛏 *84 units.*

WORD OF MOUTH

"Poipu—this is my personal favorite. You have easy access to outstanding (though sometimes crowded) beaches, top-notch condos and hotels, restaurants, and a resort feel." —alanwar

$ RENTAL 🏨 **Plantation Hale Suites.** These attractive plantation-style one-bedroom units have well-equipped kitchenettes and garden lanai. **Pros:** bright, spacious units; three pools; walking distance to shops, restaurant, beach. **Cons:** traffic noise in mountain-view units; coral reef makes ocean swimming challenging. **TripAdvisor:** "lovely rooms," "affordable and nice," "excellent customer service." [$] *Rooms from: $119* ✉ *484 Kuhio Hwy., Kapaa* ☎ *808/822–4941, 800/775–4253* 🌐 *www.plantation-hale.com* 🛏 *104 units.*

$ B&B/INN 🏨 **Rosewood Bed and Breakfast.** This charming bed-and-breakfast on a macadamia-nut plantation estate offers five separate styles of accommodations, including a two-bedroom Victorian cottage; a three-bedroom, two-bath home; a little one-bedroom grass-thatch cottage; a bunkhouse with three rooms and a shared bath; and the traditional main plantation home with two rooms, each with private bath. **Pros:** varied accommodations; good breakfast; attractive grounds. **Cons:** some traffic noise; no beach. [$] *Rooms from: $100* ✉ *872 Kamalu Rd., Kapaa* ☎ *808/822–5216* 🌐 *www.rosewoodkauai.com* 🛏 *One 3-bedroom home, one 2-bedroom cottage, one 1-bedroom cottage, 3 rooms in bunkhouse, 2 rooms in main house* 💳 *No credit cards.*

LIHUE

$ B&B/INN 🏨 **Garden Island Inn.** Bargain hunters love this three-story inn near Kalapaki Bay and Anchor Cove shopping center. **Pros:** walk to beach, restaurants, and shops; good for families, extended stays, and budget travel. **Cons:** some traffic noise; near a busy harbor; limited grounds; no pool. **TripAdvisor:** "quaint and personable," "unfortunate location," "charming but noisy." [$] *Rooms from: $99* ✉ *3445 Wilcox Rd., Kalapaki Beach* ☎ *808/245–7227, 800/648–0154* 🌐 *www.gardenislandinn.com* 🛏 *22 rooms.*

$$$$ RESORT 👶 🏨 **Kauai Marriott Resort on Kalapaki Beach.** An elaborate tropical garden, waterfalls right off the lobby, Greek statues and columns, and an enormous 26,000-square-foot swimming pool characterize the grand—and grandiose—scale of this resort on Kalapaki Bay, which looks out at the dramatic Haupu Mountains. **Pros:** oceanfront setting; good restaurants; convenient location; airport shuttle. **Cons:** distant airport noise; swimming questionable at times. **TripAdvisor:** "fabulous apartment," "perfect location and stunning grounds," "gorgeous gardens." [$] *Rooms from: $399* ✉ *3610 Rice St., Kalapaki Beach* ☎ *808/245–5050, 800/220–2925* 🌐 *www.kauaimarriott.com* 🛏 *356 rooms, 11 suites.*

THE SOUTH SHORE

$$$$ RESORT Fodor's Choice ★ **Grand Hyatt Kauai Resort and Spa.** Dramatically handsome, this classic Hawaiian low-rise is built into the cliffs overlooking an unspoiled coastline. **Pros:** fabulous pool; excellent restaurants; Hawaiian ambience. **Cons:** poor swimming beach during summer swells; small balconies. **TripAdvisor:** "excellent service," "pools are gorgeous," "paradise." [$] *Rooms from: $480* ✉ *1571 Poipu Rd., Koloa* ☎ *808/742–1234, 800/633–7313* 🌐 *www.grandhyattkauai.com* *602 rooms, 37 suites.*

$$ RENTAL **Hideaway Cove.** On a quiet street ending in a cul-de-sac, Hideaway Cove is very quiet, even though it's one block from the ocean's edge in the heart of Poipu. **Pros:** high-quality furnishings; private lanai; hot tub or Jacuzzi in each unit. **Cons:** not on the ocean; cleaning fee. **TripAdvisor:** "tropical oasis," "a perfect spot," "beautiful accommodation." [$] *Rooms from: $190* ✉ *2307 Nalo Rd., Poipu* ☎ *808/635–8785, 866/849–2426* 🌐 *www.hideawaycove.com* *7 units.*

$$$$ HOTEL **Koa Kea Hotel and Resort.** This luxury boutique hotel opened in April 2009 on the grounds of the former Poipu Beach Hotel, a Kauai favorite before its destruction by Hurricane Iniki in 1992. **Pros:** incredibly comfortable beds; brand-new ambience; good food at Red Salt restaurant. **Cons:** not much for children; wind noise in hallways can be distracting. **TripAdvisor:** "nice break from monster resorts," "peaceful stay," "great getaway for romantic couples." [$] *Rooms from: $349* ✉ *2251 Poipu Rd., Poipu* ☎ *808/828–8888, 800/230-4134* 🌐 *www.koakea.com* *121 rooms.*

$$$$ RENTAL **Outrigger Kiahuna Plantation.** Kauai's largest condo project is lackluster, though the location is excellent. **Pros:** great sunset and ocean views are bonuses in some units. **Cons:** not the best place to stay if you're looking for a romantic getaway. TripAdvisor: "excellent facility," "comfortable and well appointed," "great location." [$] *Rooms from: $349* ✉ *2253 Poipu Rd., Koloa* ☎ *808/742–6411, 800/688–7444* 🌐 *www.outrigger.com* *333 units.*

$$ RENTAL **Poipu Kapili.** Spacious one- and two-bedroom condo units are minutes from Poipu's restaurants and beaches. **Pros:** units are roomy; good guest services; property is small. **Cons:** units are ocean-view but not oceanfront. **TripAdvisor:** "spacious and comfortable," "luxury in Poipu," "exceeded expectations." [$] *Rooms from: $255* ✉ *2221 Kapili Rd., Koloa* ☎ *808/742–6449, 800/443–7714* 🌐 *www.poipukapili.com* *60 units.*

$ RESORT **Poipu Plantation Resort.** Plumeria, ti, and other tropical foliage create a lush landscape for this resort, which has one bed-and-breakfast–style plantation home and nine one- and two-bedroom cottage apartments. **Pros:** attractively furnished; full breakfast at B&B. **Cons:** three-night minimum. **TripAdvisor:** "best kept secret in Poipu," "value," "great location." [$] *Rooms from: $145* ✉ *1792 Pee Rd., Poipu* ☎ *808/742–6757, 800/634–0263* 🌐 *www.poipubeach.com* *4 suites, 9 cottages.*

$ RENTAL **Poipu Shores.** Sitting on a rocky point above pounding surf, this is a perfect spot for whale- or turtle-watching. **Pros:** every unit faces the water; oceanfront pool; wildlife viewing. **Cons:** units vary widely in style; no resort amenities. **TripAdvisor:** "awesome condo," "great place," "incredible ocean views." [$] *Rooms from: $145* ✉ *1775 Pee*

5

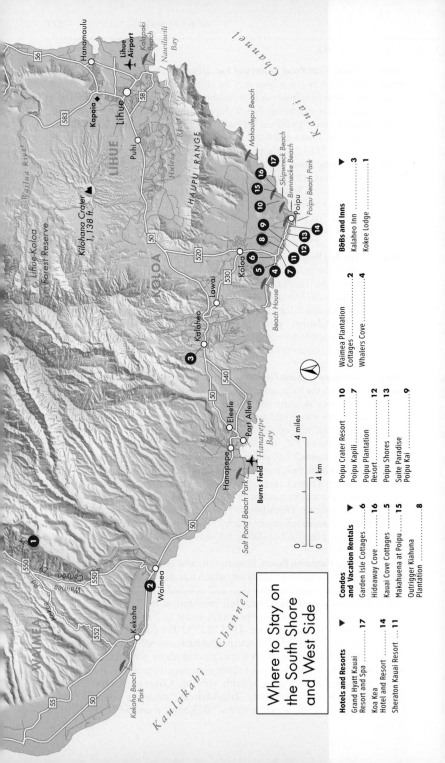

Where to Stay on the South Shore and West Side

Hotels and Resorts ▼

Grand Hyatt Kauai Resort and Spa **17**
Koa Kea Hotel and Resort **14**
Sheraton Kauai Resort **11**

Condos and Vacation Rentals ▼

Garden Isle Cottages **6**
Hideaway Cove **16**
Kauai Cove Cottages **5**
Makahuena at Poipu **15**
Outrigger Kiahuna Plantation **8**

Poipu Crater Resort **10**
Poipu Kapili **7**
Poipu Plantation Resort **12**
Poipu Shores **13**
Suite Paradise Poipu Kai **9**

Waimea Plantation Cottages **2**
Whalers Cove **4**

B&Bs and Inns ▼

Kalaheo Inn **3**
Kokee Lodge **1**

Sheraton Kauai Resort

Rd., Koloa ☎ 808/742–7700, 800/367–5004 🌐 www.castleresorts.com 🛏 39 units.

$$$$ RESORT Fodor's Choice ★ 🏨 **Sheraton Kauai Resort.** The resort's ocean-wing accommodations here are so close to the water you can practically feel the spray of the surf as it hits the rocks below. **Pros:** ocean-view pool; quiet; nice dining views. **Cons:** no swimming beach; rather staid ambience. **TripAdvisor:** "amazing view," "great beach and service," "beautiful sunsets." [$] *Rooms from: $455 ✉ 2440 Hoonani Rd., Poipu Beach, Koloa 808/742–1661, 888/488–3535 🌐 www.sheraton-kauai.com 🛏 394 rooms, 8 suites.*

$$ RENTAL 🏨 **Suite Paradise Poipu Kai.** Condominiums, many with cathedral ceilings and all with big windows overlooking the lawns, give this property the feeling of a spacious, quiet retreat inside and out. **Pros:** close to nice beaches; full kitchens; good rates for the location. **Cons:** units aren't especially spacious; beaches not ideal for swimming. **TripAdvisor:** "guaranteed comfortable," "outstanding resort," "excellent beaches within easy walking distance." [$] *Rooms from: $257 ✉ 1941 Poipu Rd., Koloa ☎ 808/742–6464, 800/367–8020 🌐 www.suite-paradise.com 🛏 130 units.*

$$$$ RENTAL 🏨 **Whalers Cove.** Perched about as close to the water's edge as they can get, these two-bedroom condos are the most luxurious on the South Shore. **Pros:** daily service; on-site staff; extremely luxurious; outstanding setting; fully equipped units (1,400–2,000 square feet). **Cons:** rocky beach not ideal for swimming. **TripAdvisor:** "unique," "best oceanfront stay," "relaxing condo." [$] *Rooms from: $349 ✉ 2640 Puuholo Rd., Koloa ☎ 808/742–7571, 800/225–2683 🌐 www.whalerscoveresort.com 🛏 39 units.*

THE WEST SIDE

$ B&B/INN 🏨 **Kokee Lodge.** If you're an outdoors enthusiast, you can appreciate Kauai's mountain wilderness from the 12 rustic cabins that make up this lodge. **Pros:** outstanding setting; more refined than camping; cooking facilities. **Cons:** very austere; no restaurants for dinner; remote. **TripAdvisor:** "rustic launching pad for hiking," "comfortable cabin," "great location." [$] *Rooms from: $105 ✉ 3600 Kokee Rd., at mile marker 15, Waimea 808/335–6061 🌐 www.thelodgeatkokee.net 🛏 12 cabins.*

$ RENTAL Fodor's Choice ★ 🏨 **Waimea Plantation Cottages.** History buffs will adore these reconstructed sugar-plantation cottages, which were originally built in the early 1900s. **Pros:** unique, homey lodging; quiet and low-key. **Cons:** not a white-sand beach; rooms are not luxurious. **TripAdvisor:** "quiet," "feels like Old Hawaii," "ultimate relaxation spot." [$] *Rooms from: $179 ✉ 9400 Kaumualii Hwy., Box 367, Waimea ☎ 808/338–1625, 800/992–4632 🌐 www.waimeaplantation.com/ 🛏 55 cottages.*

Molokai

WORD OF MOUTH

"I took the ferry and rented a car on Molokai for one day and LOVED the drive to the Halawa Valley. The winding little drive east—with virtually no traffic, then the drive down into the valley— is truly breathtaking. I'd call it a don't-miss, especially if you are going to Molokai at all."

—NeoPatrick

WELCOME TO MOLOKAI

TOP REASONS TO GO

★ **Kalaupapa Peninsula:**
Hike or take a mule ride
down the world's tallest
sea cliffs to a fascinating,
historic community that
still houses a few patients
suffering from leprosy.

★ **A waterful hike in
Halawa:** A fascinating
guided hike through
private property takes
you past ancient ruins,
restored taro patches, and
a sparkling cascade.

★ **Deep-sea fishing:** Sport
fish are plentiful in these
waters, as are gorgeous
views of several Islands.
Fishing is one of the
island's great adventures.

★ **Closeness to nature:**
Deep valleys, sheer cliffs,
and the untamed ocean
are the main attrac-
tions on Molokai.

★ **Papohaku Beach:** This
3-mile stretch of golden
sand is one of the most
sensational beaches in all
of Hawaii. Sunsets and
barbecues are perfect here.

Map labels:
Kaiwi Channel
Kawakiu Beach
Kawakiu Bay
Kepuhi Beach
Papohaku Beach
Kapukahehu Bay
Hool
Hoolehua Airport
Kaluakoi Rd.
Maunaloa Hwy.
460
WEST MOLOKAI
1
Maunaloa
Laau Point
Kalohi Channel
0   4 mi
0   4 km

1 West Molokai. The
most arid part of the island,
known as the west end,
has two inhabited areas:
the coastal stretch includes
a few condos and luxury
homes and the largest
beaches on the island.
Nearby is the fading hilltop
hamlet of Maunaloa.

2 Central Molokai. The
island's only true town,
Kaunakakai, with its mile-
long wharf, is here. Nearly
all of the island's eateries
and stores are in or close
to Kaunakakai. Highway 470
crosses the center of the
island, rising to the top of
the sea cliffs and the Kalaupapa overlook. At the base
of the cliffs is Kalaupapa
National Historical Park, a
top attraction.

3 **East Molokai.** The scenic drive on Route 450 around this undeveloped area, also called the east end, passes through the green pastures of Puu O Hoku Ranch and climaxes with a descent into Halawa Valley. As you continue east, the road becomes increasingly narrow and the island ever more lush.

GETTING ORIENTED

Shaped like a long bone, Molokai is about 10 miles wide on average and four times that long. The north shore thrusts up from the sea to form the tallest sea cliffs on Earth, while the south shore slides almost flat into the water, then fans out to form the largest shallow-water reef system in the United States. Kaunakaki, the island's main town, has most of the stores and restaurants. Surprisingly, the highest point on Molokai rises only to 4,970 feet.

Updated by
Heidi Pool

Molokai is generally thought of as the last bit of "real" Hawaii. Tourism has been held at bay by the island's unique history and the pride of its predominantly native Hawaiian population, despite the fact that the longest white-sand beach in Hawaii can be found along its western shore. Exploring the great outdoors and visiting the historic Kalaupapa Peninsula, where St. Damien helped people with leprosy, are attractions for visitors.

With sandy beaches to the west, sheer sea cliffs to the north, and a rainy, lush eastern coast, Molokai offers a bit of everything, including a peek at what the Islands were like 50 years ago. Large tracts of land from Hawaiian Homeland grants have allowed the people to retain much of their traditional lifestyle. A favorite expression is "Slow down, you're on Molokai." Although Molokai Ranch, the island's biggest landowner and employer, is closed and up for sale, residents are adapting and welcoming visitors. If you are friendly, they are friendly.

Only 38 miles long and 10 miles wide at its widest point, Molokai is the fifth-largest island in the Hawaiian archipelago. Eight thousand residents call Molokai home, nearly 60% of whom are Hawaiian.

Molokai is a great place to be outdoors. There are no tall buildings, no traffic lights, no streetlights, no stores bearing the names of national chains, and nothing at all like a resort. You will, however, find 15 parks, and more than 100 miles of shoreline to play on. At night the whole island grows dark, creating a velvety blackness and a wonderful, rare thing called silence.

GEOLOGY

Roughly 1½ million years ago two large volcanoes—Kamakou in the east and Mauna Loa in the west—broke the surface of the Pacific Ocean and created the island of Molokai. Shortly thereafter a third and much smaller caldera, Kauhako, popped up to form the Makanalua Peninsula on the north side. After hundreds of thousands of years of rain, surf, and wind, an enormous landslide on the north end sent much of the mountain into the sea, leaving behind the sheer sea cliffs that make Molokai's north shore so spectacularly beautiful.

HISTORY

Molokai is named in chants as the child of the moon goddess Hina. For centuries, the island was occupied by native people who took advantage of the reef fishing and ideal conditions for growing taro. When leprosy broke out in the Hawaiian Islands in the 1840s, the Makanalua Peninsula, surrounded on three sides by the Pacific and accessible only by a steep trail, was selected as the place to exile people suffering from the disease. The first patients were thrown into the sea to swim ashore as best they could, and left with no facilities, shelter, or supplies. In 1873 a missionary named Father Damien arrived and began to serve the peninsula's suffering inhabitants. He died in 1889 from leprosy and was canonized as a saint by the Catholic Church in 2009. Though leprosy, now known as Hansen's disease, is no longer contagious and can be remitted, the buildings and infrastructure created by those who were exiled here still exist, and some longtime residents have chosen to stay in their homes. Today the area is Kalaupapa National Historical Park. Visitors are welcome but must prebook a tour operated by Damien Tours of Kalaupapa. You can reach the park by plane or by hiking or taking a mule ride down the steep Kalaupapa Trail.

THE BIRTHPLACE OF HULA

Tradition has it that centuries ago Lailai came to Molokai and lived on Puu Nana at Kaana. She brought the art of hula and taught it to the people, who kept it secret for her descendants, making sure the sacred dances were performed only at Kaana. Five generations later Laka was born into the family and learned hula from an older sister. She chose to share the art and traveled throughout the Islands teaching the dance, though she did so without her family's consent. The yearly Ka Hula Piko Festival, held on Molokai in May, celebrates the birth of hula at Kaana.

PLANNING

WHEN TO GO

If you're keen to explore Molokai's beaches, coral beds, or fishponds, summer is your best bet for nonstop calm seas and sunny skies. The weather mimics that of the other Islands: low to mid-80s year-round, slightly rainier in winter. As you travel up the mountainside, the weather changes with bursts of downpours. The strongest storms occur in winter when winds and rain shift to come in from the south.

For a taste of Hawaiian culture, plan your visit around a festival. In January, islanders and visitors compete in ancient Hawaiian games at the Ka Molokai Makahiki Festival. The Molokai Ka Hula Piko, an annual daylong event in May, draws premier hula troupes, musicians, and storytellers. Long-distance canoe races from Molokai to Oahu are in late September and early October. Although never crowded, the island is busier during these events—book accommodations and transportation six months in advance.

GETTING HERE AND AROUND

AIR TRAVEL

If you're flying in from the mainland United States or one of the Neighbor Islands, you must first make a stop in Honolulu. From there, it's a 25-minute trip to Molokai. Molokai's transportation hub is Hoolehua Airport, a tiny airstrip 8 miles west of Kaunakakai and about 18 miles east of Maunaloa. An even smaller airstrip serves the little community of Kalaupapa on the north shore.

From Hoolehua Airport, it takes about 10 minutes to reach Kaunakakai and 25 minutes to reach the west end of the island by car. There's no public bus. A taxi will cost about $27 from the airport to Kaunakakai with Hele Mai Taxi. Shuttle service costs about $28 per person from Hoolehua Airport to Kaunakakai. For shuttle service, call Molokai Outdoors. Keep in mind, however, that it's difficult to visit the island without a rental car.

Contacts Hele Mai Taxi ☎ 808/336–0967, 808/646–9060. **Molokai Outdoors** ☎ 808/553–4477, 877/553–4477 ⊕ www.molokai-outdoors.com.

CAR TRAVEL

If you want to explore Molokai from one end to the other, you must rent a car. With just a few main roads to choose from, it's a snap to drive around here. The gas stations are in Kaunakakai. Ask your rental agent for a free *Molokai Drive Guide.*

Alamo maintains a counter at Hoolehua Airport. Make arrangements in advance because cars may not be available when you walk in. National has a desk at the Hotel Molokai. Locally owned Island Kine Rent-a-Car offers airport or hotel pickup. Be sure to check the vehicle to make sure the four-wheel drive is working before departing the agency. There is a $75 surcharge for taking a four-wheel-drive vehicle off-road.

Major Agency Alamo ☎ 877/222–9075 ⊕ www.alamo.com.

Local Agency Island Kine Rent-a-Car ☎ 808/553–5242, 877/553–5242 ⊕ www.molokai-car-rental.com.

FERRY TRAVEL

The Molokai Ferry crosses the channel every day between Lahaina (Maui) and Kaunakakai. Boats depart from Lahaina daily at 6 pm and Monday to Saturday at 7:15 am, and from Kauanakakai daily at 4 pm and Monday to Saturday at 5:15 am. The 1½-hour trip takes passengers but not cars, so arrange ahead of time for a car rental or tour at the arrival point.

Contact Molokai Ferry ☎ 808/661–3392, 866/307–6524 ⊕ www.molokaiferry.com.

RESTAURANTS

Dining on Molokai is more a matter of eating. There are no fancy restaurants, just pleasant low-key places to eat out. Try Hula Shores at the Hotel Molokai for a selection of fresh, local-style food. Other options include plate lunch, pizza, coffee shop–style sandwiches, and make-it-yourself health-food fixings.

HOTELS

Molokai appeals most to travelers who appreciate genuine Hawaiian ambience rather than swanky digs. Most hotel and condominium properties range from adequate to funky. Visitors who want to lollygag on the beach should choose one of the condos or home rentals in West Molokai. Locals tend to choose Hotel Molokai, located seaside just 2 miles from Kaunakakai. Travelers who want to immerse themselves in the spirit of the island should seek out a condo or cottage, the closer to East Molokai the better.

Molokai Visitors Association. Ask about a brochure with up-to-date listings of vacation rentals operated by this company's members. ☎ 808/553–3876.

Molokai Vacation Properties. This company handles condo rentals and can act as an informal concierge during your stay. There is a three-night minimum on all properties. The company also handles private rental properties from beach cottages to large estates. ☎ 800/367–2984, 808/553–8334 ⊕ *www.molokai-vacation-rental.net.*

COMMUNICATIONS

There are many locations on the island where cell-phone reception is difficult, if not impossible, to obtain. Your best bet for finding service is in Kaunakakai. There is in-room Internet access at the Hotel Molokai.

VISITOR INFORMATION

Contacts Maui Visitors Bureau ☎ 808/244–3530, 800/525–6284 ⊕ www. visitmaui.com. **Molokai Visitors Association** ✉ 12 Kamoi St., Suite 200, Kaunakakai ☎ 808/553–3876, 800/800–6367 ⊕ www.gohawaii.com/molokai.

EXPLORING MOLOKAI

The first thing to do on Molokai is to drive everywhere. It's a feat you can accomplish comfortably in two days. Depending on where you stay, spend one day exploring the west end and the other day exploring the east end. Basically you have one 40-mile west–east highway (two lanes, no stoplights) with three side trips: the little west-end town of Maunaloa; the Highway 470 drive (just a few miles) to the top of the north shore and the overlook of Kalaupapa Peninsula; and the short stretch of shops in Kaunakakai town. After you learn the general lay of the land, you can return to the places that interest you most. ■TIP➔ Directions on the island are often given as mauka (toward the mountains) and makai (toward the ocean).

WEST MOLOKAI

Papohaku Beach is 17 miles west of the airport; Maunaloa is 10 miles west of the airport.

The remote beaches and rolling pastures on Molokai's west end are presided over by Mauna Loa, a dormant volcano, and a sleepy little former plantation town of the same name. Papohaku Beach, the Hawaiian Islands' second-longest white-sand beach, is one of the area's biggest draws. *For information about Papohaku Beach, see Beaches.*

Kapuaiwa Coconut Grove in central Moloka'i is a survivor of royal plantings from the 19th century.

GETTING HERE AND AROUND

The sometimes winding paved road through West Molokai begins at Highway 460 and ends at Kapukahehu Bay. The drive from Kaunakakai to Maunaloa is about 30 minutes.

EXPLORING

Kaluakoi. Although the late-1960s Kaluakoi Hotel and Golf Club is closed and forlorn, some nice condos and a gift shop are operating nearby. Kepuhi Beach, the white-sand beach along the coast, is still worth a visit. ⊠ *Kaluakoi Rd., Maunaloa.*

Maunaloa. Built in 1923, this quiet community at the western end of the highway once housed workers for the island's pineapple plantation. Many businesses have closed, but it's the last place to buy supplies when you're exploring the nearby beaches. If you're in the neighborhood, stop at Maunaloa's Big Wind Kite Factory. You'll want to talk story with Uncle Jonathan, who has been making and flying kites here for more than three decades. ⊠ *Maunaloa Hwy.*

CENTRAL MOLOKAI

Kaunakakai is 8 miles southeast of the airport.

Most residents live centrally, near the island's one and only true town, Kaunakakai. It's just about the only place on the island to get food and supplies. It *is* Molokai. Go into the shops along and around Ala Malama Street. Buy stuff. Talk with people. Take your time and you'll really enjoy being a visitor. Also in this area, on the north side, are Coffees of Hawaii, a 500-acre coffee plantation, and the Kalaupapa National

Historical Park, one of the island's most notable sights.

GETTING HERE AND AROUND

Central Molokai is the hub of the island's road system, and Kaunakakai is the commercial center. Watch for kids, dogs, and people crossing the street in downtown Kaunakakai.

EXPLORING

TOP ATTRACTIONS

Coffees of Hawaii. Visit the headquarters of a 500-acre Molokai coffee plantation, where the espresso bar serves freshly made sandwiches, *lilikoi* (passion fruit) cheesecake, and java in artful ways. The "Mocha Mama" is a special Molokai treat. This is the place to pick up additions to your picnic lunch if you're headed to Kalaupapa. The gift shop offers a wide range of Molokai handicrafts, memorabilia, and, of course, coffee. Call ahead for a tour of the plantation, which costs $20. ✉ *1630 Farrington Hwy., off Rte. 470, Kualapuu* ☎ *877/322–3276, 808/567–9490* ⊕ *www.coffeesofhawaii.com* ☙ *Café and gift shop weekdays 6 am–5 pm, Sat. 8–8, Sun. 8–5.*

> **MOLOKAI VIBES**
>
> Molokai is one of the last places in Hawaii where most of the residents are living an authentic rural lifestyle and wish to retain it. Many oppose developing the island for visitors or outsiders, so you won't find much to cater to your needs, but if you take time and talk to the locals you will find them hospitable and friendly. Some may even invite you home with them. It's a safe place, but don't interrupt private parties on the beach or trespass on private property. Consider yourself a guest in someone's house, rather than a customer.

Fodor'sChoice ★ **Kalaupapa.** *See photo feature, Kalaupapa Peninsula: A Tale of Tragedy and Triumph.*

Fodor'sChoice ★ **Kalaupapa Guided Mule Tour.** Mount a friendly, well-trained mule and wind along a thrilling 3-mile, 26-switchback trail to reach the town of Kalaupapa, which was once home to patients with leprosy who were exiled to this remote spot. The path was built in 1886 as a supply route for the settlement below. Once in Kalaupapa, you take a guided tour of the town and enjoy a light picnic lunch. The trail traverses some of the highest sea cliffs in the world, and views are spectacular. ■ TIP→ Only those in good shape should attempt the ride, as two hours each way on a mule can take its toll. You must be at least 16 years old and weigh no more than 249 pounds; pregnant women are not allowed. The entire event takes seven hours. Make reservations ahead of time, as space is limited. The same outfit can arrange for you to hike down or fly in. No one is allowed in the park or on the trail without booking a tour; hikers must be down in the park by 10 am. ⇨ *See Kalaupapa Peninsula: A Tale of Tragedy and Triumph photo feature, below, for more information.* ✉ *100 Kalae Hwy., Kualapuu* ☎ *808/567–6088, 800/567–7550* ⊕ *www.muleride.com* 🖃 *$199* ☙ *Mon.–Sat. 8–3.*

★ **Kaunakakai.** Central Molokai's main town looks like a classic 1940s movie set. Along the one-block main drag is a cultural grab bag of restaurants and shops. Many people are friendly and willing to supply directions. The preferred dress is shorts and a tank top, and no

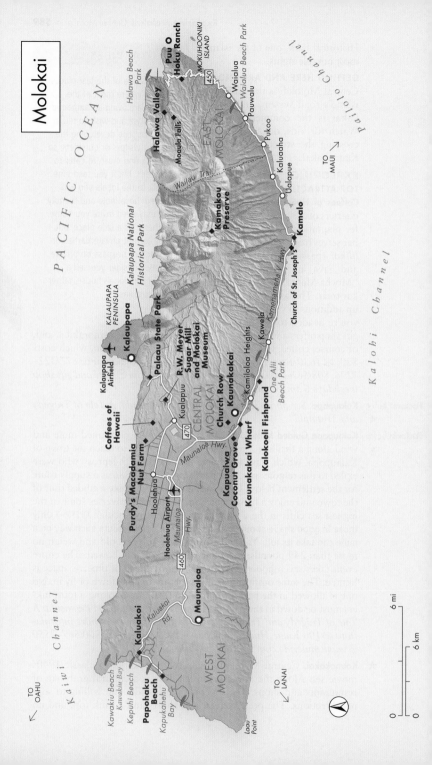

Molokai

PACIFIC OCEAN

Kaiwi Channel

TO OAHU

TO LANAI

Kalohi Channel

Pailolo Channel

TO MAUI

MOKUHOONIKI ISLAND

Puu O Hoku Ranch

450

Halawa Beach Park

Halawa Valley

Moaula Falls

EAST MOLOKAI

Wailau Trail

Wailua

Waialua Beach Park

Pauwalu

Pukoo

Kaluaaha

Ualapue

Kamalo

Kamakou Preserve

Church of St. Joseph's

Kamehameha V Hwy.

Kalaupapa National Historical Park

KALAUPAPA PENINSULA

Kalaupapa Airfield

Kalaupapa

Palaau State Park

R.W. Meyer Sugar Mill and Molokai Museum

Kualapuu

Church Row

Kaunakakai

Kamiloloa Heights

Kawela

One Alii Beach Park

Kalokoeli Fishpond

Kaunakakai Wharf

Kapuaiwa Coconut Grove

CENTRAL MOLOKAI

Coffees of Hawaii

470

Purdy's Macadamia Nut Farm

Hoolehua

Hoolehua Airport

Maunaloa Hwy.

460

Maunaloa Hwy.

Maunaloa

Kaluakoi Rd.

Kaluakoi

Papohaku Beach

Kawakiu Beach

Kawakiu Bay

Kepuhi Beach

Kapukahehu Bay

Laau Point

WEST MOLOKAI

6 mi

6 km

0

one wears anything fancier than a cotton skirt or aloha shirt. ⊠ *Rte. 460, 3 blocks north of Kaunakakai Wharf.*

Kamoi Snack-n-Go. Stop for some of Dave's Hawaiian Ice Cream at the Kamoi Snack-n-Go. Sit on one of the benches in front for a Molokai rest stop. Snacks, crack seed, cold drinks, and water are also available. ⊠ *28 Kamoi St.* ☎ *808/553–3742.*

★ **Palaau State Park.** One of the island's few formal recreation areas, this 233-acre retreat sits at a 1,000-foot elevation. A short path through an ironwood forest leads to **Kalaupapa Lookout,** a magnificent overlook with views of the town of Kalaupapa and the 1,664-foot-high sea cliffs protecting it. Informative plaques have facts about leprosy, Saint Damien, and the colony. The park is also the site of **Kauleonanahoa** (the phallus of Nanahoa)—where women in old Hawaii would come to the rock to enhance their fertility, and it is said some still do. It is a sacred site, so be respectful and don't deface the boulders. The park is well maintained, with trails, camping facilities, restrooms, and picnic tables. To get here, take Highway 460 west from Kaunakakai and then head *mauka* (toward the mountains) on Highway 470, which ends at the park. ⊠ *Rte. 470, Kaunakaki* ☎ *No phone* ⊠ *Free* ☉ *Daily dawn–dusk.*

HAWAII'S FIRST SAINT

A long-revered figure on Molokai and in Hawaii, Father Damien, who cared for the desperate patients at Kalaupapa, was elevated to sainthood in 2009. Plans call for a small museum and bookstore in his honor in Kaunakakai, and refurbishment of the three churches in the Catholic parish is currently under way. Visitors who cannot visit Kalaupapa can find information on St. Damien at the Damien Center in Kaunakakai, and may worship at Our Lady of Seven Sorrows (just west of Kaunakakai), or at St. Vincent Ferrer in Maunaloa.

6

Purdy's Macadamia Nut Farm. Molokai's only working macadamia nut farm is open for educational tours hosted by the knowledgeable and entertaining owner. A family business in Hoolehua, the farm takes up 1½ acres with a flourishing grove of 50 original trees that are more than 90 years old, as well as several hundred younger trees. The nuts taste delicious right out of the shell, home roasted, or dipped in macadamia-blossom honey. Look for Purdy's sign behind Molokai High School. ⊠ *Lihipali Ave., Hoolehua* ☎ *808/567–6601* ⊕ *www.molokai-aloha.com/macnuts* ⊠ *Free* ☉ *Tues.–Fri. 9:30–3:30, Sat. 10–2.*

R.W. Meyer Sugar Mill and Molokai Museum. Built in 1877, this three-room mill has been reconstructed as a testament to Molokai's agricultural history. Some of the equipment is still in working order, including a mule-driven cane crusher, redwood evaporating pans, some copper clarifiers, and a steam engine. A small museum with changing exhibits on the island's early history and a gift shop are here as well. ⊠ *Rte. 470, Kualapuu, 2 miles southwest of Palaau State Park* ☎ *808/567–6436* ⊠ *$5* ☉ *Mon.–Sat. 10–2.*

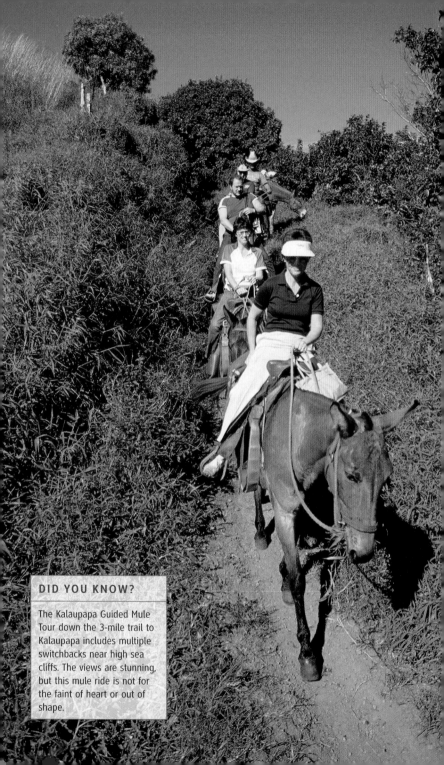

DID YOU KNOW?

The Kalaupapa Guided Mule Tour down the 3-mile trail to Kalaupapa includes multiple switchbacks near high sea cliffs. The views are stunning, but this mule ride is not for the faint of heart or out of shape.

WORTH NOTING

Church Row. Standing together along the highway are several houses of worship with primarily native-Hawaiian congregations. Notice the unadorned, boxlike architecture so similar to missionary homes. ⊠ *Rte. 460, ,Kaunakaki, 5½ miles south of airport.*

Kapuaiwa Coconut Grove. From far away this spot looks like a sea of coconut trees. Closer up you can see that the tall, stately palms are planted in long rows leading down to the sea. This is a remnant of one of the last surviving royal groves planted for Prince Lot, who ruled Hawaii as King Kamehameha V from 1863 until his death in 1872. Watch for falling coconuts. ⊠ *Rte. 460, Kaunakaki, 5½ miles south of airport.*

WORD OF MOUTH

"Visiting Kalaupapa was one of life's great moments. We took mules, but would consider flying in next time. We stayed on the very east end and enjoyed the long ride back and forth. It rivals the road to Hana and the West End Maui drives. You are literally driving beside the ocean for much of the way." —gyppielou

Kaunakakai Wharf. Once bustling with barges exporting pineapples, these docks now host visiting boats, the ferry from Lahaina, and the weekly barge from Oahu. The wharf is also the starting point for fishing, sailing, snorkeling, whale-watching, and scuba-diving excursions. It's a nice place at sunset to watch fish rippling on the water. To get here, take Kaunakakai Place, which dead-ends at wharf. ⊠ *Rte. 450, Kaunakaki, at Ala Malama St.*

6

EAST MOLOKAI

Halawa Valley is 36 miles northeast of the airport.

On the beautifully undeveloped east end of Molokai, you can find ancient fishponds, a magnificent coastline, splendid ocean views, and a fertile valley that's been inhabited for 14 centuries. The eastern uplands are flanked by Mt. Kamakou, the island's highest point at 4,961 feet and home to the Nature Conservancy's Kamakou Preserve. Mist hangs over waterfall-filled valleys, and ancient lava cliffs jut out into the sea.

GETTING HERE AND AROUND

Driving the east end is a scenic adventure, but the road narrows and becomes curvy after the 20-mile marker. Take your time, especially in the seaside lane, and watch for oncoming traffic. Driving at night is not recommended.

EXPLORING

Fodor'sChoice **Halawa Valley.** Hawaiians lived in this valley as far back as AD 650,
★ making it the oldest recorded habitation on Molokai. Inhabitants grew taro and fished until the 1960s, when an enormous flood wiped out the taro patches and forced old-timers to abandon their traditional lifestyle. Now a new generation of Hawaiians has begun the challenging task of restoring the taro fields. Much of this work involves rerouting streams to flow through carefully engineered level ponds called *loi*. The taro plants with their big, dancing leaves grow in the submerged mud of the

loi, where the water is always cool and flowing. Hawaiians believe that the taro plant is their ancestor and revere it both as sustenance and as a spiritual necessity. The Halawa Valley Cooperative leads hikes through the valley, which is home to two sacrificial temples, many historic sites, and the trail to **Moaula Falls,** a 250-foot cascade; contact Molokai Fish and Dive for information. The $75 fee supports

> **BE PREPARED**
>
> Because Molokai is not oriented to the visitor industry, you won't find much around to cater to your needs. Pick up a disposable cooler in Kaunakakai town, then visit the local markets and fill it with road supplies. Don't forget water, sunscreen, and mosquito repellent.

the restoration efforts. The 4.2-mile round-trip hike is rated intermediate to advanced and includes two moderate river crossings. ⊠ *Eastern end of Rte. 450* ☎ *808/553–5926* ⊕ *www.molokaifishanddive.com.*

★ **Kalokoeli Fishpond.** With its narrow rock walls arching out from the shoreline, Kalokoeli is typical of the numerous fishponds that define southern Molokai. Many were built around the 13th century under the direction of powerful chiefs. This early type of aquaculture, particular to Hawaii, exemplifies the ingenuity of native Hawaiians. One or more openings were left in the wall, where gates called *makaha* were installed. These gates allowed seawater and tiny fish to enter the enclosed pond but kept larger predators out. The tiny fish would then grow too big to get out. At one time there were 62 fishponds around Molokai's coast. ⊠ *Rte. 450, Kaunakaki, 6 miles east of Kaunakakai.*

OFF THE BEATEN PATH

★ **Kamakou Preserve.** Tucked away on the slopes of Mt. Kamakou, Molokai's highest peak, this 2,774-acre rain-forest preserve is a dazzling wonderland full of wet *ohia* (hardwood trees of the myrtle family, with red blossoms called *lehua* flowers) forests, rare bogs, and native trees and wildlife. Guided hikes, costing $25 and limited to eight people, are held one Saturday each month between March and October. Reserve well in advance. You can visit the park without a tour, but you need a good four-wheel-drive vehicle (hard to find on the island). The Nature Conservancy requests that you sign in at the office and get directions first. The office is at Molokai Industrial Park, about 3 miles west of Kaunakakai. ⊠ *23 Pueo Pl., Kualapuu* ☎ *808/553–5236* ⊕ *www. nature.org* ⧠ *Free. $25 guided hike.*

Kamalo. A natural harbor used by small cargo ships during the 19th century and a favorite fishing spot for locals, Kamalo is also the location of the **Church of St. Joseph's,** a tiny white church built by Saint Damien of the Kalaupapa colony in the 1880s. It's a state historic site and place of pilgrimage. The door is often open; if it is, slip inside and sign the guest book. The congregation keeps the church in beautiful condition. ⊠ *Rte. 450, 11 miles east of Kaunakakai.*

QUICK BITES

Manae Goods & Grinds. The best place to grab a snack or picnic supplies is Manae Goods & Grinds, 16 miles east of Kaunakakai. It's the only place on the east end where you can find essentials such as ice and bread, and not-so-essentials such as seafood plate lunches, bentos, burgers, and shakes. Try a refreshing smoothie while here. ⌧ *Rte. 450* ☎ *808/558–8498, 808/558–8186.*

Puu O Hoku Ranch. A 14,000-acre private ranch in the highlands of East Molokai, Puu O Hoku was developed in the 1930s by wealthy industrialist Paul Fagan. Route 450 ambles right through this rural treasure with its pastures and grazing horses and cattle. As you drive slowly along, enjoy the splendid views of Maui and Lanai. The small island off the coast is Mokuhooniki, a favorite spot among visiting humpback whales and a nesting seabird sanctuary. The ranch has limited accommodations, too. ⌧ *Rte. 450, 25 miles east of Kaunakakai* ☎ *808/558–8109* ⊕ *www.puuohoku.com.*

BEACHES

Molokai's unique geography gives the island plenty of drama and spectacle along the shorelines but not so many places for seaside basking and bathing. The long north shore consists mostly of towering cliffs that plunge directly into the sea and is inaccessible except by boat, and even then only in summer. Much of the south shore is enclosed by a huge reef that stands as far as a mile offshore and blunts the action of the waves. Within this reef you can find a thin strip of sand, but the water here is flat, shallow, and at times clouded with silt. This reef area is best suited to wading, pole fishing, kayaking, or learning how to windsurf.

The big, fat, sandy beaches lie along the west end. The largest of these—the second largest in the Islands—is Papohaku Beach, which fronts a grassy park shaded by a grove of *keawe* (mesquite) trees. These stretches of west-end sand are generally unpopulated. At the east end, where the road hugs the sinuous shoreline, you encounter a number of pocket-size beaches in rocky coves, good for snorkeling. Don't venture too far out, however, or you can find yourself caught in dangerous currents. The island's east-end road ends at Halawa Valley with its unique double bay, which is not recommended for swimming.

If you need beach gear, head to Molokai Fish and Dive at the west end of Kaunakakai's only commercial strip or rent kayaks from Molokai Outdoors at Kaunakakai Wharf.

Department of Parks, Land and Natural Resources. All of Hawaii's beaches are free and public. None of the beaches on Molokai have telephones or lifeguards, and they're all under the jurisdiction of the Department of Parks, Land and Natural Resources. ☎ *808/587–0300* ⊕ *www. hawaiistateparks.org.*

WEST MOLOKAI

Molokai's west end looks across a wide channel to the island of Oahu. Crescent shaped, this cup of coastline holds the island's best sandy beaches as well as the sunniest weather. Remember: all beaches are public property, even those that front developments, and most have public access roads. *Beaches below are listed from north to south.*

Continued on page 601

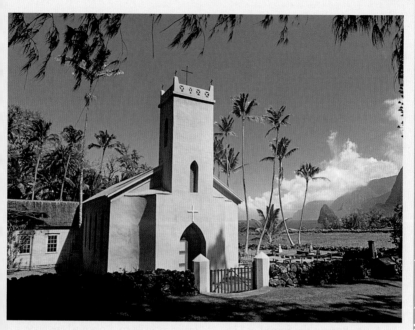

Father Damien's Church, St. Philomena

KALAUPAPA PENINSULA: TRAGEDY & TRIUMPH

For those who crave drama, there is no better destination than Molokai's Kalaupapa Peninsula—but it wasn't always so. For 100 years this remote strip of land was "the loneliest place on earth," a feared place of exile for those suffering from leprosy (now known as Hansen's Disease).

The world's tallest sea cliffs, rain-chiseled valleys, and tiny islets dropped like exclamation points along the coast emphasize the passionate history of the Kalaupapa Peninsula. Today, it's impossible to visit this stunning National Historical Park and view the evidence of human ignorance and heroism with-out responding. You'll be tugged by emotions—awe and disbelief for starters. But you'll also glimpse humorous facets of everyday life in a small town. Whatever your experience here may be, chances are you'll return home feeling that the journey to present-day Kalaupapa is one you'll never forget.

THE SETTLEMENT'S EARLY DAYS

Father Damien with patients outside St. Philomena church.

IN 1865, PRESSURED BY FOREIGN RESIDENTS, the Hawaiian Kingdom passed "An Act to Prevent the Spread of Leprosy." Anyone showing symptoms of the disease was to be permanently exiled to Kalawao, the north end of Kalaupapa Peninsula—a spot walled in on three sides by nearly impassable cliffs. The peninsula had been home to a fishing community for 900 years, but those inhabitants were evicted and the entire peninsula declared settlement land.

The first 12 patients were arrested and sent to Kalawao in 1866. People of all ages and many nationalities followed, taken from their homes and dumped on the isolated shore. Officials thought the patients could become self-sufficient, fishing and farming sweet potatoes in the stream-fed valleys. That was not the case. Settlement conditions were deplorable.

Belgian missionary Father Damien was one of four priests who volunteered to serve the leprosy settlement at Kalawao on a rotating basis. There were 600 patients at the time. His turn came in 1873; when it was

up, he refused to leave. Father Damien is credited with turning the settlement from a merciless exile to a place where hope could be heard in the voices of his recruited choir. He organized the building of the St. Philomena church (and other churches on the island), nearly 300 houses, and a home for boys. A vocal advocate for his adopted community, he pestered the church for supplies, administered medicine, and oversaw the nearly daily funerals. Sixteen years after his arrival, in 1889, he died from the effects of leprosy, having contracted the disease during his service. Known around the world for his sacrifice, Father Damien was beatified by the Catholic Church in 1995, and canonized in 2009.

Mother Marianne heard of the mission while working at a hospital in Syracuse, New York. Along with six other Franciscan Sisters, she volunteered to work with those with leprosy in the Islands. They sailed to the Kalaupapa Peninsula in 1888. Like the Father, the Sisters were considered saints for their work. Mother Marianne stayed at Kalaupapa until her death in 1918; she was beatified by the Catholic Church in 2005.

VISITING KALAUPAPA TODAY

Kalaupapa Peninsula

FROZEN IN TIME, Kalaupapa's one-horse town has bittersweet charm. Signs posted here and there remind residents when the bankers will be there (once monthly), when to place annual barge orders for non-perishable items, and what's happening around town. It has the nostalgic, almost naive ambience expected from a place almost wholly segregated from modern life.

About 17 former patients remain at Kalaupapa (by choice, as the disease is controlled by drugs and the patients are no longer carriers), but many have traveled to other parts of the world and all are over the age of 70. They never lost their chutzpah, however. Having survived a lifetime of prejudice and misunderstanding, Kalaupapa's residents haven't been willing to be pushed around any longer—in past years, several made the journey to Honolulu from time to time to testify before the state legislature about matters concerning them.

To get a feel for what residents' lives were like, visit the National Park Service

Web site (www.nps.gov/kala/history culture/) or buy one of several heart-breaking memoirs at the park's library-turned-bookstore.

THE TRUTH ABOUT HANSEN'S DISEASE

■ A cure for leprosy has been available since 1941. Multi-drug therapy, a rapid cure, has been available since 1981.

■ With treatment, none of the disabilities traditionally associated with leprosy need occur.

■ Most people have a natural immunity to leprosy. Only 5% of the world's population is even susceptible to the disease.

■ There are still about 228,000 new cases of leprosy each year; the majority are in India.

■ All new cases of leprosy are treated on an outpatient basis.

■ The term "leper" is offensive and should not be used. It is appropriate to say "a person is affected by leprosy" or "by Hansen's Disease."

GETTING HERE

The Kalaupapa Trail and Peninsula are all part of Kalaupapa National Historical Park (☎ 808/567–6802 ⊕ www.nps.gov/kala/), which is open every day but Sunday for tours only. Keep in mind, there are no public facilities (except an occasional restroom) anywhere in the park. Pack your own food and water, as well as light rain gear, sunscreen, and bug repellent.

TO HIKE OR TO RIDE?

There are two ways to get down the Kalaupapa Trail: in your hiking boots, or on a mule.

Hiking: Hiking allows you to travel at your own pace and stop frequently for photos—not an option on the mule ride. The hike takes about 1 hour down and 1½ hours up. You must book a tour in order to access the trail. **Damien Tours** ☎ *808/567–6171.*

Kalaupapa Beach & Peninsula

THE KALAUPAPA TRAIL

Unless you fly (flights are available through Pacific Wings [☎ 808/873–0877 or 888/575–4546 ⊕ www.pacificwings.com]), the only way into Kalaupapa National Historical Park is on a dizzying switchback trail. The switchbacks are numbered—26 in all—and descend 1,700 feet to sea level in just under 3 miles. The steep trail is more of a staircase, and most of the trail is shaded. Keep in mind, however, that footing is uneven and there is little to keep you from pitching over the side. If you don't mind heights, you can stare straight down to the ocean for most of the way. *Access Kalaupapa Trail off Hwy. 470 near the Kalaupapa Overlook. There is ample parking near end of Hwy. 470.*

Mule-Skinning: You'll be amazed as your mule trots up to the edge of the switchback, swivels on two legs, and completes a sharp-angled turn—26 times. The guides tell you the mules can do this in their sleep, but that doesn't take the fear out of the first few switchbacks. Make reservations well in advance. **Kalaupapa Guided Mule Tour** ☎ *808/567–6088 or 808/567–7550* ⊕ *www.muleride.com.*

IMPORTANT INFORMATION

Daily tours are offered Monday through Saturday through Damien Tours or the Kalaupapa Guided Mule Tour. Be sure to reserve in advance. Visitors ages 16 and under are not allowed at Kalaupapa, and photographing patients without their written permission is forbidden.

Kawakiu Beach. Seclusion is yours at this remote beach, accessible by four-wheel-drive vehicle (through a gate that is sometimes locked) or a 45-minute walk. The white-sand beach is beautiful. To get here, drive past Ke Nani Kai condos on Kaluakoi Road and look for a dirt road off to the right. Park here and hike in or, with a four-wheel-drive vehicle, drive along the dirt road to the beach. ⚠ Rocks and undertow make swimming extremely dangerous at times, so use caution. **Amenities:** none. **Best for:** solitude. ⊠ *Off Kaluakoi Rd.*

Kepuhi Beach. The Kaluakoi Hotel is closed, but its half mile of ivory sand is still accessible. The beach shines against the turquoise sea, black outcroppings of lava, and magenta bougainvillea blossoms. When the sea is perfectly calm, lava ridges in the water make good snorkeling spots. With any surf at all, however, the water around these rocky places churns and foams, wiping out visibility and making it difficult to avoid being slammed into the jagged rocks. **Amenities:** showers; toilets. **Best for:** snorkeling; walking. ⊠ *Kaluakoi Rd.*

Fodor's Choice **Papohaku Beach.** One of the most sensational beaches in Hawaii, Papohaku is a 3-mile-long strip of light golden sand, the longest of its kind on the island. ■TIP→ Swimming is not recommended, as there's a dangerous undertow except on exceptionally calm summer days. There's so much sand here that Honolulu once purchased barge loads of the stuff to replenish Waikiki Beach. A shady beach park just inland is the site of the Ka Hula Piko Festival, held each year in May. The park is also a great sunset-facing spot for a rustic afternoon barbecue. A park ranger patrols the area periodically. **Amenities:** showers; toilets. **Best for:** sunset; walking. ⊠ *Kaluakoi Rd., 2 miles south of the former Kaluakoi Hotel.*

Kapukahehu Bay. The sandy protected cove is usually completely deserted on weekdays but can fill up when the surf is up. The water in the cove is clear and shallow with plenty of well-worn rocky areas. These conditions make for excellent snorkeling, swimming, and boogie boarding on calm days. Locals like to surf in a break called Dixie's or Dixie Maru. **Amenities:** None. **Best for:** snorkeling; surfing; swimming. ⊠ *End of Kaluakoi Rd., 3½ miles south of Papohaku Beach.*

> ### BEACH SAFETY
>
> Unlike protected shorelines such as Kaanapali on Maui, the coasts of Molokai are exposed to rough sea channels and dangerous rip currents. The ocean tends to be calmer in the morning and in summer. No matter what the time, however, always study the sea before entering. Unless the water is placid and the wave action minimal, it's best to stay on shore, even though locals may be in the water. Don't underestimate the power of the ocean. Protect yourself with sunblock. Cool breezes make it easy to underestimate the power of the sun as well.

CENTRAL MOLOKAI

The south shore is mostly a huge, reef-walled expanse of flat saltwater edged with a thin strip of gritty sand and stones, mangrove swamps, and the amazing system of fishponds constructed by the chiefs of ancient

Lava ridges make Kepuhi Beach beautiful, but swimming is hard unless the water is calm.

Molokai. From this shore you can look out across glassy water to see people standing on top of the sea—actually, way out on top of the reef—casting fishing lines into the distant waves. This is not a great area for beaches, but is a good place to snorkel or wade in the shallows.

One Alii Beach Park. Clear, close views of Maui and Lanai across the Pailolo Channel dominate One Alii Beach Park (*One* is pronounced *o-nay*, not *won*), the only well-maintained beach park on the island's south-central shore. Molokai folks gather here for family reunions and community celebrations; the park's tightly trimmed expanse of lawn could almost accommodate the entire island's population. Swimming within the reef is perfectly safe, but don't expect to catch any waves. Nearby is the restored One Alii fishpond. **Amenities:** showers; toilets. **Best for:** partiers; swimming. ⊠ *Rte. 450, east of Hotel Molokai.*

EAST MOLOKAI

The east end unfolds as a coastal drive with turnouts for tiny cove beaches—good places for snorkeling, shore fishing, or scuba exploring. Rocky little Mokuhooniki Island marks the eastern point of the island and serves as a nursery for humpback whales in winter and nesting seabirds in spring. The road loops around the east end, then descends and ends at Halawa Valley.

Waialua Beach Park. Also known as Twenty Mile Beach, this arched stretch of sand leads to one of the most popular snorkeling spots on the island. The water here, protected by the flanks of the little bay, is often so clear and shallow that even from land you can watch fish swimming among the coral heads. Watch out for traffic when you enter the highway. ■TIP➔ This is a pleasant place to stop on the drive around the east end. **Amenities:** none. **Best for:** snorkeling; swimming. ⊠ *Rte. 450, near mile marker 20.*

Halawa Beach Park. The vigorous water that gouged the steep, spectacular Halawa Valley also carved out two adjacent bays. Acumulations of coarse sand and river rock have created some protected pools that are good for wading or floating around. You might see surfers, but it's not wise to entrust your safety to the turbulent open ocean along this coast. Most people come here to hang out and absorb the beauty of Halawa Valley. The valley itelf is private property, so do not wander without a guide. **Amenities:** toilets. **Best for:** solitude. ⊠ *End of Rte. 450.*

WATER SPORTS AND TOURS

Molokai's shoreline topography limits opportunities for water sports. Sea cliffs dominate the north shore; the south shore is largely encased by a huge, taming reef. ⚠ Open-sea access at west-end and east-end beaches should be used only by experienced ocean swimmers, and then with caution because seas are rough, especially in winter. Generally speaking, there's no one around—certainly not lifeguards—if you get into trouble. For this reason alone, guided excursions are recommended. At least be sure to ask for advice from outfitters or residents. Two kinds of water activities predominate: kayaking within the reef area, and open-sea excursions on charter boats, most of which tie up at Kaunakakai Wharf.

BODY BOARDING AND BODYSURFING

You rarely see people body boarding or bodysurfing on Molokai, and the only surfing is for advanced wave riders. The best spots for body boarding, when conditions are safe (occasional summer mornings), are the west-end beaches. Another option is to seek out waves at the east end around mile marker 20.

DEEP-SEA FISHING

For Molokai people, as in days of yore, the ocean is more of a larder than a playground. It's common to see residents fishing along the shoreline or atop South Shore Reef, using poles or lines. Deep-sea fishing by charter boat is a great Molokai adventure. The sea channels here, though often rough and windy, provide gorgeous views of several islands. Big fish are plentiful in these waters, especially mahimahi, marlin, and various kinds of tuna. Generally speaking, boat captains will customize the outing to your interests, share a lot of information about the island, and let you keep some or all of your catch.

EQUIPMENT

Molokai Fish and Dive. If you'd like to try your hand at fishing, you can rent or buy equipment and ask for advice at Molokai Fish and Dive. ⊠ *61 Ala Malama St., Kaunakakai* ☎ 808/553–5926 ⊕ *molokaifishanddive.com.*

BOATS AND CHARTERS

Alyce C. This 31-foot cruiser runs excellent sportfishing excursions in the capable hands of Captain Joe. The cost for the six-passenger boat is $550 for a full-day trip, $450 for four to five hours. Gear is provided. It's a rare day when you don't snag at least one memorable fish. ✉ *Kaunakakai Wharf, Kaunakakai Pl., Kaunakakai* ☎ *808/558–8377* ⊕ *www.alycecsportfishing.com.*

Fun Hogs Sportfishing. Trim and speedy, the 27-foot flybridge boat named *Ahi* offers half-day ($500) and full-day ($700) sportfishing excursions. Skipper Mike Holmes also provides one-way or round-trip fishing expeditions to Lanai, as well as sunset cruises in winter. ✉ *Kaunakakai Wharf, Kaunakakai Pl., Kaunakakai* ☎ *808/567–6789* ⊕ *www.molokaifishing.com.*

Molokai Action Adventures. Walter Naki has traveled (and fished) all over the globe. He will create customized fishing expeditions and gladly share his wealth of experience. He will also take you to remote beaches for a day of swimming. If you want to explore the north side under the great sea cliffs, this is the way to go. His 21-foot *Boston Whaler* is usually seen in the east end at the mouth of Halawa Valley. ☎ *808/558–8184.*

KAYAKING

Molokai's south shore is enclosed by the largest reef system in the United States—an area of shallow, protected sea that stretches over 30 miles. This reef gives inexperienced kayakers an unusually safe, calm environment for shoreline exploring. ⚠ **Outside the reef, Molokai waters are often rough, and strong winds can blow you out to sea. Kayakers out here should be strong, experienced, and cautious.**

BEST SPOTS

South Shore Reef. Inside the South Shore Reef area is superb for flat-water kayaking any day of the year. It's best to rent a kayak from Molokai Outdoors in Kaunakakai and slide into the water from Kaunakakai Wharf. Get out in the morning before the wind picks up and paddle east, exploring the ancient Hawaiian fishponds. When you turn around to return, the wind will usually give you a push home.

EQUIPMENT, LESSONS, AND TOURS

Molokai Fish and Dive. At the west end of Kaunakakai's commercial strip, this all-around outfitter offers guided kayak excursions inside the South Shore Reef. One excursion paddles through a mangrove forest and explores a hidden ancient fishpond. If the wind starts blowing hard, the company will tow you back with its boat. The fee is $69 for the half-day trip, which includes sodas and water. ✉ *61 Ala Malama St., Kaunakakai* ☎ *808/553–5926* ⊕ *molokaifishanddive.com.*

Molokai Outdoors. This is the place to rent a kayak for exploring on your own. Kayaks rent for $26 to $39 per day or $130 to $195 per week, and extra paddles are available. ✉ *Kaunakakai Wharf, Kaunakakai Pl., Kaunakakai* ☎ *808/553–4477, 877/553–4477* ⊕ *www.molokaioutdoors.com.*

6

SAILING

Molokai is a place of strong, usually predictable winds that make for good and sometimes rowdy sailing. The island views in every direction are stunning. Kaunakakai Wharf is the home base for all of the island's charter sailboats.

SCUBA DIVING

Molokai Fish and Dive is the only PADI-certified dive company on Molokai. Shoreline access for divers is extremely limited, even nonexistent in winter. Boat diving is the way to go. Without guidance, visiting divers can easily find themselves in risky situations with wicked currents. Proper guidance, though, opens an undersea world rarely seen.

Molokai Fish and Dive. Owners Tim and Susan Forsberg can fill you in on local dive sites, rent you the gear, or hook you up with one of their PADI-certified guides to take you to the island's best underwater spots. Their 32-foot dive boat, the *Ama Lua*, can take eight divers and their gear. Two-tank dives lasting about five hours cost $155 with gear, $135 if you bring your own. Three-tank dives lasting around six hours cost $275. They know the best blue holes and underwater-cave systems, and can take you swimming with hammerhead sharks. ⊠ *61 Ala Malama St., Kaunakakai* ☎ *808/553–5926* ⊕ *molokaifishanddive.com.*

SNORKELING

During the times when swimming is safe—mainly in summer—just about every beach on Molokai offers good snorkeling along the lava outcroppings in the island's clean and pristine waters. Rough in winter, Kepuhi Beach is a prime spot in summer. Certain spots inside the South Shore Reef are also worth checking out.

BEST SPOTS

Kepuhi Beach. In winter, the sea here is rough and deadly. But in summer, this ½-mile-long west-end beach offers plenty of rocky nooks that swirl with sea life. The presence of outdoor showers is a bonus. Take Kaluakoi Road all the way to the west end. Park at the now-closed Kaluakoi Resort and walk to the beach. ⊠ *Kaluakoi Rd.*

Waialua Beach Park. A thin curve of sand rims a sheltered little bay loaded with coral heads and aquatic life. The water here is shallow—sometimes so shallow that you bump into the underwater landscape—and it's crystal clear. Head to the east end on Route 450, and pull off near mile marker 20. When the sea is calm, you can find several other good snorkeling spots along this stretch of road. ⊠ *Rte. 450.*

EQUIPMENT AND TOURS

Rent snorkel sets from either Molokai Outdoors or Molokai Fish and Dive in Kaunakakai. Rental fees are nominal—$6 to $10 a day. All the charter boats carry snorkel gear and include dive stops.

Fun Hogs Sportfishing. Mike Holmes, captain of the 27-foot *Ahi*, knows the island waters intimately, likes to have fun, and is willing to arrange any type of excursion—for example, one dedicated entirely to snorkeling. His two-hour snorkel trips leave early in the morning and explore rarely seen fish and turtle sites outside the reef. Bring your own food and drinks; the trips cost $70 per person. ⊠ *Kaunakakai Wharf, Kaunakakai Pl., Kaunakakai* ☎ 808/567–6789 ⊕ *www.molokaifishing. com.*

Molokai Fish and Dive. Climb aboard a 31-foot twin-hull Power Cat for a snorkeling trip to Molokai's pristine barrier reef. Trips cost $69 per person and include equipment, water, and soft drinks. ⊠ *61 Ala Malama St., Kaunakakai* ☎ 808/553–5926 ⊕ *www.molokaifishanddive.com.*

WHALE-WATCHING

Although Maui gets all the credit for the local wintering humpback-whale population, the big cetaceans also come to Molokai from December to April. Mokuhooniki Island at the east end serves as a whale nursery and courting ground, and the whales pass back and forth along the south shore. This being Molokai, whale-watching here will never involve floating amid a group of boats all ogling the same whale.

BOATS AND CHARTERS

Alyce C. Although this six-passenger sportfishing boat is usually busy hooking mahimahi and marlin, the captain will gladly take you on a three-hour excursion to admire the humpback whales. The price, around $75 per person, is based on the number of people in your group. ⊠ *Kaunakakai Wharf, Kaunakakai Pl., Kaunakakai* ☎ 808/558–8377 ⊕ *www.alycecsportfishing.com.*

Ama Lua. The crew of this 32-foot dive boat, which holds up to 18 passengers, is respectful of the whales and the laws that protect them. A 2½-hour whale-watching trip is $69 per person; it departs from Kaunakakai Wharf at 7 am from December to April. Call Molokai Fish and Dive for reservations. ⊠ *61 Ala Malama St., Kaunakakai* ☎ 808/553–5926, 808/552–0184 ⊕ *molokaifishanddive.com.*

Fun Hogs Sportfishing. The *Ahi*, a flybridge sportfishing boat, takes you on 2½-hour whale-watching trips in the morning from December to April. The cost is $70 per person. Bring your own snacks and drinks. ⊠ *Kaunakakai Wharf, Kaunakakai Pl., Kaunakakai* ☎ 808/567–6789 ⊕ *www.molokaifishing.com.*

GOLF, HIKING, AND OUTDOOR ACTIVITIES

Activity vendors in Kauanakakai are a good source of information on outdoor adventures on Molokai. For a mellow round of golf head to the island's only golf course, Ironwood Hills, where you'll likely share the green with local residents. Molokai's steep and uncultivated terrain offers excellent hikes and some stellar views. Although the island is largely wild, all land is owned, so get permission before hiking.

Bikers on Molokai can explore the north-shore sea cliffs overlooking the Kalaupapa Peninsula.

BIKING

Cyclists who like to eat up the miles love Molokai, since its few roads are long, straight, and extremely rural. You can really go for it—there are no traffic lights and most of the time no traffic.

Molokai Bicycle. You can rent a bike from Molokai Bicycle in Kaunakakai. ⊠ *80 Mohala St., Kaunakakai* ☎ *808/553–3931, 800/709–2453.*

GOLF

Molokai is not a prime golf destination, but the single 9-hole course makes for a pleasant afternoon.

Ironwood Hills Golf Course. Like other 9-hole plantation-era courses, Ironwood Hills is in a prime spot, with basic fairways and not always manicured greens. It helps if you like to play laid-back golf with locals and can handle occasionally rugged conditions. On the plus side, most holes offer ocean views. Fairways are *kukuya* grass and run through pine, ironwood, and eucalyptus trees. Carts and clubs are rented on the honor system; there's not always someone there to assist you. Bring your own water. ⊠ *Kalae Hwy., Kualapuu* ☎ *808/567–6000* ⚐ *9 holes. 3088 yds. Par 34. Greens fee: $18 for 9 holes, $24 for 18 holes* ☞ *Facilities: golf carts, pull carts, rental clubs.*

HIKING

Rural and rugged, Molokai is an excellent place for hiking. Roads and developments are few. The island is steep, so hikes often combine spectacular views with hearty physical exertion. Because the island is small, you can come away with the feeling of really knowing the place. And you won't see many other people around. Much of what may look like deserted land is private property, so be careful not to trespass without permission or an authorized guide.

BEST SPOTS

Kalaupapa Trail. You can hike down to the Kalaupapa Peninsula and back via this 3-mile, 26-switchback route. The trail is often nearly vertical, traversing the face of the high sea cliffs. You can reach Kalaupapa Trail off Highway 470 near Kalaupapa Overlook. Only those in excellent condition should attempt it. You can also arrange a guided hike with Molokai Outdoors. ⊠ *Off Hwy. 470, Kualapuu.*

★ **Kamakou Preserve.** A four-wheel-drive vehicle is essential for this half-day journey into the Molokai highlands. The Nature Conservancy of Hawaii manages the 2,774-acre Kamakou Preserve, one of the last stands of Hawaii's native plants and birds. A long rough dirt road, which begins not far from Kaunakakai, leads to the preserve.

On your way up to the preserve, be sure to stop at Waikolu Overlook, which gazes into a precipitous canyon. Once inside the preserve, various trails are clearly marked. The trail of choice—and you can drive right to it—is the 1½ -mile boardwalk trail through Pepeopae Bog, an ecological treasure. Be aware that incoming fog can blot out your trail and obscure markers. This is the landscape of prediscovery Hawaii and can be a mean trek.

The road to the Kamakou Preserve is not marked, so you should check in with the Nature Conservancy. Let the staff know that you plan to visit the preserve, and pick up the informative 24-page brochure with trail maps. ⊠ *Molokai Industrial Park, 23 Pueo Pl., 3 miles west of Kaunakakai, Kaunakakai* ☎ *808/553–5236* ⊕ *www.nature.org.*

Kawela Cul-de-Sacs. Just east of Kaunakakai, three streets—Kawela One, Two, and Three—jut up the mountainside from the Kamehameha V Highway. These roads end in cul-de-sacs that are also informal trailheads. Rough dirt roads work their way from here to the top of the mountain. The lower slopes are dry, rocky, steep, and austere. (It's good to start in the cool of the early morning.) A hiker in good condition can get all the way up into the high forest in two or three hours. These trails are not for the casual stroller, but you will be well rewarded. There are no ranger stations and no water fountains.

GOING WITH A GUIDE

Fodor's Choice **Halawa Valley Cultural Waterfall Hike.** This gorgeous, steep-walled valley was carved by two rivers and is rich in history. Site of the earliest Polynesian settlement on Molokai, Halawa is a sustained island culture with its ingeniously designed *loi*, or taro fields. Because of a tsunami in 1948 and changing cultural conditions in the 1960s, the valley was largely abandoned. Hawaiian families are restoring the *loi* and taking

visitors on guided hikes through the valley, which includes two of Molokai's *luakini heiau* (sacred temples), many historic sites, and the trail to **Moaula Falls,** a 250-foot cascade. Bring water, food, and insect repellent, and wear sturdy shoes that can get wet. The 4.2-mile round-trip hike is rated intermediate to advanced and includes two moderate river crossings. ☎ *808/553–5926* ⊕ *www.molokaifishanddive.com* ✉ *$75.*

Molokai Outdoors. This company can arrange guided hikes that fit your schedule and physical condition. The staff will take you down into Kalaupapa and arrange for a plane to pick you up. ✉ *Kaunakakai Wharf, Kaunakakai Pl., Kaunakakai* ☎ *808/553–4477, 877/553–4477* ⊕ *www.molokai-outdoors.com.*

SHOPPING

Molokai has one main commercial area: Ala Malama Street in Kaunakakai. There are no department stores or shopping malls, and the clothing is typical island wear. Local shopping is friendly and you may find hidden treasures. A very few family-run businesses define the main drag of Maunaloa, a rural former plantation town. Most stores in Kaunakakai are open Monday through Saturday between 9 and 6. In Maunaloa shops close by 4 in the afternoon.

6

CENTRAL MOLOKAI

ARTS AND CRAFTS

Molokai Art From the Heart. A small downtown shop, this arts and crafts co-op has locally made folk art like dolls, clay flowers, hula skirts, aloha-print visors, and children's wear. The shop also carries original art by Molokai artists and Giclée prints, jewelry, locally produced music, and St. Damien keepsakes. Store hours are Monday to Friday 10 to 4:30 and Saturday 9:30 to 2. ✉ *64 Ala Malama St., Kaunakakai* ☎ *808/553–8018.*

CLOTHING AND SHOES

Imports Gift Shop. Across from Kanemitsu Bakery, this one-stop shop offers fancy and casual island-style wear, including Roxy and Quicksilver for men, women, and children. The store is open Monday to Saturday 9 to 6 and Sunday 9 to 1. ✉ *82 Ala Malama St., Kaunakakai* ☎ *808/553–5734.*

Molokai Surf. This surf shop is known for its wide selection of Molokai T-shirts and sportswear. It also sells boogie boards and surfboards. ✉ *130 Kamehameha V Hwy., Kaunakakai* ☎ *808/553–5093.*

FOOD

Friendly Market Center. The best-stocked supermarket on the island has a slogan—"Your family store on Molokai"—that is truly credible. Hats, T-shirts, and sun-and-surf essentials keep company with fresh produce, meat, groceries, and liquor. Locals say the food is fresher here than at the other major supermarket. It's open weekdays 8:30 am to 8:30 pm and Saturday 8:30 am to 6:30 pm. ✉ *90 Ala Malama St., Kaunakakai* ☎ *808/553–5595.*

No traffic lights here: Molokai's rural, uncrowded roads have wide-open views.

Misaki's. In business since 1922, Misaki's has authentic island allure. Pick up housewares and beverages here, as well as your food staples, Monday through Saturday 8:30 am to 8:30 pm, and Sunday 9 am to noon. ⊠ *78 Ala Malama St., Kaunakakai* ☎ *808/553–5505.*

JEWELRY

Imports Gift Shop. You'll find soaps and lotions, a small collection of 14-karat-gold chains, rings, earrings, and bracelets, and a jumble of Hawaiian quilts, pillows, books, and postcards at this local favorite. The shop also carries a stunning collection of Hawaiian heirloom jewelry, inspired by popular Victorian pieces and crafted here since the late 1800s. ⊠ *82 Ala Malama St., Kaunakakai* ☎ *808/553–5734.*

Molokai Island Creations. Stop here to see the store's own unique line of jewelry, including sea opal, coral, and silver pieces. ⊠ *61 Ala Malama St., Kaunakakai* ☎ *808/553–5926.*

WEST MOLOKAI

ARTS AND CRAFTS

Big Wind Kite Factory and Plantation Gallery. The factory has custom-made kites you can fly or display. Designs range from hula girls to tropical fish. Also in stock are paper kites, minikites, and wind socks. Ask to go on the factory tour, or take a free kite-flying lesson. The adjacent gallery carries locally made crafts, Hawaiian books and CDs, jewelry, sarongs, and an elegant line of women's linen clothing. ⊠ *120 Maunaloa Hwy., Maunaloa* ☎ *808/552–2364.*

FOOD

Maunaloa General Store. Stocking everything from meat, produce, and dry goods to sandwiches, beverages, and boxed meals, this shop is a convenient stop if you're planning a picnic at one of the west-end beaches. It's open Monday through Saturday 9 am to 6 pm and Sunday 9 am to noon. ⊠ *200 Maunaloa Hwy., Maunaloa* ☎ *808/552–2346.*

ENTERTAINMENT AND NIGHTLIFE

Local nightlife consists mainly of gathering with friends and family, sipping a few cold ones, strumming ukuleles and guitars, singing old songs, and talking story. Still, there are a few ways to kick up your heels. Pick up a copy of the weekly Molokai *Dispatch* and see if there's a concert, church supper, or dance.

The bar at the Hotel Molokai is always a good place to drink. It has live music by island performers every night, and Molokai may be the best place to hear authentic, old-time, nonprofessional Hawaiian music. Don't be afraid to get up and dance. The "Aloha Friday" weekly gathering here, from 4 to 6 pm, features Na Kapuna, a group of accomplished *kupuna* (old-timers) with guitars and ukuleles.

For something truly casual, stop in at Kanemitsu Bakery on Ala Malama Street in Kaunakakai for the nightly hot bread sale (Tuesday through Sunday until 10 pm, or until they sell out of bread). You'll meet everyone in town, and you can take some hot bread home for a late-night treat.

WHERE TO EAT

During a week's stay, you might easily hit all the dining spots worth a visit and then return to your favorites for a second round. The dining scene is fun because it's a microcosm of Hawaii's diverse cultures. You can find locally grown vegetarian foods, spicy Filipino cuisine, and Hawaiian fish with a Japanese influence—such as tuna, mullet, and moonfish that's grilled, sautéed, or mixed with seaweed to make *poke* (salted and seasoned raw fish).

Most eating establishments are on Ala Malama Street in Kaunakakai. If you're heading to West Molokai for the day be sure to stock up on provisions, as there is no place to eat here. If you are on the east end stop by Manae Goods and Grinds (☎ *808/558–8186*) near mile marker 16 for good local seafood plates, burgers, and ice cream.

Prices in the reviews are the average cost of a main course at dinner or, if dinner is not served, at lunch.

CENTRAL MOLOKAI

Central Molokai offers most of the island's dining options, from takeout joints to the dining room at the Hotel Molokai.

$$ ✕ **Hula Shores.** The Hotel Molokai's restaurant is *the* place to hang out
HAWAIIAN   on Molokai. The service is brisk and friendly, the food is tasty, and the

atmosphere is casual. Prime-rib specials on Friday and Saturday nights draw a crowd. Every Friday from 4 to 6 pm Molokai's *kupuna* (old-timers) bring their instruments here for a lively jam session. $ *Average main: $19* ⊠ *Hotel Molokai, 1300 Kamehameha V Hwy., Kaunakakai* ☎ *808/553–5347.*

$
CAFÉ
Fodor'sChoice
★

× **Kanemitsu Bakery and Restaurant.** Stop at this Molokai institution for morning coffee and some of the the round Molokai bread—a sweet, pan-style white loaf that makes excellent cinnamon toast. Take a few loaves with you for a picnic or a condo breakfast. You can also try a taste of *lavosh,* a pricey flat bread flavored with sesame, taro, Maui onion, Parmesan cheese, or jalapeño. $ *Average main: $6* ⊠ *79 Ala Malama St., Kaunakakai* ☎ *808/553–5855* ▭ *No credit cards* ۞ *Closed Tues.*

$
HAWAIIAN

× **Kualapuu Cookhouse.** The only restaurant in rural Kualapuu, this local favorite is a classic, refurbished, green-and-white plantation house. Inside, paintings of hula dancers and island scenes enhance the simple furnishings. Typical fare is an inexpensive plate of chicken or pork served with rice, but at dinner there's also the more expensive sautéed *opakapaka* (snapper). This laid-back diner sits across the street from the Kualapuu Market. $ *Average main: $10* ⊠ *Farrington Hwy., 1 block west of Rte. 470, Kualapuu* ☎ *808/567–9655* ▭ *No credit cards* ۞ *No dinner Sun. and Mon.*

$
HAWAIIAN

× **Molokai Drive Inn.** Fast food Molokai-style is served at this walk-up counter. Hot dogs, fries, and sundaes are on the menu, but residents usually choose the foods they grew up on, such as *saimin* (thin noodles and vegetables in broth), plate lunches, shave ice, and the beloved *loco moco* (rice topped with a hamburger and a fried egg and covered in gravy). $ *Average main: $7* ⊠ *15 Kamoi St., Kaunakakai* ☎ *808/553–5655* ▭ *No credit cards.*

$
AMERICAN

× **Molokai Pizza Cafe.** Cheerful and busy, Molokai Pizza is a popular gathering spot for local families and a good place to pick up food for a picnic. Pizza, sandwiches, salads, pasta, and fresh fish are simply prepared and served without fuss. Kids keep busy at the nearby arcade, and art by local artists decorates the lavender walls. $ *Average main: $12* ⊠ *Kaunakakai Pl., at Wharf Rd., Kaunakakai* ☎ *808/553–3288* ▭ *No credit cards.*

$
PHILIPPINE

× **Oviedo's.** Don't let the sagging front door fool you. This modest and spotless lunch counter, a Molokai tradition, specializes in delicious *adobos* (stews) with traditional Filipino spices and sauces. Try the tripe, pork, or beef adobo for a taste of tradition. Locals say that Oviedo's makes the best crispy roast pork in the state. You can dine at one of the four tables or take out. $ *Average main: $11* ⊠ *145 Puali St., Kaunakakai* ☎ *808/553–5014* ▭ *No credit cards* ۞ *Closed Sun.*

$
DELI

× **Sundown Deli.** Small and clean, this rose-color deli focuses on freshly made take-out food. Sandwiches come on a half dozen types of bread, and the Portuguese bean soup and chowders are rich and filling. It's open weekdays from 7:30 to 3:30. $ *Average main: $6* ⊠ *145 Ala Malama St., Kaunakakai* ☎ *808/553–3713* ▭ *No credit cards* ۞ *Closed weekends. No dinner.*

WHERE TO STAY

For expanded hotel reviews, visit Fodors.com.

The coastline along Molokai's west end has ocean-view condominium units and luxury homes available as vacation rentals. If you are familiar with the high-end Lodge at Molokai Ranch, please note that the resort is closed and up for sale. Central Molokai offers seaside condominiums and the icon of the island—Hotel Molokai. The only lodgings on the east end are some guest cottages in magical settings and the ranch house at Puu O Hoku. Note that room rates do not include 13.42% sales tax.

WHERE TO SPA

Molokai Acupuncture & Massage. This relaxing retreat offers acupuncture, massage, facials, waxing, herbal remedies, and wellness treatments. The professional staff also services the spa at the Hotel Molokai. ✉ *40 Ala Malama St., Kaunakakai* ☎ *808/553-3930* 🌐 *www.molokai-wellness.com.*

Note: Maui County has regulations concerning vacation rentals; to avoid disappointment, always contact the property manager or the owner and ask if the accommodation has the proper permits and is in compliance with local ordinances.

Prices in the reviews are the lowest price of a standard double room in high season. Prices for rentals are the lowest per-night cost for a one-bedroom unit in high season.

WEST MOLOKAI

If you want to stay in West Molokai so you'll have access to unspoiled beaches, your only choices are condos or vacation homes. Keep in mind that units fronting the abandoned Kaula Koi golf course present a bit of a dismal view.

$ RENTAL 🏢 **Ke Nani Kai.** These pleasant, spacious, one- and two-bedroom condos have ocean views and nicely maintained tropical landscaping. **Pros:** on island's secluded west end; uncrowded pool. **Cons:** amenities vary from unit to unit; far from commercial center; some units overlook abandoned golf course. **TripAdvisor:** "a melt away vacation," "beautiful scenery," "comfortable and affordable." [$] *Rooms from: $105* ✉ *50 Keuphi Beach Rd., Maunaloa* ☎ *808/553–8334, 800/367–2984* 🌐 *www.molokai-vacation-rental.net* 🛏 *120 units* 🍴 *No meals.*

$ RENTAL 🏢 **Paniolo Hale.** Perched high on a ridge overlooking a favorite local surfing spot, this is Molokai's best condominium property. **Pros:** close to beach; quiet surroundings; perfect if you are an expert surfer. **Cons:** amenities vary; far from shopping; golf-course units front abandoned course. **TripAdvisor:** "paradise found," "a lovely condo," "quiet." [$] *Rooms from: $125* ✉ *100 Lio Pl., Kaunakakai* ☎ *808/553–8334, 800/367–2984* 🌐 *www.molokai-vacation-rental.net* 🛏 *77 units* 🍴 *No meals.*

CENTRAL MOLOKAI

Aside from the popular Hotel Molokai, there are two condo properties in this area, one close to shopping and dining in Kaunakakai, and the other on the way to the east end.

$ HOTEL **Hotel Molokai.** At this local favorite, Polynesian-style bungalows are scattered around the nicely landscaped property. **Pros:** five minutes to town; some kitchenettes; authentic Hawaiian entertainment. **Cons:** not many frills; lower-priced rooms are small and plain; late-night live music can be loud. **TripAdvisor:** "charming," "relaxing," "fantastic time and wonderful people." [$] *Rooms from: $149* ✉ *1300 Kamehameha V Hwy., Kaunakakai* ☎ *808/553–5347, 877/553–5347* 🌐 *www.hotelmolokai.com* 🛏 *40 rooms* 🍴 *No meals.*

$ RENTAL **Molokai Shores.** Many of the units in this three-story condominium complex have a view of the ocean. **Pros:** convenient location; some units upgraded; near water. **Cons:** uninspiring basic accommodations; fussy cancellation policy. **TripAdvisor:** "the perfect place to get away," "beautiful," "charming little condo." [$] *Rooms from: $105* ✉ *1000 Kamehameha V Hwy., Kaunakakai* ☎ *808/553–5954, 800/535–0085* 🌐 *www.molokai-vacation-rental.net* 🛏 *100 units* 🍴 *No meals.*

$ RENTAL **Wavecrest.** This oceanfront condominium complex is convenient if you want to explore the east side of the island—it's 13 miles east of Kaunakakai. **Pros:** convenient location for divers; good value; nicely maintained grounds. **Cons:** amenities vary; far from shopping; area sometimes gets windy. **TripAdvisor:** "condo was fabulous," "well maintained," "great place to get away." [$] *Rooms from: $105* ✉ *Rte. 450, near mile marker 13 800/367–2984, 808/553–8334* 🌐 *www.molokai-vacation-rental.net* 🛏 *126 units* 🍴 *No meals.*

EAST MOLOKAI

Puu O Hoku Ranch, a rental facility on East Molokai, is the main lodging option on this side of the island. The ranch is quite far from the center of the island.

$ B&B/INN **Puu O Hoku Ranch.** At the east end of Molokai you'll discover these ocean-view accommodations on 14,000 isolated acres of pasture and forest. **Pros:** ideal for large groups; authentic working ranch; great hiking. **Cons:** on remote east end of island; road to property is narrow and winding. **TripAdvisor:** "a serene hideaway," "paradise on earth," "horseback riding." [$] *Rooms from: $140* ✉ *Rte. 450, near mile marker 25, Kaunakakai* ☎ *808/558–8109* 🌐 *www.puuohoku.com* 🛏 *2 cottages, 11 rooms* 🍴 *No meals.*

Lanai

WORD OF MOUTH

"We took a day trip to Lanai for snorkeling and dolphin- and whale-watching. For us, it was totally worth it. We snorkeled at Manele Bay—in addition to snorkeling off the beach here, there are some great tide pools at one end of the beach."

—Sheralyn

WELCOME TO LANAI

TOP REASONS TO GO

★ **Seclusion and serenity:** Lanai is small: local motion is slow motion. Get into the spirit and go home rested instead of exhausted.

★ **Garden of the Gods:** Walk amid the eerie red-rock spires that Hawaiians believe to be a sacred spot. The ocean views are magnificent, too; sunset is a good time to visit.

★ **A dive at Cathedrals:** Explore underwater pinnacle formations and mysterious caverns illuminated by shimmering rays of light.

★ **Dole Park:** Hang out in the shade of the Cook pines in Lanai City and talk story with the locals for a taste of old-time Hawaii.

★ **Hit the water at Hulopoe Beach:** This beach may have it all: good swimming, a shady park for perfect picnicking, great reefs for snorkeling, and sometimes plenty of spinner dolphins.

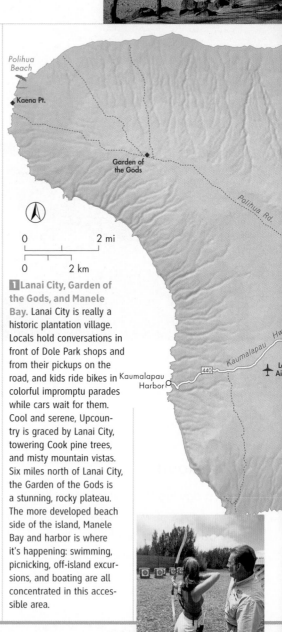

Polihua Beach

Kaena Pt.

Garden of the Gods

Polihua Rd.

0   2 mi

0   2 km

Kaumalapau Hwy

440

Kaumalapau Harbor

La
Ai

1 Lanai City, Garden of the Gods, and Manele Bay. Lanai City is really a historic plantation village. Locals hold conversations in front of Dole Park shops and from their pickups on the road, and kids ride bikes in colorful impromptu parades while cars wait for them. Cool and serene, Upcountry is graced by Lanai City, towering Cook pine trees, and misty mountain vistas. Six miles north of Lanai City, the Garden of the Gods is a stunning, rocky plateau. The more developed beach side of the island, Manele Bay and harbor is where it's happening: swimming, picnicking, off-island excursions, and boating are all concentrated in this accessible area.

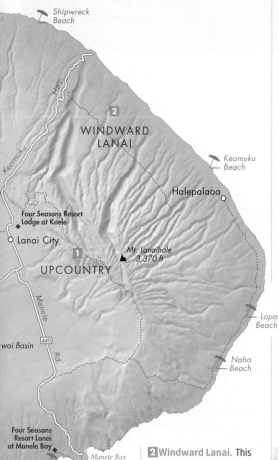

GETTING ORIENTED

Unlike the other Hawaiian Islands with their tropical splendors, Lanai looks like a desert: kiawe trees right out of Africa, red-dirt roads, and a deep blue sea. Lanaihale (house of Lanai), the mountain that bisects the island, is carved into deep canyons by rain and wind on the windward side, and the drier leeward side slopes gently to the sea, where waves pound against surf-carved cliffs. The town of Lanai City is in the center of the island, Upcountry. Manele Bay, on the south side of the island, is popular for swimming and boating.

2 Windward Lanai. This area is the long white-sand beach at the base of Lanai-hale. Now uninhabited, it was once occupied by thriving Hawaiian fishing villages and a sugarcane plantation.

By Joana Varawa

With no traffic or traffic lights and miles of open space, Lanai seems lost in time, and that can be a good thing. Small (141 square miles) and sparsely populated, it is the smallest inhabited Hawaiian Island and has just 3,500 residents, most of them living Upcountry.

Though it may seem a world away, Lanai is separated from Maui and Molokai by two narrow channels, and is easily accessed by commercial ferry from Maui. The two resorts on the island are run by the Four Seasons. If you yearn for a beach with amenities, a luxury resort, and golf course, the Four Seasons Resort Lanai at Manele Bay beckons from the shoreline. Upcountry, the luxurious Four Seasons Resort Lodge at Koele provides cooler pleasures. This leaves the rest of the 100,000-acre island open to explore. An afternoon strolling around Dole Park in historic Lanai City offers shopping and the opportunity to mingle with locals.

FLORA AND FAUNA

Lanai bucks the "tropical" trend of the other Hawaiian Islands with African kiawe trees, Cook pines, and eucalyptus in place of palm trees, and deep blue sea where you might expect shallow turquoise bays. Abandoned pineapple fields are overgrown with drought-resistant grasses, Christmas berry, and lantana; native plants, *aalii* and *ilima*, are found in uncultivated areas. Axis deer from India dominate the ridges, and wild turkeys lumber around the resorts. Whales can be seen December through April, and a family of resident spinner dolphins rests and fishes regularly in Hulopoe Bay.

ON LANAI TODAY

Despite its fancy resorts, Lanai still has that languid Hawaii feel. The island is 98% owned by billionaire David Murdock. Residents are a mix of just about everything—Hawaiian, Chinese, German, Portuguese, Filipino, Japanese, French, Puerto Rican, English, Norwegian—you name it. When Dole owned the island in the earlier part of the 20th century and grew pineapples, the plantation was divided into ethnic camps, which helped retain cultural cuisines. Potluck dinners feature sashimi, Portuguese bean soup, *laulau* (morsels of pork, chicken, butterfish, or other ingredients wrapped with young taro shoots in ti leaves), potato salad, teriyaki steak, chicken *hekka* (a gingery Japanese chicken stir-fry), and Jell-O. The local language is pidgin, a mix of words as complicated and rich as the food.

PLANNING

WHEN TO GO

Lanai has an ideal climate year-round, hot and sunny at the sea and a few delicious degrees cooler Upcountry. In Lanai City and Upcountry, the nights and mornings can be almost chilly when a fog or harsh trade winds settle in. Winter months are known for *slightly* rougher weather—periodic rain showers and higher surf.

As higher mountains on Maui capture the trade-wind clouds, Lanai receives little rainfall and has a near-desert ecology. Consider the wind direction when planning your day. If it's blowing a gale on the windward beaches, head for the beach at Hulopoe or check out Garden of the Gods. Overcast days, when the wind stops or comes lightly from the southwest, are common in whale season. At that time, try a whale-watching trip or the windward beaches.

Whales are seen off Lanai's shores from December through April. A Pineapple Festival on the July 4 Saturday in Dole Park features local food, Hawaiian entertainment, a pineapple-eating contest, and fireworks. Buddhists hold their annual outdoor Obon Festival, honoring departed ancestors with joyous dancing, dining, and drumming, in early July. During hunting-season weekends, from mid-February through mid-May, and mid-July through mid-October, it's best to watch out for hunters on dirt roads even though there are designated safety zones.

GETTING HERE AND AROUND

AIR TRAVEL

Island Air and go! Mokulele are the only commercial airlines serving Lanai City. All flights to the island depart from Oahu's Honolulu International Airport.

If you're staying at the Hotel Lanai or either Four Seasons hotel, you'll be met at the airport or ferry dock by a bus that shuttles between the resorts and Lanai City. A different shuttle will pick you up if you're renting a Jeep or minivan from Lanai City Service.

If you're not taking a shuttle, bus drivers at the ferry docks will herd you onto the appropriate bus and take you into town for $10 per person. Advance reservations aren't necessary (or even possible), but be prepared for a little confusion on the dock.

Information go! Mokulele ☏ *888/435–9462* ⊕ *www.iflygo.com.* **Island Air** ☏ *800/652–6541* ⊕ *www.islandair.com.*

CAR TRAVEL

Lanai has no traffic, no traffic lights, and only 30 miles of paved roads. Keomuku Highway starts just past the Lodge at Koele and runs northeast to the dirt road that goes to Shipwreck Beach and Lopa Beach. Manele Road (Highway 440) runs south down to Manele Bay and Hulopoe Beach. Kaumalapau Highway (also Highway 440) heads west to Kaumalapau Harbor. The rest of your driving takes place on bumpy, dusty, secondary roads that aren't marked. Driving in thick mud is not recommended, and the rental agency will charge a cleaning fee.

Renting a four-wheel-drive vehicle is expensive but almost essential if you'd like to explore beyond the resorts and Lanai City. Make reservations far in advance of your trip, because Lanai's fleet of vehicles is limited. Lanai City Service, a subsidiary of Dollar Rent A Car, is open daily 7 to 7.

Bring along a good topographical map, and keep in mind your directions. Stop from time to time and refind landmarks and gauge your progress. Never drive or walk to the edge of lava cliffs, as rock can give way under you. Directions on the island are often given as *mauka* (toward the mountains) and *makai* (toward the ocean).

Information Lanai City Service ✉ *Lanai Ave., at 11th St. Lanai City* ☎ *808/565–7227, 800/533–7808.*

FERRY TRAVEL

Ferries operated by Expeditions cross the channel four times daily between Lahaina on Maui to Manele Bay Harbor on Lanai. The crossing takes 45 minutes and costs $30. Be warned: passage can be rough, especially in winter.

Contact Expeditions ☎ *808/661–3756, 800/695–2624* ⊕ *www.go-lanai.com.*

SHUTTLE TRAVEL

A shuttle transports hotel guests between the Hotel Lanai, the Four Seasons Resort Lodge at Koele, the Four Seasons Resort Lanai at Manele Bay, and the airport. A $47.50 fee added to the room rates covers all transportation during the length of your stay.

RESTAURANTS

Lanai has a wide range of choices for dining, from simple plate-lunch local eateries to fancy, upscale, gourmet resort restaurants.

HOTELS

The range of lodgings is limited on Lanai. Essentially there are only three resort options: the two Four Seasons Resorts Lanai (at Manele Bay and Upcountry at the Lodge at Koele) and the venerable Hotel Lanai. A good alternative is looking into house rentals, which give you a feel for everyday life on the island. Make sure to book far in advance. **Note:** Maui County has regulations concerning vacation rentals; to avoid disappointment, always contact the property manager or owner and ask if the accommodation has the proper permits and is in compliance with local laws.

VISITOR INFORMATION

The Lanai Culture & Heritage Center has information and maps.

Contact Lanai Visitors Bureau ✉ *Dole Administration Building, 730 Lanai Ave., Lanai City* ☎ *808/563–0484* ⊕ *www.visitlanai.net.*

Ocean views provide a backdrop to the eroded rocks at Garden of the Gods.

EXPLORING LANAI

You can easily explore Lanai City and the island's two resorts without a car; just hop on the hourly shuttle. A small fee applies. To access the rest of this untamed island, rent a four-wheel-drive vehicle. Take a map, be sure you have a full tank, and bring a snack and plenty of water. Ask the rental agency or your hotel's concierge about road conditions before you set out. It's always good to carry a cell phone. The main road on Lanai, Highway 440, refers to both Kaumalapau Highway and Manele Road.

LANAI CITY, GARDEN OF THE GODS, AND MANELE BAY

Lanai City is 3 miles northeast of the airport; Manele Bay is 9 miles southeast of Lanai City; Garden of the Gods is 6 miles northwest of Lanai City.

Pineapples once blanketed the Palawai, the great basin south of Lanai City. Although it looks like a volcanic crater, it isn't. Some say that the name Palawai is descriptive of the mist that sometimes fills the basin at dawn and looks like a huge shining lake.

The area northwest of Lanai City is wild; the Garden of the Gods is one of its highlights.

GETTING HERE AND AROUND

Lanai City serves as the island's hub, with roads leading to Manele Bay, Kaumalapau Harbor, and windward Lanai. Garden of the Gods is usually possible to visit by car, but beyond that you will need four-wheel drive.

EXPLORING

TOP ATTRACTIONS

Fodor's Choice ★   **Garden of the Gods.** This preternatural plateau is scattered with boulders of different sizes, shapes, and colors, the products of a million years of wind erosion. Time your visit for sunset, when the rocks begin to glow—from rich red to purple—and the fiery globe sinks to the horizon. Magnificent views of the Pacific Ocean, Molokai, and, on clear days, Oahu, provide the perfect backdrop for photographs. Lanai landowner David Murdock has proposed a development plan that would transform this area into a large wind farm, but local and visitor opposition may delay the plan's approval.

The ancient Hawaiians shunned Lanai for hundreds of years, believing the island was the inviolable home of spirits. Standing beside the oxide-red rock spires of this strange, raw landscape, you might be tempted to believe the same. This lunar savanna still has a decidedly eerie edge, but the shadows disappearing on the horizon are those of mouflon sheep and axis deer, not the fearsome spirits of lore. According to tradition, Kawelo, a Hawaiian priest, kept a perpetual fire burning on an altar at the Garden of the Gods, in sight of the island of Molokai. As long as the fire burned, prosperity was assured for the people of Lanai. Kawelo was killed by a rival priest on Molokai and the fire went out. The Hawaiian name for this area is Keahiakawelo, meaning the "fire of Kawelo."

Garden of the Gods is 6 miles north of Lanai City. From the Stables at Koele, follow a dirt road through a pasture, turn right at a crossroad marked by carved boulder, and head through abandoned fields and ironwood forests to an open red-dirt area marked by a carved boulder. ⊠ *Off Polihua Rd.*

Ka Lokahi o Ka Malamalama Church. Built in 1938, this picturesque painted wooden church provided services for Lanai's growing population. (For many people, the only other Hawaiian church, in coastal Keomuku, was too far away.) A classic structure of ranching days, the one-room church had to be moved from its original Lanai Ranch site when the Lodge at Koele was built. It's open all day and Sunday services are still held, in Hawaiian and English; visitors are welcome but are requested to attend quietly. The church is north of the entrance to the Four Seasons Resort Lodge at Koele. ⊠ *1 Keomuku Hwy.*

Kanepuu Preserve. Hawaiian sandalwood, olive, and ebony trees characterize Hawaii's largest example of a rare native dryland forest. Thanks to the combined efforts of the Nature Conservancy and Castle & Cooke Resorts, the 590-acre remnant forest is protected from the axis deer and mouflon sheep that graze on the land beyond its fence. More than 45 native plant species, including *nau,* the endangered Hawaiian gardenia, can be seen here. A short, self-guided loop trail, with eight signs illustrated by local artist Wendell Kahoohalahala, reveals this ecosystem's

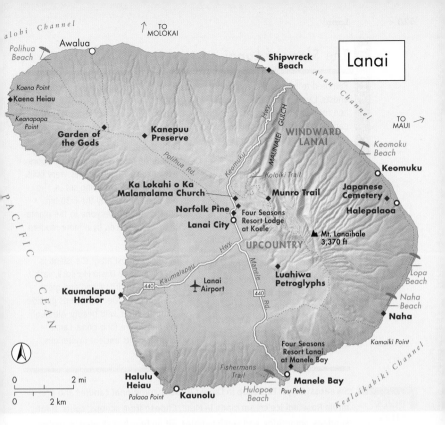

Lanai

beauty and the challenges it faces. The reserve is adjacent to the sacred hill, Kane Puu, dedicated to the Hawaiian god of water and vegetation. ⊠ *Polihua Rd., 4.8 miles north of Lanai City.*

Kaumalapau Harbor. Built in 1926 by the Hawaiian Pineapple Company, this is Lanai's principal commercial seaport. A native fishing village once thrived here. The cliffs that flank the western shore reach up to 1,000 feet tall. Water activities aren't allowed here, but it's a dramatic sunset spot. Local fishermen enjoy shore casting in the evenings. The harbor is closed to visitors on barge days: Tuesday, Wednesday, and Thursday. ⊠ *West end of Hwy. 440, 6 miles west of Lanai City.*

★ **Lanai City.** A tidy plantation town, built in 1924 by Jim Dole for his growing pineapple business, Lanai City is home to old-time residents, recently arrived resort workers, and second-home owners. A simple grid of roads is lined with stately Cook pines. Despite recent growth, the pace is still calm and the people are friendly. **Dole Park**, in the center of Lanai City, is surrounded by small shops and restaurants and is a favorite spot among locals for sitting, strolling, and talking story. Visit the **Lanai Culture and Heritage Center** to get a glimpse of this island's rich past, purchase historical publications and maps, and get directions to anywhere on the island.

The Story of Lanai

Rumored to be haunted by hungry ghosts, Lanai was sparsely inhabited for many centuries. Most of the earliest settlers lived along the shore and made their living from fishing the nearby waters. Others lived in the Uplands near water sources and traded their produce for seafood. The high chiefs sold off the land bit by bit to foreign settlers, and by 1910 the island was owned by a single family.

When the Hawaiian Pineapple Company purchased Lanai for $1.1 million in 1922, it built the town of Lanai City, opened the commercial harbor, and laid out the pineapple fields. Field workers came from overseas to toil in what quickly became the world's largest pineapple plantation. Exotic animals and birds were imported for

hunting. Cook pines were planted to catch the rain, and eucalyptus windbreaks anchored the blowing soil.

Everything was stable for 70 years, until the plantation closed in 1992. When the resorts opened their doors, newcomers arrived, homes were built, and other ways of living set in. The old pace, marked by the 6:30 am whistle calling everyone to the plantation, was replaced by a more modern schedule.

Because almost all of the island is now owned by David Murdock, vast areas remain untouched and great views abound. Deer and birds provide glimpses of its wild beauty. Although the ghosts are long gone, Lanai still retains its ancient mysterious presence.

QUICK
BITES

Sweetest Days. This shop in Lanai City sells traditional candies and premium Roselani ice cream made in Maui. Choose from scoops, splits, floats, sundaes, smoothies, and slush puppies. Sit on benches shaded by umbrellas and watch the slow world of Lanai pass by. ⌧ *338 8th St.* ☏ *808/559–6253* ⊘ *Closed Sun.*

Luahiwa Petroglyphs. On a steep slope overlooking the Palawai Basin are 34 boulders with engravings. Drawn in a mixture of styles between the late 1700s and early 1800s, the simple stick figures depict animals, people, and mythical beings. A no-longer-visible *heiau,* or temple, was used to summon the rain and was dedicated to the god Kane. Do not draw on or deface the images, and do not add to the collection. From Lanai City, head south on Highway 440, turn left on the first dirt road, and follow it for 1.2 miles. Do not go left uphill, but continue straight. When you see boulders on a hillside, park and walk up to the petroglyphs. ⌧ *Off Hwy. 440.*

Manele Bay. The site of a Hawaiian village dating from AD 900, Manele Bay is flanked by lava cliffs hundreds of feet high. Ferries from Maui and visiting yachts pull in here, as it's the island's only small-boat harbor. Public restrooms, a small café, shop, and picnic tables make it a busy pit stop—you can watch the boating activity as you rest and refuel.

Just offshore to the west is **Puu Pehe**. Often called Sweetheart Rock, the isolated 80-foot-high islet carries a romantic Hawaiian legend that is probably not true. The rock is said to be named after Pehe, a woman so beautiful that her husband kept her hidden in a sea cave. One day, the surf surged into the cave and she drowned. Her grief-stricken husband buried her on this rock and jumped to his death. A more likely story is that the enclosure on the summit is a shrine to birds, built by bird-catchers. Protected shearwaters nest in the nearby sea cliffs from July through November. ⌧ *Hwy. 440, 9 miles south of Lanai City, Manele.*

WORTH NOTING

Halulu Heiau. The well-preserved remains of an impressive *heiau* (temple) at Kaunolu village, which was actively used by Lanai's earliest residents, attest to this spot's sacred history. As late as 1810, this hilltop temple was considered a place of refuge, where those who had broken *kapu* (taboos) were forgiven and where women and children could find safety in times of war. If you explore the area, be respectful; take nothing with you and leave nothing behind. Be sure to bring along water.

This place is hard to find, and hard to reach. The four-wheel-drive-only road is alternately rocky, sandy, and soft at the bottom. From Lanai City, follow Highway 440 west toward Kaumalapau Harbor. Past the airport, look for a carved boulder on the hill on your left. Turn left on the dirt road and follow it 3 miles to another carved boulder, where you'll turn right and head downhill. ⌧ *On a dirt road off Hwy. 440.*

Kaunolu. Close to the island's highest cliffs, Kaunolu was once a prosperous fishing village. This important archaeological site includes a major *heiau* (temple), stone floors, and house platforms. The impressive 90-foot drop to the ocean through a gap in the lava rock is called **Kahekili's Leap.** Warriors made the dangerous leap into the shallow water below to prove their courage. King Kamehameha came here for the superb fishing and to collect taxes. The road is rocky, then gets soft and sandy at the bottom. From Lanai City, follow Highway 440 west past the airport. At a carved boulder on your left, turn left onto an unmarked dirt road. Continue 3 miles until you reach the second carved boulder, then go downhill 3 miles to village. At the end of the road, walk across the streambed and up the hill. ⌧ *On a dirt road off Hwy. 440.*

Lanai Culture and Heritage Center. Small and carefully arranged, this historical museum features artifacts and photographs from Lanai's varied and rich history. Plantation-era clothing and tools, ranch memorabilia, old maps, precious feather lei, poi pounders, and family portraits combine to give you a good idea of the history of the island and its people. Postcards, maps, books, and pamphlets are for sale. The friendly staff can orient you to the island's historical sites and provide directions. This is the best place to start your explorations of the island. ⌧ *730 Lanai Ave.* ☎ *808/565–7177* ⊕ *www.lanaichc.org* 🖅 *Free* ☉ *Weekdays 8:30–3:30, Sat. 9–1.*

Norfolk pine. Considered the "mother" of all the pines on the island, this 160-foot-tall tree was planted here, at the former site of the ranch manager's house, in 1875. Almost 30 years later, George Munro, the manager, observed how, in foggy weather, water collected on its foliage, dripping off rain. This led Munro to supervise the planting of Cook pines along the ridge of Lanaihale and throughout the town in order to add to the island's water supply. This majestic tree is just in front of

The calm crescent of Hulopoe Beach is perfect for swimming, snorkeling, or just relaxing.

the south wing of Four Seasons Resort Lodge at Koele. ⊠ *Four Seasons Resort Lodge at Koele, 1 Keomuku Hwy.*

WINDWARD LANAI

9 miles northeast of Lodge at Koele to end of paved road.

The eastern section of Lanai is wild and untouched. An inaccessible *heiau*, or temple, is the only trace of human habitation, with the exception of rock walls and boulders marking old shrines. Four-wheel-drive vehicles are a must to explore this side of the isle. Be prepared for hot, rough conditions. Hawaiians request that you not stack or disturb rocks. Pack a picnic lunch, a hat and sunscreen, and drinking water.

GETTING HERE AND AROUND

Once you leave paved Keomuku Highway and turn left toward Shipwreck Beach or right to Naha, the roads are dirt and sand; conditions vary with the seasons. Mileage doesn't matter much here, but figure on 20 minutes from the end of the paved road to Shipwreck Beach, and about 45 minutes to Lopa Beach.

For information about Shipwreck Beach and Lopa Beach, see Beaches, below.

EXPLORING

TOP ATTRACTIONS

★ **Munro Trail.** This 12.8-mile four-wheel-drive trail along a fern- and pine-clad narrow ridge was named after George Munro, manager of the Lanai Ranch Company, who began a reforestation program in the 1950s to restore the island's much-needed watershed. The trail climbs

Lanaihale (House of Lanai), which, at 3,370 feet, is the island's highest point; on clear days you'll be treated to a panorama of canyons and almost all the Hawaiian Islands. ■TIP➔ **The road gets very muddy, and trade winds can be strong. Watch for sheer drop-offs, and keep an eye out for hikers.** You can also hike the Munro Trail, although it's steep, the ground is uneven, and there's no water. From the Four Seasons Resort Lodge at Koele, head north on Highway 440 for 1¼ miles, then turn right onto Cemetery Road. Keep going until you're headed downhill on the main dirt road. ⊠ *Cemetery Rd., Lanai City.*

WORTH NOTING

Halepalaoa. Named for the whales that once washed ashore here, Halepalaoa, or house of whale ivory, was the site of the wharf used by the short-lived Maunalei Sugar Company to ship cane in 1899. Some say the sugar company failed because the sacred stones of nearby **Kahea Heiau** were used for the construction of the cane railroad. The brackish well water turned too salty, forcing the sugar company to close in 1901, after just two years. The remains of the *heiau* (temple), once an important place of worship for the people of Lanai, are now difficult to find through the *kiawe* (mesquite) overgrowth. There's good public-beach access here and clear shallow water for swimming, but no other facilities. Take Highway 440 (Keomuku Highway) to its eastern terminus; then turn right on the dirt road and continue south for 5½ miles. ⊠ *On dirt road off Hwy. 440, Lanai City.*

Japanese Cemetery. In 1899 sugar came to this side of Lanai. The 2,400-acre plantation promised to be a profitable proposition, but that same year disease wiped out the labor force. This Buddhist shrine commemorates the Japanese workers who died, and the local congregation comes down to clean this sacred place each year. Take Highway 440 to its eastern terminus, then turn right onto a dirt road and continue south for 6½ miles. The shrine is uphill on your left. ⊠ *On dirt road off Hwy. 440.*

Keomuku. There's a peaceful beauty about Keomuku, with its faded memories and forgotten homesteads. During the late 19th century, this busy Lanai community served as the headquarters of Maunalei Sugar Company. After the company failed, the land remained abandoned. Although there are no other signs of previous inhabitation, its church, **Ka Lanakila O Ka Malamalama,** built in 1903, has been partially restored by volunteers. Visitors often leave some small token, a shell or faded lei, as an offering. Take Highway 440 to its eastern terminus, then turn right onto a dirt road and continue south for 5 miles. The church is on your right in the coconut trees. ⊠ *On dirt road off Hwy. 440.*

Naha. An ancient rock-walled fishpond—visible at low tide—lies here, where the sandy shore ends and the cliffs begin their rise along the island's shores. Accessible by four-wheel-drive vehicle, the beach is a frequent dive spot for local fishermen. ■TIP➔ **Treacherous currents make this a dangerous place for swimming.** Take Highway 440 to its eastern terminus, then turn right onto a dirt road and continue south for 11 miles. The shoreline dirt road ends here. ⊠ *On dirt road off Hwy. 440, Lanai City.*

BEACHES

Lanai offers miles of secluded white-sand beaches on its windward side, plus the moderately developed Hulopoe Beach, which is adjacent to the Four Seasons Resort Lanai at Manele Bay. Hulopoe is accessible by car or hotel shuttle bus; to reach the windward beaches you need a four-wheel-drive vehicle. Reef, rocks, and coral make swimming on the windward side problematic, but it's fun to splash around in the shallow water. Expect debris on the windward beaches due to the Pacific convergence ocean currents. Driving on the beach itself is illegal and can be dangerous. *Beaches in this chapter are listed alphabetically.*

> ### THE COASTAL ROAD
>
> Road conditions can change overnight and become impassable due to rain in the Uplands. Car-rental agencies should be able to give you updates before you hit the road. Some of the spur roads leading to the windward beaches from the coastal dirt road cross private property and are closed off by chains. Look for open spur roads with recent tire marks (a fairly good sign that they are safe to drive on). It's best to park on firm ground and walk in to avoid getting your car mired in the sand.

Fodor's Choice ★ **Hulopoe Beach.** A short stroll down from the Four Seasons Resort Lanai at Manele Bay, Hulopoe is considered one of the best beaches in Hawaii. The sparkling crescent of this Marine Life Conservation District beckons with calm waters safe for swimming almost year-round, great snorkeling reefs, tide pools, and, sometimes, spinner dolphins. A shady, grassy beach park is perfect for picnics. If the shore break is pounding, or if you see surfers riding big waves, stay out of the water. In the afternoon, watch Lanai High School students heave outrigger canoes down the steep shore break and race one another just offshore. To get here, take Highway 440 south to the bottom of the hill and turn right. The road dead-ends at the beach's parking lot. **Amenities:** parking (no fee); showers; toilets. **Best for:** snorkeling; swimming; surfing. ⊠ *Off Hwy. 440, Lanai City.*

Lopa Beach. A difficult surfing spot that tests the mettle of experienced locals, Lopa is also an ancient fishpond. With majestic views of West Maui and Kahoolawe, this remote, white-sand beach is a great place for a picnic. ⚠ **Don't let the sight of surfers fool you: the channel's currents are too strong for swimming.** Take Highway 440 to its eastern terminus, turn right onto a dirt road, and continue south for 7 miles. **Amenities:** none. **Best for:** solitude; sunrise; walking. ⊠ *On dirt road off Hwy. 440.*

★ **Polihua Beach.** This often deserted beach gets a star for its long, wide stretches of white sand and unobstructed views of Molokai. The northern end of the beach ends at a rocky lava cliff with some interesting tide pools and sea turtles that lay their eggs in the sand. (Do not drive on the beach and endanger their nests.) However, the dirt road leading here has deep, sandy places that are difficult in dry weather and impassable when it rains. In addition, strong currents and a sudden drop in the ocean floor make swimming dangerous. Thirsty wild bees sometimes gather around your car at this beach. To get rid of them, put out water some distance away and wait. The beach is in windward Lanai, 11 miles north of Lanai City. To get here, turn right onto the marked dirt road past Garden of the Gods. **Amenities:** none. **Best for:** solitude; sunrise; walking. ⊠ *East end of Polihua Rd., Lanai City.*

Shipwreck Beach. The rusting World War II tanker off this 8-mile stretch of sand adds just the right touch to an already photogenic beach. Strong trade winds have propelled vessels onto the reef since at least 1824, when the first shipwreck was recorded. Beachcombers come to this fairly accessible beach for shells and washed-up treasures, and photographers take great shots of Molokai, just across the Kalohi Channel. It may still be possible to find glass-ball fishing floats as you wander along. Kaiolohia, its Hawaiian name, is a favorite local diving spot. ■ TIP➔ An offshore reef and rocks in the water mean that it's not for swimmers, though you can play in the shallow water on the shoreline. To get here, take Highway 440 to its eastern terminus, then turn left onto a dirt road and continue to the end. **Amenities:** none. **Best for:** solitude; windsurfing; walking. ⊠ *Off Hwy. 440, Lanai City.*

WATER SPORTS AND TOURS

The easiest way to enjoy the water on Lanai is to wade in at Hulopoe Beach and swim or snorkel. If you prefer an organized excursion, a fishing trip is a good bet (you keep some of the fish). Snorkel trips are a great way to see the island, above and below the surface, and scuba divers can marvel at one of the top cave-dive spots in the Pacific.

7

DEEP-SEA FISHING

Some of the best sportfishing grounds in Maui County are off the southwest shoreline of Lanai. Pry your eyes open and go deep-sea fishing in the early morning, with departures at 6 or 6:30 am from Manele Harbor. Console yourself with the knowledge that Maui fishers have to leave an hour earlier to get to the same prime locations. Peak seasons are spring and summer, although good catches have been landed year-round. Mahimahi, *ono* (a mackerel-like fish; the word means "delicious" in Hawaiian), *ahi* (yellowfin tuna), and marlin are prized catches and preferred eating.

BOATS AND CHARTERS

Fish-N-Chips. This 36-foot Twin-Vee with a tuna tower will get you to the fishing grounds in comfort. Friendly Captain Jason will do everything except reel in the big one for you. Plan on trolling along the south coast for ono and around the point at Kaunolu for mahimahi or marlin. A trip to the offshore buoy often yields skipjack tuna or big ahi. Whales are often spotted during the season. Fishing gear, soft drinks, and water are included. A four-hour charter (six-passenger maximum) is $700; each additional hour costs $110. Guests can keep a third of all fish caught. Shared charters on Sunday are $150 per person. ☎ *808/565–7676* ⊕ *www.sportfishinglanai.com.*

Lanai has miles of good coast for kayaking; the water is calmer in the morning.

KAYAKING

Lanai's windward coast offers leisurely paddling and miles of scenic coastline with deserted beaches to haul up on inside the reef. Curious sea turtles and friendly manta rays may tag along your kayak for company. When the wind comes from the southwest, this area is tranquil. Kayaking along the leeward cliffs is more demanding with rougher seas and strong currents. No kayaking is permitted in the Marine Conservation District at Hulopoe Bay.

Early mornings tend to be calmer. The wind picks up as the day advances. Expect strong currents along all the coasts. Experience on the water is advised, and knowing how to swim is essential. There is one other glitch: there are no kayak rentals on the island, so you need to book a tour or bring your own.

TOURS

Trilogy Oceansports Lanai. An experienced guide leads a full morning of kayaking inside the calm reef of Lanai's unspoiled northeast shore coastline. This six-hour adventure costs $181 per person and includes lunch, soft drinks, and bottled water. Trilogy also offers a 1½-hour marine mammal watch on the *Manele Kai*, a 32-foot hard-bottom inflatable raft. Book either trip at least 24 hours in advance. ✉ *Manele Small Boat Harbor, Manele Rd., Lanai City* ☎ 888/628–4800 ⊕ *www. sailtrilogy.com.*

SCUBA DIVING

When you have a dive site such as Cathedrals—with eerie pinnacle formations and luminous caverns—it's no wonder that scuba-diving buffs consider exploring the waters off Lanai akin to having a religious experience.

BEST SPOTS

Cathedrals. Just outside Hulopoe Bay, Cathedrals was named the best cavern dive site in the Pacific by *Skin Diver* magazine. Shimmering light makes the many openings resemble stained-glass windows. A current generally keeps the water crystal clear, even if it's turbid outside. In these unearthly chambers, large *ulua* and small reef sharks add to the adventure. ⊠ *Manele, Lanai City.*

Sergeant Major Reef. Off Kamaiki Point, Sergeant Major Reef is named for big schools of yellow- and black-striped *manini* (sergeant major fish) that turn the rocks silvery as they feed. There are three parallel lava ridges separated by rippled sand valleys, a cave, and an archway. Depths range 15 to 50 feet. ⊠ *Lanai City.*

EQUIPMENT, LESSONS, AND TOURS

Trilogy Oceansports Lanai. Serious certified divers should go for Trilogy's four-hour, two-tank dive. Locations depend on the weather. The $181 fee includes a light breakfast of cinnamon rolls and coffee, wet suits, and all the equipment you need. Noncertified beginners over age 11 can try a one-tank introductory dive lasting 20 to 30 minutes for $102. You can wade into Hulopoe Bay with an instructor at your side. Certified divers can choose a 35- to 40-minute wade-in dive at Hulopoe, also for $102. ⊠ *Manele Small Boat Harbor, Manele Rd., Lanai City* ☎ *888/628–4800* ⊕ *www.scubalanai.com.*

SNORKELING

Snorkeling is the easiest ocean sport available on the island, requiring nothing but a snorkel, mask, fins, and good sense. Borrow equipment from your hotel or purchase some in Lanai City if you didn't bring your own. Wait to enter the water until you are sure no big sets of waves are coming; and observe the activity of locals on the beach. If little kids are playing in the shore break, it's usually safe to enter. ■TIP➜ **To get into the water safely, always swim in past the breakers, and in the comparative calm put on your fins, then mask and snorkel.**

BEST SPOTS

Hulopoe Beach. Hulopoe Beach is an outstanding snorkeling destination. The Four Seasons Manele Resort overlooks this beach and has guest amenities. The bay is a State of Hawaii Marine Conservation District, and no spearfishing or diving is allowed. Schools of *manini* (seargent major fish) feeding on the coral coat the rocks with flashing silver, and you can view *kala* (unicorn fish), *uhu* (parrot fish), and *papio* (small trevally) in all their rainbow colors. As you wade in from the sandy beach, the best snorkeling is toward the left. Beware of rocks and surging waves. When the resident spinner dolphins are in the bay, watch them from the shore. If swimmers and snorkelers go out, the dolphins may leave and be deprived of their necessary resting place. ⊠ *Manele, Lanai City.*

Manele Small Boat Harbor. A wade-in snorkel spot is just beyond the break wall at Manele Small Boat Harbor. Enter over the rocks, just past the boat ramp. ■TIP➡ **It's dangerous to enter if waves are breaking.** ⊠ *Manele, Lanai City.*

EQUIPMENT, LESSONS, AND TOURS

Trilogy Oceansports Lanai. A 4½-hour snorkeling trip explores Lanai's pristine coastline with this company's experienced captain and crew. The trip includes lessons, equipment, and lunch served on board. Tours are offered Monday, Wednesday, Friday, and Saturday for $181 per person. ⊠ *Manele Small Boat Harbor, Manele Rd., Lanai City* ☎ *888/628–4800* ⊕ *www.sailtrilogy.com.*

SURFING

Surfing on Lanai can be truly enjoyable. Quality, not quantity, characterizes this isle's few breaks. Be considerate of the locals and they will be considerate of you—surfing takes the place of megaplex theaters and pool halls here, serving as one of the island's few recreational luxuries.

BEST SPOTS

Don't try to hang 10 at **Hulopoe Bay** without watching the conditions for a while. When it "goes off," it's a tricky left-handed shore break that requires some skill. Huge summer south swells are for experts only. The southeast-facing breaks at **Lopa Beach** on the east side are inviting for beginners. Give them a try in summer, when the swells roll in nice and easy.

EQUIPMENT AND LESSONS

Lanai Surf School. Nick Palumbo offers the only surf instruction on the island. Sign up for his "4x4 Safari"—a four-hour adventure that includes hard- or soft-top boards, snacks, and transportation to windward "secret spots." Palumbo, who was born on Lanai, is a former Hawaii State Surfing Champion. Lessons are $200 (minimum of two people). Experienced riders can rent boards overnight for $58. Palumbo also has the only paddleboard permit for Hulopoe Bay, and gives lessons and rents equipment. ☎ *808/306–9837* ⊕ *www.lanaisurfsafari.com.*

GOLF, HIKING, AND OUTDOOR ACTIVITIES

The island's two world-class championship golf courses will certainly test your skill on the green. Experienced hikers can choose from miles of dirt roads and trails, but note that you're on your own—there's no water or support. Remember that Lanai is privately owned, and land-based activities are at the owner's discretion.

BIKING

Many of the same red-dirt roads that invite hikers are excellent for biking, offering easy, flat terrain and long clear views. There's only one hitch: you may have to bring your own bike, as there are no rentals or tours available except at the resorts.

BEST SPOTS

A favorite biking route is along the fairly flat, red-dirt road northward from Lanai City through the old pineapple fields to Garden of the Gods. Start your trip on Keomuku Highway in town. Take a left just before the Lodge at Koele's tennis courts, and then a right where the road ends at the fenced pasture, and continue on to the north end and the start of Polihua and Awalua dirt roads. If you're really hardy you could bike down to Polihua Beach and back, but it would be a serious all-day trip. In wet weather these roads turn to mud and are not advisable. Go in the early morning or late afternoon because the sun gets hot in the middle of the day. Take plenty of water, spare parts, and snacks.

For the exceptionally fit, it's possible to bike from town down the Keomuku Highway to the windward beaches and back, or to bike the Munro Trail *(see Hiking)*. Experienced bikers also travel up and down the Manele Highway from Manele Bay to town.

GOLF

Lanai has two gorgeous resort courses that offer very different environments and challenges. They are so diverse that it's hard to believe they're on the same island, let alone just 20 minutes apart by resort shuttle.

The Challenge at Manele. Designed by Jack Nicklaus in 1993, this course sits right over the water of Hulopoe Bay. Built on lava outcroppings, it features three holes on cliffs that use the Pacific Ocean as a water hazard. The five-tee concept challenges the best golfers—tee shots over natural gorges and ravines must be precise. This unspoiled natural terrain is a stunning backdrop, and every hole offers ocean views. Early-morning tee times are recommended to avoid the midday heat. ⊠ *Four Seasons Resort Lanai at Manele Bay, Challenge Dr., Lanai City* ☎ *808/565–2222* ⊕ *www.fourseasons.com/manelebay/golf* ⸭ *18 holes. 6310 yds. Par 72, slope 126. Greens fee: hotel guests $210, nonguests $225* ☞ *Facilities: driving range, putting green, golf carts, rental clubs, pro shop, lessons, restaurant, bar.*

The Experience at Koele. Designed by Greg Norman in 1991, this challenging layout begins at an elevation of 2,000 feet. The front 9 move dramatically through ravines wooded with pine, koa, and eucalyptus trees; seven lakes and streams with cascading waterfalls dot the course. No other course in Hawaii offers a more incredible combination of highland terrain, inspired landscape architecture, and range-of-play challenges. Beware of the superfast greens. ⊠ *Four Seasons Resort Lodge at Koele, 1 Keomuku Hwy., Lanai City* ☎ *808/565–4653* ⊕ *www.fourseasons. com/koele/golf* ⸭ *18 holes. 6310 yds. Par 72, slope 134. Greens fee: hotel guests $210, nonguests $225* ☞ *Facilities: driving range, putting green, golf carts, rental clubs, pro shop, lessons.*

Some holes at the Challenge at Manele use the Pacific Ocean as a water hazard.

HIKING

Only 30 miles of Lanai's roads are paved, but red-dirt roads and trails, ideal for hiking, will take you to sweeping overlooks, isolated beaches, and shady forests. Don't be afraid to leave the road to follow deer trails; just make sure to keep your landmarks in clear sight so you can retrace your steps. Or take a self-guided walk through Kane Puu, Hawaii's largest native dryland forest. You can explore the Munro Trail over Lanaihale with views of plunging canyons, or hike along an old, coastal fisherman trail or across Koloiki Ridge. Wear hiking shoes, a hat, and sunscreen, and carry a windbreaker and plenty of water.

BEST SPOTS

Koloiki Ridge. This marked, moderate trail starts behind the Lodge at Koele and takes you along the cool and shady Munro Trail to overlook the windward side, with impressive views of Maui, Molokai, Maunalei Valley, and Naio Gulch. The average time for the 5-mile round-trip is two hours. Bring snacks, water, and a windbreaker, and take your time. A map is available from the concierge at the Four Seasons Resort Lodge at Koele.

Lanai Fisherman Trail. Local anglers still use this trail to get to their favorite fishing spots. The trail takes about 1½ hours and follows the rocky shoreline below the Four Seasons Resort at Lanai Manele Bay. The marked trail entrance begins at the west end of Hulopoe Beach. Keep your eyes open for spinner dolphins cavorting offshore and the silvery flash of fish feeding in the pools below you. The condition of the trail varies with weather and frequency of maintenance; it can be slippery and rocky. Take your time, wear a hat and enclosed shoes, and carry water.

★ **Munro Trail.** This is the real thing: a strenuous 12.8-mile trek that begins behind the Four Seasons Resort Lodge at Koele and follows the ridge of Lanaihale through the rain forest. The island's most demanding hike, it has an elevation gain of 1,400 feet and leads to a lookout at the island's highest point, Lanaihale. It's also a narrow dirt road; watch out for careening four-wheel-drive vehicles. The trail is named after George Munro, who supervised the planting of Cook pine trees and eucalyptus windbreaks. Mules used to wend their way up the mountain carrying the pine seedlings. Unless you arrange for someone to pick you up at the trail's end, you have a 3-mile hike back through the Palawai Basin to return to your starting point. The summit is often cloud-shrouded and can be windy and muddy, so check conditions before you start. ⊠ *Four Seasons Resort Lodge at Koele, 1 Keomuku Hwy., Lanai City.*

Puu Pehe Trail. Beginning to the left of Hulopoe Beach, this trail travels a short distance around the coastline, and then climbs up a sharp, rocky rise. At the top, you're level with the offshore stack of Puu Pehe and can overlook miles of coastline in both directions. The trail is not difficult, but it's hot and steep. Be aware of nesting seabirds and don't approach their nests. ⚠ Stay away from the edge, as the cliff can easily give way. The hiking is best in the early morning or late afternoon, and it's a perfect place to look for whales in season (December–April). Wear a hat and shoes, and take water so you can spend some time at the top admiring the view. ⊠ *Manele, Lanai City.*

HORSEBACK RIDING

A horseback ride can be a memorable experience on the island.

Stables at Koele. The subtle beauty of the high country slowly reveals itself to horseback riders. Two-hour adventures traverse leafy trails with scenic overlooks. Well-trained horses take riders (must be under 225 pounds and over 8 years old) of all skill levels. Prices range from $110 for a two-hour group ride to $250 for a two-hour private ride. Lessons are also available. Book rides at the Four Seasons Resort Lodge at Koele or with Lanai Western Adventures. ⊠ *1 Keomuku Hwy., Lanai City* ☎ *808/563–0717, 808/563–9385.*

SPORTING CLAYS AND ARCHERY

For something different, you can try your hand at shooting or archery.

★ **Lanai Pine Sporting Clays and Archery Range.** Outstanding rustic terrain, challenging targets, and a well-stocked pro shop make this sporting-clays course top-flight in the expert's eyes. Sharpshooters can complete the meandering 14-station course in 1½ hours, with the help of a golf cart. There are group tournaments, and even kids can enjoy skilled instruction at the archery range and compressed-air rifle gallery. The $60 archery introduction includes an amusing "pineapple challenge"—contestants are given five arrows with which to hit a paper pineapple target. The winner takes home a crystal pineapple as a nostalgic souvenir of the old Dole Plantation days. Prices depend on the amount of ammunition and activity. The range is just past Cemetery Road on the windward side of island. ⊠ *Off Hwy. 440, Lanai City* ☎ *808/565–4555, 808-/563–9385.*

SHOPPING

A miniforest of Cook pine trees in the center of Lanai City surrounded by small shops and restaurants, Dole Park is the closest thing to a mall on Lanai. Except for the high-end resort boutiques and pro shops, it provides the island's only shopping. A morning or afternoon stroll around the park offers an eclectic selection of gifts and clothing, plus a chance to chat with friendly shopkeepers. Well-stocked general stores are reminiscent of the 1920s, and galleries and a boutique have original art and fashions for everyone.

ARTS AND CRAFTS

Dis 'n Dat. This tiny, jungle-green shop packs in thousands of gift and jewelry items in a minuscule space enlivened by a glittering crystal ceiling. Fanciful garden ornaments, Buddhas, and Asian antiques add to the inventory. ⊠ *418 8th St., Lanai City* ☎ *808/565–9170* ⊕ *www. disndatshop.com.*

CLOTHING

Cory Labang Studio. This tiny studio shop near Dole Park reflects its owner's life-long love of vintage clothing. Cory Labang's old piano and Hawaiian family photos are a nice backdrop for her handmade bags and clutches in antique fabrics. Crystal glassware, glittering costume jewelry, and one-of-a-kind accessories complete this unique collection. ⊠ *431A 7th St., Lanai City* ☎ *808/315–6715* ⊕ *www.corylabangstudio. com.*

Lanai Beach Walk. The shop may be small, but it's crammed with many styles and colors of the now indispensable "crocs," as well as colorful resort clothing, logo T-shirts, swimwear, and classy skirts and dresses. Tropical knickknacks, souvenirs, and jewelry complete the whimsical inventory. Gail, the owner, is always up for a bit of local conversation and advice. ⊠ *850 Fraser Ave., Lanai City* ☎ *808/565–9249.*

Local Gentry. Spacious and classy, this store has clothing for every need, from casual men's and women's beachwear to evening resort wear, shoes, jewelry, and hats. A selection of original Lanai-themed clothing is also available, including the signature "What happens on Lanai everybody knows" T-shirts. Proprietor Jenna Gentry Majkus will mail your purchases. ⊠ *363 7th St., Lanai City* ☎ *808/565–9130.*

FOOD

Pine Isle Market. One of Lanai City's two all-purpose markets, Pine Isle stocks everything from beach toys and electronics to meats and fresh vegetables. The staff is friendly, and it's the best place around to buy fresh fish. The market is closed Sunday. ⊠ *356 8th St., Lanai City* ☎ *808/565–6488.*

Richard's. Along with fresh meats, fine wines, and imported gourmet items, Richard's stocks everything from camping gear to household items. ⊠ *434 8th St., Lanai City* ☏ *808/565–3780.*

Sergio's Oriental Store. Sergio's has Filipino sweets and pastries; caseloads of sodas, water, and juices; family-size containers of condiments; and some frozen fish and meat. It's open 8 to 8 daily. ⊠ *831-D Houston St., Lanai City* ☏ *808/565–6900.*

GALLERIES

Jordanne Fine Art Studio. Take a piece of historic Lanai home: Jordanne Weinstein's affordable, whimsical portraits of rural island life and gold-leaf pineapple paintings make terrific souvenirs. Greeting cards and small prints complete the offerings. Stop into her bright studio just off Dole Park, where she often paints on-site. ⊠ *850 Fraser Ave., Lanai City* ☏ *808/563–0088* ⊕ *www.jordannefineart.com.*

Lanai Art Center. Local artists display their work at this dynamic center staffed by volunteers. Workshops in pottery, photography, woodworking, and painting welcome visitors, and individual instruction can be arranged. The gift shop sells Lanai handicrafts and special offerings like handmade Swarovski crystal bracelets, whose sale underwrites children's art classes. Check with the center about occasional concerts. It's closed Sunday. ⊠ *339 7th St., Lanai City* ☏ *808/565–7503* ⊕ *www.lanaiart.org.*

Mike Carroll Gallery. The dreamy, soft-focus oil paintings of award-winning painter Mike Carroll are inspired by island scenes. His work is showcased along with those of other local artists, as well as handcrafted jewelry and Asian antiques. ⊠ *443 7th St., Lanai City* ☏ *808/565–7122* ⊕ *www.mikecarrollgallery.com.*

GENERAL STORES

International Food and Clothing Center. You may not find everything the name implies, but this old-fashioned emporium stocks goods ranging from fishing gear to imported beer. It's a good place for camping supplies and for picking up last-minute items when other stores are closed on Sunday. ⊠ *833 Ilima Ave., Lanai City* ☏ *808/565–6433.*

Lanai City Service. In addition to being Lanai's only gas station, auto-parts store, and car-rental operation, this outfit sells *manapua* (steamed buns with pork filling), hot dogs, beer, sodas, snacks, and bottled water. It's open 6:30 am to 8:30 pm daily. ⊠ *1036 Lanai Ave., Lanai City* ☏ *808/565–7227.*

SPAS

If you're looking for rejuvenation, the whole island could be considered a spa, though the only spa facilities are at the two Four Seasons properties. You can get a quick polish in Lanai City at a couple of spots, though.

Banyan Spa Suite. This simple, serene spa at the Four Seasons Resort Lodge at Koele offers a varied menu of massage treatments, including Hawaiian *lomilomi*, hot-stone massage, and the Hehi Lani Royal Foot

Treatment. Relax after your massage with herbal tea on the adjacent balcony, which has great sunset views, or return to your room in a fluffy spa robe. Two tables accommodate couples, and all massages are private. Massage services can also be enjoyed in the privacy of your room for an extra charge. The spa is open to non–resort guests with advance reservations. ⊠ *Four Seasons Resort Lodge at Koele, 1 Keomuku Hwy., Lanai City* ☎ *808/565–4555* ⊕ *www.fourseasons.com/ koele/spa* ☞ *$165–$175 50-min massage. Gym with: Cardiovascular machines, free weights. Services: Aromatherapy, hot-rock massage, guided stretching, reflexology.*

Island Images. Island Images will pamper brides and offers hair care for men and women, pedicures, manicures, waxing, and threading. ⊠ *843 Ilima Ave., Lanai City* ☎ *808/565–7870.*

Nita's In Style. Nita's In Style features hair-care services for men, women, and children. Shampoos and flashy hair ornaments are sold here. ⊠ *831 Houston St., Lanai City* ☎ *808/565–8082.*

The Spa at Manele. Granite floors, eucalyptus steam rooms, and private cabanas set the scene for indulgence. State-of-the-art pampering enlists a panoply of oils and lotions that would have pleased Cleopatra. The Spa After Hours Experience relaxes you with a neck and shoulder massage and a 50-minute treatment of your choice. You can further unwind in the sauna or steam room, or finish off with a scalp massage and light *pupu* (snacks). The banana-coconut scrub and pineapple-citrus polish treatments have inspired their own cosmetic line. Massages in private *hale* (houses) in the courtyard gardens are available for singles or couples. ⊠ *Four Seasons Resort Lanai at Manele Bay, 1 Manele Bay Rd., Lanai City* ☎ *808/565–2000* ⊕ *www.fourseasons.com/manelebay/ spa* ☞ *$165–$175 50-min massage; $360 per person 2-hr Spa After Hours Experience (2-person minimum). Gym with: Cardiovascular equipment, free weights. Services: Aromatherapy, body wraps, facials, hair salon, hair care, mani/pedicures, reflexology, waxing. Classes and programs: Aquaerobics, guided hikes, hula classes, personal training, tai chi, yoga.*

ENTERTAINMENT AND NIGHTLIFE

Lanai is certainly not known for its nightlife. A handful of places stay open past 9 pm. At the resorts, excellent piano music or light live entertainment makes for a quiet, romantic evening. Another alternative is star watching from the beaches or watching the full moon rise in all its glory.

Hale Aheahe. At the Four Seasons Resort Lanai at Manele Bay, Hale Aheahe (House of Gentle Breezes) is a classy open-air lounge with upscale *pupu* (snacks) and a complete bar. There's musical entertainment nightly from 5:30 to 9:30. Local musicians invite you to try your hula skills. Darts, pool, and shuffleboard are riotous fun. ⊠ *Four Seasons Resort Lanai at Manele Bay, 1 Manele Bay Rd., Lanai City* ☎ *808/565–2000.*

Hale Ahe Ahe. This open-air lounge at the Four Seasons Resort Lodge at Koele has a lively atmosphere. It's open until 11, so you can enjoy a late-night cocktail and plan your next day's activities. The resort also features quiet piano music every evening in its Great Hall, as well as special performances by well-known Hawaiian entertainers and local hula dancers. ⊠ *Four Seasons Resort Lodge at Koele, 1 Keomuku Hwy., Lanai City* ☏ *808/565–4000.*

Hotel Lanai. A visit to the small, lively bar here is an opportunity to visit with locals and find out more about the island. Enjoy entertainment by Lanai musicians in the big green tent on Friday nights. Last call is at 9:30. ⊠ *Hotel Lanai, 828 Lanai Ave., Lanai City* ☏ *808/565–7211* ⊕ *www.hotellanai.com.*

Trilogy Oceansports Lanai. On Tuesday, Thursday, and Saturday, Trilogy offers a Sunset Sail on a large catamaran, departing at either 3:45 (April–September) or 4:45 (October–March). This trip is perfect if you want to get out on the ocean and experience a relaxing time on the water. The two-hour sail includes hot and cold appetizers, soft drinks, two alcoholic beverages, and filtered water. If you bring your own beer and wine, the crew will put it on ice. The sunset sail costs $84 per person ⊠ *Manele Small Boat Harbor, Manele Rd., Lanai City* ☏ *888/628–4800* ⊕ *www.sailtrilogy.com.*

WHERE TO EAT

Lanai's own version of Hawaii Regional Cuisine draws on the fresh bounty provided by local farmers and fishermen, combined with the skills of well-trained chefs. The upscale menus at the Four Seasons Resort Lodge at Koele and the Four Seasons Resort at Lanai Manele Bay encompass European-inspired cuisine as well as innovative preparations of international favorites and vegetarian delights. All Four Seasons Resort restaurants offer a children's menu. Lanai City's eclectic ethnic fare runs from construction-worker-size local plate lunches to *poke* (raw fish), pizza, and pesto pasta. ■ TIP➔ **Lanai "City" is really a small town; restaurants sometimes choose to close the kitchen early, and only a few are open on Sunday.**

Prices in the reviews are the average cost of a main course at dinner or, if dinner is not served, at lunch.

MANELE BAY

Dining at Manele Bay offers the range of options provided by Four Seasons Lanai resorts, from informal poolside meals to relaxed, eclectic dining.

$$ ✕ **The Challenge at Manele Clubhouse.** A stunning view of the legendary
AMERICAN Puu Pehe island only enhances the imaginative fare of this restaurant. Spot frolicking dolphins from the terrace. Tuck into a Hulopoe Bay prawn BLT, or the crispy battered fish-and-chips with Meyer lemon tartar sauce. The fish tacos are splendid, and specialty drinks add to the informal fun. Ⓢ *Average main: $24* ⊠ *Four Seasons Resort Lanai at*

Manele Bay, 1 Manele Bay Rd., Lanai City ☎ *808/565–2230* 🌐 *www.fourseasons.com/manelebay* 🕒 *No dinner.*

$$$$ AMERICAN 🍴 **Four Seasons Hulopoe Court.** An extensive breakfast buffet and perfectly presented dinners are served in airy comfort on the hotel terrace, which overlooks the wide sweep of the bay. Retractable awnings provide shade on sunny days. Inside, comfy upholstered chairs, cream walls, wood paneling, and modern Hawaiian decor create an almost equally inviting backdrop. At breakfast, fresh-baked pastries and made-to-order omelets ensure that your day starts well. For dinner, expect serious steaks and grilled fresh fish. [$] *Average main: $40* ✉ *Four Seasons Resort Lanai at Manele Bay, 1 Manele Bay Rd., Lanai City* ☎ *808/565–2290* 🌐 *www.fourseasons.com/manelebay* ✍ *Reservations essential* 🕒 *No lunch.*

$$$$ ITALIAN 🍴 **Fresco.** Poolside at the Four Seasons Resort Lanai at Manele Bay, Fresco offers informal lunches and dinners in a setting with a stunning view of Hulopoe Bay. The big umbrellas are cool and cheerful, and upholstered chairs in yellow and green are deliciously comfortable. If you're a coffee drinker, a Kona cappuccino freeze by the pool is a must. For a satisfying lunch, try mahimahi fish-and-chips or a good old-fashioned burger. The prime offering at dinner is cioppino, a local seafood stew made with spicy shrimp broth. Braised short ribs are a meaty alternative. The service is the Four Seasons' brand of cool aloha. [$] *Average main: $40* ✉ *Four Seasons Resort Lanai at Manele Bay, 1 Manele Bay Rd., Lanai City* ☎ *808/565–2092* 🌐 *www.fourseasons.com/manelebay* ✍ *Reservations essential.*

LANAI CITY AND UPCOUNTRY

In Lanai City, you can enjoy everything from local-style plate lunches to upscale gourmet meals. For a small area, there are a number of good places to eat and drink, but remember that Lanai City closes down on Sunday.

$ HAWAIIAN 🍴 **Blue Ginger Café.** Owners Joe and Georgia Abilay have made this cheery place into a Lanai City institution with simply prepared, consistent, tasty food. Local paintings and photos line the walls inside, while townspeople parade by the outdoor tables. For breakfast, try the Portuguese sausage omelet with rice, or fresh pastries. Lunch selections range from burgers and pizza to Hawaiian staples such as saimin noodles or *musubi* (fried SPAM wrapped in rice and seaweed), and you can try a shrimp stir-fry for dinner. Phone ahead for takeout. The eatery sometimes closes early on slow days. [$] *Average main: $14* ✉ *409 7th St., Lanai City* ☎ *808/565–6363* 🌐 *www.bluegingercafelanai.com* ✍ *Reservations not accepted* 💳 *No credit cards.*

$$$$ HAWAIIAN Fodor's Choice ★ 🍴 **The Dining Room.** Reflecting the resort's country-manor elegance, this peaceful and romantic octagonal restaurant is fine dining at its best. Terra-cotta walls and soft peach lighting flatter everyone, and intimate tables are well spaced to allow for private conversations. Choose from a four-course tasting menu offering such delicacies as foie gras with pineapple-raisin chutney, bacon-wrapped scallops, and wild boar with morel mushrooms, or go à la carte with pepper-crusted ahi, lobster with cavier, or macadamia-crusted venison loin. Finish with a warm

raspberry soufflé (order in advance). A master sommelier provides perfect wine pairings, and the service is attentive. $ Average main: $59 ✉ Four Seasons Resort Lodge at Koele, 1 Keomuku Hwy., Lanai City ☎ 808/565–4580 ⊕ www.fourseasons.com/koele ⚐ Reservations essential ☾ No lunch.

$ ✗ **565 Café.** Named after the oldest telephone prefix on Lanai, 565 Café
HAWAIIAN is a convenient stop for plate lunches, sandwiches like Palawai chicken breast on freshly baked focaccia, or platters of chicken *katsu* (Japanese-style breaded and fried chicken) to take along for an impromptu picnic. Phone ahead to order pizza. Bring your own beer or wine for lunch or dinner. The patio and outdoor tables are kid-friendly, and an outdoor Saturday afternoon flea market adds to the quirkiness. $ Average main: $10 ✉ 408 8th St., Lanai City ☎ 808/565–6622 ⚐ Reservations not accepted ☾ Closed Sun.

$$$ ✗ **Lanai City Grille.** Simple white walls hung with local art, lazily turning
AMERICAN ceiling fans, and unobtrusive service provide the backdrop for a menu designed and supervised by celebrity-chef Beverly Gannon. Oysters on the half shell, pulled-pork wontons, or steamed manila clams are a great way to start the evening. Baby field greens are a special treat. The entrées are on the meaty side for Hawaii, and should satisfy serious appetites. The eatery is a friendly and comfortable alternative to the Four Seasons, and a convenient, if sometimes noisy, gathering place for large parties. $ Average main: $34 ✉ Hotel Lanai, 828 Lanai Ave., Lanai City ☎ 808/565–4700 ⊕ www.hotellanai.com ⚐ Reservations essential ☾ Closed Mon. and Tues.

$ ✗ **Lanai Coffee.** A block from Dole Park, this Northern California–style
AMERICAN café offers a nice umbrella-covered deck where you can sip cappuccinos and get in tune with the slow pace of life. Bagels with lox, deli sandwiches, and pastries add to the caloric content, while blended espresso shakes and gourmet ice cream complete the coffee-house vibe. Caffeine-inspired specialty items make good gifts and souvenirs. $ Average main: $6 ✉ 604 Ilima St., Lanai City ☎ 808/565–6962 ⚐ Reservations not accepted ☾ Closed Sun. No dinner.

$ ✗ **Lanai Ohana Poke Market.** This is the closest you can come to dining on
HAWAIIAN traditional cuisine on Lanai. Enjoy fresh food prepared by a Hawaiian family and served in a cool, shady garden. The emphasis is on *poke*, which is raw ahi tuna flavored with Hawaiian salt and seaweed. Hawaiian plate lunches and take-out *kimchi* shrimp, mussel *poke*, and ahi and aku tuna steaks complete the menu. The place also caters picnics and parties. $ Average main: $9 ✉ 834A Gay St., Lanai City ☎ 808/559–6265 ⚐ Reservations not accepted ═ No credit cards ☾ Closed Sun.

$ ✗ **No Ka Oi Grindz Lanai.** A local favorite, this lunchroom-style café has
HAWAIIAN a shaded picnic table in the landscaped front yard and five more tables
☺ in the no-frills interior. The innovative menu, which changes frequently, includes such delicacies as *kimchi* fried rice, pork fritter sandwiches, and massive plate lunches. Sit outside and watch the town drive by. $ Average main: $9 ✉ 335 9th St., Lanai City ☎ 808/565–9413 ⚐ Reservations not accepted ═ No credit cards.

$$ ✗ **Pele's Other Garden.** Small and colorful, Pele's is a deli and bistro all in
ITALIAN one. For lunch, sandwiches or daily hot specials satisfy hearty appetites.

At night the restaurant turns into a busy bistro, complete with table-cloths and soft jazz music. A nice wine list enhances an Italian-inspired menu. Start with bruschetta, then choose from a selection of pizzas or pasta dishes. An intimate back-room bar adds to the liveliness, and entertainers sometimes drop in for impromptu jam sessions. $ *Average main: $20* ⊠ *811 Houston St., at 8th St., Lanai City* ☎ *808/565–9628, 888/764–3354* ⊕ *www.pelesothergarden.com* ⚱ *Reservations essential.*

$$$$

AMERICAN

✕ **The Terrace.** Floor-to-ceiling glass doors open onto formal gardens and lovely vistas of the mist-clad mountains at this informal spot serving breakfast, lunch, and dinner. Try the hearty Hawaiian Paniolo breakfast to start the day, and pan-seared island snapper to finish it. A "design your entrée" menu lets you choose sauces for your meat, poultry, or seafood entrée as well as an appropriate side dish. The soothing sounds of the grand piano in the Great Hall in the evening complete the ambience. $ *Average main: $42* ⊠ *Four Seasons Resort Lodge at Koele, 1 Keomuku Hwy., Lanai City* ☎ *808/565–4580* ⊕ *www.fourseasons.com/koele* ⚱ *Reservations essential.*

WHERE TO STAY

For expanded hotel reviews, visit Fodors.com.

Though Lanai has few properties, it does have a range of price options. Four Seasons manages both the Lodge at Koele and Four Seasons Resort Lanai at Manele Bay. Although the room rates are different, guests can partake of all the resort amenities at both properties. If you're on a budget, consider the Hotel Lanai. Note that room rates do not include 13.42% sales tax.

Prices in the reviews are the lowest cost of a standard double room in high season.

$

B&B/INN

🏠 **Dreams Come True.** Antiques gleaned from their many trips through South Asia add to the atmosphere at Michael and Susan Hunter's four-bedroom, four-bathroom plantation home on the main street of Lanai City. **Pros:** convenient location; outdoor barbecue; nice garden. **Cons:** two-night minimum stay on weekends; on a busy street. **TripAdvisor:** "totally relaxing," "well kept," "somewhere with character." $ *Rooms from: $129* ⊠ *1168 Lanai Ave., Lanai City* ☎ *808/565–6961, 800/566–6961* ⊕ *www.dreamscometruelanai.com* ⟳ *4 rooms* ⦿ *Breakfast.*

$$$$

RESORT

☾

Fodor's Choice

★

🏠 **Four Seasons Resort Lanai at Manele Bay.** Overlooking Hulopoe Bay, this elegantly decorated retreat combines Mediterranean and Asian architectural elements: life-size paintings of Chinese court officials, gold brocade warrior robes, and artifacts decorate the open-air lobbies. **Pros:** fitness center with ocean views; teens have their own center; friendly pool bar. **Cons:** 20 minutes from town; need a car to explore the area; may seem too formal to some. **TripAdvisor:** "luxury at its finest," "remote but with resort services," "a beautiful paradise." $ *Rooms from: $425* ⊠ *1 Manele Bay Rd., Lanai City 96763* ☎ *808/565–2000, 800/321–4666* ⊕ *www.fourseasons.com/manelebay* ⟳ *215 rooms, 21 suites* ⦿ *No meals.*

Four Seasons Resort Lanai at Manele Bay

Four Seasons Resort Lodge at Koele

$$$ RESORT Fodor's Choice ★ **Four Seasons Resort Lodge at Koele.** In the highlands edging Lanai City, this grand country estate exudes luxury and romance with paths meandering through formal gardens, a huge reflecting pond, and an orchid greenhouse. **Pros:** beautiful surroundings; impeccable service; walking distance to Lanai City. **Cons:** doesn't seem much like Hawaii; can get chilly, especially in winter; not much to do in rainy weather. **TripAdvisor:** "unreal views," "magnificent natural setting," "very lovely." [$] *Rooms from: $295* ✉ *1 Keomoku Rd., Lanai City96763* ☎ *808/565–4000, 800/321–4666* 🌐 *www.fourseasons.com/koele* 🛏 *94 rooms, 8 suites* 🍴 *No meals.*

$ HOTEL **Hotel Lanai.** Built in 1923 to house visiting pineapple executives, this inn has South Pacific–style rooms with country quilts, ceiling fans, and bamboo shades. **Pros:** historic atmosphere; walking distance to town. **Cons:** rooms are a bit plain; noisy at dinnertime; no room phones. **TripAdvisor:** "perfect little corner in paradise," "fun and rustic Hawaii," "check out the cottage." [$] *Rooms from: $149* ✉ *828 Lanai Ave., Lanai City* ☎ *808/565–7211, 800/795–7211* 🌐 *www.hotellanai.com* 🛏 *10 rooms, 1 cottage* 🍴 *Breakfast.*

UNDERSTANDING
HAWAII

HAWAIIAN VOCABULARY

Although an understanding of Hawaiian is by no means required on a trip to the Aloha State, a *malihini*, or newcomer, will find plenty of opportunities to pick up a few of the local words and phrases. Traditional names and expressions are widely used in the Islands. You're likely to read or hear at least a few words each day of your stay.

With a basic understanding and some uninhibited practice, anyone can have enough command of the local tongue to ask for directions and to order from a restaurant menu. One visitor announced she would not leave until she could pronounce the name of the state fish, the *humuhumunukunukuāpua'a*.

Simplifying the learning process is the fact that the Hawaiian language contains only eight consonants—*H, K, L, M, N, P, W,* and the silent *'okina,* or glottal stop, written '—plus one or more of the five vowels. All syllables, and therefore all words, end in a vowel. Each vowel, with the exception of a few diphthongized double vowels such as *au* (pronounced "ow") or *ai* (pronounced "eye"), is pronounced separately. Thus *'Iolani* is four syllables (ee-oh-la-nee), not three (yo-la-nee). Although some Hawaiian words have only vowels, most also contain some consonants, but consonants are never doubled.

Pronunciation is simple. Pronounce *A* "ah" as in *father; E* "ay" as in *weigh; I* "ee" as in *marine; O* "oh" as in *no; U* "oo" as in *true.*

Consonants mirror their English equivalents, with the exception of *W.* When the letter begins any syllable other than the first one in a word, it is usually pronounced as a *V. 'Awa,* the Polynesian drink, is pronounced "ava," *'ewa* is pronounced "eva."

Almost all long Hawaiian words are combinations of shorter words; they are not difficult to pronounce if you segment them. *Kalaniana'ole,* the highway running east from Honolulu, is easily understood as *Kalani ana 'ole.* Apply the standard pronunciation rules—the stress falls on the next-to-last syllable of most two- or three-syllable Hawaiian words—and Kalaniana'ole Highway is as easy to say as Main Street.

Now about that fish. Try *humu-humu nuku-nuku āpu a'a.*

The other unusual element in Hawaiian language is the *kahakō,* or macron, written as a short line (ˉ) placed over a vowel. Like the accent (ˊ) in Spanish, the kahakō puts emphasis on a syllable that would normally not be stressed. The most familiar example is probably *Waikīkī.* With no macrons, the stress would fall on the middle syllable; with only one macron, on the last syllable, the stress would fall on the first and last syllables. Some words become plural with the addition of a macron, often on a syllable that would have been stressed anyway. No Hawaiian word becomes plural with the addition of an *S,* since that letter does not exist in the language.

The Hawaiian diacritical marks are not printed in this guide.

'a'ā: rough, crumbling lava, contrasting with *pāhoehoe,* which is smooth.

'ae: yes.

aikane: friend.

āina: land.

akamai: smart, clever, possessing savoir faire.

akua: god.

ala: a road, path, or trail.

ali'i: a Hawaiian chief, a member of the chiefly class.

aloha: love, affection, kindness; also a salutation meaning both greetings and farewell.

'ānuenue: rainbow.

'a'ole: no.

'apōpō: tomorrow.

'auwai: a ditch.

auwē: alas, woe is me!

'ehu: a red-haired Hawaiian.

'ewa: in the direction of 'Ewa plantation, west of Honolulu.

hala: the pandanus tree, whose leaves (*lau hala*) are used to make baskets and plaited mats.

hālau: school.

hale: a house.

hale pule: church, house of worship.

ha mea iki or **ha mea ʻole:** you're welcome.

hana: to work.

haole: ghost. Since the first foreigners were Caucasian, *haole* now means a Caucasian person.

hapa: a part, sometimes a half; often used as a short form of *hapa haole*, to mean a person who is part-Caucasian.

hauʻoli: to rejoice. *Hauʻoli Makahiki Hou* means Happy New Year. *Hauʻoli lā hānau* means Happy Birthday.

heiau: an outdoor stone platform; an ancient Hawaiian place of worship.

holo: to run.

holoholo: to go for a walk, ride, or sail.

holokū: a long Hawaiian dress, somewhat fitted, with a yoke and a train. Influenced by European fashion, it was worn at court, and at least one local translates the word as "expensive muʻumuʻu."

holomū: a post–World War II cross between a *holokū* and a muʻumuʻu, less fitted than the former but less voluminous than the latter, and having no train.

honi: to kiss; a kiss. A phrase that some tourists may find useful, quoted from a popular hula, is *Honi Kaʻua Wikiwiki:* Kiss me quick!

honu: turtle.

hoʻomalimali: flattery, a deceptive "line," bunk, baloney, hooey.

huhū: angry.

hui: a group, club, or assembly. A church may refer to its congregation as a *hui* and a social club may be called a *hui.*

hukilau: a seine; a communal fishing party in which everyone helps to drive the fish into a huge net, pull it in, and divide the catch.

hula: the dance of Hawaiʻi.

iki: little.

ipo: sweetheart.

ka: the. This is the definite article for most singular words; for plural nouns, the definite article is usually *nā*. Since there is no *S* in Hawaiian, the article may be your only clue that a noun is plural.

kahuna: a priest, doctor, or other trained person of old Hawaiʻi, endowed with special professional skills that often included prophecy or other supernatural powers; the plural form is kāhuna.

kai: the sea, saltwater.

kalo: the taro plant from whose root *poi* (paste) is made.

kamāʻaina: literally, a child of the soil; it refers to people who were born in the Islands or have lived there for a long time.

kanaka: originally a man or humanity, it is now used to denote a male Hawaiian or part-Hawaiian, but is occasionally taken as a slur when used by non-Hawaiians. *Kanaka maoli,* originally a full-blooded Hawaiian person, is used by some native Hawaiian rights activists to embrace part-Hawaiians as well.

kāne: a man, a husband. If you see this word on a door, it's the men's room. If you see *kane* on a door, it's probably a misspelling; that is the Hawaiian name for the skin fungus tinea.

kapa: also called by its Tahitian name, *tapa,* a cloth made of beaten bark and usually dyed and stamped with a repeat design.

kapakahi: crooked, cockeyed, uneven. You've got your hat on *kapakahi.*

kapu: keep out, prohibited. This is the Hawaiian version of the more widely known Tongan word *tabu* (taboo).

kapuna: grandparent; elder.

kēia lā: today.

keiki: a child; *keikikāne* is a boy, *keiki-wahine* a girl.

kona: the leeward side of the Islands, the direction (south) from which the *kona* wind and *kona* rain come.

kula: upland.

kuleana: a homestead or small plot of ground on which a family has been installed for some generations without necessarily owning it. By extension, *kule-ana* is used to denote any area or department in which one has a special interest or prerogative. You'll hear it used this way: If you want to hire a surfboard, see Moki; that's his *kuleana.*

lā: sun.

lamalama: to fish with a torch.

lānai: a porch, a balcony, an outdoor living room. Almost every house in Hawaii has one. Don't confuse this two-syllable word with the three-syllable name of the island, Lāna'i.

lani: heaven, the sky.

lau hala: the leaf of the *hala,* or pandanus tree, widely used in handicrafts.

lei: a garland of flowers.

limu: sun.

lolo: stupid.

luna: a plantation overseer or foreman.

mahalo: thank you.

makai: toward the ocean.

malihini: a newcomer to the Islands.

mana: the spiritual power that the Hawaiian believed inhabited all things and creatures.

manō: shark.

manuwahi: free, gratis.

mauka: toward the mountains.

mauna: mountain.

mele: a Hawaiian song or chant, often of epic proportions.

Mele Kalikimaka: Merry Christmas (a transliteration from the English phrase).

Menehune: a Hawaiian pixie. The *Menehune* were a legendary race of little people who accomplished prodigious work, such as building fishponds and temples in the course of a single night.

moana: the ocean.

mu'umu'u: the voluminous dress in which the missionaries enveloped Hawaiian women. Now made in bright printed cottons and silks, it is an indispensable garment. Culturally sensitive locals have embraced the Hawaiian spelling but often shorten the spoken word to "mu'u." Most English dictionaries include the spelling "muumuu."

nani: beautiful.

nui: big.

ohana: family.

'ono: delicious.

pāhoehoe: smooth, unbroken, satiny lava.

Pākē: Chinese. This *Pākē* carver makes beautiful things.

palapala: document, printed matter.

pali: a cliff, precipice.

pānini: prickly pear cactus.

paniolo: a Hawaiian cowboy, a rough transliteration of *español,* the language of the Islands' earliest cowboys.

pau: finished, done.

pilikia: trouble. The Hawaiian word is much more widely used here than its English equivalent.

puka: a hole.

pupule: crazy, like the celebrated Princess Pupule. This word has replaced its English equivalent in local usage.

pu'u: volcanic cinder cone.

waha: mouth.

wahine: a female, a woman, a wife, and a sign on the ladies' room door; the plural form is *wāhine.*

wai: freshwater, as opposed to saltwater, which is *kai.*

wailele: waterfall.

wikiwiki: to hurry, hurry up (since this is a reduplication of *wiki,* quick, neither W is pronounced as a V).

Note: Pidgin is the unofficial language of Hawaii. It is a Creole language, with its own grammar, evolved from the mixture of English, Hawaiian, Japanese, Portuguese, and other languages spoken in 19th-century Hawaii, and it is heard everywhere.

Travel Smart Hawaii

WORD OF MOUTH

"BTW—getting around the Islands is really pretty easy as the airports are small. In fact, if you want to see another island – which you can even decide to do once you are over there – you can even do it on a day trip over and back (or an overnight with a carry-on day pack)."

—Tomsd

GETTING HERE AND AROUND

■ AIR TRAVEL

Flying time to Hawaii is about 10 hours from New York, 8 hours from Chicago, and 5 hours from Los Angeles.

Hawaii is a major destination link for flights traveling between the U.S. mainland and Asia, Australia, New Zealand, and the South Pacific. Although the Neighbor Islands' airports are smaller and more casual than Honolulu International, during peak times they can also be quite busy. Allot extra travel time to all airports during morning and afternoon rush-hour traffic periods.

Plan to arrive at the airport at least 60 minutes before departure for interisland flights.

Plants and plant products are subject to regulation by the Department of Agriculture, both on entering and leaving Hawaii. Upon leaving the Islands, you'll have to have your bags X-rayed and tagged at one of the airport's agricultural inspection stations before you proceed to check-in. Pineapples and coconuts with the packer's agricultural inspection stamp pass freely; papayas must be treated, inspected, and stamped. All other fruits are banned for export to the U.S. mainland. Flowers pass except for gardenia, rose leaves, jade vine, and mauna loa. Also banned are insects, snails, soil, cotton, cacti, sugarcane, and all berry plants.

You'll have to leave dogs and other pets at home. A 120-day quarantine is imposed to keep out rabies, which is nonexistent in Hawaii. If specific pre- and post-arrival requirements are met, animals may qualify for a 30-day or five-day-or-less quarantine.

Airline Security Issues Transportation Security Administration ⊕ www.tsa.gov

Air Travel Resources in Hawaii State of Hawaii Airports Division Offices

☎ 808/836–6413 ⊕ www.hawaii.gov/dot/airports.

AIRPORTS

All of Hawaii's major islands have their own airports, but Honolulu's International Airport is the main stopover for most domestic and international flights. From Honolulu, there are flights to the Neighbor Islands almost every half-hour from early morning until evening. In addition, some carriers now offer non-stop service directly from the mainland to Maui, Kauai, and the Big Island on a limited basis. No matter the island, all of Hawaii's airports are "open-air," meaning you can enjoy those trade-wind breezes up until the moment you step on the plane.

HONOLULU/OAHU AIRPORT

Hawaii's major airport is Honolulu International, on Oahu, 20 minutes (9 miles) west of Waikiki. When traveling interisland from Honolulu, you will depart from either the interisland terminal or the commuter-airline terminal, located in two separate structures adjacent to the main overseas terminal building. The airport operates a free shuttle system between the terminals from 6 am to 10 pm every day.

Information Honolulu International Airport (HNL) ☎ 808/836–6411 ⊕ www.hawaii.gov/hnl.

MAUI AIRPORTS

Maui has two airports. Kahului Airport handles major airlines and interisland flights; it's the only airport on Maui that has direct service from the mainland. If you're arriving from another island and you're staying in West Maui, you can avoid the hour drive from the Kahului Airport by flying into the much smaller Kapalua–West Maui Airport, which is served by Hawaiian Air and Island Air. The tiny town of Hana in East Maui also has an airstrip, served by Pacific Wings and charter flights from Kahului and Kapalua. Flying here from one of the other airports is a great option if you want to avoid the long and winding drive to Hana.

Information Kahului Airport (OGG) ☎ 808/872–3830 ⊕ hawaii.gov/ogg. **Kapalua–West Maui Airport (JHM)** ☎ 808/665–6108 ⊕ hawaii.gov/jhm. **Hana Airport (HNM)** ☎ 808/248–4861 ⊕ hawaii.gov/hnm.

BIG ISLAND AIRPORTS

Those flying to the Big Island of Hawaii regularly land at one of two fields. Kona International Airport at Keahole, on the west side, best serves Kailua-Kona, Keauhou, and the Kohala Coast. Hilo International Airport is more appropriate for those going to the east side. Waimea-Kohala Airport, called Kamuela Airport by residents, is used primarily for commuting among the Islands.

Information Hilo International Airport (ITO) ☎ 808/961–9300 ⊕ hawaii.gov/ito. **Kona International Airport at Keahole (KOA)** ☎ 808/327–9520 ⊕ hawaii.gov/koa. **Waimea-Kohala Airport (MUE)** ☎ 808/887–8126 ⊕ hawaii.gov/mue.

KAUAI AIRPORT

On Kauai, visitors fly into Lihue Airport, on the east side of the island.

Information Lihue Airport (LIH) ☎ 808/274–3800 ⊕ hawaii.gov/lih.

MOLOKAI AND LANAI AIRPORTS

Molokai's Hoolehua Airport is small and centrally located, as is Lanai Airport. Both rural airports handle a limited number of flights per day. Visitors coming from the mainland to these Islands must first stop in Maui or Oahu and change to an inter-island flight.

Information Lanai Airport (LNY) ☎ 808/565–7942 ⊕ hawaii.gov/lny. **Hoolehua Airport (MKK)** ☎ 808/567–9660 ⊕ hawaii.gov/mkk.

FLIGHTS

US Airways, American, and United fly into Oahu, Maui, Kauai, and the Big Island. Alaska flies into Oahu, Maui, Kauai, and the Big Island. Delta serves Oahu (Honolulu), Maui, and the Big Island. Hawaiian Airlines flies direct into Oahu from many cities in the western United States. In 2012 it added direct service from New York's JFK Airport.

Hawaiian Airlines, go! Mokulele Airlines, Island Air, and Pacific Wings offer regular service between the Islands. All have frequent-flier programs, which will entitle you to rewards and upgrades the more you fly. Be sure to compare prices offered by all the interisland carriers. Inter-island fares have increased in recent years, but if you are somewhat flexible with your dates and times you may find a lower fare.

There are three companies that provide charter flights between the Islands. go! Mokulele Airlines services Oahu, Maui, and Molokai. Pacific Wings serves Oahu, Lanai, Maui, Molokai, and the Big Island. Services include premiere (same-day departures on short notice), premium (24-hour notice), group, and cargo/courier. The company also has a frequent-flier program. Paragon Air offers 24-hour private charter service from any airport in Hawaii. In business since 1980, the company prides itself on its perfect safety record. Should you want to explore Kaluapapa or other sites on Molokai and Maui from the air and ground, you can book tours through Paragon that depart from either the Kahului or Kapalua–West Maui airport.

Airline Contacts Alaska Airlines ☎ 800/252–7522 ⊕ www.alaskaair.com. **American Airlines** ☎ 800/433–7300 ⊕ www.aa.com. **Delta Airlines** ☎ 800/221–1212 ⊕ www.delta.com. **United Airlines** ☎ 800/864–8331 ⊕ www.united.com. **US Airways** ☎ 800/428–4322 ⊕ www.usairways.com.

Interisland Flights go! Mokulele Airlines ☎ 888/435–9462 ⊕ www.iflygo.com. **Hawaiian Airlines** ☎ 800/367–5320 ⊕ www.hawaiianair.com. **Pacific Wings** ☎ 888/575–4546 ⊕ www.pacificwings.com.

■ BOAT TRAVEL

There is daily ferry service between Lahaina, Maui, and Manele Bay, Lanai, with Expeditions Lanai Ferry. The 9-mile crossing costs $60 round-trip, per person, and takes 45 minutes or so, depending on ocean conditions (which can make this trip a rough one). Molokai Ferry offers twice-daily ferry service between Lahaina, Maui, and Kaunakakai, Molokai. Travel time is about 90 minutes each way and the one-way fare is $63.60 per person; a book of six one-way tickets costs $294.15. Reservations are recommended for both ferries.

Information Expeditions Lanai Ferry ☎ 808/214–1467, 800/695–2624 ⊕ www. go-lanai.com. **Molokai Ferry** ☎ 866/307–6524 ⊕ www.molokaiferry.com.

■ BUS TRAVEL

OAHU

While bus service is not as practical on some of the Neighbor Islands, getting around by bus is a convenient and affordable option on Oahu.

You can go all around the island or just down Kalakaua Avenue for $2.50 on Honolulu's municipal transportation system, affectionately known as TheBus. It's one of the island's best bargains. Taking TheBus in the Waikiki and downtown Honolulu areas is especially easy, with buses making stops in Waikiki every 15 minutes to take passengers to nearby shopping areas, such as Ala Moana Shopping Center.

You're entitled to one free transfer per fare if you ask for it when boarding. Exact change is required, and dollar bills are accepted. A four-day pass for visitors costs $25 and is available at ABC convenience stores in Waikiki and in the Ala Moana Shopping Center. Monthly passes cost $60.

You can find privately published route booklets at most drugstores and other convenience outlets. The important route numbers for Waikiki are 2, 4, 8, 19, 20, 58, and City Express Route B. If you venture farther afield, you can always get back on one of these.

The Waikiki Trolley has four lines and dozens of stops that allow you to design your own itinerary while riding on brass-trimmed, open-air trolleys. The Honolulu City Line (Red Line) travels between Waikiki and the Bishop Museum and includes stops at Aloha Tower, Ala Moana, and downtown Honolulu, among others. The Ocean Coast Line (Blue Line) provides a tour of Oahu's southeastern coastline, including Diamond Head Crater, Hanauma Bay, and Sea Life Park. The Blue Line also has an express trolley to Diamond Head that runs twice daily. The Ala Moana Shuttle Line (Pink Line) stops at Ward Warehouse, Ward Centers, and Ala Moana Shopping Center. These trolley lines depart from the DFS Galleria Waikiki or Hilton Hawaiian Village. The Local Shopping & Dining Line (Yellow Line) starts at Ala Moana Center and stops at Ward Farmers' Market, Ward Warehouse, Ward Centers, and other shops and restaurants. A one-day, four-line ticket costs $30. Four-day tickets, also good for any of the four lines, are $52. There are discounts when ordering online.

In Waikiki, in addition to TheBus and the Waikiki Trolley, there also are a number of brightly painted private buses, many of which are free, that will take you to such commercial attractions as dinner cruises, garment factories, and the like.

Bus Information TheBus ☎ 808/848–5555 ⊕ www.thebus.org. **Waikiki Trolley** ☎ 808/591–2561, 800/824–8804 ⊕ www. waikikitrolley.com.

MAUI

Maui Bus, operated by Roberts Hawaii, offers 10 routes in and between various Central, South, and West Maui communities, seven days a week, including all holidays. Passengers can travel in and around Wailuku, Kahului, Lahaina, Kaanapali, Kapalua, Kihei, Wailea, Maalaea, the North Shore (Paia), and Upcountry (including Pukalani, Makawao, Haliimaile, and Haiku). The Upcountry and Haiku Islander routes include a stop at Kahului Airport. All one-way tickets are $1.

For travelers who prefer not to rent a car, Maui Bus is a great way to go. It runs from early morning to late evening daily, and stops at most of the major towns and sightseeing destinations. And, you can't beat the price. Maps and schedules are available online.

Bus Contact Maui Bus ☎ 808/871–4838 ⊕ www.mauicounty.gov/bus.

KAUAI

The Kauai Bus operates a route from Hanalei (on the North Shore) to Kekaha (on the West Side) daily except Sunday. It runs once each hour from early morning until the evening, and provides a lunchtime shuttle around Lihue. The fare is $2. Children six and under travel free.

Bus Contact The Kauai Bus. ☎ 808/241–6410 ⊕ www.kauai.gov/oca/transportation.

BIG ISLAND

In Hawaii County, the Hele-On Bus provides public transportation around the island, including a four-hour trip from Kona to Hilo (each way) three times each day. The fare is $1, or $7.50 for 10 tickets. The county Transit Agency offers a shared-ride taxi program that provides door-to-door service. Participating companies charge as little as $2 per person for trips between one and four miles and as little as $4 per person for trips between four and nine miles (the longest trip covered by the program). Fares are paid with prepurchased vouchers. Maps, schedules, and taxi details are available online.

Bus Contact Hele-On Bus ☎ 808/961–8744 ⊕ www.heleonbus.org.

▌ CAR TRAVEL

Technically, the Big Island of Hawaii is the only island you can completely circle by car, but each island offers plenty of sightseeing from its miles of roadways.

Oahu can be circled except for the roadless west-shore area around Kaena Point. Elsewhere, major highways follow the shoreline and traverse the island at two points. Rush-hour traffic (6:30 to 8:30 am and 3:30 to 6 pm) can be frustrating around Honolulu and the outlying areas, as many thoroughfares allow no left turns.

Traffic on Maui can be very bad branching out from Kahului to and from Paia, Kihei, and Lahaina. Drive here during peak hours and you'll know why local residents are calling for restrictions on development. Parking along many streets is curtailed during these times, and towing is strictly practiced. Read curbside parking signs before leaving your vehicle, even at a meter.

On Kauai, the 15-mile stretch of the Napali Coast is the only part of the island that's not accessible by car. Otherwise, one main road can get you from Barking Sands Beach on the West Side to Haena on the North Shore.

Although Molokai and Lanai have fewer roadways, car rental is still worthwhile and will allow plenty of interesting sightseeing. A four-wheel-drive vehicle is best on these Islands.

Asking for directions will almost always produce a helpful explanation from the locals, but you should be prepared for an Islands term or two. Instead of using compass directions, remember that Hawaii residents refer to places as being either *mauka* (toward the mountains) or *makai* (toward the ocean) from one another.

Other directions depend on your location: in Honolulu, for example, people say to "go Diamond Head," which means toward that famous landmark to your east, or to "go *ewa*," meaning in the opposite direction, toward a town in leeward (West) Oahu. A shop on the mauka–Diamond Head corner of a street is on the mountain side of the street on the corner closest to Diamond Head. It all makes perfect sense once you get the lay of the land.

GASOLINE

Gasoline is widely available everywhere but the farthest corners of the main Islands. National chains like 76, Chevron, 7-Eleven, and Shell are ubiquitous, and accept all major credit cards right at the pump or inside the station. Prices can range from $3 to $4 for one gallon of "regular" fuel, which is sufficient for all models of rental cars. Gasoline is generally more expensive closer to the airports, where you'll need to refuel before returning your car. Neighbor Islands have higher gasoline prices than Oahu.

Information Hawaii Gas Prices ⊕ *www. hawaiigasprices.com.*

ROAD CONDITIONS

It's difficult to get lost in most of Hawaii. Although their names may challenge a visitor's tongue, roads and streets are well marked; just watch out for the many one-way streets in Waikiki. Keep an eye open for the Hawaii Visitors and Convention Bureau's red-caped King Kamehameha signs, which mark attractions and scenic spots. Ask for a map at the car-rental counter. Free publications containing high-quality road maps can be found on all Islands.

Many of Hawaii's roads are two-lane highways with limited shoulders—and yes, even in paradise, there is traffic, especially during the morning and afternoon rush hour. In rural areas, it's not unusual for gas stations to close early. If you see that your tank is getting low, don't take any chances; fill up when you see a station. In Hawaii, turning right on a red light is legal, except where noted. Use caution during heavy downpours, especially if you see signs warning of falling rocks. If you're enjoying views from the road or

need to study a map, pull over to the side. Remember the aloha spirit when you are driving; allow other cars to merge, don't honk (it's considered extremely rude in the Islands), leave a comfortable distance between your car and the car ahead of you; use your headlights, especially during sunrise and sunset, and use your turn signals.

ROADSIDE EMERGENCIES

If you find yourself in an emergency or accident while driving on any of the Islands, pull over if you can. If you have a cell phone with you, call the roadside assistance number on your rental car contract or AAA Help. If you find that your car has been broken into or stolen, report it immediately to your rental car company and they can assist you. If it's an emergency and someone is hurt, call 911 immediately and stay there until medical personnel arrive.

Emergency ServicesAAA Help ☎ *800/222–4357.*

RULES OF THE ROAD

Be sure to buckle up. Hawaii has a strictly enforced seat-belt law for front-seat passengers. Always strap children under age four into approved child-safety seats. Children 18 and under are also required by state law to use seat belts. The highway speed limit is usually 55 mph. In-town traffic moves from 25 to 40 mph. Jaywalking is very common, so be particularly watchful for pedestrians, especially in congested areas such as Waikiki. Unauthorized use of a parking space reserved for persons with disabilities can net you a $150 fine. All four Hawaii counties have implemented bans on hand-held cell phone use by drivers. If you must use the phone, pull to the side of the road to avoid a costly ticket.

CAR RENTAL

If you plan to do lots of sightseeing, it's best to rent a car. Even if all you want to do is relax at your resort, you may want to hop in the car to check out a popular restaurant. All the big national rental car agencies have locations throughout Hawaii, but Dollar is the only company that has offices on all the major Hawaiian Islands. There also are several local rental car companies so be sure to compare prices before you book. While in the Islands, you can rent anything from an econobox to a Ferrari. On the Big Island, Lanai, and Molokai, four-wheel-drive vehicles are recommended for exploring off the beaten path. Rates are usually better if you reserve through a rental agency's website. It's wise to make reservations far in advance and make sure that a confirmed reservation guarantees you a car, especially if visiting during peak seasons or for major conventions or sporting events. It's not uncommon to find several car categories sold out during major events on some of the smaller Islands.

Rates begin at about $25 to $35 a day for an economy car with air-conditioning, automatic transmission, and unlimited mileage, depending on your pickup location. This does not include the airport concession fee, general excise tax, rental vehicle surcharge, or vehicle license fee.

When you reserve a car, ask about cancellation penalties and drop-off charges should you plan to pick up the car in one location and return it to another.

In Hawaii you must be 21 years of age to rent a car and you must have a valid driver's license and a major credit card. Those under 25 will pay a daily surcharge of $15 to $25. Your unexpired mainland driver's license is valid for rental for up to 90 days. Request car seats and extras such as GPS when you make your reservation. Hawaii's Child Restraint Law requires that all children three years and younger be in an approved child-safety seat in the backseat of a vehicle. Children ages four to seven must be seated in a rear booster seat or child restraint such as a lap and shoulder belt. Car seats and boosters range from $5 to $8 per day.

Since many island roads are two lanes, be sure to allow plenty of time to return your vehicle so that you can make your flight. Traffic can be bad during morning and afternoon rush hour. Give yourself about 2½ hours before departure time to return your vehicle.

Car Rental Resources

AUTOMOBILE ASSOCIATIONS

U.S.: American Automobile Association	☎ 315/797–5000. Most contact with the organization is through state and regional members.	⊕ www.aaa.com
National Automobile Club	☎ 800/622–2136. Membership is open to California residents only.	⊕ www.thenac.com

LOCAL AGENCIES

Advantage Rent-A-Car (Oahu)	☎ 800/777–5500	⊕ www.advantage.com
Adventure Lanai EcoCentre	☎ 808/565–7373	⊕ www.adventurelanai.com
Aloha Campers (Maui)	☎ 808/281–8020	⊕ www.alohacampers.com
Discount Hawaii Car Rentals	☎ 800/292–1930	⊕ www.discounthawaiicarrental.com
Happy Campers Hawaii (Big Island)	☎ 888/550–3918	⊕ www.happycampershawaii.com
Harper Car and Truck Rental (Big Island)	☎ 800/852–9993	⊕ www.harpershawaii.com
Hawaii Car Rental	☎ 800/655–7989	⊕ www.hawaiicarrental.com
Hawaiian Discount Car Rentals	☎ 800/591–8605	⊕ www.hawaiidrive-o.com
Island Kine Auto Rental (Molokai)	☎ 877/553–5242	⊕ www.molokai-car-rental.com
JN Car and Truck Rentals (Oahu)	☎ 800/475–7522	⊕ www.jnautomotive.com

MAJOR AGENCIES

Alamo	☎ 877/222–9075	⊕ www.alamo.com
Avis	☎ 800/331–1212	⊕ www.avis.com
Budget	☎ 800/527–0700	⊕ www.budget.com
Dollar	☎ 800/800–3665	⊕ www.dollar.com
Enterprise	☎ 800/261–7331	⊕ www.enterprise.com
Hertz	☎ 800/654–3131	⊕ www.hertz.com
National Car Rental	☎ 877/222–9058	⊕ www.nationalcar.com
Thrifty	☎ 800/847–4389	⊕ www.thrifty.com

ESSENTIALS

■ ACCOMMODATIONS

Hawaii truly offers something for everyone. Are you looking for a luxurious oceanfront resort loaded with amenities, an intimate two-room bed-and-breakfast tucked away in a lush rain forest, a house with a pool and incredible views for your extended family, a condominium just steps from the 18th hole, or even a campsite at a national park? You can find all these and more throughout the Islands.

Most hotels and other lodgings require you to give your credit-card details before they will confirm your reservation. Get confirmation in writing and have a copy of it handy when you check in. Be sure you understand the hotel's cancellation policy. Some places allow you to cancel without any kind of penalty—even if you prepaid to secure a discounted rate—if you cancel at least 24 hours in advance. Others require you to cancel a week in advance or penalize you the cost of one night. Small inns and bed-and-breakfasts are most likely to require you to cancel far in advance. Most hotels allow children under a certain age to stay in their parents' room at no extra charge, but others charge for them as adults; find out the cutoff age for discounts.

Prices in the reviews are the lowest cost of a standard double room in high season.

BED-AND-BREAKFASTS

For many travelers, nothing compares to the personal service and guest interaction offered at bed-and-breakfasts. There are hundreds of bed-and-breakfasts throughout the Islands; many even invite their guests to enjoy complimentary wine tastings and activities such as lei making and basket weaving. Each island's website also features a listing of member B&Bs that are individually owned.

Contacts Bed and Breakfast.com. ☎ *800/462–2632* ⊕ *www.bedandbreakfast. com.* **Bed & Breakfast Inns Online** ☎ *800/215–7365* ⊕ *www.bbonline.com.* **Better Bed and Breakfasts** ⊕ *www. betterbedandbreakfasts.com.* **BnB Finder. com** ☎ *888/547–8226* ⊕ *www.bnbfinder.com.* **Hawaii's Best Bed & Breakfasts** ☎ *808/263– 3100, 800/262–9912* ⊕ *www.bestbnb.com.*

CONDOMINIUM AND HOUSE RENTALS

Vacation rentals are perfect for couples, families, and friends traveling together who like the convenience of staying at a home away from home. Properties managed by individual owners can be found on online vacation-rental listing directories such as CyberRentals and Vacation Rentals By Owners, as well as on the visitors bureau website for each island. There also are several Islands-based management companies with vacation rentals.

Compare companies, as some offer Internet specials and free night stays when booking. Policies vary, but most require a minimum stay, usually greater during peak travel seasons.

Contacts CyberRentals ☎ *512/684-1098* ⊕ *www.cyberrentals.com.* **Vacation Rentals By Owner** ⊕ *www.vrbo.com.</R>*

HOME EXCHANGES

With a direct home exchange you stay in someone else's home while they stay in yours. The exchange clubs listed below feature dozens of Hawaii homes available for exchange. Many are on the beach or have ocean views.

Exchange Clubs HomeExchange. com. $119.40 for a one-year membership ☎ *800/877–8723* ⊕ *www.homeexchange. com.* **HomeLink International.** $119 annual membership fee. ☎ *800/638–3841* ⊕ *www. homelink.org.* **Intervac.** $99.99 for one-year membership. ☎ *800/756–4663* ⊕ *www. intervac-homeexchange.com.*

HOTELS

All hotels listed have private bath unless otherwise noted.

■ COMMUNICATIONS

INTERNET

If you've brought your laptop with you to the Islands, you should have no problem connecting to the Internet. Major hotels and resorts offer high-speed access in rooms and/or lobbies. In some cases there will be an hourly or daily charge billed to your room. If you're staying at a small inn or vacation home without Internet access (a rarity these days), ask for the nearest café or coffee shop with wireless access.

Visitors can also access the Internet at any Hawaii State Public Library. You can reserve a computer for 60 minutes once a week, via phone or walk-in. You'll need to sign up for a library card, which costs $10 for a three-month period.

Contacts Cybercafes. Cybercafes lists more than 4,000 Internet cafés worldwide. ⊕ *www. cybercafes.com.* **Hawaii State Public Library System** ⊕ *www.librarieshawaii.org.*

■ EATING OUT

Whether you're looking for a dinner for two in a romantic oceanfront dining room or a family get-together in a hole-in-the-wall serving traditional Hawaiian fare like *kalua* pig, you'll find it throughout the Islands. When it comes to eating, Hawaii has something for every taste bud and every budget. With chefs using locally grown fruits and vegetables, vegetarians often have many exciting choices for their meals. And because Hawaii is a popular destination for families, restaurants almost always have a children's menu. When making a reservation at your hotel's dining room, ask about free or reduced-price meals for children.

MEALS AND MEALTIMES

Breakfast is usually served from 6 or 7 am to 9:30 or 10 am.

Lunch typically runs from 11:30 am to around 1:30 or 2 pm, and will include salads, sandwiches, and lighter fare. The "plate lunch," a favorite of many locals, usually consists of grilled teriyaki chicken,

beef, or fish topped with a big ladle of gravy and served with two scoops of white rice and two side salads. The phrase "broke da mouth," often used to describe these plates, refers not only to their size, but also their tastiness.

Dinner is usually served from 5 to 9 pm and, depending on the restaurant, can be a simple or lavish affair. Stick to the chef specials if you can because they usually represent the best of the season. *Poke* (marinated raw tuna) is a local specialty and can often be found on *pupu* (appetizer) menus.

Meals in resort areas are pricey but often excellent. The restaurants we include are the cream of the crop in each price category. Unless otherwise noted, the restaurants listed are open daily for lunch and dinner. *Prices in the reviews are the average cost of a main course at dinner or, if dinner is not served, at lunch.*

For guidelines on tipping, see Tipping.

RESERVATIONS AND DRESS

Hawaii is decidedly casual. Aloha shirts and shorts or long pants for men and island-style dresses or casual resort wear for women are standard attire for evenings in most hotel restaurants and local eateries. T-shirts and shorts will do the trick for breakfast and lunch. We mention dress only when men are required to wear a jacket or a jacket and tie.

Regardless of where you are, it's a good idea to make a reservation if you can. In some places, it's expected. We only mention reservations specifically when they are essential or when they are not accepted. For popular restaurants, book as far ahead as you can (often a month or more), and reconfirm as soon as you arrive. Large parties should always call ahead to check the reservations policy.

WINES, BEER, AND SPIRITS

Hawaii has a new generation of microbreweries, including on-site microbreweries at many restaurants. The drinking age in Hawaii is 21 years of age, and a photo ID must be presented to purchase alcoholic beverages. Bars are open until 2 am; venues with a cabaret license can stay open until 4 am. No matter what you might see in the local parks, drinking alcohol in public parks or on the beaches is illegal. It's also illegal to have open containers of alcohol in motor vehicles.

▍ HEALTH

Hawaii is known as the Health State. The life expectancy here is 79 years, the longest in the nation. Balmy weather makes it easy to remain active year-round, and the low-stress aloha attitude certainly contributes to general well-being. When visiting the Islands, however, there are a few health issues to keep in mind.

The Hawaii State Department of Health recommends that you drink 16 ounces of water per hour to avoid dehydration when hiking or spending time in the sun. Use sunblock, wear UV-reflective sunglasses, and protect your head with a visor or hat for shade. If you're not acclimated to warm, humid weather, you should allow plenty of time for rest stops and refreshments.

When visiting freshwater streams, be aware of the tropical bacterial infection leptospirosis, which is spread by animal urine and carried into streams and mud. Symptoms include fever, headache, nausea, and red eyes. If left untreated, it can cause liver and kidney damage, respiratory failure, internal bleeding, and even death. To avoid this, don't swim or wade in freshwater streams or ponds if you have open sores and don't drink from any freshwater streams or ponds, especially after it has rained.

On the Islands, fog is a rare occurrence, but there can often be "vog," an airborne haze of gases released from volcanic vents on the Big Island. During certain weather conditions such as "Kona Winds," the vog can settle over the Islands and wreak havoc with respiratory and other health conditions, especially asthma or emphysema. If susceptible, stay indoors and get emergency assistance if needed.

The Islands have their share of bugs and insects that enjoy the tropical climate as much as visitors do. Most are harmless but annoying. When planning to spend time outdoors in hiking areas, wear long-sleeve clothing and pants and use mosquito repellent containing DEET. In very damp places you may encounter the dreaded local centipede. On the Islands they usually come in two colors, brown and blue, and they range from the size of a worm to an 8-inch cigar. Their sting is very painful, and the reaction is similar to bee- and wasp-sting reactions. When camping, shake out your sleeping bag before climbing in, and check your shoes in the morning, as the centipedes like cozy places. If planning on hiking or traveling in remote areas, always carry a first-aid kit and appropriate medications for sting reactions.

▍ HOURS OF OPERATION

Even people in paradise have to work. Local business hours are generally weekdays 8 to 5. Banks are usually open Monday through Thursday 8:30 to 3 and until 6 on Friday. Some banks have Saturday-morning hours. Grocery and department stores, as well as shopping malls and boutiques, are open seven days a week.

Many self-serve gas stations stay open around the clock, with full-service stations usually open from around 7 am until 9 pm. U.S. post offices are open weekdays 8:30 am to 4:30 pm and Saturday 8:30 to noon. On Oahu, the Ala Moana post office branch is the only branch, other than the main Honolulu International Airport facility, that stays open until 4 pm on Saturday.

Most museums generally open their doors between 9 am and 10 am and stay open until 5 pm Tuesday through Saturday. Many museums operate with afternoon hours only on Sunday and close on Monday. Visitor-attraction hours vary throughout the state, but most sights are open daily with the exception of major holidays such as Christmas. Check local newspapers upon arrival for attraction hours and schedules if visiting over holiday periods. The local dailies carry a listing of "What's Open/What's Not" for those time periods.

Stores in resort areas sometimes open as early as 8, while shopping centers open at 9:30 or 10 on weekdays and Saturday, a bit later on Sunday. Bigger malls stay open until 9 pm weekdays and Saturday and close between 5 and 6 pm on Sunday. Boutiques in resort areas may stay open as late as 11.

MONEY

Prices are given for adults. Substantially reduced fees are almost always available for children, students, and senior citizens.

ATMS AND BANKS

Automatic teller machines for easy access to cash are everywhere on the Islands. ATMs can be found in shopping centers, small convenience and grocery stores, and inside hotels and resorts, as well as outside most bank branches.

CREDIT CARDS

It's a good idea to inform your credit-card company before you travel, especially if you're going abroad and don't travel internationally very often. Otherwise, the credit-card company might put a hold on your card owing to unusual activity—not a good thing halfway through your trip. Record all your credit-card numbers—as well as the phone numbers to call if your cards are lost or stolen—in a safe place, so you're prepared should something go wrong. Both MasterCard and Visa have general numbers you can call if your card is lost, but you're better off calling the number of your issuing bank, since MasterCard and Visa usually just transfer you to your bank; your bank's number is usually printed on your card.

PACKING

Hawaii is casual: sandals, bathing suits, and comfortable, informal clothing are the norm. In summer, synthetic slacks and shirts, although easy to care for, can be uncomfortably warm. Only a few upscale restaurants require a jacket for dinner. The aloha shirt is accepted dress in Hawaii for business and most social occasions. Shorts are standard daytime attire, along with a T-shirt or polo shirt. There's no need to buy expensive sandals on the mainland—here you can get flip-flops for a couple of dollars and off-brand sandals for $20. Golfers should remember that many courses have dress codes requiring a collared shirt. If you're not prepared, you can pick up appropriate clothing at resort pro shops. If you're visiting in winter or planning to visit a high-altitude area, bring a sweater or light- to medium-weight jacket. A polar fleece pullover is ideal.

One of the most important things to tuck into your suitcase is sunscreen. Hats and sunglasses offer important sun protection, too. All major hotels in Hawaii provide beach towels.

You might also want to pack a light raincoat or folding umbrella, as morning rain showers are not uncommon. And on each of the Islands' windward coasts, it can be rainy, especially during the winter months. If you're planning on doing any exploration in rain forests or national parks, bring along a sturdy pair of hiking boots.

SAFETY

Hawaii is generally a safe tourist destination, but it's still wise to follow common sense safety precautions. Hotel and visitor-center staff can provide information should you decide to head out on your own to more remote areas. Rental cars are magnets for break-ins, so don't leave any valuables in the car, not even in a locked trunk. Avoid poorly lighted areas, beach parks, and isolated areas after dark as a precaution.

When hiking, stay on marked trails, no matter how alluring the temptation might be to stray. Weather conditions can cause landscapes to become muddy, slippery, and tenuous, so staying on marked trails will lessen the possibility of a fall or getting lost.

Ocean safety is of the utmost importance when visiting an island destination. Don't swim alone, and follow the international signage posted at beaches that alerts swimmers to strong currents, man-of-war jellyfish, sharp coral, high surf, sharks, and dangerous shore breaks. At coastal lookouts along cliff tops, heed the signs indicating that waves can climb over the ledges. Check with lifeguards at each beach for current conditions, and if the red flags are up, indicating swimming and surfing are not allowed, don't go in. Waters that look calm on the surface can harbor strong currents and undertows, and not a few people who were just wading have been dragged out to sea.

Be wary of those hawking "too good to be true" prices on everything from car rentals to attractions. Many of these offers are just a lure to get you in the door for time-share presentations. When handed a flier, read the fine print before you make your decision to participate.

Women traveling alone are generally safe on the Islands, but always follow the same precautions you would use in any major destination. When booking hotels, request rooms closest to the elevator, and always keep your hotel-room door and balcony doors locked. Stay away from isolated areas after dark; camping and hiking solo are not advised. If you stay out late visiting nightclubs and bars, use caution when exiting nightspots and returning to your lodging.

TIPPING GUIDELINES FOR HAWAII	
Bartender	$1 to $5 per round of drinks, depending on the number of drinks
Bellhop	$1 to $5 per bag, depending on the level of the hotel and whether you have bulky items like golf clubs, surfboards, etc.
Hotel Concierge	$5 or more, depending on the service
Hotel Doorman	$1 to $5 if s/he helps you get a cab or helps with bags, golf clubs, etc.
Hotel Maid	$2 to $5 a day, depending on the level of the hotel (either daily or at the end of your stay, in cash)
Hotel Room-Service Waiter	$1 to $2 per delivery, even if a service charge has been added
Porter/Skycap at Airport	$1 to $3 per bag
Spa Personnel	15% to 20% of the cost of your service
Taxi Driver	15% to 20%, but round up the fare to the next dollar amount
Tour Guide	10% of the cost of the tour
Valet Parking Attendant	$2 to $5, each time your car is brought to you
Waiter	15% to 20%, with 20% being the norm at high-end restaurants; nothing additional if a service charge is added to the bill

TAXES

There's a 4.16% statewide sales tax on all purchases, including food (it's actually half a percent higher on Oahu to pay for a proposed rail project). An additional hotel room tax, combined with the sales tax, equals a 13.42% rate added onto your hotel bill on most Islands, and a 13.96% rate on Oahu. A $3-per-day road tax is also assessed on each rental vehicle.

▮ TIME

Hawaii is on Hawaiian Standard Time, five hours behind New York, two hours behind Los Angeles, and 10 hours behind London.

When the U.S. mainland is on daylight saving time, Hawaii is not, so add an extra hour of time difference between the Islands and U.S. mainland destinations. You may also find that things generally move more slowly here. That has nothing to do with your watch—it's just the laid-back way called Hawaiian time.

▮ TIPPING

As this is a major vacation destination and many of the people who work in the service industry rely on tips to supplement their wages, tipping is not only common, but expected.

▮ TOURS

Globus has seven Hawaii itineraries ranging from 7 to 13 days, including an escorted cruise on Norwegian Cruise Lines' *Pride of America*. Perillo Tours offers a 7-day two-islander tour to Oahu and Maui and a 10-day three-islander tour to Oahu, Maui and Kauai. Tauck Travel and Trafalgar offer several land-based Hawaii itineraries with plenty of free time to explore the Islands. If you want to stay longer, YMT Vacations has a 15-day, four-island tour.

Atlas Cruises & Tours sells more than a dozen Hawaii trips ranging from 7 to 12 nights, operated by various guided-tour companies including Globus, Tauck, and Trafalgar.

Recommended Companies Atlas Cruises & Tours ☎ 800/942-3301 ⊕ www. escortedhawaiitours.com. **Globus** ☎ 866/755-8581 ⊕ www.globusjourneys.com. **Perillo Tours** ☎ 800/431-1515 ⊕ www.perillotours. com. **Tauck Travel** ☎ 800/788-7885 ⊕ www. tauck.com. **Trafalgar** ☎ 866/544-4434 ⊕ www.trafalgar.com. **YMT Vacations** ☎ 800/922-9000 ⊕ www.ymtvacations.c om.

SPECIAL-INTEREST TOURS
BIRD-WATCHING

There are more than 150 species of birds that live in the Hawaiian Islands. Field Guides has a three-island (Oahu, Kauai, and the Big Island), 11-day guided bird-watching trip that focuses on endemic land birds and specialty seabirds. Victor Emanuel Nature Tours offers two eight-night birding trips to the Islands: "Kauai and Hawaii in March" and "Fall Hawaii" to Oahu, Kauai, and the Big Island. The guide for both tours is Bob Sundstrom, who has been leading birding tours in Hawaii and other destinations since 1989.

Contacts Field Guides ☎ 800/728-4953 ⊕ www.fieldguides.com. **Victor Emanuel Nature Tours.** Birding tours ☎ 800/328-8368 ⊕ www.ventbird.com.

CULTURE

Road Scholar—formerly Elderhostel—offers several guided Hawaii tours for older adults that provide fascinating in-depth looks into the culture, history, and beauty of the Islands. "Tall Ship Sail Training: Sailing the Hawaiian Islands" is a six-night sailing adventure aboard a 96-foot, three-mast schooner; the 11-night "Paradise Adventure from Mountains to Sea" tour includes everything from river kayaking and hiking to surfing; and the nine-night "Snorkeling Hawaii's Spectacular Marine Environments" tour lets you immerse yourself in Hawaii's fascinating marine life.

ContactRoad Scholar ☎ 800/454-5768 ⊕ www.roadscholar.org.

HIKING

"Hawaii Three Island Hiker" is a seven-night hiking tour to Kauai, the Big Island, and Maui offered by The World Outdoors, which has been organizing and leading adventure trips around the world for more than 20 years.

Contacts The World Outdoors ☎ 800/488-8483 ⊕ www.theworldoutdoors.com.

TRIP INSURANCE

Comprehensive trip insurance is valuable if you're booking a very expensive or complicated trip (particularly to an isolated region like Hawaii) or if you're booking far in advance. Comprehensive policies typically cover trip cancellation and interruption, letting you cancel or cut your trip short because of illness, or, in some cases, acts of terrorism in your destination. Such policies might also cover evacuation and medical care. Some also cover you for trip delays because of bad weather or mechanical problems as well as for lost or delayed luggage.

Another type of coverage to consider is financial default—that is, when your trip is disrupted because a tour operator, airline, or cruise line goes out of business. Generally you must buy this when you book your trip or shortly thereafter, and it's available to you only if your operator isn't on a list of excluded companies.

Always read the fine print of your policy to make sure that you're covered for the risks that most concern you. Compare several policies to be sure you're getting the best price and range of coverage available.

Insurance Comparison Info Insure My Trip ☎ 800/487–4722 ⊕ www.insuremytrip.com. **Square Mouth** ☎ 800/240–0369 ⊕ www. squaremouth.com.

Comprehensive Insurers Access America. Travel insurance ☎ 800/284–8300 ⊕ www. accessamerica.com. **AIG Travel Guard** ☎ 800/826–4919 ⊕ www.travelguard.com. **CSA Travel Protection.** Travel insurance ☎ 800/711–1197 ⊕ www.csatravelprotection. com. **Travelex Insurance** ☎ 888/228–9792 ⊕ www.travelex-insurance.com. **Travel Insured International** ☎ 800/243–3174 ⊕ www. travelinsured.com.

VISITOR INFORMATION

Before you go, contact the Hawaii Visitors & Convention Bureau for general information on each island. You can request

via phone or online, "Islands of Aloha," a free visitor guide with information on accommodations, transportation, sports and activities, dining, arts and entertainment, and culture. The website has a calendar section that allows you to see what local events are in place during the time of your stay.

You might also want to check out ⊕ www.ehawaii.gov, the state's official website, for information on camping, fishing licenses, and other visitor services. Each island has its own website as well: ⊕ www.bigisland.org (Big Island Visitors Bureau); ⊕ www.visitmaui.com (Maui County Visitors & Conventions Bureau); ⊕ www.visit-oahu.com (Oahu Visitors Bureau); ⊕ www.kauaidiscovery. com (Kauai Visitors Bureau); ⊕ www. visitlanai.net (Lanai Visitors Bureau); and ⊕ www.molokai-hawaii.com (Molokai Visitors Association).

Visit ⊕ www.honoluluweekly.com for a weekly guide to the arts, entertainment, and dining in Honolulu; ⊕ www. honolulu.gov, from the City and County of Honolulu with calendar of events for Blaisdell arena and concert hall and the Royal Hawaiian Band; ⊕ www. hawaiimuseums.org, the website of the Hawaii Museums Association. Be sure to check out ⊕ www.nps.gov for information on the eight parks managed by the National Park Service.

The Hawaii Ecotourism Site (⊕ www. alternative-hawaii.com), provides listings of everything from eco-culture events on the Islands to Hawaii Heritage tour guides, and the Hawaii Ecotourism Association (⊕ www.hawaiiecotourism.org) has an online directory of more than 100 member companies offering tours

and activities. The Hawaii Department
of Land and Natural Resources (⊕ *www.
hawaii.gov/dlnr*) has information on hiking, fishing, and camping permits and
licenses; online brochures on hiking safety
and mountain and ocean preservation; as
well as details on volunteer programs.

**Contact Hawaii Visitors & Convention
Bureau** ☎ *808/923–1811, 800/464–2924*
⊕ *www.gohawaii.com.*

INDEX

PHOTO CREDITS

1, Douglas Peebles / eStock Photo. 3, J.D.Heaton/Picture Finders/age fotostock. Chapter 1: Experience: 6-7, SuperStock/age fotostock. 8, J.D.Heaton/Picture Finders/age fotostock. 9 (left), SuperStock/age fotostock. 9 (right), Big Island Visitors Bureau. 12, Kaua'i Visitors Bureau. 13, (left) Hawaii Tourism Japan (HTJ). 13 (right), Hawaii Tourism Japan (HTJ). 14, (left) Danita Delimont/Alamy. 14 (top center), Oahu Visitors Bureau. 14 (bottom center), David Schrichre/Photo Resource Hawaii. 14 (top right), Andre Nantel/Shutterstock. 14 (bottom right), Deborah Davis/Alamy. 15 (top left), Stephen Frink Collection/Alamy. 15 (bottom left), Polynesian Cultural Center. 15 (bottom center), Lee Foster/ Alamy. 15 (top center), Photo Resource Hawaii/Alamy. 15 (right), Robert Coello/Kauai Visitors Bureau. 16, Skip ODonnell/iStockphoto. 17 (left), Jarvis grey/Shutterstock. 17 (right), Jess Moss. 18, James Michael Kruger/Stockphoto. 19 (left), Mark Pinkerton/iStockphoto. 19 (right), chris driscoll/Stock- photo. 20, Amy Kuck/Stockphoto. 23 (left), Luca Tettoni/viestiphoto.com. 23 (right), SuperStock/age fotostock. 24, iStockphoto. 25, James Michael Kruger/iStockphoto. 26, Ray Kachatorian/Starwood Hotels & Resorts. 27 (left), iStockphoto. 27 (right), muhawi001/Flickr. 28, Dwight Smith/iStockphoto. 29, Kauai Visitors Bureau. 30, Jose Gil/Shutterstock. 31 (left), Cheryl Casey/Shutterstock. 31 (right), Katja Govorushchenko/iStockphoto. 32, iStockphoto. 33 (left), nicole waring/iStockphoto. 33 (right), iStockphoto. 35 (left), Kuai Visitors Bureau. 35 (right), Hawaii Tourism Authority (HTA)/ Ron Dahlquist. 36, Jess Moss. 37, Jay Spooner/iStockphoto. 38, Patrick Roherty/iStockphoto. 39 (left), Jay Spooner/iStockphoto. 39 (right), Amanda Ostrom-Eckelbarger, Fodors.com member. 40, Michael Brake/iStockphoto. Chapter 2: Oahu: 41, Polynesian Cultural Center. 42 (center), Michael S. Nolan/age fotostock. 42 (bottom), SuperStock/age fotostock. 42 (top), Ken Ross/viestiphoto.com. 43, Oahu Visi- tors Bureau. 45, Rory Hanrahan. 46, Drazen Vukelic/Shutterstock. 63, J.D.Heaton/Picture Finders/age fotostock. 64, Oahu Visitors Bureau. 65 (left and center), Walter Bibikow/viestiphoto.com. 65 (right), Douglas Peebles/age fotostock. 66, Stuart Westmorland/age fotostock. 67 (left), The Royal Hawaiian. 67 (center), Atlantide S.N.C./age fotostock. 67 (right), Liane Cary/age fotostock. 71, U.S. National Archives. 73 (top), Corbis. 73 (bottom), NPS/ USS Arizona Memorial Photo Collection. 74 (left), Army Signal Corps Collection in the U.S. National Archives. 74 (right), USS Missouri Memorial Association. 75, USS Bowfin Submarine Museum & Park. 77, Rory Hanrahan. 81, Polynesian Cultural Center. 85, Rory Hanrahan. 94, Hawaii Tourism Authority (HTA)/Tor Johnson. 97, SuperStock/age fotostock. 99 (left and right), Pierre Tostee. 100 and 101, ASP Tostee. 102, cunninghamphotos.com. 106, Photo Resource Hawaii/Alamy. 112, Hawaii Tourism Author- ity (HTA)/Tor Johnson. 114, Hawaii Tourism Authority (HTA)/Tor Johnson. 118, Blue Hawaiian Helicopters. 124, Photo Resource Hawaii/Alamy. 137, Ann Cecil/Photo Resource Hawaii/Alamy. 141, Polynesian Cultural Center. 142, Robert Cravens/iStockphoto. 149 and 158, Rory Hanrahan. 169(top and bottom), Kahala. 170 (top and bottom), Halekulani. 174 (top and bottom), Turtle Bay Resort. Chapter 3: Maui: 177, Lee Prince/Shutterstock. 178 (top), Chris Hammond/viestiphoto.com. 178 (bottom) and 179 (top), Walter Bibikow/viestiphoto.com. 179 (bottom), Douglas Peebles/age fotostock. 181, The_seeker, Fodors.com member. 185, tmdave, Fodors.com member. 194, Jay Spooner/ istock.202, kjkltz, Fodors.com member. 205, Chris Hammond/viestiphoto.com. 207, Ron Dahlquist/ Maui Visitors Bureau. 208, Chris Hammond/viestiphoto.com. 211, Richard Genova/viestiphoto.com. 212, SuperStock/age fotostock. 213, Chris Hammond/viestiphoto.com. 219, Aurora Photos. 224, Robert Plotz/iStockphoto. 228, SuperStock/age fotostock. 236, SUNNYphotography.com/Alamy. 243, Michael S. Nolan/age fotostock. 246, Max Earey/Shutterstock. 250, Bart Everett/Shutterstock. 255, National Park Service. 258, Maui Visitors Bureau. 259, Photodisc. 260, Maui Visitors Bureau. 261, Brent Wong/iStockphoto. 271 (top), Linda Ching/HVCB. 271 (bottom), Sri Maiava Rusden/HVCB. 272, Michael Soo/Alamy. 273 (top), leisofhawaii.com. 273 (second from top), kellyalexanderphotography. com. 273 (third, fourth, and fifth from top), leisofhawaii.com. 273 (bottom), kellyalexanderphotography. com. 279, Hiroyuki Saita/Shutterstock. 283, LukeGordon1/Flickr. 291, RoJo Images/Shutterstock. 297, tomas del amo/Shutterstock. 303 (top), Westin Resort Maui. 303 (bottom left), Outrigger Hotels Hawaii. 303 (bottom right), Ho'oilo House. 309 (top), Ritz Carlton Kapalua. 309 (bottom left), Ron Dahlquist. 309 (bottom right), Images by Jesse Francis courtesy of Luana Kai. 314 (top), Four Seasons Maui at Wailea/ Vitale, Peter. 314 (bottom), Old Wailuku Inn at Ulupono. 318 (top), Rough Guides / Alamy. 318 (bottom), Hana Kai Maui Resort Condominiums. Chapter 4: The Big Island: 321, Walter Bibikow/viestiphoto. com. 322 (top left), PhotoDisc. 322 (top right and bottom), Big Island Visitors Bureau. 325 (left and right), Hawaii's Big Island Visitor Bureau (BIVB). 338, BVIB. 341, Hawaii Tourism Authority (HTA)/ Kirk Lee Aeder. 348, Russ Bishop/Alamy. 356, Big Island Visitors Bureau. 357, Russ Bishop/age fotostock. 359, Photo Resource Hawaii/Alamy. 360, Cornforth Images/Alamy. 361 (top), Big Island Visitors Bureau. 361 (bottom), Linda Robshaw/Alamy. 362, Nicki Geigert, Fodors.com member. 367, Cornforth Images / Alamy. 368, Luis Castañeda/age fotostock. 378, Andre Seale/Alamy. 381, Ron Dahlquist/HVCB. 382, Pacific Stock/

NOTES

ABOUT OUR WRITERS

Karen Anderson is a Kona resident who enjoys horseback riding in the hills of the Big Island. She is the managing editor of *At Home, Living with Style in West Hawaii* magazine and has written for a variety of publications. She's also the best-selling author of *The Hawaii Home Book: Practical Tips for Tropical Living*. Her favorite assignment is profiling island restaurants for her monthly magazine. For this edition, Karen updated the Big Island Shopping, Spas, Entertainment and Nightlife, Where to Eat, and Where to Stay sections.

Kristina Anderson has been writing professionally for more than 25 years. After working as an advertising copywriter and creative director in Southern California for more than a decade, she moved to Hawaii in 1992. She's written for national and regional publications, most notably for *At Home in West Hawaii Magazine*, which profiles a variety of homes—from coffee shacks to resort mansions—and for USAToday.com Travel Tips. For this book, Kristina updated the Big Island Golf, Hiking, and Outdoor Activities section.

Melissa Chang is a lifelong Honolulu resident and has worked in public relations for more than 20 years, representing a range of travel, retail, and restaurant clients. She is also a food reviewer for Honolulu's ⊕ *Metromix.com* and is a regular contributor to the *Honolulu Advertiser,* the state's most popular daily newspaper. Melissa updated the Shopping, Spas, and Where to Eat sections of the Oahu chapter.

Lois Ann Ell is a writer and journalist who lives on Kauai. She updated the Shopping and Spas sections of the Kauai chapter.

Eliza Escaño-Vasquez was raised in Manila, Philippines, and lived in California before falling deeply in aloha with Maui in 2005. She is a contributing writer for *Maui Concierge* and *Modern Luxury Hawaii.* For this edition she updated the Maui Water Sports and Tours, Shopping, Spas, and Entertainment and Nightlife sections. Eliza currently resides in Maui with her family, who make living in paradise even more blissful than it sounds.

Bonnie Friedman, a native New Yorker, has made her home on Maui for almost 30 years. A well-published freelance writer, she also owns and operates Grapevine Productions. She traveled around Maui to get the latest news for the Maui Exploring, Where to Eat, and Where to Stay sections, adding some of her favorite places. She also updated the Experience Hawaii and Travel Smart chapters of this guide.

Michael Levine is a reporter-host for ⊕ *CivilBeat.com*, a Honolulu-based investigative news service. He covers city government, politics, and local issues, with a focus on the City Council and the mayor. For this book, he updated the Oahu Exploring, Beaches, and Golf, Hiking, and Outdoor Activities sections.

Heidi Pool is a freelance writer and personal fitness trainer who moved to Maui in 2003 after having been a frequent visitor for the previous two decades. An avid outdoor enthusiast, Heidi enjoys playing tour guide when friends or family members come to visit. She updated Beaches and Golf, Hiking, and Outdoor Activities for the Maui chapter; and Molokai.

Charles E. Roessler is a long-time Kauai resident who was an editor for the *Japan Times* and the *Buffalo News* after teaching English and journalism for 10 years. He regularly contributes to the *New York Times* as a stringer/freelancer and loves Kauai, especially playing tennis and swimming daily at Anini Beach. Charles updated the Kauai Exploring, Beaches, Where to Eat, and Where to Stay sections of this guide.

David Simon is a Kauai resident who was the sports editor for the *Garden Island* newspaper and is a featured columnist for *MidWeek Kauai*. After graduating from Penn State University, he has worked as a sports journalist for both print and online media outlets, including as an editor at *NBA.com*. For this edition, David updated the Kauai Water Sports and Tours; Golf, Hiking and Outdoor Activities; and Entertainment and Nightlife sections.

Over the past 10 years, **Cynthia Sweeney**'s work has appeared in numerous Big Island publications including *Keo Ola Magazine*, *West Hawaii Today*, and *Hana Hou Magazine*. She writes about everything from arts and entertainment to science and technology, and the exceptional lives of the people who live here in Hawaii. Cynthia updated the Exploring, Beaches, and Water Sports and Tours sections of the Big Island chapter.

Born and raised on Oahu, **Catherine E. Toth** has worked as a newspaper reporter in Hawaii for 10 years and continues to freelance—in between surfing, hiking, and eating everything in sight—for such print and online publications as *Haute Living*, *Modern Luxury Hawaii*, *HAWAII*, and *Alaska Airlines Magazine*. For this edition, she updated the Oahu Water Sports and Tours, Entertainment and Nightlife, and Where to Stay sections.

Joana Varawa has lived on Lanai for more than 35 years and is editor of the *Lanai Times Community Email*, an online newspaper. She has authored three books and many magazine and newspaper stories, and continues to explore her island with her beloved dog, Honey Girl. For this edition, Joana updated—no surprise—Lanai.